Reading India

Reading India

The *Reading India* series is meant to disseminate a selection of scholarly research work that has been published in the *Economic and Political Weekly* and the *Economic Weekly* over the decades. The three volumes, spanning 1949 to 2017, give an overview of important issues relating to India's economy, politics and society. Each set of readings is compiled by three senior academics who have also written an introductory chapter for the volume. *EPW* also thankfully acknowledges the contributions made by the authors to the volume. This series has been produced with the help of a grant from the Tata Trusts. *EPW* is grateful to the Tata Trusts for supporting this venture.

Reading India

Selections from *Economic and Political Weekly*

Volume 2: 1966–1991

Edited by

Gurpreet Mahajan
Surinder S. Jodhka
Ila Patnaik

TATA TRUSTS

Orient BlackSwan

READING INDIA: SELECTIONS FROM *ECONOMIC AND POLITICAL WEEKLY*—VOLUME 2: 1966–1991

ORIENT BLACKSWAN PRIVATE LIMITED

Registered Office
3-6-752 Himayatnagar, Hyderabad 500 029, Telangana, India
e-mail: centraloffice@orientblackswan.com

Other Offices
Bengaluru, Bhopal, Chennai, Guwahati, Hyderabad,
Jaipur, Kolkata, Lucknow, Mumbai, New Delhi,
Noida, Patna, Visakhapatnam

First published by Orient Blackswan Pvt. Ltd. 2019

030224

ISBN 978-93-5287-749-2

Typeset by
Le Studio Graphique, Gurgaon
in Adobe Garamond Pro 11/13.5

Printed in India at
Yash Printographics, Noida

Published by
Orient Blackswan Private Limited
3-6-752 Himayatnagar, Hyderabad 500 029, Telangana, India
e-mail: info@orientblackswan.com

Contents

PART III

Economy

[illegible]

Tables and Figure

Tables

Figure

List of Abbreviations

AERC	Agro-Economics Research Centre
AIR	All-India Reporter
ASI	Annual Survey of Industries
BA	Bachelor of Arts
BHEL	Bharat Heavy Electricals Limited
BICP	BIM Innovation Capability Programme
BJP	Bharatiya Janata Party
BSc	Bachelor of Science
CAD	Constituent Assembly Debates
CAS	Credit Authorisation Scheme
CBI	Central Bureau of Investigation
CCI	Competition Commission of India
CDs	Certificates of Deposits
CIF	Cost, Insurance and Freight
CITU	Centre of Indian Trade Unions
CMIE	Centre for Monitoring of Indian Economy
CPI	Communist Party of India
CPI(M)	Communist Party of India (Marxist)
CRISIL	Credit Rating Information Services of India Ltd
CSO	Central Statistical Organisation
DAVP	Directorate of Advertising and Visual Publicity
DFHI	Discount and Finance House of India
DFIs	Development Finance Institutions
DGTD	Directorate General of Technical Development
DIG	Deputy Inspector General
DMK	Dravida Munnetra Kazhagam
DRCs	Domestic Resource Costs
EEC	European Economic Community

EIL	Engineers India Limited
ELK	Election Law Reports
EP	export-promotion
EPW	*Economic and Political Weekly*
EXIM	Export-Import Bank of India
FAO	Food and Agricultural Organization
FCI	Food Corporation of India
FERA	Foreign Exchange Regulation Act
FPIs	Foreign Portfolio Investments
FYP	Five-Year Plan
GDP	Gross Domestic Product
HMT	Hindustan Machine Tools
IBM	International Business Machines Corporation
ICMR	Indian Council of Medical Research
ICSSR	Indian Council of Social Science Research
IIP	Index of Industrial Production
IIT	Indian Institute of Technology
ILO	International Labour Organization
IMF	International Monetary Fund
IRDP	Integrated Rural Development Programme
IS	import-substitution
ISC	Indian School Certificate
JCOs	Junior Commissioned Officers
LDCs	Least Developed Countries
LLB	Bachelor of Laws
LSE	London School of Economics
MASA	Maintenance of Internal Security Act
MBA	Master of Business Administration
MLA	Member of Legislative Assembly
MNCs	Multinational Corporations
MODVAT	Modified Value Added Tax
MP	Madhya Pradesh
MP	Member of Parliament
MRTP	Monopolistic and Restrictive Trade Practice
NAS	National Accounts Statistics
NCL	National Commission on Labour
NCOs	non-commissioned officer
NHB	National Housing Bank
NNMB	National Nutrition Monitoring Bureau
NRIs	Non-Resident Indians
NSS	National Sample Survey

NSSO	National Sample Survey Organisation
OBCs	Other Backward Classes
OECD	The Organisation for Economic Cooperation and Development
OGL	Open General License
PFY	Polyester Filament Yarn
PMP	Phased Manufacturing Programme
PMP	Project Management Professional
PSEs	Public Service Employee Survey
PSF	Polyester Staple Fibre
PSU	Public Sector Unit
R&D	Research and Development
RBI	Reserve Bank of India
RCSCST	Reports of the Commissioner for Scheduled Castes and Scheduled Tribes
RPI	Republican Party of India
RR	Rural to Rural
RSS	Rashtriya Swayamsevak Sangh
RU	Rural to Urban
SAIL	Steel Authority of India Limited
SC	Scheduled Caste
SDP	State Domestic Product
SEBI	Securities and Exchange Board of India
SEEUY	Self-Employment Programme for Educated Unemployed Youth
SGPC	Shiromani Gurdwara Parbandhak Committee
SITC	Standard International Trade Classification
ST	Scheduled Tribe
TADA	Terrorism and Disruptive Activities (Prevention) Act
TDA	Tribal Development Agency
UK	United Kingdom
UN	United Nations
UP	Uttar Pradesh
USSR	Union of Soviet Socialist Republics
UTI	Unit Trust of India
UU	Urban to Urban
WDR	World Development Report
WHO	World Health Organization

Introduction

Gurpreet Mahajan, Ila Patnaik and Surinder S. Jodhka

The *Economic and Political Weekly*, as we know it today, was born in mid-1966. On 20 August of that year, the first issue (volume 1, issue 1) of *EPW* was published. This was the new incarnation of the *Economic Weekly*, and it signalled an important shift in our understanding of independent India and the challenges facing it. By the 1960s, it was evident that the task of development could not be apprehended in purely economic terms. The dynamics of the political and the social had also to be analysed systematically. The processes engendered by democracy had an independent trajectory which could not be reduced directly to the economic or the social: the transformations occurring in society due to state interventions, political consciousness and technological changes had also to be included in planning for the future. The social was a powerful force that had the capacity to throw up new agendas and compel attention from the planners and the political leaders. The task of renaming the *Weekly* signified, in this sense, the coming of age of the social sciences in India.

When we began work on this volume, we wanted to present a snapshot of the issues that social scientists engaged with and the analysis they offered of politics, society and economy from 1966 until 1991. This representation of India which surfaced through the lens of *EPW*—a journal that occupies an unparalleled position in the intellectual history of the country—would, we believed, mark our journey to the present, giving us insights about the public and political life of the nation.

This was our avowed intention, but as we read and revisited the pages of *EPW*, issue by issue (50–52 issues each year), from August 1966 to July 1991, it was evident that this was an ambitious task which we (and perhaps anyone) could not hope to accomplish successfully. Every year *EPW* undertook a review of Management/Industry/Economy and Agriculture, in addition to bringing out an annual number which looked at the central issues in the domain of politics and society. Major debates on planning, development, mode of production, poverty measurement, caste and gender occurred in the pages of this journal, with contributions from scholars in India and outside. This is where Amartya Sen wrote about utilitarianism and inequality, poverty and unemployment; Andre Gunder Frank discussed issues of debt, economic crisis and social movements; V. M. Dandekar and Nilakantha Rath discussed poverty in India; and Rajni Kothari and Andre Beteille elaborated on issues of democracy, state and citizenship. Every number carried special articles that presented primary research, detailed micro-level studies were supplemented by macro-level analysis, ethnographic work stood side-by-side with statistical data and analysis. Every week *EPW* offered a brief account of the current social and political events, and for much of the identified period (1966–91) eminent scholars discussed and traced "roots" of a concept, a movement, or a policy proposal. The range and depth of scholarship was thus enormous, and we knew that no selection could do justice to what *EPW* offered.

Nevertheless, we had to take a decision on what to select. This itself posed many questions. At the most immediate and practical level we had to decide whether we should draw only from the pool of special articles or include perspectives, reports and commentaries in the selection. We then had to ask how much consideration should be given to various ideological perspectives; if debates rather than individual articles should be included; if the focus should be on scholarship from India; whether we should include discussions of major political and economic events from the world, from the end of the New Left in Europe to Reaganite politics. Eventually, we decided to give greater weightage to special articles as they offered detailed research and analysis, but we made space for other kinds of interventions to be included. Given the limitations of space, it is individual articles rather than complete debates that have been included here, but an effort has been made to bring in scholarship from different locations and perspectives. The focus is on India-related articles rather than commentaries on political events in the world.

These were the relatively easy decisions. In making this selection we faced deeper methodological questions, which were more difficult to settle. For instance, what was the purpose of revisiting the past? What should a selection of articles seek to accomplish? Should it be celebratory and present the most influential voices of that time? Should it be a record of the past, presenting a picture of the period gone by and an account of the issues that occupied the intelligentsia at the time? Or, should we assume a link between the past and the present, and see how the roots of the present lay in the past? Most of our discussions in the social sciences today tend to view the 1990s as a point of departure, which brings with it a whole new set of concerns: liberalisation, privatisation, rejection of the Nehruvian principles, secularism, urbanisation, migration. But can we pinpoint a point of rupture or do we see gradual shifts and changes? If we lean towards the latter, we could focus on writings that pre-empt some of our more recent concerns or identify articles that contribute significantly to our present understanding and discussions. However, that might leave out issues that galvanised the society at a certain time, but appear somewhat distant to us now.

Collectively and individually, we grappled with these questions as we made the selections for the three sections of the volume—politics, society and economy. As social scientists, we began with the understanding that we are located in history: we cannot escape the issues and concerns that matter to us in the present or the manner in which the past has been presented to us. It has shaped our sensibility and our intellectual curiosity. Yet, while reading the first 25 volumes of *EPW*, we realised that there is some difference between the present construction of the past and the writings of that period. That difference needed to be captured through the selections, and this could be achieved if we could identify themes that were significant for the authors then but had simultaneously the capacity to resonate with us in the present.

This volume, like the two others in this series, is divided into three sections. Although it is difficult to place the political, social and economic in separate compartments with tightly drawn boundaries, they represent three fields of inquiry, revolving around a set of core concerns, institutions and processes. In this sense we have worked with the disciplinary frameworks that shaped the social sciences in the twentieth century. *Economic and Political Weekly* was not, however, limited by these frames of thought. It included discussions around questions of environment, feminism, education, science and technology that pushed towards a more interdisciplinary perspective. But all selections are, by their very nature, partial and incomplete. Nevertheless, we hope that they will offer a glimpse of the scholarship that *EPW* placed before us and give us reason to fill in the gaps by returning to these older volumes for the knowledge they offer in the identified fields and those areas of inquiry that could not be accommodated in this volume.

POLITICS

The period 1966–91 was full of political challenges and turmoil. The death of Pandit Jawaharlal Nehru in 1964 had left a political vacuum. While there were many stalwarts in the Congress and several leaders who wielded considerable influence in their own regions, the towering figure of Nehru had been able to hold them together and build a consensus on major organisational and policy issues. His absence fuelled factional politics, and the full might of it was felt as the Congress Party split in 1969. Factional politics represented some of the social cleavages that existed in society but it revolved, more firmly, around personalities. The mid-70s saw the most tumultuous time in the history of Indian democracy. Prime Minister Indira Gandhi's declaration of a state of emergency from June 1975 to March 1977 led to the arrest of several opposition leaders and severe curtailment of the fundamental rights of citizens. But it also brought the gamut of opposition parties together (for at least long enough to defeat Gandhi in the next general election) and subsequently energised the civil rights movements in the country.

The 1970s saw the emergence of a new brand of politics and leadership: more centralised, personality-driven and "populist" in nature, relying heavily on the language of national security and integrity of India. Preventive detention laws existed in India and had been used in the first few years after Independence, but their use had been steadily declining. However, a whole new regime of such laws, giving extraordinary and special powers to the executive and coercive apparatuses of the state, was promulgated from the 1970s. The Maintenance of Internal Security Act (MISA) was passed in 1971, and the Terrorism and Disruptive Activities (Prevention) Act (TADA) in 1985. References to internal and external "threats" and presence of a "foreign hand" were common in political speeches and campaigns; through all this *EPW* struck a cautionary and critical note. India had been attacked twice in the 1960s, so matters of territorial integrity and unity were duly noted and reported upon. But looking at the research published in *EPW* at this time, it is evident that the Indian intelligentsia and the middle classes were not overwhelmed by security-related anxieties. Nor were they unduly preoccupied with the personalities and lives of political leaders. Instead, they reflected on issues that confronted India, brought them to the public attention, so that the promises made at the time of Independence were not lost in the buzz created around commemorations and political events.

From the late 1960s until the 1990s, two concerns dominated the discussions in the *EPW*: democracy and equality. These were not entirely unrelated concerns: democracy was the chosen form of government, representative and accountable to the people, equality was the normative principle on which democracy was anchored and the expressed value that democratic India was to pursue. Both these were related in the minds of the Constituent Assembly that deliberated on the Constitution of India, and in the issues of *EPW* an engagement with these twin concerns was articulated in a variety of ways. How was the Indian democratic system functioning? How representative was this system? How did the people vote? How were the candidates selected by political parties? What was happening with the system of "reservations"? Questions of this nature dominated discussions of the political and were, in a way, precursors of what are called election studies. The one significant difference between these studies and the more familiar media-propelled election studies was that they were not focused on predicting the result of electoral battles. These were analyses of elections, trying to understand the choices made by the parties as well as the people.

The working of the parties attracted a great deal of attention. Scholars tried to spell out the distinctiveness of the Indian party system: they recognised that India was not a one-party system, but could it be identified as a multi-party system, given the preponderance of the Congress Party at all levels of the federal system? If opposition to this party was weak, could India be characterised as a democracy? What was puzzling was that the presence of social cleavages should have thrown up new parties and a viable opposition. But that did not happen for the first two decades. So, how was Congress able to create a political, administrative and ideological consensus?

Studies of individual parties revolved around questions of their ideology, social base, selection of candidates, mode of campaign and strategies adopted for purposes of elections.[1] It would be presumptuous to offer a summary of these complex studies, but as they engaged with the mindset of the parties going to polls they revealed that winning elections mattered, and that parties were willing to go beyond their known social base by winning over other segments of the population, particularly from among the marginalised sections. Akali Dal, for instance, might put up a candidate from the lower castes to neutralise the advantage that the Congress had with this group in a district.[2] The relationship between caste and voting was neither simple nor direct, as is often assumed even in recent times.

Other institutional aspects of democracy—such as the judiciary, the role of the governor, bureaucracy and other local administration—also figured, but not as centrally as in other journals of that time. Since the role of the governor and interventions by the central government in the affairs of states was a subject of much political debate, the relative neglect of this is somewhat difficult to explain. What can, however, be said is that the volumes of *EPW* share the intellectual pursuits of foreign scholars working on India in the 1960s and 1970s: both focus on the working of political parties, albeit from somewhat different perspectives. The exchanges between these scholars raise several methodological questions that need to be considered seriously even though they are not pursued in their writings in *EPW*.

Foreign scholars began self-consciously with their methodological framework and drew heavily upon interviews with the political elite, party leaders, prominent administrators at different levels of the administration. The Indian writing on the same subject rarely quotes from this elite. One can reasonably assume that the latter also had access to this elite but they relied more on what day-to-day political events revealed to them. Living in a society, listening to the varied analyses and representations of what has happened, or is happening, also provides a basis of knowledge, and the Indian writings tend to lean on this.[3] Over the years the Indian scholars also shift their perspective: they offer numbers and statistics to back their assertions. They undertake voter analysis, region by region, constituency by constituency, and while this analysis explains the moment, the event under consideration, it offers limited understanding of the political system—something that had been the forte of the earlier writings.

A striking aspect of the *EPW* is that it accommodates diverse methodological and political orientations to the study of the political. Analyses of the party system, Centre–state relations, planning and administration mostly rely on the institutional (not historical or behavioural) approach; contributors analyse the Planning Commission, its budgetary allocations, proposals of the five-year plans, and the recommendations of the Finance Commission, to understand Centre–state relations and the working of the federal system.[4] At the same time, others analyse the nature of the state in terms of class formation and pursuit of class interest.[5] These twin approaches run through the issues of *EPW*, even after the Emergency. We have discussion about the legal and institutional changes that are needed to strengthen basic freedoms, particularly freedom of the press and civil liberties, published simultaneously with analyses that relate this period to the crisis of accumulation inherent in capitalism. We have, as a consequence, an indirect dialogue running through the issues, compelling the reader to consider if democracy (in its procedural form and as a form of government) can be studied in terms of the constitutional framework, existing independently of all other structures, or if democracy is a form of government that is sustained only when it is able to protect the interests of the ruling classes.

While these two discourses run concurrently in the 1970s and early 1980s, gradually it is the former that seems to trump the latter. Democracy is increasingly viewed as being intrinsically valuable, and discussions revolve around making it stronger and deeper. In the post-Emergency period, it is questions of accountability, greater participation of the people, the nature of grassroots movements and their involvement in the democratic process,[6] institutions of decentralised governance, especially panchayati raj, that occupy the centrestage.

All along, questions of equality are woven into discussions of democracy. The Constitution made provision for separate representation for previously excluded populations, so that they could be included and be equal participants in the democracy. What was happening in these reserved constituencies? How effective were the programmes of affirmative action? Were the Scheduled Castes and Scheduled Tribes adequately present in educational institutions or government jobs? The sociological and legal status of the Backward Classes had always been a concern in Indian politics, which was reflected in the contributions to *EPW*; and as the Mandal Commission recommendations came to be accepted, reservation policy became a subject of considerable interest.

There were two other axes along which the question of equality surfaced. First, in relation to discussions on poverty, existing economic inequalities, policies of land reform, regional inequalities; and second, in terms of religion, language, caste and gender equality. Within the latter, the issue of communal violence loomed large, and gradually women's studies and the feminist perspective surfaced as a sustained concern to which a special section would, from time to time, be dedicated. Studies on communal violence spanned a range of empirical and analytical questions. *EPW* was unique in giving space to reports on incidents of communal violence, and accounts presenting the voices of the victims. There were case studies examining not only what happened but how the people immediately affected or witnessing the riot understood it; along with such anthropologies of riots there was statistical data on the frequency of riots and theoretical discussions about communalism, as "false consciousness" or contrary to the spirit of nationalism. Some of these discussions were triggered by the Punjab crisis and how we might make sense of community identities and the hardening of these identities.

From the Marxist perspective, communal violence had been analysed in terms of clash of economic interests; on the other side, a deep cultural divide was projected as the cause of such clashes. The Punjab case could not be easily explained in these terms, and this prompted a relook at the nature of identity formation, including a fresh reflection on such a superstructural phenomenon from within the Marxist paradigm.[7]

The studies on communal violence were a reminder of the failure of democracy, of its inability to check violence and protect the basic rights of all citizens. Although glimpses of identity politics, of appealing to specific groups by selectively picking up religious, linguistic or cultural concerns, were emerging by the mid-1970s, it was not the framework within which political affairs were discussed in *EPW* during the same period. On the Marxist as well as the liberal sides, interests were taken as the defining category—albeit for the former these were identified as the interests of the bourgeoisie, the industrial class, the rich peasants and so on, while the others often spoke of factions and their group interest, organised lobbies and professional groups.

Discussions on inequality invariably brought together the political, social and economic. This was not prompted by any deep commitment to interdisciplinarity but was a corollary of the analysed subject. The links between caste and class, landlessness, exploitation and marginality, targeted central schemes and their impact on poverty alleviation, placed these three dimensions in relationship with each other. Together they offered a framework for evaluating policies and programmes as well as explaining the emerging violence and unrest in different parts of the country. They also made gender and caste relevant variables in any assessment of the social and the economic, and in a way, set the trend for research over the next few decades.

Thus far, we have touched upon the over arching concerns of the *EPW* (1966–91) that deal with what is most commonly identified as the political (the state, government institutions, political processes, policies, protests and movements). This is a limited reading of the political, and one could argue that all spheres of collective life where power is exercised, or negotiations occur, from the home to the workplace, a factory or a university, a sports club or art exhibitions, constitute the political. Indeed, there are a few articles that work with this understanding and write about what is happening in the science institutes or schools, to draw our attention to the need to democratise these spaces.[8] But, given the limitations of space, and in the interest of marking some kind of boundary, however fluid that might be, between the political, social and the economic, the first section operates with a narrower understanding of politics, and, to a considerable extent this is in keeping with the view that dominated the pages of *EPW* at that time.

This overview will not be complete without noting what is absent, and rarely visible, in the articles that were published during these 25 years. Since *EPW* publishes articles from among what is submitted it tells us something about disciplinary interests and paths taken, rather than a "lack" on the part of the journal. There is hardly any writing on history of concepts or engagement with the thought of prominent political leaders, even those who shaped the Indian imagination of democracy and the concern for equality. Gandhi,[9] Ambedkar, Tagore, Aurobindo, Tilak and even Nehru rarely figured, and their ideas remained unexamined during the identified period. Political affairs were discussed but not the conceptual imagination from which they emanated or departed. This has been, in a way, the limitation of political science until the last decade of the twentieth century. The discipline compartmentalised, with concepts and political theory constituting one unit and actual study of political affairs a separate part, and international affairs and foreign policy yet another. Theory entered obliquely through the question asked or debates identified but discussions of voting behaviour and election analysis was not linked to theories of representation or accountability, or reservations to ideas of affirmative action and equality, or panchayati raj institutions to notions of participatory democracy. Conceptual histories and textual analysis remained invisible; on a rare occasion they surfaced when literary works, such as those of Premchand, were studied.

It seems that the generation of scholars who contributed to these issues of *EPW* were consumed by the desire to understand the present. Perhaps they wished to make sense of what had gone awry, and why the commitments made at the time of independence were taking so long to realise. The idea that the failures and successes of the present had to be understood in conjunction with the choices we made—the conception of democracy and justice with which we functioned and the alternatives that were set aside—gained currency only much later.

Every discipline has a contextual history. The volumes of *EPW*, in a way, offer a glimpse of the disciplinary history of political science in India. They show how the desire to make sense of the present dominated over all else. Theory permeated this understanding, but the relevance and relative strengths of a particular theory were not directly debated in the journal. Normative theorisation did not figure here either. While many forums contained intense discussions around different isms—Marxism, liberalism, fascism, to name a few—these debates did not find their way into the pages of *EPW*. Perhaps political scientists had yet to find a way to translate their theoretical and normative formulations into the study of political institutions and subjectivities. Despite these absences, *EPW* remained the desired space for scholarly writing, reaching out to people of diverse views and ideological persuasions.

The eight chapters included in this section reflect the major political concerns of this period (1966–91), and offer an analysis that is relevant even today for understanding India. The first chapter, by Rajni Kothari, reflects on the changes that were occurring in the political arena. The year 1969 was an important point of transition; it signalled the end of one-party dominance and, with it, the consensus constructed by Nehru. Was the nature and functioning of Indian democracy going to change significantly now? Satish K. Arora examines another aspect of democratic politics: who are the decision makers in the Parliament? His analysis of the social profile of the Council of Ministers over two decades throws up some interesting facts about our parliamentary democracy. For instance, a sizeable number of Indira Gandhi's Council of Ministers were below the age of fifty (over a third in the first Council and almost half in the last two Councils), and in 1962–72 almost 40 per cent of those with Cabinet rank had never served in the Lok Sabha or the Rajya Sabha.

In a society marked by deep social cleavages, it is not surprising that different groups and communities align themselves with different political parties. And yet electoral processes have a logic of their own, often at variance with our common understanding of identities and political affiliations. Moin Shakir questions what is commonly called the idea of "vote banks." The votes of minorities, he argues, are not simply packaged and delivered by the community leaders. There are differences within the community, and electoral support may go to parties that are not perceived as being close to the community.

Studies that examine "who governs" assume, at least implicitly, that different groups and communities must be represented in the decision-making bodies. Indeed, the framers of the Indian Constitution shared this point of view, so they made provision for separate representation for the Scheduled Castes and

Scheduled Tribes—populations that had remained excluded and marginalised in Indian society. How was this system of reserved seats working? Were the representatives from these reserved constituencies striving to protect and promote the interests of the SCs and STs? Should the system of reservations to legislative bodies continue? Marc Galanter's chapter addresses these issues. It analyses the experience of the first three decades to elucidate the difference made by the presence of the representatives from these marginalised communities.

Besides mandating reservations in legislative bodies for the SCs and STs, the Constitution included an "enabling" clause that allowed governments to provide special consideration for Other Backward Classes in government jobs, and for socially and educationally backward classes in educational institutions. What was the outcome of these reservations? The chapter by Pradip K. Bose draws our attention to the intended and, more importantly, unintended consequences of reservations. Reservations were expected to provide social mobility to the marginalised sections, but what was not anticipated is that changes in the social structure would trigger inter-caste conflict and violence.

Relations between groups and communities continues to be a subject of deep concern for Indian democracy and its promise of ensuring equality for all citizens. The leadership that framed the Constitution hoped that communal violence that followed the Partition would have no place in independent India, and people of different religions and cultures would live together peacefully. Unfortunately, this was not to be. Sporadic incidents of inter-community violence marred Indian democracy. Gopal Krishna maps such occurrences of targeted violence, reminding us of the unkept promises of democracy and equality.

The chapter by Vimal Balasubrahmanyan draws our attention to the insidious ways in which women continued to be discriminated against in the public domain even after three decades of independence. The Constitution of India granted equality to all citizens, but women had to fight against existing social prejudices to make this promise a reality. To challenge customs and traditions that prevailed in the private and public domain, they had to organise themselves and seek judicial remedies. The chapter reminds us that the fight for equality is an ongoing one, as it involves challenging deeply held beliefs that have crept into our everyday lives and practices.

In the case of SCs, STs and women, inequality had a social dimension; it was a consequence of the social structures. Hence the Constitution included special "enabling" provisions for them. There were of course other sections of the population—namely, the poor—that faced deprivation on account of a variety of different circumstances. In the 1970s and 1980s, the *EPW* debated ways of identifying the rural and urban poor. Empirical data was garnered by economists to discuss if the poverty line should be defined through calorie intake or some idea of a well-balanced diet. Was the existing standard of calorie intake appropriate for India? Could some sections of the population with a lower calorie intake still be healthy and not undernourished? The discussion that carried on for more than a decade shaped the discourse on poverty and hunger, and it had significant political implications for government policy and planning. The last chapter in this section, by D. Banerji, intervenes in this debate to remind us that a narrow mechanistic reading, couched in seemingly scientific language, fails to understand the nature and magnitude of the problem of hunger and deprivation in India. While governments may be interested in reducing the numbers of those who fall below the poverty line, social scientists have a responsibility to focus on that which is conveniently set aside or forgotten. Without this input the project of democracy, of creating a more equal and just society, cannot be successfully realised.

Collectively, these chapters remind us that the pursuit of equality is never easy. Even when there is a normative consensus around the desired path for arriving at this goal, social and political reality throws up new and unexpected challenges. At the ideological plane democracies face the task of creating a consensus around what is best and desirable, but the logic of electoral politics makes that project exceedingly difficult. In all this, caste, community and region get invoked instrumentally but at grave costs to the involved subjects, particularly to women.

Society

In post-Independence India, the state considered the social sciences as technocratic instruments which would offer valuable inputs for realising the goal of development. The economists were to be the "engineers" of development, advising the national government and working out models for India's economic growth. Their place in the state system and the policy-making process was formally institutionalised through the setting-up of the Planning Commission by the Government of India in March 1950, just a few months after the country adopted its constitution and declared itself to be a republic. Sociology and social anthropology were expected to assist the economists in this task and help the state actors to deal with perceived problems confronting the nation and its diverse populace. Although this was the dominant perception of the state, social science scholarship could not be so narrowly limited.

The sociologists, engaged in the study of cultures, ways of life and norms that guide and shape a society, did not see themselves as mere technocrats, engaged in the task of restructuring society rationally. Those analysing the given social reality were questioning popular perceptions and received accounts of the social; and those who were persuaded by the need for change recognised that understanding the complexity of what exists is essential for prescribing what should be done. For all these sociologists, *EPW* offered a platform for articulating critical voices representing diverse realities of the new nation, particularly of those who had historically been on the margin, and discussing policy-relevant subjects from a non-statist perspective.

In the imagination of the nation, the "economic" and the "political" were the sites of progressive action and transformative interventions; by comparison, the "social" was often seen as a site of inertia, a source of problems that the young democracy had to deal with. In the newly emergent development-driven thinking, the "social" represented regressive traditions which had kept the country economically stagnant, politically divided and culturally conservative.

Even when the argument of colonial plunder was invoked to explain India's "backwardness," the mainstream nationalist leadership and the western-educated middle-class elite accepted much of the colonial view of India's pasts. Borrowing uncritically from the orientalist formulations of the region, they associated the "social" with "village,""caste" and "patriarchal family": namely, particularistic ties that were taken to be a hindrance to the development of a pan-Indian identity and development.

There were, of course, alternative representations of the village. Mahatma Gandhi, for instance, attributed a positive value to India's village and its caste-based division of labour; his notions of such "native realities" also drew upon the colonial and orientalist imaginations, which were of little value in actual policymaking. For example, the planners of India's future drew upon his notion of village community to initiate the Community Development Programme in 1952. They were soon to realise that the programme was not producing desired results because the rural landscapes in India were fundamentally divided in terms of interests and identities. The failure of the Community Development Programme was a useful learning experience.[10] While it did not alter the assessment of the social as the "problem" domain, it underlined the value of sociological work and analysis. It showed that planning for economic development could not be indifferent to the given realities of social life on the ground; if anything, it needed a more nuanced and detailed idea of those "backward" realities on the ground than that provided by the stereotypes and generic views offered by the available constructs. Thus, the economists advising the government lobbied for state investments in collecting statistics around various development variables. The research and evaluation wing of the Indian Planning Commission also encouraged and funded qualitative empirical studies of India's "village communities."

Independently of state incentives and push, a large number of young anthropologists from western universities, including some Indians, travelled to India's villages to empirically explore the dynamics of community life and its diversities.[11] Inspired by new disciplinary trends, they produced rich case studies of Indian villages. Sachin Chaudhary, editor of the *Economic Weekly*, actively encouraged these young field researchers to submit short reports from their fieldwork for the newly launched journal. Though the words "social" and "culture" do not appear in the titles of either the *Economic Weekly* or the later *Economic and Political Weekly*, both journals have been important for the publication of research by sociologists and social anthropologists.

The village studies, as they came to be called, turned out to be so popular that one of the authors, M. N. Srinivas, collected them in a single volume, titled *India's Villages*, which was published by the Government of West Bengal and Asia Publishing House in 1955 with its editions appearing from Bombay, London and New York. Empirical studies of village life and its dynamics have continued to appear in the journal ever since, including in its Special Issues, first as Review of Agriculture (from 1968 to 2011) and then as the Review of Rural Affairs.[12]

Publication of field-based village studies helped the journal to diversify beyond economics and politics. Through their detailed first-hand fieldwork carried out in a single village, social anthropologists were able to show how the ground reality was very different from the views of rural life popular with the urban elite.[13] More importantly perhaps, the publication of village studies in *EPW* popularised the method of intensive fieldwork in the Indian social sciences. The practice of undertaking field studies of a single village did not remain confined to the social anthropologists. Several economists undertook studies of the rural economy, many of which were published in *EPW* and have been regularly revisited by later generations of scholars.[14]

Publication of village studies in *EPW* helped sociology and social anthropology gain visibility in Indian academic life. Even though both disciplines had established their own journals, being in the company of economists and political scientists helped them acquire space in the institutional mainstream of the Indian social sciences.

The self-perceived mandate of village studies was to explore the demographic setting of the rural settlement. The village, for them, had a design that reflected the realities of the larger world. It was a microcosm of India.[15] With time, village studies gave way to studies of the agrarian change. Given that nearly 85 per cent of India lived in rural settlements, the Indian state initiated a wide range of development schemes and programmes directed towards increasing productivity of land and enhancing quality of rural livelihoods. The Indian State also intervened through legislative measures, including land reforms. The success of Green Revolution technology in select pockets pointed to some significant changes taking place in the rural economies of the country. The nature of changes taking place in the Indian agrarian economy and village life spawned many interesting debates in the *EPW* throughout the 1970s. While the economists took a lead in most of these debates, sociologists and social anthropologists also contributed quite meaningfully through their empirically grounded research work.[16]

In the period under consideration, the sociologists and social anthropologists expanded and diversified their research to other areas of social life, some of which had been completely ignored during the earlier phase. The gradual spread of education, growing mobility of various sections, the increasing reach of democratic polity (sometimes unleashing violent conflicts), all attracted their interest. Writing on these subjects, they diversified their methodologies to include surveys and archival work, and through the *EPW* reached out to scholars working in related social science disciplines, social activists and policy makers.

The chapters included in this section of the volume focus on the concerns that emerged during the period 1966–91. The opening chapter is a 1968 article by A. M. Shah on the Indian family. Through his empirical work and a reading of some colonial reports and other research, he questions the widely held assumption that the joint family was the norm in the pre-colonial period. It was commonly believed that the processes of change brought in by westernisation and modernisation and increasing migration to urban centres led to the breakdown of the Indian joint family. Using historical evidence, he shows that the size of a typical household during the pre-colonial period was no different from what it was in the 1960s. It had seen virtually no change over time. Similarly, the average size of an urban household was no different from its counterpart in the rural setting.

Published in 1969, the second chapter in this section is an extremely perceptive piece by Hira Singh on the emerging strains in rural leadership in a village of eastern Uttar Pradesh. Based on his ethnographic fieldwork, he shows how even after the abolition of the zamindari land tenures and extension of citizenship rights to all, the three erstwhile dominant families of the Rajput caste continued to monopolise power dynamics in the village. Despite cases of resistance from non-Rajput "lower castes," they were able to capture all the new formal institutions put in place by the state. However, their authority was not going to persist forever. They could no longer take their position of authority for granted. As their legitimacy was challenged from below, the dominant landed families altered their strategy. They aligned with other "upper castes" to hold on to their position in the rural power structure. Most importantly, Singh's fieldwork revealed that local power structure was on its way to acquiring a "pluralist character," where the erstwhile dominant members of the Rajput caste would have to share power with the aspiring groups. This indeed has been the case in most of rural India today. Only the degree of change differs.

In the context of the Green Revolution's success, the nature of economic and social changes taking place in India's rural economy became a major empirical and theoretical concern. During the 1970s, a diverse range of scholars passionately argued these issues in the pages of *EPW*. The next chapter in this section is an abridged version of a summary of the famous "mode of production debate" in India. The summary, by Alice Thorner, was published in *EPW* in 1982. As is evident from the title, the scholars participating in the debate worked with categories derived from Marxist theory. Drawing heavily on their empirical studies of the changes occurring in the agricultural sector in different parts of the country, they debated the nature of these changes, a conceptual framework adequate for representing these processes, emerging class relations in Indian agriculture and their implications for revolutionary politics in India. Could they now identify the dominant mode of production in India's agriculture as capitalist, pre-capitalist, semi-feudal, colonial, post-colonial or perhaps a dual mode of production?

Although economists took the lead in the early stages of this debate, sociologists, social anthropologists, historians and philosophers contributed significantly to it. This attempt to link various empirical studies, recording the changes that were occurring in the rural landscape, attracted readers and contributors from across the world, including the well-known Latin American scholar Andre Gunder Frank.

The chapter by C. Rajagopalan and Jaspal Singh, published in 1968, provides an interesting sociological survey of those studying in the newly established Indian Institutes of Technology. The authors used a primary survey to analyse the social background of those enrolled in these institutions, showing that no students belonging to any of the Scheduled Castes or Scheduled Tribes could find a place in the IITs. It was very similar for those coming from rural and agricultural backgrounds. They made for less than 3 per cent of all the students in these premier institutions. A large majority of the students came from the urban upper castes, Brahmins, and castes and communities traditionally identified with trade and business. The survey was carried out at a time when the IITs were yet to introduce mandatory quotas for SCs and STs and more than 80 per cent of the Indian population still lived in rural areas. The chapter raised the important question of who gained in mobility from quality education in engineering.

Among the most marginalised sections of Indian society have been the communities officially designated as the Scheduled Tribes, those who live closer to forests and often depend on "primitive" sources of livelihood. Even though many of them had been peasantised by the early twentieth century, they remained relatively isolated from the mainstream. The chapter by K. S. Singh provides a brief introduction to the manner in which the post-Independence Indian State evolved a perspective on making them part of the Indian nation while not expecting them to completely assimilate with the mainstream. However, their social life had been undergoing significant changes over time given their growing participation in democratic processes, access to education and jobs reserved for them, and their growing migration to urban centres in search of livelihoods.

The policy of affirmative action, institutionalised in the form of quotas and reservations in educational institutions, government jobs and legislative bodies, has enabled a section of the ex-untouchable, the Scheduled Castes, to move out of their position at the lower end of caste hierarchies to "secular" occupations in the state system. The quotas have also enabled some of them to become political leaders and members of legislative bodies at the provincial and national levels. What does it mean to be an administrative or political "elite" for a person from an ex-untouchable caste? Based on biographical interviews with members of the Indian Parliament (MPs) and of the Bihar Legislative Assembly (MLAs), Oliver Mendelsohn's chapter provides a perceptive view on the subject. He shows that while being elected to legislative bodies implies an extremely important change, both for the individual and their larger social context, it remains "extraordinarily difficult to be an effective untouchable politician in India."

Besides the STs and SCs, women have remained on the margins of India's political system. The 1970s saw an important new trend in the Indian social sciences with the articulation of the women's question as a subject for social science enquiry. Through an article published in 1979, Vina Mazumdar and Kumud Sharma passionately argue for recognition of the valuable role that women play in everyday life of any society. They also explore the "historical and ideological dimension of women's roles and statuses in Indian society." The article calls for the Indian Council of Social Science Research (ICSSR) to recognise the subject and incentivise social science research on women. This plea was certainly heard by the *EPW*. Beginning with 1985 the journal has been publishing Review of Women's Studies bi-annually. The review issues have become an important academic platform for scholars working on the subject.

India's religious minorities experience marginality and discrimination too. This is particularly true of the Indian Muslims. However, research on Muslim marginality had to wait until the turn of the century. Most of the articles published during the period covered in this volume highlight the cases of communal violence and religion-based conflicts. One of the most significant conflicts around religious identity during this period was the rise of the Khalistan movement in Punjab. Unlike the Muslims, Sikhs had never been on the margins. They also did not see themselves as being a minority in India. However, the decade of the 1980s was a period of "crisis" for the region, the community and the nation. In an important piece published in 1985, at the peak of the Khalistan movement, Dipankar Gupta discusses how "minority consciousness" emerged among the Sikhs. The violence in Punjab and Sikh killings in 1984 were not simply a "political crisis." He argues that they also needed to be looked at from a sociological and anthropological perspective.

The decades of the 1960s, 1970s and 1980s were also times when the question of population control had become one of the most pressing concerns with the state. India's growing population was seen virtually as the sole cause of all its problems. The chapter by Mahmood Mamdani provides a critique of the neo-Malthusian argument, which tends to put the burden of persistent poverty in a country like India exclusively on demographic explanation. Such an explanation completely ignores the historical and relational aspects of poverty, which lie in the regional regimes of political economy.

Continuing with questions of demographics, the final chapter in this section is by Amitabh Kundu on the patterns of migration and urbanisation during the first four decades after Independence. For demographers and development studies scholars (and practitioners), migration from rural areas to urban centres was not simply a matter of population movement but also an important indicator of the unfolding of a positive change, an indicator of the pace of development. However, the national level demographics of the 1981 Census indicated a slowing down of the migrations process, and the chapter discusses its implications. Kundu also looks at the interregional variations in demographic processes and presents them as emerging socio-political challenges for the development planners.

During 1966–91 sociologists and social anthropologists were also writing on social conflict, movements, cities and industrial economy, but these subjects become popular areas of research in the post-1990 period.

ECONOMY

Economics is not a single field. It includes the fields of industry, agriculture, the financial sector and exports-imports, to name just a few. Within these fields we have writings on manufacturing, foreign and domestic investment, small enterprises, research and development, power, mining and labour reforms, land reforms, irrigation, tenancy, subsidies, fertilisers, crop prices, minimum support prices and procurement, insurance, bank nationalisation, monetary policy, inflation, growth, interest, trade policy, multinational corporations (MNCs), exchange rates, foreign direct investment and capital controls. In addition, we have important issues relating to development strategy, poverty, urbanisation, tax evasion, decentralisation, Centre–state finances, federal structure and the tax system. Each of these subjects was fiercely debated in the *EPW* and some of the most thoughtful interventions came in the pages of this journal between 1966 and 1991.

Major contributions in each of these fields could not, however, be accommodated in this volume. Given the limitations of space, this section showcases trends in economic thinking during the identified period. India's economic journey can be broadly summarised as a highly intrusive state apparatus from the 1960s until the mid-1970s, the beginning of liberalisation in 1977 while retaining autarky, opening up to the world in 1991, and the quest for domestic institution building and state capacity thereafter. When we look back at the pages of the *EPW* in 1966–91, we see a fascinating journey of ideas about the economy. While there was a dominant traditional view that argued for pursuing the policies of the 1960s, there were those who questioned this, and their ideas fed into the post-1977 policy evolution. These could be found in almost all areas including agriculture, industry, trade, Centre–state finances, foreign investment and development strategy.

The seven chapters selected for this volume, among many more that can be found in the *EPW* in this period, question the command and control economic policies of the era. They point to the emerging concerns about the Indian economy and, in a way, lay the foundations of the reforms that followed later. They show what was broken, so that when the opportunity arose, policy makers could step in and try to fix the problems in the system. The debates that occurred in the pages of *EPW* on this and other related subjects were so influential that many articles have been subsequently published in other collections. The selection of chapters here presents some thoughtful statements on the Indian economy that were not a part of the dominant view of the time: ideas which infact appeared heretical in an era of socialism but are nevertheless significant, particularly as we look back from the present vantage-point.

We could have approached our task by asking which articles contributed to academic work on Indian economics. Instead, in the hope of presenting what has been at times sidelined, we asked which articles, and thinking, contributed and gave direction to the Indian economy in the following years. These were articles which shaped the thinking about reforms in India, influenced policy making and helped India move to a higher growth trajectory; they stood for opening up the economy to markets and to foreign capital. *EPW* provided space to all these differing voices of discontent, and this also needed to be presented.

The first chapter in this section is by Arun Shourie. He looks closely at the working of the system of state intervention in India. The issues he raises regarding the difficulties posed by the system were of immense importance in inducing India to change its economic course. It is today widely recognised that the frailty of controls influences everything that is attempted in the Indian State, from industrial licensing to financial sector controls to capital controls. This chapter remains relevant even after 45 years; it is indeed fascinating to note that Arun Shourie anticipated Anne Krueger's famous article on the same subject (published in the *American Economic Review*) by one year.

These ideas were supported in the 1984 article by Bhagwati and Srinivasan. They claim that inefficient allocation of resources has resulted in poor growth rates for the economy despite a sharp increase in the savings and investment rates during the period 1968–84. They argue that this is primarily due to failure of policy or lack of policy, most importantly due to a slowdown in public investment that affects demand in general and for capital goods in particular.

Kelkar and Kumar's chapter argues that government policies had tended to create a bias in favour of chemical-based industries as opposed to the metal-based sector, though the latter was more suited to the country's development objectives; it was more in line with the economy's comparative advantage and had a better prospect for international competitiveness. The chemical industries are process industries with vast potential for automation. Consequently, these industries while being skill intensive do not generate employment. The basic metal-producing and metal-based industries are relatively more employment generating and also offer greater technological flexibility in terms of factor proportions, which can be changed to some extent in response to relative factor prices.

Kelkar and Kumar propose a number of policy reforms. First, the incentive signals in terms of effective rate of protection, relative profitability and mark-ups in administered prices may be changed to become neutral or in favour of metal-based industries. Internal competition has to be coupled with tariff-based import policy for a wide range of industries, i.e., rapid removal of non-tariff barriers. Second, the share of indirect taxes should be brought down and their incidence on basic goods and intermediates sharply reduced. Third, the long-term fiscal policy needs to be modified so as to encourage savings by a further sharpening of incentives and moving towards effectively taxing expenditure. Export incentive structures need to be reformed so as to link imports of capital goods and intermediate goods to actual export performance and not export obligation. The exchange rate needs to be reviewed to follow an "undervalued" exchange rate policy. There is a need to provide a "free trade like" regime to domestic manufacturers of capital goods so that they can source their inputs either domestically or through imports. Excessive entry in new and emerging industries must be prevented. This can be prevented by facilitating exit of unviable firms.

The conservative positions on autarky were contested in the field of capital account openness. A pioneering article by C. K. Prahalad in 1977 unveiled the now familiar argument that trade integration and financial integration were not separable. The article demonstrated the dominance of MNCs in international trade and argued that it was in India's interest to welcome MNCs into India. It came out at a time when George Fernandes was ejecting IBM and Coca-Cola from India. Prahalad narrated how India operated its export drive with several disadvantages, while also possessing some under-exploited strengths. Additionally, Indian companies were miniscule compared with the enormous financial strength and size of MNCs, with the largest Indian corporation reporting a sale of merely $1.25 billion in 1974. He argued that Indian corporations, with an insignificant share in world markets, imported technology and made negligible investment in R & D; with quality management and support skills nearly absent, they lacked the financial strength or the freedom to move resources across countries.

Writing in 1986, Errunza argues in favour of gains for India by harnessing international capital markets. Errunza's chapter is more finance focused. He argues that there are overall three broad effects of foreign portfolio investments (FPIs): the development effect, the resource effect and the welfare effect. Under the development effect, increased FPIs would result in demand for more efficient markets by foreign investors and development of institutions; it would dampen speculative movements and imperfections in the market, thereby increasing domestic investors' confidence. Increased domestic confidence in turn would prevent capital flight, thereby augmenting total domestic savings and increasing net external resources, creating a resource effect. Removal of barriers and integration with the world markets would improve overall investor welfare. Errunza argues that tapping foreign investor savings would be mutually beneficial to both India and foreign investors and that the time is ripe to pursue policies in this direction. He proposes setting up of a task force with the directive to develop a long-term strategy that would facilitate portfolio flows into the Indian market under terms and conditions most beneficial to India.

In his chapter, Mujumdar asks whether the financial system should be developed by market forces or state intervention. He argues that there should be three phases of development of the financial system. The first phase is characterised by active state intervention with a view to building institutional infrastructure. This is because developing countries are in a hurry to catch up with modern banking and developments in money and capital markets; hence they cannot afford to wait for the spontaneous and autonomous growth of the financial system to take place. This process of hurried growth may give rise to some distortions and the second phase would be one of deregulation, rationalisation and simplification of controls, a phase in which distortions inherited from the first phase would be corrected. It is only after the system settles down to a new equilibrium in an environment of a good degree of autonomy that one can begin to think of the third phase of complete liberalisation.

M. Govinda Rao, in his influential article of 1977, reviews the performance of the six finance commissions of India in terms of fulfilling the objective of equity through federal fiscal transfers. Federal transfers are intended to be corrective for the differences in relative fiscal capacities and expenditure needs of the state. The commissions have various handles to achieve this objective—mainly assigned taxes, shared taxes and statutory grants. Despite this, the working of the finance commissions presented a dismal picture. Some rich states ended up with sizeable surpluses in their non-plan revenue account. In deciding upon the criteria for fiscal devolution through shared taxes, population was the predominant criterion. Rao argues that such an approach provides only a patchwork and does not consider comprehensively the needs of the states. The method for determining the gap between projected revenue and expenditure forecasts as adopted by the finance commissions is fraught with significant weaknesses. First, the states are not required to adopt a uniform methodology or concepts to forecast their expenditure, and hence the forecasts are not comparable across states. The second important weakness is that time is treated as the only determinant of the revenue and expenditure of states. A host of other factors—economic, social, political and cultural—determine the revenue and expenditure of states, and subsuming all these into a single variable may not explain the changes. Another issue is the assumption of price stability, which might not be realistic due to continuous increase of price levels.

The major weakness, however, was the fact that budgetary gap had been taken to be the bedrock of statutory grants. As noted by Rao, there was nothing in the Constitution that called upon the finance commissions to recommend grants to cover budgetary gaps. The finance commissions did not take into account the tax effort and economy in expenditures of the states as well as the level of public services provided satisfactorily while determining the grants-in-aid revenue.

The pages of the *EPW* in the years prior to 1991 show a vigorous Indian policy community that was deeply grounded in the practical realities of India, one which diagnosed problems and debated answers. Many of the persons who wrote these articles mattered in the translation of the reform ideas into action. As an example, Arun Shourie was a key person in India's privatisation process. R. H. Patil, Ashok Desai and L. C. Gupta (whose work could not be included here due to limitations of space) played a decisive role in the establishment of the National Stock Exchange. Vijay Kelkar led the Petroleum and Finance Ministries, and then the finance commission. We hope the selection of chapters can give the reader a glimpse into how this community shaped the direction and nature of the post-1991 reform process.

As the discussion above reminds us, scholars working on India and South Asia who have mined the resources of *EPW* know there is so much more that this journal has to offer. We had a mandate to choose around 150 *EPW* print pages for this collection, so there are many omissions. Yet, the chapters here may be a reminder of the value of *EPW*, of the range and depth of the scholarship on India, of the political paths pursued and the course corrections needed, policies desired and pushed for by people's organisations and movements—all of which made Indian democracy vibrant and strong.

Notes and References

[1] C. P. Bhambhri, "Ideology and Political Parties in India," *Economic and Political Weekly* 3, no. 16 (20 April 1968): pp. 643–46; Ramashray Roy, "Selection of Congress Candidates," part 1, *Economic and Political Weekly* 1, no. 20 (31 December 1966): pp. 833–40; Ramashray Roy, "Selection of Congress Candidates," parts 2 and 3, *Economic and Political Weekly* 2, nos. 2 and 6 (14 January and 11 February 1967): pp. 17–24 and pp. 371–76.

[2] Baldev Raj Nayar, "Religion and Caste in the Punjab: Sidhwan Bet Constituency," *Economic and Political Weekly* 14, no. 31 (4 August 1962): pp. 1267–76.

[3] Indian writings on India, particularly Indian politics, have often been accused of being theoretically naïve and methodologically weak. From the perspective of normative political theory as well as behavioural and post-behavioural approaches, this might seem to be the case, as neither of these frameworks takes the category of day-to-day experience, direct and indirect, seriously. Living in a society, and being even a distant bystander, listening to different views and events as they unfold themselves, produces a political judgement that can be richer than the insights provided by a short-term participant observer. This needs also to be factored into our discussions of methodology. In recent times we have recognised the value of lived experience of the concerned agents, but we have not sufficiently valued judgements produced by experience among members of that society, even as distant bystanders. The latter seems to have no epistemic significance; relatively greater consideration is given to the statements of the decision-makers. It is perhaps time to bring the category of "informed opinion" back into our methodological discourses—something that the authors of *EPW* did in the 1960s and 1970s.

[4] V. K. R. V. Rao, "Rationalization of Centre-State Financial Relations—Issues Before the Sixth Finance Commission," *Economic and Political Weekly* 8, no. 44 (3 November 1973): pp. 1961–71.

[5] Kalyan K. Sanyal, "Accumulation, Poverty and State in Third World: Capital/Pre-Capital Complex," *Economic and Political Weekly* 23, no. 5 (30 January 1988): pp. 27–30.

[6] D. L. Sheth, "Grass-roots Initiatives in India," *Economic and Political Weekly* 19, no. 6 (11 February 1984): pp. 259–262.

[7] Randhir Singh, "Theorising Communalism: A Fragmentary Note in the Marxist Mode," *Economic and Political Weekly* 23, no. 30 (23 July 1988): pp. 1541–48.

[8] Krishna Kumar, "Quest for Self-Identity: Cultural Consciousness and Education in Hindi Region, 1880–1950," *Economic and Political Weekly* 25, no. 23 (9 June 1990): pp. 1247–55; Dhruv Raina, "Commoditised Science or Science for Consumption?" *Economic and Political Weekly* 25, no. 40 (6 October 1990): pp. 2245–47.

[9] Gandhi figures more often than others, in relation to the women's question and to offer a critique of the Indian government's development strategy.

[10] B. Moore, Jr., *Social Origins of Dictatorship and Democracy* (Middlesex: Penguin, 1966).

[11] Following the Second World War, the discipline of social anthropology had reinvented itself by shifting its focus from the study of "primitive" tribes to researching peasant communities in the emerging developing world. See Andre Beteille, *Six Essays in Comparative Sociology* (Delhi: Oxford University Press, 1974); Sydel Silverman, "The Concept of Peasant and the Concept of Culture," in *Social Anthropology of Peasantry*, ed. Joan P. Mencher (Bombay: Somaiya Publications, 1987); S. S. Jodhka, "From 'Book-View' to 'Field-View': Social Anthropological Constructions of the Indian Village," *Oxford Development Studies* 26, no. 3 (1998): pp. 311–32.

[12] See S. S. Jodhka, "Agrarian Changes in the Times of (Neo-liberal) 'Crises': Revisiting Attached Labour in Haryana Agriculture," *Economic and Political* Weekly 47, no. 26–27 (30 June 2012): pp. 5–13; S. S. Jodhka, "Rural Change in Times of 'Distress,'" *Economic and Political Weekly*

53, no. 26–27 (30 June 2018): pp. 5–7; S. S. Jodhka and Edward Simpson (ed.), *India's Villages in the 21st Century: Revisits and Re-visions* (Delhi: Oxford University Press, forthcoming).

[13] The elite also likes to think of the rural people as being "ignorant, tradition bound and resistant to progress." M. N. Srinivas,"Village Studies, Participant Observation and Social Science Research in India," *Economic and Political Weekly* 10, no. 33–35 (1975): pp. 1387–94.

[14] See S. S. Jodhka,"Emergent Ruralities: Revisiting Village Life and Agrarian Change in Haryana," *Economic and Political Weekly* 49, no. 26–27 (28 June 2014): pp. 5–17; Himanshu, Praveen Jhaand Gerry Rogers, *The Changing Village in India* (New Delhi: Oxford University Press, 2016); Jodhka and Simpson, *India's Villages in the 21st Century*.

[15] M. N. Srinivas, "Village Studies, Participant Observation and Social Science Research in India," in *Village Studies in the Third World*, ed. B. Dasgupta (Delhi: Hindustan Publishing, 1970), Andre Beteille, "The Indian Village: Past and Present," in *Peasants in History: Essays in Honour of Daniel Thorner*, ed. Eric J. Hobsbawm et al. (Calcutta: Oxford University Press, 1980).

[16] A. Thorner, "Semi-Feudalism or Capitalism: Contemporary Debate on Classes and Modes of Production in India," *Economic and Political Weekly* 17 (1982): published in three parts: no. 49 (pp. 1961–68), no. 50 (pp. 1993–99) and no. 51 (pp. 2061–66).

PART I

Politics

1

India's Political Transition*

Rajni Kothari

The fourth general election gave an electoral stamp to the process of disintegration of the Congress system of power that had been under way for the last five years.[1] An alternative system of stable power relations, however, was not available when the need arose. Politicians on all sides had got so used to working under, or through, the system of one-party dominance and its internal structure of factions that they were all taken unawares when the curtain fell upon the old system and the need arose for a new institutional articulation. It is characteristic of transitional political systems that they change their framework of power without corresponding changes in organisational capabilities and elite attitudes. In the case of India, precisely because of the sustained development of one set of organisations and attitudes represented by the Congress system of dominance and internal opposition, alternative models were not adequately anticipated and worked towards. And this in spite of the fact that the situation in certain states had for long demanded from political parties, groups and individuals alternative strategies of conflict and co-operation. The reason for this is that a party system in a federal polity is essentially a system of vertical consensus in which regional constellations are made part of a national framework of power. And it is this dimension of our politics that remained largely undisturbed for a long time and even now has not been sufficiently shattered.

[This article and the study of the election to the Madhya Pradesh Assembly by R. Chandidas, which appears later in this issue, are sponsored by the Centre for the Study of Developing Societies, Delhi.]

* This edited article was originally published in *Economic and Political Weekly* 2, no. 33–35, Special Number (19 August 1967): pp. 1489–97.

An important consequence of this organisation of party politics around the Congress centre-piece is that the post-election political picture has found its major stimulus from the fragmentation of the Congress itself rather than from the emergence of any viable alternative to it, although undoubtedly alternative alignments have emerged in certain regions (like Madras and Gujarat alongside Kerala which has all along provided the country with an alternative model). Thus, it is noteworthy that in five out of seven coalition governments the leadership of the united fronts has gone to dissident Congressmen rather than to leaders of traditional non-Congress parties. Indeed it is difficult to see how the new alignments would have been possible at all without the fragmentation of the Congress monolith. Even the hopes of "toppling" the Congress government upon the availability of a Congress leader at the Centre who would follow in the footsteps of his counterparts in UP, Haryana, MP and other states. This fact of the fragmentation of the Congress party dominates the entire politics of the post-Independence era and has made leaders in the Jan Sangh and the Swatantra party retrospect that if only the Congress had accepted Mahatma Gandhi's advice of winding itself up, a "two-party system" led on the one side by Nehru and on the other by Sardar Patel would have emerged long ago. Seen in this perspective, however ironical it might appear at first sight, it is the shifts in the internal politics of the Congress that have shaped the political picture of 1966–67 and after. And it is precisely the capacity of the other parties and groups to influence the internal politics of the Congress party that had characterised the pre-1966–67 picture also.

Let us be clear, however, that the two patterns of intra-Congress politics—one before and the other after 1966–67—are of radically different types. The great watershed in Congress history, for long in the making, has clearly arrived with the fourth general election and has been stamped with nothing less than the verdict of the electorate itself, now fully reflected in party and legislative realignments. The process of realignment has clearly begun and will soon lead the country towards a new type of party system, and indeed in some ways to a new type of political system. All that is being emphasised here is that the transition towards such a new system is marked by a process of power that was developed under the Congress system not only in terms of the continuation and accentuation of the politics of dissidence and defection within the Congress party but also in terms of the personnel provided through such a process to the non-Congress combinations that have now developed into ruling teams in so many areas.

Congress Style Continues

So much for the continuation of old patterns of power in the emerging structure of Indian politics. One can go further. Even the style of politics initiated under

Congress rule is still very much there. First, not only is there more than one "Congress" party in so many states, there are also two (now three) Communist parties; two (in some states, three or four) Socialist parties; several fronts of the depressed sections and the Harijans; different tribal parties; the RSS extremist and the non-RSS moderate fronts among the Jan Sangh; the ex-Congress and non-Congress groupings within the Swatantra party, not to speak of the numerous splinter groups at the state level and the legion of independents which is on the increase in several states as well as at the Centre. Second, the "coalitional pattern" in the states consists of at least as, if not more, amorphous and diverse an assortment of groupings and policy positions as in the Congress. Third, the very attempt at forging a non-Congress alternative has led to a diversion from policy issues for fear of losing support of one or more constituents of the coalitional structures. This is the same "coalitional" and "consensual" style as was found for so long in the Congress pattern of politics. Hence the appearance of united front governments as "pale shadows" of their Congress predecessors. The most noticeable decline in policy positions is to be found in the Swatantra and the Communist parties which had boasted for so long of clear-cut ideological positions. Fourth, the attempt to consolidate numerical positions within the legislatures by weaning away members from "across the floor" is also reminiscent of the long-established Congress style of politics. Fifth, even Centre–state relations exhibit not a new pattern, as would be expected from the rise to power of different parties in the states, but rather a continuation of personalised and factionalised interactions reminiscent of the federal structuring of the Congress before 1967. Finally, already there are signs of considerable differences in approach, and consequently factional rumblings, in the non-Congress parties and "fronts" just as there were in the Congress—between the "organisational" and "ministerial" wings, between the state parties and the central "high commands," and between the Chief Ministers and other ministers.

All in all, then, there seems to be greater continuity in the patterns and styles of politics as well as in policy positions (or lack of them) than would appear at first sight. The somewhat different picture of West Bengal politics, explained largely by the internal politics and differences over political strategy within the communist movement, only confirms the general pattern. (It should not be forgotten that Bengal politics even under the Congress was all along characterised by greater open dissidence and fissure than was the case in the other states. Even the recent trend of all-out dissidence in the Congress throughout the country was pioneered by the actions of prominent Congressmen in West Bengal who, as early as in May 1966, split the Congress and organised another Congress party, taking with them considerable organisational and affiliative resources of the parent party. The "Kerala Congress" phenomenon, which began much earlier, was of an altogether different type.)

But the Framework Has Changed

Having made these points on continuity in the power process of Indian politics, we must return to the point made earlier, that the continuities are found to operate in a radically different framework of political organisation. The Congress system of power consisted not simply in the "consensual" accommodation of various groups and in the factional interactions between them: it also provided a single framework of power, a degree of policy commitment, and a certain measure of internal consistency and discipline which at the same time provided a "system" of politics for the whole country. While the former features may still continue to inform the present phase of our politics, the latter (the "framework") is clearly disintegrating; and this constitutes a major shift in the nation's political environment. It cannot, therefore, be doubted that with the 1967 elections the country has entered a new phase of political realignment in which the one-party system is being gradually replaced by another. It is not easy to "replace" party systems in a short time (as a "party system" consists of various levels of organisational and attitudinal consolidation), and hence the process of realignment appears to be fluid and uncertain. But there can be little doubt that the process has started and that we are launched into an era of transition from one system to another.

It is in this context of emerging political realignments that the contemporary problems of party defection, so-called "floor crossing,"[2] and the invoking of dormant constitutional provisions for dissolutions and "mid-term polls"[3] have to be seen. The attempt to moralise about these phenomena and even the various calls for "codes of conduct" among parties will not help in understanding what is essentially a dynamic and long-term shift from one system of power relations to another. It is the pain of this transition and the malignant symptoms that appear in the process—kidnapping of legislators and so on—that give rise to such moralising but the transition itself cannot be easily arrested by such political or constitutional panaceas. The country is set on a long transition through an unstable pattern of politics during which the whole system of parliamentary democracy is likely to be put to severe test and its image probably further tarnished. It is the "crisis of confidence" in the system, to which the Prime Minister has been frequently referring in her public statements, that provides the more disturbing aspect of the present process of change; the extent to which the crisis can be faced, contained, or submitted to, will depend upon the ability of the elite groups in society—including the intellectuals, the industrialists and the military—clearly and constructively to understand what is perhaps an inevitable stage in our development as a nation, and to assist the process of rearticulation on the basis of such an understanding. We have arrived at a stage when one can afford to be an optimist only if the agents of national development are willing to understand, learn, reassess, think, decide and do what is minimally needed. Political transitions constitute those twilight zones from where it is possible either to open out towards fresh thresholds of development or to get checkmated by forces of chaos and disruption. It is precisely at such a crossroads of development that the fourth general elections have placed this country.

II

What, then, is to be done? Before answering that question it is necessary to realise one important point regarding the context in which whatever steps are suggested must be viewed. The point is that the functional efficacy of Congress type of politics, described above, can no longer be taken for granted. As already argued, lacking the framework of power as well as the minimal consensus that the Congress traditionally represented, both the factional and "coalitional" structuring[4] of individual and group relationships, and the style that is sustained by such a structuring, may prove dysfunctional to the fulfilment of political and economic goals which are no longer "long-term," which have gradually taken on the character of pressing tasks, and which, if not fulfilled in time, can lead to serious disaffection and pose a grave threat. The crisis that faces the country is two-fold: a performance crisis—there is a minimum that must be achieved at all costs—and a crisis of legitimacy of the system which can soon take on alarming proportions if the minimum is not achieved.

There is no need here to dilate upon the content of this minimum; it is clear that it is essentially economic and administrative, but it also requires that a high level of internal order and confidence and external security be guaranteed. All of this calls for (i) a considerable strengthening of central political authority, (ii) an autonomous and non-political functioning of the bureaucracy and the economic technocracy (no matter what the political complexion of the transitional period), and (iii) a clear ordering of federal relations around the goals set by the central decision-making authority, the developmental bureaucracy and the economic technocracy (the councils of which must of necessity include the top leaders from the states and from other autonomous bodies who must be prepared, however, to adhere to a certain minimum level of discipline and performance).

This is clearly a tall order for any system working under the strain of an unstable political transition. It is futile to wish away the character of this transition; indeed, ways and means must be found to short-circuit it. Two descriptive hypotheses and a third corollary may be advanced to characterise different levels of this political transition. First, the greater the threat to a ruling party (or front) at the State level, the more its chances of breaking up. This is contrary to a prevailing generalisation on party politics and stems from the low salience of party identities and loyalties in Indian politics and the increasing blurring of party boundaries consequent on the breakup of the dominant party system. Lacking a clear clustering of individual loyalties around party labels, the tendency towards internal cohesion is outweighed by the eagerness to join the critical marginal force in a new alignment. Second, the Central Parliament will continue to present a site of considerable fragmentation of parties, thanks to the cumulation and aggregation of various state fragments at the national level. Thus, in spite of the narrow margin of the ruling party at the Centre over the combined opposition at present, the startling fact is that the second largest party in the Lok Sabha has less than 15 per cent of the seats of the first party (and secured less than 20 per cent of the valid votes polled). This is a very different situation from that prevailing in the states. Third, as argued in the beginning of this chapter, in a party system in a federal polity like India, it is the nature of the "vertical consensus" of the system that determines its character. Lacking any homogeneity in party positions between the Centre and the states, the decision-making processes of the nation are likely to be even less articulated and clear-cut between levels than is likely to be the case at either the Central or any of the state levels.

The Character of the Transition

The upshot of these three aspects—the state, the Central, and the Centre–state—of the current transition is general fluidity in political alignments and a low level of boundary maintenance in the party system. The "transition" could well prove wholly negative to the system, but if it is to be positive it must be towards a stable realignment of political forces. As already argued, all the other symptoms such as large-scale party defections and so-called "political horse-trading" are all part of this process of realignment, and the question is how to bring it to a stable point without undue social cost and indeed without great delay. For, if it takes too long, the solution of other problems—economic, administrative and the like—will also suffer, and the fact is that there is not much time for this. Thus the question, "what is to be done?" must be addressed essentially with a view to articulating this process of realignment and stabilising the new pattern for facing the urgent tasks at hand.

Constitutional Changes Will Not Help

What then, is to be done? Many suggestions have been advanced, ranging from a lot of moralising to a lot of "fundamental" panaceas. It has been argued, with some strength no doubt, that the need of the moment is for a "code of conduct" among parties on different aspects of political behaviour, but especially on arresting the present tendency of political defection and "floor-crossing." A variant of this argument has been a legalistic demand that all those who change their parties should be obliged to seek re-election as they are supposed to be carrying a mandate based on the manifesto of the party on whose ticket they contested the election. The question of the right of a Chief Minister to demand a dissolution when faced by "opportunistic" defections from his party with a view to toppling his government has also been raised and intensely debated. The difficulty with all these arguments is that, induced essentially by moral indignation against the phenomenon of defections, they do not examine either the cause of this phenomenon or the possibility of the different parties agreeing to the solutions that are advanced. The other group of solutions advanced calls for a basic change in the constitutional position: replace federalism by a unitary system, introduce a presidential form of government at the state level but retain the parliamentary form at the Centre, introduce a system of "recalls" whenever a member changes his party and so on. Again the question remains: how does one do this, by a Presidential fiat or by a two-thirds majority in the Parliament?[5] If it is to be the latter, how does one mobilise the requisite support? More basic than all this, however, is the point that a mere change in institutions will not solve the problems that have arisen as a result of the disintegration of the Congress system and lead to the realignment that is needed for political stability and administrative performance.

To me it seems that the only way to bring about this realignment is to force its pace by compelling the constituent units in the system—including the Congress—consciously to make their choices both in respect of policy perspectives and in terms of the national electorate they want to appeal to. This can only be achieved if the parties are forced to crystallise their own autonomous organisational bases, their legislative strength, and electoral viability, or to take such steps, alone or in combination, as would enable them to achieve such viability and strength. Even the consolidation of "coalitions" on a durable basis requires such viability—all the more if some of the political parties are to emerge as suitable alternatives on their own. There is only one way of achieving this in a democratic polity based on adult franchise. It has been the process of electoral competition that has articulated party bases, their support networks in the districts and the constituencies, and their mobilisation patterns in the various demographic and economic bases of society. And it will be only through a further election that the process of realignment, started with the fourth general elections, can be further crystallised and consolidated.

There is a considerable misunderstanding in the country on the role of elections in political decision-making. It is still widely believed that elections must be held only every five years, that there must be very special reasons if an election has to be held before the five-year "term" is over, and we (including the Election Commission) prefer to call such an election a "mid-term poll." This belief is held in spite of the fact that our Constitution prescribes only a maximum, but no minimum, period for either the Central or the state legislature, and in spite of the clear provision for dissolution of the legislatures any time during their tenure. This wholly erroneous belief has led to considerable inflexibility in the governance of the country, it has neutralised the ruling party's disciplining powers over the members, and has led to lack of decisiveness in the executive and to its considerable exposure to fragmented opinion; and above all it has taken away the system's ability to revitalise and restabilise itself through recourse to the people and above the heads of the narrow coterie of "politicians." The result has been disproportionate power wielded by legislators at the expense of governmental stability, party discipline and political conventions.

Speeding Up Polarisation

This perhaps gives the clue to one way of dealing with the present situation. The attention of political parties has to be diverted from legislative offensive and defensives to articulating stable bases of political support in the constituencies. There are some states where a high level of articulation already prevails: Madras with its virtual two-party configuration with the DMK well-entrenched in power, Gujarat with a similar configuration but the Congress in power on the basis of a smaller margin, Maharashtra and Mysore where the Congress system of dominance still continues quite efficiently, and Kerala where, over many more elections than elsewhere in the country, the Communists and the Congress have been able to articulate their bases in the various regions, constituencies, and even lower down in the panchayats and villages. Of other states, including Andhra Pradesh and Orissa, where apparently stable governments are in office, this cannot be said. Speaking of parliamentary constituencies, the Congress is still better organised than other parties, but has quite considerably weakened of late; it must put its house in order before it is too late. As for the other parties, the organisational task is still greater, but some of them have shown a remarkable capacity for sustained field-work and have in many places reaped the rewards of such work. There is no doubt that this process will continue and soon get better articulated with another election or two.

The problem at the moment is to expedite this process, to force the major parties to develop their legislative strength on the basis of genuine and sustained electoral organisation, to discourage legislative behaviour in vacuo, to weed out the marginal groups, and to hasten the essential processes of political polarisation, of a stable and homogeneous executive, of relative autonomy in the functioning of the administration, and of party understandings based on a clear awareness of one another's real strengths and weaknesses. Second, parties have to be forced to cultivate autonomous bases of power instead of relying on pockets of patronage and feudal or communal loyalties. Third, the electorate also has to be forced to realise the state and national consequences of their parochial behaviour and to cast their vote against such an understanding: the process of "secularisation" of voting behaviour must be carried further. Finally, weak and fragmented parties must be forced both to close their own ranks and, under threat of extinction, to merge with other similar parties. Although for all of these to be realised in full measure two or three elections will be needed, a considerable step towards them can be achieved by even one election at this critical juncture in national development.

CASE FOR AN EARLY ELECTION

What I am suggesting, then, is the need for an early election—say within a year from now—with a view to force the developments mentioned above in the various states as well as at the Centre. I would myself prefer this election to be nationwide. I would expect party positions to be consolidated as a result of the election; in certain states single-party governments may be possible, in other states coalitions will emerge but these will be coalitions based on more stable electoral positions and very likely on the basis of a Madras-type or Kerala-type electoral alliance. I would not rule out such alliances between the Congress and like-minded parties, and I would predict that what will emerge will be a better polarisation of parties with some approximation to policy perspectives rather than the present situation of "Congress versus non-Congress" in which the "non-Congress" has little in common within itself and its aggressive style threatens to take away the cohesion that remains in the Congress.

III

Holding elections like this involves obvious costs: there is the evident economic cost and there is also the administrative cost of gearing the machinery of government at lower levels to the tasks of holding an election. (The latter would, however, mean much less dislocation if the time between the announcement and the holding of the election were shortened as it must be if the dissolution is to serve its purpose.)

Consider, however, the "costs" involved in continuing the present state of affairs, with its considerable political fluidity and insecurity in office for various governments, with the consequence that a good part of the initiative and resources of political and governmental personnel is spent on maintaining individual and group positions rather than on pursuing bold and vigorous policies and implementing them, spending of parliamentary time on political offensive and defence rather than on urgent legislation and on legislative approval of executive programmes, and slowing down—in some cases stalling—of the administrative and technocratic processes of government. Even the Central government feels considerably hamstrung, acting as it does under the compulsions of both containing the tensions of federal politics and fashioning group and party positions to maintain a precarious majority in the Lok Sabha. As far as the state governments are concerned, they are found to vie with each other in "playing to the gallery" and aiming at short-term goals of retaining the support of all the marginal groups by resorting to such short-sighted and callous decisions as abolition of land revenue, irrigation cesses and urban taxes, engaging in irrelevant linguistic jingoism and other ideological confrontations, endangering industrial peace by adopting conciliatory postures towards strikes and *gherao*s even in critical sectors of the economy and public administration, and constantly precipitating a wage-price spiral in the urban middle class sectors and thus adding to the economic difficulties of the nation and almost bringing to a dead end the planning and implementation processes of economic government. Surely all this involves far more economic and social costs than forcing governments and political parties to seek their mandates from the electorate on the basis of alternative party lines and policy positions. The fourth general election did not do this for the simple reason that it was essentially directed to crystallising the first steps towards a new political alignment. The six months since the election have shown the lines on which the new alignment can be further articulated and consolidated, and only through yet another election can the process be crystallised.

More Stable Coalitions

It is possible that a single election may not do the trick; parties may not yet be ready. But it would ensure at least a degree of stability to the major parties and force them to approximate their legislative positions to actual support in the country. The Congress can hope to reap in this election the advantage of its nation-wide organisation; the major opposition parties can hope to develop autonomous bases of power in place of their present precarious grounding in drifting legislative coalitions. Indeed, even the coalitions—which in some states may be unavoidable—will be based on more long-term agreement and commitments on policies rather than on the questionable posture of simply "destroying the Congress." Coalition governments need not necessarily be unstable governments; indeed, in some countries they are found to be even more stable than single-party governments. But in order to be stable, the compacts on which they are based ought to have a measure of policy agreement which is jointly presented to the public; and these coalitions need not necessarily exclude the Congress, especially in regions where the latter is no longer able to offer a governmental alternative by itself.

Even the fourth general election and the months that followed have forged such compacts in some states: witness the remarkable stability of Kerala and Madras on the "non-Congress" side, and of Maharashtra on the Congress side where an "understanding" with the Republican Party has further consolidated the stability of the government. In Gujarat the Swatantra Party has emerged as a viable alternative government. This has not happened in other states and at the Centre, partly because the Jan Sangh, the Swatantra Party and the SSP were not confident enough of their own strength, partly because the phenomenon of Congress defections was not integrated into clear-cut patterns of realignment, and partly because the Congress itself was badly divided. The next election should provide an opportunity for consolidation of alternative positions and would take the process of realignment considerably further, thus providing the country with a much more stable governmental pattern. In Orissa the Swatantra Party's alliance with the Jana Congress may provide one united pole in a polarised situation. In West Bengal, too, a new polarisation may emerge with the communist and non-communist parties pitched against each other. In UP and Haryana, and probably in MP too, Congress versus Jan Sangh and in Bihar a SSP–Jan Sangh alliance versus the Congress may provide opposite poles of political competition. Other such possibilities in the various states can be discussed, but there is no need to do this except to add that such a consolidation will also get reflected at the Centre in the form of fewer parties of fairly sizeable proportions, thus making for a clearer alignment of political positions and policy perspectives.

....

IV

Finally, it must be admitted that whereas even the holding of a new election, and the stabilisation of the governmental teams after it, would take some time, the problems of the economy and the administration are rather urgent. This brings us to a proper approach to the question of evolving a "code" between parties. Here I would suggest that, rather than think of a code on party defections and "floor-crossing" on which it would be hard to arrive at an agreement, it would be better to direct the attention of an all-party convention to an optimal conduct of the institutions of economic decision-making and implementation, at both state and national levels, as well as to a Centre–state consultative apparatus. There is likely to be considerable agreement on such things as speedy implementation of certain immediate economic tasks, non-interference with the bureaucracy in carrying out its day to day functions, devoting more legislative time to government-sponsored and non-controversial legislation, and approval of the measures brought forward by the executive in pursuance of agreed economic policies, speeding up of unfulfilled projects and targets, and the setting up of expeditious devices of consultation between opposite parties for ironing out differences and misunderstandings. Apart from minimising the influence of "political" factors in the fulfillment of economic and governmental tasks, such a code would also bring about the development of a "climate" of consensus and understanding which is so vital in a period of transition from one type of political system to another. The consensus apparatus so astutely built by Prime Minister Shastri, involving all the elements in his own party as well as in the opposition and the civil service, is still recalled by many with nostalgia. The need for such an apparatus is even more clear today when the party system is no longer dominated by the consensus framework of even the Congress party. (Even within the Congress party, charges of arbitrariness and failure to take the rank and file of the parliamentary party into confidence are on the increase. This is ominous in the present context when political differences can easily turn into the threat—or actuality—of defection.) A code on regular consultations within and between parties, agreements on urgent tasks and their speedy pursuance, and non-interference in the day-to-day functioning of the administration and of professional bodies like the Planning Commission, should go a long way in mitigating the uncertainties and dilatoriness of the transitional period.

By itself, of course, such a code will not ensure results. Forcing the pace of the process of political realignment through an election is needed to consolidate the framework within which such a code is to operate.

Political Engineering

There are no "mid-term" elections in a parliamentary democracy. And there is no necessity of holding elections only at five-year intervals. Elections are a major instrument of both political legitimacy and efficient governmental performance. Parliamentary terms have no sanctity about them; indeed it is necessary to cut them short from time to time to arrest unnatural and unhealthy trends in legislative politics and to restore the proper framework of democratic functioning by confronting both political parties and the electorate with situations of real choice based on secular and programmatic lines. I have argued in this chapter that contemporary Indian politics demands such a confrontation and that the Prime Minister and the Central Cabinet will be well advised to hold another general election. The political stakes of the present situation are very high and only a decisive leadership can shorten the transition to the process of political realignment on which we have clearly entered with the fourth general elections.

Allowing the transition to go on too long and pursuing an ad hoc approach to important issues of political engineering can only give rise to mounting frustration, may well shake the confidence of the people in the democratic system and pave the way for political adventurism. The cost of the solution suggested here—a general election and a "code" for the pursuance of urgent programmatic goals—is very low indeed when compared with this other alternative which is slowly threatening the great political experiment on which we have staked our fortunes as a nation.

NOTES AND REFERENCES

[1] For a somewhat detailed analysis of the causes of this disintegration, see the author's "Congress and Consensus," *Seminar* 94, June 1967. The characteristics of the system and the conditions that kept it going were laid out in "The Congress System in India," *Asian Survey* 4, no. 12, December 1964.

[2] The term "floor-crossing" is borrowed from parliamentary systems with polarised party positions where there is a government and an opposition party. In India with a multiparty situation in most states and where defections are not confined to movements from government to opposition and vice-versa, it is a misnomer.

[3] "Mid-term polls" are an even greater misnomer. They apply to systems with a fixed legislative term and not to parliamentary systems where the term can be brought to an end by a simple dissolution. The fact that the Indian government has never objected to a dissolution and the further fact that in some states a poll had to be ordered while the Central Parliament was still in session has given rise to this nomenclature. Its continued use, however, inhibits thinking on parliamentary dissolutions, an important instrument for the stabilisation of Cabinet government.

[4] It should be remembered that even the coalitional pattern of the non-Congress parties (the Congress is yet another type of "coalition") is not like the traditional coalitions of Western Europe. The latter are essentially based upon stable structures of support in the constituencies and owe their fragmented character in the legislatures to a combination of a pluralistic system of franchise and a pluralistic network of support based on regional and ethnic diversities. Our coalitional structures so far, on the other hand, are essentially based on unstable support bases in the constituencies and a legislative patchwork resulting from this.

[5] In this case of introducing a presidential system in the states, the concurrence of half of the states will also be needed. Will state governments be willing to dissolve themselves?

2

Social Background of the Indian Cabinet*

Satish K. Arora

This study attempts to analyse the social composition of the formal political elite at the apex of the national power structure. In this attempt to draw a composite profile of those who have been ministers of the Government of India we have limited ourselves to the period of the last decade, 1962–72, a span covering at least some of the cabinets of all three Prime Ministers of the country.

The Constitution does not refer to the Cabinet as such, but to the Council of Ministers. In fact, however, the Council of Ministers is a rather large body which does not meet frequently. It is the Cabinet, composed of the prime minister and senior colleagues, which meets together more often, although pressures are such that even the Cabinet as a body is divided into elastic and functional groups to cope with the extraordinary and serious affairs of state.

To what extent may we consider the particular composition of a team of ministers as a reflection of the personal choice and orientation of the Prime Minister? Article 75 of the Constitution states that:

> (1) The Prime Minister shall be appointed by the President, and other ministers shall be appointed by the President on the advice of the Prime Minister.
> (2) The Ministers shall hold office during the pleasure of the President.

In practice, what really matters is whom the Prime Minister chooses. What other potential constraints operate upon a Prime Minister with respect to his freedom of choice? Political pressures are obviously in operation, but they tend to vary

* Originally published in *Economic and Political Weekly* 7, no. 31–33 (5 August 1972): pp. 1523–32.

from one Prime Minister to another. Lal Bahadur Shastri denied that any other person had a hand in his appointments:

> I can say without any disrespect to any other colleague that I have not consulted a single person in so far as the formation of my Cabinet was concerned. Even additions and alterations were my own. In the matter of appointment of Ministers of my Government I have been secretive.[1]

There are examples, however, which seem to indicate that Prime Ministers often work under pressure from among those individuals who are within or aspiring to the Cabinet. T. T. Krishnamachari made known his refusal to join the Cabinet unless he was given the Finance portfolio; when attempts were made to shift S. K. Patil from the portfolio of Food to Railways, serious objections were raised at the time; Manubhai Shah, even after his appointment, refused to take the oath unless he was given the rank of Cabinet Minister instead of Minister of State—although this was a case where the Prime Minister won out, and the appointee reneged a few days later.[2] But the constraints of one Prime Minister are not necessarily those of another, and only a careful analysis of the specifics of a particular political situation can permit the documentation of realities of this order. This chapter does not deal with these issues.

Nor does it deal with the issue of the Cabinet's powers. The locus of formal political power is not always, of course, a point where decisions are taken: not all important national decisions are necessarily taken by the Cabinet. A number of decisions, while attributable to the Cabinet, apparently have been taken either by the prime minister alone, or by the prime minister in consultation with persons and bodies other than the Cabinet. For instance, according to testimony delivered before the Lok Sabha by former Minister for Food and Agriculture, A. P. Jain, it was the National Development Council which decided to introduce state trading in foodgrains, as well as increase the food target in the Second Five-Year Plan by over 25 per cent: the concerned ministry had not been consulted on these moves. C. D. Deshmukh, upon his resignation as Minister of Finance, similarly decried the fact that the Cabinet had not been appropriately consulted with respect to the decision to keep Bombay centrally administered for a five-year period. He told Parliament that there was "no record even of a meeting of the committee of the Cabinet, and... no authoritative text of the so-called decision is available to the members of the Cabinet."[3] Regardless of this, one scarcely need labour the point that in dealing with the Cabinet we are undoubtedly dealing with the most powerful group of individuals in the state.

REGIONAL REPRESENTATION

Who are these men? And where do they come from? The first fact worth observing is that while 80 per cent of our people live in a village, less than half of our cabinet ministers were born in rural India.[4] Over the decade of 1962–72, the 20 per cent of India that is urban contributed slightly more than half of all cabinet ministers; and of these, almost two-thirds were from cities with over 100,000 population. Two ministers had been born abroad: one in Cannes, France, and another in London.

The degree to which the various regions of the country and the various states have found representation has often been a focus of concern. But one can overdo this type of analysis. While important—regional representation is certainly a politically relevant consideration—the composition of cabinets is, justifiably, subject to other compulsions as well. It is apparent from our data that, by and large, all important regions of the country have been well represented in the Cabinet (Table 2.1).

TABLE 2.1: REGIONAL REPRESENTATION IN CABINET, 1962–72

(in percentages)

Zone	Per Cent of Population (Census 1961)		Representation in Cabinet	
Central Zone	2.2		18.4	
Uttar Pradesh		16.8		18.4
Eastern Zone	25.9		22.4	
Assam		2.7		4.1
Bihar		10.6		8.2
Tripura		0.3		1.9
West Bengal		8.0		8.2
Northern Zone	10.9		10.2	
Haryana		N.A.		2.0
Jammu and Kashmir		0.8		2.0
Punjab		4.6		2.0
Rajasthan		4.6		4.1
Southern Zone	25.2		28.6	
Andhra Pradesh		8.2		10.2
Kerala		3.8		2.0
Mysore		5.4		10.2
Tamil Nadu		7.7		4.1
Pondicherry		0.1		2.0
Western Zone	13.7		22.4	
Gujarat		4.7		8.2
Maharashtra		9.0		14.3

Our data does not support, for instance, the often alleged domination of Uttar Pradesh: with almost 17 per cent of the population, it has accounted for almost exactly the same proportion of the Cabinet. It does not appear that the eastern zone, and especially West Bengal, has been grossly underrepresented; the northern zone is equally matched; the southern states are slightly over-represented; and the western zone is the most over-represented in the profile of the decade's cabinet ministers.[5] Another finding on the subject of the representativeness of our cabinet ministers is that with respect to the largest minority in our population, Nehru, Shastri and Indira Gandhi all appear to have acted similarly: Muslims have been represented in the cabinets of all in about the same proportion as they are in the general population. Whereas the 1961 Census figures indicate Muslims were a little over 10 per cent of the population, they constitute about the same percentage of the cabinets under study.

TRAINING AND EXPERIENCE

The criteria for selection to a cabinet position are obviously many and crosscutting. Thus far we have discussed what are essentially political criteria: the need to satisfy particularistic claims for power by various sections of the society. Inevitably, selection utilising such criteria will be rationalised by the argument that all sections require representation in order that their interests are not overlooked. But while this argument is probably valid with respect to the legislature—the very *raison d'etre* of which is representation of multitudinous interests—the Cabinet presents us with a different case. This body is the one institution which must conduct its deliberations from the standpoint of the national interest; the notion of collective responsibility of the Cabinet enhances the need for such an orientation. The power which resides in this body would seem to demand recruitment of individuals whose training, experience and personality can best facilitate the objective exercise of this power. It is to the distribution of these two qualities—training and experience—that we now turn.

By any measurement, the Indian Council of Ministers as a whole, and the Cabinet in particular, are probably among the most highly educated group of political leaders in power anywhere in the world (Table 2.2). Only 2–4 per cent of any Council during the last decade had never attended university. Post-graduate degrees were distributed among about two-thirds of the members of every Council and Cabinet under study: and in the last Council under study, almost four out of every five had post-graduate degrees. Looking at the Cabinet in particular, we find that at least half of their members have held, in addition to one or two university degrees, a law degree as well; and almost three out of four members of Indira Gandhi's latest Cabinet were trained in the legal profession.

TABLE 2.2: EDUCATION OF MEMBERS OF CABINET AND COUNCIL OF MINISTERS

Cabinet	No Degree (per cent)	BA (per cent)	Postgraduate Degrees MA (per cent)	PhD (per cent)	Law* (per cent)	N
Nehru	13	17	4	4	62	(23)
Shastri	23	12	–	–	65	(17)
Indira Gandhi (1st)	25	12	–	–	63	(16)
Indira Gandhi (2nd)	8	17	8	17	50	(24)
Indira Gandhi (3rd)	13	7	–	7	73	(15)
Council of Ministers						
Nehru	11	19	14	7	49	(61)
Shastri	14	20	11	5	50	(56)
Indira Gandhi (1st)	16	21	15	6	43	(53)
Indira Gandhi (2nd)	10	12	17	10	42**	(69)***
Indira Gandhi (3rd)	9	15	18	9	51**	(55)

Notes: * Those who hold a master's degree in addition to their law degree are included under "Law."

** This category includes one member who has a PhD in addition to a law degree.

*** No information was available for six members of this Council of Ministers.

The educational levels of our cabinet members are perhaps even more remarkable in comparison with the low literacy rates of the general population. But the gap between educational qualifications of the central executive on the one hand, and the national legislature on the other, are not very dissimilar: almost three fourths of the members of the Lok Sabha, for instance, hold university degrees. The fact, then, that the education gap between parliamentarians and cabinet members is reasonably narrow may be interpreted as an indicator of a fair degree of integration between the central loci of power.

Less than 30 per cent of the cabinet members received their training abroad; but it may be worth noting the countries in which they studied. Eleven out of the fourteen who went abroad attended institutions of higher learning in England, two studied in the United States, and one in West Germany. At least four received their law training at one of the London Inns. The London School of Economics has been often cited as the training ground for many among the leadership of former British colonies, but only two of our cabinet members of this past decade attended this institution.

DISTRIBUTION OF OCCUPATIONS

A glance at the distribution of occupations among members of the Council of Ministers indicates that members are drawn from a number of occupational bases (Table 2.3). The legal profession represents the single largest base; the proportion of agriculturists has remained fairly constant at about 17 per cent. There are also representatives from the teaching, medical and engineering professions. The occupational structure of the Council of Ministers is scarcely comparable to the occupational distribution among the general population; but as in the case of education, there may be some value in comparing it with members of the Lok Sabha. Comparison of Indira Gandhi's second Council of Ministers with the members of the Lok Sabha of the same period, for instance, reveals a great deal of similarity (Table 2.4). The most significant difference seems to lie in the representation of lawyers and agriculturists: compared to the legislature, the Council contained over 12 percentage points more lawyers, and 13 percentage points less agriculturists.

A comparison of the two bodies as presently constituted would appear to reveal a slightly different pattern. Although the evidence must be utilised with some caution, there is some indication that the gap between the proportion of agriculturists in these institutions has almost been closed (largely due to a drastic cut in their numbers in the legislature). On the other hand, the gap between the proportion of professionals in the two bodies would appear to have greatly widened, with almost 60 per cent of the Council of Ministers being drawn from the intellectual and professional strata, as compared to only 36 per cent of the Lok Sabha.[6]

Compared to the Council of Ministers, as a whole, the Cabinet reveals a striking lack of diversity in the occupational experience of its members. There is decreasing variety as we move through the decade of the 1960s, amounting to what almost appears to be a professionalisation of the apex by 1971. In the decade prior to 1971, for instance, agriculturists had made up between 13 and 18 per cent of the Cabinet; in the Cabinet constituted in 1971 we find an absence of agriculturists. In the latest Cabinet, the absolute number of lawyers remained constant, but almost all other categories of occupation were either reduced or eliminated altogether.

The strong domination of lawyers in our cabinets is not an unusual phenomenon. Cabinets in the United States and Canada, for instance, have had 70 and 60 per cent of their members, respectively, who came from the legal profession;[7] in Germany, whether before, during, or after the Nazi period, lawyers have constituted half of its cabinets.[8] The legal profession is often considered to be a logical one from which political leadership may be drawn: not

TABLE 2.3: OCCUPATION OF MEMBERS OF CABINETS AND COUNCILS OF MINISTERS

(per cent)

	Agriculture	Business	Engineering	Medicine	Law	Education	Social and Political Work	Journalism	Other	No Information
Cabinet										
Nehru	17	4	–	–	30	4	34	9	–	–
Shastri	18	6	–	–	35	–	29	12	–	–
Indira Gandhi (1st)	13	–	–	–	38	–	50	–	–	–
Indira Gandhi (2nd)	13	–	–	–	38	13	29	–	8	–
Indira Gandhi (3rd)	–	–	–	–	60	–	27	7	7	–
Council of Ministers										
Nehru	16	7	3	7	33	5	18	7	5	2
Shastri	18	7	4	7	32	4	14	9	4	2
Indira Gandhi (1st)	17	8	4	4	32	–	25	4	4	4
Indira Gandhi (2nd)	18	13	3	–	29	10	19	1	7	–
Indira Gandhi (3rd)	15	9	4	–	37	15	15	4	4	–

TABLE 2.4: COMPARATIVE OCCUPATIONAL DISTRIBUTION

(per cent)

	Fourth Lok Sabha	Council of Ministers (1967–70)
Lawyers	17	29
Teachers and educationists	7	10
Journalists	5	1
Engineers, doctors, former civil and military servants	7	3
Businessmen	8	13
Agriculturists	31	18
Political and social workers	23	19
Others	2	7

only are the talents required for success in this profession remarkably similar to those required of a minister—for example, the ability to argue a case (even if one does not personally agree with it), draw up briefs, persuade an audience—but also, law is one of the few professions which one can leave for a period of time and then return to, with perhaps even an enhancement of the chances of success in the vocation. It has thus been of mutual advantage to both the party and the political aspirant himself. Indeed, there have been a number of ministers, trained in the law, who only upon retirement from the Cabinet began what apparently have been rather successful legal careers.[9]

TENDENCY TOWARDS YOUTHFULNESS

In terms of social characteristics, perhaps the most impressive difference between the Council of Ministers under Indira Gandhi and those which preceded it relates to age. Only about a quarter of Nehru's as well as Shastri's last Councils were below fifty years of age. Indira Gandhi's first Council contained over a third below the age of fifty; over half the members of the last two of her Councils were under fifty.

As might be expected, in comparison with cabinet ministers, and even ministers of state, deputy ministers in all Councils have tended to be considerably younger. This is especially the case under Indira Gandhi. Over a third of the deputy ministers in Indira Gandhi's last Council were appointed in their thirties.

The pattern of age distribution of the Cabinets is considerably different from that of the Councils. Even in Indira Gandhi's last Cabinet under study—and the youngest—there were no ministers below 40.

The overall age distribution of Cabinets and Councils is, in general, of limited value in helping us to understand the nature of these bodies, because this factor is intimately related to the degree of turnover within these bodies. Obviously the longer the duration of a minister's tenure, the older each Cabinet will tend to become; this is an important factor when one party has remained dominant throughout a quarter of a century. The fact that Indira Gandhi's appointees appear younger than those preceding them is then all the more significant.

A more useful measure may be the age at which members first enter the Council. This data clearly demonstrates the propensity of the present Prime Minister to recruit younger personnel. If one looks only at the Council of Ministers, we find a substantial increase in recruitment of lower ranking ministers who are below the age of fifty; they constituted less than half of the Councils under Nehru and Shastri; but almost 70 per cent of Indira Gandhi's third Council. Even with respect to the Cabinet, the proportion which has entered below the age of forty has doubled since Shastri's time.

A tendency toward youthfulness in the highest offices of the land may be of significance in terms of policy which such a body is likely to make. But it also signifies something more. It gives an indication of how long a future such individuals are likely to have: given normal turnover, and continuation in power of the Congress party over a long period of time, it might be predicted that some optimum point will be reached when cabinets may tend to get older. The youthfulness of a Cabinet also gives us an idea of the degree of openness within a party: advancement to the highest echelons these days may not completely hinge upon seniority alone, but may reflect rather the operation of factors, such as exceptional talent and political capabilities demonstrated within the various levels of the political hierarchy, and even outside of it.

In general, when compared with some nations for whom data is available, Indian cabinets appear rather on the older side (Table 2.5). It should be noted,

TABLE 2.5: INTERNATIONAL COMPARISON OF AGE OF FIRST ENTRY TO CABINET*

(per cent)

Nation	30–39	40–49	50–59	60 plus
India (1962–72)	2	22	47	29
United States (1900–58)	1	33	37	28
Canada (1946–57)	5	43	34	18
Great Britain (1922–60)	7	26	46	21
France (1947–58)	13	42	38	7
Australia (1946–57)	11	48	37	4

Source: * Data for United States, Canada, Great Britain, France and Australia is based on data in Joseph A. Schlesinger, "Political Careers and Party Leadership," in *Political Leadership in Industrialised Societies: Studies in Comparative Analysis*, ed. Lewis J. Edinger (New York: John Wiley and Sons, 1967), p. 289.

however, that the Indian data utilised is the average age over the decade; as we have already noted, there is a distinct trend in the direction away from patriarchism. The span of years considered for cabinets in countries other than India also seems dated in some cases, and covers different periods. In fact one wonders if cabinets of the world may be moving in a younger direction. To establish this, of course, would require further research on a cross-national basis.

ROUTES TO THE CABINET

In a Parliament system, the Constitution requires that cabinet members belong to the Parliament. The expectation usually is that a Cabinet is constituted primarily from among those already serving in Parliament and especially in the directly elected lower house. This appears to be the case for several parliamentary systems.[10] But it is not quite the case for India (Table 2.6). Indeed, we find that only 12 per cent of the ministers of the cabinets under study were directly recruited from the pool of ordinary members of the Lok Sabha; another 12 per cent came directly from the Rajya Sabha. Does the route to the Cabinet lie more via a career line stemming from service as deputy minister or minister of state? The answer is that this is the case for only about one out of every three cabinet ministers. Perhaps the most significant finding is that over 40 per cent arrive at Cabinet rank without ever having served in either the Lok Sabha or the Rajya Sabha.

TABLE 2.6: ROUTES TO THE CABINET, 1962–72

	Recruitment Source	Cabinet Members N = 49 (per cent)
(1)	Promotion from ranks of Council of Ministers	32.6
(2)	Directly from Parliament	24.4
	(a) Lok Sabha (12.2)	
	(b) Rajya Sabha (12.2)	
(3)	Outside Parliament and the Council of Ministers	42.9

For the earlier periods of independent India, this situation would be logical since cabinets were in existence before an elected Parliament was constituted. Indeed, Prime Minister Nehru himself had never served at any level of government higher than the Allahabad Municipal Council prior to his Prime Ministership; so indeed was the case with most of his colleagues. Overtime, however, the expectation would be that the earlier, and necessarily unique, situation would be substantially reversed. Our data for 1962–72 illustrating the main routes to membership in the Cabinet must be understood in light of the fact that the first elected Parliament dates only from 1952.

Apparently, Prime Ministers' talent hunts continue to go beyond the Lok and Rajya Sabhas; cabinet members continue to be inducted into the national legislature after rather than prior to their selection by Prime Ministers. They may be recruited from among political leaders from the states, or they may originate from outside regular political institutions. The basic point here is that the net of recruitment to cabinet office is cast wide and the selection process has sufficient flexibility to induct talent from a nationwide base rather than only the two houses of the Parliament.

Cutting across the now conventional categories of developed and developing nations is the central problem of political leadership. Even when the various indices for measuring polities have been utilised, and nations have been arranged along continuums of various sorts, the qualitative dimensions of leadership seem to be of crucial significance. Because policies are available within certain ranges, it has always been important to gain insight into what kinds of men of power are likely to opt for what kinds of policy options. Those concerned with sociopolitical analysis have been intrigued by the intractability of this problem; analysts from the polar extremes of psychoanalysis and Marxism have continued to demonstrate the importance of understanding the personal autobiography and class position of those at the levers of power.

In the area of our concern, several basically unanswered questions remain. One is: Can we possibly predict anything about the opinions, attitudes and, ultimately, behaviour of political elites from an understanding—however comprehensive—of their social background? Or, put in less ambitious terms, does an analysis of the social composition of elites, at any political level, guide us in any way as to their likely intentions and actions? This problem of the validity of inferring future and present behavioural patterns from what are essentially static data from the past remains what it has been so far—a problem.

Our purpose is a more modest one. We have merely addressed ourselves to providing a partial answer to the question: Who governs? Answers to this question may take a variety of descriptive forms. What they reveal can be of only limited utility if they are presented for a single point in time, or for only a particular level of leadership. The value of social background data depends upon the degree to which such data is available over significant spans of time, and for the various rungs of the national pyramids of social and political power. Social background data are less useful as snapshots; their significance is revealed when the notion of time has been captured, and the comparative dimension utilised.

Another basic question is: Can the composition of the political elite at the apex of the national power pyramid be related to the social structure of a nation, especially when the data is as limited as what we have presented here? It would appear that even when the range of background data is more comprehensive and wide-ranging than our Indian data are, inter-state and intra-state differences are elusive. One carefully done analysis concludes that in both Great Britain and the United States "those ranking near the top of the society's system of stratification possess the best political opportunities." The certitude of this finding must, however, be confronted with the same study's conclusion that: "Paradoxically the more rigid and inegalitarian British society seems to have a larger proportion of the working class in positions of political authority than the more mobile and open society of the United States."[11]

SOCIOPOLITICAL STRUCTURE

Yet, perhaps it is possible to understand shifts in the sociopolitical structure through an analysis of elite social background data, provided the range of the data is sufficiently large to record transition periods, and the analytical arrangement of this data is sufficiently imaginative. Let us consider examples from two different societies. In Great Britain, while representatives of the aristocracy in cabinet ranks declined by only 6 per cent between the periods 1868–86 and 1935–55, working class representation increased from zero to 21 per cent.[12] Data since 1955 would perhaps equally forcefully illustrate the changes in the curves of power.

Consider now Germany, an even more impressive example of the kind of politically relevant data that can emerge from an analysis of the political apex. The counter-revolutionary character of the Nazi regime emerges vividly from an examination of the trend data on the social class composition of German cabinets for the period 1890 to 1945: in spite of the German National Socialist Party's vigorous propaganda to the contrary, the increasing trends towards egalitarianism in the German political elite were in fact reversed by the Nazis (Table 2.7).

TABLE 2.7: CLASS BACKGROUND OF THE GERMAN CABINET

(per cent)

Class	Monarchy 1890–1933	Republic 1918–1933	Nazi 1933–1945
Aristocracy	64.5	11.5	27
Middle Class	35.5	78	70
Working Class	0	11	3

Source: Donald R. Mathews, *The Social Background of Political Decision-Makers* (New York: Doubleday, 1954), p. 49.

Does our Indian data illustrate any such lessons? Even such limited data as we have presented here illustrates the homogeneity which continues to characterise the members of our cabinets, and distinguishes them from the greater part of our population. But the available data is still far too limited with respect to time period, scope and depth. Some of the needs for further research are clear: for instance, we need to acquire more information about the parental background of our cabinet ministers—information seldom contained in the standard biographical references relied upon for this study. We also need to structure data over a longer time period, despite the fact that the formal structure of our democracy is young.

Discussion of the social composition of elites can take us still further; for when the descriptive profiles of social reality—and especially the reality of leadership—are linked to the normative concerns of democratic theory, other enduring questions open up before us. Chief among these are those that pertain to political life chances: who in fact ought to lead; and to what extent can, or should, the closing of the elite–mass gap be of continuing concern to political leaders, theorists and citizens.

Notes and References

[1] Quoted in R. J. Venkateswaran, *Cabinet Government in India* (London: George Allen and Unwin, 1967), p. 141.

[2] Ibid., pp. 59–60.

[3] Quoted in ibid., pp. 82–83.

[4] Most of the data regarding social background is derived from Lok Sabha and Rajya Sabha *Who's Whos*, and is supplemented by material from newspapers. Members of two bodies are considered: (1) the Cabinet, consisting only of ministers of cabinet rank; and (2) the Council of Ministers, consisting of cabinet ministers as well as ministers of state and deputy ministers. Data pertaining to members of the following units is presented (classified according to the prime minister in power at the time):

Unit and Duration

(a) Jawaharlal Nehru 10-4-1962–27-5-1964
(b) Lal Bahadur Shastri 9-6-1964–11-1-1966
(c) Indira Gandhi (1st) 24-1-1966–3-3-1967
(d) Indira Gandhi (2nd) 13-3-1967–27-12-1970
(e) Indira Gandhi (3rd) 23-3-1971–1-7-1972

Each unit consists of *all* individuals who entered it—for however brief a period, and regardless of the date of entry—within the duration cited.

The two new cabinet ministers appointed in the second half of July 1972—D. P. Dhar and T. A. Pai—were not included in the analysis of Indira Gandhi's third cabinet, since insufficient data was available at the time of writing this chapter.

[5] The zonal divisions are derived from the classification followed in the 1961 Census.

[6] In contrast to the statistics on the composition of the Fourth Lok Sabha, which are from *Lok Sabha Souvenir, 1967–70* (New Delhi, 1971), data on the Fifth Lok Sabha is based only on an 80 per cent sample of its members, published by *Times of India,* 31 March 1971.

[7] Data on Canada and the United States is derived from Rosalio Wences, "Electoral Participation and the Occupational Composition of Cabinets and Parliaments," *American Journal of Sociology* 75, no. 2 (September 1969), p. 185.

[8] Ralf Dahrendorf, *Society and Democracy in Germany* (London: Doubleday, 1967), p. 234.

[9] *Times of India*, 27 July 1972.

[10] Joseph A. Schlesinger, "Political Careers and Party Leadership," in *Political Leadership in Industrialised Societies: Studies in Comparative Analysis*, ed. Lewis J. Edinger (New York: John Wiley and Sons, 1967), p. 287.

[11] Donald R. Mathews, *The Social Background of Political Decision-Makers* (New York: Doubleday, 1954).

[12] Ibid.

3

Electoral Participation of Minorities and Indian Political System*

Moin Shakir

The victory of Indira Gandhi in the recent Lok Sabha polls is attributed to the solid support extended to her by the minorities all over the country. Earlier, in 1971 and in 1977, the minority vote to a great extent decided the outcome of the Lok Sabha polls. Social scientists have been trying to offer plausible explanation of this phenomenon. If the minorities' vote is of such critical importance, what is the significance of the majority vote? Why does the majority vote not determine the final result of the elections? What is the profile of the majority voter and a minority voter? Before we answer these questions, let us ask who the minorities are and who forms the majority in this country.

India, as any other country, has no perfectly homogeneous population. It is, therefore, essential to make an effort to achieve cohesion and unity and introduce common symbols of identity among the various segments of the population. If the people are of a mixed character, there are bound to be social differences, ethnic or cultural variations, political discords, economic rivalries and historical antagonisms. The minorities are the product of this situation. There is no sovereign remedy to eliminate the majority-minority problem in order to bring about a uniform pattern of thinking and behaviour. One way is to live with these differences and see that they do not lead to the disintegration of society.

In the context of nation-building, the problem of minorities is at the centre of politics and it cannot be tackled piecemeal and without a definite perspective.

* Originally published in *Economic and Political Weekly* 15, no. 5–7, Annual Number (16 February 1980): pp. 221–26.

The problems of the minorities are the problems of particular sections of the Indian people. They are considered to be minorities because they perceive themselves as minorities. Really speaking, they constitute a notional category. From the standpoint of theory no concept of a "minority" and a "majority" is tenable. No definition of "minority" can be taken as wholly satisfactory. Those who constitute less than 50 per cent should be called a minority. But the difficulties arise when one asks the question, 50 per cent of what? In India, the Hindus are a "majority," since they constitute 82.72 per cent of the total population. But they are not a majority in Jammu and Kashmir, Punjab and Nagaland, where Muslims, Sikhs and Christians constitute more than 50 per cent of the total population. Besides, the so-called Hindu society is characterised by fragmentation, rigid stratification and hierarchy. The vertical and horizontal divisions of the Indian social structure show that the "majority" and the "minority" are both fictitious. As a polyglot country India displays a diversity of religion and culture. Fortunately or unfortunately, there is no all-India language or all-India culture. Owing to these diversities and some subjective perceptions, a section of people may choose to be a "minority," a nationality, a nation, a sub-nation or a ritually superior group. This is not to deny the existence or the validity of the minority groups as the Hindu chauvinists do; on the contrary, it may be argued that India is a "confederation of minorities" and a conglomeration of different communities and sub-communities.

One should also take into account the wrong assumptions about the well-knit character of the so-called minority groups. The fact is that every minority is divided, socially, politically and economically. Take the example of the Muslim community. It consists of a number of sub-communities and small fanatic groups. Apart from the Shia and Sunni sects there are many prominent groups like the Bohras, the Khojas, the Memons, etc. The same is the case with the Scheduled Castes (SCs) and the Scheduled Tribes (STs), and other minorities. The social and economic divisions in these minorities are bound to be expressed in different and conflicting political postures. But the problems of minorities like the Parsis, the Jains or even the Sikhs are different from those of the SCs, STs and the Muslims, an overwhelming majority of whom are deprived and impoverished. In fact, in the Indian context these are the core minorities.

The SCs, STs and the Muslims constitute (according to the 1971 Census) 14.60 per cent, 6.90 per cent and 11.21 per cent of the total population, respectively. One wonders as to how 32.71 per cent of the total population is instrumental in determining the fate of any political party in the elections. The political scientists have been arguing that these minorities, in practically every election, cast their votes en bloc. Their vote, therefore, is communal and casteist. What is wanting in this argument is the analysis of the reasons for such block voting and a national perspective. (Even before 1967, these minorities in

Kerala and West Bengal have been supporting leftist and non-Congress fronts.) It should be noted that unlike the STs, the SCs and the Muslims are scattered all over the country. There are constituencies where the Muslims form more than 50 per cent of the voters but this is not the case with the SCs. Then there are no reserved seats for the Muslims.

It is strange but true that the leadership of these minorities is invariably in the hands of selfish persons. This is an important aspect of the electoral and political behaviour of the minority voter. Here it should be emphasised that the votes of the minorities are not purchased as is generally believed. The experience of the elections of 1971, 1977 and 1980 bears it out. Not that the candidate or the party leaders do not give money; but it is given to the local leaders and not to the voter. In fact there has always been a gap between the voters and the vote "contractors." There has been no correlation between the promises made by these "contractors" and the voting behaviour of the common man. The voting pattern of the minority communities' voters is determined by their limited perception and certain concrete situations—security of life and property, and bread-and-butter issues. In 1977 such issues made them vote against the Congress party. The programmes of forcible sterilisation, demolition of huts and houses under the guise of beautification, rising prices and the scarcity of the essential commodities adversely affected poor sections in general and the minority communities in particular. The permanentally of the minority communities is the rural and urban poor who perhaps think and act with the minority voter on a similar wavelength.

The Janata rule did not provide any relief to these minority groups. The party, in practice, has been the party of traders, former zamindars and the kulaks who are the exploiters of the SCs in the villages. The innumerable caste and communal riots alienated the minorities from the Janata party.

The biggest asset of the Janata party for capturing the votes of the minority communities was the leadership of Jagjivan Ram and the promise to make him Prime Minister if the party secured a majority in the Lok Sabha. On this basis many political organisations of the SCs asked the voters to support the Janata party. In Maharashtra, one group of the Dalit Panthers was with the Janata party and another group led by Arun Ramble was with the ruling Progressive Democratic Front which believed in the one-point programme of defeating Indira Gandhi's candidates. One faction of the Republican Party of India (RPI; Gavai group) contested about half the total Lok Sabha seats in Maharashtra independently. But the SC voters neither supported the Janata nor the PDF, nor the Dalit Panthers nor the RPI. They overwhelmingly voted for Indira Gandhi's Congress.

The Janata party lost heavily in all the ST constituencies even though the erstwhile Jana Sangh had some support in certain tribal belts because the Janata party was opposed to the eviction of traders and others who had settled down on Adivasi lands; the party could win only five seats out of the 101 it contested, while the Lok Dal which is described as the anti-Harijan party won 10 reserved seats. In contrast, Congress(I) won 79 of 116 reserved seats. Neither the influence of the village bania nor of the Maghi (village headman) could "cloud the political vision" of the tribal voters.

The Muslim leaders and the Muslim organisations did attempt to confuse the Muslim voter. The main role was played by the Jamaat-e-Islami which has been extremely friendly to the RSS since 1977. It was the inspiring force in the establishment of the National Muslim Front, comprising the Muslim Majlis, the National Muslim League, the Ittehad-al-Muslameen and the Maharashtra Muslim Democratic forum, under the leadership of Zulfiqarullah. The National Muslim Front voiced the same demands which other Muslim leaders too have been articulating—reservation in services, Police, PAC restoration of the minority character of the Aligarh Muslim University, and an assurance of not changing the Muslim Personal Law. Zulfiqarullah asserted that the Janata party was the only political organisation which commanded the confidence of the minorities and that the Front's support to the Janata would strengthen the forces of communal harmony. The Muslim National Front was also backed up by the renounced Islamic scholar and theologian, Maulana Abul Hasan Ali Nadvi. Of the other Muslim leaders and organisations, one faction of the Jamaat-al-Ulmaie-Hind led by Syed Ahmad Hashim rejected the Congress(I) as well as the Janata and supported the Lok Dal-Congress (U) alliance. The Shahi Imam secured some assurances from Indira Gandhi and supported the Congress(I).

When the results were out, it was seen that all the candidates of the Muslim National Front were defeated in UP and its leader Zulfiqarullah forfeited his deposit. But the Lok-Dal-Congress (U) alliance did attract a part of the Muslim vote, and the Left also claimed sizeable Muslim support. In 64 constituencies where Muslims constitute between 20 and 50 per cent of the voters, the Congress (I) polled 36.48 per cent of the votes while the Lok-Dal, Congress(U) and CPI(M) together polled 57 per cent of votes.[1] Of these 64 constituencies, 24 are in Uttar Pradesh, 21 are in West Bengal, five each are in Kerala and Andhra Pradesh, four are in Bihar, two each are in Gujarat and Assam, and one is in Rajasthan.

The foregoing argument makes it clear that the voters belonging to the different minority groups did not exercise their votes on the basis of caste and community. Their vote was neither communal nor casteist, nor was it cast en bloc. It should also be noted that right from 1967, the pattern of the minority voters' behaviour has been the same, although this fact has not been recognised by the political parties, the community leaders and the social and political scientists.

In spite of the fact of the employment of the Maulanas to do election work for Rs 50 to Rs 100 per day and the use of communal tricks by most political parties, the recent Lok Sabha polls have once again proved the non-sectarian and non-particularistic character of the minority voters.[2] What is the gain? What effects will it have on the political system as such? This involves many questions regarding the political and economic system in the country. In a bourgeois democratic framework electoral participation perhaps cannot mean much unless it can be an instrument to exert effective pressure to bring about structural changes in the political and economic system. Here the minorities are trapped. The one basic aspect of the politics of the minorities is its elite character. The minority communities are overwhelmingly rural but their representatives are urban, illiteracy is rampant among them but their leaders are highly educated, their spokesmen in Parliament are on a par with the high-caste members in terms of educational qualifications, occupational affiliations and places of residence. Consequently, they are not the persons who voice the real grievances of the communities. The performance in Parliament of the SCs and STs and the Muslim MPs is terribly dismal if not shocking.[3] Their representation in the Parliament is in proportion to their population; yet they have been quite ineffective in influencing the legislative process. They invariably play second fiddle to the ruling party. Whether it is a question of the atrocities on the dalits or giving justice to the lowest of the low or incidence of communal violence, these leaders have never been in the forefront. Even in the national parties to which they belong, they do not command much respect and position, being not much more than "show boys" of these parties. With the exception of the left parties, no other political party seems to be sincere about the real problems of the minorities. The minorities' leaders have failed to comprehend the realities of the bourgeois landlord domination in the country.[4] The role of the leaders of the minorities is to strike a compromise with this ruling class. The ruling class is always ready to accommodate this leadership of the minorities for maintaining the appearance of "consensus." The electoral participation of the minorities is to provide legitimacy to the system.

The entire politics of the SCs and STs revolves around the issue of reservation. The fact is that reservation has not solved and cannot solve the problems of backwardness and unemployment of the members of these communities. It is the device of the ruling class to produce a small elite group and keep the people backward. The ruling class and the minority elite group now have a vested interest in perpetuating the backwardness of the community. Even the left parties ignore that the reservations create a tendency among the educated and the activists to refuse sacrifice for any social cause. So long as reservations continue, there is no hope for any revolutionary polities in the backward communities.

In the case of the Muslims, the gulf between the elite and the masses is equally wide. The so-called Muslim politics is dominated by all sorts of non-issues like the protection of Muslim Personal Law and the minority character of the Aligarh Muslim University. On these issues, the Muslim leaders have been supporting and opposing the undivided Congress, the Janata party and the Indira Congress. These are the issues which divert the attention of the masses from the real issues. The most important issue is of changing the system of which no Muslim leader speaks.

In the recent Lok Sabha election, the minorities, on the whole, voted out the Janata party and supported the Congress (I). But is the Congress (I) really secular?

Indira Gandhi's first spell as Prime Minister was characterised by all sorts of atrocities on the minorities (Tables 3.1 and 3.2).

Even the representation of the various minorities in Central government services was extremely low, in spite of the reservation provision. According to the Report of the Commissioner for Scheduled Castes and Scheduled Tribes, the percentage breakdown of these sections in Central government services in 1975 was: Class I (Senior Administrative) 3.42; Class II (Other Administrative) 4.98; Class III (Clerical) 10.34; and Class IV (Attendants, Peons excluding Sweepers) 18.64. The low representation shows that even from the point of view of elite politics—let alone the real question of economic emancipation of the oppressed and suppressed ones—the performance of the system is absolutely unsatisfactory.

Indeed, the communal tinge can be discerned in the behaviour pattern of all bourgeois parties. The fate of the minorities is doomed in this framework of politics and economics where no emancipation is possible. The reactionary ideological influence of Gandhism on one wing of bourgeois politics and of casteism and Hinduism on another provides the "disarming power for illusion" for the survival of class society in India.[5]

The solution lies in socialist agrarian revolution. The agrarian policies of the Indian bourgeois-landlord State has been to encourage "peasant agriculture" and community development programmes which have "the remotest connection of Marxist socialism."[6] Indeed, Indian democracy simply created an atmosphere of action which became "a substitute for action" for Nehru, for Morarji Desai and for Indira Gandhi. Atrocities on the weaker sections cannot be brought to an end unless the class bias of the bureaucracy, army and the police, which is the basis of the perpetuation of the system, is eliminated. Against such a background, more electoral participation of the minorities will not really help them to decide and follow their rational goals. The social, economic and cultural constraints are so overpowering that they vitiate the political process almost beyond remedy.

TABLE 3.1: COMMUNAL CLASHES, 1967–76

Year	Number of Incidents
1967	198
1968	346
1969	519
1970	521
1971	321
1972	240
1973	242
1974	248
1975	205
1976	169
Total	3,009

Source: *New Nation* (Dacca), 23 September 1979.

TABLE 3.2: INCIDENTS OF VIOLENCE AGAINST SCHEDULED CASTES AND SCHEDULED TRIBES, 1973–78

	SC	ST
1973	NA	362
1974	8,860	864
1975	7,781	NA
1976	5,867	1,067
1977 (till Sept)	9,225	1,138

Source: Report of the Commissioner for Scheduled Castes and Scheduled Tribes, 1977–78.

The concept of the unity of the country, stability, national security and socio-economic justice may deceive them for some time, but their class content may prove the nightmare for the minorities. The political slogans and resort to religious politics on the part of the bourgeois-landlord class and the talk of cultural security and benefits to the higher strata of the minority groups must disillusion the dalit masses, oppressed tribal peasants and the poor Muslims. One need not be pessimistic on this count of minority leaders' communal solidarity or assertiveness and the theory of counterproductive "Hindu backlash."[7] "Whatever the degree of ideological manipulation, whatever the degree of state repression, whatever the degree of cultural inertia, whatever the forces—and it is substantial—of family, or caste, or religion, there is nothing illusory about food and clothing and shelter."[8]

NOTES AND REFERENCES

[1] *The Times of India*, 16 January 1980.

[2] *The Times of India*, 16 December 1979. Sec also N. K. Thakur, "New Caste Equation in Bihar," *Hindustan Times*, 16 January 1980; Salahuddin Usman,"Little Congress(I) Upswing in UP," *Patriot*, 19 January 1980; N. C. Chowla,"Muslim did not Vote en block," *The Times of India*, 26 January 1980; and *Patriot*, 17 January 1980.

[3] G. Narayana, "Social Ground of Scheduled Castes Lok Sabha Members, 1962–1971," *EPW* 13, no. 37 (16 September 1978): pp. 1603–08. G. P. Parvathamma and T. Jangam, "India's Scheduled Castes MPs: A Socio-Economic Profile," *Journal of Karnataka University* (April 1969): pp. 1–14. Jagannath Pathy, "Reserved Seats Bring SC and ST Poor Gains," *The Times of India*, 11 October 1979. Moin Shakir, "Muslim Electoral Behaviour," *Mainstream*, 12 February 1977: pp. 11–25; Moin Shakir,"To What Purpose?" *EPW* 15, no. 3 (19 January 1980): p. 85.

[4] Ajit Roy, *Political Power in India* (Calcutta, 1975), pp. 4–21.

[5] David Selbourne, "State and Ideology in India," *Monthly Review* (December 1979): p. 36; Barrington Moore (Jr.), *Social Origin of Dictatorship and Democracy* (Penguin Books, 1973), pp. 370–8.

[6] Barrington Moore (Jr.), *Social Origin of Dictatorship*, p. 392.

[7] Girilal Jain, "Role of Indian Muslims," *The Times of India*, 26 September 1979; and A. B. Shah, "Minority Segments in Indian Polity: A Comment," *EPW* 13, no. 46 (18 November 1978): pp. 1910–12.

[8] David Selbourne, "State and Ideology in India," p. 37.

4

Compensatory Discrimination in Political Representation

A Preliminary Assessment of India's 30-Year Experience with Reserved Seats in Legislatures*

Marc Galanter

The Indian effort to secure equality by means of preferential treatment or compensatory discrimination is unique in scope and extent. As Lelah Dushkin observes, "nowhere else is so large an underprivileged minority granted so much special treatment."[1] Preferences are of three basic types: first, reservations, which provide easier access to valued positions within important social institutions. The most important preferences of this type are reserved seats in legislatures, reservation of posts in government service, and reservation or places in academic institutions (especially coveted higher technical and professional colleges). To a lesser extent, the reservation device is also used in the distribution of land allotments, housing and other scarce resources. Second, there are expenditures of government resources on behalf of the beneficiaries—scholarships, grants, loans, land allotments and provision of other special facilities such as legal aid. Third, there are special protections, such as measures designed to protect "untouchables" from discriminatory treatment and exemption from liability to having one's land subject to execution.

The benefits of "compensatory discrimination" are extended to three major classes of beneficiaries.[2] First, there are those castes designated as Scheduled

* This edited article was originally published in *Economic and Political Weekly* 14, nos. 7–8 (February 1979): pp. 437–54.

Castes (SCs) on the basis of their historic connection with "untouchability." They numbered nearly 80 million (14.6 per cent of the population) according to the 1971 Census. Second, there are the Scheduled Tribes (STs) who are distinguished by their tribal culture and physical isolation and many of whom are residents of specially protected scheduled areas. They numbered more than 38 million (6.9 per cent of the population) in 1971. Third, there are the "Backward Classes" (or, as they are sometimes called, "Other Backward Classes", or OBCs), a heterogeneous category, varying greatly from state to state, comprised for the most part of castes (and some non-Hindu communities) low in the traditional social hierarchy, but not so low as the SCs.[3]

For the most part, these preferences have been distributed on a communal basis. Members of specified communities are the beneficiaries of a given scheme and all members of the community, however prosperous, are entitled to the benefits. However, some schemes use a means test to supplement the communal one—only members of the listed communities with incomes below the specified ceiling are eligible. In a few instances, the communal test has been replaced by an economic one—income or occupation or a combination of the two—and a few schemes use tests neither communal nor economic.

I

LEGISLATIVE RESERVATIONS

The Constitution specifically provides reserved seats for the SCs and STs in the Lok Sabha (lower house of Parliament)[4] and the Vidhan Sabhas (lower houses of the state legislatures).[5] No seats are reserved in the upper houses, central or state. There are no reservations in legislatures for the Other Backward Classes or for any minority groups.[6]

All of the other Constitutional provisions for preferences are merely authorisations empowering the state to make special provision for disadvantaged groups. But legislative reservations are specifically provided in the Constitution itself.[7] Seats are reserved in proportion to the population of SCs and STs to the total population of each state. Thus in 1976, 78 (14.4 per cent) of the 542 seats in the Lok Sabha were reserved for SCs and 38 seats (7 per cent) for STs. Of the 3,997 seats in the Vidhan Sabhas, 540 (13.5 per cent) were reserved for SCs and 282 (7 per cent) for STs.[8]

These reservations do not involve "separate electorates," i.e., the representation of a particular group by legislators chosen by an electorate composed solely of members of that group.[9] The seats are "reserved" in the sense that candidates who stand for them must belong to the specified groups, but the entire electorate participates in choosing among candidates so qualified. Separate electorates for

Parliament and the state legislatures are specifically outlawed by Article 325, which provides that no person shall be excluded from any electoral roll on grounds of religion, race or caste.[10]

TABLE 4.1: PERCENTAGE OF SCHEDULED TRIBE POPULATION BY LOK SABHA CONSTITUENCIES (1962)

ST as Percentage of Population	Type of Seat			
	ST Seats	SC Seats	General Seats	Total
0–9.9	0	71	330	401
10–19.9	1	3	29	33
20–29.9	4	1	16	21
30–39.9	3	0	6	9
40–49.9	5	0	3	8
50–59.9	9	0	2	11
60–69.9	4	0	1	5
70+	5	0	0	5
Total	31	75	387	493

Source: Hart Data.

TABLE 4.2: PERCENTAGE OF SCHEDULED CASTE POPULATION BY LOK SABHA CONSTITUENCIES (1962)

SC as Percentage of Population	Type of Seat			
	SC Seats	ST Seats	General Seats	Total
0–9.9	4	22	113	139
10–19.9	25	8	210	243
20–29.9	33	1	61	95
30–39.9	10	0	3	13
40–49.9	3	0	0	3
50+	0	0	0	0
Total	75	31	387	493

Source: Hart Data.

The Constitutional provision of reserved seats is complemented by statutory provision to enhance political participation by SCs and STs. Smaller election deposits are required from members of these groups and candidates for reserved seats enjoy more permissive residence requirements.[11]

Unlike the general authorisation of special treatment and the provision for reserved posts in government service, the reserved seats in legislatures are subject

TABLE 4.3: COMPARISON OF CONCENTRATION OF SCHEDULED CASTES AND SCHEDULED TRIBES IN LOK SABHA CONSTITUENCIES RESERVED FOR THEM

Percentage of SC or ST in the Constituency	Percentage of Constituencies with Concentration of the Group between	
	SC Constituencies	ST Constituencies
0–9.9	5.3	0
10–19.9	33.3	3.2
20–29.9	44.0	12.9
30–39.9	13.3	9.7
40–49.9	4.0	16.1
50–59.9	0	29.0
60–69.9	0	12.9
70–1000	0	16.1

Source: Hart Data.

to a constitutional time limit. It was originally provided that such reservations should expire 10 years after the commencement of the Constitution.[12] In 1959 these provisions were extended for another 10 years,[13] and in 1969 for yet another 10.[14]

Ten years ago, during the debate on the last extension, M. R. Masani regretted the absence of "a scientific study of the effects of [reservations] for the past 20 years."[15] As it becomes 30 years there is still no comprehensive study of these effects. This chapter attempts to assemble some of the information that is available, to identify the problems of drawing conclusions from that information, and to formulate a tentative assessment of the working of the reserved seats.

Reserved Constituencies

During the 1950s, most of the reserved seats were in double-member constituencies, in which one of the seats could be filled only by a member of the "privileged" group and the other was open to general competition.[16] Double-member constituencies were abolished in 1961.[17] This abolition seems to have been inspired principally by the concern of politicians with the greater difficulty and expense of campaigning in a double-sized district.[18] This was compounded by some resentment of the infrequent but well-publicised instances in which the unreserved "general" seat as well as the reserved seat were won by SC or ST candidates,[19] who were able to compete for both seats, while their opponents could compete only for the unreserved seat.[20] New single-member constituencies were designated for the 1962 elections.[21]

The demarcation of constituencies and designation of those reserved for SCs and STs are entrusted to a Delimitation Commission, which consists of a retired Supreme Court Judge, a sitting High Court Judge and the Chief Election Commissioner.[22] In each state, the Commission is assisted by ten non-voting associate members (five Members of Parliament and five Members of the Legislative Assembly) nominated by their respective Speakers.[23] The Courts are constitutionally barred from intervening in the process of delimitation or allotment of seats.[24]

Generally, constituencies are formed on the basis of contiguity, communications, absence of natural barriers, and cultural and ethnic homogeneity. After they are formed, certain constituencies are selected as reserved. In the case of the ST seats there is a single standard for selection—concentration of the ST population.[25] Since typically the tribal population lives in areas of concentration, the constituencies reserved for them contain a high proportion of STs.[26] In 1962, the STs comprised more than 50 per cent of the population in 18 of the 31 Lok Sabha constituencies reserved for them.[27] Conversely, most of the major concentrations of ST population are located in reserved constituencies. Of the 29 constituencies in which ST comprise over 40 per cent of the population, 23 are reserved. Thus, the reserved seats encompass the bulk of the ST population—perhaps close to 70 per cent. These constituencies are, not surprisingly, more isolated and much less urban than are the general constituencies.

In the case of seats reserved for SCs, the Commission is instructed to apply two standards—concentration of SC population and dispersal of reservations. The Delimitation Act instructs the Commission to locate seats reserved for SCs "in different parts of the State and ... as far as practicable, in those areas where the proportion of their population to the total is comparatively large."[28] The Delimitation Commission achieves this by first reserving the constituencies with the highest concentration of SCs—usually not much more than 20 per cent—and then selecting the others by the dispersal criterion. Since the SC population, unlike the tribes, is rather evenly dispersed, the constituencies reserved for them contain far fewer SC members. Among the 76 Lok Sabha constituencies reserved for SCs in the 1962 elections, there was none in which they comprised a majority of the population and only 13 in which they comprised as much as 30 per cent.[29] The bulk of SCs constituencies contain between 10 and 30 per cent of SCs. Thus, the vast majority of SCs—perhaps 75 per cent—live outside the constituencies reserved for SCs. Of the 111 Lok Sabha constituencies where SCs comprised more than 20 per cent of the population, in 1961 only 46 were reserved, while 29 constituencies with less than 20 per cent were reserved.

TABLE 4.4: ELECTION OF SCHEDULED CASTES AND SCHEDULED TRIBES TO NON-RESERVED SEATS IN LOK SABHA

Election	Total Seats	Reserved for SC	Reserved for ST	Non-Reserved	Non-Reserved Filled by SC	Non-Reserved Filled by ST	
1952	489	72	25	392	5(1)	1(0)	1955: 1, 95
1957	494	76	31	387	*7(3)	3(2)	1959–60: 11, 24
1962	494	76	31	387	*2	2	1961–62: 11, 75
1967	520	77	36	407	0	1	1966–67: 26
1971	522	77	40	405	1	4	1971–73: 244
1977	542	78	38	426	2	1	1975–77: 20–22

Note: Figures in parentheses are the number of non-reserved seat victories which were general seats in double-member constituencies.
* Total includes one Buddhist (not eligible for reserved seat nor listed in RCSCST). Other Buddhists may have occupied general seats subsequently.

Source: Chandidas, et al. 1968: 253 and RCSCST, as below.

Like the ST constituencies, those reserved for SCs tend to be political backwaters—slightly less urban, with less newspaper circulation and a slightly greater percentage of agricultural labourers.

The same pattern of concentration of STs and dispersion of SCs reappears in the reserved seats in the state legislatures. In Andhra Pradesh, for example, SCs make up only 21 per cent of the population of the constituencies reserved for them (and 13 per cent of the population of the general constituencies). But STs comprise 43 per cent of the population of the constituencies reserved for STs and only 2 per cent of the general constituencies.[30]

Designation of a constituency as reserved usually encounters opposition.

> While everyone expressed anxiety that the Scheduled Castes and the Scheduled Tribes should get their full quota of reserved seats, very rarely indeed would anybody (unless he himself belonged to any of these castes or tribes) agree to any seat being reserved for them in a constituency in which he was personally interested.[31]

The selection of reserved constituencies gives rise to the bulk of the objections to the proposed delimitation. As the Election Commissioner reports,

> generally speaking the vocal sections of the public objected to their own areas becoming part of a reserved constituency and put forward ingenious suggestions for reshaping two or more constituencies so that some particular constituency would be a general constituency.

However, these objections rarely bring about a change. The courts will not provide any relief so long as the Delimitation Commission has taken into account the factors specified by the Delimitation Act.[32] Proposals for rotation of reserved constituencies have been rejected and their location has remained relatively stable.[33]

Non-Reserved Seats

Of course, SC and ST candidates may stand for non-reserved seats. However, they have been notably unsuccessful in winning elections to them. In the first six Lok Sabhas, only a handful of candidates from SCs or STs filled unreserved seats.[34] In the lower houses of the state legislatures, the record is no more heartening, even though the smaller constituencies mean that local concentrations of population and resources should offer more opportunities for political success. An approximate count of SC and ST victories in unreserved seats is given by Table 4.5.

There is no reservation of seats in the indirectly elected upper houses at both Centre and states. The Rajya Sabha at the Centre is elected by proportional representation by the members of the State Legislative Assemblies.[35] The number of SC and ST members in the Rajya Sabha is shown in Table 4.6.

TABLE 4.5: ELECTION OF SCHEDULED CASTES AND SCHEDULED TRIBES TO NON-RESERVED SEATS IN VIDHAN SABHAS

Election	Total Seats	Reserved for SC	Reserved for ST	Non-Reserved	Non-Reserved Filled by SC	Non-Reserved Filled by ST	
1952	3,234	471	192	2,571	5*	2*	1953: 107
1957	3,201	470	221	2,411	7*	9*	1958–59: 1, 13
1962	3,296	480	262	2,553	12(16)**	13	1962–63: 11
1967	3,467	496	248	2,723	4(20)**	8	1966–67: 26
1969–70	3,563	503	262	2,798	0	1	1969–70: 92
1970–71	3,625	510	262	2,853	3	2	1970–71: 122
1971–73	3,771	516	321	2,943	0	14	1971–73: 244
1973–75	3,800	517	325	2,958	4***	–	1974–75: 194
1975–77	3,977	540	282	3,155	NI	NI	1975–77: 20

Notes: * Figures noted in source as correction from earlier report.

** Dushkin 1972: 197 gives these higher estimates including Buddhists who would not be included in the RCSCST count.

*** Noted in source as previously elected.

Source: Chandidas, et al. 1968: 717 and RCSCST, as below.

TABLE 4.6: NUMBER OF SCHEDULED CASTES AND SCHEDULED TRIBES IN RAJYA SABHA

Year	Total Seats	SC	ST	
1953	216	7	4	1953: 107 (1953: 160)***
1954		6	5	1954: 158–9
1955		7	5	1955: I, 96
1956		5	3	1956–57: II, 17
1957–58		6	3	1957–58: II, 25
1958–59	220 (1958)	7	4	1958–59: I, 13 (1958: 49)***
1959–60		10	3	1959–60: II, 11–12
1960–61		11	3	1990–61: I, 273
1961–62		11	2	1961–62: II, 75
1962–63		12	2	1962–63: I, 152
1963–64	224 (1963)	12	3	1963–64: I, 162 [1963: 35]***
1964–65		13	3	1964–65: 143
1965–66		13	3	1965–66: 180
1966–67		10	2	1966–67: 26
1967–68		10	2	Desai 1969: 91
1968–69	228 (1968)	13	5	Do. (1968: 42)***
1969–70		13****	5****	1969–70: 92
1970–71		NI*	NI*	
1971–72		NI	NI	
1972–73		NI	NI	
1973–74	243 (1973)	31**	1**	1973–74: 279 (1973: 38)***

Notes: * According to RCSCST the House discontinued the keeping of records of SC and ST members. No subsequent information available except as noted.

** As reported by the Minister of State for Home Affairs. Noted as partial information including members from major parties only.

*** Figures on total seats are taken from Ministry of Information and Broadcasting, *India: A Reference Annual*, as shown in brackets.

**** No led in sources as previous years' figures.

Source: RCSCST except where noted

The upper houses (Vidhan Parishads) in those state legislatures that have them are chosen by a more complicated formula, combining election by the lower house, special qualified constituencies and governmental nomination.[36] Here, too, the number of SCs and STs has remained fairly small, as shown in Table 4.7.

TABLE 4.7: NUMBER OF SCHEDULED CASTES AND SCHEDULED TRIBES IN VIDHAN SABHAS

Year	Total Membership (No. of States)	SC	ST	
1953	509 (10)	5	1	1953: 107 (1953: 160)*
1954		8(2)	1	1954: 158–9
1955		8(2)	1	1955: I, 96
1956		8(2)	1	1956–57: II, 17
1957		9(3)	4	1957–58: II, 25
1958–59	780 (10) [1958]	14(4)	4	1958–59: II, 56 (1958: 64)*
1959–60		16(3)	4	1959–60: II, 12
1960–61		19(3)	5	1990–61: I, 274, II, 290
1961–62		10(5)	5(1)	1961–62: II, 276
1962–63		12	3	1962–63: I, 152
1963–64	750 (10) [1963]	12	7	Desai 1969: 91 (1963: 51)*
1964–65		17	7	1964–65: 143
1965–66		12	9	1965–66: 63
1966–67		15	10	1966–67: 26
1967–68		16	10	Desai 1969: 91
1968–69	703 (9) [1968]	16	10	Do. (1968: 43)*
1969–70		18	9	1969–70: 92
1970–71		10(3)	6(1)	1970–71: 122
1971–72		12(3)	6(1)	1971–73: 244
1972–73	534 (7) [1972]	NI	NI	1973: 44*
1973–74	(Bihar only)	5(2)	2(1)	1973–74: 79
1974–75	(Four states only with 294 seats)	23(3)	3(1)	1974–75: 194

Notes: Figures in parentheses indicate nominated numbers where this is known.
* Figures on membership are taken from Ministry of Information and Broadcasting, *India: A Reference Annual*, as shown in brackets.

Source: RCSCST except where noted.

There is no constitutional requirement or statutory provision for reservations of political appointments within the legislatures or the government, such as cabinet ministerships[37] or membership on standing committees. However, it became a convention to have at least one SC cabinet minister at the Centre and in each of the states. The number of SC ministers at the Centre and the number of ST ministers in the states has slowly risen, as indicated in Table 4.8.

Reservation of seats on elective bodies at the local level is not specifically provided by the Constitution, but such arrangements are allowed by Article 15(4) and nearly all the states provide such reservations by election, co-optation or nomination in various local bodies and in panchayats. In 1963, seats in local bodies were reserved for SCs on the basis of population in Assam, Gujarat, Kerala, Maharashtra, Mysore, Punjab, Rajasthan and Uttar Pradesh. All of the other states except for West Bengal provided for some other form of representation in these bodies.[38] There is little data available on the extent to which these reservations have been implemented, much less on how effective they are.

Similarly, most of the states have made some provision for representation of SCs and STs in panchayat bodies. In 1966 all the states except Bihar, Jammu and Kashmir, Orissa and West Bengal reserved seats in gram panchayats, and most states provided for reservation or co-optation of members of these groups in the higher tiers of panchayat institutions.[39] But again there is no information about the extent to which these have been implemented or their effectiveness.

II

Assessing the Benefits and Costs

There is no lack of assertions about the beneficial or detrimental effects of the reserved seats, and of the whole policy of compensatory discrimination. Yet any attempt to evaluate the working of reserved seats quickly flounders for lack of evidence. Reliable data on the effects of these measures are sparse and scanty. But if the evidence is insufficient for a definitive evaluation, it does permit us to make a tentative assessment of the working of reservations in the legislatures.

I propose to begin this assessment by sketching the main arguments for and against legislative reservations. By sensitising us to the full range of issues at stake, this listing permits us to sort out the available evidence and helps us to formulate the questions that would provide information for a more conclusive account. Table 4.9 presents an illustrative array of the full range of claims that are made as to the various ways in which the reserved seats allegedly help or hurt the protected groups, others, and India as a whole. This list may be thought of as a specification of more general assertions about the costs and benefits of the whole policy of compensatory discrimination.

TABLE 4.8: SCHEDULED CASTE AND SCHEDULED TRIBE MINISTERS

	Centre								States								Source (RCSCST)
	M		DM		PS		Total		M		DM		PS		Total		
	SC	ST	SC	ST	SC	ST	SC	ST	SC	ST	SC	ST	SC	ST	SC	ST	
1948	2	0	*	*	*	*	*	*	10	3	0	0	*	*	*	*	1951: 179
1949	2	0	*	*	*	*	*	*	10	3	1	0	*	*	*	*	1951: 179
1950	2	0	*	*	*	*	*	*	10	3	1	0	*	*	*	*	1951: 179
1951	2	0	*	*	*	*	*	*	10	3	4	0	*	*	*	*	1951: 179
1952	*	*	*	*	*	*	*	*	*	*	*	*	*	*	*	*	1951: 179
1953	1	0	1	0	1	1	3	1	14	5	4	0	4	3	22	8	1953: 252, 4
1954	1	0	1	0	1	1	3	1	13	4	7	2	4	3	24	9	1954: 336, 7
1955	1	0	1	0	1	1	3	1	15	2	7	3	4	3	26	9	1955: II, 26ff
1956–57	1	0	2	0	0	1	3	1	*	*	*	*	*	*	*	*	1956–57: I, 9
1957–58	1	0	1	0	1	1	3	1	14	3	7	5	4	8	25	16	1957–58: II
1958–59	1	0	2	0	0	1	3	1	14	3	10	6	2	5	26	14	1959–60: I, 1
1959–60	1	0	2	0	0	1	3	1	14	4	8	4	2	5	24	13	*Do.*
1960–61	1	0	2	0	0	1	3	1	*	*	*	*	*	*	26	15	1960–61: II, 1 1961–62: I, 1
1961–62	*	*	*	*	*	*	5	2	*	*	*	*	*	*	28	11	*Do.*
1962–63	*	*	*	*	*	*	5	2	*	*	*	*	*	*	30	14	1962–63: I, 1
1963–64	1	0	4	0	2	2	7	2	18	18	7	7	0	2	25	27	1963–64: I, 16
1964–65	*	*	*	*	*	*	7	2	*	*	*	*	*	*	24	24	1964–65: 144

Key:
M = Ministers
DM = Deputy Ministers
PS = Parliamentary Secretaries
* = Information not available

TABLE 4.9: ASSERTED BENEFITS AND COSTS OF RESERVATION OF LEGISLATIVE SEATS FOR SCHEDULED CASTES AND SCHEDULED TRIBES

	Benefits		Costs
(1)	Redistribution Reservation of seats effects a direct channeling of valuable resources to SC and ST. Good jobs, patronage, personal influence, access to high places, prestige and all the benefits that go with being a legislator are provided to the SC and ST in a much greater measure than they would otherwise enjoy.	*vs.*	Diversion The resources provided directly by reservations do not spread to the benefit of the SC and ST, but are confined to a small privileged group within them, narrowing and distorting the representative character of the reserved seat holders.
(2)	Representation Reserved seats cause the presence of those who effectively represent the interests of the SC and ST, interests that would otherwise be underrepresented and neglected. Especially, the presence of the reserved seat legislators helps to insure that resources and attention are deployed to attend to the special needs of SC and ST.	*vs.*	Misrepresentation Reserved seat legislators do not represent the interests of the SC and ST accurately or effectively. New narrower interests which average from those of the SC and ST are created by legislative reservations.
(3)	Integration Reservation of seats affords a level of participation in political life that engenders among the SC and ST feelings of belonging and of having a stake in the system, thus promoting their political and social integration into Indian society.	*vs.*	Alienation By emphasising their separateness, reserved seats school SC and ST to regard themselves as outside Indian society and reduce their feelings of (and opportunities for) common participation.
(4)	Acceptance Reserved seats induce in others an awareness that SC and ST are significant actors in Indian public life, who are capable of acting in responsible roles and whose interests must be taken into account.	*vs.*	Rejection Frustrated and alienated by what they regard as unwarranted preference, others are educated to regard SC and ST as separate and distinct sections of the population who enjoy their own facilities and have no claim on general public facilities and opportunities.
(5)	Integrity Reserved seats promote pride, self-respect and a sense of self-sufficiency that will enable SC and ST to participate fully in public life as willing partners.	*vs.*	Manipulation Reserved seats subject the SC and ST to manipulation by others aggravating their sense of dependence. By singling them out for special treatment, reserved seats undermine their sense of dignity, self-sufficiency and political efficacy.

(Contd)

Table 4.9 (Contd)

(6)	Incubation By providing an area protected from outside competition, temporary reservations stimulate the acquisition of political skill, experience, confidence, ties and other resources. Reservations thus help to promote the kind of vigorous and skilled leadership needed by the SC and ST leadership capable of flourishing in open competition.	*vs.*	Overprotection The artificially protected sanctuary of reserved seats blunts the development of political resources by protecting politicians from vigorous competition.
(7)	Mobilisation Reserved seats provide an institutional base for organised action, enhancing the capacity of the SC and ST to engage in concerted efforts to address their common problems.	*vs.*	Enervation The artificial protection of reserved seats and the relations of dependence they foster reduce initiative, blunt the development of skills and reduce capacity for sustained, organised effort by the SC and ST.
(8)	Stimulation The presence of reserved seat legislators promotes awareness of and creates political incentives for responsiveness to the needs of the SC and ST.	*vs.*	Sedation The presence of a reserved seat holder encourages others to disavow direct responsibility for the well-being of the SC and ST.
(9)	Self-Liquidation These benefits may be viewed as mutually reinforcing. Their cumulative effect will be to render unnecessary any special provision for reserved seats. In this view, representation (assisted by redistribution) by amplifying mobilisation and stimulation will promote the advancement of these groups to the point that their interests converge with those of the wider public; incubation will promote a vigorous political leadership capable of representing them without special insulation from competition; as they become politically self-sufficient and more integrated, they will gain acceptance and enjoy integrity that will make it possible for them to function without reservation.	*vs.*	Self-Perpetuation Alternatively, reserved seats may be viewed as producing a set of mutually reinforcing negative effects. In this view, misrepresentation and diversion create new narrow vested interests; overprotection and enervation blunt the development of political leadership that could supply effective representation; these arrangements promote divisiveness, preventing integration, promoting rejection by others and undermining the integrity of the SC and ST. *(Contd)*

(Contd)

Table 4.9 (Contd)

(10)	Fairness Reserved seats redistribute opportunities for participation on a scale that would be unimaginable in their absence, offsetting a mal-distribution of such opportunities stemming from accumulated and unjust past disadvantages.	*vs.*	Unfairness Reserved seats bestow and restrict opportunities for participation in ways that are arbitrary and unconnected with deserts or culpability.
(11)	Secularism By reducing invidious disparities between communal groups, reserved seats lead over the long run to the reduction of the salience of communal identity in public life.	*vs.*	Communalism Reserved seats, by recognising and stimulating claims based on communal identity, increase the salience of communal identity in public life.
(12)	Development Reserved seats contribute to national development by promoting the incorporation of excluded groups into national life.	*vs.*	Stagnation Reserved seats impede development by skewing legislative priorities from development tasks to ineffectual redistributive measures.

Rough and redundant as it is, this anthology of claims will provide us with a checklist that will help in devising appropriate standards for evaluating specific schemes. For convenience, each claimed benefit is paired with the opposite claim of cost. It would simplify matters if each of these pairs represented points on a single dimension that could be unambiguously measured. Unfortunately, the most that can be claimed for them is that each is a composite of sometimes reinforcing but occasionally conflicting qualities that may conveniently be grouped together. Since the lines between the claimed effects are not always distinct, some overlap and redundancy are unavoidable. It was necessary, for convenience in labelling, to devise some rubrics that are not found in ordinary talk of these matters, imparting a somewhat stilted quality to the list. These claims are listed here in an order that proceeds roughly from the most focused and immediate to the most capacious and remote, from those which speak of impacts primarily on the beneficiary groups to those which concern the shape and career of the whole society.

....

The remainder of this chapter is an attempt to assemble information relevant to these arguments. The heavy emphasis on representation is not meant to attribute an overwhelming primacy to that factor. Nor is it implied that all of these dimensions are to be accorded equal weight in evaluating legislative reservations in themselves or the overall working of compensatory discrimination on policies. Presumably specific schemes in different fields (education, housing, etc.) or for different groups (SCs, STs, OBCs) have a different mix of intended effects. And, presumably, the relative weight to be assigned to those effects (and to unintended by-products) will vary among various participants and observers. These standards may help us to identify divergent goals as well as common ones.

Representation vs. Misrepresentation

We may safely conclude that the presence of the SCs and STs in legislative bodies is accounted for largely by the provisions for reserved seats. Very few members of these groups have been successful in open competition (see Tables 4.4 and 4.5). Even their presence in bodies where there is no reservation (upper houses, cabinets) is due largely to the political base provided by reservations. Thus, reservations do provide for a substantial quantitative presence that would otherwise be lacking.

We cannot infer that without reservations, representation would be reduced to the present level of success in non-reserved seats. Their geographical concentration would assure the STs at least a modicum of representation even in the absence of reservations. The more dispersed SCs would undoubtedly obtain far fewer seats than they now enjoy, but we should not conclude that they would have none at all. If there were no reservation some of the political talent among the SCs now competing for reserved seats would compete for non-reserved seats. Parties would then need appealing candidates in areas with heavy concentrations of SCs; perhaps state-makers would be less moved by the sense of "they already have their share" that now seems to affect the giving of tickets. (And of course, some representation would be provided by legislators from other groups who would be accountable to constituencies with sizeable numbers of SC voters.)

Perhaps the best indication of the scale of representation that might be expected in the absence of reserved seats is provided by some data on elections to local bodies where no reservations were in force. In the early 1960s local bodies in West Bengal, with a total of 1,081 members, contained only 11 SC members (3.8 per cent) and 16 ST members (1.5 per cent).[40] Among the 66 Presidents and Chairmen there were three SC members and one ST. (According to the 1960 Census, 19.84 per cent of the population of West Bengal were SCs and 5.91 per cent were STs.)[41] A similar picture is presented by some fragmentary data from Gujarat, where only 35 (0.5 per cent) of 6,863 sarpanches were from the SCs.[42] The electoral experience of India's other large and (mostly) low status minority, the Muslims, does not offer additional reassurance.[43]

The effect of reservation of seats on the quality of representation is even more difficult to assess....

No investigator has undertaken such an assessment. Hence, we have to attempt to piece together a tentative picture from the fragmentary evidence that is available.

From a handful of studies we may draw a composite portrait of the Members of Parliament who occupy reserved seats.[45] They are younger and more rural in residence than their fellow legislators, fewer have professions (other than landholding), and they have less formal education. The median age of reserved seat MPs is in the early forties; that of their fellows in general seats is in the early 1950s. The disparity in age has remained constant over successive Lok Sabhas, but the gap in educational attainments has narrowed appreciably. In the Third Lok Sabha, for example, roughly 60 per cent of occupants of general seats held bachelor's or higher degrees, compared to 30 per cent of SC MPs and 35 per cent of ST MPs. In the Fifth Lok Sabha, 53 per cent of SC and 37 per cent of ST MPs were degree holders, while the general seat MPs remained at about 60 per cent.[46] Similarly, the occupational and residential profile of reserved seat legislators seems to be becoming more like that of the MPs in general seats. But those in reserved seats continue to be younger. They are younger when they are first elected to Parliament and, unsurprisingly, come there with less legislative experience at the state level.[47] From a single study we may surmise that similar disparities might be found in state legislatures.[48]

It is widely believed that reserved seat legislators are less articulate, less assertive and less independent than their fellows. From data on the Third Lok Sabha collected by Henry Hart, we may distil a tentative picture of the parliamentary activity of reserved seat Members of Parliament. Even apart from the limitations of the present analysis,[49] it would of course be illegitimate to take this picture as reflective of current conditions. And it should also be emphasised that we would be on shaky ground generalising from data on Parliament to conclusions about the working of reserved seats in the state legislatures. Nevertheless, the data does enable us to see the legislative reservation device in action, and it may provide a useful baseline for comparison with later or state data.

The Hart data supplies some evidence for the view that reserved seat holders were as a group less active parliamentarians than those elected to general seats. Lok Sabha members in reserved seats were less likely to hold party office (Table 4.10) or to serve on select or standing committees (Tables 4.11 and 4.12) or to hold ministerships. During any one of these years, an average of 12.5 per cent of the general seat legislators were ministers, compared to 8.9 per cent of the holders of SC seats and 2.2 per cent of holders of ST seats.

TABLE 4.10: LOK SABHA MEMBERS HOLDING PARTY OFFICES

Number of Party Offices	Type of Seat		
	General	SC	ST
1	15.0	9.3	12.9
2	14.5	2.6	6.5
Total	29.5	11.9	19.4

Source: Hart Data.

TABLE 4.11: MEMBERSHIP ON SELECT COMMITTEES OF LOK SABHA

Number of Select Committees	Type of Seat		
	General	SC	ST
0	43.2	53.3	64.5
1	30.0	40.0	25.8
2	26.9	6.7	9.7

Source: Hart Data.

TABLE 4.12: MEMBERSHIP ON STANDING COMMITTEES OF LOK SABHA (MEAN FOR YEARS 1962–64)

Number of Standing Committees	Type of Seat		
	General	SC	ST
0	69.1	74.5	71.0
1	16.5	15.1	12.9
2	14.4	10.6	16.1

Source: Hart Data.

The reserved seat legislators participated less in debate—indeed, almost half were silent, compared to a quarter of the general seat holders (Table 4.13). On Hart's index of overall parliamentary activeness, the ST reserved seat holders were somewhat less active and the SC reserved seat holders far less active than the occupants of general seats (Table 4.14). Together, the SC and ST representatives occupied over 21 per cent of the seats, but they made up only 10.1 per cent of the most active stratum of the Lok Sabha—and 35.3 per cent of the least active stratum.

However, these forms of participation do not offer a full measure of the way in which legislators work to shape government action. It appears that the reserved seat holders had as much contact with constituents, both by touring and (except for ST legislators) by letter. There is no indication, though, that

TABLE 4.13: PARTICIPATION OF DEBATE BY OCCUPANTS OF GENERAL AND RESERVED SEATS IN LOK SABHA, 1962–64

Frequency of Members Who in Any Year Participated in Debate	Type of Seat		
	General	SC	ST
Not at all	27.4	44.9	47.3
Once	15.6	25.3	22.6
2–5 times	29.6	19.1	23.7
6 or more times	27.4	10.7	6.4

Source: Hart Data.

TABLE 4.14: PARLIAMENTARY ACTIVENESS (HART SCALE)* OF MEMBERS OF LOK SABHA

Parliamentary Activeness Score (4 = most active)	Type of Seat			
	General	SC	ST	Total
1	33 (8.5)	10 (13.3)	8 (25.8)	51 (10.3)
2	130 (33.6)	34 (45.3)	10 (32.3)	174 (35.3)
3	135 (34.9)	27 (36.0)	7 (22.6)	169 (34.3)
4	89 (23.0)	4 (5.3)	6 (19.4)	99 (20.1)
Total	387 (100)	75 (100)	31 (100)	493 (100)

Notes: Figures in parentheses are percentages.
* This scale is a weighted composite of data on participation in debate and question period; committee membership and holding of party office; cabinet membership; and seniority.

Source: Hart Data.

they had any particularly large amount of contact with SCs or STs outside their constituencies. Reserved seat holders were themselves more oriented to issues of SCs and STs. The demands of their constituents, as reserved seat legislators reported them, were more intensely "communal" than those reported by other members of Parliament. But the pattern, as Table 4.15 shows, is a very mixed one, for a sizeable minority of SC legislators report no "communal" demands at all.

We have seen that they were less likely to transmit these demands in formal debate or committee work. They also had less contact with ministers (Table 4.16). When they did transmit demands, to a far greater extent than other legislators, they dealt almost exclusively with constituency matters rather than with general issues, as shown in Table 4.17.

We may conclude that the occupants of reserved seats were probably less influential than other legislators in shaping policy. This is confirmed by their

TABLE 4.15: SUBJECTS RAISED BY CONSTITUENTS IN CONTACTS WITH MEMBERS OF LOK SABHA

Subjects Raised	Type of Seat		
	General	SC	ST
"Communal" only or first	4 (3.1)	7 (35)	7 (53.8)
Some "communal" but not first	108 (82.4)	7 (35)	6 (46.2)
No "communal"	19 (14.5)	6 (30)	0 (0)
Total	131	20	13

Note: Figures in parentheses are percentages.
Source: Hart Data, Interview Sample.

TABLE 4.16: AMOUNT OF LOBBYING OF MINISTERS BY MEMBERS OF LOK SABHA

Contact with Ministers	Type of Seat		
	General	SC	ST
Does not talk to ministers	11 (9)	3 (15)	3 (25)
No more than once per session	63 (52.2)	14 (70)	7 (58.3)
More than once per session	47 (38.8)	3 (15)	2 (16.7)
Total	121 (100)	20 (100)	12 (100)

Note: Figures in parentheses are percentages.
Source: Hart Data, Interview Sample.

TABLE 4.17: SCOPE OF MATTERS COVERED IN LOBBYING MINISTERS BY MEMBERS OF PARLIAMENT

Matters Covered	Type of Seat		
	General	SC	ST
Constituency only	54 (49.1)	16 (94.1)	8 (88.9)
Constituency and larger	34 (30.9)	1 (5.9)	0 (0)
Larger only	22 (20)	0 (0)	1 (11.1)
Total	110 (100)	17 (100)	9 (100)

Note: Figures in parentheses are percentages.
Source: Hart Data, Interview Sample.

own subjective impression—far fewer of them felt that they were effective advocates of their views (Table 4.18).

Obviously, one must be extremely cautious in extrapolating from this data about the Third Lok Sabha to more recent performance under changed conditions, much less to conditions that might prevail in the future. Since

TABLE 4.18: FEELING OF EFFECTIVENESS IN HAVING VIEWS CONSIDERED

Member's Estimation of His Effectiveness	Type of Seat		
	General	SC	ST
Ineffective; do not try	1 (13.2)	2 (10)	3 (25)
Partially effective	50 (41.3)	13 (65)	6 (50)
Effective	55 (45.4)	5 (25)	3 (25)
Total	121 (100)	20 (100)	12 (100)

Note: Figures in parentheses are percentages.
Source: Hart Data, Interview Sample.

the reserved seat legislators have come to resemble their fellows in terms of education, occupation and urban residence, there may also be a convergence in legislative behaviour. Or it may be that changes in political alignments have accorded reserved seat legislators a greater voice and elicited new patterns of participation. And one may, of course, wonder whether the most important sorts of representation are accurately depicted in terms of the measures of participation that we have employed.[50]

Low rates of participation do not imply a proportionate absence of effective representation of the interests of SCs and STs. Presumably the activities of reserved seat legislators are concentrated on matters which affect these groups,[51] and their effectiveness in representing the interests of these groups should be most evident in dealing with matters which contribute directly to their welfare: (1) establishing programmes of which they are the beneficiaries; (2) ensuring deployment of resources to these programmes; (3) pressing for better administration of these programmes; and (4) resisting cut-backs and premature termination of such programmes. Although I have no systematic data, there is impressionistic evidence to suggest that, in the Lok Sabha at least, reserved seat legislators have been prominent and influential in matters concerning the working of the preference policy. Expenditures for SC and ST schemes have continued to rise—in contrast to those for the OBCs. The reserved seat legislators demonstrated their political prowess by killing the 1965 Lokur Committee report, which called for the descheduling of some tribes and castes. The dissatisfaction of the reserved seat members was instrumental in bringing about the government's first defeat in the Lok Sabha in 20 years, a stunning snap vote on a 1967 motion that the constitutional safeguards for SCs and STs were not being fully implemented.[52]

This new assertiveness was followed by government's repudiation of the Lokur recommendations, appointment of new deputy ministers from among the SCs, liberalisation of the rules for reservations in promotions in government services, increasing the reservations in direct recruitment, and (after years of promises) making converts to Buddhism and Christianity eligible for post-matriculation scholarships and increasing the reservations in direct recruitment.[53]

The presence of the reserved seat legislators, if not in itself likely to raise the level of benefits, does seem to serve as a warrant of the continuation of those programmes at their existing levels. Furthermore, their presence in such numbers provides a quantitative basis for SC and ST participation in leadership at the cabinet level; it is unlikely that there would be many persons from these groups in cabinets were it not for the reserved seats. It appears that the initiation and expansion of programmes for these groups is associated with the presence of group members in cabinet posts. The first reservations in government service were established by the efforts of the first SC member of the Viceroy's cabinet. Job reservations were first extended from initial appointments to the promotion stage under the auspices of the next SC politician who became a minister. Similarly, at the state level, the first extension of reservations to the promotion stage occurred when a SC politician became chief minister of Andhra; the ascension of a SC Home Minister in Madras was followed by a dramatic increase in the vigour of prosecution under the Untouchability (Offences) Act.[54]

The potential leverage enjoyed by the occupants of reserved seats varies with the balance of party power in the legislatures. The more evenly balanced the party alignment, the greater the potential impact of the reserved seats.[55] The erosion of single party dominance and the trend toward more evenly balanced legislatures seems to portend an increase in the potential of the reserved seat legislators to influence public policy.

Incubation vs. Overprotection

While available data do not allow us to draw any conclusions about the degree of successful incubation, they suggest there is little overprotection. Reserved seat legislators, as we noted before, are younger and less educated. They have proved able to retain their seats in successive elections; this may reflect not only increased political skill but the still limited supply of political resources to challenge them—an explanation which accords with the fact that there are fewer candidates in reserved seat contests. There has been no increase in the success of SCs and STs in competition for non-reserved seats (which reflects rejection by others as well as the fact that to those eligible to stand for them, reserved seats represent an attractive return for limited political resources). If incubation is taking place—and there is some indication that there has been a great growth in political skills, experience, ties etc.—it is very doubtful that it has reached a point where many could successfully compete without the reservations.

Redistribution vs. Diversion

Reserved seats clearly have a substantial distributive effect. Not only through their law-making activities, but through their ability as legislators to intercede, obtain contracts and distribute patronage, reserved seats produce a substantial flow of resources to these groups.[56] Not least among these resources is official attention. As one of the respondents in Aggarwal and Ashraf's Haryana study expressed it,

> If reservation in elections is withdrawn Harijans will lose influence. Today if I have any serious problem I can go to a Harijan MLA or MP. He understands our problems fully. Officers listen to our problems only when they know that our MLA or MP is a Harijan.[57]

If one doubts that the effects are consistently so dramatic it is certainly plausible that they are significant. I have no basis for estimating how widely these benefits are spread or whether they are, as often alleged, confined to a narrow segment within the more numerous and politically dominant SCs and STs.[58] The demands put forward by SC legislators are disproportionately attentive to those of their fellows who already have something[59] (for example, the great attention to higher government posts) and are in a position to make demands on them, but there is no evidence that this is more the case with them than with their fellow legislators.

Stimulation vs. Sedation

In the 1969 debate on extension of the Constitutional provisions for reserved seats, M. R. Masani made the interesting observation that "this reservation ... has put the conscience of the upper class and the upper castes to sleep."[60] Reserved seats, as the most visible component of the policy of compensatory discrimination, may indeed be responsible for some diminution of non-governmental concern for the SCs and STs. Thus Lelah Dushkin reports a general tendency to assign responsibility for these groups to government, absolving other elites of any responsibility for their betterment.[61] The educated public vastly overestimates the amount and effectiveness of preferential treatment, and the viability of legislators in reserved seats may reinforce this perception of indiscriminate indulgence and erode the support that compensatory discrimination formerly enjoyed.[62] While it is plausible that there would be more non-governmental action in the absence of institutionalised compensatory discrimination, it seems highly unlikely that the total resources diverted to these groups would be as great. (The mix might be less favourable to the upper end of the scale, though, and it is arguable, but unproven, that such "voluntary" aid would be more effective than that afforded by the government.) And if reserved seats erode public support for preferential treatment, they must be credited with one massive accomplishment: the presence of SCs and STs in every legislative setting in sufficient numbers so that issues of concern to them cannot be dismissed or ignored indefinitely.

Integration vs. Alienation

Reserved seats are clearly integrative in several ways. The holders of reserved seats tend to be members of national political parties. Those who aspire to fill them are constrained to campaign for the votes of those outside their group—this is especially the case with SCs. Satish Saberwal observes that reserved seats do not promote separatism since they require candidates to aggregate broad multi-caste support. (He finds separatist sentiment associated with despair of gaining acceptance.)[63]

Rank and file members of the SCs and STs, it is sometimes asserted, are alienated by being treated separately in the administration of compensatory preferences. There is undoubtedly some distress associated with identifying oneself as recipient, although it is not clear whether it is because of the existence of separate facilities or from the personal rejection that is expected to follow upon such identification. This is probably less so with reserved seats in legislatures than with educational and job benefits. Whatever sense of alienation is conveyed by reserved seats surely pales into insignificance beside such manifestations of hostile feeling as the much-publicised assaults and atrocities perpetrated on SCs. All systematic evidence suggests that the recipient groups welcome the extensive symbolic participation that reserved seats afford and regard them as a useful safeguard of their interests.[64]

Acceptance vs. Rejection

Reserved seats are more offensive to non-members of the SCs and STs than to members of these groups.[65] This is evidenced by resistance to the placement of reserved seats and by massive withdrawal of voters from participation in elections for reserved seats, particularly in Legislative Assembly contests.[66] Apparently, large numbers of people do not feel represented by these legislators and do not care to participate in choosing them.[67] This parallels the unwillingness to have representatives from these groups in unreserved seats (see Tables 4.4 and 4.5). Reservations may aggravate rejection, but rejection obviously exists independently. The aggregate evidence gives little indication of acceptance by voters. Unfortunately, we are almost entirely in the dark about the attitudinal effects upon a constituency of being represented by a SC legislator.[68]

But at the policy-making level, reserved seats have secured the acceptance of SCs and STs as groups whose interests and views must be taken into account.

In every legislative setting they are present insufficient numbers so that issues affecting these groups remain on the agenda. Anything less than respectful attention to their problems, even if only lip service, is virtually unknown.[69] Overt hostility to these groups is taboo in legislative and many other public forums.

Integrity vs. Manipulation

The reserved seat device entails considerable potential for manipulation. Candidates, dependent on parties for funds and organisation, may be selected on grounds of their acceptability to others rather than by virtue of forceful representation of the interests of the preferred groups. This dependence is compounded in the SC constituencies, with their overwhelmingly non-SC population. In his study of UP politics, Paul Brass observes that

> For the most part, the Scheduled Castes in Uttar Pradesh have accepted the patronage of the Congress government and have given their votes to the Congress Party in return. The Scheduled Caste leaders who have been given Congress tickets in the reserved constituencies are non-militant and have no power in the local or state Congress organisations.[70]

This portrayal is confirmed by Narayana, who concludes that reserved seats tend to produce "accommodating leaders who draw significant support from the upper castes" rather than candidates who identify with the interests of the SCs and are supported by them.[71]

The participation afforded by reserved seats is in some eyes outweighed by the sacrifice of integrity (and representation) they entail.[72] Thus by 1955, Ambedkar, who had fought so long against Congress opposition to obtain the reserved seats, called for their abolition[73]—a call that has been echoed by others since. Apparently, the doubts about reserved seats that assail thoughtful SC activists are not widely shared by the rank and file.[74] Of course, the attraction of termination depends on one's estimate of the quantity and quality of representation that could be secured in an open political arena without any safeguards.

Mobilisation vs. Enervation

Reserved seats help develop political skills among the SCs and STs and bring forth a cadre of political leaders. One wonders whether reserved constituencies produce more unified action,[75] more effective bargaining or more dynamic leadership than emerges from participation in coalitions in non-reserved constituencies.[76] The subordination and dependence of reserved seat legislators presumably limits the extent to which they serve as vigorous organisers of their communities. Yet their visible presence in top positions, produced by the reservations, may have some mobilisational effects even outside the reserved constituencies. Again, we quickly reach the limits of available knowledge.

Reserved seats afford SCs and STs a presence in the legislatures that is disproportionate to their share of political life. Yet their share of political life is probably greater than their share of any other sector of activity. Anil Bhatt's report of a four-state survey (done in 1966–67) is suggestive of the level of political activity among SCs.[77] He finds that although they are less interested in political matters and less knowledgeable, they vote slightly more and are as likely to have partisan affiliations.[78] They perceive themselves as less politically efficacious than others, which comports with a general perception that they are not influential.[79] They are less politically active in non-elective as well as elective settings: they initiate fewer contacts with government and the political elite (whom fewer SC people feel able to approach if needed).[80] Although they scored low on political activity, interest and perceived influence, there was a pronounced increase on all these measures among younger age cohorts.[81] A recent study by Eldersveld and Ahmed, based on 1967 and 1971 national surveys, confirms this portrait. They find SCs and STs less interested and knowledgeable, but on a rough parity in party membership and portion of party activists.[82] These groups, they report, "constitute an increasingly large proportion of political participants as one moves along the scale from least to most [politically] involved."[83]

Shares in political power reflect social status and economic prowess, but the translation is not exact. Calculating the disparities between socio-economic status and political participation, Bhatt concludes that differences in political participation are far narrower.[84] This is so for many groups, but it is markedly so for SCs. More than any other stratum, their political participation far outruns what would be expected if political activity reflected socio-economic standing. There is no direct evidence to connect this to the reservation of seats in legislative bodies. But one may speculate that the reserved seats operate as a kind of forced draft inclusion of SCs in the political system beyond what would flow from their resources. Generally, the structures of democratic politics shrink disparities among caste groups to a smaller magnitude than is found in ritual, social, educational or economic settings. That this equalising tendency is amplified by reserved seats is suggested by Bhatt's conclusion that the disparity between political participation and socio-economic standing is far greater for the SCs than for the "low castes" just above them in the traditional hierarchy.[85]

Self-Liquidation vs. Self-Perpetuation

Reservations of government posts or university admissions often operate as guaranteed minimums rather than as allotments of places over and above those gained on merit. Therefore, the net amount of preference they confer automatically declines as members of the preferred groups gain places on merit. Reservations in the legislatures do not have this automatic self-liquidating feature. However, unlike other preferences, they alone are subject to a constitutional time limit—this limit has been twice extended. Since the presence of the reserved seat legislators undoubtedly contributed to this result, these reservations are in a literal sense self-perpetuating in a way that others are not. Furthermore, their presence helps to perpetuate other forms of preference. Indeed, that is their purpose. They can only perpetuate preferences to the extent that they are influential, so self-perpetuation is a mark of some success in fulfilling their function of representation. Thus, self-perpetuation is not to be accounted a negative feature in itself. The case against reserved seats gains no added strength from their self-perpetuating quality, unless the whole system of compensatory preference is thought to be unjustified or to have outlived its justification.

....

Fairness vs. Unfairness

The fairness argument is of course based on the principle of historical restitution: more specifically on the notion that due to the cumulative effect of past unjust deprivations, members of these groups on the whole have fewer resources (skills, standing, wealth, etc.) with which to obtain the benefits that flow from the presence of their groups in legislative bodies. There are at least two separate arguments of unfairness: (1) that which rejects the principle of collective recompense for historical injustice; and (2) that based upon the unequal distribution of the burden of compensation.

The latter takes the form of a charge that it is unfair that the representation (and chances of political careers) of some should be impaired to provide such compensation, when there is no reason to suppose that those who are discomfited are more responsible for past invidious deprivations than are those whose representation and careers are undisturbed. Reserved seats are thus seen as the conscription of an arbitrarily selected group of citizens to discharge a debt, an obligation from which equally culpable debtors are excused.

The factual assumption of equal culpability might be challenged by an argument that there is some rough justice to the selection since the non-tribal population in constituencies with heavy ST populations benefited from the past exploitation of the tribals and (even more tenuously) in areas with higher proportions of SCs, the rest of the population were disproportionately beneficiaries of the exploitation of these groups. In the absence of a persuasive marshalling of evidence along these lines, it must be conceded that the reserved seat device does involve some unfairness of this second kind. Rotation might be a cure, but at a high cost: by rendering impossible the accumulation of experience, seniority and political strength, it would vitiate much of the value of the reserved seats. Separate electorates would avoid both arbitrariness of burdens and the drawbacks of rotation, but at a cost in integration that has been thought too high.

Even unfairness admits of more or less. Just how much of it there is, is not clear. For politicians, the burden is mitigated somewhat by the absence of restrictive residence requirements, but clearly there is a barrier to novices. How much are inhabitants of reserved constituencies deprived of representation? Lower voter turnouts (see Table 4.19) suggest perceived deprivation is not negligible.[86] But it says nothing about how well non-SC constituents are served by their reserved seat legislators. Along with so much else, this question has remained immune from research.

The broader fairness argument that rejects the policy of historic compensation may take the form of objection to any attempt to distribute present benefits to remedy historical injustices. Or the notion of historical compensation may be accepted but objection taken to the distribution of benefits on the basis of group membership rather than individual deserts. Compensatory programmes in India, such as reserved seats, have typically identified as beneficiaries members of castes (or tribes) on the ground that such groups are the carriers of the heritage of cumulative disadvantage which must be offset. This leads us to the question, implicated deeply in the design of compensatory discrimination policies, of the role of descent groups in Indian society, which we can take up under the heading of secularism vs. communalism.

Secularism vs. Communalism

The use of caste groups to identify the beneficiaries of compensatory discrimination has been blamed for perpetuating the caste system, accentuating caste consciousness, injecting caste into politics and generally impeding the development of a secular society in which communal affiliation is ignored in public life.

This indictment is open to doubt at a number of points. First, it is not clear that the use of caste to designate beneficiaries has played such a preponderant role in the marriage of caste and politics. It is surely vastly overshadowed by the franchise itself, with its invitation to mobilise support by appeal to existing loyalties. But the avowed and official recognition of caste in compensatory discrimination policy makes it a convenient target for those offended and dismayed by the continuing salience of caste in Indian life.

Caste ties and cast-based political mobilisation are not exclusive to SCs and STs. The political life within these groups is not necessarily more intensely communal in orientation;[87] nor is the caste politics of greatest political impact found among these groups. Intellectual dismay at the unforeseen durability of caste has fastened on the reserved seats as the villains of the tale,[88] but the link has never been convincingly established.

The overestimation of the influence of reserved seat arrangements matches the overestimation of the amount of preference afforded to the SCs and STs. The widespread perception of ubiquitous and unrestrained preferment for these groups derives from several sources. First, there is the chronic overstatement of the effects of reservation: large portions of reservations (especially for cherished higher positions) are not filled; of those that are filled, some would have been gained on merit, so the net effect is often considerably less than popularly perceived. Second, ambiguous nomenclature and public inattention combine to blur the distinction between measures for SCs and STs and those for OBCs. The resentment and dismay engendered by use of the OBCs category to stake out massive claims on behalf of peasant-middle groups (particularly in some southern states) are readily transferred to discredit the more modest measures for SCs and STs.

Vigorous mobilisation of groups, it is now realised, is not necessarily inimical to democracy or secularism (unless these are defined in terms of an austere individualism that does not admit of any group presence in the political arena). Indeed, mobilisation along group lines among the SCs and STs may make a positive contribution to the realisation of the profoundly secular goals of compensatory discrimination—the dismantling of the traditional religiously sanctioned hierarchy of groups in Indian society. Elderveld and Ahmed found that among Harijans and tribals a high level of caste consciousness seemed connected with higher participation in public life.[89]

....

One wonders whether this association of strong caste identification and high levels of political participation can be connected with reserved seats, either as a structural effect observable in reserved constituencies or generally as a mobilisational effect of the reserved seats.

Development vs. Stagnation

As a forced draft programme of inclusion of SCs and STs within national life, compensatory discrimination has been a partial and costly success. Although few direct benefits have reached the vast mass of landless labourers in the villages, it has undeniably succeeded in accelerating the growth of a middle class within these groups—urban, educated, largely in government service. Members of these groups have been brought into central roles in the society to an extent unimaginable a few decades ago. There has been a significant redistribution of educational opportunities to them; there is a sizeable section of these groups who can utilise these opportunities and confer advantages on their children;

TABLE 4.19: VOTER TURNOUT BY TYPE OF SEAT

(in percentages, rounded)

	Lok Sabha			Legislative Assemblies		
	General	Scheduled Caste	Scheduled Tribe	General	Scheduled Caste	Scheduled Tribe
1962	57	54	44	59	48	42
1967	62	61	49	64	54	46
1971–72	57	51	43	63	53	45

Sources: 1962 and 1967 from Dushkin (1972, 195). Data for 1971–72 from Election Commission 1973, 184; Election Commission 1976, 294.

their concerns are firmly placed on the political agenda and cannot readily be dislodged. But if reserved seats are part of this self-sustaining dynamic of inclusion, there is at the same time a lesser counter-dynamic of resentment, rejection, manipulation and low self-esteem. And these gains are an island of hope in vast sea of neglect and oppression. The general pattern of the past decades might crudely be summarised as development at the upper end and stagnation at the bottom. Compensatory discrimination means that a section of the SCs and STs has been incorporated into the modern class manning the organised sector. What does this portend for the bulk of untouchables and tribals who remain excluded and oppressed? Are they better or worse off by virtue of the fact that some members of their descent group have a share in the benefits of modern India? The meaning of reserved seats and of compensatory discrimination policy ultimately depends on how one visualises the relation of this new elite to the masses of SCs and STs.

III

Conclusion

This year will see a new debate over the further extension of the reserved seats. During the 1969 debates there were undertones of opposition, but the final vote for extension was unanimous. Resentment of SC "privileges" is more overt, more intense now. It seems unlikely that the debate will be as subdued as that of ten years ago. Although Indian intellectuals, including some eminent social scientists, have passed severe judgements on compensatory discrimination policies, it is only in the last few years that systematic research on their effects has been undertaken. And unfortunately very little of it has touched on the reserved seats. Thus it seems unlikely that this year's debate will be informed by the comprehensive "scientific study" called for ten years ago.

The absence of more ample data is especially regrettable because one can so easily imagine feasible studies that would be immensely revealing about the benefits and costs of reserved seats. Perhaps more studies (including re-analyses of existing data) will surface before the year is out. But it should be remembered that for purposes of deciding whether reserved seats should be extended or terminated, the collection and analysis of data about their performance is only a first (though essential) step. The policy decision involves at least three major sorts of questions beyond the estimation of costs and benefits up till now.

First, once a pattern of costs and benefits is ascertained, there is the question of whether it can be expected to continue in the future. Is there any reason to think that one or another benefit or cost might be amplified or diminished during the next period for which reserved seats are to be extended? Are there reasons to expect that the coming period would be one to reap cumulative benefits or one in which there would be diminishing returns?

Second, since the goals and dangers of the compensatory discrimination policy are multiple and incommensurable, an evaluation of costs and benefits requires that some kind of weights and priorities be assigned to these goals or dangers. These can be supplied only by a vision of a future society that unites the desirable with the possible.

Third, evaluation must be comparative. Acceptance or rejection of the package of benefits and costs believed to be associated with reserved seats must be compared with the costs as well as the benefits anticipated to arise from any alternative that is believed preferable—a regime of income-tested preferences, or double votes, or a separatist solution. And, of course, it is necessary to make the case for the feasibility as well as the preferability of any alternative.

NOTES AND REFERENCES

I would like to acknowledge the capable assistance of Robert M. Hayden, Catherine Meschievitz and Hugh A. Ross, Jr. I am especially indebted to Henry C. Hart of the University of Wisconsin, Madison for generously allowing me to utilise data that he collected. Obviously, he shares no blame for my interpretation of them. I am grateful to Thomas Hone of Indiana University for computing the Hart data and helping me to understand it.

The following abbreviations are used for frequently cited material:

AIR	All-India Reporter
CAD	Constituent Assembly Debates
ELK	Election Law Reports
RCSCST	Reports of the Commissioner for Scheduled Castes and Scheduled Tribes

[1] Lelah Dushkin. "The Backward Classes: Special Treatment Policy," *Economic Weekly*, 13, no. 43 (28 October 1961): pp. 1665–68, 1695–1705, 1729–38; see p. 1667.

[2] Temporary preferences for yet another group, the Anglo-Indians, were not based on their backwardness but were designed to cushion the loss of the privileged position they had earlier enjoyed.

[3] On the identity and size of the Other Backward Classes, see Marc Galanter. "Who Are the Other Backward Classes? An Introduction to a Constitutional Puzzle," *Economic and Political Weekly*, 13, nos 43–44 (28 October 1978): pp. 1812–28.

[4] Article 330.

[5] Article 332.

[6] The Constituent Assembly definitively rejected political safeguards for religious and other minorities (Constituent Assembly Debates 12: p. 299). See Granville Austin, *The Indian Constitution: Cornerstone of a Nation* (Oxford: Clarendon Press, 1966), pp. 146–56. The Constitution does, however, provide for nominated representatives of the Anglo-Indian community in the Lok Sabha (Art. 331) and in the Legislative Assemblies (Art. 333). On the implementation of these provisions, see RCSCST 1975–77, 37.

[7] The Constitution contains no similar provision for representation in other political bodies. However, such political safeguards may lie within the scope of Article 15(4), which is apparently broad enough to authorise the reservation of seats in elective bodies on a local level.

[8] Election Commission, *Report on the General Elections to the Legislative Assemblies in India, 1970–72* (Delhi: Government Press, 1976a), pp. 3–6.

[9] By separate electorates is meant the representation of religious (or other) minorities by legislators chosen by an electorate composed only of members of that minority. The provision and extent of such representation was an extremely troublesome political issue in India during the forty years preceding Independence. The Government of India Act, 1909 gave separate electorates to Muslims: the Government of India Acts of 1919 and 1935 provided separate electorates for Muslims, Sikhs, Indian Christians, and other groups. Proposals to give separate electorates to the Scheduled Castes under the 1935 Act were withdrawn after adamant resistance by M. K. Gandhi. See B. R. Ambedkar, *What Congress and Gandhi Have Done to the Untouchables* (Bombay: Thacker, 1946, 2e). They were given instead reserved seats in the legislatures—i.e., only they could be candidates for these seats, but the whole general electorate chose among the candidates. Separate electorates were a constant focus of dispute between Hindus and Muslims. See Reginald Coupland, *The Indian Problem: A Report on the Constitutional Problem in India* (New York: Oxford University Press, 1944); M. N. Dalai, *Whither Minorities* (Bombay: D. B. Taraporevala Sons & Co., 1940).

[10] The Supreme Court has indicated that Article 15 prohibits communal electorates in local bodies. *Nain Sukh Das v State of UP*, AIR 1953 SC 384.

[11] Representation of the People Act, 1951 (Act 43 of 1951). The smaller deposits apply in contesting non-reserved as well as reserved seats. A proposal by Panjabrao Deshmukh, leading spokesman for the Other Backward Classes, to extend the smaller deposits concession to that category elicited a gruff dismissal from Ambedkar, then the Law Minister:

> [T]his is the first time that I hear that such a concession should be extended to the Backward Classes. Hitherto the concessions that have been spoken of as being necessary for the upliftment of the Backward Classes are educational concessions and concessions in the services of the country.... [S]o far as the Members representing the Backward Classes in this House... they are capable of paying not only their own election deposits, but also the election deposits of many others.

The government refused to accept the amendment and it was withdrawn. *Parliamentary Debates,* vol. 12–13, part 2 (19 May 1951): cols. 9141–49.

[12] Article 334.

[13] Constitution (Eighth Amendment) Act, 1959.

[14] Constitution (Twenty-third Amendment) Act, 1969.

[15] *Lok Sabha Debates*, Fourth Series, vol. 34, no. 16 (8 December 1969): col. 299.

[16] In 1952, all of the SC seats and half of the ST seats in the Lok Sabha were in double-member constituencies. In 1957, 467 out of 470 SC seats in the Vidhan Sabhas and 115 of the 221 seats reserved for STs were also in double-member constituencies. On the functioning of the double-member constituencies and their abolition, see Lelah Dushkin, "Scheduled Caste Politics," in *The Untouchables in Contemporary India*, ed. Michael Mahar (Tucson: University of Arizona Press, 1972), p. 189ff.

[17] The Two Member Constituency (Abolition) Act, 1961 (Act 1 of 1961).

[18] There were also complaints from administrators about the difficulty and expense of counting the ballots in double-member constituencies. Election Commission, *Report on the Third General Elections in India, 1962*, 2 Vols (Delhi: Manager of Publications, 1966), p. 17.

[19] In actuality, this did not happen very often. In nearly 200 double-member constituency contests for Lok Sabha seats in 1952 and 1957, the general seat was won by a reserved seat candidate in one in 1952 and five in 1957. It was apparently even less frequent in the legislative elections, as indicated by the very small number of non-reserved seats occupied by SCs and STs (see Table 5).

[20] In a well-known 1959 decision, the Supreme Court upheld the right of a Scheduled Tribe candidate to take the unreserved seat, sealing the defeat of the Labour Minister (*V. V. Giri v D. Sura Dora,* AIR 1959 SC 1318). For adverse comment, see S. S. Nigam, "Equality and the Representation of the Scheduled Classes in Parliament," *Journal of the Indian Law Institute* 2 (1960): pp. 297–320. Lelah Dushkin, "Scheduled Caste Politics," p. 192, says this decision triggered the move for abolition. The Delimitation Commission had taken some pains to avoid double-member constituencies with a minority tribal population (Election Commission, *Report on the First General Elections in India, 1951–52*, 2 Vols [Delhi: Manager of Publications, 1955], p. 151).

[21] In most cases, this was done simply by dividing the double-member constituency and allotting the reserved seat to the one with the greatest proportion of Scheduled Castes or Tribes in its population (Election Commission, *Report on the Third General Elections in India, 1962*, 2 Vols [Delhi: Manager of Publications, 1966], p. 18).

[22] Delimitation Act, 1972 (Act 76 of 1972). General information in the following paragraphs is based on an interview with a member of the previous Commission in 1966.

[23] Section 5. The associated members from each state are consulted after tentative delimitation. After changes at this stage, the proposed delimitations are published and objections invited. Where there are objections, hearings are held. The location of reserved seats is the most frequent source of objections, but they are rarely shifted.

[24] Article 329.

[25] Section 9 (I) (d).

[26] In the following pages, comparisons of the reserved seat holders in the Lok Sabha with the occupants of general seats are based on data made available to me by Henry C. Hart of the University of Wisconsin. This data consisted of (1) coded cards on all 497 members of the Third Lok Sabha from 1962–65 and (2) coded cards based on his interviews with 189 members of the Lok Sabha in 1963–64. Of the sample, 108 were a random sample (30 per cent) of Congress members. The remaining 79 were 60 per cent of the opposition and independent members. The sample of the latter is not random but is weighted slightly toward those active in the affairs of the Lok Sabha. In the sequel a source given simply as "Hart Data" refers to the larger set of cards on all members; the smaller set is referred to as the "Interview Sample." Other data from the Hart study is presented in Henry C. Hart, "Parliament and Nation-Building: England and India." In *Modern Parliaments: Change or Decline?* ed. Gerhard Loewenberg (Chicago: Aldine, Atherton, 1971).

[27] Gopal Krishna. "One Party Dominance—Development and Trend," in *Perspectives*, supplement to *Indian Journal of Public Administration* 12, no. 1 (January–March 1966): p. 28, reports 19.

[28] Section 9 (1) (c).

[29] My figures are taken from the Hart data. Krishna, "One Party Dominance—Development and Trend," p. 28, gives slightly different figures, but the overall picture is not very different.

[30] Election Commission, *Delimitation of Parliamentary and Assembly Constituencies Order, 1976* (New Delhi: Government Press, Lok Sabha, 1976b), II-A: 26. Inspection of the Election Commission tables reveals that Andhra is not atypical in this regard.

[31] Election Commission, *Report on the Second General Elections in India, 1957*, 2 Vols (Delhi: Manager of Publications, 1959), I:57. But for an instance of alleged manipulation in the opposite direction, see Satish Saberwal, "The Reserved Constituency: Candidates and Consequences," *Economic and Political Weekly* 7, no. 2 (8 January 1972): pp. 71–80; see p. 74.

[32] Election Commission, *Report on the Fourth General Elections in India, 1967*, 2 Vols (Delhi: Manager of Publications, 1968), I:12.

[33] *Mastanaiah v Delimitation Commission*, AIR 1969 AP 1. The Court rejected the argument that the Delimitation Commission was required to locate a reserved constituency in an adjoining district with a slightly higher percentage of SCs.

[34] The Election Commissioner characterised a proposal for rotation (on the ground that no area should be permanently burdened with a reserved seat) as "mere lip service to the principle of reservation", and concluded that the "real purpose of such reservations would be largely defeated if the proposal be adopted" (Election Commission, *Report on the Second General Elections in India, 1957*, I:75). In the 1969 debate preceding extension for the third ten-year period, an amendment proposing rotation, supported by a disingenuous plea to afford opportunities for election to Harijans in other localities, was negatived without a division of the House. See *Lok Sabha Debates*, Fourth Series, vol. 34, no. 17 (9 December 1969): cols. 361, 379.

[35] Of these few victories, a share resulted from the double-member constituency arrangement which obtained in the first two elections. Six of the sixteen unreserved seats (one in 1952, five in 1957) won by SC and ST candidates in those two elections were the general seats in double-member constituencies where one seat had been reserved.

[36] Article 80.

[37] Article 171. It should be noted that in only seven of the larger states is there a second chamber. Article 168.

[38] Article 164 (1) provides that the states of Bihar, Madhya Pradesh and Orissa shall have a minister in charge of tribal welfare who may in addition be in charge of SCs and Backward Classes or any other work.

[39] RCSCST 1962–63, L 153.

[40] Ministry of Food, 1966, 955, 12ff.

[41] RCSCST 1963–64, 1:163.

[42] The population figures here are somewhat overstated since SCs and STs are less urban than the general population. But offsetting this, the small territorial constituencies ought to give these groups an advantage. Also, Bengal is reputed to be less resistant to the mobility of these groups than many other areas.

[43] RCSCST 1969–70, 51.

[44] The percentage of Muslims (who make up about 11 per cent of the population of India) in legislative bodies is small and declining. Muslim membership declined from 7.2 per cent of the Lok Sabha in 1952 to 4.6 per cent in 1971 (K. L. Gauba, *Passive Voices: A Penetrating Study of Muslims in India* [New Delhi: Sterling Publishers, 1973], p. 245). Muslim participation in the

State Assemblies is at roughly the same level and has been undergoing a similar decline (ibid., pp. 262–65; Gopal Krishna, "Electoral Participation and Political Integration," *Economic and Political Weekly* 2, annual number (4 February 1967): pp. 179–90; see p. 187.

[45] My account is drawn from comparisons of the occupants of reserved and general seats found in D. N. S. Chauhan and S. L. Chopra, "A Comparative Study of the Socio-Economic Background of the Members of the Lok Sabha Elected From the Reserved and the General Constituencies," *Journal of Constitutional and Parliamentary Studies* 111, no. 2 (1969): pp. 94–100; Ratna Dutta, "The Party Representative in Fourth Lok Sabha," *Economic and Political Weekly* 4, nos 1 and 2 (Annual Number 1969): pp. 179–89; G. Narayana, "Social Background of Scheduled Caste Lok Sabha Members, 1962–71," *Economic and Political Weekly* 13, no. 37 (16 September 1978): pp. 1603–08; Manindra Kumar Mohopatra, "The Scheduled Caste Members of the Indian Lok Sabha in 1977: An Empirical Study of Developmental Change in Legislative Recruitment," Paper presented to Seventh Annual Conference on South Asia, University of Wisconsin, Madison, 3–4 November 1978. These accounts comport with the profile of Scheduled Caste MPs in C. Parvathamma and R. T. Jangam, "India's Scheduled Caste MPs: A Socio-Economic Profile," *Journal of Karnatak University—Social Sciences*, 5 (1969): pp. 153–66.

[46] Narayana, "Social Background of Scheduled Caste Lok Sabha Members," p. 1605. Mohopatra ("The Scheduled Caste Members of the Indian Lok Sabha in 1977," p. 4) shows even higher educational attainments for SC representatives in the Sixth Lok Sabha, but a renewed disparity due to even more degree-holding general members.

[47] Mohopatra, "The Scheduled Caste Members of the Indian Lok Sabha in 1977."

[48] Mohopatra's useful study of the Orissa Legislative Assembly in 1969 (n=85 of 139) found that SC and ST legislators were younger, less educated, came from more agricultural backgrounds, and fewer of them had independent professions. See Manindra Kumar Mohopatra, "The Scheduled Caste and the Tribal Political Elites: An Empirical Exploration of the Attributes, Ascent and Role Perceptions of Token Elites in an Indian State," *International Behavioural Scientist*, 5, no. 4 (1973): pp. 1–23.

[49] The data referred to here is that described in note 26 above. The reader should be warned that this data has not been subjected to refined analyses to see, for example, if the differences can be explained by other factors—like political experience or party affiliation. The interview sample (utilised in Tables 4.15–4.18) has additional problems of representativeness, but the picture there seems fully consonant with the data drawn from the whole membership.

[50] They provide no measure, for example, of the vision or sustained energy whose absence is marked by Saberwal (1972, 79) when he notes that the Harijans in the reserved constituency that he studied had no leaders who understood the larger institutional mechanisms which underlay and renewed the current inequalities, nor any who had the stamina for changing the larger system so that its processes would generate effective ... equality. He does not argue that this absence is produced by the reservation of seats, but such an argument is made in connection with some of the criticism of dependence of reserved seat legislators (discussed below under the heading of "Integrity vs. Manipulation").

[51] Stanley A. Kochanek, "The Relation between Social Background and Attitudes of Indian Legislators," *Journal of Commonwealth Political Studies*, 6, no. 1 (1968): pp. 34–53; p. 48, found Harijan MPs in 1960 among the strong supporters of land ceilings, urban income ceilings, and generally giving "higher than average support for any process of levelling." But cf. Mohopatra's ("The Scheduled Caste and the Tribal Political Elites," p. 22) finding that reserved seat holders in Orissa displayed no overwhelming concern for these groups. The pattern in state legislatures may differ sharply from that in the Lok Sabha, as suggested by Dushkin ("Scheduled Caste Politics," p. 210).

[52] On 8 August 1967. See *Journal of Constitutional and Parliamentary Studies* 1, no. 4: 55. See Dushkin, "Scheduled Caste Politics," p. 206.

[53] Ibid., pp. 207–08.

[54] Marc Galanter, "The Abolition of Disabilities: Untouchability and the Law," in *The Untouchables in Contemporary India* ed. Michael Mahar (Tucson: University of Arizona Press, 1972). [An earlier version appeared in *Economic and Political Weekly*, 4, nos. 1–2 (Annual Number): 131–70.]

[55] For example, Krishna, "One Party Dominance," p. 32, notes that in 1962, Scheduled Caste legislators in reserved seats supplied the entire Congress plurality in 8 of 13 state legislatures. Dushkin, "Scheduled Caste Politics," p. 205, calculated that in March 1967, at least nine state governments were dependent on reserved seat legislators.

[56] They are, in Saberwal's ("The Reserved Constituency," p. 78) term, "boosters" that help amplify other modes of upward mobility.

[57] Pratap C. Aggarwal, and Mohd. Siddiq Ashraf. *Equality through Privilege: A Study of Special Privileges of Scheduled Castes in Haryana* (New Delhi: Shri Ram Centre for Industrial Relations and Human Resources, 1976), p. 114.

[58] There is some evidence that the mobile minority that utilise educational benefits and job reservations is not evenly spread among the Scheduled Castes and Tribes, and it is possible that a similar clustering is found in the enjoyment of benefits directly tied to political reservations. In all these cases, the question is how much spillover is there from the direct recipients to others in the beneficiary groups.

[59] Cf. Dushkin's ("Scheduled Caste Politics," p. 211) observations that Scheduled Caste legislators:

> tend to concentrate their efforts on those items of the protective discrimination system that are of most concern to their more prosperous caste constituents, more ministries for themselves, more scholarships and reservations in higher educational institutions, and above all, more government jobs.

[60] *Lok Sabha Debates*, Fourth Series, vol. XXMV (8 December 1969): col. 299.

[61] Dushkin, "Scheduled Caste Politics," p. 213.

[62] Lelah Dushkin, "Backward Class Benefits and Social Class in India, 1920–1970," Paper delivered at the Annual Meeting of the Association for Asia Studies, Chicago, April 1978.

[63] Saberwal, "The Reserved Constituency," p. 80.

[64] Aggarwal and Ashraf, *Equality through Privilege*, p. 145; Santosh Singh Anant, *The Changing Concept of Caste in India* (Delhi: Vikas Publications, 1972), p. 97.

[65] Anant's (*The Changing Concept of Caste in India*, p. 97) useful study of three north Indian localities in 1968 reveals a consistent pattern of sharp division over preferential treatment, with urban, higher caste and more educated respondents being most opposed. Harijans were the only caste group who favoured extension of reserved seats upon their expiration in 1970.

[66] Myron Weiner and John Osgood Field, "How Tribal Constituencies in India Vote," in Jagdish Bhagwati et al., *Electoral Politics in the Indian States: Three Disadvantaged Sectors*, vol. 2 of *Studies in Electoral Politics in the Indian States*, eds M. Weiner and J. O. Field (Delhi: Manohar Book Service, 1975, p. 89ff, observe that the lower turnout in constituencies reserved for STs represents both lower voting rates among tribals and reluctance of non-tribal voters to vote for tribal candidates.

[67] Other evidence of this reluctance to have SC representatives is provided by Dushkin, "Scheduled Caste Politics," p. 191, who calculates that in the 1957 elections in double-member constituencies, SC candidates came in first in only 34.2 per cent of the Lok Sabha contests and 28.5 per cent of the Legislative Assembly contests.

[68] On the basis of his field observations Saberwal, "The Reserved Constituency," p. 77, argues that reserved seats help weaken ideas concerning the low social status of Scheduled Castes, their general lack of competence and their inherited pollution.

[69] Barbara Joshi, "Scheduled Caste Political Reservations: Who Benefits?" Preliminary draft of paper presented to Annual Meeting of Association for Asian Studies, Chicago, April 1978.

[70] Paul Brass, *Factional Politics in an Indian State: The Congress Party in Uttar Pradesh* (Berkeley: University of California Press, 1966), p. 105.

[71] G. Narayana, "The Political Elite among the Scheduled Castes," *Journal of Constitutional and Parliamentary Studies*, 8 (1974): pp. 214–19; see p. 217. Instances of this pattern are described by Owen M. Lynch, *The Politics of Untouchability: Social Mobility and Social Change in a City of India* (New York: Columbia University Press, 1969), p. 101, and Khadija A. Gupta, "General Elections of 1967 in a Small UP Town," *Economic and Political Weekly*, 6, no. 35 (28 August 1971): pp. 1881–86.

[72] But cf. Henry C. Hart, "Parliament and Nation-Building: England and India," in *Modern Parliaments: Change or Decline?* ed. Gerhard Loewenberg (Chicago: Aldine, Atherton, 1971), pp. 134–35, who observes that India has erected a system of "co-optative, representation like that which merged the Scottish into the British elite", and surmises that "to keep these voters docile ... any government will have to maintain, even accelerate, the employment of these subject peoples in government."

[73] Eleanor Mae Zelliott, "Dr. Ambedkar and the Mahar Movement," Unpublished dissertation, University of Pennsylvania, 1969, p. 279.

[74] Lynch, *The Politics of Untouchability*, p. 107ff, describes the division within the Republican Party on this issue. But cf. the overwhelmingly supportive views reported by Anant, *The Changing Concept of Caste in India*, p. 97, and Aggarwal and Ashraf, *Equality through Privilege*, p.143ff.

[75] On the basis of her case study Gupta, "General Elections of 1967 in a Small UP Town," p. 1886, concludes that "reserved constituencies tend to intensely caste tensions among ...[the groups] for whose benefit the reservation ... has been provided."

[76] An interesting portrait of SC political activity in a general constituency may be found in Veena Dua, "Elections in a Scheduled Neighbourhood: A Punjab Town," *Economic and Political Weekly*, 6, no. 46 (13 November 1971): pp. 2323–27. Revealing glimpses of SCs offering electoral support for tangible collective benefits may be found in reports of election disputes. For example, *Tirlochan Singh v Kurnal Singh*, AIR 1968 Pand H 416 (promise of Rs 1,500 to construct a Harijandharamsala); *Buluant Rai Tayal v Mshan Saroop*, 17 ELK 101 (Punjab High Court, 1958) (promise to help Harijans retain temple site and get land for building houses); *Magan Lal Bagdi v Hari Vishnu Kamat*, AIR 1960 MP 362 (promise to dig well for Harijans).

[77] Anil Bhatt, *Caste, Class and Politics: An Empirical Profile of Social Stratification in Modern India* (Delhi: Manohar Book Service, 1975, analyses a sample of 1,757 male Hindus in 100 rural and 20 urban localities in four states (Andhra Pradesh, Gujarat, Uttar Pradesh and West Bengal).

[78] Ibid., pp. 79, 82, 84, 98.

[79] Ibid., pp. 87–92.

[80] Ibid., pp. 104–07.

[81] Ibid., pp. 112ff., 150.

[82] Samuel J. Eldersveld and Bashiruddin Ahmed, *Citizens and Politics: Mass Political Behaviour in India* (Chicago and London: University of Chicago Press, 1978), pp. 109, 198.

[83] Ibid., p. 197.

[84] Bhatt, *Caste, Class and Politics*, Ch. 4.

[85] Ibid., p. 179ff.

[86] Cf. Gupta's ("General Elections of 1967 in a Small UP Town," p. 1884) description of the "general resentment among the higher caste Hindus against Sasni being part of a 'reserved' constituency." The feeling that others could not really be represented by a SC representative was echoed in a distinction drawn by an (early) Election Tribunal in *B. R. Ambedkar vs. A. Dange*, 1 ELR 364 (Election Tribunal, Bombay, 1952). Urging voters to give both of their votes to a single candidate to avoid SCs being elected to both seats in a two-member constituency was not, found the tribunal, the systematic appeal on ground of caste forbidden by the election law since the emphasis was not on the undesirability of both the seats going to the Scheduled Castes but on the possibility that as a result of the reservation, voters other than the Scheduled Caste voters might go unrepresented.

[87] In their study of Indian political participation, Eldersveld and Ahmed, *Citizens and Politics*, p. 205, report that the overwhelming majority of... activists are politically conscious of caste. They know how the caste leader voted. Among upper castes the ratio is 6 to 1 that activists are aware of caste, in the middle castes it is better than 8 to 1, and for the lower castes and Harijans it is 3 to 1 that activists are caste conscious.

[88] Thus, K. Santhanam, *Transition in India and Other Essays* (Bombay: Asia Publishing House, 1964), p. 13, for example, speculates that reserved seats for SCs provided moral legitimation for caste politics.

[89] Eldersveld and Ahmed, *Citizens and Politics*, p. 205.

5

Social Mobility and Caste Violence

A Study of the Gujarat Riots*

Pradip Kumar Bose

Caste riots are not uncommon in India and, especially in the last decade, there have been a number of such riots in various parts of the country. But they were mainly located in rural areas and were primarily rooted in disputes over land and wages. In these riots caste and class converged to a certain extent. Caste riots took place in Bihar also on the issue of reservations but the immediate reason for those riots was a policy of reservation which amounted to reserving 44 per cent of government jobs on the basis of caste alone.

Before the present riots in Gujarat, no such move was in sight; in fact, the present reservation policy has been in force for quite some time. Compared to many other states, the reservation of jobs in Gujarat is just 7 per cent for Scheduled Castes (SC) and 14 per cent for Scheduled Tribes (ST), whereas in states like Uttar Pradesh 36 per cent of the class four jobs, 25 per cent class three jobs and 18 per cent of all services are reserved for SC.[1]

How is it that such an insignificant issue of reservation of seats in the postgraduate medical courses (which has also been in force for the last three years) could trigger such violent caste riots, mainly in the urban areas of Gujarat? In this chapter we shall try to show that this outbreak of violence is primarily related to the mobility of SC in the state. We shall confine our analysis to SC because the ST are not involved in this agitation, nor are they the target of attacks.

Social mobility can have two consequences on the stability of social structure. The possibility of social mobility can sustain a belief in the availability

* Originally published in *Economic and Political Weekly* 16, no. 16 (18 April 1981): pp. 713–16.

of opportunity which may have a stabilising influence on a society and polity. But in India, where the role of caste and inherited status have for long influenced the monopolising of available jobs by the upper castes, the mobility of lower castes is viewed as dangerous by vested interests and is hence disruptive of social stability. It is true that the traditional system also allowed the mobility of castes, but they were changes in the hierarchical arrangement of castes and not in the structure. The present mobility of SC which we have witnessed in the last thirty years is in a sense caste-free, where the opportunities are, theoretically, made available to all. In the first twenty years following Independence, it was the upper castes who took greater advantage of the opportunities because of their already privileged position in society. It is only since then, when the new generation of SC entered the job market with an additional backing of reservations, that tensions have started building up in the system. In other words, the strain was the result of the ambiguity of the means by which different sections of society competed for resources sanctioned by the social and legal structure—that is, what groups get how much of the political, economic and prestige resources available. The strain in the structure was also engendered by the ambiguity stemming from the difference between how one performed and how one was rewarded. This is related to a host of problems like admission in professional courses, appointment and promotion in jobs, etc. It is obvious that a structure will not be free of strain and tension while a large number of individuals perceive themselves to be deprived; and it is significant that a slight improvement in the status of SC has produced a sense of deprivation among the upper castes belonging to the middle class.

The caste conflict in Gujarat is thus related to deep-rooted caste prejudices among the upper castes on the one hand and to social mobility of SC on the other. A study of untouchability in sixty-nine villages in Gujarat has shown that in 90 per cent of the villages, entry into temples and the houses and shops of high castes is not permitted. In 64 per cent of the villages there are separate sources of water supply and in 47 per cent of the villages untouchability prevails even in panchayat meetings.[2] It would be naive to assume that these prejudices are confined only to rural areas and that urban dwellers are free from them. A study of highly placed bureaucrats at Gandhinagar and Ahmedabad—who are in charge of developmental activities—observed that more than 50 per cent believed that efficiency in the administration has gone down due to the job reservation policy; they believed that SC/ST lacked what they called appropriate background, basic work discipline, etc.[3]

Politically, too, caste is a force to be reckoned with.

> In the 1950s the Congress party gave more weightage to party commitment, party work, etc. than to the candidate's caste in distributing party tickets. If other things were equal, the party gave preference to a candidate's caste. In the sixties

> and thereafter the party gave more weightage to caste of a candidate. Quite fresh and not even primary members of the party till the day of the selection were given Congress tickets primarily because they belonged to a particular caste. This practice started from 1967 elections. For instance, Kshatriya applicant was recommended by the State Congress Election Committee to the Central Congress Election Committee on the ground that "this is a constituency where only a Kshatriya candidate could be put up. Looking to their considerable population and backwardness, this section of society should not feel neglected." Such a consideration seems to have appeared for the first time in the Gujarat Congress Election Committee record. In the seventies the party distributed party tickets on caste considerations without any inhibition.[4]

SC in Gujarat, constituting only 6.8 per cent of the total population, has the highest literacy (27.74 per cent) among all the states except Kerala (Table 5.1).

TABLE 5.1: INDICATORS OF MOBILITY AMONG SCHEDULED CASTES

States*	Literacy**	Urbanisation**	Percentage of Job Seekers***	Total of Columns 1 and 2
	(1)	(2)	(3)	(4)
Gujarat	27.74	27.25	3.08	54.99
Maharashtra	25.27	24.68	5.29	49.95
Kerala	40.21	9.68	3.49	49.89
Tamil Nadu	21.82	17.30	1.85	39.12
Assam	25.79	9.39	1.36	35.18
Punjab	16.12	14.76	1.30	30.82
Karnataka	13.89	16.81	1.30	30.70
West Bengal	17.80	8.20	1.34	26.00
Madhya Pradesh	12.49	12.55	1.43	25.04
Himachal Pradesh	18.82	4.61	2.00	23.43
Rajasthan	9.14	14.28	0.87	23.42
Haryana	12.60	10.41	2.53	23.01
Andhra Pradesh	10.66	11.82	1.39	22.48
Orissa	15.61	6.27	0.81	21.88
Uttar Pradesh	10.20	7.56	1.12	17.76
Bihar	6.53	6.47	1.25	13.00

Notes: * States and Union Territories having less than 1 per cent of total SC population of India are omitted from the table.

** Percentages are computed on the basis of total SC population in the states.

*** *Report of the Commissioner for Scheduled Castes and Scheduled Tribes (15th Report) 1977–78*, Part II (Delhi: Government of India Press, 1979), p. 11.

Source: *Census of India* 1971, Series 1, *Scheduled Castes and Scheduled Tribes*, part 5A, p. 2.

The percentage of urban population among SC in Gujarat is the highest among all the states. While states like Himachal Pradesh, Uttar Pradesh, West Bengal, Orissa, Bihar, Tripura, Kerala and Jammu and Kashmir have a higher proportion of SC than Gujarat, urbanisation among them is less than 10 per cent. In Haryana, Tamil Nadu, Rajasthan, Andhra Pradesh, Madhya Pradesh and Karnataka it does not exceed 18 per cent; but in Gujarat it is 27.25 per cent. If we take literacy and urbanisation as indicators of social mobility and put equivalent scores in terms of high and low we find that Gujarat scores highest with 54.99 and leaves behind even Kerala, which has a very low rate of urbanisation among SC (Table 5.1). This mobility of SC in Gujarat is further indicated by the fact that while the percentage of job seekers among SC on the live registers at the end of 1977 does not go beyond 2.0 in most of the states, in Gujarat it is 3.08—a percentage exceeded only in Maharashtra and Kerala. The percentage of reserved vacancies filled by SC is also the highest in Gujarat. All these indicate that SC in Gujarat have performed relatively better than in other states. The state which comes closer to Gujarat in almost all these respects and has similar characteristics is Maharashtra, which witnessed violent caste riots three years ago.

The distribution of SC in Gujarat shows that the advanced sections of the SC community, such as Mahyavanshi and Bhambi, live mostly in north, central and south Gujarat, whereas the backward communities like Meghval live mostly in peninsular Gujarat (Table 5.2). Even the section of Vankar who live in peninsular Gujarat are backward. Historically, untouchables of both the north and central Gujarat and south Gujarat were exposed to various welfare and progressive measures much earlier than those in peninsular Gujarat, which comprised numerous small princely states ruled by unenlightened rulers. Hence, during the post-Independence era, SC belonging to these two regions took advantage of various governmental and non-governmental measures to improve their lot. The only exception among the untouchables in these two regions are the Bhangis who, though highly urbanised, are mainly scavengers or unskilled workers. Studies have shown that SC of north and central Gujarat make greater use of employment exchanges than SC of peninsular Gujarat.[5]

The present caste riots are mainly confined to the four districts of central Gujarat: Ahmedabad, Mehsana, Kaira and Baroda. In districts like Jamnagar, Rajkot and Bhavnagar there have been minor disturbances for two to three days; and in the rest of the state almost nothing has happened.

The disturbances and violence in these districts are related to two factors: (1) Mobility, i.e., the extent of literacy and urbanisation among SC; and (2) the concentration of SC in these districts. Again, if we add the scores of literacy and urbanisation and multiply the sum with the percentage of SC to total SC population in each district, we get a score which accurately reflects the occurrence

TABLE 5.2: DISTRICTWISE DISTRIBUTION OF IMPORTANT CASTES IN GUJARAT

(percentage)

District	Mahyavanshi	Vankar, Dhed	Bhambi Chamar	Bhangi	Meghval	Garoda
Jamnagar	–	19.18	16.71	7.19	50.88	1.78
Rajkot	–	37.44	20.05	12.33	26.43	1.23
Surendranagar	–	48.98	25.18	10.66	4.00	2.10
Bhavnagar	–	39.08	23.84	18.86	9.34	1.34
Amreli	–	52.82	13.63	10.52	17.10	1.12
Junagadh	–	49.64	11.17	8.78	21.21	0.79
Kutch	–	–	2.92	2.67	87.19	1.04
Banaskantha	26.15	–	30.94	15.52	13.54	5.11
Sabarkantha	40.32	–	36.01	7.55	0.24	4.44
Mehsana	35.17	–	33.47	10.51	0.05	5.61
Ahmedabad	51.58	–	24.87	12.81	0.32	2.71
Kaira	42.99	–	25.03	23.17	0.09	2.48
Panchmahals	42.83	–	17.58	29.26	1.29	1.49
Baroda	52.64	–	16.42	24.67	0.09	1.56
Bharuch	58.14	–	19.14	19.46	0.27	1.08
Surat	66.52	–	15.14	7.04	4.13	1.00

Source: Computed from *Census of India*, 1961, Vol. V, Gujarat, *General Notes on Scheduled Castes and Scheduled Tribes* (Delhi: Manager of Publications, 1969), pp. 34–35.

of violence in the particular regions of the state (Table 5.3, Column 4).[6] This reflects the mobility factor as related to caste riots. The reason for total absence of any disturbances in Valsad, where SC have higher mobility than in Kheda and Mehsana, is the lower concentration of SC in this district. Similarly, the district of Banaskantha, which has a higher concentration of SC than Baroda, has also not seen violence because of very low mobility among the SC. In Surat there were some disturbances, but the reason for the anti-reservation movement not taking off the ground was the low concentration of SC, both in terms of total SC population of the state and total population of the district. An additional reason for the relatively subdued violence in Surat and Valsad is the very high percentage of ST in these two districts. In both the districts more than 45 per cent of the population are tribals who are not in competition with SC for jobs. Finally, as I. P. Desai's study on untouchability has shown, the practice of untouchability is least prevalent in south Gujarat.

TABLE 5.3: INDICATORS OF MOBILITY IN DIFFERENT DISTRICTS

Districts	Literacy	Urbanisation	Percentage of SC to Total SC Population	Total of Columns 1 and 2 Multiplied by Column 3
	(1)	(2)	(3)	(4)
Ahmedabad	37.77	66.57	17.42	1,818
Mehsana	4.86	16.82	10.27	531
Kaira	37.68	16.29	8.12	438
Baroda	35.52	24.98	6.29	381
Surat	42.34	45.23	3.48	305
Rajkot	17.45	24.41	5.44	228
Junagadh	13.71	17.50	6.71	209
Surendranagar	18.68	20.49	4.81	188
Jamnagar	14.76	31.84	3.94	183
Bhavnagar	19.95	29.22	3.47	171
Valsad	40.95	21.54	2.35	168
Sabarkantha	24.59	4.98	5.60	166
Bharuch	34.27	18.16	2.93	154
Kutch	11.80	21.25	4.40	145
Panchmahals	22.74	13.67	3.73	136
Banaskantha	11.61	7.57	6.83	131
Amreli	17.78	11.90	3.47	103
Gandhinagar	43.22	15.09	0.72	–
The Dangs	43.27	0.0	0.03	–

Note: Literacy and urbanisation percentages are computed on the basis of total SC population in the district.

Source: Computed from *Census of India, 1971: Scheduled Castes and Scheduled Tribes*, p. 10.

In Ahmedabad, where SC have a very high urbanisation (66.57 per cent), high literacy (37.77 per cent) and high concentration (17.42 per cent), the conflict took the most violent turn and continued for the longest period. Whereas in Ahmedabad the riots were mainly confined to the city itself, in Mehsana it took the most violent form in Unjha in Sidhpur taluka and spread to places like Kalol, Kheralu, Visnagar and Patan. In Kaira the riots were mainly confined to Anand, Nadiad and Pellad. Though there were many local factors which influenced the intensity and violence of riots, in both the districts most of the affected talukas have more than average literacy rate, urbanisation and concentration of SC. The agitation first began in Ahmedabad in late January and within days took a violent turn. In Baroda it began within a week of the agitation in Ahmedabad, and in Mehsana and Kaira it started during the second and third weeks of February. If police firing is taken as one of the indicators of the intensity of violence then we find that it was most intense in these four districts (Table 5.4).[7] But in all four districts there was some resistance from SC which again was because they are mobile, urban and conscious. The textile workers of Ahmedabad, more than half of whom are Harijans, went on strike as a part of their protest against what they considered as continuous atrocities on Harijans in the state. However, it would be a mistake to conclude from this that there was greater solidarity between different untouchable castes.

TABLE 5.4: INTENSITY OF VIOLENCE IN DIFFERENT DISTRICTS

District	Killed in Firing	Injured in Firing	Days of Continued Disturbance
Ahmedabad	18	29	30
Mehsana	8	11	12
Kaira	5	12	7
Baroda	2	7	11
Surat	–	–	7
Sabarkantha	1	–	1
Jamnagar	–	–	3
Rajkot	–	–	3
Bhavnagar	–	–	3

Source: *Times of India* (Ahmedabad edition), 24 January–13 April 1981.

At the district level the targets of attack were mainly the upwardly mobile castes and not those who are menially occupied and have low mobility. In Ahmedabad Bhangis, who are generally occupied in menial jobs as scavengers and whose literacy rate is quite low, were not the target of attacks; but Vankars, who are generally occupied in blue or white collar jobs in the city, were attacked. In Kaira, too, a large number of Vankars are Christians who belong to a general co-operative society and have better opportunities for education and employment in towns.

Within the Vankar caste two groups are concentrated in different areas, broadly according to the two natural divisions of peninsular and mainland Gujarat. Thus, among them the section Mahyavanshi, Dhed or Vankar is found only in Baroda division—in the districts Banaskantha, Sabarkantha, Mehsana, Ahmedabad, Kaira, Panchmahals, Baroda, Bharuch and Surat—while the other group of Vankar or Dhed are found in Rajkot division, where Mahyavanshi are not scheduled according to the Presidential order (Table 2). Though the combined literacy of this caste is 33 per cent, the section which lives in Baroda division has a much higher literacy of 41 per cent and urbanisation of 32 per cent.

Nearly 62 per cent of the Mahyavanshis live in Ahmedabad, Mehsana, Kaira and Baroda. As Table 5.5 shows, the growth in literacy of just two sections of this caste combined is higher than that of the total population.

TABLE 5.5: LITERACY OF IMPORTANT SCHEDULED CASTES IN GUJARAT

(percentage)

Scheduled Castes	Percentage to Total SC	Literacy 1961	Literacy 1971	Growth
Mahayavanshi, Dhed, Vankar, etc.	41.10	27.66	33.34	5.68
Bhambi, Chamadia, Chamar, Rohit, etc.	22.75	21.49	26.20	4.80
Bhangi, Rukhi, Mehtar, etc.	12.76	17.79	21.13	3.34
Meghval, Menghvar, etc.	8.17	9.12	12.54	3.42
Garoda, Garo	2.51	40.48	46.72	6.24
General Population		30.45	35.79	5.34
Scheduled Castes		22.46	27.25	4.79

Source: Computed from *Census of India 1971: Scheduled Castes and Scheduled Tribes*, pp. 49–51; and *Census of India 1961*, Volume V, Gujarat, *General Notes on Scheduled Castes and Scheduled Tribes*, p. 21.

In Ahmedabad they consist of 52 per cent of the total SC population in the district; in Baroda, Kaira and Mehsana their percentage is 53, 43 and 35, respectively. It is obvious that this caste will be the target of attacks. Finally, it is these four districts which have shown greater degree of economic development and hence provide greater competition for scarce jobs.

There is a close parallel between the current caste riots in Gujarat and the Marathwada riots. We have already seen that the SC in Maharashtra and Gujarat inherit similar characteristics. Due to greater mobility of SC there are Dalit organisations in both the states, absent in places like Bihar or UP, which have much a higher proportion of SC than these two states. While analysing Marathwada riots Dipankar Gupta has similar observations to make.

> In the three affected districts (Nanded, Parbhani and Aurangabad), the number of scheduled castes enrolled in schools and colleges as proportion of their total population is much more than in Bhir and Osmanabad. Secondly, urban migration of scheduled castes in search of jobs is greater from the rural to the urban areas in these districts. Finally, these three districts have exhibited a greater degree of economic progress and development, in terms of industrial, urban and bureaucratic structure. It is therefore in these three districts that competition over scarce jobs between caste Hindus and Maharsis most developed.[8]

As in the Marathwada riots, where Mangs and Dhors were untouched and refused to join with the Mahars, in Gujarat also Bhangis did not play an active role in support of other SC. It is a well-known fact of Indian life that a member of a mobile low caste establishes the same distance with his immediate "inferiors" as the caste Hindu with him. In Ahmedabad, for instance, the Bhangis refused to join with the Vankars because they felt that they received the same kind of treatment from the Vankars as the Vankars got from caste Hindus. In short, both these caste riots point towards a pattern where we find that the greater mobility of SC when opportunities are becoming increasingly scarce has given rise to strain and tension culminating in caste riots. This also points towards the low level of tolerance of one section of the society where even a marginal improvement in the status of SC is not tolerated.

The fact that the main centres of the riots are located in the urban areas of the four districts clearly indicates that the riots were mainly over the scarce resources and employment opportunities. Hence, it was directed against the mobile section of the SC and flared up in regions where they are concentrated.

Notes and References

[1] *Report of the Commissioner for Scheduled Castes and Scheduled Tribes, 1977–78*, Part II (Delhi: Government of India Press, 1979), p. 15.

[2] I. P. Desai, *Untouchability in Rural Gujarat* (Bombay: Popular Prakashan, 1970).

[3] Y. G. Mankand, "Bureaucrat as Agent of Change: A Study in Role Perception," (Mimeo) (Surat: Centre for Social Studies, 1979).

[4] Ghanshyam Shah, "Rural Politics in Gujarat," *Teaching Politics* (forthcoming).

[5] B. V. Shah and J. D. Thaker, "Occupational Status of the Scheduled Castes in Gujarat," in *Removal of Untouchability*, ed. Vimal P. Shah (Ahmedabad: Gujarat University, 1980).

[6] This is an approximate indicator of the districts which are more prone to caste violence. Here, we have taken the percentage of literacy and urbanisation as sources varying from 0 to 100 and, to take account of SC concentration, multiplied the sum of two scores by the SC concentration in the district.

[7] These figures are computed from newspaper reports and we have taken only the number of persons killed and injured in police firing. We have deliberately omitted the figures of persons killed in stabbing, etc., as they are not very reliable. In fact, newspaper reports on the number of persons killed and injured in police firing are not always very accurate and are sometimes even contradictory. However, the table at least reflects the variations of intensity of violence in the districts.

[8] Dipankar Gupta, "Understanding the Marathwada Riots: A Repudiation of Eclectic Marxism," *Social Scientist* 7, no. 10 (May 1979): p. 12; See also, S. P. Punalekar, "Aspects of Class and Caste in Social Tensions: A Study of Marathwada Riots," (mimeo.)(Surat: Centre for Social Studies, 1981).

6

Communal Violence in India

A Study of Communal Disturbance in Delhi*

Gopal Krishna

Introduction

> A diversification among human communities is essential for the provision of the incentive and material for the Odyssey of the human spirit. Other nations of different habits are not enemies; they are godsends. Men require of their neighbours something sufficiently akin to be understood, something sufficiently different to provoke attention, and something great enough to command admiration.
>
> A. N. Whitehead, *Science and the Modern World*

That heterogeneity is a good thing because of the creative possibilities through constructive interaction it offers is the dominant liberal view in contemporary India. This view informs the public rhetoric of "unity through diversity" as the primary characteristic of Indian culture and of the cultural and historical processes at work in this country. That this is a humane and pragmatically sensible position to adopt for a society as heterogeneous as our own is self-evident. And yet it is obvious to any student of our society and history that heterogeneity has produced a great deal of conflict and violence, which has had the effect of accentuating divisions, impeding the processes of

* This edited chapter was published in two parts. The first part, consisting of Section I, is reproduced here. It was originally published in *Economic and Political Weekly* 20, no. 2 (12 January 1985): pp. 61–74.

** Sections II and III were published in *Economic and Political Weekly* 20, no. 3 (19 January 1985): pp. 117–31.

social integration, and inhibiting creative interaction. The immediate post-Independence trend towards national integration received a setback in the early part of the 1960s, and since then inter-group conflict has increased, whether it is conflict between the higher castes and the Harijans, between Hindus and Muslims, and between Hindus and Sikhs.

Inter-group conflict seems to be an inescapable aspect of public life in heterogeneous societies. The stability of such societies is precarious. The medley of peoples constituting them, in the words of J. S. Furnival, "mix but do not combine. Each group holds by its own religion, its own culture and language, its own ideas and ways. As individuals they meet, but only in the market place, in buying and selling."[1] The heterogeneity of a plural society has but few creative possibilities. It is held together by regulations, not by integration, and "lacking a common social life, men in plural society became decivilised."[2] The governing principle ordering the relations between the constituent groups in such societies is power, and there is a structural necessity for domination by one of the groups, acquiesced into by others, in order to sustain the political order.

India is a halfway house between the plural society as described by Furnival and a differentiated but coherent society envisaged in Whitehead's observation cited above. It is appropriately characterised as an "agglomerative" society by the late Irawati Karve in her illuminating essay.[3] An agglomerative society is loosely held together, has a historically evolved shared value framework, and therefore not brute power but shared culture forms the basis of the minimum necessary cohesion for an ordered collective life. Its social structure changes extremely slowly because it is grounded in an essentially stagnant agrarian political economy. When the economy begins to be transformed radically the social structure experiences great strain and the inevitable change in group status may well be accompanied by social violence. We have seen something of this happening in India in recent decades. But essentially the process can be viewed as one of creative adjustment, leading to a new form of integration of society.

The phenomenon of communal violence, on the other hand, seems to me to be qualitatively different. Hindu–Muslim relations have had the dual character of being governed by power and accommodation, and consequently the tension between the two communities is endemic, sometimes, though only rather infrequently, spilling over into mutual violence. A careful study of history would confirm that over a long period power was the dominant factor in ordering Hindu–Muslim relations, and the role of religion in fashioning our different civilisations has been so profound that it has precluded mutual influence at the higher level of culture. But the shared division of labour and a shared popular culture made for social accommodation, minimising communal conflict, especially in the rural society.

Incidents of communal disturbance have been recorded at least since the early eighteenth century. There was a riot in Ahmedabad in 1714, centering round the Holi celebration and cow slaughter questions. There was a Hindu–Muslim riot in Kashmir in 1719–20, in Delhi in 1729, in the Vidarbha region of Maharashtra in 1786, occasioned by an attack on a religious procession. During the first half of the nineteenth century there were several communal disturbances in north India. C. A. Bayly, of Cambridge University, reports that these occurred at Banaras (1809–15), Koil (1820), Moradabad, Sambhal, Kashipur (1833), Shahjahanpur (1837), Bareilly, Kanpur and Allahabad (1837–52), among other places.[4] Among the causes of these clashes was the downgrading of the Muslim state functionaries, and the consequent decline of Muslim dominance, following the British conquest of the area.[5]

Among the common causes of Hindu–Muslim conflict have been cow slaughter and religious processions playing music before mosques. Thus in 1871 Rama-Navami and Muharram celebrations coincided and led to riots in Bareilly and Pilibhit. In 1893 major disturbances took place in Azamgarh district over cow sacrifice. Behind these was the Hindu movement for the protection of the cow. The cow question has been important at least since the middle ages. Akbar had prohibited cow-slaughter in his empire, and the local successor rulers to the Mughal empire had also prohibited it. In 1847 the British banned cow-slaughter in Amritsar, and Bahadur-Shah Zafar did so during the 1857 rebellion. The cow protection movement had been started around 1870 in Punjab by the Namdhari Kuka sect of Sikhs, which later spread to north-west India as well as to UP and Bihar. In 1893 in Mau (Azamgarh) a dispute arose between Hindus and Muslims over the interpretation of the government order prohibiting "all cow sacrifices." The riots that followed spread over a very wide area, encompassing UP, Bihar, Gujarat and Bombay, and claimed 107 lives. There were 22 riots in Bihar, affecting the districts of Saran, Patna and Gaya. The largest number of deaths occurred in Bombay.[6]

Elsewhere in India riots took place in the Malabar area in 1873, 1885, 1894 and 1896; in the Central Provinces in 1889; in Nasik district of Maharashtra in 1894; in Porbandar in 1895. In Punjab between 1881 and 1893 nine disturbances of differing degrees of severity occurred, of which the Multan riot of 1881 was particularly severe.

But communal disturbances were not a regular feature of life in India in the nineteenth century. In the twentieth century the picture has gradually changed. In its memorandum to the Indian Statutory Commission (1930),[7] the Government of India mentions riots in East Bengal in 1907, Peshawar in 1910, Ajodhya in 1912, Agra in 1913, Shahabad in 1917 and Katarpur in 1918. The frequency of riots increased during the 1920s and every province was affected.[8]

The Moplah rebellion of 1921 had strong communal aspects. There were riots in Malegaon (1921) Multan (1922), Lahore, Amritsar, Shaharanpur (1923). The year 1924 saw some major outbreaks, in Allahabad, Calcutta, Delhi, Gulburga, Jubbalpore, Kohat, Lucknow, Nagpur and Shahajahanpur among others. From 1925 on a new cause, namely religious conversion, came to be added to the existing sources of conflict. New militant organisations of Hindus, such as Shuddhi and Sangathan launched by the Arya Samaj, and Tanjeem and Tabligh among the Muslims added to the scale of communal violence. The major riots of Calcutta and Bombay, of 1926 and 1928 respectively, resulted in a very large number of casualties and damage to property; in Calcutta, in a series of three riots 141 persons were killed and 1,296 were injured; in Bombay in 1928 the death toll was 117 and the injured 791. The story of the 1930s and the 1940s is, if anything, more depressing. The 1931 riot in Kanpur resulted in the killing of 294 persons and injuring of 2,529. In the Bombay riot of 1932, 214 persons were killed and 2,686 injured; in the riot of 1936, 65 were killed and 509 injured. If we take only the major riots between 1924 and 1940, the total number of persons killed was 1,175, and the injured 7,615. In the 1940s the major riots were part of the movement for partition and the scale of violence enormous. By then communal riots had become an instrument of politics.[9]

Communal riots are accompanied by acts of individual violence, commonly stabbing, and looting and burning of property. More revealingly, they take the form of mass warfare: in accounts of communal riots mobs of different sizes, varying from 100 to 10,000, confronting each other, throwing stones at each other and generally keeping an adversary at bay, are reported. There are also frequent cases of groups of people attacking weakly defended areas of the adversary community. The most endangered lives are of those people living in the midst of or close to the adversary community. In the attacks the targets chosen are mosques and temples, shops and establishments, and private houses. Neither women nor children are spared. And although in nearly all the riots there are instances of humanity, courage and mutuality, the legacy they leave behind is one of bitterness, hostility and suspicion.

Why do communal riots occur? What purposes, if any, do they serve? What conditions aggravate communal conflict? These are extremely difficult questions to which Indian social science has not addressed itself with the requisite degree of seriousness. The Indian discussions of this subject have been simplistic and moralistic. The simplistic explanation of communal conflict in the pre-Independence period was in terms of the imperialist conspiracy of divide and rule. This is now being replaced by a Marxist equivalent: the capitalist conspiracy. At a more sophisticated level communal conflict is sought to be explained by Marxists as an inevitable consequence of the contemporary capitalist order.[10] Among the non-Marxists there are at least four strands. The first one could be said to represent the view that communal conflict is in truth a result of mutual ignorance; only if the Hindus and the Muslims knew that all religions were "fundamentally" one, and if they approached each other with goodwill, there will be no conflict. This is a Hindu religiously-oriented point of view which characterised the reflections of the late Bhagwandas.[11]

The second strand is represented by the power theory of communal conflict. This holds that given the strongly developed communal identities Hindus and Muslims were bound to conflict over the question of who is to control the state because control over state power is of primary importance in preserving the culture and identity of the community and promoting the welfare of its members. This theory lay at the source of the Muslim League's demand for partition, which Jinnah believed to be in the interest not only of the Muslims but also of the Hindus.

The third strand takes communal conflict, in the post-Independence context, to be a part of the competitive political process, except that it ought to be rendered free of violence. The argument here is that democracy flourishes when there is group competition, that in India we have a group structure primarily consisting of religious communities and competition between them as well as the constraints they might succeed in imposing upon the state are likely to strengthen democracy. This is the view advanced by Humayun Kabir.[12]

Lastly there is the Hindu communalist theory that views minorities as enemies of the nation and communal violence as deliberate acts intended to humiliate and injure the Hindus. Its counterpart is the Muslim communalist theory which views communal violence as well-organised, pre-planned Hindu attacks designed to terrorise the Muslims, then depress them, to drive them out of their own areas, to reduce them to second-class citizens.

....

Communal conflict does not seem to me to originate in the ignorance of "true religion" but in the struggle for autonomy on the part of one or more groups, and there is an inescapable conflict between their drive for autonomy and the cohesion of the state in a multi-religious society. Politicisation of religion, conditions of extreme scarcity, and a particularly divisive style of politics aggravate the problem which appears to be basic to heterogeneous societies. The institutional structure for overcoming the pluralist impediments to integration is in place in India. It is well-conceived. But the dangers to it are now serious. The re-emergence of the Muslim League and the recent events in Punjab should leave no one in doubt about the outcome of the political process since Independence, especially over the past two decades.

The communal problem encompasses social, economic, religious, political, cultural and intellectual spheres—indeed, nothing escapes it because it is concerned with the collective, and through it the individual, life of every member of the community. The solidarity sentiment runs along religious lines because of the shared traditions and culture. A perceived threat to them causes anxiety. It is not only that men identify themselves with the community as the bearer of those traditions and culture that define them but that they see a danger to themselves in the weakening of it. There are therefore no measures they would not employ to defend it, and in normal circumstances there is nothing they would consent to place above it. When they find themselves placed in a plural society, culturally well-formed communities exert themselves to carve out zones of autonomy, define the plural society in such a manner that it makes no demands on them in the cultural sphere, and carefully delimit areas requiring common actions. The communal mentality expresses itself in these, essentially defensive, exertions on the part of minorities. The majority, no less well defined and no less concerned with preservation and extension of its own culture, reacts negatively to the efforts of the minorities to place limits on its power, which it views, not incorrectly, as inimical to the growth of the nation. The minorities and the majority have radically different, sometimes incompatible, ideas about the form and substance of the nation.

In India, Partition appeared to have resolved the communal problem through the drastic solution of creating a separate state for the Muslim majority areas. It was, however, not a complete solution to the problem because the residual India still remained a pluralistic collectivity. While Partition was the solution to one aspect of the problem, secular democracy was envisaged as the solution to the structural problem of plurality within the Indian Union. This still remains our best hope. But if we are ever to overcome this problem it would require pursuit of a well-conceived policy which takes into account the contradictory pulls and pressures in our public life but does not make damaging compromises with communal forces for short-term benefits, which protects minority rights but does not undermine the integrative process. The Hindu communalist ideology reflects a failure to grasp the nature of the communal problem; its hostility towards Muslims hinders the integrative process and, if persisted in, could undermine the democratic state.

While communal violence raises larger issues of grave national importance, it also represents the straightforward law and order problem. The primary responsibility of providing security of life and property of all has not been satisfactorily discharged in the past two decades, and this failure has greatly aggravated the problem. The remedy does not lie in the communalisation of the administrative machinery but making administration more effective. The decommunalisation of politics is a task for the political leadership—here there is a need for greater responsibility rather than empty rhetoric. Nothing less than the future of the nation is at stake in the way the communal problem is handled in the years ahead.

I

Communal Violence in India

The Extent

Although communal violence had become an endemic feature of Indian life before Independence, it declined markedly after 1947. There are no adequate data on communal incidents between 1947 and 1954, but there is good ground for believing that there were not many of them. Such information as is available shows that for India, except Bihar and Uttar Pradesh, there were only 20 incidents in 1950 (11 of them in West Bengal), 7 in 1951, 12 in 1952 and 4 in 1953. Their numbers were not large for the subsequent decade. The great divide in the history of communal riots in India is 1964. This is borne out by the statistical compilation put together by the Ministry of Home Affairs. Whereas the total number of reported communal incidents over the period 1950–1963 was 1,141, giving an average of 81.5 per year, in 1964 it had risen to 2,115. Admittedly, 1964 was a particularly bad year for communal violence, but there is no mistaking the fact that it represented a major change in the communal climate in the country. For the seven years between 1964 and 1970 the average number of incidents per year was 1,025, as against 81.5 for the preceding fourteen years.

Not only had the number of incidents increased, but the area affected by communal violence had steadily expanded. In 1961 there were 61 districts in the country which had experienced communal troubles in that year; by the end of the decade their number had gone up to 216, representing about 70 per cent of the basic administrative units. Again, viewed as an administrative task, whereas in 1961, 61 district authorities had to contend with communal violence, by the end of the decade their number had risen to 116. The number of districts affected in the various states over the years are given in Table 6.1.

It is evident that communal conflict has progressively emerged as one of the major problems in most of the states, and increasing administrative and political resources have to be applied to its containment.

There are three states with very low incidents of communal violence, namely Haryana, Jammu and Kashmir, and Punjab. The primary factor accounting for it is the population composition of these states. In Haryana and Punjab the Muslim population is small and consequently the potential for Hindu–Muslim conflict is much less. In Kashmir the situation is reversed—there the Hindu population is small and consequently there is less potential for Hindu–Muslim conflict. The situation in Jammu is rather different. Here the Hindus enjoy preponderance in the population. The communal situation in Jammu has deteriorated over the past fourteen years.

TABLE 6.1: NUMBER OF DISTRICTS AFFECTED BY COMMUNAL VIOLENCE, 1961–1970

State	1961	1962	1963	1964	1965	1966	1967	1968	1969	1970	Total No. of Districts	Total No. of Districts Affected
Andhra Pradesh	–	2	2	–	3	2	3	6	3	4	20	11
Assam	4	2	4	5	6	3	3	4	2	8	11	9
Bihar	1	4	9	12	9	11	14	15	16	14	17	17
Gujarat	2	3	4	7	5	3	1	2	14	5	17	16
Haryana	–	–	1	–	1	–	–	–	–	–	7	1
Jammu and Kashmir	–	–	–	–	–	–	–	–	–	1	9	1
Karnataka	2	1	2	2	4	2	2	4	4	6	19	14
Kerala	2	2	–	1	3	2	2	4	5	4	9	8
Madhya Pradesh	8	4	1	7	5	2	6	6	9	12	43	29
Maharashtra	4	5	3	10	13	11	7	9	12	17	26	25
Orissa	1	–	1	5	3	3	2	2	4	5	13	10
Punjab	–	–	–	–	–	–	–	–	–	1	11	1
Rajasthan	–	1	–	1	2	3	3	3	2	7	26	11
Tamil Nadu	2	1	1	5	2	2	2	2	3	4	11	11
Uttar Pradesh	13	11	6	9	12	9	10	14	9	16	54	31
West Bengal	10	9	5	11	8	5	7	5	10	8	16	15
Delhi	1	1	1	–	1	–	–	1	1	1	1*	1
Manipur	–	–	–	–	–	–	1	–	–	–	1*	1
Arunachal Pradesh	–	–	–	–	–	–	–	1	–	–	1*	1
Tripura	1	1	–	1	–	–	–	1	–	1	1*	1
India	61	47	40	71	77	58	63	79	94	116	316	216

* Treated here as a single administrative unit.

From the territorial spread of communal violence we move to examining its actual incidence in different states during 1961–70. We shall subject the available data to detailed scrutiny with a view to determining the rural-urban distribution of incidents, the areas of repeated violence, the intensity of violence and identification of the riot-prone towns and districts. Table 6.2 gives state-wise distribution of communal incidents for the 1961–70 period.

Communal violence occurs in areas of mixed population. There are fewer incidents in districts with small proportion of Muslim population; they also appear to correlate with the size of the Muslim population as a proportion of the urban population in several districts. While a precise relationship between communal incidents and the proportion of Muslim population in rural/urban areas cannot be established, available data do suggest a broad pattern; more riots occur in districts with Muslim population varying between 10 and 30 per cent and above. Table 6.3 supplies the details for all the states.

In the following pages a detailed state-wise analysis of these data is presented, first for urban areas and then for rural areas.

Andhra Pradesh

Town Classes	No. of Towns	No. of Incidents
I	3	119
II	1	587
III	6	23
IV	2	3
V	1	5
VI	–	–
Total	13	737

(1) Towns with persistent violence: Hyderabad experienced riots in eight out of ten years. The 1968 riots were serious, lasting for as long as 36 days, 1967 for 9 days, 1970 for 11 days. Nizamabad town experienced riots successively for three years—1965, 1966 and 1967—lasting for 4, 4 and 6 days respectively. The number of incidents was unusually large in 1967: 510 spread over 6 days. Of the total 100 days of communal violence in the state, spread over 10 years, Hyderabad accounted for 65 and Nizamabad for 14, and the other 21 days by the remaining 11 towns, giving the average duration of riots less than two days per town over a ten-year period.

(2) The number of incidents may be similarly analysed. Of the total 737 incidents reported, Hyderabad accounted for 115 and Nizamabad 587, leaving 35 incidents to the remaining 11 towns, averaging 3.2 incidents per town over a ten-year period.

(3) The rural/urban distribution of incidents: 737 urban, 22 rural.

TABLE 6.2: COMMUNAL VIOLENCE, 1961–1970 RURAL/URBAN DISTRIBUTION

States	1961		1962		1963		1964		1965		1966		1967		1968		1969		1970		Total	
	R	U	R	U	R	U	R	U	R	U	R	U	R	U	R	U	R	U	R	U	R	U
Andhra Pradesh	–	–	1	4	1	6	–	–	15	34	–	54	–	528	4	77	–	13	2	23	22	737
Assam	9	1	4	3	31	11	15	4	8	6	9	1	9	6	27	3	8	2	37	20	157	59
Bihar	24	10	5	2	12	8	97	331	25	7	2	5	337	315	55	20	48	21	66	120	691	839
Gujarat	–	2	1	4	2	17	5	37	4	26	1	2	1	–	–	4	94	578	6	15	114	685
Haryana	–	–	–	–	3	–	–	–	–	1	–	–	–	–	–	–	–	–	–	–	3	1
Jammu and Kashmir	–	–	–	–	–	–	–	–	–	–	–	–	–	–	–	–	–	–	3	1	3	1
Karnataka	1	7	1	1	–	4	2	1	22	17	–	4	5	–	4	20	1	26	3	17	39	97
Kerala	3	–	6	–	–	–	3	–	4	–	4	–	1	1	6	–	8	1	4	4	39	6
Madhya Pradesh	53	180	5	6	–	1	9	12	3	4	2	15	1	19	–	14	7	148	11	38	91	437
Maharashtra	10	7	5	27	1	14	10	67	16	210	8	238	2	163	6	29	5	35	153	194	216	984
Orissa	–	2	–	–	–	2	252	440	1	6	6	4	–	2	2	4	6	2	2	7	269	569
Punjab	–	–	–	–	–	–	–	–	–	–	–	–	–	–	–	–	–	–	2	–	2	–
Rajasthan	–	–	–	2	–	–	–	1	–	5	–	42	–	4	–	6	–	8	5	9	5	77
Tamil Nadu	2	–	1	–	3	–	3	4	8	–	2	–	2	1	2	–	2	2	9	3	34	10
Uttar Pradesh	15	76	14	17	7	5	14	7	12	27	8	121	21	26	10	147	11	18	15	38	127	482
West Bengal	35	–	66	34	9	1	456	339	23	1	13	12	15	11	5	26	63	17	78	32	763	473

(Contd)

Table 6.2 (Contd)

States	1961		1962		1963		1964		1965		1966		1967		1968		1969		1970		Total	
	R	U	R	U	R	U	R	U	R	U	R	U	R	U	R	U	R	U	R	U	R	U
Delhi	–	1	–	1	–	1	–	–	–	4	–	–	–	–	–	1	–	2	–	5	–	15
Manipur	–	–	–	–	–	–	–	–	–	–	–	–	1	–	–	–	–	–	2	–	3	–
Arunachal Pradesh	–	–	–	–	–	–	–	–	–	–	–	–	–	–	4	–	–	–	–	–	1	–
Tripura	4	–	1	–	–	–	6	–	–	–	–	–	–	–	–	2	–	–	6	–	14	2
India	153	286	110	101	6	70	872	1,243	141	346	75	498	395	1,076	122	353	253	873	403	526	2,592	5,372

TABLE 6.3: MUSLIM PROPORTION IN THE RURAL/URBAN POPULATION OF DISTRICTS (1961) AND THE NUMBER OF COMMUNAL INCIDENTS, 1961–1970

(percentage)

States	5		5.01 to 10.00		10.01 to 15.00		15.01 to 20.00		20.01 to 30.00		30.01 and Above		Total No. of Incidents		Total
	R	U	R	U	R	U	R	U	R	U	R	U	R	U	
Andhra Pradesh	1	–	21	–	–	4	–	3	–	607	–	123	2	737	757
Assam	7	2	7	3	–	36	5	2	–	14	138	–	157	57	214
Bihar	178	–	95	–	354	429	12	365	–	45	15	–	691	839	1,530
Gujarat	38	1	70	–	6	99	–	477	–	108	–	–	114	685	799
Haryana	–	1	–	–	–	–	–	–	3	–	–	–	3	1	4
Jammu and Kashmir	–	–	–	–	–	–	–	–	–	–	3	1	3	1	4
Karnataka	20	–	12	–	7	67	–	9	–	7	–	14	39	97	136
Kerala	–	–	3	–	8	4	–	1	12	1	16	–	59	6	45
Madhya Pradesh	71	–	20	126	–	213	–	2	–	66	–	29	91	437	528
Maharashtra	124	–	79	223	3	187	–	116	–	409	–	39	206	994	120
Orissa	269	26	–	441	–	–	–	–	–	2	–	–	269	569	838
Punjab	2	–	–	–	–	–	–	–	–	–	–	–	2	–	2
Rajasthan	1	–	4	3	–	3	–	65	–	1	–	5	5	77	82
Tamil Nadu	34	–	–	5	–	5	–	–	–	–	–	–	34	10	44
Uttar Pradesh	–	–	58	–	16	–	21	15	17	260	10	207	127	482	609
West Bengal	1	18	27	15	17	397	23	–	589	43	106	–	763	475	1,236
Delhi	–	–	–	15	–	–	–	–	–	–	–	–	–	15	15
Arunachal Pradesh	1	–	–	–	–	–	–	–	–	–	–	–	1	–	1
Tripura	–	–	–	–	–	–	–	–	14	–	–	–	14	–	14
India	746	48	396	833	411	1,444	61	1,055	635	1,562	288	438	2,592	5,372	7,964
	794		1,229		1,855		1,116		2,197		726		7,964		

(4) Hyderabad emerges as the single major centre of communal trouble in Andhra Pradesh. Hyderabad has been a centre of communal politics. It has a large Muslim population, a part of which has experienced reverse social mobility. There was a considerable Arya Samaj activity in the city over a long period. In recent years the growth of communal organisations has contributed to the accentuation of communal tension in the city.

Assam

Town Classes	No. of Towns	No. of Incidents
I	2	2
II	1	4
III	5	37
IV	2	3
V	4	4
VI	4	7
Total	18	57

(1) The district capital Silchar shows incidents more persistently: in five out of 10 years, Silchar, Dhubri and Karimganj, all class III towns, recorded 12, 11 and nine incidents over the decade, leaving 25 incidents distributed over the remaining 15 towns. The class I towns, namely Gauhati and Shillong, recorded only one incident each throughout the decade—Gauhati in 1965 and Shillong in 1970. In both cases the trouble lasted for only one day.
(2) Of the 42 days of communal riots in the state, Silchar, Karimganj and Dhubri accounted for 21 days, leaving 21 days of rioting in the remaining 15 centres. Of these, another class III town, Tinsukia, experienced two riots, lasting two days each.
(3) The main towns of communal trouble seem to be three, possibly four (all of them class III): Silchar, Karimganj, Dhubri and Tinsukia.
(4) In Assam the incidence of communal violence is much greater in rural than in urban areas: 157 against 57 incidents.

Bihar

Town Classes	No. of Towns	No. of Incidents
I	9	609
II	4	17
III	10	184
IV	20	20
V	8	8
VI	1	1
Total	35	839

(1) Of the 839 incidents, 84 per cent are accounted for by two industrial centres:(a) Ranchi and (b) Jamshedpur and its adjacent areas Chaibasa and Chakradharpur.

(2) Ranchi and Bihar Sharif have had recurring riots: in seven out of 10 years in Ranchi and six out of 10 years in Bihar Sharif. The Jamshedpur-Chaibasa area had riots in five out of 10 years.

(3) Of the 171 days of rioting, Ranchi accounted for 33, Bihar Sharif 10, and Jamshedpur 28; Chaibasa and Chakradharpur accounted for eight and 18 days respectively. Thus the three centres of riots accounted for 97 out of 171 days, i.e., about 57 per cent. Bhagalpur appears to be another centre of rioting: it experienced riots in three out of 10 years, and in 1967 had nine days of rioting. The worst years for riots were 1964, 1967 and 1970, which accounted for 766 of the 839 incidents, and 117 of the 171 days of rioting. In Bihar class I towns are the worst affected.

(4) There were a large number of incidents in rural areas in this state—691 over the 1961–70 decade.

Gujarat

Town Classes	No. of Towns	No. of Incidents
I	3	420
II	10	139
III	13	77
IV	14	40
V	5	9
VI	–	–
Total	45	685

(1) Most of the riots in Gujarat took place in 1969. Of the total 685 incidents over the 10-year period, 578 took place in that single year. Only two towns, namely Ahmedabad and Godhra, show a recurring pattern. During the decade Ahmedabad had riots in six years, and Godhra in five years.

(2) Of the 152 days of riots 98 were during 1969, and Ahmedabad, Baroda and Godhra accounted for 59 of the total number of days (i.e., about 40 per cent of the total). The remaining 42 towns experienced communal violence of varying duration, totalling 93 days over the decade. Even in Ahmedabad the duration of riots was not more than two or three days before 1969.

(3) Communal disturbances in Gujarat have been mainly in urban areas. The state capital, Ahmedabad, has had an old legacy of communal trouble, going back to 1714. In the decade under review the urban areas accounted for 685 incidents, while the rural areas accounted for 114 incidents.

Haryana

The state experienced a communal riot only once, during 1965, at Nuhin Gurgaon district. There was only one incident and it lasted only for one day.

The place affected was a class VI town.

Jammu and Kashmir

Jammu and Kashmir experienced a communal riot of one day's duration in 1970. The affected town Kistwar (in Doder district) is a class VI town.

Karnataka

Town Classes	No. of Towns	No. of Incidents
I	4	12
II	3	9
III	5	25
IV	4	45
V	3	5
VI	1	1
Total	20	97

(1) There were no places except one, Bidar, which experienced repeated rioting in Karnataka. Bidar had riots in four out of 10 years under review.
(2) The number of days of rioting for the decade was 33, and the worst year of rioting was 1970 when six towns had riots; in 1968 there were five.
(3) The number of incidents in the rural areas was 39 for the decade.

Kerala

Town Classes	No. of Towns	No. of Incidents
I	2	4
II	–	–
III	1	1
IV	1	1
V	–	–
VI	–	–
Total	4	6

(1) Throughout the decade Kerala experienced communal rioting only in four places, and each had only one riot. Of the six incidents, three occurred in Trivandrum, and of the five days of rioting, Trivandrum accounted for two.
(2) There were many more rural incidents than urban: 39 as against six in the towns.

Madhya Pradesh

Town Classes	No. of Towns	No. of Incidents
I	11	281
II	4	29
III	13	72
IV	5	38
V	8	17
VI	–	–
Total	41	437

(1) 328 of the 437 incidents took place in two years: in 1961 (180) and 1970 (148).
(2) Indore had riots in four out of 10 years, but every year beginning 1967. Jabalpur had riots in three out of 10 years, and so did Bhopal and Satna. Vidisha had riots in four out of ten years.
(3) Of the 119 days of riots, Indore accounted for 25, Jabalpur 14, Bhopal six and Vidisha five, leaving 69 days to 37 towns.
(4) Indore is the prime centre of communal violence in Madhya Pradesh. The worst year in Indore was 1969, with 114 incidents spread over 11 days.

Maharashtra

Town Classes	No. of Towns	No. of Incidents
I	14	484
II	7	87
III	11	320
IV	12	83
V	5	10
VI	–	–
Total	49	984

(1) The worst year for communal violence in Maharashtra was 1970, when the state experienced 85 days of rioting, out of the total of 193 days for the decade. Twenty-two towns had communal riots in 1970, as against 12 in 1968, and 16 in 1966, the previous peak year.
(2) The towns experiencing repeated rioting were: Greater Bombay, Poona, Sholapur, Malkapur, Aurangabad, Ahmednagar, Akola, Bhiwandi and Malegaon. The first four of these had communal riots in five out of the 10 years, while the remaining ones had them for four years out of 10.
(3) Bhiwandi, Poona, Aurangabad, Thana, and Greater Bombay experienced intense rioting in 1970. Bhiwandi had 20 days of rioting in that year, Poona had 10 days, Thana 13 days, Aurangabad eight days and Greater Bombay six days—together 57 days out of the total of 85 days of rioting during that

year. Washim in Akola district and Malegaon in Nasik district are two other towns which experienced communal rioting of the same scale in 1966 and 1967 respectively. Poona had its worst riots in 1965 when 201 incidents occurred over six days.

(4) There was substantial communal violence in rural areas of Maharashtra, accounting for a little over one-sixth of all the incidents over the decade.

Orissa

Town Classes	No. of Towns	No. of Incidents
I	1	14
II	2	388
III	3	20
IV	7	41
V	2	6
VI	–	–
Total	15	469

(1) In Orissa the main incidents of communal violence occurred in 1964. In that year riots took place in 11 of the 15 towns in which riots have occurred during the 1961–70 decade.

(2) There is only one town—Cuttack—with a recurring cycle of communal violence. Here riots have taken place in six out of 10 years.

(3) Of the 62 days of rioting, Rourkela accounted for 17 (15 in 1964, 2 in 1970), and Cuttack 13, leaving 32 days for 13 other towns, averaging two and a half days of rioting over a 10-year period.

(4) There was a large number of communal incidents in rural areas during the decade—264 were reported. They were mostly part of the 1964 outbreak.

Rajasthan

Town Classes	No. of Towns	No. of Incidents
I	4	66
II	1	1
III	3	4
IV	3	4
V	–	–
VI	–	–
Total	11	75

(1) The main centres of communal violence in Rajasthan were the cities of Jaipur, Jodhpur and Udaipur. They all experienced rioting in four out of 10 years. Udaipur had its worst riot in 1966 when 40 incidents took place in two days of rioting.

(2) The three cities accounted for 19 days of rioting, leaving 12 days of it to the remaining eight towns, thus averaging for them one and a half day's rioting for each over the decade.
(3) The incidents of communal violence in the rural areas of the state was negligible.

Tamil Nadu

Town Classes	No. of Towns	No. of Incidents
I	1	4
II	1	2
III	3	3
IV	1	1
Total	6	10

(1) The decade recorded very few communal incidents in the state. No town, except Madras, had more than one riot over the period; and Madras had only two of them, in 1964 and 1969.
(2) No riot lasted beyond one day.
(3) There were 34 rural incidents, 3.4 times more than the urban ones.

Uttar Pradesh

Town Classes	No. of Towns	No. of Incidents
I	14	311
II	8	12
III	10	115
IV	5	40
V	2	4
Total	39	482

(1) Fourteen class I towns account for 311 incidents out of the total of 482 for the decade. Of these 311, Allahabad, Meerut and Aligarh account for 208, i.e., over 67 per cent.
(2) Aligarh and Meerut have had riots in seven out of the 10 years under review. Moradabad has had riots for eight out of 10 years. Agra and Bareilly had them for six out of 10 years, and Allahabad and Varanasi had them for five years.
(3) Of the 179 riot days, Allahabad accounted for 32, Meerut 25, Aligarh 20, Moradabad 19, Agra, Bareilly and Varanasi 11 each—together 129, representing just over 75 per cent of the total, leaving 50 days to 32 towns for the whole decade.
(4) The number of rural incidents were relatively few, 127 out of the total of 609.

West Bengal

Town Classes	No. of Towns	No. of Incidents
I	9	235
II	15	174
III	13	60
IV	3	4
Total	40	473

(1) The major outbreak of communal violence in West Bengal was in 1964: 339 of the 473 incidents occurred in that one year in 32 towns, most of which have had no riots afterwards in the decade under review.
(2) Calcutta city has suffered communal violence on a modest scale every year since 1964.
(3) Of the 150 days of rioting, 86 were in 1964, and Calcutta accounted for 30 more in the subsequent years of the decade.
(4) The rural incidents of communal violence were substantial, accounting for over 60 per cent of all the incidents.

Delhi

Delhi experienced communal incidents every year during the decade except in 1964, 1966 and 1967. The total number of incidents were 15, resulting in 15 days of communal violence for the decade.

Tripura

Tripura reported two incidents in 1968, resulting in two days of violence.

From the analysis of the data on communal violence available to us, it would appear that the following urban centres are prone to periodic rioting:

1.	Andhra Pradesh	Hyderabad Nizamabad
2.	Assam	Silchar Dhubri Karimganj Tinsukia
3.	Bihar	Bhagalpur Bihar Sharif Jamshedpur (with Chaibasa) Ranchi
4.	Gujarat	Ahmedabad Godhra Baroda
5.	Madhya Pradesh	Indore Jabalpur Bhopal Vidisha

(Contd)

Table (Contd)

6.	Maharashtra	Bombay
		Poona
		Sholapur
		Malkapur
		Aurangabad
		Ahmednagar
		Akola
		Bhiwandi
		Malegaon
7.	Rajasthan	Jaipur
		Jodhpur
		Udaipur
8.	Uttar Pradesh	Agra
		Allahabad
		Meerut
		Aligarh
		Varanasi
		Bareilly
		Moradabad
9.	West Bengal	Calcutta
10.	Delhi	Delhi

Table 6.4 presents in a summary form the data on all the 335 towns which together recorded 5,766 communal incidents over the 1961–70 decade:

While the average number of incidents per town affected is a little over 17 for the decade, it is 33 for class I towns, 25.4 for class II towns, 9.80 for class III towns, 4.82 for class IV towns, 1.94 for class V towns, and 1.5 for class VI towns.

Taking the 1971 town classification, we find that 10.77 per cent of all the towns in the country experienced communal violence. The percentage figures for different classes of towns are: I: 15 per cent; II: 25.45 per cent; III: 15.33 per cent; IV: 7.71 per cent; V: 5.13 per cent; VI: 3.37 per cent.

The pattern of violence in rural areas:

(1) *Andhra Pradesh*: Of the 22 rural incidents reported, 14 occurred in Nizamabad district in 1965. Medak reported three rural incidents in 1968.

(2) *Assam*: Of the 157 rural incidents, 88 were reported from Cachar, 31 from Goalpara and 11 from Kamrup. The years 1963, 1968 and 1970 accounted for 95 of the 157 incidents.

(3) *Bihar*: Of the 691 incidents, Muzaffarpur accounted for 245, Ranchi 107, and Singhbhum 62—a total of 414, about 60 per cent. Of these, 304 took place in Muzaffarpur and Ranchi in 1967, and 60 in Singhbhum in 1964.

(4) *Gujarat*: Of the 114 rural incidents reported, 94 took place in 1969: 45 in Kaira, 16 in Mehsana, nine in Baroda.

TABLE 6.4: COMMUNAL VIOLENCE 1961–1970, CLASS OF TOWNS AND NUMBER OF INCIDENTS*

States	I		II		III		IV		V		VI		Total	
	1	2	1	2	1	2	1	2	1	2	1	2	Towns	Incident
Andhra Pradesh	3	119	1	587	6	23	2	3	1	5	–	–	13	737
Assam	2	2	1	4	5	37	2	3	4	4	4	7	18	57
Bihar	9	609	4	17	10	184	8	20	3	8	1	1	35	839
Gujarat	3	420	10	139	13	77	14	40	5	9	–	–	45	685
Karnataka	4	12	3	9	5	25	4	45	3	5	1	1	20	97
Kerala	2	4	–	–	1	1	1	1	–	–	–	–	3	6
Madhya Pradesh	11	281	4	29	13	72	5	38	8	17	–	–	41	437
Maharashtra	14	484	7	87	11	320	12	83	5	10	–	–	49	984
Orissa	1	14	2	388	3	20	7	41	2	6	–	–	15	469
Rajasthan	4	66	1	1	3	4	3	4	–	–	–	–	11	75
Tamil Nadu	1	4	1	2	3	3	1	1	–	–	–	–	6	10
Uttar Pradesh	14	311	8	12	10	115	5	40	2	4	–	–	39	482
West Bengal	9	235	15	174	13	60	3	4	–	–	–	–	40	473
Delhi	1	15	–	–	–	–	–	–	–	–	–	–	1	15
	78	2,576	57	1,449	96	941	67	323	35	68	6	9	336	5,766

Notes: 1. No. of towns.
2. No. of incidents.

* Haryana, Jammu and Kashmir and Tripura are excluded from the Table. They reported four incidents between them over the decade, spread over four towns (two class V and two class VI).

(5) *Karnataka*: Of the 39 reported incidents, 16 took place in Mandya in 1965. The rest were spread over the remaining 13 districts over the decade.
(6) *Kerala*: Of the 39 reported incidents, 11 took place in Kozhikode, which experienced communal rioting in six out of 10 years of the 1961–70 decade. The rest were scattered over the remaining seven districts.
(7) *Madhya Pradesh*: Of the 91 reported incidents, Sagar accounted for 25 and Jabalpur for 20. They took place in 1961.
(8) *Maharashtra*: Of the 216 incidents, 104 took place in Thana, and of these 101 occurred in 1970; 38 in Kolaba (34 in 1970); 10 in Greater Bombay (all in 1970); a total of 152 (of which 145 in 1970), representing 70 per cent of the cases.
(9) *Orissa*: Of the 269 incidents, 223 took place in Sundargarh and 21 in Sambalpur in 1964, which represents over 83 per cent of the cases.
(10) *Tamil Nadu*: Of the 34 incidents, nine were reported from Tiruchirapalli, which experienced communal riots in four out of 10 years of the 1961–1970 decade.
(11) *Uttar Pradesh*: Of the 127 incidents reported, 20 were from Gorakhpur, 17 from Allahabad, 10 from Bareilly, and 9 from Meerut.
Allahabad reported riots in rural areas in six years of the 1961–70 decade, Gorakhpur four, and Meerut five.
(12) *West Bengal*: Of the 763 reported rural incidents, 395 were from 24 Parganas, 138 from Nadia, 63 from Murshidabad, 53 from Cooch Behar, 23 from Malda, 20 from West Dinajpur. Of the 763 incidents, 456 took place in 1964, and 424 of them in two districts, 24 Parganas and Nadia.

There are 30 districts in the country which can be identified as being prone to communal violence in rural areas:

Andhra Pradesh	Nizamabad, Medak
Assam	Cachar, Goalpara, Kamrup
Bihar	Muzaffarpur, Ranchi, Singhbhum
Gujarat	Kaira, Mehsana, Baroda
Karnataka	Mandya
Madhya Pradesh	Sagar, Jabalpar
Maharashtra	Thana, Kolaba, Greater Bombay
Orissa	Sundargarh, Sambalpur
Tamil Nadu	Tiruchirapalli
Uttar Pradesh	Gorakhpur, Allahabad, Bareilly, Meerut
West Bengal	24 Parganas, Nadia, Malda, West Dinajpur, Murshidabad, Cooch Behar

Causes of Communal Violence

Most inquiries into communal riots find that their immediate causes are almost always trivial. The remarkable feature of communal incidents is, however, not that they begin with trivial friction, but that once begun they acquire a collective aspect. The riots in Delhi in 1973 and 1974 started over petty personal quarrels, but soon developed into group conflict, leading to much loss of life and property and increased communal hostility. The major riots of the 1960s had insignificant beginnings. Of the 841 incidents over the 1961–70 period whose causes have been identified by the Ministry of Home Affairs, the details are given in Table 6.5.

A little over half of the total number of disputes relate to private causes (52.66 per cent), while the rest relate to religious/public causes. The largest category of incidents, 6,815 out of 7,964, representing 81.80 per cent of the total, are identified by the Ministry of Home Affairs as "chain incidents"—they have no independent cause/s, but result from some major outbreak and are in the nature of a spillover. Almost three quarters of these "spillover" incidents occurred in four years, namely 1964, 1967, 1969 and 1970, and were related to the wave of violence that swept eastern India in 1964, Bihar in 1967, Gujarat in 1969 and Maharashtra in 1970. These together accounted for 54 per cent of the "chain incidents" of the decade. The state-wise distribution of incidents by identified public causes is given in Table 6.6.

(1) Bihar leads in having the higher number of public causes for communal violence, followed by Maharashtra, Uttar Pradesh and West Bengal. Between them these four states account for over 70 per cent of the cases.
(2) The cow slaughter question is important in Bihar, Uttar Pradesh and West Bengal.
(3) The incidents of desecration of religious places is most important in Maharashtra, and to a small extent in Bihar and Uttar Pradesh.
(4) The graveyards issue is of importance in Bihar, and to a lesser extent in Uttar Pradesh.
(5) The festivity/celebration occasions have occasioned communal violence in all the states save Punjab, Haryana and Tripura (also in Jammu and Kashmir, and Manipur).
(6) Here too Bihar takes the lead, followed by Maharashtra, Uttar Pradesh, Andhra Pradesh and West Bengal. Between them these five states account for 72.88 per cent of the cases of communal violence on this score.

The rural-urban distribution of these incidents shows that 55 per cent of them occurred in rural areas. The rural-urban and state-wise distribution is provided in Tables 6.7 and 6.8.

(1) As is to be expected in predominantly rural Bihar, there are more incidents on every count in the rural areas as compared with the urban areas. This is

TABLE 6.5: CAUSES OF COMMUNAL VIOLENCE

	No. of Incidents	Percentage
Festivity/celebrations	225	26.75
Private property disputes	162	19.26
Quarrels over women	142	16.89
Personal transactions, enmities, etc.	139	16.53
Cow slaughter	121	14.39
Desecration of religious places	34	4.04
Disputes over graveyards	18	2.14
Total	841	100.00

TABLE 6.6: CAUSES OF COMMUNAL VIOLENCE, 1961–1970

State	Cow Slaughter	Desecration of Religious Places	Festivity/ Celebrations	Graveyards	Total	Chain Incidents
Andhra Pradesh	–	1	21	1	23	680
Assam	7	1	11	–	19	106
Bihar	56	4	64	8	132	1,199
Gujarat	6	2	6	–	14	724
Haryana	–	–	–	–	–	2
Karnataka	1	1	8	2	12	100
Kerala	–	1	4	1	6	9
Madhya Pradesh	6	–	11	–	17	429
Maharashtra	8	18	35	2	63	1,022
Orissa	5	–	9	–	14	699
Punjab	–	–	–	–	–	1
Rajasthan	–	–	4	–	4	51
Tamil Nadu	–	1	5	1	7	17
Uttar Pradesh	17	4	27	3	51	425
West Bengal	15	1	17	–	53	1,040
Delhi	–	–	2	–	2	–
Arunachal Pradesh	–	–	1	–	1	–
Tripura	–	–	–	–	–	11

Note: Jammu and Kashmir and Manipur have had none of these types of incidents and are, therefore, excluded from this table.

especially so with regard to cow slaughter. This issue is also important in rural Uttar Pradesh and rural West Bengal. In Maharashtra, on the other hand, it has been an entirely urban problem.

(2) Festivities/celebrations give rise to communal incidents in rural areas in every state except Andhra Pradesh and Delhi, and in urban areas in all states except Kerala. In rural incidents of violence on account of festivity Bihar takes the lead, followed by West Bengal and Uttar Pradesh, while in urban disturbances on this count Maharashtra takes the lead, followed by Andhra Pradesh, Uttar Pradesh and Bihar.

(3) The largest number of incidents of desecration of religious places was reported from Maharashtra, where they were recorded in seven out of ten years under review. Here they were predominantly in urban areas.

(4) Incidents related to graveyards occurred mainly in rural Bihar.

TABLE 6.7: RURAL/URBAN DISTRIBUTION OF CAUSES OF COMMUNAL INCIDENTS

	Rural	Urban
Cow slaughter	88	33
Festivity/Celebrations	104	121
Desecration of religious places	16	18
Graveyards	11	7
Total	219	179

TABLE 6.8: STATE-WISE DISTRIBUTION OF CAUSES OF COMMUNAL INCIDENTS

States	Cow Slaughter		Festivity		Religious Places		Graveyards		Total
	R	U	R	U	R	U	R	U	
Andhra Pradesh	1	4	–	21	–	1	–	1	28
Assam	4	3	4	7	1	–	–	–	19
Bihar	44	12	48	16	3	1	6	2	132
Gujarat	3	3	5	1	2	–	–	–	14
Karnataka	1	–	3	5	1	–	1	1	12
Kerala	–	–	4	–	1	–	1	–	6
Madhya Pradesh	3	3	2	9	–	–	–	–	17
Maharashtra	–	8	7	28	4	14	1	1	63
Orissa	4	1	2	7	–	–	–	–	14
Rajasthan	–	–	1	3	–	–	–	–	4

(Contd)

Table 6.8 (Contd)

States	Cow Slaughter		Festivity		Religious Places		Graveyards		Total
	R	U	R	U	R	U	R	U	
Tamil Nadu	–	–	4	1	1	–	1	–	7
Uttar Pradesh	14	3	11	16	2	2	1	2	51
West Bengal	15	–	13	4	1	–	–	–	33
Delhi	–	–	–	2	–	–	–	–	2
India	88	33	104	121	16	18	11	7	398

The identified private causes of communal violence related to women, private property and personal transactions, feuds etc., over the 1961–70 decade numbered 443 in total. Their distribution for rural and urban areas is given in Table 6.9.

TABLE 6.9: RURAL/URBAN DISTRIBUTION ON PRIVATE CAUSES ON COMMUNAL VIOLENCE

Issues	Rural	Urban
Women	65	77
Private property	134	28
Personal transactions, etc.	55	84
Total	254 (57.33 per cent)	189 (42.67 per cent)

It should cause no surprise that more communal incidents occur in rural areas than in urban areas given that almost 80 per cent of the Indian population still lived in the rural areas in 1961.

The proportions between rural and urban incidents alter dramatically when we come to the "chain incidents." Here the rural areas account for only 28.77 per cent of the total number of such incidents reported for the 1961–70 decade. Riots in rural areas are sporadic and generally do not spread.

Our understanding of the "causes" of communal violence can now be deepened somewhat with the help of the findings of the various Commissions of Inquiry that have reported on some of the major riots. There are six reports of the Raghubar Dayal Commission reporting on six riots that took place between August and October 1967, the Reddy Commission's report on the Gujarat riots in 1969, the D. P. Madon Commission's report on the Maharashtra (Bhiwandi, Jalgaon and Mahad) riots of 1970, the Tandon and Prasad reports on riots in Delhi in 1973 and 1974, and the Jitendra Narain Commission's report on the Jamshedpur disturbances of April 1979.

....

All the inquiry commissions have rejected planning as a cause in any of the riots they investigated.

....

It is difficult to determine who participates in the disturbances. Communal disturbances entail both group activity as well as individual acts. Group activity is demonstrative while individual acts pertain to arson, stabbing or use of firearms against the adversaries. The various inquiry commissions, to whose reports reference has been made above, speak of riotous crowds of 100 to 10,000 or more. The figures of those arrested by the state authorities in the course of controlling riot situations, either before, during or immediately after a riot, provide a very poor guide to the scale of participation and no guide at all to the social background of the participants. The inquiry commissions' reports are also of little help here. But it is obvious that in Ranchi and Jamshedpur, Ahmedabad, Bhiwandi, Malegaon and Sholapur, the participants were mainly industrial workers; there was some student participation in the Ranchi and Ahmedabad riots. In Sursand (Muzaffarpur district, Bihar) and in Jainpur and Suchetpur (Gorakhpur district, Uttar Pradesh) the participants were agriculturists. In Delhi they were factory workers, petty traders and local gundas. In all urban riots the gunda element is strongly represented.

The available data on arrests (see Table 6.10), though of only limited value, throw some light on the scale of comparative participation in riots in different states by different communities (in this case Hindus and Muslims). Unfortunately, the "not-known" category is too large (71.30 per cent of the total).

TABLE 6.10: COMMUNAL VIOLENCE—ARRESTS, 1961–1970

State	Hindus	Muslims	Non-known	Total
Andhra Pradesh	256	166	315	727
Assam	31	398	899	1,628
Bihar	2,005	1,560	2,076	5,641
Gujarat	122	241	6,713	7,076
Haryana	–	4	–	4
Jammu and Kashmir	9	7	–	16
Karnataka	11	29	580	620
Kerala	47	9	31	87
Madhya Pradesh	3,266	1,292	1,216	5,774
Maharashtra	34	356	9,591	10,281
Orissa	26	39	1,013	1,078

(Contd)

Table 6.10 (Contd)

State	Hindus	Muslims	Non-known	Total
Rajasthan	24	71	266	361
Tamil Nadu	58	75	15	148
Uttar Pradesh	1,375	1,797	2,801	5,973
West Bengal	2,756	618	17,567	20,941
Delhi	31	34	16	81
Arunachal Pradesh	–	–	4	4
Tripura	17	–	42	59
India	10,668	6,696	43,145	60,509

....

The Cost

The human, material and spiritual cost of communal violence is very high. Its cost to the nation in terms of negative impact on national integration is even greater.

The data available to us enable us to consider the human cost in terms of casualties, and, somewhat less adequately, the damage of property. For the decade 1961–70 communal riots caused 3,195 deaths and injuries to 12,155 persons. The details for the different states are given in Table 6.11. Of the 7,964 incidents, 5,022 involved damage of property. Among the places attacked were religious shrines, markets, factories and private dwellings. There are no estimates of losses suffered in these attacks for the country as a whole, but the inquiry commissions provide details for the cases they investigated, and these must suffice as illustrations for our purpose.

One of the distressing aspects of casualties in communal violence is the marked preponderance of Muslims killed and injured. Among those identified by religion—numbering 2,679 killed and 9,272 injured—2,397 among the killed and 5,138 among the injured were Muslims. A scrutiny of the data shows that in all states save Haryana, Karnataka, Punjab and Tamil Nadu more Muslims were killed than Hindus; among the injured, Muslims preponderated in all states except Andhra Pradesh, Assam, Jammu and Kashmir, Madhya Pradesh, Maharashtra, Karnataka and Delhi. To a student of communal violence communal proportions among the killed and the injured can hold no intrinsic interest, but the disparity between the two communities in this horrible count exerts profound negative influence on the community which suffers a comparatively larger loss of life, and hence, this aspect of the data needs to be seriously noted.

TABLE 6.11: CASUALTIES, 1961–1970 (KILLED AND INJURED)

States	1961		1962		1963		1964		1965		1966		1967		1968		1969		1970		Total	
	K	I	K	I	K	I	K	I	K	I	K	I	K	I	K	I	K	I	K	I	K	I
Andhra Pradesh	–	–	–	3	–	44	–	–	–	66	–	63	13	160	3	211	–	19	3	28	19	594
Assam	2	24	–	6	14	128	2	18	1	67	1	8	–	43	10	98	2	14	7	91	39	497
Bihar	6	86	1	24	1	96	339	417	5	92	–	48	197	346	15	295	12	170	34	196	610	1,670
Gujarat	–	5	–	14	1	63	1	187	8	101	–	15	–	16	4	58	469	1,083	1	46	484	1,588
Haryana	–	–	–	–	2	–	–	–	–	25	–	–	–	–	–	–	–	–	–	–	2	25
Jammu and Kashmir	–	–	–	–	–	–	–	–	–	–	–	–	–	–	–	–	–	–	–	7	–	7
Karnataka	–	23	–	–	1	24	1	16	1	11	–	8	–	16	4	107	3	75	–	46	10	326
Kerala	–	31	3	53	–	–	–	15	–	16	–	15	2	21	1	22	–	28	–	13	6	214
Madhya Pradesh	85	205	2	38	–	1	20	38	–	24	5	22	–	51	–	22	15	368	8	155	135	924
Maharashtra	1	65	5	61	6	122	–	111	3	216	29	213	9	188	3	185	2	168	220	783	278	2,122
Orissa	–	3	–	–	–	4	985	257	–	17	–	20	–	1	–	4	4	14	–	9	989	329
Punjab	–	–	–	–	–	–	–	–	–	–	–	–	–	–	–	–	–	–	–	2	–	2
Rajasthan	–	–	–	19	–	–	–	–	1	32	1	26	–	13	–	6	1	10	1	9	4	115
Tamil Nadu	–	28	–	–	–	–	–	26	1	28	–	10	1	42	1	18	–	25	1	69	4	251
Uttar Pradesh	40	185	10	56	2	31	6	60	8	94	3	62	23	247	42	380	14	309	8	69	156	1,493
West Bengal	5	90	21	114	3	53	349	958	2	29	3	78	8	158	4	69	49	213	12	153	456	1,915

(Contd)

Table6.11 (Contd)

States	1961		1962		1963		1964		1965		1966		1967		1968		1969		1970		Total	
	K	I	K	I	K	I	K	I	K	I	K	I	K	I	K	I	K	I	K	I	K	I
Delhi	–	1	–	7	–	3	–	–	–	21	–	–	–	–	–	–	–	11	–	2	–	45
Manipur	–	–	–	–	–	–	–	–	–	–	–	–	–	6	–	–	–	–	–	–	–	6
Arunachal Pradesh	–	–	–	–	–	–	–	–	–	–	–	–	–	–	–	2	–	–	–	–	–	2
Tripura	–	9	–	–	–	–	–	2	–	–	–	–	–	–	–	–	–	–	–	–	–	11
India	139	755	42	395	30	569	1,703	2,110	30	870	42	588	253	1,308	87	1,377	572	2,507	297	1,676	3,195	12,155

The available data disclose a similar tale regarding damage of property. Of the 3,167 incidents identified as involving damage to property, 2,609 resulted in damage to the properties of Muslims, 558 resulted in damage to the properties of Hindus, and 14 to the properties of both.

For the extent of damage suffered by the Hindus and the Muslims we have to turn to the reports of the inquiry commissions. The incidents they investigated could in no sense be considered representative, but the data have an illustrative value and convey something of the magnitude of the losses suffered by the affected communities. The details are presented in the following paragraphs.

(1) *Ranchi-Hatia* (1967): The estimated total losses come to Rs 14,20,000. Arson affected 78 houses and 65 shops, and 195 houses and 128 shops and businesses were affected by looting or damage. The Raghubar Dayal Commission's report on this riot does not give a community-wise breakup of the estimated losses, but if one is to go by the rehabilitation grants made by the Government of Bihar to the victims, it would suggest that Muslims' losses were perhaps 90 per cent of the estimated total.
(2) *Sholapur* (1967): Sixteen properties were damaged. The losses suffered by the owners, all Muslims, were relatively small, aggregating to a sum of Rs 15,427.
(3) *Ahmednagar* (1967): The Raghubar Dayal Commission report on this riot noted that "[d]amage to property was fairly heavy" but provided no estimate of actual losses suffered by the victims. The claims for compensation made by 46 persons (42 Muslims and four Hindus) came to Rs 1,37,000. Of this the Hindu claims came to Rs 6,875, and Muslim claims to Rs 1,30,125.
(4) *Malegaon* (1967): According to government reports 21 shops belonging to Hindus were burnt and 57 were damaged or looted; 22 shops belonging to Muslims were burnt and 22 were looted or damaged. Damage to the property of Hindus was estimated at Rs 8,21,153, and of Muslims at Rs 6,51,500.
(5) *Jaipur-Suchetpur* (1967): The Raghubar Dayal Commission report notes that there were 11 cases of looting in various villages during the course of the riots. No estimates of the losses suffered by the victims is provided.
(6) *Sursand* (1967): Almost the entire Muslim population of the village was rendered homeless on account of the riot. The total number of houses burnt was 214, out of which 205 were of Muslims, and nine were of Hindus. The total damage suffered by the Muslims was estimated to be Rs 1,06,906,
(7) *Bhiwandi* (1910): The losses suffered by the Hindus and the Muslims, according to the estimates made by the District Police, were Rs 70,39,560 and Rs 82,80,603, respectively. In the damage suffered by industry and

trade, amounting to Rs 89,79,202, of which the Hindu losses accounted for Rs 46,63,653 and Muslim losses for Rs 43,15,549.

(8) *Jalgaon* (1970): 386 properties (six Hindu-owned, 380 Muslim-owned) were completely or partially burnt, or damaged otherwise, or looted. The estimated loss was Rs 34,74,722, of which the Muslims' share came to Rs 33,90,997, and the Hindus' to Rs 83,725.

(9) *Mahad* (1970): Here the total loss on account of arson, looting and other damage to property came to Rs 3,00,063, of which the Muslims' share was Rs 2,82,493, and the Hindus' Rs 17,570.

(10) *Ahmedabad* (1969): According to the information supplied by the state government to the Reddy Commission, the total number of houses, godowns, factories and huts burnt was 4,799, and the total number of such properties burnt with kits taken out and burnt was 1943, which together comes to 6,742. Out of the 4,799 properties, the number of Hindu properties was 573, and of Muslims 4,226, and out of 1,943 properties, the number of Hindu properties was 98 and of Muslim properties 1,845. The damage to property, both movable and immovable, was estimated to be of Rs 4,23,24,069.54, out of which the damage to Hindu property was Rs 75,85,845 and to Muslim property was Rs 3,47,38,224.54.

(11) *Baroda* (1969): According to the statement submitted by the District Magistrate to the Reddy Commission, the loss suffered by Muslims was Rs 33,26,006, and the loss suffered by the Hindus was Rs 4,58,210.

(12) *Delhi* (1973): Eight shops and a wooden *khokha* (kiosk) were burnt and a few others damaged. Of these, 6 shops belonged to Hindus and 2 to Muslims. Another house of a Hindu was partly damaged and yet another shop in the local market was partly burnt. According to the police sources, Hindus suffered a loss of Rs 3,22,145 and Muslims, Rs 1,68,815. There was a fire in yet another market in which 250 shops were destroyed, and the estimate of loss varied from Rs 1–2 crore. This fire was not specifically connected with the communal disturbances.

(13) *Delhi* (1974): The total damage to property was estimated to be Rs 12,00,450. No details for Hindu and Muslim losses are available. Of the 355 applicants to whom relief assistance was extended, 266 were Muslims and 89 were Hindus. From the data on applications for assistance it is evident that both Hindus and Muslims had suffered business losses, the latter perhaps more than the former.

The inquiry commissions have not systematically reported on attacks on and the damage done to religious places. Yet it is a recurring feature of communal riots. In the Ranchi–Hatia riot of 1967 three religious places were either burnt or otherwise damaged. The Ahmednagar riot of the same year began with the disfigurement of idols in the local temple of Markandeya. In the course of the disturbances 20 (possibly 29) mosques and tombs of pirs were damaged. According to the statement of the district magistrate submitted to the Raghubar Dayal Commission, "Muslim religious places were the main target of attack." In three years preceding the 1967 disturbances, according to police sources, there were 100 cases of desecration of Hindu temples and 77 holy places of Muslims. In the Ahmedabad disturbances of 1969, 37 mosques, 50 durgahs, six burial grounds, and three temples were damaged. In Baroda 12 mosques, 35 durgahs and four graveyards were damaged or destroyed during the disturbances of that year. One Hindu temple was also damaged. In the Bhiwandi riots of 1970, five mosques and four temples were damaged. In the Jalgaon disturbances of the same year, two mosques were attacked.

It is a very puzzling and deeply disturbing feature of many of the communal incidents that they were started or aggravated by a section of the Hindus. This is the evidence of most of the inquiry commissions' reports. The data on communal incidents compiled by the Ministry of Home Affairs for the period 1961–70 show that of the 5,189 incidents for which "first resort to violence" by Hindus or Muslims could be identified, Hindus accounted for 3,888, i.e., 75 per cent of the cases. While the "first resort" data carry no explanatory value for making sense of communal riots, they nevertheless betray a profound feeling of hostility among the Hindus towards Muslims.

Detailed data are not available for the period since 1970, but overall figures are available for the decade 1971–80. From them it is evident that during that decade the number of communal incidents were fewer than for the preceding decade. Between 1971 and 1980, there were 2,572 communal incidents, against 7,964 for 1961–70. This could be a misleading statistic in that the definition of incident employed for the 1971–80 decade might be different from the one employed for the preceding decade. There were no "major" riots during the 1971–80 period, and consequently the number of persons killed in riots is much smaller: 1,185 against 3,195 during 1961–70. Table 6.12 gives comparative data for the two decades.

TABLE 6.12: COMMUNAL INCIDENTS AND CASUALTIES (KILLED AND INJURED), 1961–70 AND 1971–80

Decade	No. of Incidents	Casualties Total	Killed				Injured			
			Hindus	Muslims	Not Known	Police	Hindus	Muslims	Not Known	Police
1961–70	7,964	K 3,195 I 12,155	282	2,397	515	1	4,134	5,138	1,888	995
1971–80	2,572	K 1,185	373	766	33	13	6,674	5,683	1,072	1,772

The figures reflect greater violence in the 1970s than in the 1960s despite the fact that the latter were characterised by at least six major riots, namely Rourkela, Jamshedpur, Calcutta in 1964, Ranchi in 1967, Ahmedabad-Baroda in 1969, Bhiwandi-Jalgaon-Mahad in 1970. The death toll per incident in the 1961–70 decade was 0.40; in the next decade it was 0.46. The difference on account of injuries is much greater: the number of injured per incident was 1.52 in 1961–70 period; it was 5.94 for the next decade. The number of policemen killed had risen from 1 in 1961–70 to 13 in 1971–80 period, and the number of policemen injured had gone up by 78 per cent for almost a quarter of the incidents.

The scale of communal violence has increased over the years. The states which were once free of it have now been affected. The issues continue to be those which agitated the rival communities in the past, i.e., music before mosques, cow slaughter, affront to women. To these has been added the new source of economic competition. Communal confrontations result in loss of life and property and damage to sacred places. Nearly all social groups, except the elite, seem to participate in one way or another in these communal conflicts. They bear the characteristics of a semi-permanent group warfare which erupts without prior warning, the eruption often sparked off by some trivial incident and leaving everyone injured, impoverished, embittered and confirmed in their hostilities.

Notes and References

[The study was made possible by a grant of Rs 25,000 made to the Centre for the Study of Developing Societies by the Gandhi Peace Foundation.]

[1] J. S. Furnival, *Colonial Policy and Practice* (Cambridge: Cambridge University Press, 1948), p. 304.

[2] L. Kuper and M. G. Smith (eds.), *Pluralism in Africa* (Berkeley and Los Angeles: University of California Press, 1971), p. 11.

[3] Irawati Karve, *Hindu Society: An Interpretation*, second edition (Poona: Deshmukh Prakashan, 1968).

[4] C. A. Bayly, *Rulers, Townsmen and Bazars* (Cambridge: Cambridge University Press, 1983), p. 335.

[5] Ibid., pp. 335–38.

[6] For the details of the story see J. R. McLane, *Indian Nationalism and the Early Congress* (Princeton: Princeton University Press, 1977), pp. 314–21.

[7] Indian Statutory Commission, 1930, Report, Vol IV, Part I, pp. 97–107.

[8] The major riots of the 1920s are considered in G. R. Thursby, *Hindu–Muslim Relations in British India* (Leiden: E. J. Brill, 1975).

[9] For a detailed treatment of the Partition-related riots see Richard D. Lambert's "Hindu–Muslim Riots," Ph.D. dissertation in Sociology, University of Pennsylvania, Philadelphia, 1951.

[10] A. A. Engineer, "Developing Theory of Communal Riots," *Mainstream*, 20 August 1983.

[11] See the report of the committee set up by the All-India Congress Committee, presided over by Bhagwandas, *Roots of Communal Politics*, ed. N. G. Barrier (New Delhi: Arnold Heinemann Publishers (India), 1976).

[12] H. Kabir, *Minorities in a Democracy* (Calcutta: Firma K. L. Mukhopadhyay, 1968).

[13] Zerah Banu, "Emerging Class Relations among Caste Hindus," in *Inter-Religious Perceptions of Hindus and Muslims*, ed. K. S. Durany (New Delhi: Indian Institute of Islamic Studies, 1982).

7

Biology and Gender Bias

Some Issues in Discrimination against Women at the Workplace*

Vimal Balasubrahmanyan

Over thirty years ago, the Constitution of India had proclaimed certain far-reaching concepts to ensure equality of the sexes. This was long before the various ILO and UN conventions to promote equality and prevent sex discrimination were adopted by the nations of the world. And yet, the continued deeply-entrenched existence of sex discrimination at the Indian workplace reflects what Justice Krishna Iyer described as "the distance between Constitution in the Book and Law in Action."

What does the Constitution guarantee? Article 14 ensures equality before the law. Article 15 prohibits discrimination on basis of sex. Article 16 guarantees equality of opportunity in matters relating to employment. Article 39 guarantees equal pay for equal work. Article 42 says it is the duty of the state to provide for maternity relief.

All this gives an impression that equality and protection from sex discrimination have been handed on a plate to Indian women without their even demanding it—leave alone fighting for it. What, on the other hand, is the reality?

I shall first cite three recent court cases which reveal the tip of the iceberg of gender bias. Next I shall give some examples of sex discrimination which

* Originally published in *Economic and Political Weekly* 20, no. 20 (18 May 1985): pp. 876–77. This chapter was read at a seminar on "Women and Employment" on 31 March 1985, organised by Mahila Abhyudaya Samastha and ICSSR in Hyderabad.

have *not* been taken to court and which provoke the question: why do women continue to endure such bias in employment? And finally, I shall give some facts which show that prevalent patriarchal attitudes are so deep-rooted and so totally at variance with the radical constitutional norms that something substantially more than legal battles is called for to achieve fundamental change in the work environment.

First, the three court cases. In 1979, C. B. Muthamma, the first woman to serve as an Indian Foreign Service officer, filed a writ petition in the Supreme Court on the grounds that two IFS service rules violated Articles 14 and 16. One rule required female employees to take permission before marrying. It also gave the government the right to ask any married woman officer to resign if it was felt that her family responsibilities would interfere with her efficiency. The second rule totally denied employment to married women. As soon as the petition was filed, the government itself repealed the two obnoxious rules and Justice Krishna Iyer, before whom the case came up, said he was "dismissing the petition but not the problem." He directed that Muthamma's seniority should be reviewed because in the meantime some of her juniors had been promoted over her. And he urged the Union government to overhaul all service rules and delete all discriminatory clauses without waiting for "ad hoc inspiration from writ petitions."

The second case is the much-publicised petition of the air hostesses of Air India and Indian Airlines in 1981. They were fighting against discriminatory service conditions and demanding parity with male cabin crew. They won some gains but lost on several crucial issues—which means that this legal battle is not yet over. The air hostesses won the right to continue in service beyond the age of 35, up to 45. The rule which made them resign on first pregnancy was struck down as unconstitutional. However, their demand to retire at 58 like male cabin crew was rejected, and the rule which required them to remain single for the first four years of service was also upheld. Many progressives had at the time expressed surprise that these biased rules were retained—but of that more later.

The third case was in 1983 when the Kerala High Court held that denial of jobs to women in class IV government service was discriminatory and unconstitutional. The court directed the state government to consider the two women petitioners for the next two immediate vacancies and also alerted both state and Union governments to initiate affirmative action against sex discrimination.

These are three important precedent-setting court rulings and one would have imagined that following these initiatives the Supreme Court and the High Courts would have been simply flooded with petitions from other women employees similarly victimised by gender bias. That this has *not* happened suggests two things. First, most women workers are unaware of the constitutional provisions and unaware that they can take such issues to court. Second, even if they have become aware, it has not been easy for them to get involved in lengthy legal battles. Nor do such issues find priority with male-dominated trade unions.

Even in the advanced EEC countries which have stronger legislation and more streamlined procedures to deal with complaints on gender bias, such discrimination on the basis of sex is far from being wiped out. A recent ILO report on this topic offers two reasons: one, few women use the law to fight back, and, two, rising unemployment and fear of dismissal prevent many of them from pursuing such complaints.

I shall give three recent examples where service and recruitment rules are patently discriminatory and yet have not been challenged in court, to the best of my knowledge.

Last year, there was much media coverage of married women house surgeons of Lady Hardinge Medical College who were required to take pregnancy tests at the time of appointment. They were offered jobs only if they were *not* pregnant. After six months they had to repeat the test, and if pregnant, were told to *abort or quit.* These women had protested against this rule to the hospital authorities, the Health Minister and even the Prime Minister. But they have so far not petitioned the court.

The second example is a news item from the *Hindustan Times* in 1981 which reported that a Home Science College in Coimbatore has a standing order for married women lecturers: "Have your baby in the vacation." One lecturer had to undergo an abortion because the delivery date would not coincide with the vacation and the college would not give her maternity leave. This rule too has so far not been challenged in court.

The third example is even more devious. It is an advertisement issued by the Directorate of Advertising and Visual Publicity (DAVP) of the Government of India for a midwifery course in Delhi's Safdarjung Hospital. The notice specifically excludes married women, and women with children, by offering the course only to "unmarried women" or "widows without encumbrances." This too remains an unchallenged criterion.

I have specifically chosen examples which show how women employees and job applicants are literally penalised for their biological function of childbearing and the social role of motherhood, the assumption being that children, to quote the DAVP advertisement, are an "encumbrance," interfering with the efficiency of women. The rules are also specifically aimed at avoiding payment of maternity benefits as required by the law. Two of the examples are of government departments which, more than anyone else, ought to be setting the standards for upholding constitutional norms. (I am not dealing here with violations of the Maternity Benefits Act and the ploys used by employers to prevent women from qualifying for benefits under the Act. Also, there is no scope in a short chapter like this to discuss the many other equally pernicious areas of gender bias which cover access to professional training, concentration of women in certain low-paid jobs, discrimination through sex-segregation of jobs, loopholes in the Equal Remuneration Act, how protective legislation is used to deny jobs to women, etc.)

Coming back to the framework of this chapter, the third issue which I wish to raise is that prevailing sexist attitudes are so deeply entrenched that legal remedies alone will obviously not be enough.

In the very first chapter of its 1975 report, the Committee on the Status of Women in India had recalled how in 1970, when Charan Singh was Uttar Pradesh Chief Minister, the state government had written to the Centre that women should *not* be appointed to the Indian Administrative Service and that if this was not possible, at least women officials should not be sent to Uttar Pradesh. In the Army Medical Service, until 1972, women had to quit on marriage. At the time the committee was preparing its report, neither doctors nor nurses were entitled to paid maternity leave. The committee also noted that despite the constitutional directives, there were instances in Tamil Nadu and Madhya Pradesh where the state government itself had fixed unequal wage rates for male and female agricultural sowers. When such are the attitudes in government circles, sexist norms in the private sector need hardly be elaborated upon.

Further, it appears that according to the current judicial interpretation, the constitutional norms are *not* binding on the private sector. In his 1982 lectures on "Gender Justice," Justice Krishna Iyer drew pointed attention to what he called the "conservative" attitude of the courts in this regard, which have ruled that the private sector can "lawfully discriminate against women." The Supreme Court, he said, had been liberal in interpreting the word "state" to cover public sector undertakings and it was time that private units were compelled to abide by Articles 14 and 16.

In the Kerala case which I mentioned earlier, Justice Potti had flayed the state government for denying class IV jobs to women and he had said that it was *not* for a male-dominated legislature or a male-dominated bureaucratic machinery to decide whether women may be allowed to do certain jobs or not. The Muthamma and the Kerala rulings are a welcome sign of a change in judicial attitudes—certainly a sign that there are some judges at least who reject old-fashioned views on women and employment.

These rulings certainly come a long way from the occasion in the early 1970s when the Supreme Court upheld a rule excluding women lawyers from applying for a short service commission in the army judicial service. In another case, quoted by Vimal Ranadive of CITU, girls working in several drug multinationals had challenged the rule which terminated their services as soon as they married. As far as I am aware, this was under the Industrial Disputes Act, and the Bombay

High Court had *upheld* the rule. The Supreme Court, however, struck down the rule "in the interests of social justice." But it did not order reinstatement of those already sacked under the rule.

Incidentally, Article 11 of the UN Convention for Eliminating All Discrimination against Women specifically prohibits dismissal on grounds of marital status, pregnancy or maternity. It came into force in 1981, and as of March 1983, forty-seven nations had ratified the convention. India is *not* one of these.

One of the most serious and disturbing features of this whole issue is the reactionary attitude of the government itself. When the air hostesses' case was filed, two women MPs, Margaret Alva and Ambika Soni, had initiated a debate in the Rajya Sabha and demanded that all discriminatory service conditions be removed. The then civil aviation minister, far from using this as an opportunity to promise a review of the offending rules and ensure justice, went out of his way to defend the existing conditions and deny that they were discriminatory. He went to the extent of making a statement that air hostesses could very well have their babies after retiring at thirty-five, and saying that it was a question whether an air hostess would attend to her professional duty or her child. It is shocking that a minister can give such replies with impunity in this time and age. This was in 1981, six years after the International Women's Year was celebrated with much fanfare and thirty-four years after the Constitution had been formally adopted.

Even the highest court's judgment in this case had evoked considerable surprise. A Supreme Court advocate writing in *India Today* had earlier suggested that the air hostesses' case was so strong that it was a foregone conclusion that the Court would take this opportunity to "teach the Maharajah some modernity." Commenting later, the journal regretted that the Court let slip an opportunity to articulate what it described as a "unisex" view of the Constitution. It was all the more disappointing because the Court had in recent times pronounced so many progressive landmark judgments in favour of deprived sections. Even Indira Gandhi had at that time expressed a sexist and traditional view by declaring that forty-five "is too old" for an air hostess, thereby equating their work qualification with youthful beauty—a criterion which the Supreme Court itself had rejected in strong language, while passing severe strictures on the airlines' management for defending such sexist norms.

In both the Muthamma and air hostesses' cases much amazement had been expressed by commentators that it had taken *three decades* for women employees to challenge their blatantly biased service conditions. In fact one of the arguments of the airlines management was that a rule left unquestioned for so long automatically acquired immunity from legal challenge!

Again, when the Lady Hardinge doctors' case figured prominently in the press, the health minister, in answer to a question in Parliament, had tabled the following reply: "Pregnancy is not a bar for Lady Hardinge doctors except in the case of first year married junior residents". Thus, instead of trying to set right an injustice brought to his notice, the minister offered a highly unsatisfactory reply which neither explains nor justifies the discrimination against the junior women doctors.

It may be added here that according to an ILO compilation of maternity legislation, although many countries have made dismissal during maternity leave illegal, very few have abolished dismissal during *pregnancy*. The Lady Hardinge rule is a clear instance of the authorities wriggling out of payment of maternity benefits by the simple strategy of refusing to employ junior doctors who are pregnant.

To this I may add a little tailpiece from the *International Socialist Review* (March 1974). At one point of time in the US, employers were going so far as to require female job applicants to take pregnancy tests before being hired. A laboratory engaged in doing pregnancy slide tests ran a series of advertisements in major papers and journals with copy that went like this: "Before the company hires her, make sure she is not pregnant. Make pregnancy testing a routine part of your pre-employment physical. And find the pregnant before your company gets involved in costly training programmes as well as health and sick pay coverage!"

QED about sums it up. The only saving grace is that the health minister did not quote this item and defend the Lady Hardinge rule as a "sophisticated management technique" for "cost-efficient hospital administration"! Though that, of course, is what it really is. Most discriminatory practices against women employees boil down to a method of saving money for the employers.

To conclude, women must first become fully aware of their legal, constitutional and human rights at the workplace. They must work to get these incorporated into and protected by their service conditions. And they must demand an appropriate machinery for redressal when these rights are violated. And side by side with all these safeguards, equally important though probably far more difficult—is the intensive education of people, both men and women, at all levels of policy planning and decision making, to remove old-fashioned, sexist notions of women and their work.

8

Measurement of Poverty and Undernutrition*

D. Banerji

It is good that some of the top names in the country in the fields of economics, statistics and planning are so deeply involved in a prolonged and very vigorous debate on the vital subject of poverty and undernutrition in the country. In their numerous thrusts and counter-thrusts, they have raised issues which cover a wide range of disciplines. Paradoxically, however, in so intensively dealing with the problem in many of its interdisciplinary dimensions, there has been a tendency to take a rather restricted view of data obtained from some of the concerned disciplines. Worse still, the debate has tended to overlook altogether some other critical dimensions, perhaps because of the inability to conceptualise all the critical issues involved. As such, the symbols that have been used to describe the reality have been derived on the basis of assumptions which suffer from serious limitations. Unfortunately, the zeal to play mathematical games with these symbols has become so strong that the symbols have been used to signify far more than their symbolic character. They have often taken the place of the reality and the reality is projected in terms of the image that emerges through the cracked lenses of distorted symbols;"the medium thus becomes the message," with all its far-reaching implications for the objects which are the "targets."

The picture that emerges from this intense involvement of the scholars is frightening. It is frightening not simply because the problem is of such overwhelming dimensions, but because those who are concerned with drawing this picture could so effectively clothe it in an aura of scientific competence,

* Originally published in *Economic and Political Weekly* 16, no. 39 (26 September 1981), pp. 1579–82.

while taking such a narrow view of a life-and-death problem like poverty and hunger among the masses of people of the country. What emerges is chillingly mechanistic, aseptic, impersonal and aloof. What is even more agonising is that it cannot be dismissed merely as a sterile academic exercise.

One is reminded of a similar exercise by scholars like Lewis, Moynihan and Glazer,[1] who forcefully propounded the theory (which received wide acclaim from certain circles) that there is poverty in the United States, not because there is anything basically wrong with the sociopolitical system of that country, but because the poor are victims of the very culture in which they grow up: "it is the culture of poverty which is responsible for persistence of poverty in the United States and, therefore, the former President Johnson's drive to remove poverty is utterly misplaced." In the course of the current debate on poverty and hunger, one can hear deafeningly loud whispers to the effect "No, all of them are not poor or hungry. As a nutritional phenomenon, many have much more efficient metabolic systems so that they manage well even when they consume fewer calories." This gives scientific respectability to the clamour of some politicians who say: "Where is poverty in India? I move around the villages all over the country. I do not see that much of poverty. People look better fed and better clad. Some academics seem to have developed a vested interest in giving an exaggerated account of poverty in India."

The most outstanding flaw in the debate on poverty and hunger is that the scholars have not adequately realised that there is an enormously wide range of categories between those who just somehow manage to satisfy their physiological need in the form of hunger and those who die of starvation or of starvation-related diseases. When a human being is unable to satisfy his hunger, apart from this being a problem having considerable social, cultural, economic and political implications, it also becomes a stark biological problem of survival. When he finds himself worsted in the struggle for existence, the human biological being "fights" back to survive in an effort to stop the downward slide and also to regain the lost ground. Therefore, in terms of biological survival, apart from the two categories consisting of those who are able to regain the lost ground and those who continue to slide down right up to the point of death due to hunger, there are numerous individuals in other categories of the hungry who continue to slide down or climb up or remain for varying periods in a steady state while remaining within the very wide range provided by the two extremes. The position of an individual in this wide spectrum is determined by the number of days in a year he/she has to suffer from varying degrees of hunger. Therefore, the number of days in a year an individual suffers from varying degrees of hunger is a point of central concern for those who want to have a sensitive tool for measuring the degree of undernutrition in a population. The question of the degree to which a human body economises on whatever it is able to eat—by lowering its

TABLE 8.1: DEGREE OF HUNGER SATISFACTION

Villages	Fully Satisfied	Not for 1 Month or Less	Not for 1 to 3 Months	Not for 3 to 6 Months	Not for More than 6 months	Irregular	Total
Andanga (24-Parg)	41.0 (16)	7.7 (3)	33.3 (13)	15.4 (6)	0.0 (0)	2.6 (1)	100.0 (39)
Bajaguli (Nadia)	38.8 (31)	6.3 (5)	28.8 (23)	17.5 (14)	2.5 (2)	6.3 (5)	100.0 (80)
C'mannam (Palghat)	39.2 (20)	0.0 (0)	0.0 (0)	39.2 (20)	21.6 (11)	0.0 (0)	100.0 (51)
J'hally (Bangalore)	67.5 (54)	0.0 (0)	3.8 (3)	20.0 (16)	5.0 (4)	3.8 (3)	100.0 (80)
Kachhona (Hardoi)	55.1 (38)	1.5 (1)	2.9 (2)	34.8 (24)	1.5 (1)	4.4 (3)	100.0 (69)
P'kode (Palghat)	13.8 (8)	0.0 (0)	0.0 (0)	70.7 (41)	13.8 (8)	1.7 (1)	100.0 (58)
P'badi (Trichy)	29.9 (29)	0.0 (0)	7.2 (7)	57.7 (55)	6.2 (6)	0.0 (0)	100.0 (97)
Rupal (Sabark)	77.7 (45)	1.7 (1)	13.8 (8)	6.9 (4)	0.0 (0)	0.0 (0)	100.0 (58)
Rohat (Pali)	75.0 (54)	0.0 (0)	1.4 (1)	11.1 (8)	4. 2 (3)	8.3 (6)	100.0 (72)
Rohala (Meerut)	70.1 (69)	0.0 (0)	8.1 (7)	13.8 (12)	0.0 (0)	8.1 (7)	100.0 (87)
Yelwal (Mysore)	25.0 (14)	1.8 (1)	17.9 (10)	44.6 (25)	3.6 (2)	7.1 (4)	100.0 (56)
Kalur (Mysore)	11.8 (2)	0.0 (0)	23.5 (4)	58.8 (10)	5.9 (1)	0.0 (0)	100.0 (17)
Amavali (Meerut)	47.4 (18)	2.6 (1)	10.5 (4)	34.2 (13)	2.6 (1)	2.6 (1)	100.0 (38)
Bilaspur (Karnal)	72.2 (13)	0.0 (0)	11.1 (2)	16.7 (3)	0.0 (0)	0.0 (0)	100.0 (18)
D'Duttapara (Nadia)	77.8 (420	5.6 (3)	5.6 (3)	5.6 (3)	1.9 (1)	3.7 (2)	100.0 (54)
Gambhoi (Sabark)	71.4 (10)	0.0 (0)	14.3 (2)	14.3 (2)	0.0 (0)	0.0 (0)	100.0 (14)
Kapur (24-Parg)	59.5 (25)	0.0 (0)	19.1 (8)	11.9 (5)	4.8 (2)	4.8 (2)	100.0 (42)
Rampura (Pali)	66.7 (14)	0.0 (0)	9.5 (2)	14.3 (3)	9.5 (2)	0.0 (0)	100.0 (21)
Sunni (Hardoi)	61.1 (22)	0.0 (0)	0.0 (0)	27.8 (10)	0.0 (0)	11.1 (4)	100.0 (36)
Total	52.3 (516)	1.5 (15)	10.0 (99)	27.8 (274)	4.5 (44)	4.0 (39)	100.0 (987)

Note: Figures within brackets denote frequencies.

basal metabolic rate or by otherwise increasing the efficiency of utilisation of the calories in performing work—is of secondary importance and this should not be allowed to cloud the central fact—that the individual is hungry.

Thus, quite apart from the various statistical and non-statistical errors that can creep in during data collection for a survey, the findings of a survey provide a snapshot of the flux at any given point of time—or within a given period if the survey covers a given period. It is desirable to have systematic, quantitative data on the number of days an individual suffers due to varying degrees of hunger and to process such data through the use of different statistical and mathematical methods. However, not only should greater emphasis be laid on the limitations of such survey data, but the limitations of these data should be highlighted at least against a conceptual background of the entire dynamics of the biological, social, cultural and economic consequences of hunger and deprivation among human beings in the country.

Indeed, considerable direct information concerning the degree of hunger at a point of time is available through the activities of the National Nutrition Monitoring Bureau (NNMB), which is administered through the National Institute of Nutrition, Hyderabad. Admittedly, the data suffer from some limitations. But these limitations certainly are not any more serious than the known limitations of the National Sample Survey (NSS) data. The NNMB has carried out an elaborate nutrition survey,[2] following the specifications laid down by the National Institute of Nutrition. As a measure of "abundant precaution," it adopted the mean of the 1968 recommendation of ICMR *minus twice the standard deviation* to define nutritional inadequacy. On this basis, the NNMB came to the conclusion that, "Considering all the states together, 58 per cent of the total [rural] households fall into the category of households consuming adequate amounts of protein and calories" (p. 13). Forty-one per cent consumed inadequate calories. This is much lower than the estimated undernutrition given by one of the scholars involved in the debate. While ignoring the findings of the NNMB, this scholar had dug out certain data on basal metabolic rates (which, as he himself says, are extremely fragile) to support his case for a low estimate of undernutrition in the country because of intra- and inter-individual variations.

The present writer's own studies of poverty[3] in terms of the degree of hunger satisfaction in the course of a long-term study of poverty, class and health culture in 19 Indian villages, located in eight states, tend to reinforce the conclusions of the NNMB. The villages were selected purposefully in terms of location of a primary health centre and these were above average villages. Careful anthropological field work was conducted in each of these nineteen villages. The field work data formed the basis of construction of a schedule to obtain quantitative data on certain parameters from a stratified, random sample (8 to 50 per cent, depending on the population). By measuring poverty in terms of the degree of hunger satisfaction, it was possible to avoid the raging controversy about various versions of nutritional recommendations by the Indian Council of Medical Research or by the various joint committees of the World Health Organisation/Food and Agricultural Organisation. It was also possible to avoid the scholarly controversies concerning variations from the recommended norm, consumer unit per capita consumption or per capita income and cost of a recommended food basket. Those who were unable to obtain two square meals (of any composition) all round the year were defined as "poor." A detailed report on this study is in the process of publication. The table reproduced here is from the manuscript of the publication.[4]

When each village is a discrete, purposefully selected entity in itself, an average has very limited significance. But it does show that, taken as a whole, almost half of the population is unable to satisfy its hunger all round the year, with more than a third remaining hungry for three months or more. More significant is the extent of variations in the prevalence of hunger in different villages.

It may be emphasised that, to avoid controversies regarding definitions of the poor, very rigorous criteria were adopted for defining the poor for this study. The proportion of the poor in the population will increase sharply if, instead of adopting merely the criterion of "two square meals all round the year," the definition is changed to "two square wholesome meals all round the year" by including even a small quantity of dal, ghee or oil and iron in the meal of the adult and a small quantity of milk for children in the definition. The extent of poverty goes up still further if minimum norms of housing in terms of space and hygiene are also included. If, in addition, a minimum standard of environmental sanitation and quality of drinking water are taken into account, very few people will be able to escape being labelled as "poor."

In their preoccupation with a debate which gets painfully restricted because of adoption of a very narrow definition of poverty and hunger in India and which was also at times associated with stretching of certain selected data to justify certain pre-conceived notions, the participants in the debate have managed to ignore altogether an aspect of the question which has considerable epidemiological and demographic significance with far-reaching political and social implications. It is significant that this issue has indeed been raised on earlier occasions,[5] but was not considered worth noticing.

As late as in 1977, the Union Ministry of Health and Family Welfare had categorically stated that as much as four-fifths of rural populations have virtually no access to health services—either government or private.[6] One can also make an epidemiological analysis to demonstrate without much difficulty that the much trumpeted public health measures against diseases such as malaria, smallpox, cholera, tuberculosis, diphtheria, etc., have had a marginal impact on death rates. One can also safely assert that during the last three or four decades there has not been any significant improvement in the levels of living of the lower two-thirds of the population in the country. How then can one explain the rise in the expectation of life at birth in the last three or four decades, particularly a fall in the infant mortality rates[7] among the poorer sections? Obviously, the category of human beings who were earlier being weeded out in the struggle for existence (as they passed beyond the minimum threshold, "the floor," for survival), now manage to survive. In the absence of any systematic study to answer this question one can only conjecture that due to some hitherto undefined changes in the human ecology, there is a lowering of the "floor" of survival. An increase in life expectancy among the lower segments of the population which is not accompanied with improvement in socio-economic conditions and improvement in health services results in a further addition of persons to the category of the poor and the destitute, who are even weaker and who are even more vulnerable to diseases as also to exploitation and control by the rich. But though in social and political terms these people come even nearer to a vegetative form of existence, they cannot, nevertheless, be labelled as dead, biologically. This gives an additional propaganda platform to the ruling rich to claim that under their benevolent rule, they have brought about a significant increase in life expectancy among the poor people.

"Launching" of the concept that severe malnutrition during infancy causes permanent brain damage provides an instance of active involvement of "scientists" in politically motivated activities. Nutrition scientists from the Massachusetts Institute of Technology used data from field studies in Guatemala to form the concept.[8] The idea was sold to the United Nations.[9] Taking up the refrain, it becomes an article of faith with some key nutrition scientists of the Third World.[10] These "scientists" were so "mentally conditioned" by the Voice from Above, that they failed to check the validity of the concept by comparing the current status of mental health of the cohorts who were exposed to the Bengal Famine of 1941 (or Bihar Famine of 1967 or those of the Russian Revolution Famine or hunger of concentration camps of World War II) with corresponding cohorts of matched controls, who escaped these calamities. As late as in 1979, an eminent social pediatrician from the UK,[11] has asserted that there is now "irrefutable evidence that prolonged periods of malnutrition occurring in the last trimester of pregnancy and within first two years will have a serious effect on the intellectual potential of the individuals and is, therefore, of great political importance in national development."

The scientists who sold this concept never showed any concern about the danger of its political misuse by the ruling rich. In this concept, the rich will find a "scientific" justification for keeping political power, arguing that chunks of population are mental cretins, because they suffered from malnutrition when they were infants so only those born to well-off families possess the intellectual capability to hold positions of responsibility in different walks of life; others do not possess mental capabilities beyond being "hewers of wood and drawers of water."

Indeed, nutrition scientists are particularly vulnerable to manipulation by political forces and the market forces which control the political forces. Unlike physical scientists, it is often difficult for them to be very precise about issues concerning human nutrition. This limitation is exploited by the market forces which use nutrition "science" to promote their products. Why did it take such a long time for the eminent nutritionists in India to realise that rather than protein deficiency, it is calorie deficiency which is of central concern? Why did they hitch the individual minimum protein requirements so high on earlier occasions? Why were they so vociferous about superior attributes of animal proteins—the so-called first-class proteins? Why did they overplay the importance of essential amino-acids and vitamins? Why is it that such a huge market has been created for many "tonics" which obviously have no nutritional value? What about the high-pressure salesmanship of baby foods? Why did not the nutrition scientist pay enough attention to basing their research on people as they exist in the community? Instead, why did they attach undue importance to nutrition research in the animal house or in the laboratory?

As one follows the heated debate among "eminent and senior" scholars, one senses that these giants harbour a feeling of awe and reverence towards whatever the nutrition experts recommend, be it calorie requirements, protein requirements or the elaborate list of a balanced diet. One tends to suspect that because of this worshipful attitude, the participants in the debate have not made adequate provision for the waywardness of the recommendations of nutrition experts, while they have been unsparing in their arguments about inter- and intra-individual differences, statistical variations,"paradoxical findings" in the NSS, and so on.

NOTES AND REFERENCES

[1] Oscar Lewis, *La Vida: A Puerto Rican Fimily in the Culture of Poverty—San Juan and New York* (New York: Random House, 1966); D. P. Moynihan, "The President and the Negro—The Moment Last," *Commentary*, vol. 43 (1967), pp. 31–45; N. Glazer and D. P. Moynihan, *Beyond the Melting Pot—The Negroes, Puerto Ricans, Jews, Italias, and Irish of New York City* (Cambridge, MA: MIT Press and Harvard University Press, 1963).

[2] National Nutrition Monitoring Bureau, *Report for the Year 1979* (Hyderabad, National Institute of Nutrition, 1980).

[3] D. Banerji, *Poverty, Class and Health Culture in Rural India*, vol. one (New Delhi: Prachi Prakashan, in press).

[4] D. Banerji, "Political Issues in Health, Population and Nutrition," *Social Scientist* 7, nos. 73–74 (August/September 1978), pp. 159–68.

[5] D. Banerji, "Epidemiological Issues in Nutrition," *Indian Journal of Nutrition and Dietetics*, vol. 16 (1979), pp. 189–94.

[6] Government of India, *Health Care Services in Rural Areas*, Draft Plan (New Delhi: Ministry of Health and Family Welfare, 1977).

[7] T. McKeown, *Role of Medicine: Dream, Mirage or Nemesis?*(London: Nuffield Provincial Hospitals Trust, 1976).

[8] J. Cravioto et al., *Indian Journal of Medical Research*, vol. 59 (1971): pp. 192–215.

[9] United Nations, *International Action to Avert the Impending Protein Crisis* (New York, 1968).

[10] Glaxo Symposium on Nutrition, Growth and Development, Session IV, Nutrition and Mental Development, *Indian Journal of Medical Research* 59, no. 6, Supplement (1971): pp. 177–220.

[11] D. Morley, "IYO: A Time to Look at Child Health," pp. 85–86, in A. DeSouza (ed.), *Children in India: Critical Issues in Human Development* (New Delhi: Manohar, 1979).

PART II

Society

9

Changes in the Indian Family

An Examination of Some Assumptions*

A. M. Shah

"From joint family to elementary (or nuclear or individual) family." This has been a slogan to summarise changes in the family in India during modern times. Recently, some sociologists have pointed out that the change implied by the slogan is not taking place. What is emerging, they say, is not the elementary family but a new form of the joint family. Even these sociologists, however, do not question the correctness of describing the traditional family system of India as the joint family system. This belief about the traditional Indian family subsumes a set of some other beliefs:

(a) traditional India was village India, and the joint family was therefore a characteristic of village India;
(b) contrariwise, urban areas are new and characterised by the elementary family; and
(c) urbanisation, therefore, leads to disintegration of the joint family.

Some sociologists have pointed out that urbanisation does not lead to disintegration but only to transformation of the joint family. They do not, however, question the belief that the joint family was always a characteristic of village India. This chapter attempts to examine these beliefs about the traditional Indian family because a proper understanding of social change requires a proper understanding of the past. It is concerned with the beliefs about the traditional family only insofar as they refer to its household aspect. It has now become

* Originally published in *Economic and Political Weekly* 3, annual number (6 January 1968): pp. 127–34.

commonplace in sociology and social anthropology to distinguish between "household" and "family." In common English parlance the word "family" has several different meanings, including "household"; the common Indian word for the family, *kutumb*, has likewise several different meanings but, for the sake of technical analysis, "household" should be distinguished from the other referents of "family." For example, two brothers and their wives and children may live in two separate households, but they may be bound by a number of relationships of many kinds. For the sake of clarity, it is necessary to consider such inter-household relationships as distinct from relationships within the household. Although the aim of the study of the family should be to study it in all its aspects, a beginning has to be made with the study of the household. An examination of ideas about the past of the Indian household is, therefore, crucial in a comprehensive study of changes in the Indian family.

II

If we take a census of households in any section of Indian society—a village, town, or caste—and examine their numerical and kinship composition, we find a number of types of composition, ranging from the most simple single-member household to a very complex household of many members. A "simple" household is composed of a complete elementary family or a part of an elementary family. A "complex" or "joint" household is composed of two or more elementary families, or of parts of two or more elementary families, or of one elementary family and parts of one or more other elementary families.[1]

Types of Composition

One of the first tasks in an analysis of households is to formulate the types of composition. The structure of the household becomes more complex as more categories of relatives are included. In a one-member household there is no relationship; in a two-member household there is one relationship; but beyond this the addition of one relative means an addition of more than one relationship. For example, the addition of a son's wife to a household of father, mother and son, means the addition of relationships not only between the son and his wife but also between father-in-law and daughter-in-law and between mother-in-law and daughter-in-law. Addition of relationships tends to create conflict between roles. For example, the conflict between a man's loyalty to his wife and loyalty to his parents is proverbial. Each person in a household is involved in a complex pattern of behaviour with every other member. Everyone in a household has his own likes and dislikes, habits, tastes and idiosyncracies. Life in a household is marked by sentiments and emotions, and cooperation as well as conflict. Therefore, if our aim is to understand household life in its entirety, the formulation of types of household composition should take into account all the various members of a household. After the types have been formulated, it is necessary to examine the frequencies of households of various types.

Classification of households according to types of composition is not, however, an end in itself. The types are not discrete and haphazard but are interrelated in a developmental process. This process may be in progression or in regression. Progressive development of a household takes place due to increase in membership, mainly by birth and marriage, while regressive development takes place due to decrease in membership, mainly by marriage, death and partition. It may be mentioned in passing that there is always some pattern in the developmental process, but it is not cyclical in nature as considered by Fortes and his associates.[2]

PRINCIPLES OF AGGREGATION

One of the determinants of the developmental process is a set of explicitly stated rules or norms governing the formation of households. In most sections of Indian society, the bride after marriage leaves her parental home and goes to live in her conjugal home. A son and his wife are required not only to start their married life in his parental home but also to continue to live there afterwards. This norm has a number of implications. For instance, if a man has more than one son, each of the junior sons and his wife will have to live not only with his parents but also with his senior brothers and their wives and children. In fact, frequently people state that a man and his wife should live with his brothers and their wives. Furthermore, they say that brothers and their wives should live together not only during the lifetime of the (brothers') parents but also after their death, and the brothers' sons and their wives should also live in the same household. Sometimes the norm is extended still further.

Taking all these norms together, the central idea is that while female patrilineal descendants of a male ancestor go away to live with their husbands, the male patrilineal descendants and their wives should live together. The wives should be so completely incorporated into their husbands' kin-group that they should not be divorced and that even after their husbands' death they should stay on in the same household. Unmarried children should be with their parents; in the event of divorce or death of their mother, they should stay with their father or his male patri-kin. I would call the central idea behind these norms briefly the principle of residential unity of patri-kin and their wives. It is necessary to clarify that this principle is normative in nature, and that there are always deviations from it as in the case of all norms. The measurement of conformity to and deviation from the principle is therefore, an important problem of inquiry.

Variations from Norms

While the principle is common to almost the entire Hindu society, there are differences between sections of the society in the extent to which it is observed. First of all, there are differences in the maximum extent to which the developmental process goes in progression along the path set by the principle. For example, in a Gujarat village I have studied, there is no case of two or more married brothers living in a single household after the death of their parents. In a nearby village, on the other hand, there is a considerable number of households of this type. Such differences in the maximum extent may also exist between villages and towns, between one caste and another caste, and between one region and another region.

Second, while the maximum extent of the developmental process may be the same in two sections of the society, there may be differences in the frequencies of the cases in which the norm is observed within this extent. For example, in the Gujarat village just cited, only about 5 per cent of the total number of households are composed of one or both parents and two or more married sons and their wives and children, while 19 per cent of the households are composed of one or both parents and one married son. This is mainly due to the fact that married sons tend to live separately from parents even before the death of parents. Out of 41 cases of parents having two or more married sons, only in 12 cases (29.26 per cent) do all the sons live with the parents in a single household, while in 29 cases (70.73 per cent) all or some of the sons live in separate households (in the village itself). And out of 50 cases of parents having one married son, in 38 cases (76 per cent) the parents and the son form a joint household, while in 12 cases (24 per cent) the parents and the son live in separate households.

One of the factors affecting the degree of extension of the principle of residential unity of patri-kin and their wives appears to be the degree of Sanskritisation of a caste. This is due to the great emphasis which the Hindu scriptures lay on the high degree of observance of this principle. The ritually higher castes, who are under the greater impact of the scriptures, tend to have a higher degree of extension of the principle. Another factor affecting the degree of extension of the principle appears to be the institution of cross-cousin and uncle-niece marriages.

Family beyond Household

Whatever be the maximum extent to which the principle goes in progression in a particular section of the society, it is important to note that the processes of progressive and regressive developments go on simultaneously in the society taken as a whole. One household may be undergoing progression, another may be undergoing regression. As a result, there are always households in the society which are small and simple in composition, along with households which are large and complex in composition.

When a complex household, say, of two or more married brothers, is partitioned, two or more separate households come into existence, but at the same time a number of other relationships continue to operate. They would cooperate in economic pursuits, hold and manage property jointly, help each other on many occasions, celebrate festivals, rituals and ceremonies jointly, and so on. This is also a normal process, which highlights the importance of technical distinction between "household" and "family" mentioned at the outset. Thus, two or more households may be separate but they may constitute one family.

III

For a long time, students of the Indian family have used ancient Indian literature for information about its past. This information is of two main kinds: (a) pertaining to the property aspect of the family, which is generally included in the study of Hindu Law, and (b) pertaining to certain family rituals, such as the *shraddha*.[3]

DEFINITION OF JOINT FAMILY

The Hindu legal text Mitaksara first defines a coparcenary: it comprises only those males who are entitled by birth to an interest in the joint or coparcenary property, i.e., a person himself and his sons, son's sons, and son's grandsons. As each son acquires by birth an interest in coparcenary property, even a father and his unmarried son are sufficient to constitute a coparcenary. Under the Dayabhaga, there is no coparcenary between a man and his son(s), married or unmarried, even though they may be living in a single household. The legal definition of the joint family is based on that of the coparcenary: it consists of all males included in the coparcenary, plus their wives and unmarried daughters. The latter are not coparceners but have only a right to maintenance.

There are two main points here. First, the legal definition of the joint family is a highly specialised one and has nothing to do with the sociological distinction between elementary family and joint family. A joint family of the legal conception can exist even within an elementary family of the sociological conception. For example, a father and an unmarried son, or a widow and her unmarried son, are sufficient to constitute a joint family according to law. Second, the law does not lay down the rule that the joint family of the legal conception should always be a joint household. A son may live separately from his father, and one brother from another, but they continue to be members of their respective joint property group. In brief, the law is concerned primarily with the rights of constituting a property-holding group and of maintenance therefrom, but not with the constitution of the household group.

In the sacred texts (Shastras), the question as to who should hold and inherit property is discussed usually in relation to the question as to who should perform the shraddha ritual for whom. In other words, the legal definition of the constitution of the joint family tends to coincide with and is sanctioned by the definition of the circle of persons required to perform the shraddha. This circle of persons need not live in a single household, just as the persons constituting the joint property group need not live in a single household. It seems to me that it was because of the coincidence of the legal and the ritual definitions of the joint family that the definition given in the Shastras came to be accepted as the general definition of the Hindu joint family. I shall call it the Indological definition. As most of the early studies were carried out by Indologists (including historians, Sanskritists and Orientalists) on the basis of sacred literature, and as both Indologists and lawyers were dominant in the academic field in India, the Indological idea of the joint family carried a lot of weight and gained popularity.

The Indological-cum-legal material on the Indian family was used by Henry Maine in his general theory of the evolution of the family. He compared and contrasted the joint family of India with the individual family of the West, and considered the latter as later in evolution than the former. He thus laid the foundation of the sociological study of the Indian family, and through him the Indological view of the Indian family came to be accepted in sociology.

I just now pointed out the fact that the Indological definition is not concerned primarily with the composition of the household. Insofar as it was concerned with the household, it laid down only the definition of the ideal household, or in my terms, only the maximum extent of progression of the developmental process of households. The Indological literature does not provide any information on the various types of households, nor on the frequency of households of each type. Obviously there was no census of households, in any section of Hindu society, at any period of time. Furthermore, the literature provides information more about the Brahmins and a few other higher castes whose property relations and rituals were governed by the sacred texts. With regard to the household also, the ideal that the texts emphasised was high—a household of four generations[4]—and it seems only the higher castes tried to emulate the ideal to a higher degree. The texts do not provide any idea of differences in the family life of different sections of the society.[5]

IV

We begin to get more precise data on the household only with the beginning of the British administration in India. The Office of the Census Commissioner of India has planned to publish a series of volumes on population estimates for the period from the eighteenth century to 1871 on the basis of censuses conducted in different parts of India during the period. The first volume in this series, dealing with the decade 1820–30, was published recently.[6] It seems to me that it will be extremely useful if attempts are made to find and then analyse the original schedules of all these censuses. My experience in Gujarat indicates that such attempts are likely to be fruitful. During my search for sources for the study of social history of villages in central Gujarat, I found in the taluka headquarters the original schedules of a census carried out by Captain Cruikshank and his associates,[7] the same schedules that he used in compiling general reports on different parts of Gujarat, which have in turn been used by the Bhattacharyas in their volume on population estimates for 1820–30 mentioned above. In this census of Gujarat, a census register was prepared for every village, in which were listed the names of heads of households in the village according to their religion and caste and against each name were given the following details: (i) houses and huts, (ii) men, (iii) women, (iv) servants and slaves, and (v) total number of persons.

HOUSEHOLDS IN GUJARAT

I have made a detailed analysis of the 1820–30 census data on the household composition in a Gujarat village.[8] It shows (a) that the average size of the household was 4.5, and (b) that progressive development of households rarely, if ever, went beyond the phase of co-residence of two or more married sons during the lifetime of their parents. It is significant that census data of a village in Maharashtra of the same period, which Professor Ghurye has presented in his book *After a Century and a Quarter*,[9] shows the same average size of the household as in the Gujarat village. The early nineteenth century data, thus, indicate that we cannot start the study of changes in the family in India with the assumption that villagers in traditional India always lived in large and complex households of three or four generations. We need a more realistic base line, and the early nineteenth century census data are a very useful source for reconstructing such a base line.

As regards differences in the family between rural and urban areas also, it is important to keep in view the position at the beginning of the nineteenth century. The early nineteenth century census data indicate that there was a higher proportion of the population of higher and more Sanskritised castes in towns than in villages. The bulk of the population in villages consisted of lower and less Sanskritised castes. If this point is related to my earlier point that the higher castes were under the greater impact of scriptures and there was, therefore, a higher degree of observance of the principle of residential unity of patri-kin and their wives among higher castes, it follows that there was a higher degree of observance of this principle in towns than in villages. The reality was, thus, quite the reverse of the widely prevalent belief that there was a greater emphasis on joint households (i.e., on the principle of residential unity of patri-kin and their wives) in villages than in towns in traditional India.

V

Although the censuses upto 1871 had certain obvious drawbacks—they covered only small areas in the country, and even within a small area the census was not taken simultaneously in all the villages and towns—it is remarkable that they collected and recorded a great deal of information of demographic and sociological value. The later censuses covered wider areas and became uniform in techniques, terminology and classification, but there was retrogression in the case of information concerning the household. In all the censuses from 1867 to 1941, the distinction between "household,""house" and "building" was not followed uniformly in all the provinces and states and sometimes even in all the parts of a single province or state, and hardly any attempt was made to collect information either on the kinship or on the numerical composition of households. Nevertheless, even the meagre information they provided is highly suggestive.

False Belief

All of these censuses show that the average size of the household was rather low, between 4.5 and 5. The Census Commissioner for 1911, E. A. Gait, stated the position very succinctly: "The average population per house is 4.9 or much the same as in European countries. In the British Isles it ranges from 4.8 in Scotland to 5.2 in England and Wales."[10] This suggests that the people in India lived mostly in small and simple households. It is noteworthy, however, that almost all the census officials interpreted their figures unrealistically. They assumed that Indians in pre-British days always lived in large households, and therefore, they concluded from their figures that the traditional household system was disintegrating due to modernisation. The assumption about the past was a great obstacle to a realistic interpretation of the figures before them.

In a recent paper, Henry Orenstein[11] has used the census data to examine the usual general idea about changes in the Indian household. He has posed the problem as follows: If the widespread belief that the modern processes of industrialisation, Westernisation, etc., of traditional societies such as India lead to smaller households is true, then the increasing industrialisation, Westernisation, etc., should be reflected in a decreasing average size of the household. He presents figures to show that the average size of the household has not only not decreased from the 1867 to the 1951 Census, but there has been on the contrary a slight tendency—very slight indeed—towards increase. This suggests that the modern processes of industrialisation, Westernisation, etc., have not brought about the so-called disintegration of large and joint households. Orenstein conjectures, I think quite rightly, that the belief about the wide prevalence of large and joint households in pre-British India is false.

VI

During the last thirty years or so, professional sociologists and social anthropologists have studied the problem of changes in the family in India. Some of these studies are concerned only with the household and some with the household as well as other aspects of the family. I would refrain from commenting here upon those studies which are not concerned with the household, as well as upon those studies of the household which are not concerned with the problem of change.[12] As far as the studies of changes in the household are concerned, I submit that most of them have suffered from the assumptions I have examined in this chapter. It seems to me that we need a new and more sophisticated framework for our study.

First of all, we have to distinguish the normal developmental process from change. This is a difficult task, but we have to face it. Studies of the early nineteenth century data on the household seem to me to be very necessary for this purpose.

Second, there is no point in postulating a single line of change for the entire Indian society. I suggest that it would be profitable to bring into the study of the household Srinivas's ideas on Sanskritisation and Westernisation. In this context it is worthwhile to recall the slight increase in the average size of the household indicated by Orenstein. It is possible that this increase may be due to some demographic factor. Orenstein himself has suggested that it may be due to a rise in the average number of children or in the average number of adults per household. (If the latter is true, it strengthens the argument in favour of an increasing overall emphasis on large and joint households.) Notwithstanding the influence of demographic factors, it seems worth inquiring whether the Sanskritisation of lower castes and Adivasi tribes that has been taking place on a massive scale in the country has contributed anything to an overall greater emphasis on the principle of residential unity of patri-kin and their wives. It cannot be denied that Westernisation of the higher castes has contributed to a lesser emphasis on the principle, but the countervailing influence of Sanskritisation might have led to an overall tendency in favour of greater emphasis on it. What I plead is that let us not assume that there has been an inevitable trend from large and complex (or joint) to small and simple households.

Finally, we need to have a fresh look at the problem of the impact of industrialisation and urbanisation on the household. It has already been pointed out that the situation in the past was possibly quite the reverse of what we have been assuming it to be. That is to say, there was greater emphasis on large and joint households in towns than in villages. Migration of rural people to towns, therefore, does not necessarily mean migration from a social environment of large and joint households to that of small and simple households. It seems to me that the study of the long-established population of older towns and cities is extremely important. I have in mind, for example, the walled cities of Delhi, Agra and Ahmedabad, certain sections of the population of even Bombay, Calcutta and Madras, and the large number of small towns. We should also examine the extent to which migrants to a town tend to be its permanent residents, and whether they practise the old norms when they are permanently settled. The whole question of relation between migration and the household in India seems to be complicated. In any case, we begin to understand it better if we get rid of the old established assumptions.[13]

Notes and References

[1] The terms "simple household" and "complex household" are not discussed here in detail for want of space. However, it may be noted that (i) "elementary family" is not the same as "simple household"—actually, a household composed of a complete elementary family is only one of the several types of "simple households"—and (ii) "joint household" is only a convenient alternative of "complex household." The background for discarding the usual dichotomy of elementary and joint family is provided in my paper, "Basic Terms and Concepts in the Study of Family in India," *Indian Economic and Social History Review* 1, no. 3 (January–March 1964): pp. 1–36. I have dealt with most of the points of this chapter at length in my forthcoming book on the family in India.

[2] See Jack Goody (ed.), *The Developmental Cycle in Domestic Groups* (Cambridge: Cambridge University Press, 1958).

[3] For a fuller discussion of this literature as well as for citations, see my paper, "Basic Terms and Concepts in the Study of Family in India," pp. 10–14.

[4] The definition of the household composition on the basis of generations is also confusing. For a discussion of this point, see my paper, "Basic Terms and Concepts in the Study of Family in India," pp. 5–6.

[5] The Indological literature is wider than the literature I have considered here, but I doubt if the other literature also provides the kind of data the sociologist needs for the study of the household.

[6] D. Bhattacharya and B. Bhattacharya (eds.), *Census of India 1961: Report on the Population Estimates of India (1820–30)* (Delhi: Office of Registrar General, 1965).

[7] For a detailed description of these records, see A. M. Shah, R. G. Shroff and A. R. Shah, "Early Nineteenth Century Village Records in Gujarat," in *Contributions in Indian Economic History, Vol. II*, ed. Tapan Raychaudhuri (Calcutta: Firma K. L. Mukhopadhyay, 1963), pp. 89–100.

[8] See my PhD dissertation, "Social Structure and Change in a Gujarat Village," in the library of the University of Baroda, Baroda, 1964, pp. 76–86.

[9] G. S. Ghurye, *After a Century and a Quarter: Lonikand Then and Now* (Bombay: Popular Book Depot, 1960), p. 14.

[10] E. A. Gait, *Census of India 1911, Vol. 1 (India), Part I—Report* (Calcutta: Government Printing), p. 47.

[11] Henry Orenstein, "The Recent History of the Extended Family in India," *Social Problems* 8, no. 4 (Spring 1961): pp. 41–50.

[12] I have dealt with the terminological and conceptual aspects of some of the other studies in my paper, op. cit., and my forthcoming book on the Indian family includes a rather lengthy review of the literature on the subject.

[13] I thank all those who commented upon my paper at the seminar on "Trends of Socio-economic Change in India—1871–1961," Indian Institute of Advanced Study, Simla; a seminar in the Department of Sociology, University of Delhi; and a panel discussion on "Industrialization and Its Social Consequences: The Family," Conference of Indian Sociologists, 1967, Bombay. I thank Dr. R. D. Sanwal for his comments on the penultimate draft of the paper.

10

Strains in Leadership Structure

From Status Group to Pluralism in an East UP Village*

Hira Singh

Recent changes, particularly the abolition of zamindari and the extension of franchise to all adults, have legitimised the leadership aspirations of all the castes in the village. The legitimisation of the leadership aspirations of the traditionally dominated groups has many far-reaching implications for the village political structure. These implications have been conspicuously ignored in the mushrooming studies of rural leadership in India in the last decade.[1] Hence, there has been a misplaced emphasis on the continuity of traditional leadership.[2] This chapter is an attempt to look beyond the apparent continuity of the traditional leadership by analysing the strains and stresses in the leadership structure of an East UP village.

The leadership structure in the village under study exhibits an elemental continuity in that it has been and is being ruled over by a status group[3]—the one-time zamindar Rajput caste. This status group is exposed to an unprecedented challenge from the leadership aspirations of the traditionally subservient and disprivileged groups. This challenge, being persistent, is likely to alter not only the relative positions of the different groups in the leadership structure, but also the entire complexion of the village polity.

* Originally published in *Economic and Political Weekly* 4, no. 18 (3 May 1969): pp. 759–64. The author is grateful to Yogendra Singh for his valuable comments.

THE VENUE OF OBSERVATION

Some 22 miles from the district town of Jaunpur in East UP, the village Mahuari is situated in a relatively isolated locale. Surrounded by paddy fields on three sides and bordered by a small rivulet on the fourth side, the village is absolutely inaccessible to traditional or modern means of transport, save elephants and palanquins, particularly during rains.

Its total population of 1,125 makes it larger than an average UP village, which has 527 heads. It is a multicaste village consisting of fourteen castes, divided into 156 families (Table 10.1).

TABLE 10.1: NUMBER OF FAMILIES AND PERSONS BY CASTE IN VILLAGE MAHUARI

Caste	Number of Families	Total Strength
Ahir	54	400
Chamar	42	294
Brahmin	19	137
Pasi	16	105
Nai	9	59
Thakur	3	30
Teli	2	25
Kahar	2	10
Lohar	2	15
Dhobi	2	14
Gareria	2	14
Kumhar	1	10
Gosain	1	7
Kayastha	1	5
Total	156	1,125

LEADERSHIP

In the past the leadership of the village, both formal and informal, was in the hands of three zamindari Rajput families. The scope of formal leadership was formerly extremely limited. There was in the village a statutory Gaon Panchayat—an administrative-cum-judicial body. The head of this body was known as the Mukhiya. Both judicial and administrative powers were vested in the Mukhiya. In his judicial capacity, he had to hear petty suits that fell within the jurisdiction of the Gaon Panchayat. Most of the cases brought before the Gaon Panchayat were, it is said, decided informally. In his administrative capacity the Mukhiya had to act as an intermediary between the government and the villagers, but such occasions were few. Being hereditary, the office of the Mukhiya was always held by a member of a single Rajput family.

The scope of informal leadership during zamindari days was quite large, pervading all aspects of village life—economic, political, social and cultural. As noted by R. D. Singh[4] and Yogendra Singh[5] among others, zamindari, though essentially an economic phenomenon, had established itself as an all-pervasive pattern. The zamindar commanded the economic, political, social and cultural sanctions in the village. The zamindars thus had two interconnected features, namely traditional authority[6] and an all-pervasive informal leadership.

Two changes of major importance in the post-Independence period deserve mention. The abolition of zamindari ended the officially sanctioned economic and the political hegemony of the traditionally dominant group. The other significant change has been the extension of citizenship to all adults, followed by the introduction of new formal political institutions like the Gram Panchayat, the Adalat Panchayat Samiti and the Zilla Parishad.

Simultaneously, there have been some important changes in the relative economic and educational positions of the non-Rajput castes. Due to the sheer weight of numbers, they accounted for the bulk of the exodus to urban industrial towns in search of employment and thereby improved the economic position of their families. The number of school-going Rajput boys is proportionately smaller than that of the other castes. Rajput boys are seriously lagging behind even in educational performance.

Leadership Structure and Function

The new political institutions have widened the scope of formal leadership. The main formal institutions in the village are the Gram Panchayat, the village co-operative society, and the managing committee of the school. Besides, the Adalat Panchayat, the Panchayat Samiti and the Zilla Parishad provide for new formal leadership positions.

The most important formal position of leadership in the village is that of the Pradhan—the head of the Gram Panchayat. Since the inception of the Gram Panchayat some 15 years ago the office of the Pradhan has been held by a Rajput of the ex-zamindar family. There has never been any contest for this post and this Rajput has been a unanimous choice each time. The village co-operative society is an exclusively Rajput body. The membership of the Adalat Panchayat and the Panchayat Samiti is decided predominantly by the Rajputs. Many in the village are not even aware of the existence of the Panchayat Samiti or the Zilla

Parishad. The primary school of the village was started by the Rajputs, and until recognised and aided by the government, it was financed and looked after by them. Now, a government grant is available and the Rajputs, though absolved from their financial burden, still continue to have a major say in the constitution and working of the school.

In brief, formal leadership is still in the hands of the old rulers of the village.

Informal Leadership

The formal political institutions have not, however, been able to do away with the popularity and sanctity of informal leadership in the village. If we take a day-to-day or problem-to-problem view, we find that the occasions for informal leadership greatly outnumber the formal ones. The informal leadership is exclusively in the hands of three ex-zamindar Rajput families. The members of these families are the most "reputed" ones in the village; they have a dominant role in decision-making and despite a general setback in their position following the abolition of zamindari, they are the most influential persons in the village.

The scope of informal leadership is very wide. The crucial role of informal leaders lies in the settlement of disputes relating to economic, political, social and moral issues. Economic issues figure prominently at the time of the fission of a family when the joint property is to be divided. These divisions are always informal in the first instance; nevertheless, they are more or less binding. The moral issues involving kidnapping, illicit sex relations and cheating, etc., are decided by the informal leaders. Deviations in respect of social relations are brought to the notice of the informal leaders. If a young man, for instance, does not treat his parents properly or if a man behaves atrociously towards his wife or children, the informal leaders try, frequently with success, to correct the deviant.

Except for the Rajputs and the Brahmins, each caste in the village has its caste panchayat. The caste panchayats operate today almost as efficaciously as they did during zamindari days. But they have never been effective for the whole village. Vertically the jurisdiction of each caste panchayat is confined to its respective caste, while horizontally it has always extended along caste lines far beyond the village boundaries—which weakened its effectiveness as a village unit.

The present leadership of the traditional leaders does not, however, represent a smooth continuity from the past to the present. The age-old authority of the Rajputs was seriously challenged by non-Rajputs, particularly the lower castes of the village, immediately after the abolition of zamindari in the early 1950s. Two incidents are especially relevant to our purpose. In one case, one Bachai Ahir used to cultivate a piece of land of a zamindar Rajput, Thakur Kshatra Pal Singh, and the revenue for the same was paid to the latter. After the abolition of zamindari, Bachai refused to pay the revenue to Kshatra Pal Singh, and the latter asked him to quit the land. In reaction to this all the Ahirs of Mahuari and the surrounding villages[7] got together and took possession of the land in dispute by force. They also sent a message to Thakur Bans Gopal Singh, the oldest and most respected Rajput of the village, that the Rajputs could come for a trial of strength, if they so wished. This infuriated the Rajputs of the village and in a short time all the Rajputs of Mahuari and also of some nearby villages got together to face the challenge. As soon as the Rajput party marched towards the disputed spot the Ahirs fled away. Subsequently, Kshatra Pal Singh filed a suit in the Adalat Panchayat of the village which was headed by a Brahmin. The Rajputs and the Brahmins joined hands and heavy fines were imposed on the Ahirs.

The other incident took place a year later, when Thakur Basdeo Singh, a landowner, asked one of his tenants, Pasi by caste, to quit a piece of land under the latter's cultivation, which he refused to do. One day while the tenant was ploughing the land in question, Basdeo Singh along with a few other Rajputs went there to stop him. No sooner did the Rajputs reach the spot than the Pasis combined with some of the Ahirs of the same hamlet and attacked them from three sides. In the fierce fight that followed, both parties sustained injuries. The next morning, the Rajputs and the Brahmins of the village organised a raid on the residence of the tenant. The Pasis and the Ahirs involved in the dispute had already left the village out of fear. The Rajput party burnt the house of the Pasi tenant in broad daylight. The Pasis reported the case to the police and also filed a suit against the Rajputs in the District Court, but it was dismissed as the Pasis failed to produce any evidence against the Raiputs. On the other hand, Basdeo Singh filed a suit against the Pasis in the Adalat Panchayat and once again the Brahmin head of the Panchayat helped the Rajputs by imposing heavy fines on the Pasis.

Structural Factors

These two incidents re-established the authority and dominance of the Rajputs in the village. Besides, they brought together three Rajput families which were split into three open factions during zamindari days. They also brought the Rajputs of Mahuari closer to the Brahmins and the Rajputs of the neighbouring villages, since they came to realise that they could defend themselves better against the other castes if they stood united. This new unity in addition to the Rajputs' major share in the village lands appears to be the main force behind their dominant position in the village.

Our findings indicate that structural factors play a deterministic role in the recruitment of leaders. Right from the beginning village leadership has been in the hands of the Rajputs. Belonging to the Rajput caste is the most important factor behind an individual's leadership position. A Rajput is invariably preferred to a non-Rajput. In other words a Rajput is always a leader for a non-Rajput in the village. The situation is essentially similar to that described by Oscar Lewis in his study of a north Indian village, where, "every jat is a leader for a non-jat."[8]

The individual attributes are important, nevertheless, even if they cannot transcend the limits set by the group. There are some criteria, only conventionally implied, which individual leaders or families are expected to fulfil. Thus, among Rajput families, the family which stands higher in terms of wealth, social reputation and social contacts has a greater say in leadership matters. On the other hand, individuals who are supposedly honest, truthful, humble, loyal, hospitable and of known moral integrity become more popular and are easily accepted as leaders. We therefore agree with Wolfe,[9] that the legitimacy of authority or dominance of a particular group in the village cannot be explained exclusively or even mainly in terms of coercion or a major share in the lands. On the contrary, as pointed out by A. K. Singh,[10] the legitimacy of a leader's role is recognised largely to the extent that he fits into the cultural image of a leader held by the people.

General Role

The role of leaders in the village is not specific but of a general kind. Leadership does not consist in the performance of any particular task or in the attainment of any specific goal, but in the resolution of issues of a wide variety, ranging from the economic, political and social to the moral and cultural spheres. They are not the products of any crisis situation but are ones which normally arise in day-to-day dealings. These issues, if not satisfactorily resolved, pose serious threats to the village social order. To the extent that the leaders succeed in solving these problems they contribute to the maintenance of the village social order, and that is the function of leadership.

It follows that the leadership is in the hands of a group of persons who constitute the social core of the village. They perform for the village society a set of multiple functional roles in the economic, political, social and cultural fields. Functionally, they are analogous to Keller's "strategic elites"[11] although structurally they are the latter's exact antithesis.

Thus, there is an apparent continuity in village leadership from the past to the present insofar as the leaders are the same—the Rajputs—and the nature of leadership is the same, in that the authority is traditional and the informal leadership is more pervasive than the formal one.

Here, we are confronted with a question of fundamental importance: who will lead in the future? And what will the nature of leadership be? The abolition of zamindari and the extension of citizenship with its corollary, civic incorporation of the masses, assume a special significance in this context. Formerly, the zamindar was one class, the non-zamindar was another, and between them there was an abyss, the leadership being the prerogative of the former. The abolition has done away with the traditional gap between the zamindars and the non-zamindars, thereby ending the leadership prerogative of the former. The antiquity of blood, to use a popular phrase, is finished for good. The inference that the leadership is no more ascribed but achieved is only too obvious.

Theoretically Possible

On the other hand, the extension of citizenship and the civic incorporation of the masses have made it theoretically possible for all to participate in the village polity on an equal footing. It implies, above all, that the non-Rajput castes can now legitimately aspire for leadership positions in the village. Any such aspiration in the past was illegitimate. The legitimisation of the aspirations of the other castes for leadership is the single most important factor in the context of the village leadership in future. The continuance of old rulers does not mean that they are the accepted leaders for ever. And even if they succeed in retaining the leadership, the nature of leadership will change, simply because the different castes will now compete with one another for leadership in which wealth, education, personal attainments and numerical strength will play a decisive role. The group which excels others in regard to these factors will stand a higher chance for leadership. As these opportunities are open to all, the village polity is more likely to acquire a pluralistic[12] character. The leaders will have to take into consideration the interests of the different competing groups, resulting in a constant shifting and reshuffling of interests. This will give rise to and make room for the accommodation of new interest groups and cliques in the village politics.

The changing economic, social and educational conditions are prone to create a climate conducive to the growth and development of pluralistic tendencies in the village polity. Outside employment is improving the economic lot of the non-Rajput castes. Education is making them more politically conscious. Growing contact with the outside world is breaking through their apathy. With adult franchise numerical strength has already become a major political power.

Under these circumstances, a fundamental change in village leadership is not a mere theoretical plausibility. The process has already set in. Formerly, the Rajputs looked at the non-Rajputs as their subjects, thinking of themselves as the latter's natural masters. Now, on the contrary, they look at others as their legitimate competitors and try, consciously, to retain their hold through "politicking." This conscious effort to attain and retain the leadership on the part of the traditional leaders implies a major breakthrough.[13]

In this chapter, we have examined the structure and the function of leadership in an East UP village. We have found that in the recruitment of leaders the structural factors play a decisive role. The role of the leaders is not confined to any specific problem or field. On the contrary, they perform multiple roles which are functional to the entire village social system as a whole. The structure of village leadership exhibits an elemental continuity in that for the past few centuries the village has been governed by the three "reigning families"—to borrow Lynd's phrase[14]—of a status group, the one-time zamindar, Rajput caste. Our observations, however, suggest that this continuity is ephemeral: it is a mere survival of the past. Exposed to the new political, economic and cultural factors, the village polity is experiencing novel strains in response to which it is on its way to acquiring a pluralistic character in which there will be more accommodation between the interests of the different groups legitimately competing with one another for leadership positions, and more important than that, the leaders will have to be accountable to their followers.

NOTES AND REFERENCES

[1] Cf. R. Park and I. Tinker (eds.), *Leadership and Political Institutions in India* (Oxford, 1960); *Emerging Patterns of Rural Leadership in Southern Asia* (Hyderabad: National Institute of Community Development, 1965); Udai Pareek (ed.), *Rural Leadership in India* (New Delhi, 1966); L. P. Vidyarthi (ed.), *Leadership in India* (London: Asia Publishing House, 1967).

[2] Cf. Prabhat Chandra,"Rural Leadership in India," *The Eastern Anthropologist* (September–November 1959); John T. Hitchcock,"Leadership in a North Indian Village: Two Case Studies," in *Leadership and Political Institutions in India*, eds R. Park and I. Tinker (Oxford, 1960); Brij Raj Chauhan,"Phases in Village Power Structure and Leadership in Rajasthan," in *Leadership in India*, ed. L. P. Vidyarthi (London: Asia Publishing House, 1967).

[3] Status group is used here in the Weberian sense. In Weber's usage, a status group has three distinct features: (a) peculiar style of life; (b) hereditary charisma, concretised in a claim to a position of prestige by birth; and (c) monopoly of political power. See Max Weber, *The Theory of Social and Economic Organisation* (n.p.: Free Press, 1964), p. 342.

[4] R. D. Singh,"Social Change in a UP Village," *Far Eastern Quarterly* (December 1956).

[5] Yogendra Singh,"Changing Power Structure of Village Community: A Caste Study of Six Villages in Eastern UP," in *Rural Sociology in India*, A. R. Desai (Bombay, 1961).

[6] Traditional authority, as used by Max Weber and Talcott Parsons, refers to a situation where the area of personal influence is not clearly separated from that of the official authority.

[7] Mahuari is surrounded by a few villages where the Ahirs are not only numerically strong, but also known for their notorious activities against the upper castes, the Rajputs and the Brahmins.

[8] Oscar Lewis, *Village Life in Northern India* (n.p.: University of Illinois Press, 1958).

[9] A. W. Wolfe,"Concepts of Authority: An African Study," in *Leadership in India*, ed. L. P. Vidyarthi (London: Asia Publishing House, 1967).

[10] A. K. Singh,"Unconscious Image in Indian Leadership," in *Leadership in India*, ed. L. P. Vidyarthi (London: Asia Publishing House, 1967).

[11] Keller's usage of "strategic elites" refers to the persons selected on the basis of individual motivation and capacity. Structurally they are diverse in the sense that they may be selected from any class and in this respect they are opposite of the leaders selected from one single caste. See S. Keller, *Beyond the Ruling Class* (New York, 1963), pp. 30–35.

[12] Pluralism is used in the same sense as used by Wildavski. The core feature of pluralism is that in this system the dominance is essentially persuasive rather than coercive in nature. See A. Wildavski, *Leadership in a Small Town* (n.p.: Bedminster Press, 1964).

[13] Opler has taken full cognisance of the changing nature of the village society. In his study of Senapur he concludes with the remark: "For the first time in the history of the village a respected village elder has gone out to seek honour and support rather than to assume that it would accrue to him in due course. This is a temper that will introduce new blood and will effect a transition from old village administrative structure to the new." Morris Edward Opler,"Factors of Tradition and Change in a Local Election in Rural India," in *Leadership and Political Institutions in India*, ed. R. Park and I. Tinker (Oxford, 1960).

[14] Robert Lynd,"Power in American Society as Resource and Problem," in *Problems of Power in American Democracy*, ed. A. Kornhauser (Detroit: Wayne State University Press, 1957).

11

Semi-Feudalism or Capitalism?

Contemporary Debate on Classes and Modes of Production in India*

Alice Thorner

For more than a dozen years Indian and foreign Marxists have been arguing with passion, subtlety and an abundance of statistics about the existing mode of production in Indian agriculture or, more broadly, in India. There have been proponents of capitalism, pre-capitalism, semi-feudalism, colonial and post-colonial modes, and recently, a dual mode. Authors of important contributions to this debate include economists: Ashok Rudra of Visvabharati University in Shantiniketan, West Bengal; Utsa Patnaik, Amit Bhaduri and Dipankar Gupta, all now of Jawaharlal Nehru University in New Delhi; Nirmal Chandra and Ranjit Sau of the Indian Institute of Management, Calcutta; Amiya Bagchi of the Centre for Studies in Social Sciences, Calcutta; Pradhan Prasad and Nirmal Sen Gupta of the A. N. Sinha Institute of Social Studies in Patna; Jairus Banaji of Bombay; Paresh Chattopadhyay and Sharat G. Lin, both teaching in Canada; and John Harriss of the University of East Anglia; social anthropologists: Kathleen Gough of Vancouver who began work in South India in 1947; and Joan F. Mencher of the University of the City of New York; and sociologists: Hamza Alavi of the University of Manchester and Gail Omvedt, an American who has adopted residence in Maharashtra. But this listing is not exhaustive.

* This edited article was originally published in *Economic and Political Weekly* 17, no. 49 (4 December 1982): pp. 1961–68.

The second and third parts were published in *Economic and Political Weekly* 17, no. 50 (11 December 1982); and *Economic and Political Weekly* 17, no. 51 (18 December 1982).

In very large part, the successive formulations, presentations of data, critiques and rebuttals have appeared in the *Economic and Political Weekly* of Bombay. Two other journals which have published substantial contributions are *Frontier*, Calcutta, and *Social Scientist*, Trivandrum. Although a handful of relevant books have been published in India and elsewhere during the period, the cut and thrust of the argument has been carried almost exclusively in the periodicals.

The framework and terminology of the discussion are explicitly Marxist. References to classics by Marx, Engels, Kautsky, Lenin and Mao Tse-tung (Mao Zedong) abound. Our authors are also familiar with the current international Marxist literature. They cite European and Latin American writers including Louis Althusser, Étienne Balibar, Charles Bettelheim, Samir Amin, Ciro Cardoso, Andre Gunder Frank, Michał Kalecki, Jean-Loup Herbert, Joan Martinez-Alier, Ernest Mandel, Nicos Poulantzas, Pierre-Philippe Rey, Claude Meillassoux and Rodolfo Stavenhagen, some of whose works have not been translated into English.

Gunder Frank actually intervenes briefly in the debate. But the focus remains Indian, and the concrete evidence brought forward in support of the various theses is drawn primarily from Indian experience. Thus the different participants in the debate deal with the same body of subject matter, and they share a common theoretical commitment to Marxism. But they are very far from agreement as to how Marxist methodology should be applied to the Indian case. It is taken for granted that Marxist historical models exist; there is no consensus as to the nature of these models. In fact, questions of the Marxist legitimacy of this or that position are argued elaborately and with considerable vehemence. Despite the intrinsic interest of these strictures, we shall leave them to one side and concentrate on the substantive agreements and disagreements with regard to the nature of Indian reality.

What, then, are the main issues at stake?

(1) Is there capitalism in Indian agriculture? To a significant degree? In some parts of the country only? Is it a recent phenomenon? Is it spreading? Is it the dominant tendency? Is it a guarantee of agricultural progress? By what criteria can the existence of capitalism in agriculture be proved or disproved?
(2) On the contrary, is the dominant form of production relations in agriculture not capitalist but pre-capitalist or semi-feudal? What are the salient features of semi-feudal relations? Are they a brake on the productive forces? Do they resist change?
(3) Can India today be characterised with one or another of Marx's well-known modes of production: slavery, feudalism, capitalism and the Asiatic mode? Is it necessary to modify one of Marx's original concepts or to bring in a new mode (or modes) to take account of Indian (or more largely, colonial) specificity? Can there be more than one mode of production in the same

country at the same time? If so, are these modes necessarily in conflict, or may they be articulated in some fashion?

(4) What was the mode of production or the prevailing form of production relations in India during the colonial period? At the moment of Independence in 1947?

(5) What are the principal rural classes? The basis for their demarcation? Their respective shares of the rural population?

(6) What are the main lines of conflict, the contradictions in rural India today? In India as a whole? What is the role of the government?

(7) What implications for political action by left parties follow from the answers given to the above questions?

....

From the beginning, the debate is carried on simultaneously at several levels: that of the individual cultivating unit, that of the agricultural sector of a particular region (e.g., Punjab-Haryana or Eastern India) or of India as a whole, that of the entire economy of a region or of India as a whole; that of the colony–metro pole relationship or of the imbrication of India in the world economy. A number of authors (Rudra, Patnaik, Bhaduri, Prasad, Nirmal Chandra, Mencher, Harriss) bring in freshly gathered field data at the first and second levels to buttress their arguments. Others (Sulekh Chand Gupta, Kotovsky, Omvedt, Cough, as well as some of these who conducted their own rural enquiries) draw upon the vast stock of data available from official sources such as the Farm Management Studies, the National Sample Survey, the Rural Credit Surveys, the Censuses and Agricultural Censuses, the Rural Labour Surveys. Banaji and Bagchi use historical sources to document their analyses of nineteenth century developments. Several of the economists (Patnaik, Rudra, Bhaduri, Nirmal Chandra, San and Lin) employ mathematical models. A handful (Chattopadhyay, Sen Gupta, Dipankar Gupta, and Lin) restrict themselves to purely theoretical exercises.

....

The Precursors

Sulekh Chand Gupta, G. G. Kotovsky, Daniel Thorner

As early as 1962 Sulekh Chand Gupta, then on the staff of the Agricultural Economics Research Centre of the Delhi University, offered an estimate of capitalist farming as of 1953–54. Taking as his point of departure the concentration of hired labourers on larger-acreage units shown in the Farm Management Studies, he noted that in the state of Uttar Pradesh the element of hired labour exceeded that of family labour on farms with 20 or more acres. Extrapolating in a conservative fashion to India as a whole, in parts of which the size of holdings operated mainly with year-round farm servants was as low as 7.5 acres, he proposed to take the number of households operating 20 acres or more as a rough approximation of the number of capitalist farms. Applying this procedure to the figures from the 1953–1954 Census of Land-holding, he came up with an estimate of less than 6 or 7 per cent of all operational holdings, amounting to about one-third of the total area under cultivation.

A similarly constructed estimate was proposed by G. G. Kotovsky of the Institute of the Peoples of Asia, Moscow. In Kotovsky's judgement the area cultivated wholly or mainly by hired labour in 1953–1954 amounted to 25 or 30 per cent of the total for India. His conclusion was that the capitalist sector represented the leading tendency in Indian agriculture, but that it did not yet dominate.[1]

Neither of these estimates appears to have provoked any wide discussion. Quite the contrary was the case with the series of four articles published in *The Statesman* (Calcutta and Delhi), on four successive days in November 1967, by Daniel Thorner. In these lively journalistic pieces Thorner related what he had just seen in a village tour which had taken him through seven states in the North-west, North, West, South and East of India. Whereas fifteen years previously his impression had been of rural stagnation,[2] this time he found alert, enterprising cultivators, eager to experiment with new scientific methods: quick to switch to power for traction and pumping; ready to invest in improvements; preferring to cultivate themselves with hired labour rather than, or in addition to, giving out their land on rent in small parcels; and able to obtain substantial increases in output. He wrote:

> What we are witnessing in India is the emergence of an advanced sector in agriculture that is broadly comparable to the advanced sector in modem industry. This new agriculture has been tested, has proved profitable, and is rapidly expanding.[3]

Some of the new-style cultivators whom Thorner came across on his rural swing turned out to be present or former industrialists, merchants, moneylenders, civil servants, army officers, doctors, lawyers and similar persons of high economic status and caste. Thorner dubbed these agriculturists "gentleman farmers," and pointed out that their command over funds, their education and their connections in the right places all facilitated their farming activities. He concluded that the unprecedented wave of capitalist farming foreshadowed new social and political as well as economic developments:

> Before the 1960's there used to be in the plains of India only a few pockets of genuinely capitalistic agriculture—parts of the Punjab and Western UP, Central Gujarat, Coimbatore, and Coastal Andhra. Now for the first time there has come into being in all parts of the countryside in India, a layer, thick in some regions, thinner in others, of agricultural capitalists.... These capitalistic farmers seem

> to be the most rapidly growing group in rural India; they may already be the most powerful element. The implications of this are far-reaching, not only in the economic field, but for the structure of society and the future shape of politics.[4]

....

THE ORIGINAL PROTAGONISTS

Ashok Rudra and Utsa Patnaik

The debate proper opens with a report on a sample survey of big farmers in the Punjab by Ashok Rudra and two of his colleagues in the same Agro-Economic Research Centre of the University of Delhi where S. C. Gupta had earlier worked.[5] Rudra explained that the study was undertaken to find out what was really happening in Indian agriculture, particularly in the Punjab.

The sample chosen through a three-stage process included 261 farms above 20 acres in size in all eleven districts of the Punjab; and the survey was carried out in 1968–69. Why 20 acres? Rudra tells us:

> What we have been after, being more interested in the Red Revolution than the Green one, is really to get at what may be called the "capitalist farmers".... Most of the capitalist farmers, we have presumed, would have at least 20 acres of cultivated land. The rationale ... was merely to enclose in it a very large portion of what may eventually qualify as being capitalist farms.

With regard to gentleman farmers, Rudra's initial findings were negative. Lurid pictures, he informs us, have been painted of farm households with air-conditioners and motor cars, of farmers' sons in drain-pipe trousers. True enough, says Rudra, such phenomena are blatantly present in the countryside. But their very conspicuousness blinds the observer to the surrounding, very different, reality. In his sample 92 per cent of the large-farmer respondants claimed that cultivation was the only occupation they ever had. As many as 97 per cent denied pursuing any subsidiary calling. A bare 3 per cent were former government servants or military men. Only 1 per cent could boast of college-level education, while 69 per cent had remained illiterate.

So far as their agriculture was concerned, the land owned by these big farmers had increased by 9.5 per cent over twelve years, with those in the largest size group registering the most substantial increases. Rapid rates of capital formation were evident from the substantial rise in value of tractors, pumping sets and tubewells, draught cattle, agricultural implements, etc.

Warmly welcoming Rudra's report, Thorner observed that if his own impressionistic account had helped to stimulate the Punjab study, it had achieved one of its principal aims.[6] With regard to the "intriguing but secondary question" of gentleman farmers, whose significance lies "not in their absolute numbers but in the dynamism which they have brought to the countryside," Thorner enquired about the occupations followed by the fathers, brothers and adult sons of the respondents. As to revolutions of different hues, he wrote:

> The colour of the revolution which I have seen in one area after another of India in the 1960s is steel-grey. I call it an industrial revolution. Since Independence, hundreds of new industrial centres have sprung up. Thousands of plants using advanced technology ... have been put into operation. Millions of men have gone to work in the new factories and the auxiliary workshops.... Construction contracts and new jobs have showered purchasing power on households in city and countryside. The resulting demand for raw materials and foodstuffs has sent agricultural prices soaring ... investment in farm production has become unprecedentedly profitable. To the lure of great gain from actual farming (rather than from rural rents and usury) has responded the rise of a class of enterprising agriculturists ... their emergence as a significant group in every State is one of the facets of the industrial revolution which is today changing the face of India.[7]

Thorner's query about the occupations of family members is, in fact, answered in the second instalment of Rudra's survey report in the very same issue of the *Economic and Political Weekly*.[8] It turns out that, as Thorner had suspected, in 39 per cent of the cases one or more adult males other than the head of the household are indeed involved in work outside of agriculture. This figure gives a clear notion of the extent to which the big-farm families had, in Thorner's words, "diversified their interests either from urban activities to agriculture or *vice versa*".[9]

It is also in this instalment that Rudra takes up the subject of classes among the peasantry. He does so in the context of whether or not he finds continuities in the values for each variable (e.g., ratio between land owned and land rented out, or percentage of sales to production) when distributed according to size-groups of land owned. Farm economists as well as rural sociologists, Rudra remarks, have the habit of referring to "three categories of farmers: small peasants, middle peasants and big farmers." But he is not at all sure this categorisation is warranted. He continues,

> Marxists in particular are wont to talk in terms of there being such subclasses among the peasantry. Now if all the important variables relating to farm economies are representable by continuous functions of size, then these concepts of big, small and middle must be quite vacuous.[10]

In his third and final instalment, Rudra at last sets forth his criteria for identifying capitalist, as distinguished from merely big, farmers. These are similar to Thorner's earlier descriptions. Rudra expects that the capitalist in Punjab would:

(a) tend to cultivate his land himself rather than to give it out on lease;
(b) tend to use hired labour in a much greater proportion than family labour;

(c) tend to use farm machinery;
(d) market an important share of his produce; and
(e) so organise his production as to yield a high rate of return on his investments.[11]

As surrogates for these five characteristics Rudra uses data thrown up by his field enquiry with respect of five variables:

(1) percentage of land rented out to total land owned;
(2) wage payment in cash for acre of farm size (X_2);
(3) value of modern capital equipment per acre of farm size (X_3);
(4) percentage of produce marketed to total produce (X_4); and
(5) cash profit per acre (X_5).

He explains that X_1 is productivity defined as value of output per acre of farm size.

Rudra then argues that if indeed there existed a category of farmers who were capitalists, that is, who filled all of the listed conditions, then there should be strong positive correlations between each pair of Xs (i.e., between X_2 and X_3, X_2 and X_4 etc.). His field data, however, "fail to indicate any strong association between any of these pairs." Hence, he concludes, there is no evidence that such a category exists.

A year later Utsa Patnaik demolishes Rudra's statistical argument in a hard-hitting article which raises a great many of the points central to the subsequent discussion. She terms Rudra's method of analysis of his data "un-historical." His criterion of high positive association between pairs of variables, she pronounces, "would make sense only in an unreal idealised world in which different classes existed only in their purest form"; it could be satisfied "only if the process of capitalist development has been carried out to its limit so that capitalism is already the dominant mode of production".[12] Historically, she contends, the capitalist is a former landlord or rich peasant. He does not suddenly appear out of the blue as a clearly defined "pure" socio-economic type: he develops within the pre-existing non-capitalist economic structure.

Utsa Patnaik prefers the term "non-capitalist" to "pre-capitalist" since it does not imply that capitalism has made no headway at all. On the contrary, Patnaik believes, "ex-colonial countries like India are characterised precisely by a limited and distorted development of capitalism which does not revolutionise the mode of production." In what sense, she asks, is there today a tendency toward capitalist development which was not present earlier? The answer, she suggests, is to be found neither in the employment of hired labourers nor in production for the market. Each of these, she states, is a necessary but not a sufficient condition of capitalist organisation. Both were widely prevalent in India during the colonial period. The large force of rural wage labourers arose from the pauperisation and proletarianisation of the "poorer majority of the peasantry" under the impact of imperialism. The choice of operating with this cheap hired labour or of leasing out to tenants represented for landowners "a purely contingent, reversible decision taken on the basis of current circumstances," that is, the comparative terms on which labourers and tenants were available in the particular locality at a particular time. Similarly, the colonial period saw a growing commercialisation of agriculture with increasing regional specialisation in cotton, sugarcane, etc. But this also was not capitalist production.

The characteristic of the genuine capitalist, Patnaik proposes, is not merely appropriation of surplus value generated by wage labour nor the sale on the market of a high proportion of produce, but also—and indispensably—accumulation and reinvestment of surplus value in order to generate more surplus value on an even-expanding scale. The capitalist in agriculture can be recognised by the "degree of capital intensification"—i.e., growth of outlay on both constant and variable capital with respect to a given land area and, over time, a tendency towards a higher than average organic composition of capital, leading to higher productivity of land and labour.

This process was under way in India from the mid-1950s onward, in Patnaik's view, because of the expanding domestic market created by the large governmental outlays under the five-year plans. In a clear break with the situation in the colonial past, it had become profitable to invest in irrigation, to turn off tenants so as to operate with hired labour, to go in for double and triple cropping rather than simply to continue with the classical pre-capitalist uses of surplus value such as trade, usury and purchase of more land to let out on tenancy.

Citing the results of her own field survey carried out in 1969 and covering 66 big farmers in five states—Orissa, Andhra, Mysore, Madras and Gujarat—Patnaik reported her conviction that a new class of capitalist farmers was indeed emerging. Whereas she started her enquiry with an extreme scepticism about the existence of any significant new trend outside of the Punjab, she was persuaded after going through her data that capitalist development was on the way, *albeit* in varying degrees, throughout the regions which she had studied.

Since Patnaik is not satisfied with wage labour alone as a criterion of capitalist production, she rejects S. C. Gupta's and G. G. Kotovsky's calculations. Despite Rudra's own negative conclusion, she suggests that his results show clearly the process of capitalist development in the Punjab.

She deals severely with Rudra's attempt to define peasant classes in terms of statistical discontinuities, as incompatible with a Marxist analysis:

> The Marxist distinction between classes within the peasantry is not derived from such a superficial statistical criterion but is a structural one based on the relations of production. The rich peasant is distinguished from the poor peasant by the fact that the former hires wage-labour to a considerable extent along with engaging himself along with family members in cultivation, while the latter is forced to hire

himself out as a laboureror lease in land on onerous terms in addition to working with family labour on his own land. The middle peasant operates mainly with family labour, neither exploiting much wage labour, nor being exploited himself.[13]

In his reply, Rudra defends strongly his scepticism about the existence of peasant classes and his insistence on their being statistically separable within a Marxist framework.

> I suggest that the concept of discontinuities is the direct translation of the Marxian concept of "quantities into qualities".... If one has to undertake measurements and test hypotheses arising from Marxian analyses, one will have to undertake such translations as I have done. And for me, the Marxian concept of three classes in agriculture remains a hypothesis to be tested.[14]

He also stands firm on his position that the failure of his variables taken in pairs to show strong positive association indicates that there has not yet appeared a "readily identifiable group" of capitalist farmers in the Punjab. He brings in at this point a new term: polarisation. His data, states Rudra, indicate that:

> There has not yet been among the farmers of Punjab any strong *polarisation* and I have expressed doubt whether it serves any important purpose to talk about capitalist development before polarisation has reached a sufficiently high degree.... In a situation of capitalist development one should expect to find a polarisation developing such that not only would the values of the variables tend to increase among the farmers undergoing the transformation but increase *conjointly*. As long as such conjoint movement has not taken place to a considerable extent—that is, as long as there is no polarisation—we cannot say that capitalist development has taken place.[15]

In a rapid riposte Patnaik returns to her charge that Rudra has hopelessly confused two quite different propositions: (1) that there exists within the prevailing non-capitalist economy a small but growing class of capitalists, and (2) that Indian agriculture is characterised by sharp polarisation into two main classes, capitalists and wage labourers. In disproving the second one, she says, he thinks he has disproved the first, since "he treats proposition 2 as a necessary condition for proposition 1." This, she declares, "is certainly not Marxist theory".[16]

With regard to indications of peasant classes, Patnaik insists that size of holding is not a satisfactory guide. Since the available Farm Management Studies data, which are grouped by size, show that above a certain level of acres owned hired labour predominates over family labour, with regional variations (e.g., 10 acres in Bengal, 40 in Punjab), it has seemed reasonable to take the farms above these limits as roughly corresponding to rich peasant holdings. But this is a very crude procedure.

> My argument is that size of farm even as a rough indicator of rich peasant status is no longer good enough in the present situation when techniques are changing

> and intensive cultivation by some groups is taking place. If production techniques are intensified (more irrigation, triple cropping, mechanisation) then a farm may get smaller in terms of area, and *at the same time* get bigger as an economic unit, expand in terms of output and the extent of use of hired relative to family labour.[17]

At this point Paresh Chattopadhyay enters the debate in the role of a self-appointed arbiter of Marxist orthodoxy, distributing plaudits and blames to Sulekh Chand Gupta, Ashok Rudra and Utsa Patnaik. Gupta's analysis was "on the whole in the right direction," but he overestimated the development of capitalism in India and underestimated "the strength of the pre-capitalist modes of production still prevalent in our agriculture". As for Rudra, his work "is full of interesting empirical data" but theoretically weak. "Most of his theoretical shortcomings have been fairly ably pointed out by Utsa Patnaik (though perhaps not in the most desirable manner)." Patnaik is criticised for offering "a new notion of capitalism... not in the spirit of Marxism." Here Chattopadhyay cites Lenin's definition of capitalism as "the highest stage of commodity production where labour-power itself becomes a commodity." There is no need, pontificates Chattopadhyay, to specify separately accumulation and re-investment of surplus value since they already "fall within this definition." Elaborating this argument, he writes, reproaching Rudra as well as Patnaik:

> The existence of a sophisticated instrument of production is not necessary for identifying a capitalist. Given the capitalist mode of production, for which capital as a relation is only required, the existence of modern equipment would only indicate a higher level of capitalism.[18]

Answering Chattopadhyay, Utsa Patnaik restates her objection to taking wage labour as a sufficient condition for establishing the existence of capitalism in Indian agriculture. The bourgeoisie which battened upon the surplus value produced by agricultural labour in India, she argues, was not Indian but British. She suggests that Chattopadhyay's proposal "of regarding generalised commodity production as *necessarily* implying capitalist productions relations (regardless of the uniqueness of the colonial situation)" would lead, carried to its logical conclusion, to an extreme position like that of Andre Gunder Frank's, with whom, she assumes, Chattopadhyay is not in agreement:

> Namely, all countries dominated by imperialism entered the network of world capitalist exchange relationships (and also thereby experienced generalised commodity production to a greater or lesser degree). Therefore all these countries are "capitalist." Therefore the only possible immediate programme of a revolutionary political party in each of those countries must be *socialist* revolution. I believe the fallacy in this chain of reasoning lies at the starting point, in the failure to distinguish between capital in the sphere of *exchange* and capital in the sphere of *production*.... I am sure P. C. will not choose to draw the extreme

> conclusion which Gunder Frank has done; but his theoretical premise does seem to be quite close to Frank's.[19]

Jairus Banaji comes in as a professed supporter of Patnaik "in her brilliant polemics with A. Rudra, particularly concerning the identification of capitalist development, and with P. Chattopadhyay, concerning the 'specificity' of the colonial economy." It is this second aspect, the search for a "Marxist characterisation of the colonial economies prior to the growth of a local industrial bourgeoisie," which particularly interests Banaji. He rejects both the thesis that conditions in the colonial world were feudal, a thesis "once maintained by most of the Communist parties of the colonial world who used the struggle against 'feudalism' as a means of postponing the struggle for a socialist programme," and the more recent position arising from the work of Gunder Frank to the effect that all the colonies were capitalist because of their "umbilical ties to a world market dominated by the capitalist mode of production." The most striking aspect of the colonial period, according to Banaji, was precisely the "absence of a process of capitalist expansion, for some six decades at least in manufacturing, and for about a century in agriculture." Banaji's own proposal is to "accept the reality of colonial modes of production with their own coherence and laws of development," with, however, the proviso that they could not have come into being except within the sphere of capitalist production. Their chief historical function was to finance primary accumulation *outside* the colonial world. They served as "the circuits through which capital was drained out of the colonies in the form of bullion, consumption goods, raw materials and so on." They transmitted to the colonies "the pressures of the accumulation process in the metropolis without unleashing any corresponding expansion in the forces of production".[20]

Paresh Chattopadhyay returns to his disagreements with Utsa Patnaik in a substantive article published at the end of 1972. He takes issue with her treatment of the role of imperialism as exclusively "destructive" and "negative." In his view, "the British preserved as well as destroyed the conditions of India's pre-capitalist economy, accelerated as well as retarded the development of capitalism in India." On the one hand, Chattopadhyay cites evidence to the effect that the essential aspects of capitalism—*generalised* production for sale and a predominantly free class of wage labourers—were *not* present in Indian agriculture in colonial times. On the other, he holds that agricultural production "did increasingly show its commodity character at least since the last quarter of the nineteenth century." As proof he brings to bear statistics of the growth of non-foodgrains, the degree of differentiation among the peasantry, the percentage of cultivators engaged in money-wage relationships and the expansion of capital stock in agriculture in the years preceding Independence. "Capitalist development," he concludes, "was a reality in India during the British period." But he insists upon "all the ups and downs, advances and retreats of this development," as well as "the contradictions engendered by capitalism's co-existence and co-presence with the still dominating pre-capitalist relations".[21] Not so far, after all, from Patnaik.

Apparently piqued by Patnaik's reference to his position as a logical extreme, Gunder Frank attacks her "far-out definition of capitalism in agriculture." While taking no exception to her statement that "extended reproduction and accumulation is a criterion of capitalism," he argues that she is incorrect in defining capitalism so narrowly as to require that surplus value be invested on the very spot where it is produced, i.e., in agriculture itself, or in agriculture in the same geographical area. He charges Patnaik with confusion of levels of analysis:

> UP looks for the criterion of the mode of production on the individual farm!... No wonder if the UP method is to "extend" the criterion of extended reproduction, accumulation and reinvestment of them in each of the impoverished farms of India, that she is hard put to recognise the capitalist mode of production when she sets it.

With regard to the political implications of Patnaik's method of analysis, Frank asks how long she is presented to put off the socialist revolution:

> Well, what conclusion will UP choose to draw from her other extreme method? That socialist revolution will not become the programmatic order of the day until capitalism by her criterion—reinvestment of surplus value produced by farm labourers on the same farm itself—has penetrated each and every one of her individual farms?[22]

Semi-feudalism, an Eastern India Syndrome

Amit Bhaduri, Pradhan Prasad Nirmal Chandra, Ranjit Sau and, once again, Rudra

The first standard-bearer for semi-feudalism in the framework of the debate—the concept of course, being much older—is Amit Bhaduri, who published articles in 1973 in both *Frontier* and the *Economic Journal* in England. On the basis of a survey which he had conducted in 26 West Bengal villages in 1970 Bhaduri concluded that the "dominant character of existing production relations" could best be described as semi-feudal in that they "have more in common with classic feudalism of the master-serf type than with industrial capitalism." He listed four prominent features of these semi-feudal relations: sharecropping, perpetual indebtedness of the small tenants, concentration of two modes of exploitation—usury and land ownership—in the hands of the same economic class, and lack of accessibility to the market for the small tenant. Indebtedness arises from the continual need for consumption loans. In the typical situation the creditor is the landlord, locally known as the *jotedar*. The tenant cannot move away without settling his debt, and he has no alternative source of credit. The rate of interest on these consumption loans is extraordinarily high: Bhaduri cites figures ranging from 25 to 200 per cent for a period of about four months. Usury is thus an important additional source of income to the semi-feudal landowner. The continuation of the double exploitation requires that the available balance of paddy with the *kishan*, the sharecropper, must always fall short of his family's consumption requirements. Therefore, technological improvements which might raise the productivity level of the *kishan* are *undesirable* to the landowner, since they would weaken the political and economic power of the landlord based on his being able to keep his tenant constantly indebted. In this way "semi-feudal production relations operate as a barrier to the introduction of improved technology".[23]

Bhaduri envisages four possible developments for the future: continued stagnation, adoption of new technology together with rent increases, gradual development of capitalistic relations, or even a peasant revolt:

(1) low productivity and stagnation in agriculture will continue to maintain the existing power structure at the village level in eastern India.
(2) the semi-feudal production relations themselves will be modified to accommodate profitable use of improved technology.
(3) and (4) It is also possible that semi-feudal production relations will gradually give way to capitalistic production relations based on wage labour or will be simply overthrown by the desperate poor unless a radical land reform is carried out by the State.[24]

Pradhan Prasad furnishes support for Bhaduri's thesis with data from another area of eastern India: Purnea, Saharsa and Monghyr districts of Bihar, in which he surveyed over 2,000 households in a couple of dozen villages in 1970 and 1972. In these villages utilisation of available irrigation facilities declines with increase in the size of holdings, larger landowners (10 acres and above) who cultivate with hired labourers, prefer "attached" workers, indebtedness is widespread, sharecropping is a common feature, and daily wages are so low that even households with two workers employed throughout the year are forced to take consumption loans at exorbitant rates of interest. These debts run on indefinitely since the creditors "do not expect ever to get the stipulated interest and principal from such rural poor'".[25] Usury, Prasad continues, "is thus practised mainly to perpetuate the indissoluble bond between the direct producer and his overlord." Low utilisation of resources such as irrigation and low demand for labour by big landowners are essentially directed towards "preventing the strengthening of the economic condition of the direct producer rather than maximisation of their rate of profit or rate of return." In the same way as Bhaduri, Pradhan insists that big landowners fear that the introduction of new agricultural practices might serve eventually to free their tenants from their semi-feudal bondage.

> The essential feature of the model is thus reflected in the big landowning classes... approaching the whole process of production and distribution with a view to strengthening their control over land and their hold on the rural masses, resulting in a set-up (which we may call semi-feudal) ... essentially characterised by the two modes of appropriation, namely sharecropping and usury. This results in semi-servile condition of living and a low level of consumption ... low productivity of land and labour (which is understood mainly in terms of disguised unemployment), under-utilisation of resources and almost negligible net investment in the agricultural sector.[26]

In a subsequent article, Prasad argues from the evidence of various sample surveys conducted from 1951 through 1971 that his "semi-feudal model (but for variations in details) is, by and large, valid for the most part of rural India".[27]

Another partisan of the semi-feudal thesis, Nirmal Chandra makes use of official data for West Bengal and explicitly links agricultural development with industrial development at the national level. He recalls the laws of motion for agriculture formulated by Kautsky and Lenin in the context of a national economy undergoing capitalist transformation: increasing returns to scale, increasing concentration of landholding, increasing proportion of agricultural labourers, decreasing extent of sharecropping, and increasing orientation of agricultural production towards the market rather than towards self-consumption by the cultivator. On the basis of data for 250 farms in five districts of West Bengal for each of the six years from 1962–1963 through 1967–1968 published by the state government, Nirmal Chandra finds no unmistakable trends along these lines. He is led to suspect that "our country has not been going through a capitalist transformation at all, and that there are important socio-economic forces impeding such a transformation".[28] He assigns a large share of blame for the stifling of incipient capitalism to imperialism:

> During the British Raj colonial rule undoubtedly constituted the biggest single obstacle. As a natural ally it greatly strengthened feudal or semi-feudal elements in the countryside that are primarily responsible for the indifferent progress in the post-colonial era even though the imperial yoke has been lifted.[29]

The basic features of semi-feudalism in the West Bengal countryside, in Nirmal Chandra's view, have been most lucidly and cogently set forth by Bhaduri. But Nirmal Chandra offers two emendations. First, he feels that Bhaduri has exaggerated the effect of semi-feudal relations in holding back the productive forces:

> For, technological improvements have taken place on share-tenanted land in different parts of West Bengal with working capital often provided by the

> landowner. If one allows for a variable share-cropping ratio, then semi-feudal relations of production can persist even after the new high-yielding varieties of crops have been introduced. By lowering the tenant's share, the landowner can keep him as poor as he always was.[30]

Even more important, according to Nirmal Chandra, is Bhaduri's omission of the effect of "massive underemployment in our countryside." In several ways this critical un- and under-employment factor helps to explain the stability of semi-feudalism:

(a) The value of labour power is pegged at the lowest possible levels so that the real income of a share-tenant is no greater than that of a hired agricultural worker.
(b) From the landowner's point of view the net surplus to be extracted is the same under the one or the other system.
(c) Given the weak bargaining position of labour, the landowners can arbitrarily alter the share-ratio in their own favour in case new production possibilities appear.[31]

Moving to the national scale, Nirmal Chandra argues that large-scale rural employment "greatly delimits the market for industrial products." After the saturation of export markets, military demand, and the consumption requirements of an urban middle-class, stagnation becomes inevitable.

> We may then infer that labour surplus on a scale that is probably unparalleled in human history is perpetuating the semi-feudal set-up. Limited progress along the road to modernisation cannot be ruled out. Without vigorous measures to reduce considerably that surplus, we fail to see how one can get out of the vicious circle or how capitalism can strike deep root.[32]

Nirmal Chandra does not have much faith in the ability of industrial capital in India to break out of the shackles of semi-feudalism:

> Industrial capitalism in this country, including the forces of State capitalism, is extremely weak in the relative sense. It seems to have no option but to rely on foreign capital and foreign technology, which themselves create almost insuperable barriers to industrialisation on a wide front.... Since we cannot envisage how (within the confines of the present socio-economic formation) things might radically improve either on the industrial front or in respect of surplus labour, we cannot visualise when productive capital will dominate over usury capital in our agriculture or when the pre-capitalist crop-sharing eastern will disappear.[33]

Accordingly, he believes it would be more useful to characterise agrarian production relations in India as "semi-feudal" rather than "lumpen-bourgeois" or "rickety capitalist." But he takes a guarded position as to the proper designation of the mode of production:

> But one needs to explore many more facets of history, economics, politics, etc., before one can positively assert that semi-feudalism is the dominant mode of production in Indian or West Bengal agriculture.[34]

Ranjit Sau expresses agreement with Nirmal Chandra's "characterisation of the mode of production in Indian agriculture as semi-feudal" and also with the argument that "the presence of enormous unemployment weakens the impulse of capitalist growth in agriculture." He adds another explanatory factor to account for the stubborn persistence of semi-feudalism: the determination of small peasants to continue cultivation, no matter how meagre the returns, because of the lack of other possibilities:

> Why does not urban industrial capital penetrate agriculture and transform the semi-feudal mode? There are certain early signs of such a shift. The celebrated "gentleman-farmers" are indeed descending upon the countryside.... This trend also would not go very far.... In the absence of alternative job opportunities in industry, the small peasants would hold on to their land by reducing consumption to an unbelievable minimum. Increasing returns to scale or no increasing returns to scale, the capitalist farmers would face insuperable barriers in ousting the small farms.[35]

Returning to the subject in a series of three articles in *Frontier*, Nirmal Chandra brings in evidence from his own study of three villages in a rice-producing tract in Burdwan district, the most advanced area of West Bengal outside of the Calcutta conurbation, which had been chosen in the 1960s as one of the 1.6 districts in the country to benefit from the Intensive Area Development Programme. He found production relations in these villages had undergone some changes since Independence. On old *zamindar* (non-cultivating landlord, often absent) family was still on the scene and still affluent although not at the top of the economic pyramid. Otherwise the villages were dominated by *jotedar*s (formerly occupancy right tenants holding large blocks of land which they either leased out or got cultivated by agricultural labourers; to a varying degree involved in moneylending and trading in agricultural commodities), a class which for over 100 years before the formal abolition of the zamindari system in Bengal in 1953 had been slowly replacing the *zamindar*s as the leading group in the countryside.

Nirmal Chandra found land ownership to be highly skewed; tenancy arrangements were predominantly of a traditional kind, with tenants taking one half of the gross output when they bore the costs of production but only one-third to one-fourth otherwise; "the corresponding legal ratios are three-fourths and one-half respectively." In social terms "most lessors come from the upper classes." Except for one village, the vast majority of tenants came from the poorer sections, belonged to the backward castes and were personally dependent on their landlords. Individual landlords had up to eight tenants under them. One of the methods through which control is exercised is the threat of eviction:

> In the ten years prior to our survey in 1974 the number of households evicted was as high as one-fifth of the total or nearly two thirds of the tenant households.... Nearly every one of the poor tenants was evicted at one time or another over this period.[36]

The overall economic status of the poor peasants, Nirmal Chandra calculated, was no better than that of the agricultural labourers for whom wages were the only source of livelihood. Most workers were employed on a daily basis. Only about a quarter of the total number (from both agricultural labour and poor peasant households) had annual contracts with their masters. The casual workers were employed on an average for only 126 days in the year. Landlords almost invariably charge high interest on loans given to their tenants; this exaction is not always apparent:

> Sometimes, formally speaking, the interest rate is zero. But since paddy loans are usually made in monsoon months when the price is double the post-harvest level, in effect the tenant repays a great deal more in kind. Similarly, workers for their wage advances have to repay with labour services. Taking into account both the wage cut as well as the seasonal price variations, the employer may make up to 300 per cent profit in his wage advance.[37]

Landlords are also able to extract various types of *begar* (un- or underpaid labour services), often taking the form of non-productive work in the landlord's house. Workers are typically afraid of their landlords, some of whom do not hesitate to assault them physically for slackening in their work.

In sum, Nirmal Chandra argues that because of their "activity pattern," it is the top eight to ten families in each of his villages which constitute "the main bottlenecks to the development of productive forces," in effect, the chief obstacles to the growth of capitalism. Specifically, he charges, these families hold land in excess of legal ceilings, contribute little to paddy levies, crowd out the small farmers by obtaining an unfair proportion of institutional credit, engage in usury or usurious wage advances, and funnel their savings into the tertiary sector.[38]

Meanwhile, in a dramatic reversal of his previous position, Ashok Rudra announces his conviction that there are increasing manifestations of characteristic features of capitalism in the agriculture of eastern India. Turning on the proponents of semi-feudalism, Rudra centres his attack on Pradhan Prasad and Nirmal Chandra. As against Prasad's claim of "intimate contact with some of the rural areas of Bihar",[39] Rudra, who had shifted from Delhi to Shantiniketan, puts forward his own "direct first-hand knowledge of conditions prevailing in West Bengal."[40] In particular, he asserts, he has carried out during the past year an enquiry into agrarian relations in the different districts of the state.

Nowhere in these districts, Rudra reports, has he encountered the landowners whom Prasad and Nirmal Chandra describe—a class "that finds it more in its economic and social-power interests to resort to usury rather than to capital investments." On the contrary, he has found in many parts of the state landowners "who are very much engaged in capital investments in the form of irrigation, fertilisers and high-yielding variety seeds." This is equally true of "landowners who give their land out on lease to sharecroppers and those who cultivate it themselves with the help of hired labour." The practice has become almost universal in Bengal, Rudra discovered, "of owners paying for the irrigation costs and advancing the tenant's share of the costs of seed and fertilisers." These advances are repaid "by the tenant in terms of crops at the time of the harvest. No interest is charged."[41]

Similarly, although poor tenants, farm servants and casual labourers are typically bound to landlords by consumption loans, such loans "when taken by a tenant from the landowner from whom he has leased in land or by a farm servant from the landowner for whom he works" are free of interest. They are usually repaid not in cash but in labour at the time when the leader calls for it, the amount of labour "being calculated at a wage rate somewhat lower than the ruling wage rate".[42]

Interest at 10 per cent or more per month is charged whenever a loan is taken from a landowner or moneylender "other than the one with whom the borrower has an attachment relation as tenant or farm servant." Thus usury does exist, and may serve as the "the subsidiary source of income of the land owning class." But it does not appear to Rudra that "the land owning class in West Bengal is *primarily* dependent on usury".[43]

Against Nirmal Chandra, who questioned the development of capitalist relations in West Bengal because he found no clear trend toward concentration of landholding, Rudra uses Utsa Patnaik's argument that concentration should be measured not in acres but in the value of land held. In this sense he is sure that it has been increasing sharply "as a result of investments on land carried out by the large land-owners".[44]

Criticising also Nirmal Chandra's insistence on labour surplus, Rudra asserts that although there is indeed a great deal of unemployment during the lean seasons, there exists in many parts of West Bengal "a scarcity of actual labour supply in relation to labour demand during the peak periods." It is this high-season labour shortage, argues Rudra, which "provides the economic incentive to the landowners to go in for arrangements that guarantee supply of labour during periods when they need it most".[45]

From the labourer's or tenant's point of view, his being bound by debt and other obligations to a particular landowner means that he cannot sell his labour-power freely. If this is a characteristic of feudalism, opines Rudra, "then such feudalistic features continue to exist in various forms both in farms cultivated by tenants and farms cultivated by hired labourers." Rudra announces cautiously that he prefers to postpone until after he presents his new survey findings any full-dress discussion of "the concepts that have been used by Prasad and Chandra, e.g., capitalism, semi-feudalism." But in the balance it is clear that his 1974 intervention weighs heavily on the side of capitalism as against semi-feudalism.[46] Although he had earlier failed to discern capitalism among big farmers in the Punjab, he now strongly suspects it in wide areas of West Bengal.

Re-entering the discussion to sharpen some of his original formulations and to comment on positions taken by Ashok Rudra, Ranjit Sau and Hamza A'lavi, Paresh Chattopadhyay insists notably on the "dual role of capitalism with regard to pre-capitalism." That it seeks both the destruction and the preservation of older forms, Chattopadyay holds, "is a universal Phenomenon and not confined to what is usually considered as 'colonies or 'semi-colonies'."[47]

A two-part article by Sharat G. Lin puts forward a new term, "a dual mode of production", for post-colonial India. Citing Banaji, Sen Gupta and Brian Davey, Lin finds overall agreement that there is a superposition of more than one mode of production. In Lin's formulation, "the two primary modes (pre-capitalist and capitalist) interpenetrate", generating "a single mode with dual character having, at once, both accommodating and conflicting internal dynamics." State power "must be shared by two, historically opposed ruling classes" since it is "based on two historically opposed primary modes"; hence it cannot remain forever stable. Yet, Lin opines, it may last longer "than has been the case elsewhere in the world". This is because the pre-capitalist mode is so well-entrenched, because of wide regional variation in the strength of capitalist forces, because of the social inertia of sheer size, and because of the role of cultural factors.[48]

With regard to the possibilities for revolutionary action, the oppressed classes must struggle against whichever of the two modes and elements of state power "holds trend-dominance in the process of transition to holding status-dominance." The enemy must be carefully chosen, since a struggle against the feudal aspect which does not take into account the bourgeois aspect will lead by default to strengthening the position of the latter and "to the type of class collaboration exercised by various left parties". However, it is not yet the moment for "a stage of struggle for the socialist revolution since the Indian bourgeoisie has not completed and cannot complete the bourgeois democratic revolution." This democratic revolution can only "be completed through an alliance of the proletariat and impoverished peasantry who together constitute some 90 per cent of the population."[49]

Two recent articles concentrate on elements of the current rural scene which have been identified as "feudal". Dipankar Gupta considers the nature of sharecropping and contends that it is "not a feudal institution but rather appears only in formations where feudal institutions have been undermined by capitalism and where capitalism has not yet appeared in all its virility." He prefers to view the Indian economy as "a capitalist one when capitalism has not developed uniformly." Although capitalism is the main enemy, a revolutionary takeover "is not yet in the offing," so that the prospect is of a "long period of struggle ahead." The Left should not rush to raise the cry of immediate socialisation of the land since slogans such as "land to the tiller" can still motivate the majority of the peasants.[50]

Similarly, Aparajita Chakraborty attacks the idea that tenancy as an institution is necessarily a feature of pre-capitalist modes of production, in particular the feudal mode, and that "capitalist development necessarily calls for its disappearance." She names Utsa Patnaik, Nirmal Chandra and Amit Bhaduri as having subscribed to this erroneous and, in her opinion, un-Marxist notion. On the contrary, Chakraborty presents the view that tenancy is a flexible arrangement which "takes different forms and embodies different mixtures of capitalist and precapitalist relations under different historical conditions." In India, until very recent times, tenancy has been characterised by "very regressive features", and even today in many cases peasants are subject to "exploitative rents" and "exorbitant rates of interest." In this way, agricultural surplus is being diverted into non-productive channels, and the development of capitalism in agriculture is held back. The relations of production embodied in this process, Chakraborty concedes, "are no doubt pre-capitalist in nature." But this does not mean that tenancy itself is feudal or semi-feudal:

> In India, until recently, tenancy was an institution which was very much a part of the precapitalist relations of production that characterised agriculture. But it is getting changed along with changing conditions to the point of becoming compatible with emerging capitalist relations.[51]

For his part, Ashok Rudra denies the usefulness of feudalism as a concept for analysing any period at all in Indian history. He points out that while political economists who use the term "semi-feudal" presumably believe that the mode of production in India during some previous period was feudal, much influential opinion among historians rejects the thesis that there was ever feudalism in Indian history. After reviewing the historical debate, Rudra castigates the participants for paying insufficient attention to "social, cultural and religious institutions." Whereas the "European genius" forged the features and rituals of feudalism (such as commendation, homage and fealty), the "Indian genius" invented the caste system, the Hindu ethos. He advances the hypothesis that whereas in the Western world the hierarchic structure of society is maintained, in the ultimate analysis by violence, "*this particular role in Indian history was played not by violence but by ideology.*"[52]

This thesis, Rudra insists, "has an extremely important implication for practice." The political lesson that he draws is that "the struggle against the reactionary elements of the Brahmanic ideology" should constitute an important element "in any struggle for progress in this country."[53]

This proposal of Rudra's is very close to the recommendations of a left-wing Maharashtrian organisation, the Atyachar Virodh Samiti, at the end of a report on riots in Marathwada in which caste Hindus wreaked violence upon members of Scheduled Castes. The Samiti contends that the caste system functions as "an extremely effective method of economic exploitation." Caste hierarchies reflect economic power and ownership of land. As bourgeois relations develop, the argument continues, the institution of caste starts to disintegrate, but the process is not smooth. It is at this point that caste riots, reflecting a conflict of class interests, take place. In the "mixed capitalist economy" of today, caste persists "as a part of feudal ideology." But it also serves the bourgeois system since one of its functions has been "to prevent formalisation of consciousness and struggles on class lines." The Samiti calls upon all progressives and Leftists to take up issues around specific caste questions, and to support unconditionally autonomous Dalit (oppressed) movements with democratic demands against caste discrimination. "To establish a link between fights against caste-oppression and class exploitation," the report concludes, "is the need of the hour."[54]

In a major review of the evidence which has become available during the 1970s, Gail Omvedt gives an unequivocally affirmative answer to the question as to whether India's agriculture is now dominantly capitalist. Harking back to Daniel Thorner's 1969 formulation that the emergence of capitalist farming represented one facet of the industrial revolution which was transforming India, she stresses "the links between agriculture and industry, city and countryside."[55]

At the time of Independence, Omvedt believes, Indian agriculture was "predominantly feudal in character, though important elements of capitalism had risen." This was a "caste-structured" form of feudalism which existed before the British period. When the colonial State no longer officially enforced the caste system, "caste" and "class" began to represent separate social phenomena, "but there was still a near-absolute correlation between them." Because of the particular caste aspect of Indian feudalism, Omvedt affirms, "the anti-feudal movement was expressed not only through peasant revolts but also in the radical anti-caste movements of Phule, Ambedkar and Periyar."[56]

For the present, Omvedt's arguments for the dominance of capitalism can be summed up as follows:

(1) over half of the rural population depend upon wages;
(2) all cultivators are forced to sell to some extent in the market, and their production is governed by the laws of the market;
(3) the means of production in agriculture are now, to a large extent, produced industrially and acquired through the market;

(4) there has been a substantial growth in the use of capital inputs such as fertilisers and oil engines;
(5) there has been a genuine, if halting, growth in agricultural production;
(6) generalised commodity production, including the sale of labour power, prevails;
(7) the primary aspect of the relationship of the rural rich with the rural poor is as exploiters of labour power;
(8) the rural semi-proletariat is, by and large, an increasingly mobile, migrant and free class, whose differences with the urban working class "seem more those of quantity than of quality."[57]

Despite the evidence that she marshals to prove the reality of capitalist development in agriculture, Omvedt emphasises her assessment that this development "is not leading to any increased overall welfare for the rural (or urban) masses." She disparages the assumption of some authors that "immiserisation, pauperisation, growing landlessness, etc, are themselves signs of 'semi-feudalism' or the lack of capitalist development."[58]

Omvedt's prescription for political action rests upon her faith in the revolutionary potential of the rural proletariat. She is persuaded that the agricultural labourers and poor peasants are capable "of forming a centre around which middle peasants and other oppressed sections can be united." Accordingly, she deplores the tendency of the major parliamentary left parties to call for alliances including the rich peasants, who, she contends, are in effect "the village rulers and capitalist farmers." The apparent weakness of the rural semi-proletariat, Omvedt tells us, is belied by "vast numbers of diverse and unreported or under-reported clashes" involving "agricultural labourers and other labourers as well as poor and middle peasants." Since "class exploitation is compounded with caste and national oppression", many struggles assume forms which are difficult to identify as class conflicts, as for example those of the Jharkhand Mukti Morcha in the tribal area of Bihar or the Dalit Panthers in Maharashtra. Although up to now the "rural toiling masses have not yet found their own revolutionary party," Omvedt confidently foresees for the future "tumultous political developments."[59]

Balance-Sheet

What, we may now ask, has been clarified in the course of the past dozen years of debate, and what remains controversial? First of all, there would no longer appear to be any doubt that capitalism today dominates Indian agriculture, as it already was generally seen to dominate industry at the time the discussion began. Does this mean that the mode of production which prevails in contemporary

India is capitalist, and subject to the Marxist laws of motion of capitalist development? Here, the answer is less evident, since India's capitalism has emerged in a particular colonial setting, markedly different from the conditions in the metropolitan countries where capitalism was born.

By what criteria has the prevalence of capitalism been established? It has been abundantly shown that the existence of widespread tenancy and/or sharecropping does not necessarily indicate the presence of feudal relations of production; nor does the concentration of landholding together with the cultivation of small units by large numbers of peasants. By the same token, the use of wage labour cannot by itself be taken as a sure sign of capitalist relations. Yet the shift from exploitation through tenants to large-scale or intensive farming by means of hired labour is significant.

The growth of capitalist farming in India has been accompanied by—in fact, amounts to—a transformation of the relations of production and forms of exploitation. Servile, debt-bonded, and/or traditionally tied labour has been largely supplanted by free, relatively mobile wage labour, paid (if meagrely) for the most part in cash. Investment in modern, scientific agriculture has enormously expanded, and has resulted, on the whole, in enhanced production, at least of certain crops in certain areas. Tenancy and sharecropping arrangements have, in many regions, been adapted to the new economic and technical requirements.

Yet master-servant types of behaviour, extra-economic constraints, rack-renting and usury have by no means disappeared. A particular feature of the Indian scene is the vast mass of un- or under-employed who, if they cannot emigrate and find jobs outside of agriculture, exercise upward pressure on the rental price of land, and downward pressure on wage rates. The school of thought which tried to take account of these aspects by labelling Indian agriculture semi-feudal has withdrawn from the debate after about the middle of the 1970s, but there is still talk of the persistence of feudal and semi-feudal relations of production. Similarly, the original proponents of a colonial mode have themselves dropped the term, while the term 'dual mode' has, to my knowledge, attracted no followers. But the concepts of the preservation/destruction of earlier modes of production by capitalism, and of the articulation of different modes within a single social formation continue to figure in the discussion.

Several authors who accept the leading role of capitalism nonetheless express grave doubts as to the likelihood of its further and full development. They point out obstacles to capitalist progress on a national scale, such as the relative narrowness of India's industrial base in terms of the size of the country, the dependence of this industry on foreign technology, the very limited amount of employment provided by the secondary sector, and the extreme modesty of the economic demand for consumers' goods. There is agreement that capitalism in agriculture cannot be depended upon to solve the crucial problems of access to land and to food of the entire rural population.

The set of rural classes proposed by the various authors ranges from Ashok Rudra's drastic duality to Nirmal Chandra's six-fold grouping, and the even larger number of categories used by Joan Mencher and Utsa Patnaik. This lack of accord on the array of rural classes should not surprise us. Apart from marked regional differences, it would seem that the class configuration which one sees depends primarily on one's point of view. Researchers trying variously to explain why a land reform has or has not actually been implemented; when agricultural development programmes work and when they do not; why particular candidates or parties receive the votes of specific village groups; where reform or revolutionary movements arise and spread, or where they are nipped in the bud; should obviously not be expected to come up with identical lists of classes. Under the circumstances, efforts to attach numerical values to particular classes are even less comparable. There is not even a consensus as to the identity of the typical producer; is he an independent middle peasant—or, to the contrary, is he an impoverished tenant, sharecropper or agricultural labourer?

Cut-off points in size of landholding terms are clearly inadequate for marking off agricultural classes. Combinations of landholding categories with other characteristics (such as labour relations) become unwieldy in practice. In the course of preparing this chapter, I tried to make up a table showing the relative shares of the rural population attributed to each class by the different authors who have attempted this exercise (Bhaduri, Nirmal Chandra, Prasad, Mencher, Rudra, Omvedt) and to include the one-shot estimates of this or that class by other writers (for example, Alavi and Lin). But the rubrics utilised by these writers proved so disparate that I had to give up the attempt.

The various discussions of colonial India have all emphasised the detrimental effect that its involuntary integration into the world capitalist circuit had upon the older Indian economy (whether characterised as Asiatic, feudal or pre-capitalist). For some authors, British transformation of its Indian colony into a market for manufactures and a source of primary products such as wheat, cotton and jute served to establish dominant capitalist relations in late nineteenth-century India, or in certain regions of the country. For others, imperialism in its own interest shored up feudal elements in Indian economy and society. All agree that India is still a tributary to a large degree to the international market; some refer to this as a semi-colonial status. Others prefer to speak of India's peripheral capitalism in relation to metropolitan centres.

Early interventions in the debate were largely limited to economic issues. Later papers have paid increasing attention to elements of consciousness and culture, with special reference to caste. One of the weaknesses of Marxist studies on India has been precisely a failure, perhaps even an unwillingness, to deal adequately with this basic facet of Indian society. This is one of the directions which future debate can most fruitfully explore. Another is a more detailed analysis of the role of the State.

NOTES AND REFERENCES

[1] G. Kotovsky, *Agrarian Reform in India* (Moscow: Progress Publishers, 1964).

[2] Daniel Thorner. *The Agrarian Prospect in India* (New Delhi: Allied Publishers, 1976 [1956]).

[3] Daniel Thorner. "Capitalist Stirrings in Rural India," *The Statesman*, Calcutta, 1–4 November 1967. Reprinted in Daniel Thorner, *The Shaping of Modern India* (New Delhi: Allied Publishers, 1980).

[4] Ibid.

[5] Ashok Rudra, A. Maiid and B. Talib. "Big Farmers of the Punjab: Some Preliminary Findings of a Sample Survey," *Economic and Political Weekly*, IV, no. 39 (Review of Agriculture, 1969): pp. 143–46.

[6] Daniel Thorner. "Capitalist Farming in India," *Economic and Political Weekly*, 4, no. 52 (27 December 1969): pp. A-211–12.

[7] Ibid.

[8] Ashok Rudra. "Big Farmers of Punjab: Second Instalment of Results," *Economic and Political Weekly*, IV, no. 52 (Review of Agriculture, 1969): pp. 213–19.

[9] Thorner, "Capitalist Farming in India."

[10] Rudra. "Big Farmers of Punjab: Second Instalment of Results."

[11] Ashok Rudra. "In Search oi the Capitalist Farmer," *Economic and Political Weekly*, V, no. 26, (Review of Agriculture, 1970): pp. 85–87.

[12] Utsa Patnaik. "Capitalist Development in Agriculture," *Economic and Political Weekly*, VI, no. 39 (Review of Agriculture, 1971a): pp. 123–30.

[13] Ibid.

[14] Ashok Rudra. "Capitalist Development in Agriculture: Reply," *Economic and Political Weekly*, VI, no. 45 (1971): 2291–92.

[15] Ibid.; emphasis in original.

[16] Utsa Patnaik. "Capitalist Development Agriculture: A Note," *Economic and Political Weekly*, VI (1971b): 123–30.

[17] Ibid.; emphasis in original.

[18] Paresh Chattopadhyay. "On the Question of the Mode of Production in Indian Agriculture: A Preliminary Note," *Economic and Political Weekly*, VII, no. 13 Review of Agriculture, 1972a): 39–46.

[19] Utsa Patnaik. "On the Mode of Production in Indian Agriculture: A Reply," *Economic and Political Weekly*, Vll, no. 40 (Review of Agriculture, 1972a): pp. 145–51.

[20] Jairus Banaji. "For a theory of Colonial Modes of Production," *Economic and Political Weekly*, VII, no. 52 (1972): pp. 2498–2502.

[21] Paresh Chattopadhyay. "Mode of Production in Indian Agriculture; An Anti-Kritik," *Economic and Political Weekly*, VII (Review of Agriculture, 1972b): pp. 185–92.

[22] Andre Gunder Frank, "On 'Feudal' Modes, Models and Methods of Escaping Capitalist Reality," *Economic and Political Weekly*, VIII, no. 1 (1973a): pp. 36–37.

[23] Amit Bhaduri. "A Study of Agricultural Backwardness under Conditions of Semi-feudalism," *Economic Journal*, LXXXVI, no. 329 (1973a): pp. 120–37.

[24] Ibid.

[25] Pradhan Prasad. "Reactionary role of Usurers' Capital in Rural India," *Economic and Political Weekly*, IX, nos 32, 33 (1974): pp. 1305–08.

[26] Pradhan Prasad. "Production Relations: Achilles' Heel of Indian Planning," *Economic and Political Weekly*. VIII, no. 19 (1973): pp. 869–72.

[27] Prasad. "Reactionary role of Usurers' Capital in Rural India."

[28] Nirmal K. Chandra. "Farm Efficiency under Semi-Feudalism: A Critique of Marginalist Theories and Some Marxist Formulations," *Economic and Political Weekly*, IX, nos 32, 33, 34 (1974): pp. 1309–31.

[29] Ibid.

[30] Ibid.

[31] Ibid.

[32] Ibid.

[33] Ibid.

[34] Ibid.

[35] Ranjit Sau. "Farm Efficiency under Semi-Feudalism: A Critique of Marginalist Theories and Some Marxist Formulations: A Comment," 10, no. 13 (29 March 1975): pp. A 18–A 21.

[36] Nirmal K, Chandra, "Agrarian Transition in India," *Frontier*, VII, nos 28, 29, 30 (1975a, b, c).

[37] Ibid.

[38] Ibid.

[39] Cited in Prasad. "Reactionary role of Usurers' Capital in Rural India."

[40] Ashok Rudra, "Semi-Feudalism, Usury Capital, Etcetera," 9, no. 48 (30 November 1974): pp. 1996–97.

[41] Ibid., but compare with the remarks about zero interest rates in Chandra, "Agrarian Transition in India."

[42] Rudra, "Semi-Feudalism, Usury Capital, Etcetera."

[43] Ibid.; italics in original.

[44] Ibid.

[45] Ibid.

[46] Ibid.

[47] Paresh Chattopadhyay. "Mode of Production in Indian Agriculture: An Afterword," *Economic and Political Weekly*, XV (Review .of Agriculture, 1980): pp. 85–88.

[48] Sharat G. Lin. "Theory of a Dual Mode of Production in Post-Colonial India," *Economic and Political Weekly*, XV, nos 10 and 11 (1980): pp. 516–29, 565–73.

[49] Ibid.

[50] Dipankar Gupta. "Formal and Real Subsutnption of Labour under Capital: The Instance of Share-Cropping," *Economic and Political Weekly*, XV, no. 39 (Review of Agriculture, 1980): pp. 98–106.

[51] Aparajita Chakraborty. "Tenancy and Mode of Production," *Economic and Political Weekly*, XVI, no. 13 (Review of Agriculture, 1981): pp. 5–14.

[52] Ashok Rudra. "Against Feudalism," *Economic and Political Weekly*. XVI, no. 12 (1981): pp. 2133–46; emphasis in original.

[53] Ibid.

[54] Atyachar Virodh Samiti. "The Marathwada Riots: A Report," *Economic and Political Weekly*, XIV, no. 19 (1979): pp. 845–52.

[55] Gail Omvedt. "Capitalist Agriculture and Rural Classes in India," *Economic and Political Weekly* (Review of Agriculture, 1981): 140–59.

[56] Ibid.

[57] Ibid.

[58] Ibid.

[59] Ibid.

12

The Indian Institutes of Technology

Do They Contribute to Social Mobility?*

C. Rajagopalan and Jaspal Singh

As the IITs enjoy a special status, are endowed with a constitution and organisation different from that of the other engineering colleges in the country, and have been declared institutes of national importance by an Act of Parliament, it may be of interest to know something about the students who succeed in securing entry to these institutes. There is a great demand for admission to the IITs, as evidenced by the number of applications for admission, but only a small percentage are eventually admitted. In 1965, the total number of applications for admission to the five IITs was 25,719. The number of students who appeared for the entrance examination was 22,776. Of these only 2,133 or 9.37 per cent were qualified. The number of applicants in 1966 was higher than that in the earlier years. Admission to these institutes is based on an all-India joint entrance examination and is apparently free from all discriminations. Yet, in a vast country like India, the great range in social and economic conditions may have the unintended effect of making it difficult for certain sections of society to qualify for the facilities of education provided in these institutes. For instance, the localisation of educational facilities may itself have the unintended consequence of actually restricting their use to that region. Or the existence of certain educational facilities may not be known to most people. Also, as schools vary widely in the facilities they offer and consequently in the standards they maintain, belong to different denominations, and use different media of

* Originally published in the *Economic and Political Weekly* 3, no. 14 (6 April 1968): pp. 565–70.

instruction, students from certain schools may be automatically eliminated in the competition for admission owing to no fault of their own. This is especially so when the competitive examination is modelled on the basis of standards maintained by the best schools. It is far from our intention to suggest that the standard of the competitive examination be brought down to enable the weak students to get through. Our aim is only to examine whether there is evidence that any such disabling factors are in operation against certain sections of society. How these factors can be eliminated is an altogether different question, and is in any case beyond the scope of this chapter.

SOCIAL BACKGROUND

A study of the social background of these students is of interest for another reason. It is assumed that the IITs, by virtue of their unique status and numerous facilities, can attract the most suitable and talented students and train and convert them into engineers who are bound to be superior to the ones being turned out by the ordinary engineering colleges. If this is true, it is likely that the students graduating from these institutes will have a definite edge over their counterparts from other engineering colleges in matters of employment. Consequently, in a few years most of the important and top positions in the field of engineering and technology in the country may be controlled by them. In a country which has embarked on a process of rapid industrialisation, therefore, what amount of power and influence the products of the IITs might wield can easily be imagined. If the IITs are engaged in producing a potential elite which is bound to play a very crucial role in the industrial and technological development of the country, the whole question of recruitment and of the elite becomes a matter of profound interest. A study of the social background of these students would disclose the social strata from which they come and the extent to which the recruitment conforms to the accepted goals of social transformation of our society.

The term social background has been used in this study in a very comprehensive sense and includes factors such as religion, caste, family, the rural or urban character of the native place of the students, the income, education and occupation of their parents, and the students' school background, i.e., the type of school attended, its media of instruction and the final qualifying examination passed before being admitted to the IIT. Factors like caste, religion, family and rural/urban background have been included because they are important principles of stratification in Indian society which has yet to completely shed its traditional character. As Indian society undergoes a change from its traditional orientation to a modern one, these principles of stratification are bound to lose their importance and be eventually replaced by criteria of achievement for social stratification; hence the relevance of factors like parental education, occupation and income being included in this study. The analysis of the school background is designed to discover whether certain kinds of schooling tend to act as a handicap in securing admission.

Of the 237 students interviewed, as many as 87.8 per cent were from urban areas, and only 8.1 per cent from rural areas. The remaining 4.1 per cent did not indicate the rural/urban character of their native place. It is clear that the bulk of the students belong to urban areas.

The rural/urban background refers to the student's native place, defined as his traditional home community. In actual fact, however, the student may be alien to his home community insofar as he may have been born and brought up in an urban area where his parents have been permanently employed. Further analysis of the data shows that this is substantially true. Out of 8.1 per cent of the students whose traditional home community is rural, as many as 5.5 per cent are more or less permanent residents of the city where the institute is located (this will hereafter be referred to as the "city area" and students from it as "local students"). It is possible that the remaining six students too, whose parents are not settled in the city, are in fact residents of an urban area other than the city, so that not more than 2.6 per cent of the students belong to the rural areas.

Table 12.1 shows the nativity of the students in terms of the state of origin and rural/urban background. It will be seen that 59.5 per cent are local students, and of these all but two are urbanites. The actual number of people belonging to the city, however, is more if we add the 5.5 per cent from the rural areas whose parents have actually settled down in the city. In other words, as many as 65 per cent of the students are from the city itself. Another 22.4 per cent come from the three states adjacent to the city. Students coming from other states in northern and southern India form 8.0 and 5.1 per cent respectively of the students interviewed. It is quite clear that, judged by the state or origin of the students, the Institute caters mostly to students from the city.

TABLE 12.1: STUDENTS BY THE STATE OF ORIGIN AND RURAL/URBAN BACKGROUND

State of Origin	Urban	Rural	No Response	Total
The City	137	2	2	141
Three Adjacent States	36	15	2	53
Rest of Northern India	17	2	–	19
Southern India	9	–	3	12
Foreigner	3	–	–	3
No Response	6	–	3	9
Total	203	19	10	237

In the course of the interviews it came to light that of the five branches of engineering in which courses are offered at the Institute, mechanical and electrical engineering were the most sought after. This is also borne out by the preferences expressed by the students in their applications for admission to the Institute. When the students were asked why they chose the particular discipline, virtually all the students reading mechanical and electrical engineering replied that they were genuinely interested in these branches of engineering, while many of the students from the other three disciplines said that they did not choose these disciplines but had opted for them after having been refused places for mechanical and electrical engineering on the basis of the merit entrance examination. This is also attested by the fact that students on the top of the merit list are generally admitted to mechanical and electrical engineering courses except when their own preference is for some other discipline.

In view of the different degrees of prestige attached to the different branches of engineering, it may be interesting to see whether the rural/urban background and nativity of the students are factors that have helped or hindered them in getting admission to the preferred branches of engineering. The relevant data are presented in Table 12.2. It is clear from the table that while the percentage of students not belonging to the city is as low as 17.5 in some of the more highly preferred disciplines, their percentage rises to 42.3 in the least preferred discipline. As a matter of fact, the total intake of students is much smaller in the least preferred discipline compared to that in the other disciplines. In other words, students from the city have not only a better chance of getting admission into the institute, but also of getting admission into courses of higher prestige.

TABLE 12.2: STUDENTS CLASSIFIED BY ENGINEERING DISCIPLINE AND PARENTS' PRESENT RESIDENCE

Parental Residence	Engineering Discipline			Total
	Mechanical	Electrical	Three Other Disciplines	
The City	44	47	91	182
Three adjacent States	3	5	22	30
Rest of northern India	2	2	9	13
Southern India	1	1	–	2
Foreigner	2	1	–	3
No response	4	1	2	7
Total	56	57	124	237

A religion-wise breakup shows that 90.3 per cent of the students are Hindus, 8.4 per cent Sikhs and the remaining 1.3 per cent Muslims. Of the three Muslim students, one is a foreigner. And the two Indian Muslim students are in the least preferred branch of engineering. It is also significant to note that there is no Christian student. Thus the vast majority of the students are Hindus.

In view of the fact that the students come from different states, some of which have unique systems of caste nomenclature, it is difficult to make any comparisons of caste unless they are reduced to the Brahman/non-Brahman/ Scheduled Caste (SC) classification. This is an over-simplification which may overlook differences between castes comprised within any of the categories.

However, the fact that the vast bulk of students come from the city and other adjacent states, where the caste systems are comparable to a certain extent, permits us to analyse caste by excluding the small proportion of students who belong to other states. Similarly, since only two religious groups are represented adequately in the sample, the analysis of caste can be done in the context of religion. This is presented in Table 12.3.

TABLE 12.3: STUDENTS CLASSIFIED BY RELIGION AND CASTE

Caste	Religion			Total
	Hindu	Sikh	Muslim	
Brahman	52	–	–	52
Trading castes	142	6	2	150
Agricultural castes	2	6	–	8
Artisan castes	–	6	–	6
Miscellaneous	12	–	–	12
No response	6	2	1*	9
Total	214	20	3	237

* Foreigner.

It is significant that there is not a single student from any of the SCs or Scheduled Tribes (ST). Brahman castes are represented to the extent of 21.9 per cent. The vast majority of the students are from the trading castes,[1] which account for 63.3 per cent of the aggregate, and artisan castes have a numerically small representation. In terms of religion, however, the agricultural castes have a much higher percentage among the Sikhs than amongst the Hindus. All students from the artisan castes belong to the Sikh religion and none to the Hindu. Thus, while the Hindu students are almost exclusively from the Brahman and trading castes, the Sikh students are more or less evenly distributed among the trading, agricultural and artisan castes. The two Indian Muslim students are also from a trading caste (Bohra).

Most of the students, 67.9 per cent, come from nuclear families. The second largest category, 22.8 per cent, are from potentially nuclear, residually joint families. Only 9.3 per cent come from joint families. That a large number of students come from nuclear rather than joint families, is quite consistent with the earlier finding that practically all the students come from urban areas and particularly from the city itself.

Significantly again, all the students are males, with no girl getting admission in the year under review, although there is no bar against the admission of girls.

The educational level of the parents of the students is shown in Table 12.4. It shows that the largest number of students, 39.6 per cent, have fathers who have had college education. Next come those whose fathers have a postgraduate degree, and they number 18.5 per cent. Students with fathers whose educational level is that of matriculation account for 17.7 per cent. The fathers of 10.6 per cent of the students have professional education, such as a degree in engineering or medicine. Only a small number of students, 5.1 per cent, have fathers who are not even matriculates. A vast majority of the students, therefore, have fathers with varying degrees of college education, ranging from graduation to doctorates and professional degrees.

TABLE 12.4: STUDENTS CLASSIFIED ACCORDING TO THEIR PARENTS' EDUCATION

Fathers' Education	Mothers' Education					Total
	Below Matric	Matric	College Education	Post-Graduate	No Response	
Below matriculation	9	–	–	–	3	12
Matriculation	23	11	1	–	7	42
College education	23	26	22	2	21	94
Postgraduate	6	10	12	6	10	44
Professional degree	5	7	8	2	3	25
No response	3	6	1	2	8	20
Total	69	60	44	12	52	237

As regards the education of the mothers, with the exception of three cases, their educational level is lower than that of the fathers. As against 5.1 per cent of fathers with education of below the level of matriculation, the percentage of mothers with this level of education is 29.1. As a rule, the difference between the education of couples is not too wide insofar as in only 4.6 per cent of the cases of cohorts the father has the highest education, such as a postgraduate or professional degree, and the mother the lowest, viz., below matriculation. Our analysis thus conclusively proves that most of the students have parents who are fairly well if not highly educated.

The fathers of the students are engaged in a variety of occupations and these have been classified under six heads. The fathers of the largest number of students, 32.9 per cent, are clerks, assistants, stenographers, accountants, section officers, superintendents, etc. The next largest number, 18.9 per cent, are in higher administrative occupations such as gazetted officers, company managers, executives, secretaries to government, etc. Third comes business, with 15.2 per cent of the fathers engaged in it. This includes retail as well as wholesale dealers, contractors, commission agents etc. The next largest category is the professions, which includes engineers, doctors, lawyers and chartered accountants, who account for 13.9 per cent of the fathers. There are only 5.1 per cent and 4.6 per cent students whose fathers are in teaching and in the armed forces, respectively. It may, however, be pointed out that of the 12 teachers six are school teachers, while the rest are college or university teachers. Among those in the armed forces, except for one who is a junior commissioned officer, all the rest are commissioned officers of various ranks. The residual category consists of 10 fathers of whom three are non-cultivating landowners residing in the city, one is an ex-Cabinet Minister, two are artists, one is a cabin man in the railways, one a traffic inspector and two railway inspectors. It may be pointed out that there is not a single student whose father is a farmer, labourer, artisan, craftsman, soldier, or in any other low-paid occupation. So, occupational background again indicates that insofar as occupation is an index of social stratification, practically all the students come from the middle or upper strata of society.

TABLE 12.5: STUDENTS CLASSIFIED ACCORDING TO THEIR FATHERS' OCCUPATION

Occupation	Number of Cases
Clerical	78
Higher administrative	45
Business	36
Professional	33
Teaching	12
Armed forces	1
Others	10
No response	12
Total	237

Another index of social position is income. We have sought to find out the incomes of the fathers of the students from their occupations and the total family income including the income of other earners in the family to get an idea of the per capita monthly income in the family. Both these provide some idea of the economic background of the students.

The incomes of the fathers vary widely between Rs 100 and Rs 6,000 per month. The largest number of fathers, 34.2 per cent, have monthly incomes ranging from Rs 251 to 500.[2] Another 16 per cent of the fathers have incomes between Rs 501 and 750, 11.4 per cent of the fathers from Rs 751 to 1,000, 17.3 per cent from Rs 1,001 to 2,000, and 3.8 per cent above Rs 2,000 per month. There are only 5.1 per cent of the students whose fathers have an income below Rs 250 per month. The distribution of fathers by income thus corresponds to a considerable extent with the occupational distribution. During the course of our investigation we found that in many families there are earning members other than the father. Since the majority of the students are members of nuclear families, it was thought that family income would provide a more accurate measure of the economic condition of the students than the father's income alone. However, in view of the fact that the families may vary in size, we thought it better to analyse the families in terms of the average per capita monthly income of its members so as to give due weightage to such variations. We have calculated the per capita monthly income by dividing the total income from all sources by the total number of members in the family. This is presented in Table 12.6. It is seen that in the case of 3.4 per cent of the students their families have a per capita monthly income of over Rs 500 per month. In 36.7 per cent cases it is up to Rs 100—which includes 9.3 per cent cases with income of less than Rs 50. Judged by the national per capita income[3] all the students except very few come from families which have a per capita income much higher than the national average, and this reinforces our earlier finding regarding the social class status of the students.

TABLE 12.6: STUDENTS CLASSIFIED ACCORDING TO THE PER CAPITA FAMILY INCOME FROM ALL SOURCES

Income in Rs/month	Number of Cases
Up to 50	22
51–100	65
101–250	77
251–500	51
501–750	2
751–1,000	3
1,001–1,500	3
No response	14
Total	237

It is clear that in terms of the objective criteria of education, occupation and income of their parents, virtually all the students belong to the upper and middle class. That this is substantially true is also attested by the students' own assessment of their class position. The students were asked two questions:"How would you yourself rank the overall esteem of your family" and "In your opinion, in what esteem is your family held in the place where you habitually live?" The results of their responses recorded on a three-point scale are as shown in Table 12.7. It is clear that by either standard of assessment, not more than 1.3 per cent of the students can be said to identify themselves with lower class. Thus, even according to their own self-image as well as their conception of their image others have about them, virtually all of them belong to the upper or the middle class.

TABLE 12.7: STUDENTS CLASSIFIED BY THEIR SUBJECTIVE CLASS IDENTIFICATION

Response	How would you rank the overall esteem of your family?	In what esteem is your family held in the place where you habitually live?
High	105	117
Neither high, nor low but in between the two	123	113
Low	3	–
No response	6	7
Total	237	237

In our study we made an attempt to find out how many of the students come from families in which someone or the other is already an engineer. We tried to collect this information at two levels of family organisation. At the widest level the information refers to a maximum of four degrees of relationship with the student considered as the ego, and at the narrowest level the first-degree relations, viz., the students' fathers and brothers.

At the widest level our data show that 70.5 per cent of the students have some relative within the range of four degrees who is an engineer and the maximum number of relatives in the engineering profession which any student has is 10. In all, 167 students have a total of 451 relatives in the engineering profession, which works out to an average of 2.7 relatives per student. In view of the fact that nearly three-fourths of the students already have one or more relatives in the engineering profession, it is clear that the tendency for self-recruitment in terms of the wider family unit is quite pronounced.

With regard to first-degree relatives, we find that only 15.6 per cent of the students have such relatives in the engineering profession. In the case of 8.4 per cent, the relative in the engineering profession is his own father, and in 7.1 per cent it is his brother. There are, however, only two cases where both the father and one or more brothers are in the engineering profession. At the level of the nuclear family, therefore, the tendency for self-recruitment is much less marked than at the wider family level.

We may now turn to an analysis of the educational background of the students themselves with a view to finding out whether students educated in certain types of schools and with a certain language as the medium of instruction have an advantage over others in securing admission to the Institute. This is important in view of the fact that there are different types of schools in the country employing different languages as media of instruction, especially up to the high school level. Since the medium of instruction in the institute is English and the joint entrance examination is being conducted in English, it is likely that students educated through the medium of regional languages are handicapped in securing admissions. We have, accordingly, tried to analyse the educational background of the students in terms of the type of school in which they were educated, the medium of instruction, and their maximum educational attainments before being admitted to the Institute.

Table 12.8 shows the highest examination passed by the students before they were admitted to the Institute. Three-fifth, or 60.3 per cent, of the students have passed the Higher Secondary examination. The remainder consist of those who have passed the Indian School Certificate examination and Pre-Engineering FSc, in more or less equal ratio. As compared to the proportion of students passing the Indian School Certificate examination to that passing the Higher Secondary or Pre-Engineering FSc in the country as a whole, or even within the city, it seems that the former have a definite edge over the latter for admission to the Institute. It is also interesting to note that 77.3 per cent of those who have more than the required minimum in education, such as FSc Pre-Engineering, are from outside the city. Thus, in order to successfully compete for admission, students from the rest of the country are required to have higher education than students from the city.

TABLE 12.8: STUDENTS CLASSIFIED ACCORDING TO THE EXAMINATION PASSED AND THE UNIVERSITY

Examination	ISC	City Board	Other Boards/ Universities	No Response	Total
Higher Secondary	–	131	9	5	145
Indian School Certificate	45	–	–	1	46
FSc, Pre-Engg, First Year of Diploma in Engg	–	6	34	4	44
No Response	–	1	–	1	2
Total	45	138	43	11	237

Table 12.9 shows the type of schools attended by the students. It is found that public schools contributed the single largest number of students to the Institute—26.6 per cent. The percentage of students from privately managed schools (may be aided by government, and other than public schools) is 24.5. Schools run and managed by government or municipal committees, etc., got in 18.9 per cent of the students. Another 29.0 per cent were from a mixed school background, having moved between government, private and/or public schools at primary, middle and higher levels of study. Judged by the proportion of public schools to the total number of educational institutions in India, or in the city itself, the higher percentage of students from the public schools indicates that the former have relative over representation.

TABLE 12.9: STUDENTS CLASSIFIED BY THE TYPE OF SCHOOLS THEY WENT TO

Schooling	Number of Cases
Public throughout	63
Private throughout	58
Government throughout	45
Mixed (Public/Private/Government)	69
No Response	2
Total	237

Table 12.10 indicates that 60.3 per cent of the students were from schools with mixed media of instruction, one medium invariably being English. They may have received instruction in English and Hindi, or in English and their own regional language, or in English, Hindi and the regional language. Another 33.3 per cent had all their education in English only. Only 6.3 per cent were from vernacular medium schools. Thus, schools with English medium have contributed more than five students to every student from schools employing vernaculars as media of instruction.

TABLE 12.10: STUDENTS CLASSIFIED BY THE MEDIA OF INSTRUCTION IN SCHOOL AT DIFFERENT LEVELS

Level of schooling	Medium of instruction			Total
	English	Vernacular	English + Vernacular	
Primary	94	143	–	237
Middle	92	142	3	237
Higher	213	16	8	237
Throughout	79	15	143	237

It is evident from the foregoing analysis that the students represent, by and large, a homogeneous group insofar as their general social background is concerned. More specifically, in terms of cultural factors like religion and caste, there is a preponderance of the Hindus belonging to the Brahman and the trading castes. As regards the social class background, they represent preponderantly the urban upper and middle classes. The educational background reveals that students from public schools, with English medium, and qualifying for the Indian School Certificate examination generally preponderate over others.

CONCLUSIONS

This finding seems to fit into a certain pattern. Even though admission to the Institute is based on an all-India competitive examination and no artificial restrictions have been imposed on any section from seeking admission, in actual practice admission appears to be determined by a set of socio-cultural factors. Among these, the awareness of the existence of technological education, appreciation of its importance, and—perhaps more importantly—the ability to afford that education as well as the quality of education previously received seem to be crucial. These factors are not isolated, however, but are closely related to one another. Awareness of new educational opportunities holding possibilities of a good career is bound to be higher in the urban areas where these opportunities are generally concentrated. And within the urban areas awareness is bound to be higher at the upper rungs of the social hierarchy since individuals so placed are more educated than those at the lower rungs. For the same reason people from the upper strata are also in a position to select the best schools for their children. Since these schools are more expensive than the government-managed and other aided schools, they tend to draw their students from a select segment of society who can afford them.

In other words, even though no student is intentionally precluded from securing admission there are certain disabling and debilitating factors inherent in the structure of society which prevent certain sections from taking advantage of the new educational opportunities.

It has already been pointed out that the IITs are engaged in producing what may be termed a class of potential elite, and our findings have established that this potential elite is itself being recruited from the higher strata of society almost to the neglect of the lower strata. Accordingly, IITs as educational institutions seem to make only a limited contribution to social mobility.

Notes and References

[1] Bania, Arora, Bhatia and Sood are undisputedly trading castes. Khatri have been classified by Hutton as trading castes. See J. H. Hutton, *Caste in India* (London: Oxford University Press, 1961), p. 284.

[2] The report of the Education Commission (p. 119) has pointed out that the fathers of 57.5 per cent of the students of the IITs in India have income exceeding Rs 500 per month. According to our data the percentage of students whose fathers have similar incomes is 48.5. According to another study, the family income of 57 per cent of the sample was above Rs 1,000 a month and only 7.1 per cent came from the income group below Rs 500. The authors of this survey have pointed out that, "Considering the fact (given by the last Census) that the average income of families in Delhi is approximately Rs 300 a month, it is not impossible that the education in the Delhi University is the prerogative of the more affluent." See A. Ghosh, T. C. A. Rangachar and S. Chatterjee,"Sample Survey of Delhi University," *Yojana* (2 April 1967): pp. 23–24.

[3] According to the NCAR, per capita income of an average Indian is Rs 334.50 (quoted by the Education Commission Report, p. 126).

13

Transformation of Tribal Society

Integration vs. Assimilation*

K. S. Singh

Social anthropology has moved away from the stereotype of a tribe as an isolate, and has focused on interaction and interdependence of tribes and peasants.[1] Speaking in 1973 on a similar theme, the transformation of tribal society in modern India, Surajit Sinha delineated the process of assimilation of tribes into the caste-peasant base of Indian civilisation through the adoption of agricultural technology and linguistic and cultural norms of the peasant castes. The *varna-jati* model of absorption has given way to the search for political status as an ethnic minority within a constitutional framework informed with an egalitarian democratic ideology. This inspired the rise of ethnicity-based solidarity movements led by an educated elite, there being a broad correlation between the intensity of the separatist solidarity movements and the degree of spatial and cultural isolation from the regional caste/peasant society.[2] The social historian has seen this process of integration within the framework of the political economy of feudalism and colonialism.[3] What Nirmal Kumar Bose described as the Hindu mode of absorption was neither Hindu nor absorption, but a process of integration into the production system of colonialism.[4] This secular process has sometimes been oversimplified; the transition of tribes into peasants and of peasants into depeasantised working class is generally described as a unilinear process.[5] Such studies of a tribe as a class or one ethnic community overlook the complexities of tribal social formations and situations, such as the

* This edited article was originally published in *Economic and Political Weekly* 17, no. 33 (14 August 1982): pp. 1318–25.

pull of ethnicity amidst growing differentiation. G. S. Ghurye, who propounded his anti-isolation and pro-assimilation viewpoint regarding tribals in 1942, has recently not only reiterated his views but has also questioned the related policy and programmes and the social anthropologists' commitment to the concept of integration instead of assimilation of tribes into the larger society.[6] What irks him is that the American model of ethnic-cum-cultural pluralism has been unabashedly applied to the Indian situation, even though it has failed in relation to the American Indians. Ghurye notes that while the Russians have set out to Russianise their nationalities, the Chinese have Sinified their minorities and the Americans did try to Americanise their ethnics once upon a time, there is also a case for the assimilation of the Scheduled Tribes (ST), a process which has been held up by the faulty policies of the government out to appease the tribals.

Therefore, it will be appropriate to set the "tribal transformations" in a wider perspective. I will first deal with the perspective and ideology, economic transformation and social stratification in tribal society in India. I will then discuss how these processes are reflected not only in ethnicity-based solidarity movements but in a whole range of movements.

Perspective and Ideology

We are by now familiar with the stories of the annihilation of indigenous peoples and the formation of the reservations for the "Red Indians" in the New World, under various treaties concluded between their chiefs and the colonisers' governments, continuing encroachment on reservations and restrictions of the native's rights in them, etc. The encounter with the white settlers and Christianity gave rise to many a movement the study of which has generated a good deal of information and stimulated a lot of theoretical model-building. The United States has an Indian population of 800,000, divided into 300 tribes living in 300 reservations. About 40 per cent of them live below the poverty line. This is in spite of the fact that the Federal Government spends an incredibly large amount on their welfare and the Indians enjoy full rights as American citizens. The Indians have refused to be assimilated and to give up their identity in spite of the Americanisation of their lifestyle. The process of grabbing of the Indian land continues. In a damning indictment, the World International Tribunal at Rotterdam (Holland) in November 1980 held the governments of the United States and Canada guilty of stealing the land of the Indians and charged them with following a systematic policy of genocide against the Indians, of having illegally deprived them of their lands and of unleashing violent repression against their protest movements. The tribunal also condemned the activities of various multinational corporations in the Indian settlement areas which have resulted in reckless mining, deforestation, despoiling of the land and utter callousness in waste disposal. These activities have caused serious environmental and health hazards leading to innumerable diseases and, in the long run, physical deformities and deaths.[7]

The North American model of reservations travelled to Latin America. A recent study of the policy, legislation and administration of welfare measures for these people, conducted by the International Labour Organization, shows that they were still governed by the nineteenth century attitude of complete assimilation and denied the right to a share in administration of their affairs. In Brazil the Indians who are not integrated with national life are held under tutelage and thus denied the exercise of full civic rights. Of the 180,000 Indians under tutelage none has applied for emancipation. In Columbia the general law of the State does not apply to the "savages" who are being reclaimed to civilisation by the missions. In general the picture which emerges is dismal.[8]

In Australia, too, the aborigines were pushed off their ancestral land and herded on to reservations, and continued to be exterminated until 1928 when the last official killings were reported. Their number fell from 300,000 in the late eighteenth century to 67,000 in 1901, and has been slowly increasing since then, having reached 161,000 today. It was not until 1967 that equal citizenship rights were given to the aborigines, their languages were recognised, and the Commonwealth assumed concurrent jurisdiction over matters relating to them which earlier fell within the purview of the state regimes. Other administrative changes have been the creation of a Department of Aboriginal Affairs, an Aboriginal Development Commission and an elected National Aboriginal Conference. The aborigine customary law is being integrated into Australian Jurisprudence. The ownership of land, however, remained the key issue, and it was not until 1977 that the government enacted a law whereby the aborigines could lay claim to any crown land not already occupied. It is reported that about 25,000 aborigines acquired freehold title to roughly 28 per cent of Northern Territory's 523,620 square miles of rock and shrub. Similarly, the Government of South Australia handed over to the Pitjantiatiara tribe title deeds to about 40,000 square miles of territory.[9] Complications have, however, arisen in this regard as Australia has struck rich oil and mineral deposits in the aborigines' homeland.

Alongside the reservations, there is also the model of incorporations established for indigenous people. There are Maori incorporations in New Zealand in which the Maori landowners have become shareholders, farming is determined by a managing committee and profits are disbursed annually as dividends. While they have carried out expensive farming operations, which have contributed significantly to the overall growth and productivity, they hardly claim to be a vital link of New Zealand's economy.[10]

Against the capitalistic models of reservations and incorporations based on the concept of the assimilation of indigenous peoples could be pitted the socialistic concept of self-determination of nationalities. It was formulated as part of the debate on the national question in the second and third decades of the present century. Soviet ethnographers recognise ethnicity as a process of social consolidation working at a level lower than nationality and as a key element in socialist reconstruction. At the time of the foundation of the USSR the right of the nationality and national minority to determine its political and economic status was recognised and their union into the great family was considered a voluntary act. In consonance with this principle the ethnic boundaries were rigorously demarcated and made co-terminus with the administrative boundaries of republics and autonomous territories. The policy has been to promote the full development of cultural autonomy of the nationalities while integrating them fully within the politico-economic system of socialism. While describing this process the Soviet ethnographers have noted that the pre-Revolution social system of many of these national minorities was characterised by the rise of private property and social differentiation, alienation of the upper crust from the working populations, etc. With the growth of the socialist economy, the primitive communities have been generally urbanised and their pastoral or agrarian economies have been integrated into the macro-level industrial complexes leading to a phenomenal rise of productive forces.[11] At the same time there have also been strong centralising influences at work—for example, the widespread use of the Russian language as the medium of communication. Once the choice of self-determination has been exorcised at the time of the formation of the state or the nation-state, secessionism is out of question and is seen as the handiwork of neocolonial forces.

The third world under the colonial system was generally spared the traumatic experiences of the reservations. The colonial encounter with the indigenous population was not as direct and as bloody. The colonial system in the countries of tropical Africa and South Asia preferred direct or indirect rule or a combination of both for the indigenous population. These countries shared the experiences of national oppression, ethnic conflicts and contradictions, the role of the ethnic factor or factors in their freedom struggles. After attaining independence, many of the African states faced the task of forming a nation out of myriad tribes, and the euphoria over the unity of ethnic communities forged in the course of the freedom struggles gave way to a mature understanding of inter-ethnic relationship and the need for its development in the process of national consolidation. Although many African states had passed the stage of tribal formation, tribal forms and prejudices survived. Therefore, while ethnic groups were exhorted to give up their tribalism, it was generally understood that the solution of ethnic problems is linked with the socio-economic transformation of the nation-state.

Secessionism has no place in the system. As Jomo Kenyatta said: "Nationhood and familyhood must and can be contrived out of our many tribes and cultures."[12] This is also echoed in one of the objectives of the Tanganyika African National Union, which is "the creation of a nation out of more than 120 tribes, out of peoples of different religious and different social groups, and a nation in which race is of less importance than a record of service and an expected ability to give service."[13]

Of particular interest is President Julius Nyerere's socialistic experiments in a tribal milieu:

> In the past, when our population was divided into different tribal groups, the land belonged to the particular tribe living on it. In future, however, our population will be united as one nation, and the land will belong to the nation. And today, just as one man cannot prevent another man from his tribe from using land, so also tomorrow one tribe will not be able to prevent another tribe from using land that is actually the property of the nation as a whole.[14]

Many of these countries are grappling with colonial backlog of discrepancies between ethnic and political boundaries, inter-tribe conflicts, movements of separatism and secessionism.

The African experience is relevant because we too are faced with the problem of consolidating a nation-state and have inherited the colonial backlog of ethnic conflicts which have sharpened as the process of development intensifies. Our founding fathers too sought to create and consolidate a nation-state out of a congeries of communities, including tribes. However, India is not the best example of a plural society, because while pluralism stresses cleavages and discontinuities between the sections of people differentiated by race, ethnicity, religion or culture, there has been an all-pervasive sense of cultural unity, a wide-ranging sharing of its idioms and symbols, in spite of diversities in our country. Tribals were not aliens: their isolation was relative, never absolute; they have been part of the Indian civilisational universe. However, as a nation-state in the process of consolidation, we too are confronted like others with ethnic problems.

To go back to the colonial experience of the subcontinent, unlike Africa, which adopted the system of indirect rule, namely rule through the traditional chiefs of territories, a large part of the tribal region and most of the tribal population in India were integrated within the administration of the provinces of British India or within that of the Indian State, where the British Resident kept a watch on the tribal situation and, in some cases, even acted as the agent for the tribal regions. There were areas of tribal concentration which were enclaved to "reclaim to civilisation" the tribes who had rebelled or were difficult to pacify. It was in these enclaves that the concept of protection of the tribes as an ethnic community developed in stages. The Agency system established with the objective of quelling rebellions was the earliest mode of protective administration. The Agency settled tribes, opened up the tribal world, laid lines of communication, established *chatties* along highways to supply the army, which brought in merchants, traders and peddlers, and set up cantonments and centres of administration and trade. The colonial system ended the relative isolation of the tribal society; brought it into the mainstream of the new administrative setup, policy and programmes; put an end to the political dominance of the tribes in the region; and roped the tribal communities which had been spared the strain of surplus generation by their states into a new system of production relations. The colonial system, as elsewhere, followed the dual policy of strengthening the feudal crust of the tribal societies, formed by the rajas, chiefs and zamindars, and simultaneously created conditions in which their economy and political system were undermined by the rampaging market forces.[15]

That the normal laws should not automatically apply to the tribal areas was the principle that underlay the passage of the Scheduled Districts Act (1874) and shaped the concept of the backward areas in the Government of India Act of 1919. Whether or not this principle should continue to be applied was a matter that figured in a most lively debate in the early 1930s. While one school contended that the aborigines formed a distinct element in India and should be placed in the British government's charge, the nationalists saw in this proposition the continuation of the imperial policy of divide and rule. However, the tribal and non-tribal areas were both partly and fully "excluded" in the Government of India Act of 1935.

Gandhi reacted sharply to the segregation of various communities, particularly the tribals, under the dangerous spell of the policy of the "isolation and status quo." The Act of 1935, he would recall, separated tribals from the rest of the inhabitants. The "Excluded Areas" were placed under the government's direct administration: the Adivasis were put into watertight compartments and classified as tribal people by the government. "It was a shame," he told social workers, "that they had allowed them to be treated like that. It was up to them to make the Adivasis feel one with them." In strategically situated Assam, in 1946, he reminded the people that "it was their shame that the Adivasis should be isolated from the rest of the nation of which they were an inalienable part." While including Adivasis' welfare as the fourteenth item the Mahatma said:

> Adivasis have become the fourteenth item in the construction programme. But they are not the least in point of importance. Our country is so vast and the races are so varied that the best of us, in spite of every effort, cannot know all there is to know of men and their condition. As one comes upon layer after layer of things one ought to know as a national servant, one realises how difficult it is to make

good our claim to be one nation whose every unit has a living consciousness of being one with one another.[16]

On the eve of the transfer of power the most scathing indictment of the colonial policy of isolation and status quo for tribals came from the last British Governor, T. G. Rutherford of Bihar:

> While we [the British] have been in power we have not done much for them beyond a certain amount of protective legislation which functions effectively when the officers responsible are really sympathetic and—largely with the aid of missionaries—we have done a little to educate them. The tendency on the whole has been to treat them as delightful primitives whose simplicity and customs are a welcome relief from the sordid details of administration among the ordinary Hindus and Muslims.[17]

The need to provide adequate safeguards for the tribal was again extensively discussed in the Constituent Assembly, and the nationalist opinion favoured incorporation of far more radical provisions for the safeguards of the tribals' interests in the forms of the Fifth and Sixth Schedules of the Indian Constitution. This was an index of the profound change that had come over the nationalist opinion in regard to the tribal question owing to the efforts of Gandhi and Thakkar Bapa, among others, the unfolding of the profound humanism of the freedom movement, and the liberalism of the tribal leaders themselves. This appreciation of the uniqueness of the tribal factor within the framework of Indian nationalism and the extension of political rights to tribals were beyond the expectations of the colonial administrators and anthropologists.

Short of providing a measure of protection for tribals in middle India under the Fifth Schedule and of autonomy in the North-East under the Sixth Schedule, it was neither possible nor practicable to create a tribal state out of the adjoining tribal majority areas of the provinces at the time of the transfer of power. India had inherited the boundaries of the provinces fixed with an eye on administrative convenience. Language and not ethnicity determined the reorganisation of states in the 1950s. It was within the political and cultural system of the states that the tribals in middle India were sought to be integrated, even though they were divided between more than one state. Ethnicity influenced the formation of the states in the North-East in the 1960s and 1970s, even though certain ethnic areas are still to be integrated. However, the application of the principle of tribal ethnicity elsewhere in middle India is fraught with difficulties because nowhere except in two districts and a few talukas are the tribals in majority. However, the Chotanagpur Development Authority presents an interesting model of regional autonomy. Its performance deserves to be watched for some time before the concept of regional autonomy is examined for application elsewhere in middle India.

The process of decolonisation which began after the transfer of power involved enfranchisement and granting of full citizenship rights to tribal communities and setting up of democratic institutions. This resulted in the curtailment and abolition of the power of the tribal chiefs who had acted as the natural leaders of their community. The chiefs enjoyed a great deal of power in the Mizo and Khasi hills and therefore, when threatened with loss of power, they joined hands with the anti-national forces in the early 1950s, while the educated tribal elite favoured union with India. In middle India, tribal chieftainship was abolished with the zamindari and intermediary interests in the first flush of land reforms. As a corollary to this a new leadership came up through elections and as agents of the development process. It controls the apparatus of political power and corners a good bit of development benefits today. Almost all over the country this class of tribal elite exploits the national stereotypes of tribal society to secure benefits and acts as the mediator with the government; it has more in common with the middle class elsewhere than with its own people.

Second, while isolation was equated with the status quo in the colonial society, a new strategy of development was drawn up combining the twin elements of protection and development. Seen in the perspective of the third world, the Indian strategy of tribal development, in spite of its limitations, has been acclaimed as a unique experiment.

Jawaharlal Nehru's philosophy and vision shaped the tribal policy in the 1950s, particularly in the North-East. He avoided the extremes of the two standpoints; namely, the anthropological approach which sought to treat the tribals as museum specimens to be kept apart for study and observation; and the other approach which sought to destroy their individuality, distort the process of their development and absorb them in a culture and way of life that was alien to them. That they should be "engulfed by the masses of Indian Humanity" was a prospect that appalled Nehru.

> I am alarmed when I see not only in this country but in other great countries too—how anxious people are to shape others according to their own image or likeness, and to impose on them their particular way of life.... I am not at all sure which is a better way of living. In certain respects I am quite certain theirs is better. Therefore, it is grossly presumptuous on our part to approach them with an air of superiority or to tell them what to do or not to do. There is no point in trying to make them a second rate copy of ourselves.[18]

Therefore, while tribal identity should be preserved, tribals should develop in their own way without let or hindrance. As Nehru admitted, these reactions were, to begin with, instinctive and not based on any knowledge or experience. Gradually and towards the close of the 1950s, outlines of a policy emerged.

(i) People should develop along the lines of their own genius and we should avoid imposing anything on them. We should try to encourage in every way their own traditional arts and culture.
(ii) Tribal rights in land and forests should be respected.
(iii) We should try to train and build up a team of their own people to do the work of administration and development. Some technical personnel from outside will, no doubt, be needed, especially in the beginning. But we should avoid introducing too many outsiders into tribal territory.
(iv) We should not over-administer these areas or overwhelm them with a multiplicity of schemes. We should rather work through, and not in rivalry to, their own social and cultural institutions.
(v) We should judge results not by statistics or the amount of money spent, but by the quality of human character that is evolved.

In consonance with this philosophy a strategy of tribal development was framed. The Nehru era laid the foundation of tribal policy. The Scheduled Areas and Scheduled Tribes Commission (1961) evaluated the working of constitutional safeguards for the tribals and tribal development programmes. It noted the changes of far-reaching character introduced in tribal areas by the development process. The Commission, while endorsing Jawaharlal Nehru's approach, made wide-ranging recommendations involving protection of tribals' land, of their right in forest, their rehabilitation etc., all within the framework of the Nehruvian policy.

The framework of policy and strategy imbued with Nehru's humanism held the ground for about 15 years. It still provides the sheet anchor of India's tribal policy, though in recent years there has been a considerable broadening and deepening of the structure of the policy and programmes. We enter upon a more intensive phase from mid-60s. The formulation of the Fifth and Sixth Five-Year Plans showed perception of (a) the deleterious effects of the disturbance of the environment consequent upon the intensive exploitation of the natural resources of tribal regions on the tribal communities, (b) the growing incidence of exploitation of the tribal people, their loss of land, their indebtedness, their transformation from peasants into labour, particularly in the zones of intensive industrial activities, and (c) the diversities of tribal situations, which called for a more area-specific approach to planning and development. This means a gradual moving away from the schematic pattern of the earlier plan and formulation of a more integrated approach to the tribal problems. More backward communities have been identified as tribes, Uttar Pradesh appeared for the first time on the tribal map of India, and areas of tribal concentration were enlarged to bring within the ambit of planned development the populations ranging from 50,000 to 10,000. Each tribal region prepares its own sub-plan, which forms a part of the plan of the state. Each project in the sub-plan region—there are 180 intensive tribal development projects—prepares its own project report with reference to the special needs of the areas; these are compiled into the sub-plan, which is a part of the plan prepared by the state. A plethora of legislation has been enacted to prevent alienation of land, regulate money-lending, abolish the bonded labour system, and organise labour. The new package of programme seeks to tackle more effectively on a wide front the programmes of credit and marketing, application of a simple and relevant technology to agriculture, development of a programme of social forestry under which the tribals could become the owners rather than remain workers in forests, and further development of communications, health and education, which have already made an impact. The resources being mobilised for the development of the tribal regions from many sources, outlay in the state plan, investment of the Central government ministries, institutional finance and the special central assistance for development of tribal areas have reached an all-time high. The funds allocated for tribal development by successive governments since Independence might not have been commensurate with the proportion of the tribal population, and they were very low up to the Fourth Plan, but they did rise to 3.01 per cent in the Fifth Plan and 4.37 per cent in the Sixth Plan, thus inching very close to their share in the plan efforts. The development experience shows that even where ample funds are available, the administration in tribal areas has to be so reoriented and the technology of development so evolved that the tribals are able to absorb and take advantage of the development programme.

To sum up, while the Indian experiment with tribal development has been hailed as unique in the third world perspective of the treatment of the indigenous peoples, one has to take a balanced view of its processes. On the positive side the tribes who are full citizens have, barring a couple of islandic communities, maintained their demographic growth rate. They have also maintained their identity, their distinct way of life, although they have not remained unaffected by the storms blowing around their country. They have also remained in good parts of the North-East and a large part of middle India an agrarian community in possession of their lands, even though the incidence of land alienation has sharply increased in and around urban areas. From almost the zero level in the 1930s progress in education and literacy, health care and communication has been remarkable, though critical gaps exist in the utilisation of these facilities by tribals as compared to non-tribals. They have also participated in the democratic processes and have a share in the control of the apparatus of political power. Therefore, there is no substance in the allegation that their population has declined and that they have been prevented from acquiring real political powers.[19] On the negative side, however, they remain the most backward, under-developed and, next only to the Harijans, the most exploited community.

II

Economic Development and Change

We now turn to an analysis of the processes of economic transformation. Both economic and non-economic criteria determine the definition of the "tribes," which is an administrative category. The traditional criteria are tribals' relative isolation, homogeneity, and settlement in a well-defined habitat. To these are added criteria influenced by administrative convenience and the compulsions of rural development: primitiveness, economic backwardness and treating the community as a whole notwithstanding the levels of advancement of its strata as a unit of development planning. Thus, the more primitive groups have been distinguished from the less primitive; the former are characterised by low literacy rate, pre-agricultural technology and small population. Implicit in this two-fold division has been the recognition of the fact that there is not one tribal system but many, that there is not one but several tribal economies. Before we turn to the spatial distribution of tribal economies, it should be noted that except for a few isolated and small communities, no tribe in India today subsists on a single techno-economy of production. The primitive technology of hunting, food gathering, shifting and terrace cultivation is confined to the heavy monsoon zone covered by tropical forests in the North-East, part of Eastern and Central regions, the Nilgiris and the Andaman Islands. While there is historical evidence of the practice of shifting cultivation having prevailed in western India, it is no longer practised in the arid and semi-arid regions. The hunting and food-gathering tribes are the Onges and Jarwas of the Andaman Islands and the Shompens of Nicobar Island; the Sulung in the North-East, who are now taking to shifting cultivation; the Cholanickans in Kerala; and the Birhors in Bihar and Orissa. Food gathering is now generally a subsidiary and, during the lean months, a primary source of food for most of the primitive tribes on the mainland. Shifting cultivation is being practised by 2.6 million tribals, who constitute 8.7 per cent of the tribal population. A firm indication of the extent of dependence on this mode of production will emerge after the completion of the Anthropological Survey of India's current project on shifting cultivation. Wet terrace cultivation has developed in the western Himalayas, North-East India and in a couple of pockets in Bihar and Orissa. Pastoral economy, which constitutes about 10 per cent of the tribal population, survives in the high altitude of the sub-Himalayan regions, the arid zones of Gujarat and Rajasthan, and in a small pocket in the Nilgiris. All over tribal India settled dry cultivation has emerged as the primary mode of food production, involving nearly 60 per cent of the tribals.

The major thrust of change has been from tribes into peasants. We are in a position today to trace the process of transfer of technology from peasants to tribes in the pre-colonial and colonial societies. By the end of the 18th century communities of peasantised tribals had emerged in Assam, Rajasthan, middle India, etc. The colonial period witnessed an accentuation of this trend as movements of peasants into tribal regions continued. The colonial administration built up a hierarchy of tenures for the upper crust of the tribal society, which consisted of the tribal chiefs, and recognised the occupancy rights of tribal peasants. The colonial system followed the policy of reclaiming the tribes to civilisation through the adoption of plough culture and integration into market. The survey and settlement operations introduced in unsurveyed tribal regions acted as an instrument for the transformation of tribes into peasants. They identified different categories of land, determined tribals' rights in land, fixed rent and thus grafted the concept of private property in land on to the tribal system. Transition to settled agriculture was also helped by the conservation of forest resources for commercial exploitation, which pushed the tribals off their land in reserved forests.

Since Independence this process of transformation has intensified. Pressure of tribal population on land has grown as the carrying capacity of land has diminished. There has been diffusion of improved agricultural technology by government agency. Of particular interest is the extension of agriculture technology into the tribal economies of the North-East because, unlike middle India, there was no transfer of technology from peasants to tribes, no inter-ethnic participation in production. Separation of craft from agriculture occurred within the tribal community itself and its economy was integrated with the market system across the Inner Line. With introduction of new technology the shifting cultivation is being increasingly combined with terrace and wet cultivation in the foothills and low-lying areas, iron implements have replaced the wooden tools, and a variety of new crops is grown to suit the market. The technological innovations have brought about a change in social relationships. Hunting, food gathering and shifting cultivation technologies were associated with the system of communal or collective ownership of land and use of labour. The systems of terrace and wet cultivation are associated with the emerging trends of private ownership of land, increased use of inputs and labour, and the role of the market. In the North-East, while collective and private ownership exist side by side, evidence suggests that the latter preponderates in areas of wet cultivation.

Much the same kind of technological structural change is taking place, though on a smaller scale, in the regions of dry cultivation. As the dry farming technology is developed and applied to settled agriculture, the pace of the transformation of tribal agriculture is quickened. At present, much of settled cultivation is at subsistance level and the majority of the tribals produce not a marketable surplus but "marketed surplus," which they are forced to do to buy their necessities. However, pockets of modernised agricultural farming are emerging among the Munda and Oraon of Chotanagpur, the Gonds and Korkus of middle India, the Badagas and Mullu Kurmbas of the Nilgiris. Cash cropping of coconut has turned the Nicobarese into an affluent community. Incidence of cash cropping has been reported from parts of tribal Gujarat, Rajasthan, Andhra, Orissa and Chotanagpur.

This process may be discussed at some length. In Chotanagpur, particularly in Ranchi, tribals have taken up cultivation of wheat as a second crop, aided by minor irrigation. Helped by voluntary agencies and the government, they have constructed thousands of wells. About one-third of the area under the improved variety of crops and a substantial area under the high yielding varieties is owned by tribals. The increase in production of cereals and vegetables has not resulted in generation of surplus; it has only shortened the tribals' hunger period.

In this connection, the findings of two micro-level case studies in the transformation of tribal economy are interesting. The first is based on the study of the working of the Tribal Development Agency (TDA), Chakradharpur (1972–78), which embraces remotely situated tribal regions lying on the borders of Ranchi and Singhbhum, and peopled by the Ho and Munda communities. During the last six years the TDA spent Rs 1.80 crore, a major part of which went into developing a minor irrigation system in the undulating terrain and application of the new agricultural strategy. Over 52,000 out of 70,000 families participated in the programmes. There has been a noticeable increase in the area under cultivation and consumption of fertilisers by farmers has gone up. There has been a rise in the production of vegetables and wheat and summer crops, the areas under which have multiplied. As tribal economy is traditionally deficit in draught cattle, their distribution helped boost agriculture. The application of the techniques of dry land farming has substantially helped agricultural development. The upland was treated for acidity and cropped with high yielding varieties which became instantly popular, covering about 30 per cent of the area. It is however in the area of wheat cultivation that the most spectacular results could be seen. Tribal peasants have taken to double and, in some cases, even triple cropping instead of the traditional mono cropping, and the area under both is progressively being extended. This would not have been possible without the reorientation of irrigation policies. The emphasis has shifted from the construction of weirs and large irrigation works to the exploitation of underground and surface water resources through a chain of intake wells constructed in river beds, big dia-wells, a few of which were energised with pumps in rivulets and streams. As the tribal economy is starved of credit because of the legislative restriction on the transfer of land, a major innovation has been the arrangement for easy flow of credit from co-operative institutions and banks on furnishing personal or collective security by tribal farmers, thus reducing their dependence on moneylenders. Tribals have always been responsive to the programmes concerning rearing of pigs, ducks and goats; and aided by subsidies this programme has become very popular, enabling a tribal family to earn an additional yearly income of Rs 2,500 to Rs 4,000. An evaluation of the impact of this intensive programme of development suggests (i) that the traditional lean and hunger period has been shortened; (ii) that surpluses which have emerged are being used for creating productive assets, or meeting higher consumption requirements; and (iii) that there has been visible affluence among a few middle-level tribal peasants who have benefited most from the development process.

The other project, the Indo-German Project, smaller in size, was started in April 1979. It covers 709 families in the Simadega block. They mostly belong to the primitive Kharia tribe. The project has spent Rs 40 lakh, which works out to a per capita investment of Rs 4,000, making it an essentially capital-intensive project. It introduced the new agriculture strategy, supported by a vigorous irrigation programme. Like the TDA, it constructed big dia-wells (160) and set up lift irrigation schemes (4); there were also mobile pumping sets. Altogether, they irrigated 700 hectares owned by tribal families. Thus mono crop areas were brought under double (525 ha) and triple cropping (100 ha), accounting for a total production of 26,400 quintals. The average family income has thus gone up. They have used the increased income to buy land and fancy goods, repay debt, acquire assets, etc. There is no starvation. Out-migration has stopped.

There are many such success stories, which suggests that the first "green revolution" has spread to the backward tribal tracts and created pockets of affluence. The technology of the second green revolution in pulses and seeds, maize and minor millets has been developed and is being introduced. The plateau regions of Orissa have reported a substantial rise in the yield of these crops benefiting tribals. The small peasant sector in tribal areas has become dynamic, as part of the overall process of the transformation of rural society.

As a result of the introduction of the new agricultural technology, and methods of farming suited to the north-eastern region, foodgrain production rose by 16 per cent between 1972–73 and 1977–78; the area under various crops increased during the same period from 30.88 lakh hectares to 31.39 lakh hectares, while the average production rose to 1,130 kg from 989 kg in 1972–73, an increase of 14 per cent. Manipur reported the highest yield (1.626 kg per hectare), while the corresponding figures for Meghalaya and Tripura were 1,152 kg and 1,224 kg respectively. For the country as a whole, about 7.44 lakh acres of tribal land was brought under various improved agricultural techniques in all eight tribal development agencies. The other dimensions of the agricultural strategy for the tribals who subsisted on agriculture and forest produce comprised (a) allotment of land for cultivation (18,253 acres), (b) land-development and soil-conservation programmes (23,531 acres), (c) extension of minor irrigation

(60,000 acres) through wells (5,600), (d) construction of tanks, roads and arterial loads and (e) distribution of plough bullocks (12,800 pairs) and saplings and grafts (7.3 lakh). Around 71 per cent of the targeted beneficiaries (3.36 lakh) have benefited from these programmes. In fact, the entire thrust of the programme appears to be to peasantise the tribals, draw them closer within the network of the new agricultural policy and programme, to improve productivity of land, bridge the food gap, increase earnings from land etc. Financing of the Scheduled Tribes/Castes by the commercial banks as on 31 December 1978 was of the order of Rs 36.78 crore. The inflow of institutional finance explains the success of the new agricultural strategy in the tribal areas. A critical study of the physical achievements of their programmes during the Fifth Five Year Plan shows that notwithstanding a wide range of variations in performance, the programmes have succeeded in achieving their objectives, though in a limited way.[20] Yet tribals' transition to the peasant system is not yet complete, their dependence on the forest as a source of food and earnings is in many ways as crucial as their dependence on land.

Tribal areas in middle India have witnessed a rapid growth of urban population and industrialisation. An immediate result of this has been the immigration into tribal areas of non-tribals in search of a job. In Chotanagpur the level of immigration jumped from 4,80,000 in 1951 to 10,73,920 in 1961 and to 14,29,803 in 1971. The demographic pattern has thus been disturbed and tribal population is declining. Another result has been the displacement of tribals from lands which have been acquired for setting up industries and constructing projects. In the early phase of industrialisation the tribals were given handsome compensation for land which they did not know how to use. They became nomads. The danger of displacement still haunts them. The strategy of relief and rehabilitation therefore will have to be reoriented with the objective of recreating community settlement in an appropriate environment. This means that some land will have to be given for the land to be acquired, and displaced persons will have to be assured of opportunities for employment or self-employment. Absorption into industrial culture of the indigenous people through training and education should be part of an industrial project, and a charge on it, as has been the experience of socialist countries. This is all the more necessary because there has been a steep decline of village industries and traditional crafts.[21]

SOCIAL STRATIFICATION

The political and economic processes of tribal transformation described above have been reflected in social stratification. There always existed within a tribe a measure of distinction between the high and the low in terms of social and physical distance, notion of purity and pollution, prestige and status, habits and customs, etc. The colonial system created and strengthened a threefold division with the feudatory chief zamindars at the top, the well-to-do headmen in the middle and the general mass at the bottom. As mentioned earlier, a class of insider *diku* and professional tribal moneylender also grew up as the unintended result of the anti-land alienation laws, which restricted transfer from tribals to non-tribals. A rich stratum of tribal buyers of land emerged as suggested by the data on transactions in land and moneylending in the district settlement reports.[22]

This process has developed further in the post-colonial phase. The 1961 Census Reports suggest a three-tier pattern of landholding in tribal society.[23] In a perceptive analysis of emerging stratification in tribal Gujarat, Bose identifies four distinct classes of peasants among tribals: rich peasant, middle peasant, poor peasant, and agricultural labourer.

> In no region has a single tribe solely occupied a particular class position; but they are generally distributed among all the four classes. However, some tribes are in better position than the others. For instance, in Vadodara, none of the Nayakas are rich peasants, 30.3 per cent of them are labours and 54.5 per cent are poor peasants, while all the rich peasants in this district belong to the Bhil tribe. But, from the same tribe we find 35.4 per cent are middle peasants and 1.6 per cent are rich peasant, and 10.5 per cent are agricultural labourers. Again, in Sabarkantha in which 97 per cent of the district tribal population belong to Bhil tribe, we find that 11.6 per cent are agricultural labourers, 65.1 per cent are poor peasant, 21.7 per cent are middle peasant and 1.6 per cent are rich peasants. A similar pattern has also been observed in the other districts.
>
> At the bottom of the stratificatory system are the tribal agricultural labourers. A majority of agricultural labourers are landless, a few of them have less than one acre of land of poor quality which virtually means having no land at all and like landless labourers they also live by selling their labour power.[24]

In a restudy of the Chodhras, a Gujarat tribe again, Shah tells us about the emerging differentiation based on land ownership and education which reflect in political attitudes and behaviour.

> The rich Chaudhris identify their interests with those of the non-tribal rich farmers. In fact, some of them supported the Khedut Samaj (rich peasant organisation) against paddy levy and land ceiling. Educated Chaudhri boys identify themselves with the urban middle-class boys. These attitudes reflected in the 1975 State Assembly elections to some extent. The majority of the poor peasants voted for the ruling Congress, believing that it was a party of the poor. The middle peasants got equally divided between the Congress and Janata Morcha, and the majority of the rich peasants voted for the Janata Morcha. Similarly most of the educated Chaudhris, like the urban and rural educated youths, voted against the ruling

> Congress on moral issues, considering the ruling party as corrupt. This division of votes strata wise in the tribal society also reflects the general voting pattern among the caste Hindus in South Gujarat. Thus, in perception, behaviour and life style, members of the different strata among the Chaudhris in general and educated and rich peasants in particular are becoming part of the larger society, joining hands with the similar secular strata outside the tribal society. Such process, on the one hand, disintegrates the tribal society in terms of its culture-customs, rituals, life style and economic interests and integrates some of its sections with the larger society, on the other.[25]

Mishra reports a similar process from the north-east:

> The special division of labour between tribes and the subjugation of one by the other having performed its historic role lapses into oblivion and a new phase of social karyokinesis within the members of a single tribe comes into existence. In some place, as in the Khasi hills, where private property in land is well developed, the division of labour takes a new shape. Here the first group of citizens discriminates against the second, the second against the third, and all discriminate jointly against the rest. In addition to this the law of female ultimogeniture in matters of inheritance has a built-intendency to create both propertied as also dispossessed sections of society. And it is through the forces operating in this endogenous process that the landlord, tenant and labourer come into being to perform their roles as assigned by the great social division of labour.[26]

However, it should be noted in evaluating the findings of these studies that there are also contrary pulls in the opposite direction. The bonds of ethnicity and the appreciation of the political advantages of the tribe as an ethnic minority are still strong. This has inhibited the development of tribals with non-tribals. An interesting example of intra-tribal contradictions which are overshadowed by stratification is the developing nexus between the "insider and outsider."[27] *Diku*, the alien, a creature of the colonial system, acted as the middleman, trader and moneylender. While the protective tenancy laws sought to curb this class, they had the unintended result of spawning a class of tribal moneylenders or the insider *diku*. Recent settlement operations in Chotanagpur have revealed extensive transaction in land between tribals and tribals. This process operates in the North-East also where the business and trading communities across the Inner Line have maintained close relations with their tribal agents. Therefore, it appears that no matter how strong the sentiments against these aliens in the North-East and elsewhere may be, they are far too deeply entrenched in the economic system of the region to be expelled. Their ouster will mean the collapse of the market with which the tribal economy is being increasingly linked. Even the most primitive economic system of the Cholanaickans has been drawn into the vortex of market forces.

Notes and References

[1] S. C. Dube (ed.), *Tribal Heritage of India, Volume 1: Ethnicity, Identity and Interaction* (Delhi: Vikas Publishing House, 1977).

[2] Surajit Sinha, "Transformation of Tribal Society in Modern India," Fifth Devraj Chanana Memorial Lecture, 1973 (unpublished).

[3] K. S. Singh,"Colonial Transformation of the Tribal Society in Middle India," Presidential Address, Bhubaneswar, 1977. Also see R. S. Sharma, *Indian Feudalism: c. 300–1200* (Calcutta: University of Calcutta, 1965).

[4] *Ibid.*

[5] A. B. Bardhan, *The Unsolved Tribal Problem*, Freedom Jubilee Series No. 5 (n.p.: Communist Party Publication, 1973). Also see, Sharit Bhowmik, *Class Formation in the Plantation System* (New Delhi: People's Publishing House, 1981).

[6] G. S. Ghurye, *The Burning Cauldron of North-East India* (Bombay: Popular Prakashan, 1980). Also see G. S. Ghurye, *The Scheduled Tribes* (Bombay: Popular Prakashan, 1963).

[7] "Red Indians Fight for the Right to Live on the Land of Ancestors," *The Searchlight*, 15 September 1981.

[8] See Lee Swepston, "Latin American Approaches to the 'Indian Problem,'" *International Labour Review* 117, no. 2 (March–April 1978).

[9] See Sunanda K. Datta-Ray, "New Dreams for Old," *The Statesman*, 1 and 2 December 1981. Also see Rupa Chinai, "The Alienated Aborigines," *Sunday Standard* magazine, 8 March 1981.

[10] I. H. Kāwharu, I. M. McEwen and W. Winiate, "Maori Incorporations in New Zealand," New Zealand National Commission for UNESCO (unpublished).

[11] "National Relations in the USSR: Theory and Practice, Problems of the Contemporary World," *Social Sciences Today*, Editorial Board (Moscow: USSR Academy of Sciences, 1974). Also see, Yu V. Bromley, "Soviet Ethnography: Main Trends, Problems of the Contemporary World," *Social Sciences Today*, Editorial Board (Moscow: USSR Academy of Sciences, 1978).

[12] Quoted in R. N. Ismagileva, *Ethnic Problems of the Tropical Africa: Can They Be Solved?* (Moscow: Progress Publishers, 1978), p. 122.

[13] Ibid., p. 126.

[14] Ibid.

[15] K. S. Singh, "Colonial Transformation of the Tribal Society."

[16] K. S. Singh, "The Mahatma and the Adivasis," *Man in India* 50, no. 1 (January–March 1970).

[17] Quoted in K. S. Singh, "Colonialism, Anthropology and Primitive Society: The Indian Scenario (1928–47)," Second Indo-GDR History Seminar, University of Delhi, December 1981.

[18] Quoted in K. S. Singh, "Jawaharlal Nehru: Tribals and Their Transformation," Seminar on Nehru and Village, Madras, 22–27 February 1980.

[19] Steve Jones, "Tribal Underdevelopment in India"(paper presented to UN Institute for Economic Planning and Development, Environment Training Programme, Seminar on Environment and Poorly Integrated Societies in Africa, Mauritius, April 1976). Also see a rejoinder by Bhupender Singh, *Planning Strategy for Tribal Development in Retrospect: A Mid-Term Appraisal*, Occasional Papers on Tribal Development 29 (New Delhi: Ministry of Home Affairs, 1981).

[20] K. S. Singh, "Tribal Economy in India," Indo-Soviet Symposium in Social Sciences, 22–26 February 1977, Visva-Bharati, Santiniketan. Also see, by the same author, "Transformation of Tribal Economy: Two Case Studies" (unpublished, 1978) and "Pattern of Agricultural Changes in Tribal Chotanagpur," in *Trends of Socio-economic Change in India: 1871–1961*, ed.

M. K. Chaudhuri, Transactions of the Indian Institute of Advanced Study 7 (Simla: Indian Institute of Advanced Study, 1969).

[21] N. Prasad and A. Sahay, "Impact of Industrialisation on Bihar Tribes" 1961: Census of India, 1961, "Social processes in the Industrialisation of Rourkela" 1908: L. P. Vidyarthi, "Industrialisation in India: A Case Study of Tribal Bihar, 1970." Also see Pradhan, H. Prasad and N. Sengupta, "Regional Distribution of Economic Benefits Arising from a Steel Plant: A Case Study of Rourkela Steel Plant" (mimeographed).

[22] K. S. Singh, "Colonial Transformation of the Tribal Society."

[23] "Land Tenures in India," Census of India 1961, vol. 1, India, Part XI-A (i) (1968).

[24] Pradip Kumar Bose, "Stratification among Tribals in Gujarat," *Economic and Political Weekly* 16, no. 6 (7 February 1981): pp. 191–96.

[25] Ghanshyam Shah, "Socio-Economic Condition of Chodhras: A Restudy," Centre for Social Studies, Surat, Indian Council of Social Science Research (unpublished).

[26] Rani Prasanna Misra, "Kirata Karyokinesis: Modes of Production in Tribal Societies in North-East India," in *Agrarian Relations in India*, ed. Arvind N. Das and V. Nilkant (Delhi: Manohar, 1979).

[27] K. S. Singh, "Tribal Ethnicity in a Multi-Ethnic Society: A Study in Colonial and Post-Colonial Chotanagpur," UNESCO Seminar on Trends in Ethnic Group Relations in Asia, Manila, March 1976.

14

A "Harijan Elite"?

The Lives of Some Untouchable Politicians*

Oliver Mendelsohn

The system of reservation now threatens to become a major source of social division in India.[1] Extension of reserved seats in educational institutions and public employment to the "other backwards" has occasioned violent conflict in a number of states, most disastrously in Gujarat. The high castes are outraged that their usually modest and highly contingent life-chances are snuffed out by populist programmes of reverse discrimination.

The current furore over reservation for the other backwards (the term comes from Article 16(4) of the Constitution) contrasts with the generally uncontroversial system of reservation for untouchables and tribals—the Scheduled Castes and Tribes (SC/ST)—which has been in place throughout the post-Independence period.[2] That system is more beneficial to its clientele than the recent reservation for backwards, since it includes the provision of reserved seats in the national and state legislative bodies. The guarantee of parliamentary seats in proportion to their population was designed to give the scheduled communities a broad political advantage in addition to their particular preferment in education and public employment. Why, then, has such a vast system of reverse discrimination been so relatively uncontroversial?

The answer to this question is no doubt complex and must take account of M. K. Gandhi's achievement in creating and sustaining the Harijan question over the quarter century prior to Independence. It was largely Gandhi's championing of the Harijan question that enabled the scheme of reservation

* Originally published in *Economic and Political Weekly* 21, no. 12 (22 March 1986): pp. 501–9.

to be given the force of a Constitutional mandate and removed it from the potential realm of high controversy. But these and other relevant considerations aside, the overwhelming reason for the still relatively uncontroversial reservation for untouchables and tribals is its ineffectiveness over almost 40 years of practice. In a word, reservation has failed to alter the relative prosperity between high or middle castes and untouchables or tribals. In this (though perhaps not in a more limited) sense reservation is a failure and has therefore not engendered the resentment that a more successful scheme would have.

This is not a chapter about the general progress of reservation for the SCs, so we can be content to document the sweeping observation above by citing only a few statistics. The most convenient are some figures calculated on the basis of the 32nd round of the National Sample Survey Organisation (NSSO) of 1977–78, which was the first of the NSSO surveys to separate out SCs and STs.[3] For the purpose of the exercise the poverty line was drawn at the figure of Rs 65 per capita per month in the rural areas and Rs 75 in urban areas. Of Indians who fell beneath this poverty line, 18.11 per cent were SC and 9.66 per cent ST persons. So 27.7 per cent of the poor were SCs and tribes, whereas their share of the Indian population was 21.57 per cent. But once the poverty figure is divided in half, a more dramatic picture emerges. Fully 40.60 per cent of Indians living on less than half the poverty figure are from the scheduled communities. In other words, the lower you draw your poverty line the greater the proportion of scheduled persons you will net. This, after almost 40 years of reservation.

If reservation has been quite unequal to the task of combating poverty among the scheduled communities, it is still open to perception as having had useful marginal effects on mass poverty and also as having created a group which is either actually or potentially useful in leadership roles within the communities. It is the latter question which will preoccupy us in this chapter. More specifically, we are interested in the so-called "Harijan elite." The material for this discussion comes exclusively from interviews with representatives of one branch of the presumptive elite, occupants of reserved seats in the national and state legislatures. The interviews were conducted with 20 members of the Lok Sabha and Rajya Sabha drawn from different parts of the country and with 12 MLAs from Bihar alone. The conversations took place in the period December to February 1982–83, in Delhi and Patna.

This limited study of the so-called Harijan elite arises from a more general study of the political economy of untouchables, but the question of the elite has considerable relevance to contemporary agitational politics in various parts of India. For, while we have said that reservation for the scheduled groups has been comparatively uncontroversial, it has not been entirely free of active resentment or resistance. In the Gujarat agitation and riots of 1980 and 1985 the target of high caste communalism has spilled over from the backwards to the SCs.

Both here and in other states too—Bihar, for example—admission policies in medical faculties have been a potent source of discontent. The grievance is with a system that in effect discounts the marks of high caste students in favour of less accomplished SC applicants. It seems to be the case that wherever quotas in highly prized faculties or grades of public service are taken up in considerable number by SC candidates, a strong adverse reaction can be predicted from among those who believe they are disadvantaged by the existence of such quotas. These agitations have as yet not been an important dimension of Indian politics since the cause has been minor—particularly in the higher grades of public service, the number of SC and ST persons falls far below the specified quota. But as the group of preferred professionals from these communities grows over the years and as the quotas are progressively taken up, presumably the counter-agitation will become more virulent.

My object in talking to SC MPs and MLAs was modest—essentially to see just what kind of people were being picked up and run by political parties in reserved constituencies. I was not primarily interested in them as politicians but rather as untouchables who had emerged from the impoverished background typical of their communities. Did they, for example, conform to the character depicted by Sachchidananda in *The Harijan Elite*?[4] Sachchidananda and his researchers had talked to legislators, public servants and social workers and concluded that,

> large numbers of educated Harijan elite both in the towns and in the villages have little active concern with bettering the lot of their less fortunate caste fellows. They overload political processes with petty local issues. Alienated from their own base, they have betrayed an incapacity to apply themselves to the tasks of reshaping the larger society into egalitarian structures. Their major preoccupation appears to be that of meeting the needs of the immediate family and kin. Some of the elite who have risen high in the social hierarchy have snapped their ties with their bleak past. They are largely out of tune from the mass of the community and seek a realignment with status and power groups in the wider society.

An accurate and appropriate account of the "Harijan elite" is important precisely because this group is generally the creation of the reservation system. If Sachchidananda is right, then reservation has failed not only on the general economic level but also in spawning a privileged group selfishly devoted to its own petty advancement and uncaring about the wider untouchable community. So it has failed the untouchables as well as stirring the resentment of non-untouchables.

Sachchidananda's account of the beneficiaries of reservation is not an isolated one and it should be borne in mind as we rehearse some biographial material on SC politicians. We will return to this point of view towards the end of the chapter.

BIOGRAPHICAL MATERIAL

Perhaps the most general finding to emerge from this study is that it is almost impossible for an untouchable to rise in a single generation from the ordinary condition of his people to men (very occasionally women) of Parliament. The biographies I collected reveal that no more than one or two men have risen without an older member of the nuclear or extended family having made a break from the condition of landless labour which typifies traditional untouchable poverty. (I was not able to interview any of the few women in the national Parliament; there were none in the Bihar Assembly.) Characteristically, the untouchable Member of Parliament has built on the financial and perhaps educational efforts of the previous generation, usually the father. In a very high proportion of cases, a modest piece of land acquired by the father has been the basis of the next generation's being able to produce a politician. The following is a simple example of this.

Extended Case 1: Narsing Murty,[5] Member of Lok Sabha

Narsing Murty is MP for a constituency in Karnataka and is Mang by caste.

Narsing Murty has ridden to Delhi on the back of a cow. The story goes like this. NM was one of four brothers and two sisters, the children of agricultural labourers (both father and mother). But the father was of enterprising spirit and managed to save to buy a cow for a modest sum. Now, *mirabiledictu*, this cow turned out to be a prize cow. Every year for some nine years the cow threw a beautiful calf, which was sold on the market for between 500 and 700 rupees.

NM is the eldest son of the family and until the age of 11, it was his duty to mind the prize cow. By then, the cow had made the family sufficiently prosperous to allow the contemplation of education for NM. He says that among the dominant Lingayats and Marathas in his village there were a number of "socialist minded" people who had been busy persuading his father that it would be beneficial to send NM to school. So from the age of 11 he was released from his cow minding and began schooling. Another son, of course, was detailed to the cow. At about this time NM's father determined to buy some land with savings accumulated from the earnings of the cow. He bought 11 acres of land from a Lingayat Deshmukh, paying 1,500 rupees for the land in 1956. For the next ten years the father remained at least a part-time agricultural labourer, since he initially had no capital with which to work the land. He started out hiring oxen from a neighbour in return for a one-quarter share of the crop grown in his fields. In those days there were no agricultural banks in the area.

The family of NM had by this time become the most prosperous of the 40 Mang families in the village. (There were also about 30 Mahar and 10–15 Chamar households in the village.) NM attributes this to the imagination of his father in buying the cow and being prepared to countenance education for his children. The greatness of the Mother Cow deserves mention too!

The remainder of NM's career to date is the usual hard slog, aided by reserved places in schools and hostels, a modest government scholarship, and the continuing help of the family. As to the latter, NM was able during his high school day, to bring grain from his father's land to his temporary home with a sister in the nearby town. So the land was a crucial base to allow him to study for years on end: he was for many years a drain, rather than a supplier of family income. Indeed, it is only since his election to the Lok Sabha in 1980 that he has earned an income.

NM completed a BSc but from the beginning was more interested in politics than science. From his second year of the degree he took an active interest in Sanjay Gandhi's Youth Congress. When he graduated in 1974 he became a full-time "social worker." He spent his time in the Harijan colony of the village, advising on approaches to government and on education. By this time a younger brother was engaged full-time in agriculture, and none of the family now hired themselves out as agricultural labourers.

For six years he was a full-time social worker, all the time willingly supported by the family. Among his accomplishments was the establishment of a Harijan hostel in the town where he had been educated. He became associated with Sanjay Gandhi's anti-dowry movement in 1975–76, and clearly Sanjay remains an important inspiration in his life. They did not meet, however, until after NM became an MP in 1980. NM got the Congress ticket simply by application through the mail, he says. He had no patron and made no trips to Delhi, Bangalore or anywhere else. It was his reputation as an earnest worker which secured him the ticket, he says.

As yet, NM has not sought to make his mark in the Lok Sabha. He sees himself as a party man, leaving New Delhi politics to the more experienced. He does not see himself solely, perhaps even primarily, as a Harijan leader. Rather, he sees himself simply as a young Indian leader.

NM's father and mother are still working in the fields that the cow bought. With the exception of the eldest daughter, all the children have now been educated. They attained various levels, one brother becoming a BA graduate. NM married in 1979. His wife is an orphan, a category he deliberately chose in the light of his involvement in the anti-dowry movement. He says that he was in considerable demand as a prospective son-in-law but was determined to live up to his principles. The wife has been educated up to university level, and the couple now have a son.

Comment: No life story is typical, but this one seems representative of the early career of an untouchable politician in the present period. What singled NM out from the rest of his untouchable brothers in the village and the wider district was the start that his father made. NM's achievements are those of two generations, and they are crucially bound up with creating a cash flow (the cow) and the later purchase of agricultural land. Once NM had the backing to go to school, he was borne along by the reserved places available to him. And, of course, he gained his parliamentary seat by being a plausible SC man to run as candidate in a reserved seat. But surely what stands out most clearly about Narsing Murty's story is the fineness of the line that stood between himself and the other untouchable boys in his village.

It may be objected that Narsing Murty's story is all too neat and that the usual background of a SC MP cannot be so clear-cut and dramatic. True, I found no other case where a four-legged beast made seemingly all the difference between living out a life as an agricultural labourer and rubbing shoulders with the great as an MP in New Delhi. But what is common between this story and many of the others is the painfully small income which gives that crucial "lift" to the untouchable boy. The sources of that income are various: in two cases the family "fortune" derived from a hereditary family occupation as priest to families deprived of Brahmanical rites by their untouchability. In one of these cases the father of the MP was an ayurvedic doctor as well as priest. In both cases the income derived from their services had been in part ploughed back into land, which of course in turn generated income. In a third case the father of an MP was described by him as a "quack"—indeed the grandfather before him had been this too—and the family's better than normal financial position had derived from the sale of medicines. In this case the family had not been able to buy land.

More frequent cases are where a more-or-less steady income has flowed into the family through shoe making/selling/repairing in the case of Chamars, clothes washing by dhobis in a city like Calcutta, or rickshaw pulling (in this case by the brother of a Musahar MLA and Minister in Bihar). A toddy-selling business established by a Pasi family was the origin of another MLA's career in Bihar. In most of these cases the family managed to acquire a little land along the way, and this tended to underpin the break from abject poverty.

In contrast to all cases discussed thus far, I encountered only one case of someone who rose in a single generation from a landless labouring family, without income of any kind—still the most common situation of untouchable families throughout India—to the position of parliamentarian, in this case an MLA in Bihar. The case is so singular that it merits a closer look.

Extended Case Study 2: Rameshwar Manji,* (Almost) Perfectly Self-Made Man

Rameshwar was born in October 1945. When I asked how he was so sure of this, since rural people do not usually know their exact age, he explained: there was a great flood in 1946 and his father tied him up in a dhoti and hung him on a peg so he wouldn't drown. This was about a year after his birth, which can therefore be dated.

RM is from a village in Gaya district and is from the lowliest of untouchable castes in Bihar, the Musahars. These people are chiefly associated in the public mind with rat catching—Musahars traditionally dig out from burrows and eat field rats. This represents an apparently useful source of protein, perhaps even a delicacy. But it also sets the caste off from others, who tend to look down on the humble rat catchers.

RM comes from a village of some 40 households. Eight are Bhumihar houses; 25 Yadav; three Musahar; a couple of Dusadh; and one Brahmin. The Bhumihars have three-quarters of the land, while the Yadavs are small peasants with very little land. The Musahars and Dusadhs have no land at all.

Rameshwar is fully aware of the freakish quality of his life story, and he tells it well. From a beginning that was characteristically inauspicious for a Musahar, he and his brother have emerged into some considerable prosperity. His brother is of Police Inspector rank and is currently in charge of a police station. His two sisters, by contrast, are married to agricultural labourers.

RM's mother and father were ordinary labourers and from the age of five he himself was employed as tender of animals for the large Bhumihar family to which his father was attached (bonded) as labourer. This family retained a tutor for the children's education, since there was no school in the village at that time. One day, after he had finished his work, Rameshwar sat down outside the circle of the children being taught and listened in. This became something of a habit with him and RM notes that on one occasion he intervened to give a right answer to a question wrongly answered by one of the Bhumihar boys (for which error the latter was soundly beaten by the tutor).

The tutor, a Kayasth by caste, used to take toddy in the company of RM's father at the village toddy shop. In the course of conversation one day, the tutor talked of RM's interest in learning and suggested that he be formally schooled. The father thought this over for some time and decided there would be no harm in approaching his Bhumihar masters to ask their permission for his son to join the tutor's circle after he had finished his daily chores. He was wrong. When he asked his master, the response was a sound beating for the insolence of having stepped thoroughly out of line. Education was no business of a Musahar. One of the Bhumihar brothers was of more humane disposition, however, and eventually the request was acceded to. RM was issued with a slate and chalk and allowed to join the circle—after he had finished his daily job, of course. This continued for a number of years and up to the equivalent of seventh class he had not studied in school at all. To this day he bears the mark of the tutor's deficiencies—the tutor knew no maths but was strong in literature. By the time Rameshwar got to a formal school there was only one year of compulsory maths left, so he didn't bother.

His job was very onerous. There were 14 or 15 oxen and several cows and buffaloes to mind, since the family's spread was 100 bighas or so. RM's father was much impressed with his son's faithful application to learning and eventually decided that the boy should be released from most of his duties and sent to school. So he began regular school, walking four miles, morning and afternoon. He was given a government scholarship of 10 rupees a month, and this was of great assistance. He duly passed his matriculation at this school and he then entered an intermediate college in Gaya, 25 miles from his village. He was able to stay at a very good Harijan hostel which was built shortly after he arrived there. The government scholarship had risen to Rs 50 a month, and some of this he sent home so that his brother could go to school. He also undertook some tuition in order to augment his income. In 1967 he passed his BA and went on to Magadh University to enrol for MA.

Several circumstances conspired to prevent his completing the MA. Bihar underwent a severe drought in 1967 and his mother and father were in grave difficulties in the village. Also, he had been married at age 11 and had begun to live with his wife from the age of 13. Inevitably, children had arrived; one in 1962, another in 1965 and a third in 1967. He amusedly notes that these arrivals coincided with his gaining his matriculation intermediate pass, and then his BA. The final factor was his realisation that his parents would not be able to work much longer even after the drought was over—they were growing old and tired.

So in 1967 Rameshwar took a job as a clerk in the Post and Telegraph Department. He gained the job on merit, though it was also within the reservation quota. He occupied the job until his resignation on election to the Assembly in 1980. From the beginning he had it in mind to enter politics but knew he could only do this once his brother had been educated and gained a job.

He got the Congress ticket in 1980 after travelling to Delhi and contacting the "high command" of the party. He pointed out to them that there was no Musahar representative from Gaya district, a district with a vast Musahar population.

Comment: This life history is unique among those I collected, in that Rameshwar had none but a bit of ordinary decency to help him on his way. In the other cases I encountered the legislator had derived a major aid from someone else, usually a previous generation within the family. Rameshwar did it all by himself. He cannot explain why he had such a great interest in education. It was just something in him. He was a freak.

Representation of Different Scheduled Castes

If we go beyond the uniqueness of Rameshwar's case, the fact of his particular caste might have given us a clue that his base was likely to be weaker than that of many other SC politicians. The Musahars (the name is used to include Bhuinyas) are by common consent the poorest of the major untouchable castes in Bihar and, presumably, the number of Musahars who are well off by general Indian standards must bevery low. I interviewed only one of the other five Musahars who were MLAs at the time, this one being a minister. The economic condition of his father's family was weaker than in most of the cases that came to my attention but somewhat more promising than that of Rameshwar Manji's father. There was a very small piece of land—about an acre between his father and two uncles—though in the grandfather's generation there seems to have been considerably more land that was somehow lost. And importantly, an elder brother was working as a rickshaw puller at the time when education became a possibility for the future Minister. And finally, his father had worked in the company of zamindars and had developed some mildly progressive attitudes towards education. This was the slender but crucial support for his education and advancement.

I was able to interview only one other politician from a particularly low caste, an MP from Uttar Pradesh who is Bhangi by caste. (The Bhangis are in ritual terms probably lower than the Musahars but economically they are now often better off.) His original circumstances did in fact turn out to be less favourable than many (though by no means all) of the interviewees. What distinguished the family from other Bhangis was that his father had managed to become a farm manager for a zamindar in the pre-Independence period—he was said to be earning seven rupees a day by 1947, clearly a far greater return than could be gained from sweeping (which his wife was doing at the same time). An older brother of the MP turned out to be a better than usual keeper of pigs—they kept between 20 and 30 pigs at any one time. So this income flow was able to underpin a consciousness about education that was fed by stories from uncles who were in the service of the British as sweepers in various parts of the country. In short, our MP undertook education and after a long journey through service to various embassies in New Delhi, he became a politician.

The limited sample that forms the basis of this study (and that was determined by the availability of interviewees during a three months' period) does not permit of firm conclusions on the comparative representation of the various SCs and the prosperity of individual members from the different castes. But it may turn out, for example, that the more prosperous castes have a disproportionate share of reserved seats and that the individual members tend to be wealthier than those drawn from castes lower in the hierarchy. Certainly the Bihar figures show a somewhat skewed pattern of seats relative to caste populations. Castes with a total of 10 per cent of the SC population (1971 figures) did not have a representative in the Bihar Legislative Assembly. These castes include some with quite large numbers, particularly the Dom with 1,43,144 persons and the Hari, Mehtaror Bhangi with 80,731 persons. These two groupings contain most of the Biharis traditionally engaged in sweeping and scavenging, which is particularly unclean work in the ritual hierarchy. But not too much need be made of this, since the ratio of reserved seats to population works out roughly at one to 1,55,000—slightly more than the Doms, though substantially less than the two groupings put together. And it is true that there was a Mehtar MP from Bihar at the time. Moreover, a Dom was elected (I am informed for the first time ever) to the Bihar Assembly in the 1985 election. At the same time, it would give no surprise to find a consistent all-Indian pattern of under-representation for these particularly depressed communities.

The Bihar figures do show a marked over-representation of two SCs, the Dusadhs and the Pasis. The Dusadhs are the second largest SC in Bihar, with 19,90,273 persons in 1971. This was less than 27 per cent of the SC population but their share of reserved seats was over 37 per cent—their numbers would "entitle" them to 13 seats, whereas there were 18 Dusadh members. The Pasis had 3.8 per cent of the population but 6.25 per cent of seats (3). Conversely, the third largest caste—the Musahars (including the Bhuinyas)—had 21 per cent of the population but less than 15 per cent of reserved seats—8 seats, whereas their "entitlement" would have been 10. In the case of the largest caste, the Chamars, the correspondence between population and reserved seats was almost perfect—30.5 per cent population and 31.25 per cent seats, 15 in number. Now, the sample is small and we have no time-series data but the above figures seem intuitively understandable. The Dusadhs are socially the most prominent SC in Bihar—the Rajputs of the SCs—though it is not clear whether they are much better off economically than their great rival, the Chamars. Given their characteristic boldness, it does not seem surprising that they would manage to get a disproportionate share of reserved seats. As to the Pasis, their traditional occupation of toddy tapping has sometimes given them a stronger cash flow than many SC people enjoy and the caste also has a better record in education than the other communities. By contrast, we have already noted that the Musahars (including the Bhuinyas) are by far the poorest of the three major SCs. Accordingly, their under-representation is perhaps not unexpected.

In short, the Bihari figures give some support to the notion that the richer and socially more prominent SCs have gained a disproportionate share of seats reserved for SCs. But obviously comparable data would need to be collected for other regions and over time for us to be sure that this was a pattern general throughout India. If it were the case, the phenomenon might be largely attributable to attitudes among political party leaders. Thus a former Chief Minister, Jagannath Mishra, noted that the Congress party selects candidates for reserved seats largely on the basis of two criteria—level of education and reputation in the area.[6] If the educated figures are more heavily concentrated in particular communities, then it is perhaps likely that these communities will come to be over-represented. But there is no doubt a limit to how far this will proceed—an effort is probably made by party leaders to provide some representation to SCs with a significant population.

Question of Education

What emerges from all the individual cases discussed above and indeed almost all the cases I collected is the role of education in the career of SC politicians. Of the 32 men interviewed, only three had not attended college, and one of these had undertaken a four-year technical course after finishing his schooling. A few of the others did not last long enough to get a BA but a large number have Master's degrees and law degrees. These figures confirm the general impression gained from talking to untouchables in various states of India to the effect that education is seen as an indispensable ladder on which to climb out of agrarian servitude. There is, of course, no uniqueness to this taste for education, which is spread throughout the various agricultural communities which were once marked by their almost total illiteracy.

This is not the place to explore our subjects' experience in educational institutions but it is worth saying that the experience may by unusually formative. The confidence and sense of personal power gained from education alongside high caste boys can be seen to induct untouchable boys into a different world, one where equality of opportunity is the formal ideology and even sometimes an approachable reality. The grosser practice of untouchability is no longer common in the education system, though eating in the hostel situation at school or college has provoked discrimination in the fairly recent past.[7] There is clearly a generational change. Thus, two of my older informants reported being punished as school children by the teacher throwing the punishing stick at them rather than risking pollution by being at the other end of a stick touching the flesh of an untouchable. But these experiences were up to 50 years ago—Jagjivan Ram's problems in the mess at Banaras Hindu University are still earlier—and there is no recent act so blatant as this. The overt and covert discrimination that still remains is no doubt a powerful disincentive to stay in the educational system—an economically weak base is still more of a disincentive—but none of the politicians interviewed in this study were at all deterred by their school or college experiences. Perhaps this is true almost by definition, since the subjects of my interviews were success stories.

There can be little doubt that the government programmes to encourage education among the SCs have contributed strongly to the emergence of many of the individuals interviewed in the present study. It is only in recent years that scholarship payments have been made at the primary and middle school levels, so we cannot directly attribute our subjects' basic education to "affirmative action" by government. But the scheme of payments to assist tertiary education of untouchables has been a key aspect of educational policy for most of the post-Independence era. Clearly many of our subjects would not have been able to undertake college education without such support. The political parties would still have had to field SC candidates in reserved seats, whatever their educational level. But that educational level would certainly be weaker than it is now. And the remoteness of higher education would have inhibited the broadening of the base of political recruitment among the untouchables.

As to the two politicians who did not undertake tertiary education, they had both made long careers in labour and social reform work. Naisinh Makwana, a Vankar or weaver by caste, left school after a series of fights with rich boys. He had only four years of schooling and at the ripe age of 9 or 10 became a bootblack in Ahmedabad, where his father had come to work in a textile mill several years previously. After about a year and a half he became a bearer in a hotel and finally a textile worker by the age of 15 or 16. What gradually followed was an interest in union affairs and in the Socialist party; he became a full-time union worker in 1954, 15 years after entering the mill. He contested a number of elections for the Socialist party and, after 1969, for Congress. In 1975 he won a seat in the Gujarat Assembly and in 1980 became an MP.

This career is very recognisable to a Western eye, since it parallels the career of a great many unionist/politicians. Like Makwana, the figures in the West have usually not been highly schooled in a formal way. But this figure is rare for India, with its small modern sector.

The second politician without a background in tertiary education is A. C. Das, who was at the time of interview Secretary of the Parliamentary Committee for the Welfare of Scheduled Castes and Tribes. On completing his school education he joined Vinoba Bhave's bhoodan movement and worked among tribals for 17 years. At one point he thought of going to college but Vinoba persuaded him that he was getting a better education through the life he was leading. It was only after leaving the movement in 1971 that he joined Congress and immediately got a ticket for a seat. He was successful at his first attempt and has been a professional politician since. Again, this figure stands out quite sharply from most of his fellow untouchable legislators through his long career in social reform. Many legislators claim to have been social workers prior to entering parliament, but for most this is a synonym for involvement in non-parliamentary party politics.

It is very common for SC parliamentarians to have first made their career in a reserved position in the public services. Such a position can be used to build up a financial case for their family and to make useful political contacts. Thus, Suraj Bhan told me that had his father and brother not died during his college years, he would have tried to enter politics immediately upon finishing college. But as it was, he served for 16 years in the Post and Telegraph Department before finally making the break and becoming an MP. Likewise, Rameshwar Manji (see above) worked in the same department but in another state for some 13 years before making his political move. But it is also now quite common for SC young men to set themselves for a political career as early as their college days—as Suraj Bhan did—and to go on and win a reserved seat without experience of any other job. Our cases are insufficient to point to any general trend in these career paths, though it may be the case that very early political career is becoming more common.

Three Men of the Older Generation

The general picture we have drawn thus far is of a group of politicians whose early years were far from comfortable. But if it is possible to find the rare case of Rameshwar Manji, the self-made man, on the other side can be found a considerably greater number of people whose circumstances were initially relatively affluent. We can begin with three veterans of SC politics. Two of them had promising beginnings and went on to personal prosperity as well as political success. The third had neither a promising beginning nor an affluent end—he is now dead—but represents a useful counterpoint to the others.

For many years the national symbol of Harijan success has been Jagjivan Ram, long-time Defence Minister and ultimately Deputy Prime Minister in the Janata regime. Jagjivan Babu's origins parallel those of a number of other untouchables in the later colonial period. His Bihari family had its horizons broadened through army service—his father and an uncle were both employed in a paramedical capacity in the Indian Army. A steady flow of income provided the young Jagjivan with a quite unique base in his area. The family bought land—they had 17 acres when his father died in Jagjivan's childhood—and conceived an interest in education. An elder brother became a compounder in the Calcutta Medical College and Jagjivan proceeded from village school right up to Banaras Hindu University. By the time he reached high school he was already the only Chamar boy in the school. What followed was an illustrious career built on his control of SC politics in Bihar. Obviously, Jagjivan Ram and his family are now prosperous by virtually any Indian standard.

The army connection also forms the background of the oldest and longest-serving parliamentarian in New Delhi—he is a Member of the Rajya

Sabha—Piare Lall Kureel. A great-grandfather inaugurated what became a family tradition of entering the army. What the army supplied, of course, was a perfectly secure income and therefore opportunity to acquire agricultural land, access to schooling and, importantly, an environment where caste and outcaste were concepts more remote than in the villages of India. Kureel worked closely with Ambedkar, whose career he also attributes in good part to the military background within that family. Like Kureel's father, Ambedkar's father was a Subedar Major. In the case of Kureel, generations of literacy and involvement in national institutions have culminated in the situation of his own children. One of his sons is an Indian Airlines pilot, another has an LLB, the third a BA. Two daughters are qualified doctors and the last two daughters are currently studying for a BSc, prior to undertaking graduate degrees in a technical area. Clearly the family is now well up with the middle-class standards of New Delhi, but equally Kureel's overall situation seems modest for someone so prominent in national affairs for more than 40 years. He complains of the hardships he is now facing in the matter of marrying his daughters.

But clearly Jagjivan Ram and Piare Lall Kureel had a more auspicious start to public life than did another of their contemporaries, Bhole Paswan Shastri. After J. Ram himself, Bhole Paswan had perhaps the most illustrious career of an untouchable politician in post-Independence India. He was three times Chief Minister of Bihar, though for very short periods—less than a year in total. He notes that he took his opportunities when the high caste men were disunited. Bhole Paswan's father had owned 15 or 16 bighas of land but fell into financial difficulties and finally lost the land in 1923/24, when Bhole Paswan was about 10. Thereafter, he was a sharecropper and labourer. All of his siblings died, as did his mother in 1926. But his mother had for some reason conceived of the idea that he be educated so that he would not have to work as his father had.

Bhole Paswan started his education in the village school and was awarded a free scholarship to high school. He was not able to take up this offer because he had no money for his living needs—the scholarship would not pay these. In the meantime, a nationalist school in his native Purnea district had been established in the name of Mahatma Gandhi. For four years he studied there, supported by the School Management Committee—his father was by then reduced to agricultural labourer and was unable to spare him anything. The rest of his educational career is intertwined with work in the nationalist movement and supported by progressive elements within that movement. He studied at a college in Banaras for four years—he was admitted to the institution in 1935 on the strength of an essay on football. He esteemed his teachers there as "very learned professors, good gentlemen" and by the end of the period felt that "I have learned something, I can fight, I can make my life. I had no inferiority complex now as a SC person. I was a free man!" As a free man he was gaoled by the British in the period 1942–44, which he says was later a qualification for ministerial office.

Bhole Paswan Shastri ended his political career in the Rajya Sabha and died in 1984. He had lived for years in a single room in a hostel in New Delhi, his reputation for uprightness and honesty unimpeached. Clearly he had not accumulated wealth and noted that although he had a good income there were always a lot of expenses, particularly at election time. His wife, to whom he was married as a child, lived almost all her life in her village with her brothers. Only for a short period when he was minister in Patna did she live with him. Although he did not tell it quite like this, clearly the gap in sophistication between the two was far too great to allow a normal married life. There were no children.

From the cases discussed earlier, it will be clear that Bhole Paswan's career is scarcely representative of untouchable politicians in general. There is far too much of the self-made man for that. But the example is instructive, particularly in juxtaposition to the case of Jagjivan Ram. The latter has been by far the most eminent of the post-Independence Harijan politicians but he has also been a figure who has persistently drawn fire for what are said to be his shortcomings: that he has attempted and accomplished little for his fellow untouchables and that he has been content to build up political power and money for selfish reasons. The present writer is in no position to assess these charges but it does seem that what has frequently entered into the adverse judgements is a set of standards more rigorous than those ordinarily applied to national politicians. Babuji is then condemned by reference to the standards and declared to be an arch member of the selfish "Harijan elite." But if we turn to Bhole Paswan Shastri, no such general judgement clouds this figure. He was far less eminent than Jagjivan Ram and therefore did not attract adverse attention. But there was also nothing in his life which could have led to scathing dismissal. His personal life appears to have been led with painful modesty and the obvious incompatibility in his married life was the heavy price he had to pay for his success. But he was clearly not alienated from his people in any meaningful sense. It was thoroughly clear that the problems of untouchables were at the core of this man's political preoccupations. Why must we assume, then, that the supposedly grossly flawed Jagjivan Ram is the archetype of the successful Harijan politician rather than the patently unsullied Bhole Paswan Shastri? The answer to this question may have more to do with preconceptions than with value-free facts. Bhole Paswan Shastri would perhaps be an uncomfortable model of the untouchable politician. Too good.

Another Prosperous Group

In this survey of our biographies we should finally turn to several men who are clearly among the better off in our sample. Two of those interviewed were from moderately prosperous business families which had developed their business in an urban setting. One such man is P. C. Sarkar, a CPI(M) Member of the Lok Sabha from Burdwan, West Bengal. Sarkar's caste is Sunri, which is a caste of brewers, agricultural labourers and small businessmen. Presumably it is the connection with brewing which makes the caste untouchable. His family is based in the town of Burdwan, from which the ancestral village is only some five miles distant. Apparently, among the 2,000-odd Sunri families in Burdwan town, Sarkar's family is the most prosperous. There are, however, a considerable number of other prosperous families. Literacy in Sarkar's family runs at least as far back as his grandfather. In the present generation, the family's fortune is tied up with the business concerns of Sarkar's brother, who possesses a range of distributorships; one of them is an Eveready Battery distributorship.

Untouchability appears not to have weighed so heavily in Bengal as it did further West, so the example of P. G. Sarkar as a member of a successful business family may not be so remarkable. Clearly more notable is the case of Mohan Ram. His family's fortune is based on his father having begun a charcoal business in Patna which eventually led to a multi-faceted business including bus lines, trucking and brick kilns. The father's business was initially based on supply of fuel to British officials in Patna, including the Governor of Bihar. Through the continuing efforts of the children and grandchildren of this enterprising Chamar (who was himself bolstered by his still more enterprising wife), a substantial family business has been created. The family's stature has led on to the acquisition of reserved positions in the public services and to the achievement of suitable matrimonial alliances. To give just one example, a daughter of Mohan Ram is married to a Deputy Superintendent of Police. Mohan Ram claims that at the time his father created his fuel business, there was no comparable untouchable businessman in the whole of Bihar. Whether or not this is strictly true, it is clear that Mohan Ram's family is quite distinctive in Patna. But what is not clear is the prosperity of the family relative to business families from caste Hindu or Muslim backgrounds. Mohan Ram pointed out to me that his house was modest by Patna standards, and it was. The overall feel of the household was comfortably middle-class, and no more than this. My guess is that there are many hundreds of businessmen in Bihar more wealthy than Mohan Ram, almost all of them from communities other than untouchables. And without doubt it is possible to find a great many men in national and provincial parliaments throughout India who are vastly more wealthy than this man.

A third Bihari whose background is clearly more comfortable than that of most SC politicians is Radha Prasad, a 28-year-old Member of the Legislative Assembly. The crucial work of building his family's fortunes was done by one of his great-uncles, who was himself elected MLA from Palamau district as early as 1957. Unlike the previous two examples, this family's success was achieved in the countryside rather than the town.

RP's Dusadh family prospered through close association with a Rajput family brought about, it seems, by the great-uncle himself. Dusadhs have traditionally been the untouchable community favoured by Rajputs, who employed them in a range of custodial and martial functions. The Dusadhs (or Paswans) in turn came to see themselves as the Kshattriyas of the untouchables, bolder and prouder than the others. In this case the association with the Rajput zamindar enabled the great uncle to get some education and some land. The zamindar's aid brought about a major family transformation and by now the family has acquired some 40 or 50 acres of (admittedly not very good) land.

RP's family looks remarkably like a progressive family from one of the formerly backward peasant castes—the Jats, Kurmis or Yadavs for example. (I encountered one other case—that of a Chamar MP from Punjab—which had a similar quality.) It is these elements which have sometimes not inappropriately been dubbed the post-Independence *kulak*s of India. But obviously there are few untouchable *kulak*s and, therefore, RP's family emerges as quite exceptional. RP himself had a very smooth path into the Assembly—an intelligent scion of a family such as his is almost bound to receive preferment for a reserved seat.

Before we attempt to draw together the strands of this biographical treatment of untouchable politicians, it is appropriate to look at one more extended study of an MP. Here the career is essentially city-based and one with certain affinities to that of Narsing Makwana discussed above. At the same time, this case has elements of the kind that have led to pejorative judgements by critics such as Sachchidananda.

Extended Case 3: Krishna Wada

KW was first elected to the Lok Sabha from a constituency in Maharashtra in 1957, re-elected in 1962 but lost the ticket in 1967. It was not until 1980 that he regained Congress support for the seat. KW is a Mahar whose father was originally a simple agricultural labourer, but shortly after KW's birth he moved the family to the nearby town of Nagpur and became a textile worker in a factory. KW's mother made bidis at home to supplement this income. Both parents were illiterate.

KW was the elder of two brothers and there was a sister who died. He went to school at the correct starting age for children. The reason, he says, is that this was the beginning of the era of consciousness fostered in the untouchable community by Ambedkar. It was already widely believed that education was the key to advancement for the community. KW has a BA and discontinued his studies while enrolled for an LLB. His brother did not finish college and is now in private business.

KW was aware of the problems of untouchability in the immediate post-Independence period, but they did not really affect him. He explains that he is a "city man" and hence escaped the rigours of the caste system. Immediately after his graduation he took a job as headmaster in a school. This did not lead to a career but it did to a wife—he married one of his colleagues, a Brahmin. She faced considerable difficulties with her family over the marriage but eventually they were mollified. Her family is "a little bit liberal but not really liberal."

KW made his career in the Maharashtra trade union movement. His introduction to unions was through his father and he was active even during his college days. He has been associated with various unions, including the Bidi Workers Union and the Textile Workers Union. His parliamentary career has been built on the support of the Independent Labour Parties, a union summit organisation originally established by Ambedkar. But while the unions have made his political career, KW does not seem to have taken an active part in union affairs for many years. Politically, he was considerably associated with Sanjay Gandhi. It was only after the defeat of Congress in 1977 that he came into contact with Sanjay, and the rebirth of his parliamentary career in 1980 is no doubt connected with this relationship.

KW's constituency lies between Bombay and Nagpur, and he was given it because it is a reserved seat. He has never been resident in the constituency. His own house is in Nagpur but he has been living in Delhi for some years now, since the time when one of his daughters was admitted to medical college there. The measure of KW's personal success is his sophisticated, highly polished manner, and the career of his children. The three children are identified "100 per cent" with SC people. The children are all in their early twenties. Both daughters are in medical college and the son is doing his MBA, MA and LLB simultaneously. All the children have been able to take advantage of reservation in the colleges. This has been of particular utility for the two daughters' entry into medical college, the most sought-after education in India. Understandably, then, KW sees reservation as the key to the rise of the SCs. With reservation in public employment the SCs will eventually gain social respectability, and this will be enough to end untouchability.

Comment: This case is instructive on a number of counts. Plainly, it is not a typical case—the inter-caste marriage is highly unusual, though it could be said to follow the example of Ambedkar himself. And Krishna Wada is also rare in the extent to which he is, in his own words, a "city man." He is a representative of a rural constituency without ever having lived in a village. This no doubt accounts for the special "polish" he exhibits—city men are more polished than their country cousins.

Perhaps the initial reaction of many observers would be to condemn Krishna Wada as someone who has taken advantage of the system of reservation, while being dubiously deserving of such preferment. The advantage which his children have enjoyed maybe a particular source of criticism. No doubt views of this kind have some substance—the gulf between the characteristic situation of untouchables throughout India and the comfortable life of Krishna Wada in his large government bungalow in New Delhi is truly vast. Krishna Wada is in no substantive sense a "representative" of untouchable communities. And yet if one retraces his life through the sketchy details that we have, a stance of condemnation may come to be seen as inappropriate.

KW was clearly a bright young man from an educationally unpromising background, and he made the most of his early opportunities. As a potential object of criticism his key act was to marry one of the teachers at the school in which he was a headmaster. This woman happened to be a Brahmin. Perhaps the very attraction to her was in part because she was a Brahmin, an educated woman coming from a community which had social prestige and an attachment to education. Is KW really to be condemned for such an attraction? Is Ambedkar himself to be condemned for marrying a Brahmin woman? In fact, such marriages widely provoke reactions ranging from unease to denunciation in both untouchables and high caste people. For the untouchables, Ambedkar's act is sometimes seen as consorting with the great enemy, Brahminism. And for the high castes, undoubtably such marriages often appear as acts of defilement. Not even the first attitude seems reasonable, given the intensely personal as well as social dimensions of marriage. In the case of KW, any adverse reaction to his overall situation today tends to crumble when one subtracts as irrelevant the fact that he married a Brahmin woman. The only unusual features of this case are the inter-caste marriage and the fact that the career is city-based. But the latter feature is far from unprecedented—there are several other examples in the small sample discussed in this chapter.

One other politician in our sample has also married a Brahmin. In this case it was a second marriage and apparently the first (untouchable) wife is still loud in her claims of being badly done by. And I am advised by an untouchable university lecturer that marital incompatibility is a great problem in the case of many untouchables who have been educated to a high level but have been married off in childhood to a quite uneducated girl.[8] Emotional turmoil and even divorce are apparently not uncommon in these situations. In reality, the case of KW alerts us more to the sheer arduousness of the way up for the untouchable rather than to any corruptions of the spirit. But let me hasten to add that I am not suggesting that an untouchable girl will be unfit for an untouchable boy who has been highly educated. The point is simply that to this stage highly educated untouchable girls are very few and that a highly educated man may feel the need of a mate who operates on the same cultural level that he has attained. The fact that in such a situation the man engages in an inter-caste marriage should not as a matter of course merit criticism.

The great temptation is to prescribe from the outside what an untouchable politician ought to be. No doubt, harsh evaluation of politicians is a standard occupation in almost every society, India included. But in the case of occupants of reserved seats the ordinary tendency becomes exaggerated. Perhaps there is bound to be sharp scrutiny to see whether the SC members measure up to ordinary standards applied to Members of Parliament from open constituencies. But it is plain that something more than this is at work. Either explicitly or implicitly the tendency is to posit some kind of ideal which untouchable politicians are supposed to approximate. The man is imagined to have arisen from the mainstream of untouchable society, to be a proud and unswerving leader of his people and at the same time to be a sophisticated politician capable of surviving and succeeding in the ruthless world of Indian politics. Such an ideal is unlikely to receive much fulfilment. It is difficult enough to be a leader of the most depressed group of people in India. It requires greatness to be simultaneously a leader of this kind, an effective general politician, and also a family man capable of carrying one's own family from rural subordination to educated, middle-class status.

"THE HARIJAN ELITE"

We are now in a position to try to draw together the strands of these various lives we have discussed and to comment on the applicability of previous works on "the Harijan elite." What we have found is that there is certainly no one type of untouchable politician, though there are regularities of several kinds. The most striking of these is that the untouchable legislators do not come from the characteristic untouchable situation of landless labour but tend to be at least the second generation of a family somewhat economically superior to this situation. The case of a man who rose from a completely landless family without income from outside the village to the position of parliamentarian is represented in our sample by only one man, two if you count Bhole Paswan Shastri (whose father had lost his land early in BPS's childhood).

But just how comfortable were the early circumstances of the subjects of these interviews and how prosperous have they become as a result of their careers? We have spent more time on the first of these questions and our broad conclusion is that they do not represent a privileged minority when measured by the standards of urban India or the standards of caste Hindus in general. Perhaps the appropriate comparison is with middle peasant castes—I have no data on parliamentarians from these castes but we can confidently predict that their circumstances would be greatly superior to those of SC politicians. In a word, the peasant representatives would be seen to come from families possessed of far more land than is characteristic of our group. And if the comparison were with high caste politicians from either town or country, no doubt the gap in prosperity would be still greater.

Among the sample discussed here, only two politicians came from business families and demonstrably the business interests were of minor stature. The highest reported parcel of land was some 50 acres of not very good land spread over a large extended family. Most of the group were very much less wealthy than these people, many of them being at least initially only marginally above the level of the general untouchable population in the countryside. But what happened to them and their families in the course of a political career? We have spent less time on this question and our information is indeed somewhat scanty. But by and large and unsurprisingly, the answer is that their condition has improved in proportion to the strength of their initial base—the originally more prosperous men have managed to consolidate this status whereas those whose original condition was one of relative poverty have struggled to carry their family into self-sustaining middle-class status. Many of the families now have members in reserved places in the public services, but these positions are often not in the first or second grades. Although it is difficult to make judgements of this kind, it often seems that untouchable politicians have with difficulty succeeded in carrying their family from rural semi-poverty to lower-middle-class urban status. Certainly there is a tendency for such families to be urbanised in the wake of the politician's career—sometimes the urbanisation in question is only from a village to a sub-district centre, but this is nonetheless an important transformation.

The case of Krishna Wada can be seen as somewhat exceptional to this process. Although his parents were poor and illiterate, two of his children—girls at that—are medical students. Quite clearly a key factor in this transformation is the fact that his wife is an educated Brahmin woman. Presumably her input into the education and motivation of her children has been a significant factor in their academic success. The other families discussed here have not benefited from sophisticated guidance of this sort.

There is no evidence, then, of great enrichment by the subjects of this study, though of course the families are with every year distancing themselves economically and in terms of sophistication from the ordinary untouchable villagers. Indeed, what can be argued with considerable vigour is that many of the untouchable politicians are not economically sufficiently comfortable to play the strong and independent political role which might more effectively promote their community's interests. To turn Sachchindananda's argument on its head, the argument might be that while there is scarcely a "Harijan elite" today the creation of such an elite may be in the interest of the general untouchable population.

Sachchidananda's conception of the "Harijan elite" derives no confirmation from the results of our own study. Admittedly, the two samples were different, since Sachchidananda's group included public servants and social workers as well as politicians. But this is unlikely to make a major difference to the findings. Our own conclusion is that it is at best strained to talk of an "elite" of people who turn out to have the economic characteristics described in this chapter. They are only an elite relative to the mass of their caste fellows, and even here the term is inappropriate. The term carries with it an image of isolation from caste fellows which seems unjustified by the attitudes and behaviour of the subjects of this inquiry.

Perhaps what is ultimately at issue between views such as those put forward by Sachchidananda and the arguments of this chapter, is appropriate standards of judgement rather than material facts. I would want to claim that the standards applied to untouchable politicians seem often to be different and harder than those applied to the representatives of open constituencies. And closely allied to this point, the opportunities open to the untouchable politicians are often almost illusory. It would have been miraculous if reservation of seats had been able to accomplish at one stroke the creation of a talented, highly effective group of untouchable politicians. Given what Sachchidananda aptly terms the "bleak past" that characterises the untouchable situation, such a transformation was simply not going to take place. Reservation is a symbol of the fact that the present is not so bleak as the past, but just as the untouchables (or the "ex-untouchables," the Harijans, SCs, dalits—choose your name) are still oppressed communities, so their legislative representatives reflect this subordinate condition.

Even if the untouchable parliamentarians were as a group unusually well-educated and articulate, their ability to further the interests of their communities would be limited. Reservation of parliamentary seats for the SCs was no doubt seen as a means of giving these groups political preference but it was never allowed by the national leadership to threaten its own dominance. The political parties are never controlled by untouchables even while the reservation system guarantees a large block of untouchable legislators. Jagjivan Ram controlled the large contingent of untouchable MPs from Bihar at the height of his power, but he could never have controlled the whole Congress party in Bihar. He was shut out from this degree of power by virtue of being a Chamar, irrespective of questions of talent.

The point was put simply by Radha Prasad, the young Bihari MLA. He was loud in his condemnation of the weakness of SC parliamentarians. They are at the mercy of the caste Hindu bosses, and I must say I saw considerable evidence of what he meant. Radha Prasad claims that if he supports untouchables too systematically then he will be labelled a "casteist" and will not get a Congress ticket for the next election. The untouchable legislators are not prepared to stand up as a bloc, ignoring party lines, on issues of significance for their communities—they will not do so even on the issue of "Harijan atrocities," he says. But he also says that there is now a new generation of SC politicians who are less timorous than the previous ones and who will increasingly stand up and be counted.

It is no doubt productive for young politicians like Radha Prasad to be scornful of the older generation of untouchable politicians, though the discussion in this chapter is more sympathetic than his view of his professional colleagues. And if he is right about the more radical and assertive generation of leaders coming forward, then there is reason for some hope. It is perhaps relevant that Radha Prasad himself comes from one of the better-off families in our sample. It is also relevant that he is a Dusadh, the unusually martial SC of Bihar. In this case, at least, prosperity and high status (in the sense of a more Sanskritised status) have not blunted his concern for the welfare of the SCs. Quite the reverse, it seems. And by extension, I find unconvincing the argument that SC politicians are dominated by their own immediate material concerns for their family and associates. No doubt almost all Indian politicians are to some extent dominated by these concerns, some more than others. But I can find no warrant for the assertion that SC politicians are particularly caught up in this pursuit so that they do not devote themselves sufficiently to their job. Moreover, the material striving of a SC parliamentarian on behalf of his family is perhaps to be welcomed if it makes his own and his family's position more secure. It seems positively desirable that scheduled communities begin to develop particular families which are both materially well off and also politically sophisticated; these are the kind of families out of which one can expect leadership in politics, education and business to come. (At the same time, we must bear in mind that the overall national leadership will be resistant to any push for greater power from untouchable leaders.)

There are those who argue that the current weakness of SC parliamentarians owes largely to the particular mechanism for reservation of constituencies which is now in force. Those SC politicians who can remember the two-member constituencies in the Lok Sabha which existed for the first decade of independence claim it to have been more conducive to the effective statement of priorities of the scheduled communities. Under this system, the reserved seats were located in constituencies which also returned a general member. In other words, the SC member was conceived simply as representative of the SCs, rather than of the whole population of the constituency. Suraj Bhan, a prominent member of the Lok Sabha for the BJP at the time of interview, sees in the dismantling of the two-member constituency what he calls the first great sell-out of untouchables after Independence.

But in the end it is clear that there are far more than mere technical problems in the whole system of reservation, which will progressively move to centre stage in Indian politics. The system may be intuitively unattractive in its derogation from the principle of equality which is so prized in liberal democracies. But my own view is that the maintenance of reservation at the parliamentary level (and in public employment, for that matter) is vital for the untouchable communities. There is plenty of room for criticism of the performance of untouchable politicians but there is absolutely no reason to believe that the 110 million untouchables would be better off without them. And it is entirely clear that without reservation very few untouchables would manage to gain the backing of the major political parties—there are simply too many other plausible claimants from stronger socio-economic backgrounds.

To repeat, we should be careful to avoid the imposition of special and unreasonable standards on untouchable parliamentarians. As a group they can and should be more resolute in the cause they are elected to promote but we should also recognise the pressures of working in a political environment which cannot be insulated from the patterns of economic and social dominance and subordination in the world outside the legislature. It is extraordinarily difficult to be an effective untouchable politician in India.

NOTES AND REFERENCES

[1] The interviews that form the basis of this chapter were conducted in the period December to February 1982–83 in New Delhi and Patna. For financial assistance to conduct this research I thank the Australian Research Grants Scheme. In this and other fieldwork I have incurred incalculable debts to innumerable people. For the most part I should not name these people but I am terribly grateful to them. Of course, the work would have been impossible without the generous co-operation of the MPs and MLAs whom I interviewed. They often gave hours of their time, sometimes on several occasions.

[2] There is no ideal term to denote the people who are the subject of this chapter. The term "untouchable" is legally inaccurate and conceivably offensive to some, since untouchability was abolished by the Constitution and its practice made an offence. But since ritual untouchability is what the SCs have in common, I have often used the term here. The "schedule" of castes is a list prepared under the auspices of Article 341 of the Constitution, for the purpose of nominating beneficiaries of the special schemes for disadvantaged castes. The term "Harijan" was adopted by Gandhi as a term of respect for the untouchables but in recent years it is increasingly seen as patronising and meaningless, though it is still frequently used. The term "dalit" is used in Maharashtra and somewhat more widely to denote downtrodden groups and chiefly the untouchables. But as yet the term is not used sufficiently widely throughout India to justify its employment in an article of the present kind.

The literature on untouchables is surprisingly thin though now quite fast growing. Most of the best work has been studies of individual untouchable communities in particular localities.

Many of the essays in the collection edited by J. Michael Mahar, *The Untouchables in Contemporary India* (Tuscon: University of Arizona Press, 1972), fall into this category. Michael Moffat, *An Untouchable Community in India* (Princeton: Princeton University Press, 1979) follows suit. In *Untouchable: An Indian Life History* (London: Allen and Unwin, 1979), James Freeman reduces the scope to one (fascinating) individual. Among the category of more general works, the largest in scope is Marc Galanter, *Competing Equalities: Law and the Backward Classes in India* (Berkeley: University of California Press, 1984). This work concentrates heavily on the legal dimensions of the untouchability issue and particularly on the matter of preferential treatment.

[3] The following figures are taken from S. P. Gupta, K. L. Dutta and Padam Singh, "Poverty among the Weaker Sections: A Regional Study" in *Regional Dimensions of India's Economic Development* (Lucknow: State Planning Institute, Government of Uttar Pradesh, 1983). Substantially the same point is made in an article which is at once more detailed than the above but less relevant for the present purpose, since it fails to disaggregate SCs and STs. The article is Vijay Nayak and Shailaja Prasad, "On Levels of Living of Scheduled Castes and Scheduled Tribes," *Economic and Political Weekly* 19, no. 30 (28 July 1984), pp. 1205–13.

[4] Sachchidananda, *The Harijan Elite* (n.p.: Thomson Press (India), 1977). See also G. Narayana, "Social Background of Scheduled Caste Lok Sabha Members, 1962–71," *Economic and Political Weekly* 13, no. 37 (16 September 1978), pp. 1603–08. This short article is based on a culling of several of the "Who's Who" in the Lok Sabha publications and concludes that SC Members are becoming over time educationally and occupationally less distinct from other Members and are increasingly to be seen as part of a single Indian political elite. By this logic the SC Members are therefore becoming more distinct from the mass of SC people. While there is no doubt something in this argument, we will later have reason to doubt the depth of insight that such a view can provide.

[5] Narsing Murty is a pseudonym, as are subsequent names marked with an asterisk (*) after their initial use. A number of the names used in the article have not been changed—the decision to use a pseudonym was taken simply if it was felt that there might be some (even slight) embarrassment to the interview subject.

[6] Interview with the author, Patna, 25 May 1985.

[7] For many—perhaps most—untouchable children, education can still be a humiliating, demeaning experience. See Krishna Kumar, "Educational Experience of Scheduled Castes and Tribes," *Economic and Political Weekly* 18, nos. 36–37 (3 September 1983), pp. 1566–72.

[8] Interview with S. K. Thorat, New Delhi, 5 May 1985.

15

Women's Studies

New Perceptions and the Challenges*

Vina Mazumdar and Kumud Sharma

The new academic search to organise knowledge on various aspects of women's situation, resulting in changes in perception about women's contribution to society and their needs and problems in the context of modernisation, development and social change has raised many issues. In their effort to place the contemporary situation in proper perspective, social scientists concerned with women's problems have sought explanations in (a) the historical and cultural framework of a society, (b) the evolution of policies and strategies for national development, and (c) biases inherent in the concepts and methodology of social research. It has been contended that using identical standard indicators to measure changes in the quality of life of heterogeneous segments of the population has been a constraint in understanding the complex roles of women in the context of the wider society and its various sub-systems.

Research on women is not new but the studies offer a variety of concerns with shifting emphasis and perspectives, depending on one's theoretical orientation, ideological alignments, changes in the contemporary situation and in priorities for social and national development. These shifts in emphasis and approach have much to do with trends in current thinking on specific issues relating to the total population in society as well as to women in particular. The emphasis has sometimes been on human rights and social oppression of women, on population policy and planning, the issues of poverty, unemployment,

* This edited article was originally published in *Economic and Political Weekly* 14, no. 3 (20 January 1979), pp. 113–20.

inequality and strategies for survival or on equality in education, health, political and economic participation and other opportunities for development.

Early researches on women in India were primarily done by social historians, indologists, anthropologists and sociologists. Historians and indologists investigated the position of women, mainly of the high caste and elite sections of society, reasons for the deterioration in their status and the emergence of social evils like child marriage, suttee, the general oppression of widows, purdah and illiteracy. They shared the concerns and the basic ideology of the social reform movement which sought to cleanse Indian society of institutions and practices which were believed to be deterrents to national resurgence and progress and which gave India a bad name in the eyes of the Western world.

Latent within the reform movement's humanist aims was a perception that traditional Indian culture and values must be strengthened to resist the inroads of Westernisation. As custodians of traditional values and cultures, women were viewed as potential allies in this struggle, provided their weakening influence within families could be strengthened by education and improved legal status.[1] Historians and reformers argued that customs like child marriage, purdah, the oppression of widows, and the denial of education and property rights to women were indicators of cultural degeneration, not intrinsic attributes of Indian culture. Opposition to this idea came only from one or two radical thinkers[2]—who perceived oppression of women as a traditional *instrument* for maintaining social inequality, and the high castes in Indian society.

Shift in Perspective

The merging of the social reform movement into the political movement for independence resulted in a marked shift in the perspective on women's issues. Democratic ideology and the recognition of the need to obtain women's support for the national struggle resulted in the acceptance of the principle of equality of rights, status and opportunities for participation in the process of national development. The marked increase in the participation of women in the freedom struggle from the 1920s was reflected in an increase in research and debate on women's issues. The new literature continued the earlier concerns but with the added dimension of equality in the field of political activities.

The greater involvement of women in the task of political mobilising, social reconstruction and national development through instruments of directed social change called for a fundamental redefinition of sex roles. The signal for this redefinition was given in the writings of Mahatma Gandhi. Viewing women as an oppressed group, Gandhi projected them as potential vanguards of a radical but nonviolent process of social transformation. Removal of their existing disabilities—legal, educational and social—and equality in the arena of political decision-making and individual role-choice were, in his opinion, only preconditions for women to play their historic role.[3]

It is amazing that in spite of the acceptance of the equality principle by national leadership and the Constitution-makers, the thrust for redefinition of sex roles had only a marginal impact on the work of social scientists. A trend survey of research on women[4] indicates that in the period up to 1950 the focus of research was primarily on general surveys of women's roles and status within the narrow perspective of the family, kinship and the community, with education occupying the second position. During the 1950s, which ushered in reforms in personal and labour laws, there was some increase in studies on the legal and economic status of women. The legal studies, however, predominantly focused on scriptural and statutory laws, which affected mainly the upper strata of society, especially the urban educated class, while the lives of the majority of women continued to be governed by customary laws. Serious research on customary laws by legal scholars did not begin until the 1970s, though anthropologists accumulated information on them from a much earlier period. In the economic sphere, studies concentrated on the modern sector of the economy which attracted the attention of planners as well as academic scholars. Since the participation of women in this sector, whether in blue-collared or white-collared activities, was marginal throughout this period, research on women's roles and opportunities in economic activity remained marginal. Agricultural economics began to develop rapidly from this period, though it surprisingly ignored the major role played by women in agriculture and the manners in which they were being affected by the process of modernisation.

Why did the social sciences fail to respond to the ideas articulated by the nineteenth century radicals and Gandhi? Why did the women's movement and the national debate on women's roles in society die out from the mid-1950s? Why did development planners as well as women's organisations perceive women as objects of marginal welfare services rather than as a concern in economic planning? Even the Community Development Programme, intended as a multi-dimensional instrument for both social and economic development of the rural population, originally overlooked women,[5] and included them later only as recipients of family welfare services, not of productivity programmes in agriculture.

Answering these questions calls for considerable research. Only some partial explanations have been offered recently.[6] Persistence of the urban middle-class bias in perception of social problems, inadequacy of data, over-concentration on economic at the cost of social development, complacency among educated women and women's organisations after winning constitutional and legal equality, and adoption of the Western industrial rather than the Gandhian model for development may all have contributed to the process. Another reason could be the national consensus to keep the women's question out of the sphere of political controversy, projecting it as a purely social issue of long-term changes in attitudes through education and development. There is little doubt that this consensus was the outcome of the perspective that the sources of women's oppression were all to be found within traditional attitudes and cultural institutions rather than in the socio-economic and political structures of society.

Demographers' Interest

The demographers' interest in women stemmed, first, from the population problem, and second, from the declining ratio of women in the Indian population, a trend observed from the first Census in 1872. It is amazing that with the exception of one or two scholars, the declining sex-ratio was not taken up as a major issue related to the changing status of women till the 1970s of this century. The problem of population growth, which tended to overshadow all other demographic issues, resulted in an enormous volume of research on population problems and policies, acceptance and attitude towards family planning (KAP studies) and identification of areas of success and failure with a view to reducing population growth.

A by-product of research on family planning was a renewed emphasis on women's education which was expected to improve both their access to family planning services and their general status. This view of the social scientists was in harmony with the general attitude of planners, which confined programmes for women's development to education, health and welfare. In collection of data and information regarding women, this narrow focus persisted and little attempt was made to relate these variables to other major determinants of status like employment, family income, class and caste positions, etc.

These biases prevented both social scientists and planners from noting with any serious concern the decline in women's labour force participation reported by the Census of 1951 and some sectoral studies. A few attempts by economists to examine women's role in the labour force invariably led to one or more of the following conclusions:

(a) that the data was unsatisfactory and non-comparable to that on men—therefore it could not be used for any serious analysis;
(b) that women's participation in economic activity was essentially determined by cultural attitudes and was thus beyond the purview of the economists; and
(c) that women's employment could only expand with education and change in social attitudes and could thus be dismissed as a long-term objective for which no immediate concern was necessary.

Some of the later researches in the population field did point to employment as a possible variable. But they viewed the relationship between women's employment and fertility decisions predominantly in the context of the "role conflict" theory—of women seeking jobs outside their homes and facing a conflict with their traditionally accepted roles within the home. It should be noted that in the Indian context, or that of any predominantly agrarian society, this theory is only applicable to middle-class working women, who are *new* entrants to the labour market. The preoccupation with role conflict indicates the failure on the part of scholars to recognise the importance of women's traditional economic roles in agriculture and the household economy. As stated earlier, this received only cursory attention, as an aspect of cultural variations. While anthropological studies did occasionally note rural women's economic roles, they failed to examine any changes, either quantitative or qualitative, in women's participation in economic activity.

The report of the National Commission on Labour (1969) drew attention to the problems of wage discrimination and general oppression of women workers, particularly in the rural sector, and criticised the government's failure to protect their health and working conditions. The report of the Expert Committee on Unemployment Estimates (1970) (which consisted primarily of social scientists) admitted, however, that apart from the limitations of quantitative data, the heterogeneous character of the Indian economy, the uneven rates of development in different regions and sectors, and the varying impact of modernisation on different segments of the labour force posed serious problems in examining and assessing the dimensions of the unemployment problem. The Committee recommended that it was imperative to estimate different "segments" of the labour force separately, "taking into account such characteristics as religion, sex, age, rural and urban residence, status or class of workers and educational attainments." The 28th Round of the National Sample Survey, which followed this report, attempted for the first time to estimate the size of women's unemployment, and the Report of the Committee on Unemployment (1973) admitted that unemployment among women was of a far higher order than had been hitherto suspected.

Research on women can broadly be grouped into (a) macro studies focusing on general features of socio-economic development, how sex roles are enacted and performed and the nature of the transformations which alter and affect them, and (b) micro studies that explore specific situations in which women are placed.

FIRST MAJOR ATTEMPT

The Report of the Committee on the Status of Women in India (1975) was the first major attempt to review and evaluate data on various aspects of women's status and the directions of change in women's roles, rights and opportunities due to planned development. The Committee's investigation revealed that changes in women's roles are the by products of many events: changes in the mode of production through commercialisation, capitalisation and technological developments; shifts in the value systems through the process of modernisation, urbanisation and the rising standards and costs of living; as well as legislative reforms, expansion of education, demographic transition and political developments. Some of the major questions that confronted the Committee during its investigations were:

(1) Why has the process of understanding women's contribution—social, economic and political—been shrouded in mystery?
(2) Why were women's concerns generally seen by planners and social scientists as welfare rather than development, or as peripheral rather than central to the development process?
(3) What were the historical and ideological dimensions of women's roles and status in Indian society?
(4) Do the empirical dimensions selected by social scientists to analyse women's roles and status actually represent operational indicators of women's status, and are they applicable to all groups of women?

The conceptualisation of these problems raised some substantial issues and is a challenge to researchers in the area of women's studies.

The Committee experienced a major difficulty with regard to data, particularly on the unorganised sectors of the economy and women of the poor classes, and concluded that the indicators used to measure women's position in the changing social process did not reflect Indian social realities—particularly of rural society. Identifying an interrelationship between the disturbing trends revealed by the declining sex ratio, low life expectancy, higher mortality, declining work participation and increasing migration of women, the Committee concluded that they were indicators "of a process of change that is moving in a direction opposite to the goals of our society and its plan for development." In the Committee's view, these demographic trends represented the groundswell of a process of devaluation of women. The surface manifestations of the same process were visible in the increasing volume and penetration of the dowry system, increasing commercial use of and traffic in women, and the development of social attitudes that suggested "regression from some of the norms developed during the Freedom Movement."

Studying the "Invisible Women"

The growing realisation of the inconsistencies developing between social goals and the development process has stimulated an exploration of people-oriented or specific group-oriented approaches to the study of development. The information that is now being generated by research studies on women, particularly with a "third world focus," however, has brought to the surface many issues relating to women and the development process, an important area of concern for both development planners and academics. Several streams of new thinking have also emerged in India as a result of the Committee's Report and later studies on "invisible women," which is one of the important objectives of the ICSSR's programme of Women's Studies.

Responding to the Committee's appeal that "changes in the status of women will be a long-term aspect of our social process and will require continuous examination and assessment by persons interested in social change," the ICSSR adopted a programme of sponsored research with the following objectives:

(1) generation and analysis of data in order to uncover significant trends in patterns of social and economic organisation which affect women's position in the long run;
(2) development of needed new perspectives in the social sciences, particularly through clarification of concepts like the family, household, women's work, economic activity, productivity, etc., the restrictive and ambiguous use of which has resulted in a general under-assessment of women's contribution to society.

The programme emphasises the study of women in the poor or "less visible" sections in Indian society with a view to understanding the regional and sectional differences in roles, status and problems of women and the different nature of the impact of development on their lives. This emphasis has been provided in order to correct the bias of previous research and policies for women's development which were primarily influenced by the experiences of women in the elite classes. The National Plan of Action for Women which was framed by the Government of India on the basis of the findings of the Committee on the Status of Women in India has also emphasised the need for purposive and problem-identifying research to facilitate designing of appropriate development policies and programmes, particularly for the weaker sections of women who have been adversely affected by the process of change.

The Council's programme initiated a series of critical evaluations of available sources of data and a series of micro studies on conditions of identifiable groups of women workers in the informal sector in order to explore how structural changes in the Indian economy have affected the occupational choice and the lifestyles of these women. These micro studies as well as detailed analysis of demographic data have substantially confirmed some of the findings of the Committee on the Status of Women.

A major exercise undertaken by the programme was preparation of time-series data to examine changes in the relative positions of men and women in the population, in different occupations (both traditional and modern), and in access to literacy.[7] The unit of analysis was the district, in order to highlight regional variations in these trends. The result of these studies indicate a significant parallelism between economic modernisation and changes in the relative position of women and men in the labour force and in particular occupations, in the population as a whole and in growing differentials in mortality, life expectancy and access to health services and literacy. Micro studies on women in the informal sector show that the main reason for their migration from their home villages is not the "pull" of better opportunities in the cities but pauperisation caused by the disappearance of their traditional avenues of employment.[8]

A study conducted in Calcutta[9] reports that in spite of the fact that there has been no significant increase in wage rates over the last seven years, more women are coming forward to work in the informal sector. Of the later entrants, an increasing percentage comes from families with no tradition of women working for monetary returns outside their homes. This "bottomless pool of cheap labour" and its growth in recent years, in response to newly developing manufacturing concerns using mainly female and child labour in small workshops and through the putting-out system, does nothing to reduce poverty and misery. The entrepreneurs use this labour for decentralised production, thereby avoiding the regulations of factory legislation and corporate taxation, and the process acts as an obstacle to the growth of the organised or modern high-wage industrial sector.

The study on migrant women in the slums of Delhi[10] indicates that the burden of increasing poverty falls heavily on women, particularly as migration results in the loss of support from their own family and kin groups. The study has also found that the selection of metropolitan cities for migration is invariably on the anticipation that they will offer some opportunity for employment to women in the domestic service sector or in construction work. The men in these families often remain unemployed or only casually employed for a long time and the family is dependent mainly on the women's income. When these women come from high-skilled occupations like weaving, they consider their urban occupation in domestic service as degrading and involving a loss of status. Their illiteracy and lack of other marketable skills leaves them little alternative to such low-paid unskilled work.

While these studies increasingly offer evidence of the growing burden of work, and loss of both physical and emotional support from the family among women who are moving down the social ladder through increasing poverty, there is another established process of change in the roles and status of women in upwardly mobile groups. Such upward mobility may take place from increasing prosperity, or men's access to more "socially respectable" occupations through the spread of education amongst the lowest strata in the society. M. N. Srinivas describes this as the "sanskritisation process," when lower social groups adopt the behavioural norms, lifestyles and ideology in sex roles of more dominant groups in society.[11] In rural agricultural classes, the roles of women vary at different levels of the land and caste hierarchy. Respectable status is regarded as inconsistent with women's wage work outside the family. In small and marginal farms, women work on the family farms. Increase in prosperity with agricultural development results in their withdrawal from active participation in field agriculture. The immediate consequence of this process, according to Srinivas, is a stage of "immurement of women" when they are subjected to seclusion, differential treatment in access to education and other developmental services and are increasingly regarded as tools for improvement and display of the families' social status. This is manifested in the introduction and inflation of the dowry system even in such families which had traditionally practised the opposite custom of bride price.[12] While there is evidence of a loss of relatively equal position in decision-making between men and women in such families, the area that remains to be investigated is women's perception of such changes in their roles.

WOMEN'S STATUS AND SOCIAL STRATIFICATION

Such studies clearly indicate an integral relationship between variations in women's roles and status and the nature of social stratification. It was hitherto believed that women's role in agriculture was predominantly determined by their caste position. The studies undertaken under the Women's Studies Programme suggest that there are other factors influencing this. The agrarian structure and land relations, though generally related to the caste structure, may exert independent influence on women's work roles and status. Changes in the demand and supply of agricultural labour, resulting from migration, changes in cropping patterns, the introduction of new technology or the opening up of alternative labour markets as well as landlessness have been found to affect the utilisation of female labour in agriculture.

A significant factor in these changes is women's access to particular agricultural skills. One study suggests that what has frequently been interpreted as a social taboo on women's participation in field agriculture in certain regions of the country may be a consequence of some change in the labour market situation at an earlier date. Agricultural skills are easily lost if not practised regularly. Thus women who were withdrawn from agricultural activities sometime in the past are unable to return to this occupation at a later date or to transfer the skills to their daughters.[13]

Changes in the income level of the family which have generally been found to act as a compulsion or deterrent to women's employment have recently registered some variations. As the study of Delhi slum women indicates, rural artisan families who confine women's work to unpaid processing operations within the home are prepared to push them into paid work in the cities as a means for the families' survival and security.

These studies suggest that any improvement or increase in employability of women (in domestic work in cities or dairy development in the rural areas) may not only result in the withdrawal of social taboos, but may increase women's work burden to enable males in their family to search for better employment or improved qualifications. This process is visible even among the middle classes. In the traditionally arranged marriage market in the metropolitan cities, the demand for employed brides has shown a marked increase.

Conventional approaches usually adopted literacy and education, employment, and political and legal rights as the indicators of women's status and progressive equality. Research on family planning uncovered another indicator, that of a role in decision-making, as vital in fertility choices. Recent studies suggest that the relative importance of these indicators varies according to position in the social hierarchy.

In traditional high-status families which secluded women and denied choices in marital matters, older women performed many managerial functions, and commanded considerable power in family decision-making.[14] The source of this power certainly did not originate in extra-domestic spheres or in formal education or economic independence. Younger women from this group were the first to receive access to the new opportunities opened through expansion of education, employment in various professions, other white-collared services and political careers. Many studies have reported that women's expanded roles have not necessarily increased their role in decision-making. For some there has been an improvement in status—but how much of such gain stems from individual achievement and how much from the family's status has not been examined adequately.

At lower levels of the society, women were economically active and enjoyed relatively higher degree of autonomy in marital choices and in interaction with men. Whether the absence of seclusion allowed them to play a more effective role in decision-making within and outside the family needs to be investigated. What has been observed is a loss of status and power among these women when they are moved from their traditional background into a different setting, even though they may continue to be economically active.[15]

Studies on political awareness and participation of women are challenging the older thesis—that education, employment or urbanisation *per se* result in increased political consciousness or participation of women.[16] On the other hand, the fading out of women's issues from the political arena and declining representation of women in all elective bodies from the second decade after Independence has opened up new areas for investigation which are only being explored at the moment. Why has the number of women in legislative bodies declined while voting participation increased at a faster rate than men's? Why have states with the lowest participation of women voters elected the largest number of women legislators and states with the highest political mobilisation of women selected the least? Why have political parties, trade unions, co-operatives and other politicising organisations ignored this vast source of support and treated them mainly as appendages of the family? It is only during the elections of 1977–78 that some appeals to women as separate from men have been taken up, marginally, by leaders and parties in limited areas. Has formalisation of the political process increased or decreased women's ability to participate meaningfully in politics? Why do women respond more eagerly to movements than to established political activities? Why with some women entering the highest offices without any opposition (on the ground of their sex), have women been so powerless at all levels of the political process?

The process of development in its entire complexity renders the task of understanding the meaning of such changes in different groups more difficult. It also demands a re-examination of conventional theories and strategies for women's development and the relative importance of these indicators used to determine changes in their status.

MICRO STUDIES

Realising the complexity and the magnitude of problems of women and development and the need to examine various dimensions of these problems, the ICSSR's programme sponsored micro studies to examine the differential impact of the development process and the causal and structural linkages of micro-situations with macro-variables. Some of the issues which are currently being studied at micro level are:

(i) Does a particular development strategy result in development for men and underdevelopment for women?
(ii) Do development and modernisation lead to a change in the sexual division of labour and differential in socio-economic status and income between the sexes, with women enjoying less control over and access to resources without any reduction or change in their traditional responsibilities?
(iii) How are the roles of women being affected by changing modes of production and production relations and its effect on skill generation and promotion?

(iv) How do policy choices and policy interventions in the economic sphere lead to important changes in non-economic spheres, and what is the interrelationship between the two?

Available data on rural women do not generally provide answers to questions such as how flexible is the division of labour between the sexes, what is the impact of technology and labour migration in terms of labour displacement and labour demand and its implications for women, the forms of dominance operating in the labour market and their control over the labour process and products and conditions under which women contribute their labour in the production systems. This will necessitate an examination of not only the system of stratification but the whole gamut of relationships in which women of different households are directly or indirectly involved. A study on rural households[17] is seeking to explain their response and decision regarding labour with the aid of time-disposition data.

The problem of widening women's access to the development process—both as beneficiaries and as participants, is complicated by conflicting social trends and policy choices. The claims of democratic decentralisation may conflict with the needs of women for special attention, as local authorities have often been found to be neglectful, if not hostile, to women's rights and needs. The desire to provide women with employment opportunities within the household sector, so as not to conflict with their family roles, tends to clash with other social objectives, for example:

(a) to diversify women's employment opportunities, access to new skills, knowledge and the wider society, with a view to increasing their self-reliance, bargaining power and participatory opportunities and rescuing them from their present status of unpaid family workers;
(b) to eliminate the present tendency to relegate women to low-paid, low-skilled and low-status occupations which reinforce discriminatory attitudes and practices;
(c) to promote voluntary acceptance of the small family norm, as studies have shown that household industries tend to encourage growth of large families, and the exploitation of women's health and labour;[18]
(d) even a policy to promote women's self-employment in the small-scale sector sometimes provides only a thin guise for men's monopoly over resources, and control over such enterprises, with the woman not even able to control her income.[19]

While widening opportunities for employment emerges as critical for women's development, inadequate attention to their other needs—for knowledge, health and conscious autonomous participation in decision-making—has tended to encourage their exploitation and consequent regression from the principle of equality.

The draft Five-Year Plan for 1978–83 has suggested a strategy of increasing investment in "women-preferred" industries, i.e., industries which employ a large number of women. The Working Group appointed by the Planning Commission has however pointed out that such a policy may only strengthen the trends observed in the last few decades: (a) of women's concentration in low-status occupations; and (b) their displacement with increased investment in capital intensive technology (particularly observed in textiles, jute, agriculture and agro-industries). The Group also observed that the fiscal policies and other measures favouring capital investment rather than increased employment have further strengthened this trend.

INTEGRATION WITH PLAN STRATEGIES

The uncomfortable findings of recent research, the increasing realisation among planners of the inter-linkages that exist between poverty, unemployment, inequality as well as the population problem, and the international pressure for the "integration of women in development," have combined to generate some interest in women's studies, and the search for policy measures to diversify and expand opportunities for women's participation. Attempts are being made to integrate women's needs within the Plan strategies for full employment and distributive justice. Some of the instruments being discussed by different working groups (which include development administrators, field workers as well as social scientists) are:

(a) organisations of underprivileged women to protect and generate employment, to provide access to skills and other types of knowledge, health and child care services, and above all to function as pressure groups to increase their participation in development decisions;
(b) establishment of specialised agencies at different levels to act as mobilisers and catalytic agents, in order to promote women's development and participation;
(c) development of multi-disciplinary training and orientation of development cadres and research scholars on women's issues; and
(d) introductory special protection/preferential treatment for women in all sectoral and area plans and in vocational training.

The revival of interest in problems of women owes much to the International Women's Decade and to the rather alarming findings of the Committee on the Status of Women in India. The latter contributed to a range of new perceptions which have influenced the studies sponsored by the ICSSR and a few other agencies. It must, however, be admitted that the overriding concern for improving the quality of intervention in favour of some target groups, and to arrest the trend towards devaluation of women, has resulted in a concentration of research interest in the sphere of economic participation, particularly of women in low income groups. While such research has certainly helped the search for new policy instruments, there has been neglect of some of the vital areas of theoretical concern for understanding women's roles and position in society. For example, while most of the studies perceive a linkage between women's status/ roles and the stratified structure of society and power relations, we have yet to discover the *determinants* of women's status as perceived by women, and by others, at different levels of society. A second area on which work remains to be done is the interlinkage between variations in family structure, sexroles, values and the socialisation process, leading to identity formations.

....

NOTES AND REFERENCES

[1] Vina Mazumdar, "Social Reform Movement in India from Ranade to Nehru" in *Indian Women: From Purdah to Modernity*, ed. B. R. Nanda (Delhi: Vikas Publishers House, 1976).

[2] Jyotiba Phule, "Lukhitawadi Gopal Hari Deshmukh and IsvarchandaVidvasagar" in *Indian Women: From Purdah to Modernity*, ed. B. R. Nanda (Delhi: Vikas Publishers House, 1976). Also D. N. Vora, "Liberal Thought in Maharashtra" (unpublished PhD thesis, Pune University, 1975).

[3] M. K. Gandhi, "Role of Women,""To Women," Ahmedabad, Navajivan Prakashan. Also, Sugata Das Gupta and I. N. Tewari, "Emancipation of Women: Sociological Analysis" (Unpublished paper prepared for the Committee on the Status of Women in India). A. J. Dastur and Usha Mehta, "Gandhi and the Emancipation of Women"(Bombay: SNDT Women's University, 1969, being published shortly). Vina Mazumdar, *op. cit.*

[4] Kalpana Das Gupta, *Women on the Indian Scene: An Annotated Bibliography* (Delhi: Abhinav Publishers, 1976).

[5] Reported to the authors by S. K. De, the founder and Minister-in-charge of the programme.

[6] *Towards Equality: Report of the Committee on the Status of Women in India* (Government of India, Department of Social Welfare, 1975).

[7] Ashok Mitra, (a) "Implications of the Declining Sex-ratio in India's Population," (b) "Status of Women—Literacy and Employment," (c) "Status of Women—Economic Participation in Household and Non-Household Activities." ICSSR, Programme of Women's Studies (all three in press).

[8] (a) Leela Kasturi, "South Indian Migrant Women in Delhi Slums," ICSSR, Programme of Women's Studies (ongoing).

(b) Sulabha Brahme, "Economic Plight of Hamaal Women in Pune," ICSSR, Programme of Women's Studies (ready for publication).

[9] Nirmala Bannerjee, "Women in the Unorganised Sector in the Metropolitan City of Calcutta," ICSSR, Programme of Women's Studies (ongoing). Also the same author's paper,"Women and Development," *Social Scientist* (March 1978).

[10] Leela Kasturi, "South Indian Migrant Women in Delhi Slums."

[11] M. N. Srinivas, *Changing Position of Indian Women*, Thomas Huxley Memorial Lecture, 1976 (Delhi: Oxford University Press, 1978).

[12] T. Scarlett Epstein, *South India: Yesterday, Today, Tomorrow* (New York: Holmes and Meier, 1973).

[13] G. C. Tewari, "Regional Variations in Women's Employment Patterns," ICSSR, Programme of Women's Studies (ongoing).

[14] M. N. Srinivas and E. A. Ramaswamy, *Culture and Human Fertility in India* (Delhi: Oxford University Press, 1977).

[15] Jyoti Sen, "Tribal Women and Development," ICSSR, Programme of Women's Studies (ongoing).

[16] V. M. Sirsikar, Nirmala Bannerjee, D. M. Shukla and Pathak in *Symbols of Power: Studies on the Political Status of Women in India*, ed. Vina Mazumdar (Delhi: Allied Publishers, forthcoming).

[17] Devaki Jain, "Work Participation of Women in Agricultural Households," ICSSR, Programme of Women's Studies (ongoing).

[18] Ashok Mitra, "National Population Policy in the Context of National Development," Ajit Bhagat Memorial Lecture, Ahmedabad, 1977, *Population and Development Review* (1978).

[19] Planning Commission of India, *Report of the Working Group on Employment of Women, 1978.*

16

The Communalising of Punjab, 1980–85*

Dipankar Gupta

The tragedy of Punjab today is not the making of Punjab alone. The entire nation is party to it and is implicated by definition in the emergence of a new minority consciousness among the Sikhs. Yet such an awareness has never clearly surfaced because of the uncritical acceptance that communal practices are sponsored only by communal parties. Once this readily assimilable position is taken one has almost no qualms in ethnicising an entire population such as the Sikhs as being inherently prone to fundamentalist diktats. The possibility that Sikhs may have other identities too is relegated into the background. One has also, as a consequence, no qualms, no analytical bewilderment either, with the term "Hindu backlash." Unmindful of the communal swagger that this term validates, it is freely used to explain the repeated and large-scale violations on the Sikh community by the non-Sikhs (primarily Hindus). The diacritica of this new majority consciousness should not have gone unnoticed.

The New Minority

Any attempt to comprehend the problem of contemporary Punjab should begin by first accepting the reality that a new minority consciousness has emerged. In this case, neither the ethnicised history of a community, such as the Sikhs, nor the mere existence of a communal party like the Akali Dal, can explain, singly

* Originally published in *Economic and Political Weekly* 20, no. 28 (13 July 1985): pp. 1185–90.

or jointly, the specificity of this new phenomenon. It is for anthropology and sociology to plumb the depths of this problem but only after the practitioners of these disciplines too realise the uniqueness of the event. For so many years these disciplines had only primitive communal givens to contend with and write about. This gave rise to the belief that communal mobilisations only occurred between certain culturally pre-ordained groups. It was as if every dyad of proven communalism was a pair bound by a very special and inherent tie of antagonism, such as between the Hindus and Muslims (cow worshippers *versus* cow eaters), or between Scheduled Castes (SCs) and upper castes (pollution *versus* purity). Punjab over the last six years should have changed all that. It has demonstrated that communalism does not require that its passions be always traceable to hoary traditions in order to raise dust and settle it down with blood.

This is perhaps the unkindest cut of all to scholarship, but there is no social tragedy however great from which anthropology and sociology do not happen to benefit. Undoubtedly, in this situation too these disciplines are privileged for Punjab in the last six years approximated a gigantic laboratory leavening communal passions over a slow fire. The resultant Hindu–Sikh communal dyad does not seem any the poorer, or feeble, in spite of its late nativity. The nationwide massacre of Sikhs in November 1984 should leave little doubt on this score.

That fateful day Indira Gandhi cast a long morning shadow as she walked through the opening that connected residence to party office. Home and office, domestic menials and party liege men, all merged into one which only an acute exercise in parallax separated. When she fell her shadow fell too, only it crumpled faster to form a shady and irregular hem around her. Her legacy too adjusted to this stone-cold certainty within a matter of hours and stayed true to the shady fringe that hugged her to the last. In a tutored attempt at reflexive mourning the dark margins came to life and roamed at large, displacing national shock with private griefs, and bloodshed with a blood bath. Through every slain victim the body of the 20th century *Purusasukta*—or the communal nation-state—was reconstituted amidst howls and arrhythmic chants of "*khoonka badlakhoon*." It is at dark moments such as these that the term "violation" draws deep into its etymological roots.

The massacre of the Sikhs in November 1984 was no thoughtless throwaway curve. It completed the circle of communalism with such vigour that its involuted overflow darkened every space and publicly tainted the Centre.[1] The swiftness of the xenophobic stroke conveys the superficial impression that it was primarily reactive in character, thus justifying the wide circulation of the term "Hindu backlash." Even if one were to entertain the phrase "Hindu backlash" for the time being with its reactive connotations, then of necessity one must conclude that the score is now even: action–reaction, point–counterpoint. From the time of Operation Bluestar no opportunity was lost by the Centre to humiliate the Sikhs as a community,[2] and on each such occasion it has earned greater sympathy from the Hindus. The normal divisions between the Sikhs, such as between Jats, Mazhabis, urban Khatirs and Aroras, shaded off into a single identity because in the making of communalism subtlety is positively shunned.[3] As a matter of fact it is the Sikh identity that is reactive as many Sikhs till the November massacres had other political and social identities as well.[4] The fact that neither Hindu activism recognised it in deed, nor Hindu pacifism in words, signifies first the fact of Hindu communal consolidation *vis-à-vis* the Sikhs, and second, that Sikh communal identification is not a mirror image of Hindu communalism.

The Liberal and Left Predicament

The communalising of Punjab over the last six years provides the only active historical base for the comprehension of the problem. The close infighting, feints and counter-moves making for the dense minutiae of these short years have also had the contrary effect of spreading confusion because the reportage on these events pivoted around the vivid prototype of the Sikh provocateur. Even among those resolute liberals and deliberate secularists who are still not willing to "blame the victims" for the "backlash" it is difficult to find a complete, unabashed, unquestioning, and irrevocable partisanship with the victims and potential victims. Unused also to viewing victims of communal violence as anything but poor, helpless and the traditionally persecuted, they feel that they are somehow being cheated by the sheer prosperity and the confidence of the Sikhs. So every time they raise a voice for this new minority it is hollowed by a dubiety they are unable to position. This adds to the concentricity of the Punjab problem as the victims categorically spurn the patronising hand-up.

There is, however, one cultural factor which has also contributed to this unification of the Sikh sentiment. Sikh religion is a very young religion and still retains much of the vigour of youth. It is a participatory religion in which there is one principal text, the Granth Sahab, uniformly recognised five principal *takhts*, and hardly any significant doctrinal emendations or conflicting schools of interpretation. The gulf between the laity and the hierarchy is nowhere as wide as in most other religions. The congregation do not sit back in awe and incomprehension but intone silently and knowledgeably with the *granthis* and *ragis*. But even this cultural factor does not stand alone. Sikhism has also been a vehicle in recent years for the assertion of the community's economic affluence. To be a Sikh was to be economically prosperous, independent and enterprising:[5] and that is why many bleeding heart liberals are not sure whether they should bleed with the Sikhs or not.

For the left political formations too it would have been so convenient if only the Sikhs had been poor, helpless, and had sought patronage. The left could then have reflexively, and with a clear conscience, stood by the victims without being in two minds as they are today. Confused by the concentricity of the Punjab problem, confused too by the vigour and unanimity of the Sikh response, they erroneously believe that the current intransigence in Punjab is an independent outcome of Akali politics. But this is certainly the lowest common denominator. If one works one's way through the positions that the left has taken over the years apropos of the Punjab, one finds that, on this issue at least, the entire gamut of left politics is quite rudderless. Several discordant voices pulling in different directions can be heard from the ranks of even the CPI(M). Many leftists, particularly in the CPI, even found words of praise for the Operation Bluestar which killed hundreds of innocent pilgrims in order to claim the lives of approximately fifty militants led by Bhindranwale.[6] Many among them also considered the Anandpur Sahab resolution as one potent with mischief, which only reveals that they have either not read the resolution or did not like the confident look of the Sikhs. The full story of the needless massacre at the Golden Temple has yet to be written, but in the following pages we will have occasion to return to a consideration of the Anandpur Sahab resolution only to show how its non-reading coupled with persuasive misinformation and disinformation by the Centre has created the chimeric image of the Sikh fanatic.

Still the left, particularly the Left Front government in West Bengal, gave evidence of what no-questions-asked-anti-communalism can be when they put a quick end to the anti-Sikh saturnalia in West Bengal. It must be remembered that anti-Sikh violence began in Calcutta even before the country knew that Indira Gandhi was dead. It was kicked off only after Rajiv Gandhi left West Bengal on hearing of his mother's death on a privileged basis. The rest of India, true to the old adage, thought of massacres the day after. This is why the accomplishment of the West Bengal government on this score is unparalleled. It cannot be equated with the other non-Congress states because there were no riots in these states in the first place and also because the Congress partisans here were nowhere as powerful as they were in West Bengal. The success of the Congress in the 1984 parliamentary elections in West Bengal should demonstrate that.

THE CRUCIAL YEARS: 1980–85

Even if we take the years 1980 to 1985 as the active historical base for comprehending the communalising of Punjab, one must of necessity also be willing to move vertically and horizontally, and comingle various levels of India's polity and society to provide perspective to the last six years. One must, for instance, take into account the constraints under which the new political masters of India must function as micro chips off the old block; one must also be able to fathom why the promise of breathing on the open spaces of the twenty-first century must be accompanied by ethnic marginalisation. There was an opportunity earlier during the partition of learning some truths on issues such as these, but it was pushed aside in the euphoria of political independence and on the mistaken notion that there was something very special about Hindu–Muslim antagonism.

So history has obliged by repeating itself with the communalising of Punjab. It has again demonstrated the feasibility of making points with blunt instruments. But it would be a mistake to think that when history repeats itself then it is always as a farce the second time around. Be that as it may, the political centre-stage today does not depict a single-act tragedy, or farce, but a vignette from a performance of epic proportions where climaxes heap upon climaxes leading exhaustingly to a wasted denouement. The denouement when it comes will reveal the waste, the tragedy, and possibly the farce too, but right now the unbridled need for climatic highs is still deliciously recalling the foreplay.

It helps to look back into the past to comprehend how the current passions were stoked, provided we use history and do not let history use us. The past lends itself to the present with different degrees of valency: the recall subserving current obsessions. Many commentators of the Punjab situation have viewed the recently finished Sikh identity as an outcome of Sikh traditions and history with the present only offering another occasion.[7] As a matter of fact, such inflexible uses of history are lit by spontaneous communal impulses so bright that the scholar-commentator often mistakes them for flashes of erudition. It is true that Sikh lore makes a great to-do about martyrdom, *peeri-meeri*, and so forth; and it is also true that the Akali Dal constantly returns to these evocative symbols. There are no doubts, least of all for Longowal, that the Akali Dal is a communal party, but there are grave doubts if the people of Punjab were politically always communal. If communalism were confined to the communal parties then the sluice gates of xenophobia could be jammed fairly effectively. It is only when it spills over that the circle of communalism darkens: the Centre and the periphery are equally tarred.

If one were to examine the career graph of the Akalis then it would become obvious that far from the graph depicting a steady curve riding high on lore, myths, history (mythstory), it actually features both peaks and troughs. If one wishes to go back to pre-Independence Akali politics the record would seem even shabbier. In 1946 when Master Tara Singh, prodded by the mythstory of the Sikhs, incomprehensibly lisped the demand for a separate Sikh state, he found his constituency quickly leaving the room to have a hearty laugh outside.[8] He hurriedly withdrew this demand and was only able to re-establish himself much later during the Partition by demonstrating his solidarity with India. If in those days this was accomplished by anti-Muslim bigotry, today it is accomplished by anti-Sikh xenophobia.

Incomprehensibly too, to the unreflecting scholar-commentator, some of the most outstanding Sikh Congress leaders of the past four decades had begun their political careers as Akali partisans. Their conversion to Congress did not make them apostates, nor were they declared *tankhaiya*. Swaran Singh and Pratap Singly Kairon are perhaps the best known among such men. Yet these notables did not cease being Sikhs, or even cease subscribing to the sectarian Sikh folklores and mythistory. If the Sikhs were really unable to distinguish between temporal and spiritual authority (as enunciated by the *peeri-meeri* duo) the Congress would never have won as resoundingly as it has in the past with Sikh votes, and neither would the Akali party have been in near disgrace in the 1980 elections. In the Sikh majority district of Ludhiana, for instance, the Congress won nine out of 12 seats in 1980.

CHANDIGARH, WATER AND TERRITORY: TAKE OFF OF A SECULAR MOVEMENT

If there is a historic cut-off point for the current tensions communalising Punjab, then it is 1980. That is the time around when the sluice gates of communal passions around Punjab were gradually being oiled and un-jammed, and kept in readiness to be flung open. History stood by in attendance with its records and accomplishments, but in order of the most recent first. Not Guru Gobind Singh, nor the *gailughara* (literally, bloodbath) of Abdall, nor even the Akali *jathas* of the 1920s, got precedence. Like memory, the past stretched slowly backwards from the present. Chandigarh, territorial disputes, and the sharing of river waters were the main issues then. Ironically, the martyrdom of Guru Tegh Bahadur seems all-important now. Five years of Congress rule inclusive of Operation Bluestar and the Sikh massacres of 1984 mnemonically revived the past, pushed away the present, and filled in the concentricity of a new communalism.

The demand for Chandigarh as the capital of Punjab; the demand that the sharing of river water between Punjab, Haryana and Rajasthan be adjudicated by the Supreme Court; and the demand that territorial disputes between Punjab and its neighbours be decided by the territorial tribunal, were among the principal demands of the Anandpur Sahab resolution. This resolution was passed in 1978 when the Akalishad Punjab in their grip and also a finger in the sticky Janata pie in the Centre. Yet, the adoption of the Anandpur Sahab resolution did not signal mass communal excitement in 1978. All the Akali Dal did was to file a case in the Supreme Court on the issue of interstate distribution of water. What is more, the Akalis showed no enthusiasm to implement any of the ethnic demands contained in the Anandpur Sahab resolution. Paradoxically, the Congress(I), while refusing to take heed of the secular elements in the Akali resolution, were quick to recognise and make concessions on ethnic issues. The most remarkable of these was the publicised willingness of the Congress(I) to constitute a separate Sikh code bill, thus amending Article 25 of the Constitution.[9]

Source Credibility of Akalis

Why did the Anandpur Sahab resolution come to mean so much in the years following 1980? After all, the Akalis were defeated in Punjab a scarce two years after the resolution was formally adopted. The majority of elected legislators in Punjab after the 1980 elections were Sikhs, but not Akalis. But by 1982 Sikh opinion began to give the Akali Dal a source credibility which it perhaps lacked even in 1978. To comprehend this and to plumb the depths of the communalisation of Punjab the period since 1980 deserves closer scrutiny.

The increasing source credibility of the Akali Dal can be traced to two factors. First, the apparent transparent honesty of the Akali demands. Chandigarh, the Akali Dal demanded, should be given to Punjab as it was built as the capital of Punjab at a site where the majority language was Punjabi. The Akalis further urged that disputes over water and territory be handed over to superior adjudicating bodies and that the Dal would accept the decision of these bodies. In spite of the apparent honesty of the Akali demands, that alone would not have given it its source credibility. At this point we must take into account the second factor which enhanced the Dal's credibility, *viz.*, the fact that the Congress never squarely faced the Akali demand. The Centre put off any consideration of the major issues by (a) calling the Anandpur Sahab resolution secessionist; (b) by withdrawing from the Supreme Court the case that the Akalis in 1978 had filed on water disputes; and (c) by linking Abohar and Fazilka with Chandigarh. The last meant that the only way Punjab could get Chandigarh would be if it gave Abohar and Fazilka to Haryana in return, and they are deep in Punjab. The transfer of these regions to Haryana would entail the construction of a corridor, not unlike Danzig. Instead the Akalis contended that all territorial disputes be handed to the appropriate commission/tribunal, and the matter be decided as in all territorial disputes, on the principles of contiguity and village (not block or district) level language enumeration.

Instead of responding to this position openly, the Congress(I) kept talking of Abohar, Fazilka, corridor, Chandigarh, all at once. To make matters worse, after their accession to power in Punjab the Congress(I) in 1980 withdrew from the Supreme Court the case on water distribution that was filed by the earlier Akali Dal government. When the Congress(I) withdrew the case the only reason it gave was that the Akalis were being unneighbourly and unpatriotic in moving the court.[10] If this were the case surely the Supreme Court would have given the same judgment and the well-curved Akali sail would then have hung limp.

None of these three major demands made by the Akalis were ethnic or communal. They were straightforward regional and secular issues. West Bengal, Karnataka, or Andhra Pradesh could have come up with similar demands. But unlike these states, also known for the strength of their regional political formations, the party sponsoring these demands in Punjab was a communal party, the Akali Dal. Also unlike any of the issues actually raised by West Bengal, or by any other non-Congress(I) state, there was no ambiguity in any of these three issues raised by the Akalis since 1980. Not one of these could be reasonably controverted: at least the Congress(I) did not exert itself to do so. On the contrary, it insisted on communalising these demands by raising the bogey of Sikh separatism. This immediately struck a responsive chord in Hindu hearts uneasy with forebodings of another partition.

I would further contend that the issues of water, territory and Chandigarh were not equally important nor equally transparent in their honesty in the eyes of the Sikhs. Though each of them merited a 24-carat status, it was Chandigarh that was the real solitaire—shone to resplendence by the heaviest of Congress(I) handlings. For a long time, till actually Operation Bluestar, it was the unassailable Akali position on Chandigarh that helped the Dal to get its act together *vis-à-vis* the Centre. Though the Anandpur Sahab resolution also talked of reworking Centre–state relationships, this aspect received no salience with the people. With time, however, as the Centre tossed about the issues of Chandigarh, water and territory, instead of firmly grappling with them, the validity of redefining Centre–state relationships found vindication and objectification in the eyes of an ever-growing number of Sikhs. Surely and rapidly the Akali Dal kept gaining in source credibility such that it was even emboldened to talk in terms of *Dharam Yudh* (religious war) on 4 August 1982 even though a large number of Sikhs still thought it to be quite irrelevant. Operation Bluestar and the November 1984 Sikh massacres completed the communal circle. *Dharam Yudh* suddenly became the most relevant issue.

FROM SECULAR TO COMMUNAL: HEIGHTENING OF MINORITY CONSCIOUSNESS

If Operation Bluestar was designed to smash communal extremism, nothing could have been a greater failure. Secular and regional issues went into the shade and Sikh opinion consolidated as never before behind its religious ramparts. It is not as if Sikhs objected to the necessity of using the army to weed out criminal elements from the Golden Temple. In fact they would have favoured a police action in the Golden Temple as early as in 1982 when A. S. Athwal, the Deputy

Inspector General (DIG) of Police, was allegedly murdered by extremists. The groundswell of Sikh hostility to the army action of June 1984 grew as it did primarily because the brutality of Operation Bluestar resulted in the deaths of a large number of innocent pilgrims. Bluestar was followed by similar operations in other gurudwaras too, where again, as in Dukhniwaran Sahab in Patiala, a large number of devotees lost their lives. That Bhindranwale is near canonisation in the minds of many Sikhs today is because Bhindranwale's blood mingled with the blood of at least 400 pilgrims who died during Bluestar. Other factors such as the overuse of force, mortar, HASH and tanks which devastated large portions of the temple fell in line and stoked this initial anger further. The scale of and the devastation wrought by Operation Bluestar even horrified some loyal Congress(I) members.[11] When the Bluestar showed no signs of a flagging momentum, and was followed by large scale harassment of Sikhs, young and old, men and women, more recalcitrants slipped behind fundamentalist ramparts and ideologically barricaded themselves. The November 1984 massacres successfully nationalised this tendency among Sikhs. The enemy was no longer the Congress(I) government but the Hindu *sarkar*. The source credibility of the Akalis became unassailable and their communal prognostications took on a clairvoyant character.

This is what source credibility is all about. Once an individual or an organisation wins absolutic credibility on certain issues, that individual or organisation is deemed in the public eye as a source of unimpeachable credibility such that its other pronouncements are subscribed to without scrutiny.[12] Exhortations towards martyrdom, towards traditional obeisance to the temporal authority of the *takhts*, towards the defence of Sikh religion and traditions—in short, exhortations towards *Dharam Yudh*—began to possess a credible ring. It is not as if the past heavily burdened the present in 1980, but rather it is the manner in which the Centre reacted to the Akali demands, which were initially secular, that mnemonically revived tradition as an ideological rationale for activism. If, however, we fail to take note of this and argue instead that Sikh religious consciousness was from the beginning the motivating factor then we would be making a superficial use of history, and in objective terms "blaming the victims." It needs reminding that every community is capable of creating a history full of glory, sacrifice and martyrdom. The Tamils of Sri Lanka next door are doing it right now. The Druze, the Palestinians, the Iranians, the Bengalis, the Maharashtrians, to name a few, have all demonstrated this capacity in recent times.

Hindu Communalism and Sikh Communalism

The gradual consolidation of Sikh opinion around the Akalis did not produce Hindu communalism. The two proceeded apace but were pointed in different directions. While the various Sikh factions tilted at the Centre, Hindu communalists organised against the Sikhs. The communalism of these two communities are still not mirror images of each other. Most incidents of communal violence on the streets, such as the recent ones in Hoshiarpur district, or the earlier ones in Patiala, Ambala and Panipat, as well as the Sikh massacres in November, have occurred where the Sikhs are in a minority. Rural Punjab, where Sikhs are a majority, is tense, thanks to the ruthless persecution of Sikh youth, but there has been no major communal incident in Punjab villages. It hardly needs repeating that from the early years of this century a significant section of the Hindu community in Punjab has rallied behind the Arya Samaj to deny Sikhism its separate identity. The gurudwaras too were under Hindu mahants who made every effort to efface them of any special significance to Sikhism. Hindu idols were installed in the gurudwaras to convey the impression that the Sikhs had no special claim to these shrines.[13] The Sikh resentment of this was obvious and understandable. This explains why it was necessary to take Hindu idols away from the gurudwaras in 1905 to appease the Sikhs. But the Sikhs even then were against that brand of Hindu communalism that was aimed against them and not against Hinduism as such. This is what allowed Gandhiji to talk to the leaders of the Akali movement of the 1920s like a school master.[14] Neither did Master Tara Singh receive mass approbation for his advocacy of an autonomous, sovereign Sikh state in the 1940s. This strain still characterises Sikh politics even though it has become much communalised. Already stress lines are developing and there is not much time before the mirror cracks from side to side and Sikh communalism becomes a mirror image of the Hindu one.

Time is indeed running out. Perceptions and counter-perceptions—not issues—seem to be fuelling passions increasingly. The perceptions among Hindus that the Sikhs are out for another partition is an outcome of a non-reading of the Anandpur Sahab resolution aided in no small measure by the Congress(I)'s deliberate policy to misrepresent the situation. The radio and the television flood out by sheer cusecs of verbiage any possibility of a fair assessment of the Anandpur resolution. The view has gained ground that the resolution is every bit as cretinous as Hindu communalism would wish: that in fact it is a mirror image of Hindu communalism. The fact that the Anandpur Sahab resolution of 1978 nowhere makes the claim that Punjab should be under the sway of *khalsa ka hot bata* (or Sikh fundamentalist diktat) will come as a surprise to many. The volume, consistency and intensity of government misinformation and disinformation on Punjab tightly interwove with the popular perceptions of the Sikhs among the Hindus to give the Congress(I) an unprecedented number of seats in the Lok Sabha elections of 1984.

Undercutting of Moderates

This Hindu communalism is no backlash. The raw material of popular Hindu perceptions was carefully worked upon by the Congress(I) such that in Punjab today one has two completely distinct views, one Sikh and one Hindu, on almost everything. In the years 1980 to 1984 the government portrayed the Anandpur Sahab resolution principally as a religiously inspired secessionist document, when in reality it was far from that. From 1980 to 1984 the government refused to talk to Akali leaders, breaking off talks on one pretext or the other. On three instances in these years the Akalis were ready to negotiate but had to return to Punjab in humiliation. The talks were still-born because of the abortive tactics of the government. On one occasion on the eve of a slated round of talks P. C. Sethi suddenly announced that there would be no talks till normalcy was restored. This lofty pronouncement was made without even pausing to consider why talks should be held regarding the restoration of normalcy if normalcy prevailed anyway. The fact that there was no public condemnation of Sethi's position at the national level is symptomatic of the success with which the government had won the credibility of the non-Sikhs. On a second occasion Bhajan Lal's Haryana erupted with anti-Sikh riots in several districts on 14 February 1984, forcing the Akalis to return to Punjab. On a third occasion on 18 February 1984, on the eve of another round of talks, the police unnecessarily created an incident in front of the Golden Temple, thus forcing the Akalis again to return to Punjab. But what is perhaps unknown to many is that on the eve of the inauguration of the Asiad in 1982 an agreement was actually arrived at between the Congress(I) and the Akalis, where even Harkishan Singh Surjeet of the CPI(M) was involved. While the Akali leaders, such as Prakash Singh Badal, and Congress(I) mediators were toasting this event and waiting for the official declaration from the cabinet, Indira Gandhi suddenly announced that the agreement was not acceptable to her. This not only dumbfounded the Akalis but several Congress(I) members too.

All this was cutting into the moderate and majority section of Sikh opinion. While Longowal and the Aklai Dal were gaining in source credibility they were not really prepared to carry out a fundamentalist drive. The moderates were thus shoehorned into a dilemma by the force of their own latent potentialities. Each rebuff by the Centre gave respectability, albeit in small doses, to refractory Sikhs, and any concession to these elements by the Akali Dal weakened Longowal's public commitment to the integrity of India, to the Anandpur Sahab resolution and to communal amity. The Akali Dal is careful to play only a limited-risk game of communalist politics. However, the Akalis at this juncture chose unwisely not to conduct an ideological war against Bhindranwale for a dubious kind of united frontism which publicly overlooked the enemy at the doorstep. Yet they could not help but constantly look back over their shoulders to protect their flanks against militant depredations. As a consequence the Akalis had only a blurred image of the Centre's moves and an incomplete grasp of the "Bhindranwale effect." After Operation Bluestar they were made to pay dearly for this. The meeting at Khatkar Kalian in March 1985, to commemorate Bhagat Singh's death anniversary is illustrative of this situation. Unaware of the public mood after long months in detention following Bluestar, Longowal began his speech by asking the gathering to consider issues "with a cool head." The hostility with which the *kesari* turbaned crowd reacted to this prefatory comment compelled Longowal to change gears instantly and adopt a shrill and belligerent attitude. As a consequence he had also to swallow his bile and refer to Bhindranwale as a *Sant* and a martyr. Neither did this position him advantageously *vis-à-vis* the Centre. All the latter had to do in this situation was to gloat to the rest of India with an "I told you so."

If there was any pride (*izzat*) left among the Sikhs after the massacre of their numbers in the Operation Bluestar even that was being forced out into the streets. First, the Sikh library and museum in the Golden Temple complex was set on fire a full two days after Bluestar was officially concluded. Then again, instead of allowing the Shiromani Gurdwara Parbandhak Committee (SGPC) to rebuild the Akal Takht and the bullet-marked sanctum sanctorum and recover its shame, the government handed the task to an interloper from a renegade Sikh sect, the Buddha Dal, which further aroused the ire and resentment of the Sikh masses. This was followed by the arrest and torture of hundreds of Sikhs reminiscent of the Naxalbari operation a decade ago. The crucial difference with the anti-Naxalites operation however is that in this case it is enough to be a Sikh to be worthy of suspicion. Other identities do not matter.

The country's military and paramilitary forces have come down heavily on the restless Sikh youth, both in the countryside and in urban areas. The youth who were already frustrated with the tapering-off of the green revolution were immediately incensed. Because of the pressure on land, and the decreasing returns on agriculture, they were now on the lookout for scarce jobs in urban areas, in the Middle East and elsewhere. The number of schools and colleges that came up in Punjab after the state was redemarcated, especially after 1969, is evidence of the growing need among Sikh youth for formal education as a passport for other economic opportunities. They had already lost their privileged position in the army after the British left. All this makes for a very volatile and inflammable situation. It is often believed that resentment can only be furthered by absolute deprivation and to that extent the believers of such a position are at a loss to understand why the economically prosperous Punjab should demand more water and employment opportunities. But as a matter of fact, economic deprivation is quite as often viewed relatively as well. The fact that the first thrust of the green revolution set off a standard of living and a scale of emulation which became difficult to sustain as the years went by should also be remembered. The increasing costs of agricultural inputs, the rush to buy mechanised agricultural implements that in many cases only increased the household's financial liability, queered the pitch a good deal and rubbed off some of the shine generated by the first few years of the green revolution.[15] The Sikh cultivators, of course, saw the problem as an economic one, so much so that the Bharatiya Kisan Union was able to hold a large rally even after the Bluestar operation in Punjab. Yet this has not been able to counteract the extant suspicion among the Sikhs that it is the Sikhs alone who are being singled out for persecution. The manner in which the Akali Dal slowly gained charisma and source credibility as mentioned earlier bred and fed this suspicion till it became an unshakable faith.

Army Desertions: Communalising Process in a Microcosm

The "desertions" of Sikh troops is another indicator of the level of alienation among the Sikhs today. Here, too, we find in a microcosm the national forces at work in the communalising of Punjab. Not once has it been mentioned that in Ramgarh, from where maximum desertions took place, as many as 20 out of 23 officers left their position in the Sikh Regimental Centre and sought refuge with their families elsewhere. It was only after the officers left their posts and left their troops leaderless that mass anxiety gripped the soldiers—some of whom were just raw recruits. On the following Sunday, when it is the custom that every officer of the Sikh Regimental Centre, accompanied by his family, attend the regimental gurudwara along with the soldiers, there was not a single officer present.[16] Neither did the officers ever hold a *darbar* with the soldiers on this issue. Past practices should have made the holding of *darbar* an occasion to explain to the Sikh troops the compulsions of the Bluestar operation which would have helped to assuage their feelings. The first desertions that took place were the desertions of these officers. It is a fact too that Sikh soldiers everywhere were disgruntled and disaffected after the Bluestar operation, but wherever their officers stood by them and provided leadership "desertions" did not take place. What fear, what propaganda took hold of the minds of the non-Sikh officers to desert their posts will never be known with certitude, but certainly the army command succumbed as much as did the nation at large to the persuasive typification of the bloodthirsty, disloyal, extremist and secessionist Sikh.

This continues to be evident during the court-martial proceedings too. While the soldiers under trial pleaded guilty to desertions, the prosecution is still not happy. The army prosecution wants to prove that these under trials conspired and that the conspiracy was led by their JCOs and NCOs. The prosecution is unwilling to accept that the soldiers acted spontaneously out of grief and anger and that they were provoked by the desertion of their officers. To accept this would weaken the case against the soldiers and the accusing finger would point instead at the government and the army brass. Hence the long hours of torture and deprivation to compel the prisoners to commit perjury. So far they have held out by reliving in their minds the martyrdom of Guru Tegh Bahadur.

CENTRE STRIKES BACK: ETHNICISATION IN REVERSE

Since Independence, India has constantly been embroiled in tensions between the Centre and the federating units. This has emboldened political scientists to put down in print that the cultural variations in India will soon bring down the fragile unity in the Centre which embodies the nation-state. A closer inspection at the points of conflict between the Centre and the federating units, however, reveals that cultural factors *per se* have never put any tension on the political unit of this country. In fact, it would be wrong to believe that the current tensions between the Centre and several states are actually the final efflorescence of the earlier movements of cultural assertion. If anything, there have been three distinct phases, involving three distinct kinds of political problems over this entire period with reference to unity and diversity, or cultural primordialism and political cohesion.

The first phase was with the demand for unilingual states. This was followed by nativist or "sons of the soil" movements. This, in turn, after a gap of several years, was followed by regional movements which demanded a reworking of Centre–state relationships. It would be incorrect to assume that the last is the logical culmination of the first, or that any of these political phases ever questioned the Indian Union.

The most cultural of the above three kinds of political manifestations was the linguistic movement demanding unilingual states. This movement actually demonstrated the possibility of a nation-state celebrating its differences and thus questioning both the inevitability and the inherent superiority of the western type of nation-state.

The nativist movements too always turned to the Centre for help and looked upon the Centre as the prime adjudicating body, much as the linguistic movements had done before them. The Centre yet again played the role of the arbitrator but not before it had gained some advantages for itself. Only with the regional movements of the 1970s and 1980s do we find purely secular and economic issues being raised to the forefront, and it is only now that the Centre seems most maladroit.

During the linguistic movements the Centre had to preside over the reshaping of the administrative structure and boundaries of its constituting elements, but as it did not have to deny the linguistic demands of any major linguistic group by acquiescing in the linguistic demands of another, we witnessed, as was mentioned above, a celebration of differences which defied the Western model (which is also the RSS model) of a nation-state. The nativist movements too provided no major challenge to the Centre for the ruling party in Delhi was never threatened by nativist movements. On the other hand, the latter was always willing to be co-opted into the former. There could be no better example of this than the Shiv Sena of Bombay. But with regional and secular movements the ruling party at the Centre, more particularly the Congress(I), was for the first time faced with a political formation that was hostile to it. Now was the time for the Centre to strike back. And the Centre struck back ethnically. It ethnicised secular issues in order to marginalise its opponents, one by one, from the national mainstream. The fact that the demarcation of state boundaries is superimposed by linguistic and/or religious markers provided the temptation for the regional political formations to lapse into the ethnic slot the Congress(I) was pushing them into. While Farooq Abdullah and N. T. Rama Rao came perilously close to it, the Akali Dal blundered straight into it.

The Centre's policy of ethnicising regional demands in Punjab was aided not merely by the fact that it was the Akali Dal that was playing the leading agitational role, but also because the Congress was able to place a communalising catalyst in the shape of Bhindranwale. It may be recalled that Bhindranwale's candidates were wiped out in the SGPC elections in 1979. But Bhindranwale was able to overcome this humiliation with the help of the state government. He was arrested for the murder of Lala Jagat Narain in 1981, but then the government dramatically released him. The manner in which he was arrested and released created an aura around Bhindranwale. The *Sant* had made it known that the police could arrest him only after he had spent a week in meditation in his hermitage, and he laid down the further condition that only proper *khalsa* Sikhs with open beards should be sent to take him into custody. The government acceded to this unprecedented request, and that too to a man who had, at that point, no standing in the Sikh community. His release soon after from prison added dramatically to his charisma. It was hard to believe that only a year back his candidates supported by the Congress were routed in the SGPC elections.

From then on Bhindranwale's prestige kept soaring. He bucked the Akalis to a pace and to a style of politics they were just not in the shape for. Sikh fundamentalism which did not figure even during the Master Tara Singh-led Punjabi Suba movement began to gain salience with the emergence of Bhindranwale. Operation Bluestar almost canonised him and for a while it seemed that Longowal had thrown in the towel. But he rolled with the punch and is finding his feet again.

Fortunately for Punjab, Longowal is not allowing the ghost of Bhindranwale to act as an *éminence grise* any longer. To this end he has publicly distanced himself from the faction led by Bhindranwale's father and Jathedar Talwandi. Fortunately too for Longowal, he was able to assert his leadership over the Akali Dal on 9 June 1985 in Manji Sahab. Fortunately too, there are many economic, sectional and old fashioned idealist interests left in Punjab which together, for different reasons, want the tangle to be sorted out fast and to unmake the communalising of Punjab. But unfortunately, every day of procrastination only succeeds in communally titillating the environs, every instance of unwarranted police or paramilitary atrocity only aggravates the situation further. The Sikhs are not yet used to subservience. Their economic strength and prosperity allow them the extravaganza of defying the victimisers. But once the mirror image of Hindu communalism is reflected in Sikh communalism, then in the final climax of wargasm the fundamentalist Sikhs will ride the Congress(I) and turn the clock back for a long time to come. Well, might many say, good riddance like they said to Pakistan in 1947. But just think of the devastation of lives, the profligate expenditure of mortality, and yet another crippled limb that will never grow again like the heads of cabbages and kings do. We are all prepared after a fashion, to expect a wasted denouement, but one is never prepared enough for an irrevocable and avoidable disaster.

NOTES AND REFERENCES

[I have greatly benefited from discussions with Gautam Navlakha. I alone am, however, responsible for the shortcomings of the chapter.]

[1] See *Who Are the Guilty?* (New Delhi: People's Union for Democratic Rights (PUDR) and People's Union for Civil Liberties (PUCL), 1984).

[2] See *Black Laws in Punjab* (New Delhi: People's Union for Democratic Rights (PUDR), 1985).

[3] Scheduled Caste Sikhs such as the Mazhabis are known for their anti-Jat Sikh, and hence anti-Akali Dal, political preferences. For instance, over 90 per cent of the left organisation, the Khet Mazdoor Sabha, is made up of Mazhabi Sikhs. Giani Zail Singh was also successful in mobilising a large number of Kamgarhia Sikhs into the Congress(I). He himself is a member of this community. However, the Operation Bluestar seems to have obliterated these differences. The best illustration being the SC origins of both Satwant Singh and Beam Singh, the assassins of Indira Gandhi. It is also undeniable that the Delhi Sikhs who were in the past with Congress(I) openly supported opposition candidates in the 1984 parliamentary elections.

[4] For a moving account of this, see Baljit Singh Malik, "I Dare to Belong," *Lokayan* 3, no. 1 (1985): pp. 29–41.

[5] Richard Fox, "Urban Class and Communal Consciousness in Colonial Punjab: The Genesis of India's Intermediate Regime," *Modern Asian Studies* 18, no. 3 (July 1984): pp. 459–90; see especially pp. 480–84.

[6] In two separate resolutions, the CPI(M) first praised Operation Bluestar and then criticised it. In the first resolution on 3 June 1984 they blamed the Akali Dal alone. The second resolution of 6 June 1984 blamed both the Akali Dal and Congress(I) (*Statesman*, 12 June 1984). Even H. S. Surjeet of the CPI(M) charged the Akali Dal for separatist tendencies (*Times of India*, 25 March 1984). The CPJ has been more unambiguous and consistent. It publicly proclaimed great relief that Operation Bluestar had taken place (*Times of India*, 7 June 1984) and has not found it necessary to modify this position since.

[7] Sudhir Kakkar, "Legend as History," *Times of India* (1984). M. J. Akbar also inclines towards an identical argument in his book, *India: The Siege Within* (Penguin, 1985), see especially pp. 173–200.

[8] Christopher Shackle, *The Sikhs*, Report No. 65 (London: Minority Rights Group, 1984), p. 7.

[9] The Centre declared its agreement to amend Article 24 of the Constitution as a gesture of goodwill on 31 March 1984 (*Times of India*, 1 April 1984).

[10] See also Government of India's "White Paper on Punjab" of 11 July 1984.

[11] Swaran Singh of the Congress(I) said on record that Operation Bluestar was not necessary, "especially when other solutions were available." He went on to say that the sanctity of the Golden Temple was first defiled by the extremists and then by the government. "Two wrongs," he added, "do not make a right"(*Amrit Bam Patrika*, 17 June 1984).

[12] For an understanding of source credibility see, James A. Davies, "Sociology of Attitudes," in *Knowledge and Society*, ed. Talcott Parsons (Voice of America Publications, 1968), p. 25. I have tried to demonstrate the utility of this concept in greater detail elsewhere with reference to the Shiv Sena movement in my book *Nativism in a Metropolis: The Shiv Sena in Bombay* (New Delhi: Manohar Publications, 1982), pp. 140–46.

[13] Shackle, *The Sikhs*, p. 7.

[14] See M. K. Gandhi, *Collected Works* (Ministry of Information and Broadcasting, 1960–67), Vol. 18, p. 356; Vol. 19, p. 402; Vol. 23, pp. 229–30.

[15] According to one estimate, the rate of return on wheat for Punjab farmers fell from 27.28 per cent in 1972–73 to as low as 10.89 per cent in 1978–79. In 1977–71 it was an unbelievably low 1.32 per cent. See Sucha Singh Gill and K. C. Singhal, "Punjab: Farmers Agitation—Response to Developmental Crisis in Agriculture," *Economic and Political Weekly* 19, no. 40 (6 October 1984), pp. 1728–32; see p. 1729.

[16] These facts came to light in the military court-martial proceedings at Jabalpur on 3 June 1985.

17

The Ideology of Population Control*

Mahmood Mamdani

The principal explanation for India's continuing poverty advanced by bourgeois social science over the last decade has been the theory of overpopulation, particularly in its neo-Malthusian version. Neo-Malthusianism seeks to establish a relation between national resources and national population by projecting into the future the existing development of each. Shorn of its particular trappings, substantially the argument is that the rate of population growth is outstripping the rate of resource development; the result: imminent catastrophe—hunger, starvation and social conflict—both nationally and internationally.

The left critique of neo-Malthusian thought has sought to argue that its very presentation of the problem has been *ideological*, that the national societies are class societies and in class societies appropriation has a *dual* aspect. It is the appropriation both of nature and of the producers, natural appropriation as well as social appropriation. The control over national resources is thus not as much national as by particular classes whose objective interests dictate its mode of utilisation and its future growth in size and composition. Second, the appropriation of these resources is not just within a national but primarily in an international context and thus analysis must situate itself at the level of the totality: the international capitalist system.

A critique at the level of ideology, however, is only a first step. Though a necessary step, it must be followed by a *scientific* explanation of what is a real phenomenon: the rising rates of natural increase in population in most backward capitalist countries. It is the purpose of this chapter to contribute to

* Originally published in *Economic and Political Weekly* 11, special number (7 August 1976): pp. 1141–48.

the development of such an explanation and thereby deepen the critique of neo-Malthusian thought as well as attempt a redefinition of what has been called the "population problem."

A scientific explanation is possible only if a phenomenon is located in its specificity, in this case both social and historical. Birth rates are not territorially specific as much as specific to particular social groups. Anybody familiar with the demography of a town or a village knows that the reproductive practice of land labourers is different from that of the landlords and of the petty bourgeois from that of the proletarian or the unemployed. Reproductive behaviour is not a natural but a social phenomenon. Territorial birth rates or rates of natural increase are an abstraction that do not advance as much as mystify our understanding. Second, this same behaviour is neither idiosyncratic nor accidental but is substantially *reproduced* over time. The "population problem" would only exist if there was a certain uniformity over time of the reproductive behaviour of social groups. In other words, our concern with reproductive behaviour is not in its individuality, as a subjective phenomenon, but as one both social and objective. The question that must be posed then is: What are the *social relations* that underlie these practices? Furthermore, the social relations themselves did not always exist but were historically created. The very relations must then be understood in their historical specificity.

This chapter will attempt an analysis of the reproductive behaviour of two social groups that form the bulk of the population in the Indian social formation: the working peasantry and the unemployed. Its purpose will be to delineate those historically created social relations that explain the reproductive behaviour of these groups. What we hope to show is, one, that it is not high population growth that explains India's poverty but the contrary, and two, that this poverty itself is nota natural but a historical phenomenon: its reproduction cannot be understood unless we analyse it as the result of social relations which themselves must be placed in the context of a system of oppression, imperialism.

I

The Working Peasantry

What are referred to as the underdeveloped countries today were incorporated into the world capitalist system in the last four centuries. Their incorporation, however, was not uniform but uneven. The capitalist mode of production was implanted only in the territories of colonial *settlement*; in the regions of colonial *domination*, however, capitalism did not simply destroy the pre-capitalist modes by appropriating the peasantry and transforming it into a class of wage-labourers. The process, on the other hand, was far more complex. The pre-colonial modes were partially destroyed, restructured and then incorporated into the world capitalist system as *subordinate* to the capitalist mode of production internationally[1]—to produce for it, on the one hand, cheap raw materials, and on the other, cheap labour-power, thus cheapening the elements of both constant and variable capital. Henceforth, the accumulation needs of imperialist capital would dictate the content of production in the colonies. In the emerging social formation, while capitalist production was confined to small pockets, imperialism dominated overall production through the agency of the state—at first colonial, later neo-colonial.

For our purposes, it is not necessary to go into all the ramifications of the above process, resulting in the creation of backward capitalism. Suffice it to note that in these social formations, capitalist production was confined to small pockets. Outside of these pockets, whatever the relations of production on the land, be it the small tenanted plot subject to landlord appropriation or peasant commodity production dominated by commercial/money-lending capital, the labour process remained pre-capitalist. The producer remained united to his means of production and the unit of production remained the family.

That the family is the organisational form within which social production takes place has very important implications. It means that socialisation for productive labour is also carried on within the family; the relations of work are reflected in the relations within the family and the discipline of work becomes the discipline of the family.

Family relations among the working peasantry[2] remain rigid and hierarchical. The parent is the head of the family and exercises absolute control. The parent–child relationship is simple: the parent commands, the child obeys. Age and experience are the yardsticks of merit and claim to authority. Parental chauvinism flourishes but is not simply an attitudinal phenomenon. The point is that family relations, sustained by the nature and relations of work, make it possible for adults to control the time and labour of children, including the fruits of that labour.

The qualitative difference with developed capitalism should be quite clear. There the unit of production is no longer the family but the capitalist enterprise. Similarly, socialisation for work is carried out not as much within the family as within the school or the prison. The producer is not as much a family member as a wage-labourer, a capitalist or a member of the salariat. The family here remains but a unit of consumption and procreation, *no longer a unit of production.* Thus emerges the bourgeois family, its relations being part of the material basis of the ideology of individualism and individual freedom. The ideology of the "peasant family" on the other hand, is that of loyalty and unity: it forms the ideological basis of parental authority over children.[3]

Control over children's labour, however, can be of material consequence only if the labour process allows for the productive use of child labour. In other words, what use can the family make of children's time? Another characteristic of backward capitalism is that, outside of the small pockets of capitalist production, the forces of production remain backward. The technology of production in agriculture remains low. In fact, all throughout the colonial period, there has been little change here. Unlike advanced capitalism, backward capitalism does not revolutionise production. The result is twofold. First, an expansion of total output is not the result of increased investment on land in the form of machinery (i.e., through an increase in the organic composition of capital) but the result of an increase in the total labour exerted in agricultural production, a result of an increase in both the working time of the peasant and an increase in the number of working peasants. Second, given its low technical basis, the production process is characterised by activities which include numerous tasks that are both simple and repetitive: from taking care of the grazing, cleaning and feeding of farm animals to the laborious task of weeding and, to some extent, sowing and harvesting. Outside of productive labour, the presence of children in the house can also assure a certain ease in life. The smallest children perform a variety of tasks that the adults regard as tedious, time-consuming and tiresome. When too small to do any work, they will be cared for by older children who include them in their play or carry them on their hips when doing work such as tending to farm animals. As a Punjab farmer put it:

A forest is not made of one tree.
A Jat (tanner) is not made of one son.

It is precisely because children's activity can be of considerable gain to the family that their time and their life are closely regulated by the family, more so as they become older. The very nature of childhood is affected: there is no adolescence. Adolescence is a category specific to advanced capitalism. In backward capitalist formations, on the other hand, there is only childhood and adulthood. When they grow up, children become not youths but young adults.

It might be pointed out that the extremely high levels of unemployment and underemployment in agriculture must limit the access of children to productive labour. Unemployment, however, is much more characteristic of entire families, not of individuals. In agriculture, adult and child unemployment go hand in hand as family unemployment. Without access to means of production, the family moves. The movement of the pauperised and appropriated poor peasantry will be dealt with in the next section.

The nature of what has been called "underemployment" must also be concretely grasped in the rural context. Given the low technical basis of production, the rhythm of work corresponds to the rhythm of nature and is highly uneven. Periods of intense work alternate with periods of low activity.

Harvest, weeding and sowing times—covering over half the year—are the peaks of productive activity corresponding to an acute need for labour. For example, in District Ludhiana in the Punjab, with a tractor and all the necessary implements, it takes three people to work 50 acres of land. Without a tractor, the same land requires at least fourteen people around the year, and at least twenty at sowing, weeding and harvesting times. As the "Rural Labour Enquiry" of the Ministry of Labour concluded: "What facilitates their absorption [the absorption of child labour] in the labour market is the shortage of labour in the peak agricultural seasons in the local area."[4] In these periods of high employment, while it is the family that works and saves, it is the parents who control the savings.

To grasp the relation between rural exploitation and the rural family it is important to bear in mind that the social relations of production, however reminiscent of pre-capitalist relations, derive their motion from their subordination to imperialist accumulation internationally. Peasant production which used to be petty production for use is now petty commodity production for the international capitalist market. While imperialist capital exploits the peasant producer, it does not do so directly but through the mediation of local appropriating classes. In the countryside, the appropriator in the first instance, the one that immediately pumps the surplus out of the petty producer is a *monopoly-based* commercial and/or landed class. The class struggle in the countryside pits the *monopoly* power of the merchant or the landlord against the *fragmented* producers. The result is the appropriation of the petty producer that leaves him with no more than his bare subsistence needs and certainly no surplus to expand the technical basis of his production. There is neither a movement from manual to mechanised labour nor a rise in the productivity of labour as agricultural surpluses are siphoned out—immediately by unproductive classes, and through their mediation by the local and the imperialist bourgeoisie—and not reinvested in agriculture. Whatever the form of appropriation of the direct producers and whatever the form of competition between them, the only means by which the individual producing unit, the family, can increase the physical product at its disposal is by increasing the labour-power at its disposal, i.e., through high rates of reproduction. Even the government's own "Rural Labour Enquiry" empirically grasps the significance of rural child labour: "They [children under 15] are pressed into employment mainly to supplement the meagre income of chronically poverty-stricken rural households."[5] High birth rates are not the cause of peasant impoverishment; they are the response of an impoverished peasantry.

Furthermore, the hierarchical relations within the family and adult control over children's labour means that for the producing family, with each additional child, the cost of having a child declines and the benefit rises. In the absence of a class organisation of the exploited the only possible (not necessarily effective) form of security for peasant producers, not only against social but also against natural calamities such as famine or floods, is the family. As a middle peasant in northern India put it:

A rich man has his machines, I have my children.
It's that simple.

The ideology in peasant cultures incessantly emphasises the virtue of child-bearing. In India, it is considered one's *dharma* (religiously sanctioned social obligation) to have children: to desire as many children as possible is not only in the natural order of things but also an indication of virtue. Marriage vows and blessings put emphasis on the good fortune of having many children. Folk songs, usually sung on occasions such as marriage, childbirth or the harvest, sing praises of the prolific mother and the fertile soil. A popular theme running through many stories is the love of the mother for the son: it is considered the purest form of love. Sanctions against childless women further underline the necessity of children. In other words, *ideology* reinforces the demands of reality.

II

The Appropriated Masses

That the agricultural surplus is siphoned out of agriculture has decisive consequences for the nature of class differentiation in the countryside. While the lower sections of the peasantry are increasingly pauperised, a rural bourgeoisie which could employ the appropriated peasantry fails to emerge.[6] The rural unemployed, unable to find work in the countryside, flock to the cities. The high figures of rural–urban migration in India are testimony to the existence of this process.

The ranks of these appropriated masses are swelled by another social group: the pre-capitalist craftsmen whose material base was undermined with the expanded import of metropolitan commodities during the colonial era. The craftsmen and artisans provided not only consumer goods for the cities but also the basic implements for rural labour such as the plough. Metropolitan imports of both consumer goods and implements of labour made these skilled labourers redundant in the first phase of colonialism, in fact reducing all labour to the lowest common denominator, unskilled agricultural producers engaged in the production of cash crops for export to the metropolitan markets. The bulk of the skilled crafts and artisan workers join the ranks of the appropriated urban masses.

Certainly, this same process—the appropriation of the poor peasantry and the redundancy of skilled pre-capitalist craftsmen—occurred in early western capitalism. There was, however, one critical difference. In advanced capitalism this process was followed by another: proletarianisation. What we find in backward capitalism, on the contrary, is appropriation without proletarianisation.[7] In order to understand this, we must turn to the nature of industrialisation and the structure of employment in the urban economy.

The character of industrialisation in India bears a direct relation to the limited and distorted development of the home market. That the bulk of the Indian population are petty producers on land has a dual effect: one, given the low technique of their production, agriculture provides a very limited market for industries producing the means of production; two, given that peasants produce their necessaries (food crops and dairy goods) side by side with industrial crops, agriculture provides a very limited market for industries producing consumption goods. Thus, the home market for Indian industry is defined predominantly by the consumption needs of the propertied classes.

Thus, in the Department producing means of consumption (Department 2), it is the industries producing for bourgeois consumption[8] that take the lead. The content of the first phase of import substitution is nothing but the production within the internal market of those commodities that used to be imported before: durable consumer goods. Once the Department producing means of production develops, as it did in India in the late 1950s and 1960s, its growth is organically tied to the growth of industries for bourgeois which form the leading factor in industrial development.[9]

It is the production of commodities for bourgeois consumption, durable consumer goods, that forms the objective basis for the collaboration between the Indian industrial bourgeoisie and the transnational corporations, for the latter provide the necessary technology. For our purposes, it is important to understand the consequences of this kind of industrialisation, using the capital-intensive technology of the transnationals, for the structure of employment in modern industry.

Factories and machines may multiply, but not always the workers in them. The development of the factory proletariat, workers in large-scale modern industry, is but a trickle compared to the expansion in industrial production. In India, according to official statistics, the percentage of working population living by modern industry *fell* from 5.5 in 1911 to 4.3 in 1931, registering an increase only in the 1950s, only to return to 4.3 in 1970.[10] The 1960 ILO report on India remarked that "during the first five-year plan, urban unemployment increased in spite of the rise in industrial production ... from 117 (index) in 1951 to 161 in 1956."[11]

The dominant process in the backward capitalist economy undergoing dependent industrialisation is not proletarianisation but *appropriation without proletarianisation.* An entirely new social group emerges in the urban areas, the appropriated masses, living on the fringes of respectable society, at best casually employed. It would be a mistake to see them as a lumpenproletariat or even as Marx's relative surplus population necessary to the smooth functioning of a capitalist labour market. Whenever employed, they form part of the working class since they are producers of material values from whom surplus value is appropriated in the process of production; at the same time, employment in their case regularly alternates with stretches of unemployment which throw them into the ranks of the chronically unemployed. Why do casual employment and high population growth go hand-in-hand in this case?

The most important characteristic of the structure of casual employment is that it allows for child employment to a far greater extent than does modern industry. The 1969 report of the National Commission on Labour[12] points out that, unlike in "organized industries," child employment "persists in varying degrees in the unorganised sector such as small plantations, restaurants and hotels, cotton ginning and weaving, stone-breaking, brick kiln, handicraft and road building.... Under the excuse of preparing a boy for taking up productive employment as he reaches adulthood a small child is engaged to train his fingers in the required skills." The detailed discussion in this report enables us to identify two types of industries in which child labour is common, manufacture and domestic industry, and further, to give examples to illustrate these two instances.

The Commission found "prevalence of child labour in handloom and power-loom units. Usually a weaver has as his mate a child of school-going age." Another "intricate operation where child labour is quite common is brocade work. Here, the Commission noted the employment of boys who "looked between 8 to 10 years of age or even younger." In most of these cases, "the payment of the child was the responsibility of the adult worker whom the child helped," thus compelling the adult to facilitate the exploitation of child labour by capital. "A similar arrangement," the Commission noted, "prevails in carpet-weaving." Asked to explain why the parent does not avail of free education to send the child to school, the Commission pointed to the obvious: "The low earnings of the artisans are compensated by the income of his mate," and pointed out, "For him, an uneducated child is an asset."

Domestic industry provides two examples of intensive child labour in the context of work organised along family lines: mat-making and bidi-rolling. Contractors distribute work in private dwellings "where workers take raw materials given by the employer or his contractor and hand over the finished product at the stipulated place."[13] The system of payment is by piece-rate and the nature of work allows for both female and child labour.

In urban centres proper, the centres of bourgeois consumption, children turned to shoe-shining, to cleaning cars or opening doors, to restaurant work. One form of activity in which young age is a positive asset is begging, here a regular occupation; it is *organised*, and in fact predominantly confined to children.

Denied productive employment, the poor make demands on the "conscience" of local ruling classes and their metropolitan tourist friends. For a member of the affluent classes it is difficult to walk a few yards in any of the urban centres of backward capitalism without hearing a call for "bakshish." Certainly, the family here doesn't possess the unity it does among the working peasantry: once they grow up, children might leave their families. All the same, in slum populations, it is not quite unusual to find children as important breadwinners in the family.

III

The Ideology of Population Control

The decision by a couple located within the working peasantry or the appropriated masses to have a number of children is essentially a national decision, a judgement of their social environment. Rationality does not exist in the abstract; it is concrete, the product of a particular social and historical context. The pitfall of neo-Malthusian liberalism is precisely its "rationalism," that it assumes a universal rationality and forgets that in a class society there exists class rationality.

The demand for population control may be rational in one class situation, but not necessarily in another. The "rationalism" of the neo-Malthusian universalises the situation and thus the rationality of a particular class: what is good for the bourgeoisie is good for all!

Ideological thought is not simply false. It is thought that presents an aspect of reality *as* reality and obscures the *relation* between the aspect and the totality. The specific historical relation between high rates of population growth in particular social groups and their social oppression is obscured. How a problem is defined greatly affects the formulation of the solution. When the phenomenon is defined as the "population problem," its core assertion is that people are poor because they are too many. Exploitation is reduced to poverty and the explanation of poverty become the poor themselves!

Notes and References

[1] See Charles Bettelheim in appendix to Arghiri Emmanuel, *Unequal Exchange: A Study of the Imperialism of Trade* (New York: Monthly Review Press, 1971).

[2] The formation of the working peasantry excludes that section of the peasantry which was proletarianised and refers only to small commodity producers on land. I am aware that an analysis which makes a strict separation between the two, failing to analyse the relations between them, is unscientific. For example, in Africa, large sections of the proletarianised peasants are migrant labourers who return to their families after a period of wage-labour. The wife here becomes the petty commodity producer and the structure of the peasant family itself is altered. Partial

observation leads me to think that though this alters the relation between the husband and wife it does not alter the parent–child relation. Nonetheless, in this social group as in others, only a concrete analysis of concrete social conditions can clarify to us the laws of population growth.

[3] Certainly, the "bourgeois family" can be found in the Indian social formation. Its existence, however, is class specific, located within the bourgeoisie or the urban petty bourgeoisie.

[4] Government of India, Ministry of Labour, Labour Bureau, "Rural Labour Enquiry," 1963–65, *Final Report*, p. 151.

[5] Ibid.

[6] The exception here would be the so-called "Green Revolution" in the Punjab. The tendency of monopoly capitalism to thwart the development of the productive forces in the countryside should not be interpreted in a one-sided manner. It doesn't preclude a limited and localised development of the productive forces. To explain such a development, however, we must take as our starting point the accumulation needs of capital and the concrete class struggle. Three points come to the fore so far as the "Green Revolution" in the Punjab is concerned. First, the initiative by the American oil monopolists to introduce in the Indian countryside high-yielding seed varieties that at the same time require high inputs of chemical fertilisers was an attempt by the oil monopolies to maximise their profits by creating larger markets for the by-products of oil. Second, rural Punjab, unlike large sections of semi-feudal India, was not dominated by a politically powerful landed class. Semi-feudal exploitation in rural Punjab was principally mediated through moneylenders who were both localised and whose political strength had been considerably undermined during the Independence struggle. Finally, some reports from the Punjab countryside recently on the struggle between the new rich peasantry and commercial capital in the towns points to the re-emergence of moneylending, this time coexisting with capitalist forms of exploitation.

[7] Once again, this tendency should not be interpreted in a one-sided manner. A factory proletariat, limited in numbers though of strategic importance, does develop.

[8] By industries for bourgeois consumption, we mean industries producing commodities the demand for which comes out of profits, not wages.

[9] It is useful at this point to draw attention to Samir Amin's 4-sector model, where he draws the distinction between an advanced capitalist and a backward capitalist economy (Samir Amin, "Underpopulated Africa," mimeo, Dar-es-Salaam):

(1) Export Production
(2) Capital Goods Production
(3) Mass Consumption
(4) Luxury Consumption

According to Amin, the determining relation in an advanced capitalist country is between capital goods production and mass consumption (2 and 3) but in a backward capitalist country between export production and luxury consumption (1 and 4). Even when the capital goods industries do develop in the latter case, they do in relation to the sector producing luxury consumption goods, not that producing mass production goods.

[10] Figures for 1911 and 1931 quoted in E. Mandel, *Marxist Economic Theory*, p. 473; figures for 1970 computed from *The Indian Labour Year Book, 1970* (Labour Bureau, Ministry of Labour and Rehabilitation, Government of India), p. 2 and p. 16. Under modern industry, I have included four categories: (a) Mining and quarrying, (b) Manufacture, (e) Electricity, gas, water and sanitary services, and (d) Transport, storage and communication.

[11] ILO, *Why Labour Leaves the Land: A Comparative Study of the Movement of Labour Out of Agriculture* (Geneva, 1960), p. 123.

[12] *Report of the National Commission on Labour* (Government of India, Ministry of Labour, Employment and Rehabilitation, 1969), p. 386.

[13] Ibid., p. 427.

18

Migration, Urbanisation and Interregional Inequality

The Emerging Sociopolitical Challenge*

Amitabh Kundu

The Census of 1971 had sounded a note of warning with regard to the increasing "immobility" of the Indian population. The "mobile" population, defined as those enumerated not at their place of birth, increased from 145 million in 1961 to 167 million in 1971 but its share in total population came down from 33.0 per cent to 30.4 per cent only.[1] A decline in this percentage figure was of course expected with death taking its toll during the decade of certain proportion of the international migrants coming to India during Partition. This, however, cannot explain the significant fall in the share of the lifetime migrants, the number of international immigrants in India falling from 9.5 million to 9.0 million during 1961–71. It is important to mention here that the females constitute about 70 per cent of the total migrants. The fall in the general mobility rate in India is, however, more due to the decline in the male migration rate. While the lifetime male migrant population grew by 12.36 per cent only during 1961–71, the corresponding growth figure for the female migrants was 16.55 per cent.

The migration scene in the 1970s seemed to be different from that of the previous decade. The growth rate of urban population picked up from 37.91 per cent in the 1960s to 46.02 per cent in the 1970s. Correspondingly, the rate of

* Originally published in *Economic and Political Weekly* 21, no. 46 (15 November 1986): pp. 2005–8.

migration showed an upward trend. The percentage of lifetime migrants was noted to improve from 30.4 per cent in 1971 to 30.7 per cent in 1981. This inference, however, is likely to be misleading if applied to all streams of the migrant population. The rising share of the migrant population during 1971–81 can easily be attributed to the increasing contribution made by the female migrants, which in any case had not suffered a major setback during the 1960s, as mentioned above. Female migration in India can be explained largely in terms of marriage and associational mobility, and these would change only over a long period, with changes in social norms and practices. Male migration, on the other hand, responds directly to economic factors and can, therefore, be analysed to articulate the changes occurring in the spatial structure of the economy. It may be noted that the proportion of lifetime male migrants to the total male population has gone down during the past two census decades, the figures being 20.7, 18.6 and 18.1 per cent in 1961, 1971 and 1981 (see Table 18.1), respectively.

It is important to mention that the small decline in the share of male migrants during 1971–81 cannot be explained away by attributing it to the falling number of international migrants, the figure coming down to 7.9 million only in 1981. Excluding the international migrants, the percentages of internal migrants among the male population work out to be 18.50, 16.87 and 16.83 per cent for the past three census years. One should, therefore, examine the implications of a falling or at best a stagnating male migration ratio in the context of the changing sociopolitical scenario in the country.

In order to examine the impact of the spatial structure of the economy on the migration pattern and urbanisation, the changing shares of the various streams and components of the male migrants has been analysed at the national level. The decomposition of the total migrant population into various streams is likely to provide an insight into the underlying forces responsible for the changes in its structure. Second, the chapter considers the interstate variations in the incidence of migrants in general and interstate migrants in particular in an attempt to look at the population mobility in the context of development dynamics in the country. Third, the implications of growing immobility among the Indian population in both urban and rural areas are examined in relation to the process of accentuation of regional imbalances. Although the basic discussions have been in terms of male migration only, the figures for female migrants have been considered, whenever necessary, to substantiate an argument.

Changes in Migration Pattern over Two Decades

It may be seen in Table 18.1 that male migrants as a proportion of total male population declined both in rural as well as urban areas during 1961–81. The rural and urban male population increased by 23 and 37 per cent during the

TABLE 18.1: PATTERN OF MIGRATION BY PLACE OF BIRTH AND THEIR GROWTH RATES

(in millions)

	Population	Migrant Population	Male Population	Rural Male	Urban Male	Male Migrants	Rural Male Migrants	Urban Male Migrants
1961	439	144.8 (33.0)	226	183.2	42.8	46.9 (20.7)	28.0 (15.3)	18.5 (43.2)
1971	548	166.8 (30.4)	284	225.3	58.7	527 (18.6)	30.8 (13.7)	21.4 (36.5)
1981	665	204.2 (30.7)	343	260.0	83.9	62.1 (18.1)	32.7 (12.6)	29.3 (34.9)
Growth Rate								
1961–71	24.83	15.19	25.66	22.98	37.15	12.36	10.00	15.68
1971–81	21.35	22.42	20.77	15.40	42.93	17.83	6.17	36.92

Note: The figures in brackets are percentages to the corresponding total population.

1960s. The growth rates for the corresponding migrant population were 10 and 16 per cent, respectively. Consequently, the proportion of urban migrants fell more sharply than for the rural counterpart. During the 1970s, the urban immigration rate picked up a bit (37 per cent), but was still lower than the growth rate of urban population (43 per cent).[2] The two growth figures for the total and migrant population in the rural areas are 15 per cent and 6 per cent, the gap indicating a significant fall in the proportion of the rural migrant population during the 1970s, as compared to the figures for urban areas.

The growth rate for urban population during the 1970s was historic in a certain sense as the country had never experienced as high a rate of urbanisation in any other decade in the present century. It is true that urban growth during 1941–51 was reported to be slightly higher than this, but that has been attributed to the Partition of India and the inadequacies in the application of a uniform definition of "urban place" in the 1951 Census, especially in the erstwhile Princely States. However, this historic growth of urban population during the 1970s cannot be explained totally in terms of the massive rural–urban migration. The high growth of the total urban population relative to that of the male migrant population in the urban areas must be explained in terms of (a) higher female immigration rate, (b) emergence of new urban centres, and (c) expansion of municipal limits of the existing towns and cities.

Female migrants have grown faster than the male migrants in all the streams during 1961–81. This has resulted in an increase in the sex ratio, defined as females per 1,000 male population. The increase seems to be positively related with the "distance" of migration—the highest increase occurring in case of interstate migrants (from 861 to 1,090, a growth of 27 per cent) while for the intradistrict migrants the increase (from 3,041 to 3,244, a growth of 7 per cent) is the least. This implies that male migration relative to female migration has suffered the most in case of movements across the states. On the other hand, the increase in the sex ratio for the urban to rural migrants has been the highest among the four migration streams which reflects the growing importance of family migration in this stream.

The fall in the share of the male migrants in the total male population is primarily due to the sluggish growth rate in the number of rural to rural (RR) migrants.[3] The share of RR stream has gone down among the intradistrict, interdistrict and interstate migrants during 1961–81, as may be noted in Table 18.2.

Although the ratio of interstate male migrants to the corresponding female migrants is lower in 1981 compared to 1961, as noted above, its proportion to the total male migrants improved marginally (Table 18.2).[4] This increase has occurred because the RR stream is an important component of the intradistrict migrants but this is not so for the interstate migrants. The slow or negative growth of RR stream has, therefore, affected the interstate migration component only marginally. It is important to note that the growth rates of both rural to urban (RU) as well as urban to urban (UU) interstate migrants are lower than the growth rates or urban population. Similarly, the growth rates of rural to rural and urban to rural interstate migrants are less than that of the rural population. These imply that the interstate migrants as proportions to the urban and rural populations have declined over the two census decades. It may also be noted that the interstate RU and UU streams have grown at a slower rate compared to corresponding streams in the intradistrict and interdistrict migrants during 1971–81, and consequently the proportion of male interstate migrants (to total migrants) in 1981 in the urban areas is less than the corresponding figure for 1971.

Two points thus emerge quite clearly whose implications need to be examined in greater depth: first, the slow growth of rural to rural migrants during 1960s and absolute decline in its number during 1970s, and second, the slow growth of the rural to urban and urban to urban migrants across the states—the rates being significantly lower than the corresponding interdistrict and intradistrict figures. The same is true for the 1960s as well, excepting the intradistrict urban to urban category, wherein the growth rate was negative. Also all the observations made earlier would be generally valid if one uses data on migrants by place of last residence instead of place of birth.

The figures for the *current* migrants (with duration less than one year at the place of enumeration) and *intercensal* migrants (arriving at the place of enumeration after the previous census) defined by their place of last residence, further confirm the trends noted above. Table 18.3 indicates that the percentages of current and intercensal migrants have gone down in all the streams, suggesting that male and female migration during 1970s was lower than in the previous decade.[5] Relatively faster decline in the proportion rural–urban and urban–urban interstate migrants—current as well as intercensal—further supports the point that migration into urban areas from other states is slowing down faster over time. A third interesting point that emerges quite sharply is that the proportion of current as well as intercensal migrants from urban areas are higher than those from rural areas. This is true for the migrants enumerated both in rural as well as urban areas. This suggests that relatively more people go from urban areas to villages and towns for short duration than from rural areas. Fourthly, current and intercensal male immigration rates are higher in rural compared to the urban areas. Lastly, the decline in the short duration migration rates in the urban areas is more in case of interstate migration compared to interdistrict or intradistrict migration.

TABLE 18.2: PERCENTAGE DISTRIBUTION OF BIRTH PLACE MIGRANTS IN DIFFERENT STREAMS, SEX RATIOS AND GROWTH RATES

Migration Streams	1961		1971		1981		Growth Rates of Migrants	
	Males	Sex Ratio	Males	Sex Ratio	Males	Sex Ratio	1961–71	1971–81
Intradistrict								
1. Rural to rural	73.75	3660	71.72	3613	64.75	4202	11.67	–6.12
2. Rural to urban	16.58	1198	17.58	1233	21.33	1301	21.75	33.55
3. Urban to rural	5.45	1248	4.60	1340	7.12	1399	–3.08	70.36
4. Urban to rural	4.22	1783	6.10	1998	6.79	2128	65.98	22.69
Percents total migrants	54.44	3041	53.58	2992	49.33	3244		
Interdistrict								
1. Rural to rural	42.13	2474	37.22	2701	32.66	3294	4.80	18.57
2. Rural to urban	32.86	803	33.11	849	34.80	960	19.52	42.05
3. Urban to rural	19.48	1056	22.03	1135	24.79	1252	34.15	52.09
4. Urban to rural	5.54	1457	7.64	1620	7.74	1894	63.59	36.96
Percents total migrants	26.78	1592	27.23	1660	30.84	1866		
Interstate								
1. Rural to rural	28.27	1425	25.89	1580	20.68	1981	6.84	–1.20
2. Rural to urban	41.72	504	39.36	566	41.97	674	10.07	31.91
3. Urban to rural	25.94	790	28.58	888	30.47	1006	28.54	31.91
4. Urban to rural	4.07	1057	6.17	1185	6.02	1417	16.86	20.80
Percents total migrants	18.78	861	19.19	959	19.83	1090		

TABLE 18.3: PERCENTAGE DISTRIBUTION OF CURRENT AND INTERCENSAL MIGRANTS TO TOTAL INTERNAL MIGRANTS BY PLACE OF LAST RESIDENCE CLASSIFIED BY THE PLACE OF ENUMERATION

Migration Streams (the place of last residence)	Type of Place of Enumeration							
	Rural				Urban			
	1971		1981		1971		1981	
	Male	Female	Male	Female	Male	Female	Male	Female
1. Total migrants								
a Current (rural)	11.93	5.27	9.96	3.14	7.81	5.72	5.77	4.47
Current (urban)	18.90	10.21	14.24	6.56	9.55	7.21	6.63	5.30
b Intercensal (rural)	53.05	34.49	49.47	31.50	50.44	44.33	49.65	44.43
Intercensal (urban)	67.19	49.95	63.20	46.05	56.78	52.444	52.58	49.82
2. Intradistrict								
a Current (rural)	10.30	4.80	8.32	2.73	8.46	5.17	6.61	4.18
Current (urban)	15.62	8.88	11.81	5.58	10.48	7.11	7.90	5.67
b Intercensal (rural)	51.11	33.62	47.53	30.75	53.25	41.99	52.35	42.61
Intercensal (urban)	64.30	46.83	61.30	43.89	60.00	51.38	56.38	50.21
3. Interdistrict								
a Current (rural)	16.15	6.80	13.28	4.13	7.26	6.1	5.42	4.49
Current (urban)	20.04	11.06	1,460	6.85	9.80	7.35	6.80	5.23
b Intercensal (rural)	58.42	37.16	40.09	33.32	49.59	46.22	49.83	46.35
Intercensal (urban)	69.53	52.89	64.56	47.53	59.09	53.91	54.83	51.01
4. Interstate								
a Current (rural)	16.28	8.33	16.32	6.29	7.57	6.88	4.94	5.27
Current (urban)	24.86	14.33	19.96	9.96	8.76	7.08	5.48	5.05
b Intercensal (rural)	57.55	40.42	54.83	37.20	47.52	48.01	45.32	46.16
Intercensal (urban)	70.42	57.32	65.65	51.32	52.39	51.11	46.83	47.51

Interstate Variation

The spatial variation in the percentages of lifetime male immigrants in rural as well as urban areas provides interesting insights into the development dynamics in the country. It may be seen in Table 18.4 that the backward states like Bihar, Jammu and Kashmir, Orissa, Rajasthan and Uttar Pradesh had migration rates much below the national average in the rural areas both in 1961 and 1971. The same is true for the urban areas as well with the addition of Andhra Pradesh in the list and exclusion of Orissa. It may be added that the north-eastern states generally have high rates of immigration both in rural and urban areas. Also, the relatively developed states in the south of India, *viz.*, Tamil Nadu and Karnataka, have low immigration rates in the urban areas because of language and other cultural barriers.

Table 18.5 presents the spatial profile of the rate of outmigration from rural and urban areas, in different states and union territories. The relatively backward states like Bihar, Himachal Pradesh, Kerala, Rajasthan and Uttar Pradesh have high rural as well as urban outmigration rates in 1971 and 1981. The case of Punjab and Haryana which have high outmigration rates must be considered as unique because of their being part of one state along with Himachal Pradesh till 1966. Madhya Pradesh and Orissa, on the other hand, are exceptional cases reporting very low rates of outmigration in rural and urban areas. This may be explained in terms of massive public sector investment and expansion of tertiary employment in these states that have discouraged outmigration and attracted migrants from other states.

The interstate variation in the growth rates of migrants in different streams during 1971–81 does not bring out a clear pattern. One can, therefore, discuss a few interesting cases. One, the north-eastern states have generally not attracted migrants from rural areas of other states and the absolute numbers in the rural to rural and rural to urban (interstate) streams have gone down. Two, Madhya Pradesh experienced a phenomenal increase in the number of outmigrants in all the streams, especially from the rural areas while Orissa had a fast growth in its urban to urban outmigration component. Three, Bihar, Orissa, Kerala, Rajasthan and Uttar Pradesh had a negative or almost zero growth rate in their rural to rural outmigration stream. Four, Punjab experienced negative growth rate in all but urban to urban migration stream.

Table 18.6 generally supports the observations made above. It may be noted that excepting Tamil Nadu, all the states reporting negative figures for net interstate migration are economically less developed. Madhya Pradesh was an emigrating state in 1971 but by 1981 it also joined the other outmigrating states with low per capita income. The only other backward state having positive net migration in 1981 is Orissa. It may be noted that Orissa had very few net migrants in 1971, but during the 1970s the number increased dramatically. Another interesting point is that Punjab and Haryana had very few additional net migrants during 1971–81, its decadal rate of net migration being quite low among the immigrating states. One may add that Punjab and Haryana are the only states wherein the net decadal female migration during 1971–81 is negative, with positive net migration figures in 1971. It may, therefore, be argued that the capacity of both Punjab and Haryana to attract net interstate migrants has suffered drastically during the 1970s. This is due to low inmigration rate (outmigrants declining in number) in Punjab and a high outmigration rate in Haryana. Karnataka, on the other hand, has changed its status from an outmigrating to emigrating state for females and also improved its male immigration rate. Finally, Rajasthan has experienced positive decadal growth rate of net immigrants, although the state was outmigrating in character in 1971 and 1981.

Another important observation can be made with regard to the high growth rate of short and medium distance migration from urban to urban areas. This may be explained in terms of stepwise migration from villages to smaller towns and then from smaller to larger towns. This has resulted in a fast growth of a large number of small towns and emergence of several new towns during the 1970s, especially around a few metropolitan cities. The migrants from the rural areas may not be able to go directly to the metropolitan or class I cities due to various social and economic constraints but are reaching there through a number of successive movements. Also, it may be mentioned that the percentage of lifetime interstate migrants in the urban areas by the place of last residence in 1981 is 27.5, which is lower than the corresponding figure of 28.6 by the birthplace definition. The two figures in 1971 were 29.7 per cent and 29.9 per cent respectively. This could be due to the fact that a certain proportion of the immigrants who were born outside the state had first come to another place, possibly a smaller town, in the state a decade before and consequently have not been counted as migrants by their place of last residence in 1981. One of the explanations for this phenomenon would be the stepwise migration, as discussed above.

REGIONAL IMBALANCE AND POPULATION MOBILITY

The changing migration pattern over the past two census decades raises the following question: If it is indeed true that the rate of migration is declining over time in both urban and rural areas—for males more sharply than for females—if the rural to rural stream is the worst affected by this trend, if the interstate rural to urban and urban to urban migrants have not grown fast enough compared to intrastate components or the past trend, why should these be matters of concern?

Can it not be argued, as the Census of India (1974) did that "due to the mass developmental programmes, the persons who have been previously migrating in search of job opportunities away from their places of birth may now be able to secure means of livelihood at the places of their birth. Better communication and transport facilities as existing today might have also prevented the persons to leave their homes for settling elsewhere. The improved medical facilities in the shape of more hospitals, maternity and family planning centres, both in rural and urban areas may have reduced the chances of accidental births occurring at places away from the usual residence of parents!"[6]

There is perhaps no denial of the "general development" occurring in the economy, with per capita income growing at about 1 per cent per annum in real terms. The level of infrastructure, too, has shown distinct signs of improvement over the decades. But what one is apprehensive about is the accentuation of interstate as well as intrastate inequalities that should, *ceteris paribus*, encourage migration. It has been noted above that it is generally the economically prosperous states that had a high percentage of immigrants in general and that of interstate immigrants in particular. The poorer states have, with a few major exceptions, been out-migrating in character. The neo-classical growth models that assure optimality in the spatial distribution of economic activities are based on the assumption of free movement of the factors of production. An initial accentuation of regional imbalance would ultimately lead to regionally balanced development through diffusion of growth impulses in space and movement of labour force from less developed to more developed regions. If this mechanism gets short-circuited due to certain sociopolitical factors, evidently the efficacy of the growth models in ensuring spatial optimality would be questioned even within the neo-classical framework.

In a study carried out in the late 1970s,[7] Alagh, Bhaduri and Bhalla have argued that there is already a "suction mechanism" in operation in Indian agriculture whereby the regions with high and growing land productivity are able to attract migrant workers from other regions. This, they said, results in the equalisation of labour productivity across the regions. It is possible to use the model to provide rationale for the adoption of an agricultural development strategy focused only on select regions with high growth potentials. However, with a sluggish growth in the rural to rural migration stream and also a low growth rate of interstate urban–rural migration (that too would have some component of agricultural labourers), the possibility of redistribution of the fruits of concentrated agricultural development among a larger community does not seem very promising. Unless the reasons for the increasing immobility are properly understood and the factors responsible for it are removed, it would be dangerous from the point of view of spatial equity and redistributive justice to follow the strategy of pumping in subsidised techno-chemical inputs in select districts of the country.

Relatively faster growth of intrastate rural to urban migrants compared to the interstate component suggests that urban centres are drawing larger proportions of the migrants from within the state. This is a departure from the colonial pattern. The fast rate of urban growth in the backward states of Uttar Pradesh, Orissa, Rajasthan and Madhya Pradesh can be explained by this phenomenon. It may be noted that each state has identified one or two industrial centres or regions and provided subsided inputs at these places only. A large part of the state has thus received only a small share of the total investments and labour productivity in agriculture has stagnated or gone down all around excepting a few select pockets. This has sharpened intrastate inequality and encouraged migration of people from rural to urban areas within the state. Also, a few district centres and taluka headquarters have been able to attract migrants from the immediate neighbourhood as the government investment in these centres have created certain level of infrastructure and generated some job opportunities.

The interstate inequality in various socio-economic dimensions of development are noted to be on the rise by several scholars.[8] A review of the studies on the trends in inter-state inequality in terms of per capita State Domestic Product suggests that at least since the early 1960s, the disparity has gone up significantly.[9] The Task Force on Urban Development set up by the Planning Commission (1983) reports this disparity, measured through coefficient of variation to have shot up from 23 per cent in 1961 to 26 per cent in 1971 and to 32 per cent in 1981. The values of the inequality index for agricultural productivity (labour) are 30.59 and 73 per cent at these three points of time respectively.[10] A slowing down of the interstate mobility, especially for the male population, on the face of rising disparity in terms of per capita income and labour productivity is indeed very alarming.

Studies on the inter district variation in the levels of development in different states also suggest an upward trend in the inequality index. The strategy of agricultural development in India has been to promote the seed fertiliser technology which has accentuated horizontal as well as vertical inequalities. The movement of male population within and across the district boundaries has unfortunately gone down, especially from one rural to another rural area, as noted above. This must be one of the factors responsible for the increasing disparities in terms of per capita output or labour productivity within the state.

The decreasing mobility of both the rural as well as urban population poses the major challenge for the development strategy being followed in India and the development perspective for the twenty-first century. The policy of unbalanced development if maintained despite this ominous trend, now distinctly visible, can be extremely dangerous. It is, therefore, important that the implications of the population redistribution in space are examined with empirical rigour and the measures to stall this trend, if possible, are worked out. However, if the dynamics of population distribution happens to be largely beyond the scope of governmental policies, this must be explicitly recognised in working out the strategy for future economic development.

Notes and References

[Himmat Singh Ratnoo, a doctoral student at the Jawaharlal Nehru University, assisted in the analysis of the data.]

[1] See "Migration Tables," Census of India, Part II C(ii), 1961; and "Migration Tables," Census of India, Part II, D (i), 1971.

[2] "Final Population Tables," Census of India, 1981; and "Reports and Tables Based on Five per cent Data," Census of India, 1981.

[3] See A. Kundu and Moonis Raza, *Indian Economy: The Regional Dimension* (New Delhi: Spektrum Publishers, 1982).

[4] See M. K. Premi, "Internal Migration in India: 1961–81," *Social Action* (July–September 1984).

[5] Also see ibid.

[6] See G. K. Mehrotra, "Birth Place Migration in India," Census of India, 1974.

[7] Y. K. Alagh, A. Bhaduriand G. S. Bhalla, "Agricultural Growth and Manpower Absorption in India," in *Labour Absorption in Indian Agriculture: Some Exploratory Investigation* (Bangkok: International Labour Office, 1978).

[8] The most recent comprehensive publication on the subject would be G. P. Mishra and A. Joshi (eds), *Regional Structure of Development and Growth in India* (New Delhi: Ashish Publishing House, 1985).

[9] See A. Mathur, "Regional Income Disparities in India: A Sectoral Analysis," *Economic Development and Cultural Change* 31, no. 3 (April 1983): pp. 475–505.

[10] Planning Commission, *Task Forces on Housing and Urban Development, I: Planning of Urban Development* (Government of India, 1983).

PART III

Economy

19

Controls and the Current Situation

Why Not Let the Hounds Run?*

Arun Shourie

Controls have become a habit with us. Within government circles the habit is by now so deeply ingrained that the advantages of a proposal for a fresh control have no longer to be demonstrated. They are assumed to be self-evident. Whenever the government learns that an existing control is not working well its reflex action—as well as the course of action it adopts after much thought—is to introduce yet another control to prop up the one that is not working, or to add yet another twist to the existing control.

Thus a committee is appointed to go into the leakage of foreign exchange through under- and over-invoicing of exports and imports. After deliberating for one and a half years the committee comes out with a 130-page report which proposes all sorts of new checks and examinations, new agencies, new regulations, new enactments, new amendments to existing enactments, and so on; and yet the report does not contain a word about the exchange rate. A typical recommendation of the committee is as follows. The committee discovers the fact that, among the many commodities whose invoices are manipulated, there are various kinds of capital goods which are imported into India. It recognises that as capital goods are not standardised it is extremely difficult—if not impossible—to verify the true price of a particular piece of equipment. Instead of concluding then that the only effective way of dealing with invoice manipulation, in this and other cases, is to adjust the exchange rate which currently provides the incentives

* Originally published in *Economic and Political Weekly* 8, special number (11 August 1973): pp. 1467–87.

for manipulation, it recommends that, in future, every industrialist who seeks permission to import a capital good should be asked to float international tenders and submit the results to the government. This, it believes, will enable the government to check the veracity of the price that the applicant has stated in his import application. Similarly, in expounding on the obduracy of private entrepreneurs wanting to set up fertiliser plants, a government representative tells the Estimates Committee that difficulties arise because "they do not want to fit into the pattern of the various types of fertilisers that the government would like them to produce to meet the demand of the cultivators. They would like to stick to the most profitable product-mix that they can think of. So we have to drive them towards an acceptable pattern of production and prevent them from putting up schemes which involve import of costly intermediates." We can be certain that, out of habit, the government will do everything to "drive them towards an acceptable pattern" except to alter the relative prices of different types of fertilisers or those of imported and domestic inputs.

Now is this habit confined to government officials? Outsiders, too, have become accustomed to controls. The last 15 years have conditioned them into thinking that the only natural way for the government to act is to impose controls. They are no longer surprised to read two simultaneous press reports—one, that the government will not consider floating the Rupee or devaluing it *vis-à-vis*, say, the Pound; and another saying that from now on units in priority as well as non-priority industries will be compelled to export fixed proportions of their output. It is hardly surprising, then, that in the 482-page record of evidence given by a host of officials, parliamentarians, and non-officials regarding the new Foreign Exchange Regulation Bill the role of an unrealistic exchange rate in ensuring the leakage of foreign exchange is mentioned only twice, and that too in passing.

In this chapter, I shall argue that far from being the instruments of socialism or of rational allocation that their advocates make them out to be, controls are just devices to ensure that patronage rests securely in the hands of the official and the politician. Our controls enrich individuals (and this is one of the factors that contribute to their durability), but they have disastrous effects for the productive system: they contribute to an accusatory atmosphere, they direct enterprise into unproductive channels, they perpetuate scarcities, and they militate against the collection, processing and dissemination of data. I shall briefly review the fate of reforms that have proceeded on the assumption that the machinery can be made to work better by shuffling a few organisation boxes, by rerouting slips, or by instituting special committees. I shall sketch the reasons on account of which the system works the way it does, argue that it is incorrigible, and that, therefore, we must think of achieving our objectives by instruments other than the administrative fiat.

I shall illustrate my argument by examples from various types of controls. It would be easy to confine the illustrations to one control—say, capital goods licensing. But this procedure always invites a standard response from those who administer the controls: "You may be right about capital goods licensing; but the situation is completely different in regard to the allocation of foreign exchange for raw materials—to say nothing of industrial licensing." The only way of pre-empting this—"yes, but not in the south"—kind of response, advocated by Stephen Potter, is to adduce illustrations from our experience with various controls. There is an additional reason for doing so. We are not being held back by one control or by one licensing procedure. We are being held back by the premises, the unverified assumptions, the attitudes that underlie all controls. These are the ones that have to be questioned and put out of the way; not just an individual control or an individual procedure.

I

THE PREMISES

The advocate of controls has taken textbook passages about the imperfections of the market to heart. Textbooks have told him about monopolists and oligopolists who restrict output, who collude, who prevent entry, and who indulge in other unspeakable acts. They have told him that in the real world, factors are immobile: they do not move freely between industries, between occupations, between regions. They have also told him about the market's myopia in not being able to take full account of externalities and of how—"given the free play of market forces"—the product pattern that emerges will be such as to satisfy the demands of the rich only. He has also learnt how the advantages that markets confer are cumulative—those (entrepreneurs, regions) who have, acquire more—and how this tendency can lead to the obliteration of the small man, to the emergence of Zaibatsus, and to dangerous regional imbalances. These textbook notions are combined with a particularly dismal view about entrepreneurs as a class—the view that they are ("or at any rate 99.9 per cent of them are") a bunch of scoundrels who are only interested in "profiteering" and "making a quick buck."

Many of the strictures against the market are true, and together they constitute a powerful argument for intervention, for modifying the results of the market. Nothing in the foregoing says that the only—or even that the best—method of intervention is the administrative fiat. To reach the latter conclusion the advocate of controls introduces some additional—and this time unverified—assumptions. He will assume, for instance, that the *dramatis personae* in developing countries do not respond to market signals, that something much more "direct," much more "final," is needed. He will assume that the market is too blunt an instrument, useful only for passing gross signals, whereas an economy like that of India requires detailed intervention—about product, location, process, scale, debt–equity ratio, precise items of equipment to be imported, and structure of management boards—and that administrative controls alone can achieve this degree of specificity. He will assume that a poor country cannot afford to waste resources in "unprofitable" or "uneconomic" or "sub-optimal" (the expression varies with the sophistication of the speaker) projects—that, as the Estimates Committee was in effect recently told, in an industry like electronics where the technology is changing rapidly and where demand is volatile, the government just cannot process applications quickly and must take time to consider each case thoroughly. The advocate of detailed controls and detailed intervention will also assume that the market is too ruthless, that if market forces had a free hand entrepreneurs would hurl themselves as a horde into an industry that seems profitable for the moment, that competition would subsequently kill many of them, dislocating labour and leaving a lot of capital idle—a dislocation and an idleness that a poor country cannot afford. Competition is all very well for the US and Germany and Japan, where entrepreneurs are well-informed and far-sighted, where labour can be retrained and capital can be redeployed or scrapped, we are told. But not for us. A poor country cannot afford failures. Nor, it is said, can it afford duplication.

Attitudes such as these are supplemented by a remarkable optimism about what can be accomplished through controls. It is assumed that controls can obviate the pressures of the market place on, say, the product pattern. It is assumed that systems of gathering and processing the information needed for administering controls can indeed be devised—*à la* Lange—especially now that computers have entered the picture. Finally, it is assumed that what is decreed on paper will, indeed, come to prevail in practice.

None of the premises about response to market signals, about the costs of failure, etc., nor any of the assumptions underlying the optimism about controls, is borne out by Indian experience. The whole pattern of import substitution, shifts in cropped area, and similar bits of evidence document the alacrity with which entrepreneurs respond to market signals. It has just not been possible to improve information systems within the government. Computerisation is still caught up in controversies about computers creating or eliminating jobs. Decrees and dictates continue to be violated at will. Yet the premises, attitudes and habits of thought survive. Their survival bears testimony to the power of textbooks, to the immortality of Harold Laski and others at LSE, and to the inertia that holds our minds in a groove once they stumble into it.

II

THE CONSEQUENCES

Over the years, controls have become more numerous. Most individual controls have become more detailed and a formidable volume of case-law has been built up in the administration of each control. Instruments, too, have multiplied. As these amendments and accretions have always been of a marginal nature, instances of controls and instruments working to cross-purposes abound. The government imposes export obligations and accords a high priority to fulfilling these obligations, but the Steel Priority Committee does not have any method of picking out such cases and according them the priority that other parts of the government say they should have. For two years, companies like ACC are told that they will not be allowed to expand their cement production, yet the price that is fixed for their product continues to include a factor called "expansion allowance." And so on.

The principal consequence of this gradual extension and accretion of controls has been an atmosphere of pettiness, of suspicion, of complaint and counter-complaint, of corruption and the talk of corruption. Controls are not instruments of socialism. They are a substitute for doing something really socialistic—like redistributing incomes, assets and power. With their help, we have not established socialism in India. We have instituted toll-gate socialism. We use them to set up hurdles at every passable point along a person's path, and then we charge him licit and illicit fees for attempting to jump over them. Corruption is becoming a way of life ("*bhai, seedhiungli se to ghee nikaltanahin*"), and we seem to have begun our journey back to the days of the East India Company—days in which officials were paid nominal salaries and were expected to fend for themselves. Controls are not a necessary condition for corruption—the Philippines and the US seem to do quite well without the degree of governmental intervention in the economy that we have. Nor are they a sufficient condition. But given our level of public morality, controls make corruption inevitable by concentrating patronage in the hands of the official and the politician. Talk about official and political corruption is, of course, even greater than actual corruption could possibly be. These days, if an official takes time in processing a case, many have no difficulty in convincing themselves that he is delaying matters because he has not yet received an adequate reward; if, on the other hand, he handles a case expeditiously, few will believe that he is being exceptionally efficient and the betting would be that he has received what he thought was fair compensation.

The contribution that controls make towards generating an atmosphere of suspicion, of corruption and of the talk of corruption should not be dismissed as just another one of those points that sociologists and political scientists are fond of raking up. Such an atmosphere has far-reaching consequences for the economic decision-maker, whether he is in or out of the government.

In the prevailing air of suspicion and distrust, even honest officials and politicians are compelled to procrastinate, to prevaricate, to find ways of protecting themselves from all sides, to associate as many persons as possible with every decision they take. Many features of economic administration in India today are explained by this motivation.

Consider the processing of an application for an industrial licence. Within a department the copy of an application or a file is passed around vertically and horizontally to as many functionaries as possible. A file within, say, the Ministry of Industrial Development, will thus be handled and initialled 20 to 30 times before it is disposed of. Nor is the purpose of convening meetings of groups, such as the Licensing Committee, any different. The outsider views the Licensing Committee as a haloed institution embodying the collective wisdom of various departments and agencies and thinks that the Committee deliberates long over every application, that it considers it from various angles, that at each of its sittings it is engaged in an earnest maximising exercise. This is far from true. The Committee is not engaged in maximising anything. The purposes of the exercise are to minimise complaints and to dissolve responsibility. In usual circumstances, the Committee meets once a fortnight. The agenda for each sitting runs into about 200 pages and, four or five days before a sitting, 110 copies of the agenda are circulated. Surely no one seriously thinks that 110 viewpoints have to be borne in mind while examining each case. The meeting is attended by 30 to 40 individuals and usually lasts about three hours. At each sitting, this group disposes of 40 to 50 cases—i.e., on an average, it devotes about four minutes to a case. A group of 40 individuals can do little in four minutes, let alone maximise something after the thorough examination that the outsider believes is being undertaken. The only reason for going through the ritual of the meeting—as in circulating 110 copies of the agenda papers and 180 copies of the minutes—is to associate the maximum number of witnesses with each decision so that responsibility can no longer be pinpointed on one individual or on one department.

The system has equally pernicious consequences for the entrepreneur. For, in the kind of atmosphere we have today, an individual is safe only so long as he burrows away underground like a rat. The moment he is successful and particularly if he is conspicuously successful, he becomes suspect.

The atmospherics apart, controls have encouraged within and outside the government a kind of enterprise that does not help production. Enterprise has now come to consist of acquiring quotas, agencies, licences, and selling them in black markets, of pre-empting licences, of getting the government to ban further licensing of units wanting to make one's product, of greasing palms. Within the government, too, enterprise has come to consist of pushing files, of roping others into decision, of finding ingenious ways of invoking or dodging rules. Over the years, whole armies of officials and functionaries have come into being—functionaries who have been recruited and trained and are now addicted to administering controls, statutes, rules under statutes, and sub-rules under rules. The ones who get recruited to government offices and who rise in them are those who can push files controlling the sugar industry, not those who can help cane-growers build co-operative institutions. We should not underestimate the heavy weight this imposes on the economy: it institutionalises inertia. Today, one of the principal reasons on account of which controls cannot be abandoned swiftly or completely is that the controllers cannot be transformed into managers, co-operative leaders, and constructive workers overnight.

Controls in India have perpetuated scarcities in various ways. Price controls as well as the pattern of industrial licensing illustrate some of the ways in which they have done so.

Over the years, as items have become scarce and as lamentation about their scarcity has become strident, the government has decreed "statutory," "voluntary" as well as "informal" controls over the prices of these commodities. These price controls have perpetuated scarcities by making the production of these "essential" commodities less attractive than the production of other commodities.

First, prices of other (ostensibly "non-essential") commodities have continued to rise. At the same time, the costs of producing the "essential" goods have not risen at rates lower than those of producing the non-essential ones. Consequently, the rewards from producing the non-essential goods have risen *vis-à-vis* those from producing the goods whose prices have been controlled.

Second, these controls have been imposed on the prices at which producers sell their products. The government has never had any machinery for verifying the prices at which these goods are sold by traders to consumers, or for controlling the activities of touts who procure the scarce goods for a consideration. The conviction that this policy somehow helps the consumer persists with remarkable tenacity. Just a few months ago, the representative of the Ministry of Petroleum and Chemicals told the Estimates Committee that, as "the vital interests of a very important sector of the economy" were involved, fertiliser prices could not be allowed to float—"they would inevitably go up and there would also be a tendency for profiteering." At the same time, he admitted that neither the Central nor the state governments had any machinery to verify fertiliser prices in the field.

The third reason on account of which price controls have perpetuated scarcities is the following one. Once the government decrees a control over the price of a commodity it cannot revise this price often nor can it revise it by substantial amount without inviting censure, without inviting allegations that it is abandoning the helpless consumer to the wolves. For this reason, the government has held on as long as possible to a price it has once decreed and when it has revised the price it has done so tardily and partially. Increases in capital costs—which have been dramatic in industries such as sugar and cement—have seldom been covered fully by the revised prices.

These controls over prices have never helped the non-governmental consumer, for he has had to pay the price dictated by the balance of demands and availabilities. What the controls have achieved is that the producers do not obtain the surpluses that arise out of the scarcities—surpluses that, had they accrued to the producers, would have increased the relative attractiveness of producing these commodities.

Of course, in some cases the touts have had to pass back a part of the black margins to the producers and to share part of the loot with governmental functionaries. Their cuts have enriched the functionaries as well as those who own or control the production of these commodities. But these surreptitious gains have not helped production to the extent that open increases in retention prices would have done. It is much riskier to use black money to purchase additional capital equipment than to use it for gold, diamonds, real estate or consumption. Nor can black money be used to pay higher dividends to one's shareholders. Nor, indeed, can a new entrepreneur approaching a public financial institution for assistance for setting up a factory to produce the scarce and essential commodity use the prospect of black profits to convince the institution that his actual balance sheet will be much more profitable than is suggested by the controlled prices. The government itself loses—both as tax collector and as shareholder—for many public financial institutions hold shares in these companies.

This is, indeed, a peculiar variety of myopia: one that dubs higher profits to producers as "profiteering" but shrugs its shoulders at the margins that go to touts as just the "inevitable consequences of scarcity." Because of it, new entrepreneurs have been discouraged from undertaking the production of these items and existing entrepreneurs have—whenever they could—shifted to producing other commodities.

A good example is the farcical control over the prices of essential varieties of cotton textiles. Many years ago, the government decreed prices of various types of mill-made cloth and, with much fanfare about its solicitousness for the poor man, it has often stoutly refused to revise these. Whenever the production of these varieties has become uneconomic, mills have switched to producing other varieties. As a consequence, the share of controlled varieties in total mill-made cloth fell from 25 per cent to 2 per cent at one stage and the varieties became even scarcer than they were to start with. Characteristically, the penalties for not producing the controlled varieties were kept so low that the mills happily paid the penalties instead of producing the varieties. Instead of altering the relative profitability of producing different varieties so as to make the production of controlled varieties more attractive, the government has taken to exhortation, rhetoric and prescription of percentages. As a consequence, these varieties still account for less than half the total mill output as they had till but a few years ago.

There is one superficial sense in which the government has gained. As it is often a large consumer of many of the controlled items—e.g., cement—it can console itself with the knowledge that if it had allowed producers to charge higher prices it would have had to pay more for its purchases. But this has been a pyrrhic victory. A policy that perpetuates scarcities harms every consumer, including the government. What is important from the point of view of completing the government's projects is not the notional price that it pays for cement but whether or not cement is available in ample quantities. Moreover, as every government official who has built a house knows, scarcities and interruptions in supply dislocate the government's projects much more than they do private houses and the like. If an individual is building a house and there is a sudden shortage of cement or bars or rods he can buy these from the black market. But a government department constructing godowns for grain feels much more inhibited to do so.

Controls over the setting up, expansion and diversification of industrial units, too, have perpetuated scarcities. They have done so by restricting entry and by protecting the inefficient. A new unit cannot oust an existing inefficient producer because, to enter the field, the new unit must seek the government's permission. The government, in turn, has been obsessed with crude notions of physical balances. As the cost at which, or the efficiency with which, a commodity is being produced has seldom entered its thinking, it has not allowed new entrepreneurs to enter fields merely because the existing producers are inefficient. Its view has been that as long as the physical quantity they are producing is what the government with—as we shall see later—its crude data thinks is needed, there *is* no scope for new entrants. Neither can an existing firm expand or diversify its output to the point of eliminating the inefficient producers. Competition from imports too is minimised by the application of norms such as the "indigenous angle"—the norm that, if a domestic producer says that he can supply a commodity, its import will not be allowed.

In fact, once a unit has come into being, the government has been obsessed with ensuring its survival. Once again, price controls play their part—prices are fixed so as to enable the least efficient firm to survive. The more efficient ones are not allowed to use their intra-marginal profits to expand and wipe out the less efficient.

The pattern of retention prices allowed to sugar mills provides a ready example: it retards the shift of cane cultivation to areas that have a comparative advantage for it and, within each region, it keeps the less efficient mills afloat. Thus, to cite a single instance, in computing the conversion charges that must be covered by retention prices allowed to sugar mills, the variable conversion charges allowed to mills in Madhya Pradesh are about five times those allowed to mills in Gujarat and Maharashtra. The pattern of allocating foreign exchange too ensures that every firm will get at least enough to survive.

The costs of the delays that accompany controls are indeed phenomenal. Consider the consequences of a single control: the capital goods licensing procedure. It has recently been estimated that, on an average, the government takes 390 days to process an application for importing a piece of capital equipment. Before the applicant files his application, he has to place an advertisement in a few trade journals and he has to wait for a mandatory 45 days for the responses to trickle in. Respondents suggest that it takes them three to four weeks to place their advertisement in the journals that have been designated for the purpose. Thus, in all, obtaining the licence may be said to take about 460 days. We import capital equipment roughly worth Rs 500 crores a year. Machinery prices have been increasing by about 10 per cent a year in world markets. The delay of 400 days thus costs us about Rs 60 crores just in terms of the higher prices that we must pay for eventually importing the equipment. In addition, we must reckon losses in terms of forgone output. If we assume that this imported equipment represents even three-quarters of the total value of equipment installed by the applicants, that total equipment is even 60 per cent of total investment by them, and that the capital–output ratio is a sturdy 5:1 in these industries, even then a delay of 460 days would imply forgone output of about Rs 275 crores. Much of this forgone output—as in the case of fertilisers and petroleum products—has to be made up by imports. Not even the most ardent advocate of the capital goods licensing procedure has ever suggested that the screening and processing of applications saves the country anything comparable to either the Rs 60 crores or the Rs 275 crores figure. And capital goods clearance is only one of the hurdles that the applicant must attempt to cross. I doubt if there is any other instance in which a nervous and self-protective search for the best has been so systematically made an enemy of the good as it has been in the administration of our controls.

It is an error to think that these long delays have anything to do with the care with which an application is examined, or that they imply that the system is engaged in a meticulous maximising exercise, or that the allocations, certifications and decisions that emerge from the system are economically rational.

For the outsider, institutions such as the Licensing Committee, the Capital Goods Committee and other committees that administer controls are black boxes. He does not know what goes on inside them. Over the years, he has been led to assume that officials attending the meetings of these committees possess some special wisdom, that they have access to special information, that they are able to examine each case thoroughly, that the deliberations of these bodies are suffused with economic rationality, that they have well-articulated and unequivocal objectives which enable them to place each case in a "wider context," and that they are able to assess each proposal in terms of an unambiguous "national interest." He compares all this to what he has read about rapacious capitalists and about the imperfections of the market in developing countries, and he concludes that there is no alternative to controls.

The actual state of affairs is far from what he assumes it to be. The committees are manned by over-worked amateurs. The information they have is fragmentary, and its quality can only be described as abominable. The examination that the amateurs conduct of each proposal is perfunctory. Hunches, rules of thumb and an attitude of petty bargaining mark the processing of an application as well as the final decisions. And in spite of having been at the game for 15 years, they have not been able to introduce any notions of the economic calculus into their cogitations. We should compare this state of affairs—and not the imagined one in which omniscient, rational and wise administrators pursue the "national interest"—with the imperfections of our markets.

A number of examples can be cited to illustrate this state of affairs. I shall confine myself to recounting a few instances from the way in which foreign exchange allocations were made in the 1960s.

Officials have surrounded the budgeting and allocation of foreign exchange and the approval of import licences with much mystery, and they have assiduously cultivated the impression in the public mind that there take place optimising exercises and delicate balancing of varied criteria. This is humbug. In an earlier issue of this journal I recounted how, even in the face of a major catastrophe such as the Sino-Indian clashes of 1962, when everyone was being urged to re-examine priorities and to bend every effort to urgent tasks, the allocators of foreign exchange had been able to think of nothing better than a 6 per cent across-the-board cut for all industries save seven which accounted for 9 per cent of the exchange allocated by the Economic Adviser. For these higher cuts were imposed. Almost every single half-yearly allocation period yields similar instances.

Consider allocations for a typical period: October 1964 to March 1965. In this period, as in others, the Economic Advisers' office allocated exchange between 37 categories. The categories were a heterogeneous bag. Ten represented specific raw materials (raw cotton, raw jute, wattle bark and extract, copra, palm oil, etc.). There were three categories of equipment (textile machinery and components, heavy electrical plant, jute and tea machinery); ten types of processed material (coal tar dyes, raw film, sulphur, etc.); two categories of consumer goods (drugs and medicines, all other consumer goods); four portmanteau categories of goods (scientific, surgical and optical instruments, machine tools, all other finished goods required by industry etc.); some catch-all categories for industries that fell under different administrative jurisdictions (raw materials for scheduled industries under the jurisdiction of the DGTD, non-ferrous metals for these industries, raw materials for small-scale industries etc.); and various catch-all ceilings (other chemicals to be licensed out of the CCI's ceiling, CCI's *ad hoc* ceiling, ceiling for OGL, ceiling for export promotion schemes). It would be unreasonable to expect anyone to undertake any kind of maximising exercise as between these categories. For 24 of these categories (that absorbed about half of the total exchange allocated) the Economic Adviser's office just repeated the allocations of the previous period. Of the remaining 13 a uniform cut of about 20 per cent was decreed for five. These five absorbed 70 per cent of the exchange allocated to the 13 categories.

Nor were things improved farther along the line. Tables 19.1 and 19.2 record the allocations of exchange to different directorates of the DGTD and, as but one illustration of allocations to industries under the charge of one directorate, Table 19.3 records the cuts imposed for mineral-based industries. To be sure free exchange was only 30 per cent and 70 per cent of the total exchange allocated to the engineering and chemical directorates in this period. But the Economic Adviser's team and the DGTD had much less freedom in apportioning the exchange that was available through various kinds of foreign credits than was the case with free exchange. The former was "tied" in many ways: the source of purchase, the industries for which it could be used, the units to whom it could be given—for instance, certain credits could be used only for units having collaboration with parties in the countries giving the credits. The toughest bargaining and the greatest freedom in making decisions was for free foreign exchange.

And what factors influenced inter-unit allocations within each industry? The answers of Development Officers of the DGTD as given to an official study team remind one of Alberuni's account of the jugglers of Kanauj who lectured him on chronology: "I used great care in examining every single one of them, in repeating the same questions at different times in a different order and context. But lo! what different answers did I get. God is all wise."

Some directorates said they related allocations in one period to some variable in some preceding period. This was past consumption of raw materials in some cases, past production in others, past allocation of foreign exchange in still

TABLE 19.1: FOREIGN EXCHANGE ALLOCATIONS TO CHEMICAL DIRECTORATES OF DGTD

(Allocations for October 1964–March 1965 as per cent of allocations for April–September 1964)

Directorate	Free Exchange	Total
Aromatic Chemicals	100 (1.3)	50 (0.9)
Alkalines and Allied Chemicals	90 (6.0)	90 (4.0)
Cement	88 (3.8)	88 (2.6)
Leather, including Footwear	80	80
Rubber goods industries including types	80	69
Drugs and Pharmaceuticals	80	83
Dyestuffs	80	65
Industrial Explosives	80	80
Acids and Fertilisers	80	80
Miscellaneous Chemicals including Industrial Cases	80	80
Soaps	80	80
Oil and Copra Crushing	80	80
Food	80	80
Paints	80	85
Organic Chemicals and Petrochemicals	80	80
Plastics	80	80
Insecticides	80	92
Asbestos Products	80	116
Ceramics	80	80
Glass	80	80
Rayon and other Synthetic Fibres	80	83
Paper and Paper Products	80	78
Timber and Timber-based Industries	80	80
All Directorates	81 (100)	82 (100)

Note: Figures in parenthesis indicate the share of the Directorate in total allocations for October 1964–March 1965. Allocations of free exchange represented two-thirds of the total allocations to Chemical Directorates.

others. Moreover, "past consumption of raw materials" referred to consumption in the last one year in some cases, the last six months in others, the last one-and-a-half months in still others. The base year selected for purposes of calculation was also not uniform. In one case (Oils, Food and Plastics Division: detergent soaps and cosmetic industries) the base period selected in determining the allocation for April–September 1963, for instance, was the actual consumption

TABLE 19.2: FOREIGN EXCHANGE ALLOCATIONS TO ENGINEERING INDUSTRIES ON THE BOOKS OF THE DGTD

(Allocations for October 1964–March 1965 as per cent of allocations for April–September 1964)

Industry	Free Exchange	Total
Machine Tools and Small Tools	89 (6.0)	90 (7.8)
Electrical Industries	76 (35.8)	81 (18.2)
Automobile and Ancillary Industries	75 (25.6)	94 (61.0)
Industrial Machinery	70	65
Light Mechanical Industries	70	62
Heavy Mechanical Industries	70	55
Metals and Metallurgical Industries	70	62
Instruments Industry	70	65
Medical Instruments Industry	70	28
All Industries	74 (100.0)	85 (100.0)

Note: Figures in parenthesis indicate shares in total allocations. Allocations of free exchange were about one-third of total allocations to these industries. Automobile and Ancillary industries received 60 per cent of all aid.

TABLE 19.3: ALLOCATIONS OF FREE EXCHANGE TO MINERAL-BASED INDUSTRIES

(Allocations for October 1964–March 1965 as per cent of allocations for April–September 1964)

	Industry	Percentage
(1)	Asbestos cement sheets, pipes and accessories	80
(2)	Asbestos textile industry including packing, etc., but excluding brake and clutch linings for which Auto-Directorate was to advise	80
(3)	Cement industries including RCC (hume) pipes and cement tiles	80
(4)	Ceramics including insulators, pottery, refractories, sanitary ware, glass tiles, pipes, roofing tiles and dental porcelain	80
(5)	Glass industry including enamel ware, safety glass mirrors, liquid gold, glass beads, false pearls and chatons, wired and figured glass, glass and glass ware including bottles, containers, miscellaneous glass ware, laboratory glass ware, glass tubes and glass shells for lamps	80
(6)	Carbon and graphite products including cinema arc carbons, graphite crucibles and midget electrodes	80
(7)	Pencil industry including pencils and lead slips	80
	All Mineral Based Industries	80

Note: (1) These allocations were for raw materials. Applications for spare parts were to be dealt with "on merits."

of imported raw materials in 1956–57. The Light Mechanical Engineering Division in determining allocations for the same period for units in the bicycle industry used 1958 production as the basis. Similarly, where past production was the norm this referred to production in the last financial year in some cases, the last calendar year or the last six months in others. And even after the base period was selected there were endless variations on the theme: for steel castings and aluminium industries the Metallurgical Industries directorate estimated requirements of raw material for a period of *nine* months on the basis of past and likely future production and rough norms of raw material requirements per unit of production. From these it deducted stocks in hand and likely arrivals. The remainder was taken as the next *six* months' requirements. Finally, the norms relating foreign exchange requirements to production too differed: some were physical-coefficient norms, others were value norms. And each of these was changed from period to period. For instance, the Oils, Food and Plastics Division in dealing with manufacturers of dentifrices adopted the following basis. For April–September 1963, foreign exchange was allocated on the basis of Rs 95 per tonne of production during 1962. In April–September 1964 this norm was raised to Rs 280 per tonne of the average production during 1961, 1962 and 1963.

Overriding Priority

Some directorates while taking past production into account also looked to the "installed manufacturing capacity" or the "targeted production" or the "likely production," taking into account the firm orders that the establishment already had in hand. And the use of each of these was subject to further variation because different directorates would think it fit to permit firms under their charges to utilise different proportions of their (approved, licensed or installed) capacity or to fulfil their (targeted or likely) production plans to different degrees. In addition, some directors superimposed their assessment of a firm's absorptive capacity—its ability to utilise foreign exchange. The Industrial Machinery Division, for example, in processing applications of new firms commencing production of "machinery for all types of industries" first estimated their actual requirements by taking into account factors such as orders with the party, stocks of raw materials, expected arrivals, etc. Then in all cases it limited actual allocations to 50 per cent of its estimate of actual requirements—unless the firm belonged to an industry of "overriding priority."

Some Development Officers said that they took account of stocks of raw materials in hand and of expected arrivals against import licences issued in previous periods. But "the stocks in hand" referred to the total quantity of stocks in some cases, to stocks in excess of six months' requirements in others and to stocks in excess of twelve months' requirements in still others.

In still other cases the cut in allocation was made a function of the actual value of the import licence. So that for the paints and allied industries where the face value of raw material licences was less than Rs 50,000 it was left uncut; where it was between Rs 50,000 and Rs 1,00,000 it was cut by 5 per cent; where it was between Rs 1,00,000 and Rs 3,00,000 it was cut by 10 per cent, and where it was greater than Rs 3 lakh it was cut by 15 per cent.

Other bases too were cited, ranging from the value applied for to the approved phased manufacturing programme of the firm.

The range thus extended all the way from the dictum of the Industrial Machinery Division that "there is no hard and fast rule and each case has to be decided on its own merits" to the declaration of the Oils, Food and Plastics Division that for the plastics industries, units engaged in the same industry were always subjected to the same *pro rata* cut as was imposed on the industry as a whole. Moreover, each directorate used a different mix of these principles, the relative weight attached to each norm was not clear at all and both the norm and the mix were liable to change from one period to the next.

Rules of Thumb

The foregoing account relates to the mid-1960s and the advocate of controls is liable to make much of this fact. Such evidence as I have been able to examine suggests that in spite of subsequent changes this account is not of archival interest only. In periods when foreign exchange has been more abundant than it was during most of the 1960s the degree of arbitrariness has, of course, been much less. But the ability of the system to settle matters more rationally in dealing with scarce commodities or resources has not improved nor has its addiction to rules of thumb lessened. Recent reports suggest, for instance, that in allocating the 15 million tonnes of cement that it anticipates will be produced during 1973, the government has reserved 21 million tonnes for Central Government departments and has distributed 12.2 million tonnes among all state governments and Union Territories on the basis of 110 per cent of the average level of supplies received by them during 1968–72. The remaining 8 lakh tonnes are reported to have been assigned to those states that have major irrigation and power projects underway. The only way to counter the preceding narrative and the evidence contained in Tables 19.1–19.3 is for government spokesmen to release information about foreign exchange allocations in subsequent periods.

The government's knowledge about the economic and technical characteristics of different products—the price and income elasticities of demand, the backward and forward linkages, the shape of the cost curves—continues to be so crude that it cannot but fall back on crude ratios (like market shares of two or three firms, the total amount of investment) and on rules of thumb (like allocations during the previous periods). Let us treat all units with assets (excluding land and buildings) worth less than Rs 7.5 lakhs as "small scale" units (though let us include land and buildings while computing the assets of "large scale" units); let us free investments up to Rs 1 crore from the licensing procedure; let us refer all proposals for investments above Rs 5 crores to the Cabinet Committee on Economic Co-ordination; let us ask companies that have more than 40 per cent foreign equity participation to come to us for approvals and not those who have less than 40 per cent. Most decisions in administering controls have just as much economic content as the setting of these limits. In fact, as procedures and criteria for cases above and below these arbitrary limits differ drastically the limits themselves circumscribe the extent to which economic considerations can be brought into play in administering any control.

The existence of successive hurdles—the industrial licence, the capital goods licence, approval of foreign collaboration, the MRTP clearance, import licences for materials and so on—itself dilutes the vigour with which any individual control is administered: "*Abhi jane do, sale ko CG Committee me pakdenge.*"

Compliance and Enforcement

Such rationality as the processors and allocators are able to introduce is cast to the winds by lackadaisical enforcement of decisions and allocations. Licences, quotas, scarce domestic materials and imported materials are sold and bartered at will. This journal has already drawn attention to the way in which tax laws are administered—three and four persons being convicted in 1968/69 and 1969/70 and each being let off with the mildest of punishments. The position is no different in enforcing the types of controls that we are considering here. Once again I will limit myself to one set of examples.

Prosecutions under controls over imports and exports of goods and over foreign exchange transactions in general are handled mainly by the Enforcement Directorate, the CBI and the Customs administration. Between 1968 and 1970, 5,702 cases of violation of foreign exchange regulations were registered. These led to the prosecution of 97 persons and to the conviction of 77. Fifty-five of those convicted were fined; 20 were fined or, in the event of default, were to be sent to prison; only two were sentenced to imprisonment. Table 19.4 presents some details of cases settled departmentally.

Table 19.4 shows that the fines levied were not a spectacularly high multiple of the amounts involved in the violations; that, in fact, the proportion diminished with the amount involved; and that most of the cases related to small amounts. One can safely infer that the really big operators are seldom caught and, when caught, are punished much more lightly than are the widows and orphans who get caught in the act of receiving small amounts from their relatives abroad.

Our version of the Biblical axiom seems to be: from those who have less will be taken away.

TABLE 19.4: CASES INVOLVING VIOLATIONS OF FOREIGN EXCHANGE REGULATIONS THAT WERE ADJUDICATED BY THE ENFORCEMENT DIRECTORATE IN 1972

Amount Involved	Number of Cases	Penalty as Percentage of Amount Involved	Penalty Plus Currency Confiscated as Percentage of Amount Involved
Up to Rs 10,000	1,223	20	32
Rs 10,001 to Rs 1 lakh	246	18	31
Above Rs 1 lakh	85	12	13
All cases	1,554	13	16

Note: The figures are approximate. The relevant Act provides that the adjudicating authorities can impose penalties up to three times the foreign exchange involved or Rs 5,000, whichever is more. Officials of the Enforcement Directorate cite various reasons on account of which the penalties are low; while the Indian currency involved in a violation can be determined, it is often difficult to pinpoint the amount of foreign exchange involved, with the result that the maximum penalty that can be imposed under the existing Act is Rs 5,000 only, irrespective of the amount involved; the adjudicator often feels that the person who has been implicated is just the carrier and not the real operator and so on. They also suggest that in 1973 the adjudicators have begun to impose much harsher penalties than in the past and that many of the legislative lacunae which made stricter action difficult in the past are being taken care of in the proposed amendments to the Foreign Exchange Regulation Act.

The CBI's prosecutions too are minimal. In 1970, 1971 and 1972 the CBI obtained 18, 26 and 26 convictions for misuse of Actual Users' import licences and for import licences obtained by misrepresentation or forgery. In addition it was able to punish 23, 30 and 30 firms departmentally for these offences. Its annual reports have a certain unvarying quality about them when they recall its prosecutions for violations of foreign exchange regulations. The 1970 report states that "14 such cases were pending trial from the previous year and 4 more were sent up for trial during the year under report. Three cases ended in conviction, 2 in acquittal or discharge, 7 were otherwise disposed of and 6 cases remained pending at the close of the year." The 1971 report continues the narration: "six such cases were pending trial from the previous year and 7 more were sent up for trial during the year under report. One case ended in conviction during the year and 12 cases remained pending at the close of the year." The 1972 report concludes the story *sans* one case: "11 such cases were pending trial from the previous year and 26 more were sent up for trial during the year under review making a total of 37 cases for disposal. One case was discharged while

36 cases remained pending trial at the close of the year." Thus, in 1970, 1971 and 1972 the CBI obtained three, one and zero convictions of parties violating foreign exchange regulations. In addition it punished two, six and five parties departmentally on this account.

The enforcement machinery that we have built is an effective instrument for harassing individuals, not for ensuring compliance of laws and controls. Contrast its ability to drive terror into the heart of an uncooperative businessman with its inability to apprehend persons smuggling garments as rags—smuggling them for months and years, in thousands of bales, each bale a solid 4 cubic metres, each bale examined by three officials at a port, and smuggling them when the import of rags is canalised through the State Trading Corporation.

As for the severity of the punishment, I have already cited some figures for offences under the Foreign Exchange Regulation Act during 1968, 1969 and 1970. Table 19.4 gives some idea about the cases decided in 1972. The Law Commission in its forty-seventh report has stated its strong conviction that the courts have not fully appreciated how grave the consequences of social and economic crimes are and that they have generally let the culprits off lightly. The Chairman of the Foreign Exchange Regulation Appellate Board has recently given us his—somewhat enigmatic—assessment of the punishment handed out by departmental adjudicators: "from whatever few cases I have heard and disposed of I have found that the adjudicating authority was more lenient than what it should be. The Act prescribes the amount of penalty as three times the value of the foreign exchange or Rs 5,000 whichever is more. We found that the penalty imposed in some cases was about 10 per cent of the amount which was involved. Though the Appellate Board has the power to enhance the penalty so far we have refrained from passing orders for enhancing penalty regard being had to the facts of circumstances of the cases.... There may be some evidence like this. For example, when a sum of Rs 3 lakh is received in an illegal manner, if that is established, then the Director will impose a penalty on the basis of Rs 3 lakhs. He can say that one lakh will be the penalty as the amount involved in the contravention is Rs 3 lakhs. Some such basis will be there. The whole amount is not accruing to the party. Only the differential. Sometimes we find that the penalty which is imposed is equal to the profit which the party has made. Sometimes it is only 10 per cent of the amount involved. It depends upon the discretion of the Director having regard to the facts and circumstances of each case."

It is hardly surprising then that once the allocators and Committees hand out licences and quotas these are redistributed in the bazaars at will. So that whatever "rationality" they had been able to impose on the allocations is soon swamped by the pressures of the market place.

Information Systems

One often hears it said that in one important respect controls reinforce themselves. Their proper administration requires new and up-to-date information and the rules that accompany the controls ensure that much new data will become available to the government. Controls do not only require data, it is said, they generate it. But the Indian experience shows that this is true only in the superficial sense that each control is accompanied by a host of proformas which firms have to fill in. All that happens in practice is that firms send in filled proformas and these are filed away. Far from facilitating the collection of data, controls militate against the collection, analysis and dissemination of data.

Firms find that it is more profitable for them to spend their time and resources in manipulating the system than in filling forms punctiliously. They are secure in the knowledge that the government—in the form of, say, the DGTD—has few ways of verifying the data they send. A Development Officer cannot spot misrepresentations on a tour. His reliance on consistency checks is a feeble one for it would be a rare firm that is so naive as to send inconsistent figures to different government agencies. His reliance on "industry norms" is equally feeble for in all probability these norms are based on obsolete (and equally falsified) information.

It is not often realised that far from enabling the government to collect data, in many cases the existence of a control prevents collection and processing of vital data. In an economy such as ours, controls—and *not* scarcities—inevitably lead to black markets. For various reasons our government just cannot bring itself to acknowledge the existence of these black markets. As systematic collection and analysis of data about black markets would amount to acknowledging their existence, the data are seldom collected, analysed and discussed. The consequence is that the government shuts itself off from one of the most important sources of information about current and impending economic developments.

Because of the secrecy that is associated with the administration of each control, information about the decisions and the reasons that led to the decisions as well as the data associated with the working of the control become the exclusive property of the government. Outsiders are seldom able to assess the veracity of the government's claims or to assess the working of the control in question. The government's policy of not releasing any information about the country's foreign exchange budget is perhaps the most dramatic example of this feature. Year after year the government has refused to divulge any information about this budget on grounds such as the one that the budget contains vital secrets about our defence preparations. Reasons such as this one are disingenuous. Persons who are interested in finding out the state of our defences will learn little from being told that Rs X crore of foreign exchange have been allocated to defence.

Rs X crore could mean so many airplanes of such and such variety, or so much naval equipment, or so many tanks or so many pieces of artillery equipment. This is the kind of data that will help them. Not a portmanteau figure of Rs X crore. And the defence argument does not work at all when we come to consider the decision to keep allocations made by the Economic Adviser or by the DGTD secret. Moreover, the fact of the matter is that data about the foreign exchange budget—the very data that have been withheld from the Indian Parliament and from Indian researchers by invoking ghosts such as "defence considerations"—have been given to visiting economists from international agencies and have been included in the reports of such agencies. The reports of these agencies are sent to all member governments on a routine basis. Data on the foreign exchange budget are not released merely to prevent outsiders from learning how arbitrary are the decisions that are taken, how casual is the work that goes into taking these vital decisions, and how perfunctory is the information on which the whole edifice is built. Our administrators succeed admirably in this objective: they cover the administration of each control with a shroud of secrecy; this enables them to withhold data about the functioning of the control; and this, in turn, is one of the principal reasons on account of which the control is able to ward off all efforts to reform its operation.

Such data as are gathered are seldom processed. Firms that have received letters of intent or industrial licences are expected to report the progress they have made in implementing the letters of intent or the licences by filling in the "G forms" every quarter. The data from these forms have never been aggregated by industry, by region or in any other way to assess the progress that is being made. In 1968 a Committee was set up to devise a coding scheme that would enable the government to keep track of the pace at which import licences are being utilised: the idea—a commendable one—was to develop a management tool by which the government could relate the issuing of licences to the importation of goods and, ultimately, to the outflow of exchange. Firms were asked to report a long code number with each import application, procedures were set up to have the information flow from the CCI and E and the DGCI and S to a computer centre in Delhi. Yet till early 1973 the principal officials concerned with import licensing had not begun to examine—much less use—the information that this exercise had begun to yield. For years firms on the books of the DGTD have been reporting their consumption of raw materials to the DGTD every month. Many firms have been reporting meticulously the quantity and value of as many as 150 items every single month. Yet not once have these returns been aggregated or analysed for any purpose whatsoever.

We thus have a situation in which the government is not able to collect vital bits of information, in which it does not process such information as it receives, in which it does not release data about the functioning of the control—a situation in which the right hand does not know what the right hand is doing. And yet, in spite of all this, the government continues to act as if the state of affairs were the exact opposite of this—as if it were receiving and processing all the data that the efficient administration of its numerous controls requires.

It reserves 123 products for small-scale units even though it has no information about whether, say, the capital-output and capital-labour ratios in these industries are less than in other industries or whether "small" units will have lower ratios in manufacturing these products than larger units. It sets up targets for an industry such as paints and varnishes and allows or disallows new entrants by declaring that existing capacity is or is not sufficient to meet demand for the products. Yet it has little idea of the production capabilities of "small" units manufacturing paints and varnishes which, according to the Annual Surveys of Industry, account for as much as 35 per cent of the capacity in this industry. It debates whether a fiscal levy on the sugar industry should be lowered by 1 or 1.5 per cent when it has little data about the cost profiles of different mills, about the capacity of gur and khandsari producers in the catchment areas of the mills, about the price elasticity of demand for cane of gur and khandsari producers. It refuses or grants licences by claiming that it knows how much additional capacity is needed while in early 1972 the Secretary of the Ministry of Industrial Development offers the Estimates Committee the following assessment about its ability to determine what capacity is needed: "In our own Ministry ... till about two years ago, we used to have a system of estimating what the requirement of a particular commodity is going to be and we used to restrict licences up to that limit or 10 to 20 per cent more.... A lot of shortages in various consumer items that we see today are the result of that policy of restricting licences to a certain level. After a long experience of the system of evaluating the demand of consumer items and restricting licences to that extent, we have ourselves given up this system and we have now come to the conclusion that the person who is going to invest his future in an industry should be left free to judge how much the demand is going to be and whether he should or should not make this commodity.... This kind of approach where we leave it to the entrepreneur himself to decide whether there is room for further manufacture in the particular line or not is a more effective method of arriving at an estimate of the requirements than any system of our trying to judge what the requirement would be and then trying to restrict licensing to that extent." Even as he says this the representative of the Department of Electronics maintains stoutly that his Ministry continues to refuse or grant licences according to its assessment of how much capacity is required. In any case, within a few months the Secretary moves to other pastures and estimates of required capacity come back into vogue. No official avers that the government is any more able today to assess what capacity is required than it was a few months ago: "It is just that our policy has changed."

The breezy self-confidence of our controllers leaves one aghast.

III

CAUSES

Some effort or another at reforming the system is always underway. At any given moment a study group, a working group, a committee or a commission has either just been set up and one is told that "the Government is awaiting the results of its study before rushing into action"; or the committee has just submitted its report and one is told that "the Government is examining the recommendations keeping in view all their ramifications"; or the suggestions of the committee have just been put into effect and one is told that "it is too early to assess the effects of the new procedures."

With each new Minister or each new Secretary and immediately after the report of the latest committee is received there is a flurry of activity—new proformas come into vogue, new procedures, new task forces to clear backlogs. Yet within a few months the system reverts back to the *status quo ante.*

Consider, for instance, the case of delays. Since the early 1960s a host of committees and commissions have examined this problem. And, if one goes by the written record, almost all of their recommendations have been implemented. Yet delays persist. In the mid-1960s the Mathur Committee discovered that it took the government 270 days to grant the capital goods clearance. This was regarded as unpardonable. Over the years a number of suggestions have been made to shorten this period. In a formal sense most of them have been implemented. Today, as we noticed above, the government takes 390 days to grant the capital goods clearance after the application is received.

Not only do delays persist, absurd delays persist. Of these 390 days, for instance, fifty full days are taken up in communicating the decision of the Capital Goods Committee to the CCI and E's office. The meetings of the CG Committee take place in the same building that houses the CCI and E's office. Not only that, the Chief Controller is himself a member of the CG Committee and he or one of his representatives invariably attends the meeting. And yet it takes fifty days to tell him what he and his colleagues have decided in the meeting. The existence of this particular delay is not a new discovery. Nine years ago the Mathur Committee had calculated that 54 days were being spent in notifying the CCI and E about the CG Committee's decision.

Reforms that have been attempted thus far have yielded little because they have proceeded on the assumption that the deficiencies of the system are due to ill-conceived procedures or to deficient legislation. And that the system can be improved by rerouting slips, by shuffling a few boxes on organisation charts, by adding yet another twist to an existing control or by adding another control to buttress the existing one.

Consider the fate of reforms that have started from these premises.

The Stepping-stone solution: Rule 15 of the "Registration and Licensing of Industrial Undertakings Rules" says that all applications for industrial licences must be disposed of within three months of their receipt. By 1964 the Government had concluded that it will never be able to adhere to this limit. So it decided that it would issue letters of intent speedily and after only a preliminary examination of each case. The idea was that this speedily issued piece of paper would enable the entrepreneur to start implementing his project expeditiously; he could finalize negotiations with foreign collaborators, he could raise capital, he could even start constructing his factory and so on. The Government decided that while it had not been able to issue industrial licences within three months it would certainly issue letters of intent within this period. A fact that should have been obvious from the beginning soon became apparent: once the entrepreneur had taken all these steps towards implementing his project the Government could not refuse him the industrial licence. Therefore, all the delays and the supposedly detailed scrutiny that were associated with the industrial licence soon came to characterize the letter of intent too. In early 1972 the Estimates Committee discovered that letters of intent themselves were taking much longer than three months—in many cases even more than a year. It discovered that while the rules prescribed that applications be put up to the Licensing Committee within 4 to 6 weeks and that while the Secretary of the Ministry of Industrial Development was assuring it that the letter of intent "is issued in three months time and fairly quickly", 94 per cent of the applications it examined had not been sent up to the Licensing Committee within 3 months of their receipt and 46 per cent had taken even more than 6 months. Its 19th Report records the fact that in mid-November 1971—six years after the new procedures had been introduced—933 applications were pending with different ministries. Of these, 28 had been pending for more than 3 years, 83 between 2 and 3 years and 822 between 1 and 2 years. Far from being the stepping stone it was intended to be the letter of intent has become an additional hurdle.

The special-machinery solution: Whenever it has appeared that one single committee is not able to process cases expeditiously proposals have been made to partition its functions and to allocate these to separate committees or sub-committees. Or its jurisdiction has been curtailed to one set of cases (e.g., cases involving investment or foreign exchange above a certain limit) and other sets have been allocated to newly created committees or sub-committees. The creation of the Foreign Investment Board, delineation of the responsibilities of different departments for processing applications for industrial licences, the splitting up of the CG Committee into the CG (Main) and CG (Ad hoc) Committee are illustrations of these reforms. After a while each of the departments and each of the sub-committees had acquired all the characteristics of the bodies that were originally responsible for processing the case. Whenever, on the other hand, someone has noticed that a control is being administered by too many separate committees and that, in any case, the same overworked Secretaries and Joint Secretaries are members of each of the committees, proposals have been made to integrate the functions into one special committee. This too has never worked. Thus, to cite but one example, a Special Committee of Secretaries was set up in 1966 to serve as both the Licensing Committee and the Foreign Investment Board for all proposals for fertilizer projects and on paper at least it had all the powers to process applications expeditiously. As the country has been facing a food crisis since the mid-sixties and is spending crores on importing fertilizers, one would expect that this Special Committee would have been seized by a sense of urgency. Yet we now learn that of the 52 cases that this Special Committee was able to dispose of between 1 January 1967 and 30 November 1972 two-thirds took more than 1 year and one-quarter took more than 2 years. Of the 9 cases that were pending with it in the beginning of 1973, seven had been in this state for more than a year.

The computerization syndrome: Since 1962, for instance, proposals have been made to computerize the data that lie buried in the files of the DGTD or rusts away in the heads of its Development Officers. Experts have come and gone, committees have been appointed and have reported, consultants have used up much time and money and yet the DGTD stores, retrieves and processes data in much the same way as it did in 1962.

The cut-off-rule solution: Whenever the cases a committee or a Ministry is supposed to consider have overwhelmed it because the backlog has become intolerably large, proposals have been made to raise the cut-off mark below which cases do not have to be processed. Thus, for instance, in 1970 the Government decided that investments below Rs 1 crore would not have to obtain industrial licences unless they were by foreign companies controlled by large houses. But each time this has been done, after a short while the flood has risen again. Thus, for instance, the view is now being put forward that the only way for the Licensing Committee to keep its head above water is to raise the delicensing limit to Rs 3 crores, if not Rs 5 crores. This way of lessening the work of the Licensing Committee removes road blocks for the production of even luxury items provided the investment in the project is less than the specified limits but retains the full obstacle race for even vital products merely on the ground that the investment in the project is above an arbitrary cut-off point. Moreover, as the delicensing has not been accompanied by any fiscal changes to alter the relative profitability of producing different commodities this particular "reform" has meant that the Government has completely abandoned any effort to influence the production pattern provided the investment is below a certain limit.

These and other remedies of this kind have failed because they have proceeded on the assumption that the system is corrigible, that a few O and M notions, that a computer here and a special committee there can change things. But the delays, inefficiencies and inconsistencies that characterise the administration of our controls are caused by factors that cannot be removed by tinkering with the system.

Objectives

The first reason on account of which delays and inconsistencies occur is that we have not been clear about the social and economic objectives we want to achieve with our controls and restrictions. This point is often mentioned but it should not for that reason be dismissed as being trite.

Some of this confusion in objectives can be deduced from what I have said above about price controls and about the way controls over imports and the setting up of industries have been administered. The implementation of the Monopolies and Restrictive Trade Practices Act provides yet another example. The Act was passed in June 1970. The list of industries to which the concept of dominance was to apply was not finalised till September 1971. Various Ministers continued to assert different things about the precise scope of the Act, about the objectives that the government was trying to achieve and about the criteria that the government would employ in judging applications from large houses. In mid-July 1970, for instance, the Minister of Industrial Development told the Lok Sabha that applications from large houses and foreign companies "would also deserve consideration in the middle sector (i.e., investments between Rs 1 crore and Rs 5 crores) if they are willing to establish units in industrially backward areas where other entrepreneurs are reluctant to go." In early 1972 the Secretary of the Ministry of Industrial Development was asked by the Estimates Committee to tell them what the Minister's statement meant in operational terms and his response—a year-and-a-half after the statement—was: "our own ideas on this point are not very clear at the moment. The Minister did make a certain statement of that nature but we are not clear whether it enunciates Government policy or not; we are trying to get this question clarified." He went on to assure the Committee that there was no absolute prohibition on issuing licences to larger houses and foreign companies, that if the government felt that "in the national interest" or "on merits" a licence should be given, it would certainly be given. When asked to explain what he meant by "merits" his answer was the predictable one: "what items go into merits is something which it is very difficult for me to say at this moment."

Since then concepts such as the joint sector have been floated with much equivocation and have got nowhere. Recently—as we all know—the scriptures have been reinterpreted: "interconnectedness" has taken on a new meaning so that while formerly 185 Birla firms were identified as being "interconnected" now only 35 are held to be so; the "core sector" too has been redefined to include conveniently ambiguous categories such as "industrial machinery."

As a result of these ambiguities nervous bureaucrats and apprehensive Ministers have procrastinated and they have sought shelter behind rules of thumb. The government's decisions on the MRTP cases have, as a consequence, been exactly what the most reactionary and traditional business house and what an oligopolist would want them to be.

Most Indian industries are oligopolistic only in the formal sense that a few producers account for most of the output. The essential features of oligopoly—the interdependence of profits and the consequential uncertainty in the mind of each producer about the reactions of his competitors—are seldom to be found. Given the extreme shortage of most commodities, the general inflationary situation and the restrictions that the government has imposed on the expansion of his competitors, neither are profits dangerously interdependent nor need the oligopolist be too worried about the possible reactions of his competitors. So as to ensure a completely safe and undisturbed existence for himself his primary interest is to ensure that the total supply of his product on the market remains as small as possible and his share in it as large as possible. Similarly, the traditional—one is almost tempted to say feudal—sire of a business house who is not acquainted with the mathematics of majority voting, who still does not believe the fact that given a bunch of indifferent shareholders he can control his companies without owning an overwhelming block of the companies' equity—such a sire would want to maintain his dominant share in the company's equity.

In case after case the government—out of the nervous apprehension that it may be accused of pandering to the interests of the large houses—has catered precisely to these interests. It has allowed them small expansions—expansions that will not result in such an increase in the supply of a commodity that the oligopolists have to start worrying about competition, about prices and quality and reliable delivery schedules; expansions that will not ensure the economies of scale that would reduce costs for domestic consumers and enable the enterprises to compete in export markets; expansions that are small enough to be financed out of the reserves of the company or out of the resources of the business house so that it can maintain its share in the firm's equity. The government's decision on the applications of the Bajaj and API groups for scooters, of the Sarabai group for copying machines, of Malhotra for razor blades and many others provide ready examples.

The current position seems to be—though no one will bet on this—that if a large house proposes a project to produce an item that can be identified as falling in the "core sector," if the project costs more than Rs 5 crore and if it is to be located in one of the country's backward districts then it will be considered sympathetically. One can be certain that very soon someone will point out that if we are really serious about preventing our own Zaibatsus from controlling the vital sectors of the economy then "core sector industries" are precisely the ones which we should not let the large houses enter. After all, they are the important ones, they are the heights that overlook the surrounding landscape. Moreover, someone will soon show that locating capital intensive projects producing "industrial machinery" and the like is little help to the residents of backward districts. He will be able to point to the meagre benefits that capital intensive projects have yielded to the residents of Orissa, Bihar and Madhya Pradesh and to contrast the experience of these states with that of Punjab and Haryana. Having been faulted on both the "core sector" and the "backward district" grounds, our policy makers will have to begin thinking *ab initio.*

O and M remedies are no help in a situation of this kind.

Economic Administration: Four Features

Confused and ambiguous objectives are the politicians' special contribution towards making controls ineffective and, in many cases, perverse. We should not forget that when the politicians have clear objectives—as they do at the time of elections—they are able to use the same administrative machinery to devastating effect. But the matter does not end with the politicians. The pattern of our economic administration contributes a great deal towards making our controls ineffective, dilatory and unproductive. I will illustrate this by drawing attention to four aspects of our administration.

The first of these is, of course, the fact that each of our Ministries functions as a state within the state. No Ministry has the power to override other Ministries on matters relating, for example, to approving an application for an industrial licence. Everyone is free to express his point of view on every aspect—thus, for example, we find DGTD officers raising questions about the appropriateness of the debt-equity ratio of the applicant—and everyone's point of view has to be borne in mind. Far from having the power to disregard the points raised by another department, the department that is primarily responsible for a case or a project is fairly helpless in even urging others to process the case expeditiously. As the Secretary of the Ministry of Industrial Development told the Estimates Committee recently, neither he nor his Minister could do anything beyond to "go on writing to them (the other Ministries) and remind them ... We keep on sort of asking the Ministries concerned as well as our own officers concerned to speed up the disposal of these (pending) cases." How vivid is the description of helplessness: "we keep on sort of asking." Thus everyone acquires a veto over what is going on and, in the accusatory atmosphere we have today, no one is prepared to push a case vigorously.

It is hardly surprising that in this state of affairs the award of priority status to a project or an industry by a Ministry administering one control does not mean that the project will be accorded priority all along the line. Nor is a ban decreed by one Ministry or by the government as a whole respected by all. To cite but one instance, the Administrative Reform Commission's Study Team on Economic Administration examined 349 cases disposed of by the Licensing Committee in five meetings between 12 December 1965 and 15 February 1966. Of the 44 it studied in detail, 42 had been approved. Neither of the two that had been rejected belonged to an industry on the banned list but 10 of the 42 cases which the Licensing Committee approved belonged to this list—a list that the government had finished many months before these meetings and which it was publicising at every opportunity. It is not surprising that, as we noted above, the Department of Electronics continues to reject or approve projects according to its notions of required capacity when the Ministry of Industrial Development says that the government is unable to frame reliable estimates of required capacity. Nor indeed is it surprising that while one of the reasons on account of which refineries are prohibited from using their capacity fully is said to be that part of the capacity they have set up is unauthorised while at the same time Bajaj Autos are never hauled up for setting up capacity "in anticipation of Government's approval" and are indeed allocated materials to produce scooters far in excess of their licensed capacity. (The MRTP report on the applications of API and Bajaj Autos tells us that while the sanctioned capacity of Bajaj Autos in 1966–67 and 1967–68 was for 12,000 units a year, their installed capacity was for producing 27,000 units a year and that while their sanctioned capacity in 1970–71 was for 24,000 units their actual production was about 36,000 units). Nor indeed is one surprised when one learns that the Licensing Committee continues to differentiate between "key" and "non-key" industries years after the concept has been abandoned by the government and even though, in the words of the government itself, the concept "does not seem to have any particular relevance now." Nor is one surprised to learn that even though prices of urea have shot up in world markets, even though we are spending enormous amounts on importing fertilisers, no one is prepared to say that it is absurd for the government to insist that the Kota fertiliser expansion scheme procure indigenous equipment worth Rs 31 lakhs even when this delays the completion of the project by a year and even though the country loses output worth Rs 7 crore because of this delay.

The second feature of our economic administration, as indeed of our economic system in general, is that failure invites no penalties. There is no way by which the errors, delays and the shoddiness with which, say, a licensing procedure is run can be translated into penalties for the ones who run it. Over the years deadlines have been prescribed for almost every single stage in the processing of the application for an industrial licence. As we noticed earlier, the three-month limit for issuing an industrial licence has even been included as one of the Rules framed under the Industrial (Development and Regulation) Act. Yet there isn't a single deadline that is adhered to in the majority of cases for which it is meant and no one is ever hauled up for violating the deadlines. Our deadlines are not lines on crossing which one falls dead. The result is shown in Table 19.5. In it deadlines have been underlined. Most of the activity takes place beneath the lines. There is no way in which an officer can be penalised for crossing them. Nor is there any way in which an official can be penalised for imposing a loss of Rs 7 crores on the country by his bullheaded insistence that an applicant procure indigenous equipment worth Rs 31 lakh.

The third characteristic of our administration of controls is that there are no external checks on the system. The patronage that controls have conferred on the government has enabled it to keep businessmen from shouting against the system. The shroud of secrecy with which the government has clothed the working of many of these controls has, as we noted earlier, enabled it to keep researchers from learning much about the system. In these circumstances the Parliament and its committees alone can provide effective external checks. But our Parliamentarians have shown little interest in examining economic issues systematically.

Few attend meetings of the Parliament's economic committees. In 1971–72, for instance, about 80 per cent of the Estimates Committee's 73 meetings were attended by less than two-thirds of its members, half by less than half of its members and four meetings were held in spite of the fact that the quorum of 10 was not complete. Of the Committee's 30 members only 4 attended more than three-quarters, 12 attended between one-half and three-quarters and 14 attended less than one-half of its meetings. Comparable figures for 1972–73 are not available as yet. The few that are do not suggest any improvement. Thus, for instance, the Committee devoted six meetings to fertilisers in 1972–73: two of these were attended by seven members only, one by 10 and one by 11. It considered industrial licensing in 14 separate meetings: at 11 of these 13 or fewer than 13 and at three, 10 or fewer than 10 were present. Those who attend the meetings seem to leave most of the work to the secretariat of the Committee—a secretariat that does not have, nor does it co-opt, persons who have some special knowledge about the subject that is being examined.

It is no wonder, then, that the government's representatives can get away with half-truths and with statements which, if they were made in a court of law, would be regarded as perjury. The evidence presented by the government's representatives on industrial licensing provides a typical example.

The Secretary of the Industrial Development Ministry leaves the Committee with the impression that the delays that characterised licensing procedures have been eliminated from his Ministry and that licence applications are being put up to the Licensing Committee within three months of their receipt.

TABLE 19.5: TIME TAKEN TO PROCESS APPLICATIONS FOR INDUSTRIAL LICENCES

Time Taken	Issue of Letter of Intent/Industrial Licence														Foreign Investments Board Clearance					
	Registration and Distribution of Applications by Central Licensing Policy Section		Receipt of Comments on Application from Technical Advisers		Preparation of Summary Report by Administrative Ministry for Licensing Committee		Reference of Case to Cabinet Committee in Economic Co-ordination and Department of Company Affairs after Licensing Committee Meeting		Disposal of Case by Dept of Company Affairs without Reference to Monopolies Commission		Status of Pending Cases with Dept of Company Affairs		Issue of Industrial Licence or Letter of Intent by Administrative Ministry after Licensing Committee Meeting Minutes Circulated		Applications pending without being Placed before the Foreign Investment Board		Applications Approved by Foreign Investment Board		Applications Pending with Foreign Investment Board	
	No.	%	No.	%	No.	%	No.	%	No.	%	No.	%	No.	%	No.	%	No.	%	No.	%
0–3 days	–	–	–	–	–	–	–	–	–	–	–	–	–	–	–	–	–	–	84*	19
3–7 days	1	8	–	–	–	–	–	–	–	–	–	–	–	–	–	–	–	–	–	–
1–2 weeks	11	92	–	–	–	–	–	–	–	–	–	–	1	10	–	–	–	–	–	–
2–4 weeks	–	–	–	–	–	–	5	63	–	–	–	–	2	20	–	–	–	–	1	neg
4–6 weeks	–	–	2	18	1	2	1	13	4	3.5	–	–	1	10	10	4	–	–	123	35
6–8 weeks	–	–	3	28	1	2	–	–	4	3.5	4	6	–	–	22	8	–	–	123	35
2–3 months	–	–	2	18	2	4	2	24	10	9.0	4	6	1	10	30	11	–	–	21	5
3–4 months	–	–	2	18	6	12	–	–	7	6.0	5	8	1	10	30	11	56	16	12	3
4–5 months	–	–	2	18	8	16	–	–	10	9.0	10	16	3	20	30	11	40	12	12	3
5–6 months	–	–	–	–	10	20	–	–	20	18.0	15	25	1	10	42	16	47	13	–	–

(Contd)

Table 19.5 (Contd)

Time Taken	Issue of Letter of Intent/Industrial Licence														Foreign Investments Board Clearance					
	Registration and Distribution of Applications by Central Licensing Policy Section		Receipt of Comments on Application from Technical Advisers		Preparation of Summary Report by Administrative Ministry for Licensing Committee		Reference of Case to Cabinet Committee in Economic Co-ordination and Department of Company Affairs after Licensing Committee Meeting		Disposal of Case by Dept of Company Affairs without Reference to Monopolies Commission		Status of Pending Cases with Dept of Company Affairs		Issue of Industrial Licence or Letter of Intent by Administrative Ministry after Licensing Committee Meeting Minutes Circulated		Applications pending without being Placed before the Foreign Investment Board		Applications Approved by Foreign Investment Board		Applications Pending with Foreign Investment Board	
	No.	%	No.	%	No.	%	No.	%	No.	%	No.	%	No.	%	No.	%	No.	%	No.	%
6–12 months	–	–	–	–	19	38	–	–	35	32.0	19	32	–	–	78	29	150	42	–	–
12–18 months	–	–	–	–	2	4	–	–	20	18.0	4	7	–	–	22	8	60	17	–	–
Over 18 months	–	–	–	–	–	–	–	–	–	–	–	–	–	–	–	2	–	–	–	–
Total	12	100	11	100	50	100	8	100	110	100	61	100	10	100	269	100	353	100	428	100
Reference:																				
Page, 19th Report	127		131		129		149		163		163		151		174		173		173	

(Contd)

Table 19.5 (Contd)

Time Taken	Issue of Letter of Intent/Industrial Licence							Foreign Investments Board Clearance		
	Registration and Distribution of Applications by Central Licensing Policy Section	Receipt of Comments on Application from Technical Advisers	Preparation of Summary Report by Administrative Ministry for Licensing Committee	Reference of Case to Cabinet Committee in Economic Co-ordination and Department of Company Affairs after Licensing Committee Meeting	Disposal of Case by Dept of Company Affairs without Reference to Monopolies Commission	Status of Pending Cases with Dept of Company Affairs	Issue of Industrial Licence or Letter of Intent by Administrative Ministry after Licensing Committee Meeting Minutes Circulated	Applications pending without being Placed before the Foreign Investment Board	Applications Approved by Foreign Investment Board	Applications Pending with Foreign Investment Board
	No. %	No. %	No. %	No. %	No. %	No. %	No. %	No. %	No. %	No. %
Period covered by cases	NA	NA	Week ending May 15, 1971	Minutes of LIC meeting of August 7, 1971	Up to November 15, 1971	Up to November 15, 1971	NA	For the year 1971	For the year 1971	For the year 1971
Stipulated Time:	3 days from receipt of application	3 weeks from receipt from application from CLP	4–6 weeks from receipt of application	NA	90 days from the date of reference to DCA	90 days from the date of reference to DCA	NA	2 months from the date of receipt of application	90 days from the date of receipt of application	90 days from the date of receipt of application

* Approved by FIB, orders to be issued.

Source: 19th Report: Estimates Committee (1971–72) Fifth Lok Sabha. Figures have been re-grouped where necessary for comparison.

But simultaneously the Committee discovers 259 applications that have been pending with the Ministry of Industrial Development itself for more than a year and it also notices that 94 per cent of the applications it examines have taken more than three months to get to the Licensing Committee. The Secretary tells the Committee that if technical departments and other Ministries fail to send their comments within the prescribed deadlines his Ministry sends applications to the Licensing Committee without waiting for their comments. When the Committee later tries to verify this statement it learns from the Ministry of Industrial Development that the Ministry is not in fact sending up cases in the way its Secretary said it was, that "the introduction of such a procedure is still under (the Ministry's) consideration." The Secretary tells the Committee that when an application for extending the validity of a letter of intent is rejected "a show cause notice is generally not issued." In a written reply the Ministry later alters this to say that "a show cause notice is expected to be issued and the reasons for rejection are expected to be communicated to the parties." Later still, when it tries to verify these statements, the Committee learns that the Ministry's written statement relates to applications for industrial licences and not to applications for extending the validity of the letters of intent. In telling the Committee what action it has taken on the Committee's recommendations the government thrice mentions that the DGTD information systems are being computerised and it conveys the impression that this will take care of the points raised by the Committee. It forgets to mention that the government has been trying to computerise the DGTD's information systems since 1963, that, in fact, at the very time it was making these assertions to the Committee it was extremely worried about the fact that little had come out of an expensive, three-year project to modernise the DGTD's information systems. And so on.

The fourth feature about the way our controls are administered relates to the bureaucrats who man the system. I have already mentioned how recent events and the present accusatory atmosphere have left them nervous: each is preoccupied with saving his neck and not with doing a job. Few of them have any specialised or intimate knowledge about the industries whose development they control and thwart. Few of them have the skills or aptitudes of a manager. This has at least two adverse effects for the administration of controls.

As they are not managers, as they are not directly affected by the progress or lack of progress in a plant or an industry, and as they cannot be penalised for their errors and delays they function without any notions about costs and benefits. They examine each case as it would be examined by a criminal judge—without any thought about the opportunity costs of their examination. They insist on the formal enforcement of rules and procedures without any notion of the net benefit to the economy of this compliance.

Nowhere is the lack of managerial skills and managerial aptitude more apparent than in their attitude to data. If a manager were running the industrial licensing system he would free himself from the futile burden of examining individual cases. Instead he would spend his time on policy issues and on assessing and improving the performance of the system as a whole—the pace at which it processes applications, the net benefits that result from the examination and so on. In complete contrast to this our administrators pay no attention to the functioning of the system as a whole. Most of their time is spent on chasing, hurrying or blocking individual files.

Even the most elementary aids that would help them assess the system and keep track of the consequences of their decisions remain unused. For example, as we mentioned earlier, the Licensing Committee and the Capital Goods Committee take decisions on about 40–50 and 30–35 cases at each of their sittings. One would expect that someone will be tabulating the consequences of these decisions—consequences in terms of likely investments, the likely draft on foreign exchange resources, the likely costs in terms of foregone output because of the time it has taken to process the case and so on. No tabulations of the sort are made. No one bothers to see what the consequences of these decisions are for output in different industries, for investment, for the country's net foreign exchange position. The Committees meet, devote two to three minutes to each case and adjourn. The machinery gets busy preparing minutes about the decisions regarding each case and compiling papers for the next sitting. The Secretaries and Joint Secretaries carry over to Udyog Bhavan the District Collectors' faith in the surprise visit: instead of setting up methods by which they will receive information about the controls systematically and regularly they think that they can keep everyone on his toes by occasionally asking for a particular file, by occasionally soliciting a number. Consider another example. In May 1970 the government announced that investments up to Rs 1 crore would be exempt from licensing unless they were being undertaken by a dominant undertaking or a company affiliated to a large house. As we have noted earlier, proposals are now being made to raise the relicensing limit to, say, Rs 3 crores. But the administrators do not know—and presumably have not had the aptitude or skill to set up a system that would keep them informed about—the extent to which this delicensing has enabled them to process the remaining cases more expeditiously, about the industries in which and the locations at which these new investments have been made, about the direct or indirect foreign exchange implications of the new investments and so on. Nor, as I mentioned earlier, have they been able to or felt compelled to aggregate the information they receive periodically in forms such as the G-form. They look upon each form as a potential instrument of hauling an individual up and not—as a manager would—as a means of keeping tabs on the performance of the system as a whole. In brief, our controls are being administered by overworked criminal judges rather than by managers.

Larger Issues

The controls, the confusion that envelops their formulation, the delays and the *ad hocry* that marks their administration—each of these survives because it serves a purpose. Ambiguities and contradictions enhance discretionary powers in the hands of the Minister and the official. Delays enable them to extort favours. Ambiguities and contradictions also serve the interests of the rich and resourceful industrialist for they make it easier for him to persuade and cajole the machinery into taking care of his interests. There is scarcely a control today that does not benefit an industrialist or a tout. It is the national economy that suffers. The official, the politician and the businessmen prosper. And so the system survives and is able to ward off every effort to reform it.

The persistence of these features is also due to our habits of thought and to the dilemma in which our ruling class has placed itself—its slogans have disabled it from doing the things that come naturally to it. I have mentioned some of these factors in earlier issues of this journal. Here it is necessary to note only one factor which is especially visible in the way we formulate and administer our controls. This is our obsession with form.

We are obsessed with form in two senses. First, when we perceive a difficulty we work ourselves into a verbal fever—a fever that does not abate till we have taken some token measures to deal with the difficulty, till we have set up a committee, referred its recommendations to another committee, passed a law and set up a directorate or a commission to administer the law. The second aspect of our obsession with form is that once we have taken these token measures—once we have satisfied the form—we relapse into a state of satisfaction or at least of indifference. For us form is necessary as well as sufficient. Is concentration of economic power a problem? Let us set up a Monopolies and Restrictive Trade Practices Commission. Never mind if it is not free to choose the cases it should examine, if it does not have much of a staff, if its recommendations do not have any mandatory force *vis-à-vis* the government. Should we not centralise materials planning for the industrial sector? Indeed—and especially in view of emergencies such as 1962 and 1965—we must. Let us, therefore, set up a materials planning cell; let us ask a senior research officer to look after it on a part-time basis and let us assign a research officer to assist him in the task. Shouldn't we protect the consumer? Let us impose controls over the prices at which factories sell their products. Are there many violations of the Foreign Exchange Regulations? Let us set up an Enforcement Directorate and sanction a staff of 130 men to police the entire country. Do industrialists not siphon off funds for their enrichment and that of their relatives by manipulating the sales and purchase policies of their concerns? Does X, whose product is under price control, not pay inflated prices to units from which he buys components, thereby showing that his unit yields meagre returns; and are not those ancillary units—the prices of whose products are not controlled—owned by his relatives? Let us use the substantial shares that government-sponsored financial institutions have in the units to rectify malpractices of this kind. Let us, therefore, set up a holding company of these institutions—no matter if the same overworked Joint Secretaries have to look after its affairs and, in addition to everything else they do, also sit on the boards of the industrial units; no matter if they do not have any expertise in assessing sales and purchase practices: "*arey bhai, kuch to karnahai.*"

Because of this attitude we seldom care to enquire whether the controls we institute are ever enforced and whether they achieve the purposes for which they are meant.

IV

THE MORAL OF THE STORY

The preceding passages constitute a long catalogue of ailments. It is easy to turn these around into an equally long list of "constructive" suggestions. One can urge, for instance, that the administration of controls should be entrusted to those who have managerial skills, that decision-makers should be penalised for the errors and delays they perpetrate, that objectives and policies should be clarified, that cost-benefit notions should be introduced all along the line, that information systems should be improved, that when a project is given a priority status it should be accorded priority by every department, that the examinations connected with, say, the setting up of an industrial unit should be made the responsibility of one committee so that an approval does not just mean approval to run to the next hurdle, and so on.

Suggestions such as these have been made before and many of them are being considered now. Little will come of them for the same reasons—the sort of reasons that have been sketched in section III—on account of which previous efforts at reform have failed to improve the system.

The only way to improve things is to cleanse the atmosphere, to examine and articulate the alternatives in detail, to expose the workings of the system to public scrutiny and to eliminate administrative controls.

We have already seen the ways in which the current atmosphere of suspicion and accusation hampers the administration of controls. This atmosphere also scares officials and politicians from considering alternatives to the present setup.

It is indeed a curious aspect of the current situation that one seldom comes across an officer who believes that the controls he is administering help the economy. And yet none of them raises a voice against them. Each fears that were he to propose that alternatives be examined his commitment to socialism will be called into question. Our first task must be to cleanse this atmosphere and one way of doing so is to expose the true nature of controls, to expose the fact at every occasion.

20

Indian Development Strategy

Some Comments*

Jagdish Bhagwati and T. N. Srinivasan

Sukhamoy Chakravarty's Fifth G. L. Mehta Lecture (1984) discussing India's development strategy for the 1980s is characterised by his customary erudition and lucidity of style. But its analysis of our past economic performance, and of our future prospects and the strategy for maximally improving them, raise several key questions. We can think of no better tribute to Sukhamoy Chakravarty's intellectual efforts than to address these questions and to indicate our agreements and disagreements with him. We hope that this will prompt a debate on the vital issues of Indian economic policy at this critical point in our history.

Essentially, there are two central issues raised by Chakravarty's analysis. (1) The relatively stagnant growth of the Indian economy since the mid-1960s, despite the impressive augmentation of our investment rate, needs explanation. After considering several factors, Chakravarty leans somewhat heavily on (domestic) "demand" constraints. (2) Implicit in this choice, as Chakravarty is aware, is elasticity or export pessimism which has, of course, characterised our planning and policy for most of the post-Independence era. His scenario for the future is dominated again by such pessimism. In the following discussion, therefore, we focus essentially on these two aspects of his lecture, while commenting on related themes as appropriate

* Originally published in *Economic and Political Weekly* 19, no. 47 (24 November 1984): pp. 2006–7.

I

As for the issue "where has the investment gone?," there is no denying the fact that, in the last decade or so, savings and investment rates as estimated by the Central Statistical Organisation (CSO) have risen sharply without much of an impact on the growth rate of national product.[1] If we break up the period 1950–84 into 1951 to 1965 (coinciding roughly with the Nehru and pre-wheat-revolution era) and 1968 to 1984 (omitting the two severe drought years of 1965–66 and 1966–67 and accepting a projected growth rate of real gross domestic product of 7.5 per cent for 1983–84), the trend growth rate is 3.88 per cent per year in the former period and 3.75 per cent in the latter period, there being no statistically significant difference between the two rates. The decadal average growth rate of the 1950s (3.59 per cent), 1960s (3.13 per cent) and the 1970s (3.62 per cent) are also similar. However, the fate of gross investment which was about 10 per cent of gross national product (at current prices) during the 1950s is now close to 25 per cent. We have had therefore blood, sweat and tears, but little results. Why?

Part of the explanation of this puzzle, is of course, the changing composition of investment towards more capital-intensive industries. Increasing investment and constant growth can also be reconciled somewhat if the unaccounted (or black) economy is allowed for. Estimates of the black economy vary considerably, from around 20 per cent to 100 per cent of the official estimate of national income. Whatever its extent, however, there seems to be agreement that the black economy is increasing. But to bring about a full reconciliation, the *growth* of the black economy would have to be extraordinarily large indeed. In the appendix we show that under certain plausible assumptions the black economy would have had to grow at a sustained rate of over 10 per cent per year for 25 years to bring about such a reconciliation. And this is simply not credible.

The bulk of the explanation therefore would seem to us to have to lean on the "common wisdom" (as Chakravarty describes it), attributable to the earlier work of Bhagwati and Desai[2] and Bhagwati and Srinivasan[3] on the efficiency of our trade and allocational policies, that our resource utilisation has been substantially inefficient. Chakravarty concedes this but suggests, without weighing the evidence in these works, that it is only a part of the explanation, even if a large one, and that too for some sectors.

In particular, he leans on the role instead of demand factors. Posing the question, "Is it possible to say that the rise in capital-output ratio has something to do with the operation of demand factors?" he answers affirmatively. But there are several objections to this thesis.

First, from a strictly arithmetical point of view, it is true that even if there is no capital-deepening in the sense of an increase in the ratio of investment to full capacity output, the ratio of investment to actual output can rise if the rate of capacity utilisation falls. Indeed some years ago Srinivasan and Narayana,[4] who were the earliest to analyse the growth stagnation of the Indian economy since the mid-1960s, noted that using actual output in measuring capital-output ratio in periods of falling capacity utilisation can be misleading in the sense that shortfalls in demand will get confounded with shortfalls in production efficiency. But to go beyond this arithmetic to the economics of the situation, one has to explain why capacity utilisation fell and in spite of it investment continued to increase. Bhagwati and Srinivasan cited several reasons why the prevailing capacity licensing system encouraged the tendency to create additional capacity in spite of low rates of utilisation of existing capacity. As to why capacity utilisation fell (or failed to increase). Srinivasan and Narayana identified several factors, at the sectoral and aggregate levels. But the thrust of their argument was that the shortfall in aggregate demand was not *structural* (as Chakravarty seems to imply) but a symptom of *failure of policy or lack of policy.* They identified several domestic policy failures, the most important being the slowdown in public investment that affected demand in general and for capital goods in particular. Their analysis has been updated, considerably extended and deepened by Isher Ahluwalia,[5] who confirms many of their conclusions.

Second, as Chakravarty recognises, home demand is not the only source of demand and there is foreign (export) demand as well. We would add that home production is not the only source of supply for traded goods and the other source is imports. This is important to remember because Chakravarty maintains that "the crucial factor which seemed to have led to a diversion from the (Mahalanobis) strategy in the mid-1960s was the growing proneness of the economy to inflation, in itself based on the failure of agricultural supply to match the demand that was being placed on it due, in part, to efforts at accelerating industrialisation, and to a greater extent the slow down of acreage expansion in agriculture and an increase in population growth." At the outset, we should note that, while it is true that the acreage expansion slowed down, *there is no evidence of any slowdown in the growth of agricultural output since the early 1950s.*[6] *Since the mid-1960s there was no significant increase in the rate of population growth nor was there any "accelerating industrialisation." Indeed, quite the contrary is the case.* If anything, *taken as a whole*, the post-1966–67 period is one in which agricultural supply more than matched effective demand. In any event, in an open economy, any incipient inflation because of shortfalls in the domestic supply of tradeables can be curbed through imports, and with an adequate export effort the capacity to import would have been there. Chakravarty must therefore resort to elasticity or export pessimism to support his argument. Indeed, unless such pessimism, which has characterised our policies to date, is successfully defended, the essence of the arguments based on domestic demand factors cannot get off the ground. (Whether then the *further* justifications required to link the domestic demand factors to the disappointing economic performance are, in turn, valid is something else indeed, but as we have argued above even those justifications are not as persuasive as Chakravarty seems to believe.) We must therefore turn anew to the question of export pessimism. Before we do this, however, let us note that Chakravarty asserts that India lacked entrepreneurial talent in significant measure at the time of her independence. This claim however is surely exaggerated, if not false, as is evident from India's pre-Independence economic history and indeed the presence of entrepreneurship not just in trade but also in steel, textiles and other activities in ample degree at the time of independence.

II

Chakravarty accepts the "need for stepping up our export performance" and that "our import substitution in some sectors has been extremely costly": two conclusions which were reached after detailed analysis in Bhagwati and Desai[7] and Bhagwati and Srinivasan,[8] among other contributions. But his analysis, as shown above, still reflects export pessimism. Moreover, and this is disturbing, his recommendations for future strategy are also built on such pessimism. Basically, he seems to have two arguments: one, that India simply cannot exploit external opportunities for trade expansion; two, that the external environment is not favourable anyway.

For the former, he mainly cites infrastructural difficulties which are surely remediable by policy rather than to be taken as givens and a study of Fields[9] which asserts that outward orientation has not been good for Jamaica et al. as they have had high urban wage differentials and therefore the Far Eastern export-promotion (EP) model is inappropriate. However, Fields's article fails to demonstrate that Jamaica et al. were indeed following export promoting policies (as clearly defined in the work of Krueger, Balassa and ourselves, among others) in the first place. In fact, if one had to go by casual empirical evidence, Jamaica would appear to be a prime example of what is described in the trade-theoretic and trade-policy literature as the import-substitution (IS) strategy. If we are to invoke wages in the question on developmental-strategy choice we would rather say that the countries that have had successful EP strategies, and superior economic performance, have had very good macro policies (based probably on their authoritarian political structures, though the excesses of spending and runaway inflations in Latin America have also occurred under authoritarian regimes with a far less appealing political track record) which have kept the growth of wages under wraps. Their excellent micro incentives through EP strategy have been built on sound macro foundations. India's tragedy has been that, while we have had reasonable though conservative macro policies, the micro policies (including trade strategy) have failed to exploit this fact: we have simply thrown away a splendid opportunity by resorting to unwarranted export pessimism, as far as the EP versus IS choice is concerned, by refusing to yield to reality on the question.

This brings us to the second point in Chakravarty's argumentation: the worry over the unfavourable external environment. Manmohan Singh's early and pioneering work on India's export performance, recent work by Martin Wolf,[10] and several other studies have demonstrated the fallacy of Indian export pessimism. This is hardly the place to reiterate the familiar arguments. But we must remind the readers of the *EPW* that India's share in world exports was a minuscule 0.41 per cent in 1981 and has been falling almost continuously since 1948 when it was 2.4 per cent. Other countries which began with a much smaller industrial base are not only exporting *more manufactures* than India but, what is more striking, catching up with India in the *absolute size* of their manufacturing sector. According to the World Bank's World Development Reports in 1983 and 1984, the size of Korea's manufacturing sector as measured by value added (in constant 1975 US dollars) in 1970 was $2.35 billion, less than 25 per cent of India's $10.2 billion. By 1981, Korea's figure had risen to $10.54 billion, more than 60 per cent of India's $16.9 billion. Korea's manufactured exports at current prices, which were negligible compared to India's $630 million in 1962, amounted to $15.7 billion in 1980, nearly *four* times that of India's $4.4 billion. The point is not that India should emulate Korea's political and economic system nor that Korea's success is due to 'laissez faire' policy, issues on which we have written in the 1970s, pointing to the fallacies in these *nonsequiturs*.[11] It is rather that the causes of India's unsatisfactory performance are to be sought in Indian economic policy and the fallacious premises on which it was predicated and not in the global economic system.

III

Evidently, if India is to accelerate her growth performance and also to impact more meaningfully therefore on poverty through the "pull up" process that Pitambar Pant and other planners in the 1960s envisaged, much else will have to be done, including a forceful leadership on economic issues which no longer relies on "muddling through" since what one gets in practice is "muddling under." What we would like to reiterate forcefully, however, is that such leadership will have to address precisely the kinds of issues that we have discussed above. Continuing failure to face up to the experience of the last 25 years on obviously key issues such as those Chakravarty addresses and we discuss is hardly likely to propel us in the direction of achieving our efficiency and distributional objectives.

Appendix

The following numerical example illustrates the argument. Suppose net investment as a proportion of measured income grew linearly over time from 5 per cent to 20 per cent in 25 years. Denoting by it the investment rate, this means that $i_j = .05 + .006t$ where $t = 0, 1, \ldots 25$.

Let us assume that measured income Y_t^M grew steadily at a rate $g = .035$ or 3.5 per cent per year and at $t = 0$ it was 97 per cent of the true income Y_O^* (measured plus black income). Suppose the true incremental output capital ratio was unchanged at 1/5. Then assuming an average lag of one year between investment and output we get.

$$Y_{25}^* - Y_O^* = \left(\frac{1}{3}\right) Y_O^M \sum_{t=0}^{24} (.05 + .006t)(1 + g)^1$$

$$= \frac{.97}{3} Y_O^* \left[.05\left(\frac{(1 + g)^{25} - 1}{g}\right) + \frac{.006}{g^2}\left((24g - 1)(1 + g)^{24} + 1\right]$$

Where $g = .35$.

Writing g^* as the average rate of growth of Y_1^* during the 25 years we get,

$$(1 + g^*)^{25} - 1 - \frac{.97}{3}\left[\frac{.05}{.035}(1.035)^{25} - 1 + \frac{.006 \times 1.035}{(0.035)^2}\left(.160(1.035)^{24} + 1\right)\right]$$

$$= \frac{.97}{3}(1.9475 + 3.2173) = 1.6700$$

or

$$(1 + g^*)^{25} = 2.6700 \text{ or } g^* = .04$$

Now black income equals by assumption $.03Y_O^*$ in year 0 and $Y_{25}^* - Y_{25}^M$

$$= Y_O^*\left[\left(1 + g^*\right)^{25} - 97\left(1 + g\right)^{25}\right]$$

in year 25. That is, it increases to $.3777Y_O^*$ from $.03Y_O^*$ in 25 years. Hence denoting by g_B the average rate of growth of black income we have:

$$\left(1 + g_B\right)^{25} = \frac{.3777}{.0300} = 12.5884 \text{ or } g_B = 12.5884.$$

Thus black income must grow at an average rate exceeding 10 per cent per year to keep the true marginal capital output ratio, i.e., ratio of investment to the change in true income (measured plus black income).

More generally, if we write $i(t) = \alpha_O + \alpha_1 t$ and $Y_O^M = \theta Y_O^*$ we get, for any horizon T > 0, $(1 + g^*)^T$

$$= 1 + \beta\theta\left[\frac{\left(\alpha_0 g + \alpha_1\left[(T-1)g - 1\right]\right)}{g^2}(1+g)^T + \left(\frac{\alpha_1 + (\alpha_1 - \alpha_O)}{g^2}g\right)\right]$$

$$\left(1 + g_B\right)^T = \frac{\left(1+g^*\right)^T - \theta\left(1+g\right)^T}{1-\theta}$$

and the share B(T) of black income to measured income is given by

$$B(T) = \frac{\theta}{\left(1-\theta\right)^2}\left[\left(\frac{1+g^*}{1+g}\right)^T - \theta\right]$$

Interested readers can use their own values for α_O, α_1, g and θ to analyse the resulting values of g^*, g_B and $B(T)$ for various horizons.

NOTES AND REFERENCES

[1] The methodology of CSO's estimation of national income suggests that underestimation of output due to the omission of black income is unlikely to be significant in respect of the following: agriculture inclusive of forestry and fishing, mining and quarrying, electricity, gas and water supply, railways, banking and insurance, public administration and defence and, arguably, registered manufacturing. These industries account for nearly 60 per cent of official estimates of net domestic product at current prices.

[2] J. N. Bhagwati and Padma Desai. *India: Planning for Industrialisation* (London: Oxford University Press, 1970).

[3] N. Bhagwati and T. N. Srinivasan. *Foreign Trade Regime and Economic Development: India* (New York: Columbia University Press, 1975).

[4] T. N. Srinivasan and N. S. S. Narayana. "Economic Performance since the Third Plan and Its Implication for Policy," *Economic and Political Weekly*, 12, Annual Number (9 February 1977).

[5] Isher Ahluwalia. *Industrial Performance in India, 1959–60 to 1978–79* (New Delhi: Indian Council for Research in International Relations, 1982)

[6] T. N. Srinivasan. "Trends in Agriculture in India, 1949–50—1977–78," *Economic and Political Weekly*, Special Number (August 1979).

[7] Bhagwati and Desai, *India*.

[8] Bhagwati and Srinivasan. *Foreign Trade*.

[9] G. Fields. "Employment, Income Distribution and Economic Growth in Seven Small Open Economies." *Economic Journal*, 94 (March 1984).

[10] M. Wolf. *India's Exports* (New York: Oxford University Press, 1982).

[11] Authoritarian regimes are the *overwhelming* majority in the developing world but cases of successful development are far too few!

21

Industrial Growth in the 1980s

Emerging Policy Issues*

Vijay L. Kelkar and Rajiv Kumar

I

The Context

It has been an eventful decade for industrial development in India. Changes in government policy which had been initiated in the closing years of the previous decade were further reinforced and accelerated during the 1980s. The technological somnolence of the 1970s was replaced by a spate of technological collaborations and ambitious schemes for modernisation and capacity rejuvenation. There are hints even of a reversal in the trends of industrial efficiency as reflected in estimates of total factor productivity. The industrial sector in India during the 1980s appeared to be moving towards the intensive rather than the extensive margin on which it had operated for the past three decades.

Most important perhaps was the marked upturn in industrial growth during the current decade which brought all other institutional and qualitative aspects into focus. According to the latest *World Development Report* (*WDR*) of the World Bank, Indian industry registered an average annual growth rate of 7 per cent. This was higher than the growth rate achieved in all the developed economies and in several newly industrialising countries such as Brazil, Argentina, Singapore,

* Originally published in *Economic and Political Weekly* 25, no. 4 (27 January 1990): pp. 209–22.

Indonesia, etc. Indian industrial growth during 1980–87, according to *WDR*, was lower only than that achieved in China, Pakistan and South Korea among a broadly comparable set of countries.

This merited upturn in industrial growth and an apparent shift in policy regime has expectedly generated a lively debate within the country on several aspects of this growth. The quantum of growth as reflected in the revised series of index of industrial production (IIP) has itself been questioned by some contributors.[1] The index has been criticised for containing an upward bias for growth rates in the 1980s as it overestimates output due to "arbitrary replacement" of supposedly slow-growing industries with faster growing ones.[2] Others like Nagraj[3] have argued that even when data on gross value added, as reported by the *National Accounts Statistics* (*NAS*), are considered, an upturn in industrial activity during 1980–87 (the period for which data are available) is unambiguously evident. Other contributors to the debate have expressed scepticism over the sustainability of this rate of growth.[4] Both demand constraints and likely supply (resources) bottlenecks, not necessarily together, it is argued, will work to slow down this growth in the coming years. On the demand side, it is argued that the recent performance has been possible primarily on account of rise in real incomes of the middle income categories in the organised workforce which has come about as a direct result of government's fiscal and industrial policies. This rise in incomes has generated a high demand for consumer durables and services which have been the main driving forces of industrial growth during the current decade. For various reasons, it is argued, this demand expansion may not be expected to continue in the future and as repressed demand from previous years has largely been fulfilled, rates of growth may be expected to decline. On the supply side, critics of current industrial performance point out that, due to its very nature of being import and energy intensive[5] and not generating additional employment, the current growth will soon run into severe resource constraints.[6] Seen as part of the package of new economic policy or "liberalisation," etc., which has been put into place in the present decade, industrial growth as also the entire package of economic policies, it is argued, is unsustainable and is unviable for the economy.

Most of the arguments on either side, however, falter in three important respects. First, the debate so far has been carried on either completely on an a priori or conjectural level without reference to empirical basis or at best on the basis of aggregate data on industrial growth up to the mid-1980s. This has obviously resulted in some reservations being expressed about the conclusions reached by some of these contributions. Second, none of the contributors have analysed the implications of this performance for future policy-making. Third, and perhaps most crucially, the impact of recent shifts in policy and of changes in industrial activity on future international competitiveness of Indian industry has been left unanalysed.

This chapter attempts to fill these gaps and thus help to take this important debate a step further. The evidence and results reported here are part of an ongoing exercise on analysing industrial performance and policies in the country. It was felt that, although preliminary in nature, these data and conclusions presented here will serve as timely inputs for deepening the debate on perhaps the more important economic issues facing the country in the coming decade. The chapter also suggests some policy changes for improving industrial performance during the next two plans.

The chapter is divided into five sections. The next section on empirical evidence presents and also briefly discusses the available statistical evidence on aggregate rates of growth of industrial output and of value added during the 1980s and compares them to previous decades. Disaggregated data on sub-sectoral growth rates are then discussed. The disaggregated data, derived essentially from IIP and partially from time series on prices compiled by CMIE, provides the basis for the subsequent discussion on nature and sources of industrial growth during the 1980s and its implications for future competitiveness and government policy in the coming plans. The chapter's major hypotheses, as based on and derived from the data presented here, are discussed in the latter half of the next section. This part also includes some additional data on recent trends in investment across various industrial subsections and on income distribution, in order to reinforce the hypotheses stated earlier. This core section of the chapter ends by bringing together some of the major conclusions of the discussion.

Section III is devoted to highlighting some of the implications of industrial growth during the 1980s. These implications are discussed under two broad subsections. The first subsection analyses the impact of the 1980s' industrial growth on various aspects of the domestic economy like regional concentration of industry, employment expansion in the industrial sector, performance of the non-tradable industrial section and public-sector enterprises, and capital or resource intensity of industrial activity. The second subsection examines the implications of this recent growth for international competitiveness of Indian industry. After summarily discussing the share of manufactured exports from India in global trade and the export propensity of Indian industrial output, the section goes on to examine recent evidence on some indicators of competitiveness, viz., domestic resource costs (DRCs). This is done to examine if recent industrial growth has been in line with the country's natural comparative and competitive advantage.

The penultimate section attempts to relate the industrial performance of this decade to some of the specific changes in government policy. Admittedly, the discussion here is limited to some of the major aspects of government policy affecting industrial growth in the country. Other important policy issues concerning technology imports and technological development, the role and efficiency of public sector, industrial employment, etc., have not been addressed only because of constraint of space and the rather limited scope of the chapter. The discussion in this section represents an attempt to draw some causal links between some of the policy changes and industrial growth in recent years and provides the basis for policy recommendations made by us here. Based on the major findings and conclusions of this chapter, required policy reforms are indicated in the last section.

II

THE EVIDENCE

It is important to recapitulate the relationship between the two official sources of data on industrial growth.[7] The data collected through the Annual Survey of Industries (ASI) and presented in the *NAS* pertains to gross value added by the registered, unregistered and manufacturing sector as a whole. The publication of *NAS* (1989) has made available the aggregate data on growth of sectoral GDP until 1987–88 and details of the manufacturing sector at the two-digit level until 1986–87. The second official source, i.e., the index of industrial production, presents a time series index of gross industrial production in registered manufacturing sector. The weights used to constitute the aggregate index are derived from the sectoral shares in value addition as given in the ASI-*NAS* data. IIP is available with a substantially shorter time lag and enables us to consider the growth performance for the year 1988–89 as well. Details at disaggregated (three and four digits industries specifications) levels are available up to January 1989. It was clearly established that IIP consistently underestimated industrial production as compared to the ASI, at least until the beginning of the 1980s.[8] Recently, Nagraj has shown on the basis of a preliminary analysis of *NAS* and IIP data, that even for the period up to 1986–87, IIP continues to underestimate industrial growth when compared to ASI. This is further corroborated by data for 1987–88 which show that, according to IIP, industrial growth during 1987–88 was 7.9 per cent per annum as compared to 8.33 per cent recorded by the ASI. IIP has generated a growth rate of 8.9 per cent for the year 1988–89, which is marginally lower than the average growth based on ASI data for 1981–82 to 1987–88, which was 9.78 per cent. Given the downward bias of the IIP, the 1988–89 growth rate may be reflected as a higher annual rate in terms of ASI data. Overall, therefore, it could be safely concluded that manufacturing gross domestic product during the 1980s has grown by more than 9 per cent annually.

It may be recalled that the base year for the IIP and the weighting profile has been changed in 1985–86 primarily to bring the IIP closer to the ASI estimates. Fears were expressed by some observers on an upward bias having been introduced in the IIP as a result of the revision of the base year and change in weights for different industries. We would reinforce Nagraj's conclusions that these fears are unfounded and the downward bias of the IIP compared to the ASI still continues though it is less marked as a result of the revision in 1985. Therefore, the more disaggregated evidence on industrial growth as presented and analysed later in this section is derived from the IIP to enable us to take into account the performance up to 1988–89.

Confining ourselves initially to *NAS* value added data, it is evident (Table 21.1) that the overall growth rate of the manufacturing sector during the 1980s (1981–82 to 1986–87) has been substantially higher than in earlier periods. This is confirmed by taking six-yearly moving averages for annual rates of growth and on that basis comparing average growth rates for each decade. During these years, value added in the registered manufacturing sector, at 1980–81 prices grew at 10.13 per cent per annum as compared to 5.5 per cent during 1966–67 to 1979–80 and 7.6 per cent during 1959–60 to 1965–66.[9] A comparison of the 1980s' growth rates with those achieved during the earlier so-called Mahalanobis period (1959–65) is important because it brings out the rather marked contrasts in the nature of growth during the two periods.

In the earlier period, i.e., 1959–60 to 1965–66, the fastest growing sector (apart from leather products, which is common to both) was industrial groups comprising of basic metal, metal products and machinery, both electrical and non-electrical.[10] In the 1980s, no such single interrelated groups of industries stands out as the prime mover of growth. Instead, we have the five highest rates being achieved by (apart from leather and miscellaneous) electrical machinery, food products, non-metallic mineral products, chemicals and chemical products, and rubber and petroleum products, in that order.[11] Given that electrical machinery is common to both periods and that food products also fall within the broad biochemical sector, it is clear that the role of prime movers during the 1980s was taken over by the petrochemicals, chemicals and allied industries. In contrast, the metal-based industries which provided the momentum for industrial growth during the previous period (i.e., 1959–65) grew at rates lower than the industry average. Basic metal sector grew at only 4.91 per cent, metal products by 6.49 per cent and non-electrical machinery at 9.74 per cent per annum during the 1980s. This shift, as we emphasise later, has important implications for the economy.

Estimates of growth of manufactured output in the unregistered sector during the 1980s shows that like in the earlier decades, the unregistered sector has grown more slowly than registered manufacturing. Annual rate of growth

TABLE 21.1: RATE OF GROWTH OF VALUE ADDITION DURING 80s

Sl No.	Ind	Industry/Year	1981–82	1982–83	1983–84	1984–85	1985–86	1986–87	Average Growth Rate (1981–82 to 1986–87)
(0)	(1)	(2)	(3)	(4)	(5)	(6)	(7)	(8)	(9)
1.	20–22	Food products	32.07	34.95	11.49	0.89	4.72	5.98	15.02
2.	22	Beverages, tobacco, etc.	6.10	3.45	84.07	–15.49	0.48	–12.09	11.9
3.	23	Cotton textiles	–16.02	–6.16	24.29	–5.93	8.03	–0.13	0.68
4.	24	Wool, silk, etc.	20.77	5.23	17.58	5.44	9.74	9.14	11.32
5.	25	Jute textiles	–9.57	–6.83	–25.64	–2.46	–2.02	4.12	–7.07
6.	26	Textiles products	25.00	12.12	4.86	19.07	18.18	–22.71	9.42
7.	27	Wood furniture, etc.	0.00	1.41	26.39	–4.40	3.45	10.00	6.14
8.	28	Paper, printing, etc.	9.32	–7.83	15.09	17.38	12.57	9.93	9.41
9.	29	Leather and fur products	22.08	10.64	21.15	16.67	21.09	5.62	16.21
10.	30	Rubber, petroleum, etc.	–6.03	52.51	5.68	15.48	3.91	–2.42	11.52
11.	31	Chemicals, etc.	18.82	3.54	2310	3.95	8.08	13.69	11.87
12.	32	Non-metallic products	7.17	25.20	13.52	26.45	13.69	1.93	14.66
13.	33	Basic metal industries	11.50	–7.72	8.43	–0.17	9	8.42	4.91
14.	34	Metal products	1.38	1.09	12.10	6.71	9.21	8.44	6.49
15.	35	Non-electric machinery, tools, etc.	6.90	7.03	12.60	2104	2.02	8.87	9.74
16.	36	Electrical machinery	2.72	28.53	5.28	25.94	34.79	27.01	20.71

(Contd)

Table 21.1 (Contd)

Sl No.	Ind	Industry/Year	1981–82	1982–83	1983–84	1984–85	1985–86	1986–87	Average Growth Rate (1981–82 to 1986–87)
(0)	(1)	(2)	(3)	(4)	(5)	(6)	(7)	(8)	(9)
17.	37	Transport equipment	13.21	12.54	9.20	10.42	3.17	6.58	9.19
18.	38	Other manufacturing	20.18	23.54	16.69	19.62	19.05	29.24	21.39
19.	39	Repairing services	0.00	20.33	14.61	8.76	7.95	15.22	12.81
20.	2–3	Total registered manufacturing	8.25	9.82	14.45	8.32	10.18	9.75	10.13

Source: CSO (1989).

TABLE 21.2: GROWTH RATES GROSS/NET VALUE ADDED IN REGISTERED MANUFACTURED IN DIFFERENT SUB-PERIOD AT DISAGGREGATED LEVEL

(Per Cent)

Sl No.	Industry Group	Period I (1959–60 to 1965–66)	Period II (1966–67 to 1979–80)	Period III (1980–81 to 1986–87)
1.	Food products	0.7	3.8	13.1
2.	Beverages	9.3	7.3	9.9
3.	Tobacco, etc.	1.5	1.3	
4.	Textiles	3.9	4.4	3.3
5.	Footwear, etc.	15.3	14.5	16.6
6.	Leather and fur products	0.5	3.1	
7.	Wood and cork	1.1	5.4	6.1
8.	Furniture and fixtures	11.7	6.3	
9.	Paper and paper products	11.4	7.3	9.5
10.	Printing and publishing	6.8	1.7	
11.	Rubber products	4.6	4.2	12.3
12.	Petroleum products	–5.9	6.2	
13.	Chemicals and chemical products	10.7	9.1	11.1
14.	Non-metallic mineral products	7.0	3.0	16.2
15.	Basic metal	15.0	5.1	4.1
16.	Metal products	12.0	2.5	6.8
17.	Non-electric machinery	17.9	7.5	10.3
18.	Electrical machinery	14.7	9.8	20.6
19.	Transport equipment	10.3	4.6	9.1
20.	Miscellaneous	14.2	4.5	20.6
21.	Repair services			13.3
	Total gross net value added	7.6	5.5	10.4

Source: Reproduced from Nagraj (1989), p. 1482.

during the 1980s (1981–82 to 1986–87) at 5.89 per cent was, however, higher than in the previous decades. It is also interesting to observe that even in the unregistered sector, the two fastest growing sectors, other than electrical machinery, with growth rates far higher than others, are rubber and petroleum products and chemicals.

According to the IIP, industrial output in the country grew at an average annual rate of 7.7 per cent during the 1980s (1981–82 to 1988–89 at 1980–81 = 100) (Table 21.3). The growth rate of manufacturing excluding mining and electricity was slightly lower at 7.4 per cent per annum during the same period.

TABLE 21.3: RATE OF GROWTH OF INDUSTRIAL OUTPUT DURING THE 1980s

Sl No.	Item	Index of Industrial Production (Base 1980–81 = 100)				Average of Annual Growth Rate 1980–81 to 1985–86 (*n* = 5)	Average of Annual Growth Rate 1984–85 to 1988–89 (*n* = 5)	Average of Annual Growth Rate 1980–81 to 1988–89 (*n* = 8)
		1981–82	1984–85	1985–86	1988–89			
1.	General Index	109.30 9.30	130.70 8.55	142.10 8.72	181.04 8.80	5.32	5.22	4.42
2.	Mining and quarrying	117.70 17.70	160.80 8.80	167.50 4.17	198.89 7.80	6.13	4.15	4.81
3.	Manufacturing	107.90 7.90	124.80 7.96	136.90 9.70	175.98 8.90	511	5.13	4.31
4.	Food manufacturing industries	113.50 13.50	119.00 –1.73	125.60 5.55	149.01 7.20	3.46	2.20	3.06
5.	Beverage and tobacco industries	104.30 4.30	11170 6.89	112.10 0.36	92.12 8.50	2.31	3.15	2.51
6.	Manufacture of textiles	99.01 –0.99	101.55 4.85	108.79 7.13	110.32 –.75	2.20	2.05	1.16
7.	Manufacture of footwear, other wearing apparel and made up textile goods	116.80 16.80	135.40 8.15	220.40 62.78		17.54		
8.	Manufacture of wood and cork except manufacture of furniture	153.20 53.20	216.50 29.25	223.20 3.09	171.73 6.20	17.11	7.71	11.47
9.	Manufacture of paper and paper products	108.20 8.20	131.90 20.68	148.50 12.59	171.62 3.20	8.29	7.29	5.58

(Contd)

Table 21.3 (Contd)

Sl No.	Item	Index of Industrial Production (Base 1980–81 = 100)				Average of Annual Growth Rate 1980–81 to 1985–86 ($n = 5$)	Average of Annual Growth Rate 1984–85 to 1988–89 ($n = 5$)	Average of Annual Growth Rate 1980–81 to 1988–89 ($n = 8$)
		1981–82	1984–85	1985–86	1988–89			
10.	Manufacture of leather and fur products except footwear and other wearing apparel	128.00 28.00	139.70 20.12	169.20 21.1	177.34 –4.40	13.85	7.37	8.10
11.	Manufacture of rubber products	119.20 19.20	147.20 8.16	153.00 3.94	168.84	6.26	2.42	3.91
12.	Manufacture of chemical and chemical products	116.90 16.90	142.80 9.01	154.30 8.05	232.78 16.10	6.79	6.63	6.26
	a. Manufacture of chemical and chemical products, (except petroleum)							
13.	Manufacture of non-metallic mineral products except products of petroleum and coal	106.70 6.70	138.40 13.26	157.30 13.66	184.66 16.80	6.72	8.74	6.30
14.	Basic metal industries	100.00 0.00	107.30 12.83	117.00 9.04	144.96 6.90	4.37	5.75	3.60
15.	Manufacture of metal products except machinery and transport equipment	99.60 –5.40	105.0 19.18	114.70 9.24	133.49 3.00	4.60	6.28	3.25
16.	Manufacture of machinery except electrical machinery	111.10 11.10	127.60 6.69	130.20 2.04	159.66 14.70	3.97	4.68	4.32

(Contd)

Table 21.3 (Contd)

Sl No.	Item	Index of Industrial Production (Base 1980–81 = 100)				Average of Annual Growth Rate 1980–81 to 1985–86 ($n = 5$)	Average of Annual Growth Rate 1984–85 to 1988–89 ($n = 5$)	Average of Annual Growth Rate 1980–81 to 1988–89 ($n = 8$)
		1981–82	1984–85	1985–86	1988–89			
17.	Manufacture of electrical machinery,	103.90	148.80	200.60	350.95			
	apparatus, appliances and supplies	3.90	3.98	34.81	4.70	8.54	8.70	5.92
18.	Manufacture of transport equipment	108.10	131.60	135.80	171.11			
		8.10	6.65	3.19	12.50	3.59	4.47	3.80
19.	Miscellaneous manufacturing industries	149.00	122.80	152.70				
		49.00	17.40	24.35		18.15		11.34
20.	Electricity, gas and steam	110.20	140.40	152.40	198.1			
		10.20	11.96	8.55	9.40	6.14	5.98	5.1

Source: Index of Industrial Production.

This is a marked upturn from growth rates of around 4 per cent achieved during the latter half of the 1960s and the 1970s. This performance is also an improvement upon the growth rates achieved during the First and Second Plan periods. It perhaps also marks the beginning of a new period of industrial growth in the country in as much as the strong link between industrial and agricultural growth appears to have been broken during recent years. This cleavage between industrial and agricultural growth rates could also be due to the relatively slower growth of employment in the organised sector. The agricultural constraint becomes operative as a wage-good demand constraint which did not become binding due to the high income-employment growth differentials during the 1980s.[12] As was pointed out earlier, the index consistently under-reports the rate of growth as compared to the ASI data on value addition in the registered manufacturing activity. During 1981–82 to 1987–88, according to IIP, the rate of growth is 7.12 per cent as compared to 8.14 per cent estimated on the basis of ASI's value addition data on registered manufacturing sector. At the aggregate level, thus, it is unambiguously established that the Indian industrial sector achieved rates of growth during the 1950s which were markedly higher than those recorded in the earlier periods. There have been reports that industrial activity has registered a slowdown during the current year (1989–90) which is also the last year of the decade and of the Seventh Five-Year Plan. Nevertheless, it may not be incorrect to conclude that the present decade has witnessed a decisive reversal of industrial stagnation in the country during the early 1970s which was reported by Ahluwalia and commented upon by a number of experts.[13] The highest growth rate in value added prior to the 1980s was during 1951–52 to 1964–65 at 7.8 per cent per annum. The growth rate during 1981–82 to 1987–88 of registered manufacturing at 9.8 per cent is significantly higher. On all accounts, thus, industry has moved on to a higher growth path. The more interesting question is whether this growth rate can be continued in the next decade.

An examination of industrial output data for the 1980s (1981–82 to 1988–89) further reinforces this conclusion on the shift away from metal based and machine building industries in terms of relative growth rates. As Table 21.4 reveals, the sector classified as machinery, machine tools and parts except electrical machinery (NIC 35), grew at an average annual rate of 6.15 per cent which is below the rate achieved by industry as a whole. This sector also includes the manufacture of air-conditioners and refrigeration (355), whose output expanded at 12.18 per cent per annum over the 1980s. The growth rate of the machine building sector, excluding air-conditioners and refrigeration, then comes down to 5.47 per cent annually over the period 1981–82 to 1988–89. Similarly, it is noticed that the industrial growth rate of metal products output (sector 34) is a mere 3.95 per cent over the 1980s. For basic metal and alloys (sector 33), a

TABLE 21.4: SECTORAL GROWTH RATE DURING THE 1980s

Sl No.		Index of Industrial Production (1980–81 = 100)									Average Annual Growth (1980–81 to 1988–89)
		Weight	1981–82	1982–83	1983–84	1984–85	1985–86	1986–87	1987–88	1988–89	
1.	Machinery, machine tools and parts except electrical machinery (non-electrical) 35	6.24	111.1 (11.1)	112.0 (.81)	1196 (6.78)	127.6 (6.68)	130.2 (2.03)	141.8 (8.9)	139.2 (–183)	159.66 (14.69)	6.15
2.	Basic metal and alloy industries 33	9.802	100.0 (0.0)	104.2 (42)	951 (–873)	107.3 (12.83)	117.0 (9.04)	126.8 (8.38)			4.94
3.	Chemical and chemical products 31	12.51	116.9 (16.9)	121.2 (3.6)	1310 (8.0)	142.8 (9.0)	154.3 (8.05)	175.5 (13.7)	200.5 (14.24)	232.78 (16.04)	11.19
4.	Rubber, plastic, petroleum exceptional (30-306-301)	3.433									7.87
5.	Consumer durable (355+364–364.4–364.5–364.6+374+375+376+382	5.623									2.44
6.	Consumer non-durables (20+21+22–227+23+25+26)	30.35									2.23
7.	Consumer goods (5+6)	35.97									3.82

Source: Index of Industrial Production.

growth rate of 4.94 per cent was achieved, which was partially pushed up on account of appreciably higher growth achieved by copper and copper alloys (333 and 334) at 15.88 per cent and aluminium (335) which grew at 8.9 per cent. The core iron and steel sectors (330) expanded at only 5.15 per cent over this period. And the manufacture of ferro alloys (332) actually experienced a decline of 1.73 per cent over this decade.

In contrast to this below-average performance of the metal based and machine building industries, the chemicals and petrochemicals industry experienced growth rates consistently above the industry average. Thus, chemicals' and chemical product industries' output expanded at 11.19 per cent per annum. Together with rubber and petroleum products (i.e., sectors 30 and 31 together) and excluding coal products (i.e., 306 and 307) from the group, the chemicals sector registered an average annual growth rate of 10.62 per cent from 1981–82 to 1988–89. In 1987–88 and 1988–89 chemicals have increased their output at 14.5 and 16.1 per cent.

Another interesting feature of the 1980s' industrial performance is revealed by looking at the relative growth rates of industrial output when classified by end-user categories (Table 21.5). Over the 1980s, the fastest growing segment was consumer durables whose output increased at 14.7 per cent per annum. This acceleration in rate of growth of consumer durables is further reinforced by examining the more detailed (3 digit) data which is provided as part of index of industrial production (see Table 21.4). It is seen that output of refrigeration, air-conditioners, etc. (355) increased at 12.18 per cent; of radios and television at 28.65 per cent per annum (364–364.4, 364.5 and 364.6) over the period 1981–82 to 1988–89; that of motor cycles, scooters, etc. (375) at 18.8 per cent and watches and clocks (382) at 97 per cent. For the broad group of consumer

TABLE 21.5: RATE OF GROWTH OF VALUE OF OUTPUT BY END-USER CATEGORIES

Sl No.	End Uses	Average Annual Growth Rate				
		1951–55	1955–60	1960–65	1965–76	1981–88
1.	Basic goods	4.7	12.1	10.4	6.5	8.09
2.	Capital goods	9.8	13.1	19.6	2.6	9.99
3.	Intermediate goods	7.8	6.3	6.9	3.0	5.83
4.	Consumer goods	4.8	4.4	4.9	3.4	6.86
5.	Non-durables	–	–	–	2.8	5.68
6.	Consumer durables	–	–	–	6.2	14.70
7.	General index	5.7	7.2	9.0	4.1	

Sources: (1) S. L. Shetty, "Structural Retrogression in the Indian Economy since Mid-60s," *EPW*;(2) *Economic Survey*, various issues.

durables (defined to include industries covered at the 3 digit level of 355, 364, 374, 375, 376 and 382 and excluding 364.4, 364.5 and 364.6) the growth rate over the 1980s was estimated at 12.44 per cent. It would be noticed that some of the fastest growing segments within consumer durables were those where import content has been high.

While consumer durables' output recorded highest growth rate amongst user segments, that of consumer non-durables, with a weight of 21.1 in industrial output, increased only at 5.68 per cent. It is thus clear that the demand pull on industrial growth rates during this decade originated from a rather limited segment of the population. The growth, even if it could be viewed as consumption-led growth, did not have a broad demand base in the economy.

In contrast, the intermediate industrial goods output achieved the lowest growth rate at 5.83 per cent. This was almost half of the overall growth rate of the industrial sector during the 1980s and points towards the emergence of a strong constraint on future industrial growth in the country. Output of capital and basic goods, which together accounted for as much as 56 per cent of total industrial output, increased in line with the average industrial growth at 9.9 and 8.1 per cent, respectively.

It is instructive to compare the growth rates of end user segments of industrial output across different time periods. This data is presented in Table 21.5. In the period 1955–65, which recorded the highest growth rates prior to the 1980s, the growth impulse was primarily derived from the capital goods sector which grew at rates significantly higher than those achieved by consumer durables or other consumer goods. The steep decline in growth of capital goods sector, from 19.6 per cent per annum during 1960–65 to a mere 2.6 per cent per annum between 1966–75, almost completely explains the stagnation in industrial output during the latter period.

The empirical evidence presented and analysed above yields three important conclusions. First, it is established beyond doubt that during the 1980s, Indian industry achieved an accelerated rate of growth. This rate of growth which was not a result of statistical refinements, as feared by some, was higher than the previously recorded highest growth rate during the latter half of the 1950s and early 1960s. This conclusion is based on examining the long-term growth rate of value addition in the registered manufacturing sector of the industry up to 1986–87 and also according to the index of value of industrial output up to 1988–89. It is thus incontrovertible that the 1980s marked a decisive reversal of trends in industrial output of the 1970s.

Second, the prime determinants of growth in the industrial sector experienced a radical shift. The acceleration of the 1980s has been led by the chemicals, petrochemicals and allied industries. This is borne out quite unequivocally by the evidence on disaggregated growth rates as earlier discussed. The thrust sector of the current growth have been, among others, synthetic fibres, downstream petrochemical products, plastics, inorganic chemicals, etc. This leading role of the chemicals and related sectors marks a departure from the growth performance of the "Mahalanobis period," which was premised upon metal based products and machine building.

Third, the investment-led growth of the earlier period (1955–65) is in stark contrast to the consumption-led growth of the 1980s. This change also emerges quite unambiguously from the data discussed earlier. The consumer goods segment was traditionally the slowest growing amongst the various segments of industrial output right until the end of 1970s. This has been changed completely in the current decade and, more important perhaps, the fastest growing segment of the industry turns out to be consumer durables, for which effective demand derives from a rather restricted income group within the economy. An interesting corollary to this consumer durables led growth is the high import propensity of this class of industrial goods. Although it is beyond the scope of this chapter to marshall statistical evidence in support of this corollary, it is our hypothesis that evidence on structure of imports during the 1980s will point towards an acceleration of imports of components and ready-to-be-assembled kits for these consumer durables during the 1980s.

These conclusions on the changing structure and nature of industrial growth are further reinforced by the data on investment flow in the economy during the 1980s. Data collected from CMIE publication (see Table 21.6 for details) reveals that the share of investment in the chemicals industries in total investment in the manufacturing sector increased from 31.5 per cent at the beginning of the decade (1980) to 49.7 per cent in 1986 and further to 52.7 per cent in 1988. On the other hand, metal based industry's share declined from 41.2 in 1982 to 25.1 in 1988. Investment in machine building industries (i.e., electrical and non-electrical machinery) accounted for 2.6 per cent of total investment in 1982 and only 1.4 per cent in 1988. It is interesting to note from the same source that over 1986–88 inorganic chemicals and petrochemicals together with fertilisers and man made fibres accounted for as much as 61 per cent of the increase in total quantum of investment in the manufacturing sector.[14] Due to non-availability of data on investment in terms of end-user classification of industrial activity, our other hypotheses cannot be similarly tested.

Changes in relative prices for industrial products, which have a bearing on profitability and hence on investment flows have also tended to favour chemicals and consumer durables. During the 1980s, the CMIE data on wholesale prices points out,[15] prices of chemicals and chemical products increased at an annual average rate of 5.6 per cent compared to an increase of 6.1 per cent for manufactured products in general over the same period (1980–81 to 1988–89). In contrast, prices for basic metals, alloys, etc., increased by 13.1 per cent per annum; of metal products by approximately 10 per cent; and of machinery and machine tools by 8.6 percent. Clearly, the decade has seen a worsening of the demand position for metal based products and machinery. These have become relatively dearer *vis-à-vis* chemicals and related products and with more liberal imports, as a result of government policy, they have suffered on account of competition from imports. With lower profitability, faced with an adverse price effect and having experienced a decline in the share of investment flows, metal based products and machinery industries not only lost their primacy in industrial growth in India during the current decade but also faced the prospect of further decline in future. The 1980s could, in this respect, mark an important watershed in industrial development in the country.

TABLE 21.6: AGGREGATE ANNUAL INVESTMENT—INDUSTRYWISE DISTRIBUTION

(in Rs million)

	1982	1986	1988	Per Cent Share in Investment Increase 1988–1989
Ferrous Metals	17,864 (29.1)	18,653 (22.7)	17,183 (16.6)	Decrease
Non-Ferrous metals	918 (1.5)	3213 (3.9)	2834 (2.7)	4.5
Transport equipment	3614 (5.9)	2862 (3.5)	1760 (1.7)	Decrease
Electronic and telecommunication	–	1916 (2.3)	2477 (2.4)	1.3*
Electrical machinery	879 (1.4)	537 (0.7)	773 (0.7)	Decrease
Non-Electrical machinery	712 (1.2)	534 (2.7)	688 (0.7)	Decrease
Metal ore mining	1265 (2.1)	478 (0.4)	332 (0.3)	Decrease
Total metal based	25,252 (41.2)		26,047 (25.1)	1.9
Petroleum and natural gas	1,578 (2.6)	6,897 (8.4)	8,184 (7.9)	15.6
Refineries	1,149 (1.9)	4,863 (5.9)	4,593 (4.4)	8.2
Organic chemicals and petrochemicals	4,858 (7.9)	11,678 (14.2)	21,332 (20.6)	39.0
Inorganic chemicals	1,638 (2.7)	2,786 (3.4)	2,789 (2.7)	2.7

(Contd)

Table 21.6 (Contd)

	1982	1986	1988	Per Cent Share in Investment Increase 1988–1989
Man-made fibres and textiles	2,557 (4.2)	4,681 (5.7)	6,566 (6.3)	9.5
Fertilisers and pesticides	75.5 (12.2)	8,199 (10.0)	10,442 (10.1)	7.0
Other chemicals	– –	1,722 (2.1)	736 (0.7)	Decrease
Total chemical based	19,285 (31.5)	40,826 (49.7)	54,642 (52.7)	85.6
Grand total	61,338	82,076	103,587	42249
Coal mining	5,024 (802)	5,432 (6.6)	11,504 (11.1)	15.3
Non-metallic mineral production	– –	4,478 (5.5)	4,829 (4.7)	Decrease
Paper	2,350	1,694	1,856	Decrease

Note: Figures in parenthesis are percentage share in total investment.
* Increase over 1986.
Source: CMIE, *Basic Statistics Relating to the India Economy*, Vol I, All-India for 1982, 1984, 1986 and 1989.

III

THE IMPLICATIONS

These already accomplished and ongoing changes in industrial structure have expectedly had some significant implications for the various aspects of the economy. First, the relatively poor performance of the metal based industries has further sharpened the regional imbalance of industrial economy in the country. It has been clear for a while now that the western region, comprising primarily states such as Maharashtra and Gujarat, has had a larger share of industrial investment since the latter half of the 1960s. The bias in favour of chemicals and related products has ensured that this region's industrial output grew at rates faster than in other regions. This was due both to greater accessibility to petrochemical raw material in this region as also to availability of required managerial skills and venture capital which has demonstrated a marked preference for these locations. This is especially true of MNCs, which have a greater presence in these sectors of industrial activity. The eastern region, with its greater dependence on iron and steel based industries, could not experience a similar growth in industrial output despite making available, especially in the case of West Bengal, all the preconditions for attracting investment flows. As a result, the share of the three eastern states (West Bengal, Bihar, Orissa) in total value addition in the industrial sector has come down from 23 per cent in 1968–69 to a mere 16 per cent in 1984–85. In contrast, the share of Maharashtra and Gujarat, with substantially lower population and natural resources endowments, has gone up to more than 33 per cent during the mid-1980s. It is, therefore, not surprising that between 1977–78 and 1983–84 (the period for which data are available) per capita net social domestic product (SDP) from manufacturing declined in Bengal from Rs 132.92 (at 1970–71 constant prices) in 1977–78 to Rs 121.74 in 1983–84.[16] For the country, the SDP from manufacturing rose from Rs 96.03 in 1977–78 to Rs 112.67 in 1983–84, a rise of 17.3 per cent, while for the three eastern states this increase was a mere 2.4 per cent over these six years. In contrast, per capita manufacturing SDP in Maharashtra and Gujarat, which was already more than double the national average in 1977–78, increased by 25.4 per cent over the same period.[17] The recent proving of large natural gas deposits on both off- and on-shore sites will further raise the share of these two states in the country's industrial output. Of the total number of industrial licences, registrations and location of the licensed establishments between June 1985 and December 1987, Maharashtra and Gujarat accounted for 22 per cent; Tamil Nadu, Karnataka and Andhra Pradesh for 20 per cent; and the three eastern Cinderellas for only 9 per cent. These likely trends in future expansion of industrial capacity will further exacerbate the regional imbalance which can only imply some avoidable consequences for the federal polity.

The second implication of this changing industrial structure concerns employment in the formal industrial sector. The latest *Economic Survey* (1988–89) reveals that employment in private manufacturing as also in the industrial sector as a whole has declined since 1982. After reaching a peak of 75.5 lakh in 1982–83, employment in private industry declined to 73.7 lakh in 1987. To some extent, this decline was compensated for by the increase in employment in the public sector. Overall, however, industrial employment in the country has stagnated during this decade despite the higher rate of growth and industrial output. Chemicals, petrochemicals and related activity are process industries with vast potential for automation, and application of electronic process control equipment. Value added per employee is generally always the highest in these activities (i.e., excluding some of the new software-embodied industries such as informatics). Consequently, these industries while being skill intensive are not employment generating. The relatively faster growth of these industries during the 1980s may perhaps explain the stagnation in the employment level in the manufacturing sector during the 1980s. To some extent this was also the result of a greater reliance on imported kits in the consumer durable goods industries. The basic metal producing and metal based industries are relatively more employment generating and also offer greater technological flexibility in terms of factor proportions, which can be changed to some extent in response to relative factor prices. Technological rigidity is more the rule for chemical and other process industries and these rigidities increasingly have a labour saving bias. The inability of the industrial sector to expand employment has serious implications for both equity as well as for the future domestic demand base of industrial output in the economy. It is clear that rigidities in the labour market and modernisation of existing capacities have also been responsible for stagnation in employment in the formal industrial sector. Nonetheless, a relatively faster growth of metal based, machine building and related industries would have, to some extent, ameliorated the situation.

Third, it has been argued that the industrial production structure in India as it has evolved since independence is characterised by an iniquitous distributional impact.[18] This is true only for the formal industrial sector and to an extent perhaps exaggerates the experience of industrial development until the end of the 1970s.

Patnaik's argument may perhaps be valid for the experience of the 1980s. The decade had, as discussed above, seen the evolution of a production structure which responds to demand from a restricted income group and at the same time generates low volumes of employment. Industrial growth during the 1980s may, in some sense, be seen to be based upon modernisation of consumption. It is undoubtedly true that a large number of consumer products embodying modern technological characteristics have appeared in the domestic market during the past few years. This modernisation and expansion of consumption has also been facilitated by the macroeconomic policies followed in this decade. It is clear that the large budgetary deficits as also the increasing deficits on the external account were major elements of the macroeconomic policies. As we have argued above, this may have been at the expense of the much needed modernisation of the economy's production structure that could strengthen the national economy.

Fourth, the growth of consumer durables output and demand in conjunction with the rise in consumerism has also adversely affected growth in household savings in the economy during the decade. As the *Economic Survey* reports, household savings (at current market prices) had reached a peak of 18.2 per cent of the GDP in 1978–79.[19] According to the new series (which brought down the rates as a result of the revision) household savings declined from 16.1 per cent of GDP in 1980–81 to 13.5 per cent in 1982–83 and increased to 16.6 per cent in 1987–88. Thus, over the 1980s, household savings have stagnated. Total savings in the economy have actually declined from 21.2 per cent of GDP (new series) in 1980–81 to 20.2 per cent in 1987–88. This trend in domestic savings rate does not augur well for future mobilisation of investment resources. In a situation where access to concessional external finances has appreciably declined, the safe limit for commercial borrowings has been virtually reached, and the country has already exhausted the potential for internal borrowings, a decline in household savings is bound to impose a resource constraint on future growth. To the extent that changes in industrial structure have been the cause of such a decline in the savings ratio of the economy this trend will need to be reversed in coming years.

The fifth implication of industrial growth during the past eight years has been a decline in self-sufficiency ratios in meeting the indigenous demand for capital and intermediate goods in the economy. As revealed by Table 21.5, the rate of growth of intermediate goods is noticeably lower now than in the earlier period, i.e., 1959–65. It is, however, more important to note that the difference between the rate of growth of intermediate goods and the general index of manufacturing output, with the former lagging behind, has been the highest during the 1980s. A higher percentage of growth in industrial output during this decade is thus apparently dependent upon imports of intermediate and capital goods. This conclusion may seem, at first instance, to conflict with the statistical evidence on the rate of growth of gross domestic product in manufacturing as discussed earlier. In our view, there is no such conflict for three reasons. First, the industry may itself have become more vertically integrated as a result of which value addition may register an increase without a similar rise in index of output for intermediate goods. Second, the input intensity of industrial output may have declined as a result of technological progress. Third, domestic input may have been replaced by imports without this being reflected in the quantum of value addition generated by individual industries. Thus, the aggregate value addition growth rates may not adequately reflect the decline in self-sufficiency ratios for intermediate and capital goods.

The decline in self-sufficiency ratios is also a result of relatively higher price increases experienced by capital and intermediate goods during the 1980s. BICP studies point out that price differentials is domestic and international prices for a range of intermediate inputs used in engineering goods industries has ranged between 44 and 113 per cent. These price differentials are largely a result of the administered price policy and high rates of protection being available for intermediate inputs. Both these together have pushed up the prices of these goods in the economy. This is reflected in the CMIE data discussed above. Producers of capital goods in the economy have little option but to pass on the higher costs of inputs to the consumers. In the face of easier access to imported inputs by the end-users this has effectively led to a lower demand for domestic intermediate and capital goods.[20] This decline in self-sufficiency ratios would not have been a cause for concern if the economy was not already facing a balance of payments problem. Increasing imports of intermediate and capital goods may further worsen the balance of trade.

A large proportion of these intermediate and capital goods are manufactured by public sector units. These units have faced an increasingly adverse environment for their operations during the 1980s. This is also partly a result of the implicit bias against metal based and machine building industries during this decade. Public sector units in these industries have faced a squeeze on their profitability both from the product and input markets. In the product markets their output has faced increasing competitive pressure from imports. This pressure has been due to two factors. First, import policy has been changed over the 1980s to include an increasing number of capital and intermediate goods on the open general licence category. This has effectively brought down the protection afforded to domestic producers. In fact, in some engineering goods industries the effective rate of protection became negative. Second, the World Bank and other multilateral financial agencies have insisted upon a regime of globally competitive tenders for all projects financed by them. With the tightening of the resource constraint, a large number of projects in the infrastructural sectors like power, coal, railways, steel, shipping, etc., have had to rely upon external finance. In all such projects, domestic producers have virtually faced full-fledged international competition. The domestic enterprises, largely in the public sector, have been given a 15 per cent price preference and in some cases received deemed export benefits amounting to another 10–15 per cent of costs. Thus, the decade has seen the public sector units having to face increasingly intense competition from abroad. On the other hand, these units have been severely constrained by government policy in their choice of sourcing of inputs. The Phased Manufacturing Programme (PMP) requirements have forced them to secure their intermediate inputs from domestic sources. These inputs have been available to them at prices appreciably higher than in international markets, due to high levels of effective protection afforded to them and the working of the administered price regime. This differential in domestic and international prices of inputs used by public sector engineering units has been well-documented in BICP's enquiries. Consequently, they faced negative effective rates of protection in a number of cases. In other cases, effective rates of protection for engineering and metal-based industries declined during the 1980s. The short-term effect of this worsening of effective protection rates for this sector has been the extreme pressure on capacity utilisation and on profitability of these enterprises. Internationally competitive enterprises such as BHEL, HMT and EIL have seen a marked deterioration of their order book positions as users have resorted to imports. The long-term effects could well be more adverse as investment is diverted away from these sectors. Consequently, capacities in engineering industries will not be modernised and gradually be phased out or become sick and perpetually dependent on budgetary support. This, in our view, will be out of line with the country's natural and competitive advantage. Moreover, it will also imply a steady deterioration of the balance of payments position and further worsening of the resources situation.

These implications, as discussed above, should be seen together with the impact of changes in industrial structure on the international competitiveness of the Indian industry. This would then bring out the full impact of emerging structural weakness on the future industrial growth in the country. Table 21.7 gives details of the share of manufactured goods exports from India in global trade flows for manufactured goods over the 1980s. Given the different sources for the data, the share of Indian exports as presented in column 4 should be taken as tentative and only indicative of broad trends.[21] Yet, the conclusion is inescapable that Indian exports of manufactured goods have lost even their marginal share which they had built up during the early 1970s. With the major thrust of "liberalisation" policies coming after 1984, the share of India's exports has started to decline after peaking in the mid-1980s. This lackadaisical performance of exports is further reinforced when we examine the export propensity of India's manufactured output. Table 21.8 provides annual details of the percentage share of exports in total manufactured output data (from *Monthly Statistics of Output*). Again, the absolute figures for each year are only broad estimates but the table is useful in revealing trends over the years. The first important conclusion which emerges is that the share of exports in total output of manufactured goods has consistently gone down over this decade. In fact the drop is fairly significant when the initial and terminal years are compared. The export propensity of the manufactured sector has declined by almost half. The second conclusion is

TABLE 21.7: SHARE OF INDIAN EXPORTS IN GLOBAL EXPORTS OF MANUFACTURED GOODS

(US$ million)

Year	Indian Export	World Export	Indian Export as per cent of World Export
(1)	(2)	(3)	(4)
1970	2,026	315,100	0.64
1975	4,355	875,500	0.50
1980	8,378	2,002,000	0.42
1981	8,373	1,976,733	0.42
1982	8,807	1,845,641	0.48
1983	8,713	1,811,600	0.48
1984	9,874	1,904,600	0.52
1985	8,750	1,923,400	0.45
1986	9,178	2,113,600	0.43

Source: DGCI and UN Trade Statistics.

TABLE 21.8: SHARE OF EXPORT IN MANUFACTURED OUTPUT

Year	Manufactures (Excl 20–22, 30, 31 and Repair)		Exports (ITC Classn) (DGCI and S)		Share of Export			
					(6, 7 and 8)		(5, 6, 7 and 8)	
	With Chemical	Without Chemical	(6, 7 and 8)	(5, 6, 7 and 8)	Without Chemical	With Chemical	Without Chemical	With Chemical
(1)	(2)	(3)	(4)	(5)	(4)/(3)	(5)/(2)		
1978–79	3.552	24,819	3,424.6601	3,580.1946	13.79854	11.71836	14.4521	11.20928
1979–80	36,419	29,525	3,618.57	3,826.991	12.25595	10.50822	12.96186	9.935940
1980–81	42,737	34,572	3,708.295	3,942.886	10.72629	9.225930	1.40485	8.677012
1981–82	51,696	40,863	425.537	4,610.921	10.41415	8.919299	11.28385	8.231849
1982–83	57,966	46,751	4,192.856	4,541.091	8.968484	7.834059	9.713355	7.233302
1983–84	63,087	50,133	4,623.343	4,950.335	9.222155	7.846838	9.874404	7.328519
1984–85	76,296	74,267	5,714.703	6,192.526	7.694807	8.116449	8.338193	7.490173
1985–86	90,867	73,308	7,298.368	6,336.627	9.955759	6.973518	8.643841	8.031923
1986–87			4,192.8561	7,783.326				

Sources: 1. National Account Statistics, CSO, various issues.
2. DGCI and S, various issues.

perhaps a more interesting one in the context of this chapter. With the inclusion of chemicals (Standard International Trade Classification [SITC]-5) in both exports and manufactured output, the share of exports becomes consistently lower. Moreover, the decline in exports' share between 1978–79 and 1985–86 is 40.5 per cent with the inclusion of chemicals and only 30.7 per cent when industrial sectors other than chemicals are considered. It may be noted in this context that the data above are exclusive of petroleum.

It is clear therefore that chemical goods produced in the country are less export-worthy than other industrial products. The reasons for this relative comparative advantage of non-chemicals and especially the metal-based sector derives simply from the natural resource endowment of the economy. It is well established that the country has some of the world's highest quality iron and other mineral resources. Its resources of other complementary factors like engineering skills, power-generating coal, etc., although not of the highest quality, are sufficiently available to exploit its advantage in ferrous and some non-ferrous metals. In complete contrast, the country, despite recent discoveries, continues to be deficit in basic feedstock for chemical industries, viz., petroleum and other hydrocarbons. Moreover, the economy is also actually short of both capital and energy which are the two other major inputs for chemical industries. Cost of the domestic production of chemical products thus is expectedly higher than global levels. The smaller scale of production also contributes to the rising of these costs. It is therefore not surprising that the share of Indians exports in global trade in manufactured exports as well as share of exports in total industrial output was higher during the 1970s when engineering exports were expanding rapidly and the growth of metal-based and related industries was relatively higher than that of chemicals.

In a more dynamic and competitive sense as well, the country appears to possess a stronger comparative and thus competitive advantage in metal-based and engineering industries. This is demonstrated by the DRC estimates prepared by BICP as well as by the World Bank and ICICI. It can be seen from Table 21.9 that in overall broad terms, the evidence on Domestic Resource Costs (DRCs) indicates a competitive advantage in favour of engineering goods. The domestic capital goods industry in particular appears to be internationally competitive, although this is expectedly not true for the entire spectrum of capital goods. Aluminiums manufacturing and power generating equipment emerge as having favourable DRCs, a conclusion reinforced in a very recent study on power equipment conducted by BICP. In a number of enquiries undertaken during the 1980s, auto-ancillaries, cement, sugar and paper and pulp manufacturing machinery emerged as internationally competitive on the basis of DRC estimates. In the case of auto-ancillaries, as many as two-thirds of the components being produced indigenously have favourable DRCs.[22] Expectedly, the DRCs appear

TABLE 21.9: SELECTED DRC RATIOS ESTIMATED IN BICP STUDIES

	DRC Ratio
Capital good including	
1. Radial drill	1.48
2. Surface grinder	1.51
3. Gear hobber	1.52
Electrical machinery	1 – 1.32
4. Boiler 210 M	1
5. Turbo generator set	1
6. Hydro turbine	1.14
Auto-ancilliary (1987)	
7. Radiator	.47 – .97
8. Carburetor	.8 – .9
9. Brake assembly	1.17 – 1.32
10. Starter	.95 – 1.39
11. Ignition	.54 – .74
Synthetic rubber (1984)	
12. Pbr	2.7
13. Sbr 1712*	(a) 2.65 (b) 2.44 – 2.94
Thermo plastics (1986)	
14. Lope (film grade)	
15. PP (injection moulding)	2.75 – 45
16. HDPE	0.37
17. Vinyl acetate monomer	
(a) Actual cost	6.27 – 7.55
(b) Normative cost	1.56 – 4.50
Manmade fibres	
18. Viscose staple fibre (November 1987)	1.29 – 2.12
19. Polyester staple fibre (April 1988)	1.95
20. Nylon filament yarn (August 1988)	2.45
21. Polyester filament-yarn (1988)	1.32 – 1.64
22. Benzene (1988)	.86 – 1.71
23. Paraxyelene (1988)	.61 – 6.87

Note: (a) Alcohol route, (b) Naphtha route.
Source: BICP studies as cited in references and Report on Aromatics.

to be better for exporting firms compared to non-exporting industries in case of auto-ancillaries. Export incentives were therefore effective. According to a set of enquiries undertaken by ICICI, once the DRC estimates are adjusted for higher prices for domestically supplied inputs and for exchange rate premia more than half of the product groups examined emerge as internationally competitive.[23]

In the case of steel, the basic input for machine building and metal based products, DRC estimates over the years provide an interesting case. In recent BICP studies, it emerges clearly that until 1978 the Indian steel industry remained internationally competitive. This underlines the boost in engineering exports during the previous decade. After 1978 the industry appears to have completely lost its competitiveness, with DRC ratios in the range of 2.5 (with South Korean Pohant as 1) for cold rolled sheets and above 1.6 for hot rolled sheets.

It emerges that the Indian steel industry is uncompetitive at the stage of producing hot metal but becomes more competitive as successive downstream projects are examined. The spate of licence applications for export-oriented steel manufacturing facilities in the last two years with facilities to import capital goods and raw materials at international prices further reinforces the understanding that the country possesses a natural as well as a dynamic comparative advantage in the production of basic metals and metal based products. As is argued below, government policies may have worked to nullify this advantage in more ways than one.

In case of DRCs for chemicals and chemical based products (mainly petroleum based raw materials and intermediates) the picture is also a mixed one as in the case of metal based and engineering industries. The one difference, however, is that in this case the number of products with favourable DRCs is lower than in the case of metal based industries. The second difference, perhaps more important, is that the enquiries undertaken so far do not indicate any comparative advantage in either a natural or technologically dynamic sense for this industry. According to the study undertaken in the early 1980s, it is more efficient to import kerosene and diesel than to import crude oil and produce the two derivatives domestically by putting up refining capacities.[24] In the case of fertilisers, recent studies based on the sectoral planning approach have reinforced the DRC estimate-based conclusions of the mid-1970s, that domestic production of nitrogenous fertilisers is not an efficient use of the economy's resources. It may be recalled here that nitrogenous fertilisers have been produced for a period with negative value added, as the CIF price of naphtha, the imported intermediate input, was higher than the CIF price of the final product. Although there is no explicit tariff, differentials in domestically prevailing and global prices range between 53 and 112 per cent for various grades of fertilisers. It is noteworthy that for a number of domestic units the production of urea even currently would yield negative value addition.

A similar picture emerges for the other major sector of chemical industries. In aromatics, for production of benzene and xylene, the former shows favourable DRCs, while the latter yields unfavourable DRC estimates. In case of thermoplastics, all products except polypropylene yield efficient DRC estimates. In the case of man-made fibres a range of DRC estimates is available. These estimates clearly show the extremely high rates of protection which have become necessary to maintain indigenous capacity. For polyester staple fibre (PSF) the bureau's computation of the required rate of protection was 165 per cent, while for polyester filament yarn (PFY) the proposed duty was 180 per cent as based on comparison of domestic and global costs. Even these were found to be inadequate and higher rates of 180 per cent and 205 per cent are currently operational. Given that the basic inputs for these industries are charged duties of approximately 60 per cent, these final products like PSF, PFY and NFY actually receive some of the highest rates of effective protection in the country. Explicit tariffs are higher than price differentials prevailing between domestic and global prices (implicit tariffs), thus also indicating extremely high official protection rates afforded to the industry.[25] DRC estimates for caprolactum and methanol, both important industrial chemicals, are not favourable. Overall, therefore, the group of chemicals and petroleum based industries do not demonstrate favourable DRC estimates, which would justify allocation of large investment resources to these industries. Their use as thrust sectors for accelerating industrial growth in the country can be justified only under very high effective rates of protection which will create further distortions in the economy.

The evidence cited above is of course not exhaustive. Results arrived at, therefore, should be seen as indicative of trends. We are aware of the methodological weaknesses of DRC estimates.[26] Even when used merely as broad indicators of international competitiveness and for efficient resources allocation, these estimates in conjunction with other more qualitative information do reveal that the industrial growth of the 1980s has perhaps not been in line with the country's comparative advantage whether in the Ricardian sense or in a neoclassical sense or perhaps even in the sense of the "new" theory of international trade that draws upon the theory of technological innovations and industrial organisation.

IV

GOVERNMENT POLICY

Despite recent attempts at rationalisation and harmonisation, far too many policy instruments continue to impinge directly on industrial performance. This complexity and multiplicity of instruments as also quite often their interrelated nature ensures that we cannot even attempt to provide an exhaustive appreciation of the industrial policy regime in this chapter.

To begin with, we may refer to the need for continuing with the measures for further simplifying and rationalising the policy regime. Measures which directly reduce costs in the form of managerial effort for and discourage generation of rent in securing government clearances and approvals will yield high financial returns. These measures will yield even larger quantum of non-pecuniary positive externalities. There is also a pressing need to reconcile the objectives and working of several policies, viz., technology development, industrial location, capacity expansion and modernisation, reservation, etc. Some of these involve trade-offs in their operations at present. To discuss some of these measures more specifically is beyond the scope of this chapter.

One noteworthy omission from the discussion here is lack of any reference to the role of technology policy on industrial growth during this decade. It is perhaps unquestionable that an active policy for technological development has significant influence on the pace and structure of industrial growth in any developing economy. In India, the objectives of technology policy like self-reliance, especially in the strategic sectors, preservation of repetitive technology imports, promotion of indigenous technological capability in the industrial sectors, etc., have played a role in determining the quantum and quality of technological effort in the country. The issues are, however, far too complex to be adequately discussed here. Suffice it to say that in our view, issues in technological development like selective resource allocation in identified sectors, greater coordination of user needs and activities of the R and D centres, efforts to absorb and adapt new technologies to the domestic conditions, etc., were not adequately addressed in the rush to accelerate rate of industrial growth in the economy.

The discussion here is restricted to some aspects of the package of economic policies which have come to be termed as new economic policies, liberalisation, deregulation, etc. More specifically, the impact of these policies on bringing about changes in the nature and structure of industrial growth is the focus of discussion in paragraphs below.

A number of policy measures which have been gradually implemented since the latter half of the 1970s (after the recommendation made by the Alexander and Dagli Committees) can be seen as part of a package to reduce the incidence of controls and regulations on industrial growth. This domestic or internal liberalisation package has included measures such as automatic endorsement of capacity expansion up to 25 per cent of licensed capacity, broad banding of industrial licence to enable firms to optimise a variated product mix rather than be constrained by tightly defined product specifications, dereservation of about 40 industries and thereby permitting large firms to enter them, raising the investment limits for inclusion in SSI categories, revising the turnover ceiling upwards for inclusion in MRTP classification and delicensing of several industries, especially if these capacities are to be established in designated backward areas or are dedicated predominantly for exports, etc.

In more general terms, the thrust of recent domestic economy reforms has been, first, to lower some of the institutionally created entry barriers in a number of industries, thus increasing the intensity of competition or creating the opportunities for it. Second, these reforms have attempted to offer larger discretion and decision-making to corporate managers without reference to government machinery, thereby providing more degrees of freedom for corporate planning. Third, a rather straightforward scaling up of corporate sizes has been undertaken for purposes of classification in different categories which attract differentiated incentives and taxes. The number of categories or the nature of incentives and differentiation therein have not been substantively altered. There is, however, a hint of preference in these reforms for the larger corporate entity on grounds of greater economies of scope if not scale and consequently a better chance for attaining international competitiveness. At least the overt policy bias of the past against large corporate sizes was not further strengthened. Finally, the policy reforms could be seen as the first step towards removing the pre-emptive claims of the government for undertaking production in pre-designated sectors of industrial activity. In fact some sectors hitherto reserved for public sector were opened for private investment. Although a part of the general process of lowering entry barriers in the economy, this set of dereservation measures related to the public sector may have a profound impact on the nature of core and infrastructural industries. These policy changes, in our view, have contributed directly to the acceleration in industrial growth in the economy during the current decade. These measures, in large part, were initiated prior to 1984 and were a result of some serious policy contemplation which was engendered by the stagnation of the 1970s.[27] Their effects were visible largely during the latter half of the 1980s when some of these measures were further consolidated and reinforced. A lowering of exit barriers to correspond to the scaling down of entry barriers, as already achieved, will perhaps be a logical extension of these reforms and also contribute to further acceleration in industrial growth.

These reforms have had some implications for the structure of industrial growth during the 1980s. By their very nature, they have been more favourable to private sector operations and have had a minimal positive impact on the working of the public sector. The private sector has been (due to the working of the Industrial Policy Resolution) less active in the metal based machine building sectors. The chemicals, petrochemicals, consumer durables and other consumer goods sectors have been areas of its predominance. Private sector enterprises in these sectors have expectedly grown faster than enterprises in other sectors. Second, the measures for dereservation have also tended to create greater economic spaces and lowered entry barriers for the private sector predominantly in these areas. Policy reforms for greater openness of the domestic economy, therefore, have naturally benefited the private sector with the concomitant implications outlined above.

On the other hand, as discussed above, government policy towards public sector had actively constrained their profitability by imposing on them a squeeze both in the product and import markets.[28] In recent enquiries it has emerged that in some cases technical parameters for projects supported by external financial resources have been so specified that domestic producers have been excluded in the pre-qualification stage itself. In some cases performance guarantees and working experience requirements have been so stipulated as to restrict domestic public-sector units from entering a bid in the global tenders.[29] The worst case is of projects financed through external resources received as a part of a bilateral financial package which combines concessional and commercial credit. In such cases, projects are not open for global tendering and are restricted to enterprises from countries which make these bilateral funds available. A significant number if not all of such bilaterally funded projects are in the infrastructure and capital goods sector, which are dominated by public sector enterprises. These enterprises have therefore faced a negative discrimination in their domestic market as a result of the economy dependence on bilateral funds.

Public-sector units have also had to operate in a regime of administered prices. These prices have been invariably based on historical average costs[30] and follow the actuals with varying lags. By definition this kind of policy regime generates revenue deficits for the concerned public sector enterprises. This is now conclusively established in a number of studies at BICP. As a result, the BICP has recently adopted a policy of price fixation on the basis of long-term marginal costs of production and moved away from average cost based prices. PSU also face binding administrative constraints in procuring their capital goods and raw materials. While under the new dispensation, private sector operators increasingly have easier access to imports, PSEs are still forced by government fiat to procure these supplies domestically on the basis of some phase programme of manufacturing. The public sector, unable to circumvent the PMP requirements by means legitimately open to private sector, is burdened with higher costs, longer delivery schedules and poorer quality of capital goods and raw materials while expected to compete with imports.

As a consequence of this policy stance, the public sector industries, especially other than those in the petroleum refining sector, have seen their share in industrial turnover decline over the decade. In the 1980s, this decline in performance, especially seen in contrast both to the improved performance of the private sector enterprises and publicly stated government expectations, has appeared in an even worse light than it actually merits. A predominant share of public sector activity has been in the heavy engineering, core industries and infrastructural services sectors. In many of these sectors PSEs account for the predominant share of total sectoral output. With a decline in the performance of these PSEs, the overall sectoral performance has also been adversely affected. This is reflected in the changing structure of industrial growth as described earlier.

The second set of policy reforms during the 1980s was concerned with external liberalisation. Here, the focus was on changes in the country's industrial and trade policies, with the objectives of making some sectors of the industry less protected and improving access to foreign technology and capital goods for sectors where production capacities needed modernisation. The policy package for external liberalisation included measures to rationalise import policy procedures to lay the groundwork for a gradual shift from non-tariff to tariff protection by shifting products from banned and restricted lists to OGL category, to improve export promotion measures by adopting import-export passbook and advance licensing schemes and making available inputs and raw materials at international prices and to facilitate inflow of foreign capital for investment in export-oriented ventures and hi-tech industries, especially those in backward areas where 100 per cent foreign equity participation was permitted.

The impact of the exchange rate policy has been decisive in the 1980s. Since the beginning of the 1980s, the rupee has been linked to a basket of currencies. It was only after 1985 that the rupee was steadily devalued against the major trading currencies like Japanese yen, British sterling and US dollar and the Deutsche mark. This devaluation, however, came only after a period of five years when the exchange rate for the rupee actually appreciated. The favourable balance of payment and reserves position at the end of the previous decade apparently resulted in misplaced complacency. This was revealed in an overvalued rupee during 1979–84. The rate of devaluation since then has not adequately taken into consideration the two important determinants of relative exchange rates in India *vis-à-vis* other competing countries. It was pointed out by Kelkar and Raipuria[31] that the real exchange rate for the rupee should take into consideration not only the relative rates of inflation but also the level of relative competitiveness in terms of productivity levels in India and its competing economies. When measured by these two criteria, the rupee appears to have remained overvalued during this decade. As a result, Indian exports have lost their price advantage. Macro effects of this relatively overvalued exchange rate were to substitute foreign financial resources for domestic savings and make imports somewhat cheaper and, most important, perhaps, not providing sufficient incentives in terms of relative profitability for exports *vis-à-vis* domestic sales.

Consequently, although aggregate exports as well as manufactured exports have shown considerable increase in nominal rupee terms, in US dollar and even more so in terms of constant SDRs, the expansion in export earnings has been much less spectacular. Moreover, as Bhalla[32] has pointed out, India did not improve her share in total exports of developing economies even during the latter half of the 1980s. This would demonstrate that the country could not perhaps take full advantage of the buoyancy in world trade during this decade. The balance of payments position, as is well established, has further worsened largely on account of a bunching up of repayment obligations.

The trade and industrial policy package needs to be reviewed in the context of the less-than-expected performance of our exports and even more so in the light of some important weaknesses which have emerged during the past few years. The first structural weakness which needs almost immediate attention is the marked bias in our commercial policy for chemical goods. The chemical goods industries have enjoyed exceptionally high effective rates of protection as has been well documented in the recent BICP studies on synthetic fibres, aromatics and fertilisers. A number of these products show negative value addition and yet continue to attract investment on account of attractive protection levels. On the other hand, metal based and engineering industries have seen their effective rates of protection decline and in some cases brought down to being negative. The consequences of this incentive structure for the economy and industrial growth have been brought out earlier. This bias needs to be not only neutralised but quickly restored in favour of metal based industries if some of the avowed objectives of employment, regional balance and international competitiveness have to be achieved.

The second rather critical weakness in recent trade and industrial policy measures has arisen from the attempt to foster domestic competition through delicensing of domestic industries while continuing with non-tariff measures to protect them from external competition. This policy was followed even in case of new industries like consumer and process electronics and computers. The results, in our view, have not been very encouraging. The policy has led to excessive entry in all cases with the resultant capacity fragmentation and near absence of any corporate technological capability. The non-tariff protection has enabled the industry to price their products at levels many times higher than in global markets. Even in the case of new industry such as computers, this policy has led to a situation where hardware prices in the domestic markets are in some cases four times as high as in international markets even when value added at international prices was marginal or negative. In some cases, this has prevented a fuller exploitation of growth and export potential in downstream industries. Software is a classic example. Value addition has in a number of cases been negative given that the CIF value of imported kits is higher than the CIF value of the finished product. Excessive entry has also prevented any firm from undertaking any form of vertical integration or strengthening its technological capability to compete globally. Consequently, domestic industry also lost any notion of quality competitiveness in relation to global demand. Essentially, the policy of "internal competition first and international competition later" has led to a major transformation problem for India's industrial economy, and this is one of the major structural causes of the country's present balance of payments difficulties.

In the past two years, the BICP has consistently recommended a shift from non-tariff to tariff based protection in the case of an entire range of chemical as well as engineering industries. In almost all the recently concluded enquiries, the bureau has also pointed out the deleterious effects of a non-tariff regime on prospects for technological upgrading and attainment of international competitiveness by domestic firms. Potential benefits from a shift to tariff based protection are seen to emerge in the case of a number of industries such as aluminium, electronics, computers and power generation equipment which were recently examined by the bureau. The situation can be rectified only through a policy of undertaking domestic liberalisation in conjunction with measures to shift to tariff based protection.

This policy was successfully tried in the oil field equipment[33] and services. Here was a conscious policy decision to improve the indigenous content of domestically produced equipment through delicensing of domestic industry coupled with tariff based protection at moderate level against imports. While the users—the oil sector—were allowed access to OGL imports, the domestic manufacturers of equipment were afforded only a moderate tariff protection, i.e., no non-tariff barriers. The domestic units were afforded on average a 40 per cent tariff protection along with the usual deemed export benefits. The evidence is that domestic producers have been able to improve their share significantly in the five years that this policy has been in operation. The import content of domestic output has also come down and even taking this import content into account there has been a net foreign exchange saving in this sector as a result of this policy. The example has been cited at length to draw attention to the merits of tariff based protection, even in case of newly emerging industries. Such protection is transparent, finite and well-defined. When levied at moderate levels it lays a healthy foundation for the new industry to take advantage of domestic reform while not losing sight of global cost and quality conditions. Protection levels, if moderate, also act as a deterrent to excessive entry and put a ceiling on costs that users have to pay for the particular product. It thus also limits the cost of possible errors which could be committed. Yet, this does not eschew the emergence of domestically competitive firms, which without being unduly constrained by PMP requirements and capacity regulation could grow into globally competitive corporations. The above discussion shows that the policy hitherto followed in new industries of first encouraging domestic competition in combination with non-tariff barriers and planning to expose them to external competition through tariff protection only later needs to be reviewed. Such a review of this policy of increasing spurious competition domestically will help in evolving a more effective policy for some critical newly emerging technologies like telematics, solar photovoltaics and biotechnology.

One of the important elements of the new policy will have to be to follow an aggressive exchange rate policy. Consequently, the rate at which the exchange rate is changed has to be closely monitored and periodically adjusted. It must take into account the relative inflation rates prevailing in our economy *vis-à-vis* not only developed economies but also more importantly in some of the competitor countries. Further, adjustments in exchange rates should also take into consideration the changes in relative factor productivity in specific industries in India and its competitors. An adequate adjustment in exchange rates without undue lags will perhaps be the key necessary condition for improving the external balance of the economy. Finally, the importance of reducing as rapidly as possible the host of procedural and other specific measures in the realm of EXIM policies cannot be overstated. Combined with a more efficient management of the macro parameters in the economy, these measures will provide the right signals for investment flows in future and redress the emerging imbalance.

The package of existing trade and industrial policies has not had the desired results in overall terms. Specific aspects of required policy changes are too detailed to be covered in this chapter. The changes in the past few years have had only a marginal effect so far on improving the country's balance of trade. There is now a danger of these measures being reversed in an *ad hoc* fashion, which may cause even more problems and should therefore be avoided.

Finally, government's long-term fiscal policy has influenced the pace and nature of industrial growth both from the supply and demand side. On the supply side it has improved corporate profitability through a reduction in direct taxation rates and consolidation of investment allowance and depreciator provisions. More importantly, it has had a positive impact on future expectations for returns on investment by its assurance of maintaining continuity. The switch to MODVAT, though partial, has simplified the procedures and nominally lowered the rate of indirect taxes on value added. These reforms have together improved the investment climate in the country. On the demand side, by a lowering of direct individual income tax rate levels and by completely exempting earnings from exports from direct taxes, the policy has raised disposable incomes of the tax-paying segment of the population. However, the increase in government expenditure being in the nature of transfer payments also added to this demand. This, as would be expected, has raised effective demand for consumer products and especially for consumer durables. The long-term fiscal policy has therefore provided the complementary financial signals for accelerated investment in industrial capacity and output growth.

The long-term fiscal policy has however also contributed to some of the weaknesses which have been discussed above. By reducing direct tax rates it has swelled the demand for consumer durables in the economy and reinforced consumerism in general. This has wide demonstration effects and, as pointed out earlier, could have played a role in the decline of the savings rate in the economy over the 1980s.

Ironically, however, the working of the long-term fiscal policy has tended to exacerbate the supply side problems which it sought to remove. The policy has led to a sharp reduction in the share of direct taxes in total tax revenue of the government. The contribution of personal income and corporate tax declined from 14.27 per cent in 1981–82 to 12.17 per cent in 1988–89. On the other hand, the share of three primary indirect taxes—customs duties, central excise and sales tax—increased from 69.52 per cent in 1981–82 to 73.0 per cent in 1988–89. Along with other taxes, which are also predominantly in the nature of commodity taxes, indirect taxes accounted for 87.82 per cent of total tax revenue in 1988–89. This higher share in total tax incidence of indirect taxes has led to a general cost escalation in the economy. This cost impact has been even more marked because the brunt of the increase in the rate and coverage of indirect taxes fell on capital and intermediate goods. These have become more expensive over the years as revealed by the data on relative prices in the economy. Indian manufacturers have consequently faced high costs of capital goods and also intermediates as a result of fiscal levies and taxes. In sectors such as chemicals, these higher costs have simply been passed on to consumers as the industry enjoyed high rates of effective protection. In engineering, especially the capital goods industry, however, this has led to increasing imports of final goods which were more easily accessible. The manufacturers, faced with high costs of capital and intermediate goods, and bound by Phased Manufacturing Programme requirements and inadequate levels of effective protection became uncompetitive *vis-à-vis* imports. The long-term fiscal policy may thus have reinforced some of the emerging structural weaknesses in the economy.

The discussion on some recent government initiatives has hopefully brought out the policy driven nature of recent acceleration and changes in industrial growth in the country. This is to be expected given that over the decades government policy had left few economic spaces untouched, especially in the industrial sector. Some of the recent changes in policy may lead to an enlargement of such autonomous economic spaces. The future performance of the industrial sector, in particular its private enterprise segment, will reveal whether with greater autonomy the private industry is able to retain or improve upon the existing equation between private and social gains from industrial growth. The reconciliation and if possible an optimal convergence of the two, it may be reiterated, is the *sine qua non* of government intervention in economic activity.

Government policy changes during the 1980s have tended to give wrong signals in some important aspects of industrial growth. They have tended to create a bias in favour of chemical based industries as opposed to the metal based sector while the latter is more suited to the country's development objectives, is more in line with the economy's comparative advantage and has a better prospect for international competitiveness. Policy signals have also emphasised a modernisation of consumption almost at the cost of, or at least in preference to, the modernisation of the production structure of the economy. Finally, by relying almost exclusively on non-tariff forms of protection at high rates, in conjunction with increasing delicensing of entry, the policy has led to excessive entry, high costs of production and lack of competitive quality in domestic industries. Unfortunately, this has been true of some of the new industries such as electronics and computers, which have extensive linkages both forward and backward. There is no easy method by which these industries can now be brought back to the path of international competitiveness. Yet, this has to be achieved if Indian industrialisation is not to be a saga of high costs, loss of consumer welfare and dependence on government subsidies and protection barriers. It is, therefore, perhaps incumbent to initiate a shift towards a tariff based regime of protection for industries. Policy measures should encourage industries which are in line with the country's comparative advantage and are based on broader segments of domestic demand.

V

Proposals for Policy Reforms

Towards this, some suggestions for future directions of policy may be in order. First, the incentive signals in terms of effective rate of protection, relative profitability and markups in administered prices where applicable may be changed to either become neutral or be biased in favour of metal based and related engineering industries. This means, amongst other things, internal competition has to be coupled with tariff-based import policy for a wide range of industries, i.e., rapid removal of the non-tariff barriers. Second, the incidence of indirect taxes maybe reviewed and suitably changed to reinforce the earlier suggestion. The share of indirect taxes should be brought down and their incidence on basic goods and intermediates sharply reduced. Third, the long-term fiscal policy needs to be modified so as to encourage savings by a further sharpening of incentives and moving towards effectively taxing expenditure. Fourth, an urgent reform of the export incentives structure so as to link imports of capital goods and intermediate inputs more strongly to actual export performance and not export obligation. Fifth, a review of the official exchange rate to incorporate relative inflation and productivity levels and changes in exchange rates not only of the developed economies but also that of our competitors so as to follow an "undervalued" exchange rate policy. Sixth, providing the "free trade like" regime to domestic manufacturers of capital goods and intermediate products to source their inputs either domestically or through imports in industries which are facing competitive pressure from imports in their product markets. The PMP provisions which have actually proved counter-productive, especially in case of high-tech industries, should be dispensed with. Seventh, excessive entry, especially in new and emerging industries, must be prevented. One of the ways to achieve this is to facilitate exit of unviable firms. This may be a costly method in social terms as capital assets may get locked up. A better method perhaps is to initiate a process of competitive bidding for capacity licences. The bidding is to be conducted in terms of effective protection required by applicants against imports. Firms which demand the least protection should be granted the licence.[34] The cutoff point could be determined either on the basis of domestic demand levels or, better still, on the basis of pre-selected tariff levels under which all firms are granted the licence. This procedure will do away with all other forms of non-tariff protection and also dispense with the need for a phased manufacturing programme. This will also provide transparency. In addition, if undertaken in conjunction with financial institutions this procedure will be more expeditious than the present ones. It would also ensure greater efficiency in investment allocation and minimise possibilities of wrong investment choices. Eighth, reconciling and harmonising bilateral inflows of concessional resources with the objective of maintaining domestic capability and taking into account the overall social costs and benefits of these financial flows. Finally, policy changes should be made so as to give complete autonomy to public sector enterprises for price fixation, import procurement and competitive practices while exposing them to global competition through a tariff based import regime.

The above suggestions will, in our view, consolidate the appreciable gains made during this decade in industrial development. These gains should also be extended by further simplifying and harmonising the procedures and controls which exist at present. The greater autonomy of the private sector needs to be reinforced by a similar autonomy in real terms to public sector enterprises. At the same time, incentive signals need to be changed by suitable policy measures to be in line with the country's long-term and natural comparative advantage. Such a shift in policy will also address some of the structural weaknesses which have emerged in the domestic economy during the present decade.

There is an additional point. Expansion of employment opportunities has been one of the major objectives of India's industrial policy. In this regard, the experience of the decade of the 1980s has not been encouraging. For instance, the growth rate in employment in the organised sector has been only 1.4 per cent per annum in the 1980s.[35] Perhaps the important reason for this low growth in employment has been the mix of trade, industrial, fiscal and exchange rate policy which was followed. The proposed reforms of these policies which are indicated here would not only improve the efficiency of resource allocation and productivity in the economy but also expand more rapidly industrial employment opportunities, as the economy improves its international competitiveness and thus increases its share in the world trade in manufactures.

NOTES AND REFERENCES

[These are personal views and need not reflect the views of the organisation with which the authors are associated. Inputs from D. N. Chaturvedi, Pushp Dogra, Arun Jha and Jitender Singh are thankfully acknowledged.]

[1] See C. P. Chandrashekhar. "Aspects of Growth and Structural Change in Indian Industry," *Economic and Political Weekly*, Special Number (19 November 1988); C. T. Kurien, "Indian Economy in the 1980s and on to the 1990s," *Economic and Political Weekly*, 24, no. 15 (15 April 1989).

[2] R. Nagraj. "Growth in Manufacturing since 1980: Some Preliminary Findings," *Economic and Political Weekly* (1 July 1989b): p. 1481.

[3] R. Nagraj, "Trends in India's Gross Domestic Output: Some Tentative Results," Mimeo, 1989a; and "Growth in Manufacturing since 1980."

[4] See Kurien, "Indian Economy in the 1980s and on to the 1990s"; P. Patnaik, "A Perspective on the Recent Phase of India's Economic Development," *Social Scientist* (February 1988), and "Critical Reflections on Some Aspects of Structural Change in the Indian Economy," Mimeo (New Delhi: Centre for Economic Studies and Planning, Jawaharlal Nehru University, 1989); S. Mundle, "Growth, Acceleration and Fiscal Constraint," *Mainstream* (9 September 1989).

[5] Mundle, "Growth, Acceleration and Fiscal Constraint."

[6] Ibid.; Bureau of Industrial Costs and Pricing (BICP), *Strategies for Cost Reduction: Some Issues from BICP Studies* (New Delhi: BICP, 1988): pp. 21–22.

[7] I. J. Ahluwalia, "Some Aspects of Planning Policies in India," Three lectures delivered at the Govind Ballabh Pant Social Science Institute, Allahabad, 1985; Nagraj (1989); and Uma Dutta Ray Chaudhari, "New Series on National Accounts Statistics: Some Comments," *Economic and Political Weekly* (23 July 1988) provide further details on sources of industrial data, their comparability, etc.

[8] Ibid., for details.

[9] See Table 5 in Nagraj, "Growth in Manufacturing since 1980," p. 1482.

[10] It is interesting to note that growth rates achieved by these four sectors during the Mahalanobis period were base metal: 15.0 per cent; metal products: 12.0 per cent; non-electrical machinery: 17.9 per cent; and electrical machinery: 14.7 per cent. These were all substantially higher than the growth rate of net value added (on average) in the industrial sector, which was 7.6 per cent.

[11] See Table 21.1. It should be pointed out that computers are included in the broader category of electrical machinery. We know that this segment of the industry has expanded very

rapidly during the 1980s. Thus, the factors responsible for its fast growth during the earlier periods and the 1980s may be quite different.

[12] See B. B. Bhattacharya and Anup Mitra. "Industry-Agriculture Growth Rates: Widening Disparity—An Explanation," *Economic and Political Weekly*, 24, no. 34 (26 August 1989), p. 1970.

[13] See K. N. Raj. "Some Observations on Economic Growth in India over the Period 1952–53 to 1982–83," *Economic and Political Weekly* (13 October 1984); Y. K. Alagh, "Some Aspects of Planning Policies in India," Three lectures delivered at the Govind Ballabh Pant Social Science Institute, Allahabad, 1985.

[14] As Mundle, "Growth, Acceleration and Fiscal Constraint," points out, investment during the 1980s has also gone to energy and power intensive industries. The power generation industry, which is one of the more capital-intensive industries, has accounted for a major share of public investment. These have also tended to raise capital intensity of the industrial sector and contributed to the stagnation in employment.

[15] See Centre for Monitoring Indian Economy (CMIE), *India's Economic Growth: 1950–51 to 1988–89*, December 1989.

[16] See Rakesh Mohan and Pushpa Thottan, *The Regional Spread of Urbanisation, Industrialisation and Urban Poverty* (New Delhi: Development Policy Division, Planning Commission, Government of India, 1988).

[17] Ibid., Table A-6. The authors also cite the growth of chemical industries as one of the reasons for the faster growth of industrial output in the western region.

[18] See P. Patnaik, "Critical Reflections on Some Aspects of Structural Change in the Indian Economy," Mimeo, Centre for Economic Studies and Planning, Jawaharlal Nehru University, New Delhi, 1989, for a detailed analytical exposition of this argument.

[19] See GOI, *Economic Survey* (1988–89), p. S-10.

[20] As a recent World Bank study on capital goods points out, at present there are only six categories of capital goods on restricted lists and 31 on OGL. In terms of individual items, 1,170 items are on OGL and only 154 on restricted lists.

[21] The data on Indian exports is taken from DGCI and C and converted into US dollars by using suitable exchange rates. The quantum of global trade in manufactured goods is based on UN data.

[22] See BICP, *Strategies for Cost Reduction*, Table 4, p. 10, on auto ancillary sector and also Table 1, p. 8, where ERPs of 0 and below 1 are reported for many engineering products.

[23] See ICICI, *Export Performance of ICICI Financed Companies, 1979–80 to 1980–81* (Bombay, 1984).

[24] See Ramesh Bhatia and B. Goldar, "Strategy for Industrialisation in India: Import versus Domestic Production," Mimeo, 1988.

[25] In terms of political economy, these high protection rates reveal a bias in government policy for some segments of the industry.

[26] These DRC estimates are based on data specific to a time period and often use prices which do not reflect long-term marginal costs of production. These results, as is well-established, are also fairly sensitive to international price levels and the exchange rate used. We are aware of these limitations and therefore use these estimates only to indicate broad trends in competitive efficiency.

[27] See M. A. Ahluwalia, "Mid Year Review of the Economy," Mimeo, New Delhi, 1989.

[28] Also see Vijay I. Kelkar, "On Efficiency of the Public Sector," Eighth Dr Deepak K. Merchant Memorial Lecture delivered on 23 October at IIT, Powai, Bombay, 1989.

[29] This is borne out in one of the recent enquiries into power generation equipment industry.

[30] See BICP, *Administered Price Policy: A Discussion Paper* (New Delhi: BICP, 1987a).

[31] Vijay I. Kelkar and K. M. Raipuria, "Manufactures Exports in India's Development: Policy Options for the Eighties," IDPAD, Tilburg, 1985.

[32] Surjit Bhalla. "Export Performance: Recognising Reality," *The Economic Times*, 28 July 1989.

[33] See ONGC internal review papers on the working of policy to improve indigenous content in oilfield exploration equipment.

[34] See BICP, *Report on Electronics* (New Delhi: BICP, 1987b).

[35] See CMIE, *India's Economic Growth*.

22

MNCs and Export Development*

C. K. Prahalad

The importance of multinational corporations (MNCs) in world trade, foreign direct investment and transfer of technology is well known and does not need repetition here. Suffice it to say that as of 1970, 200 of the largest MNCs operated more than 28,000 subsidiaries around the globe. These subsidiaries generated sales of $80 billion.[1] Multinational corporations have been growing at a very fast rate. In 1975, the total foreign investment of MNCs was estimated to be $300 billion and their total production was estimated to be $750 billion.[2] It is claimed that MNCs account for more than one-eighth of the gross product of the non-communist world, and that their share is growing.[3]

In managing their far-flung subsidiaries, MNCs have demonstrated their ability to build and sustain a global network involving manufacturing, marketing and financing activities; and more importantly, their ability to harmonise the skills of people everywhere. They have evolved many organisational and legal mechanisms—exports, technical collaboration agreements, joint ventures, subsidiaries—to sustain their involvement in the economic activity around the globe.

Multinational corporations have also been at the centre of worldwide debate. Their size (the smallest MNC among the world's 200 largest had a stated turnover of $400 million in 1967),[4] their employment (US controlled subsidiaries employed 49,000 Americans and 5.5 million local workers as of 1970),[5] and the consequences of their economic power, especially their ability to use economic power to cow down sovereign states, have all been debated.

* Originally published in *Economic and Political Weekly* 12, no. 9, Review of Management (26 February 1977): pp. M25–M31.

Containing the power of MNCs has become a concern of not only a few sovereign states but also of a world body like the United Nations.[6] Hence, in any discussion of the use of MNCs to augment exports, we should be sensitive to the strengths of MNCs and how we might use them to our advantage as well as the dangers they represent to political and economic sovereignty of nations.

I

MNCs in the Indian Context

Indian industry has had a long relationship with multinational corporations. For example, a study of 877 private sector companies conducted by the Reserve Bank of India (RBI) showed that during 1964–70 they accounted for 1,098 technical agreements. Of these 877 companies, 433 were minority companies, 197 were subsidiaries of MNCs, and 247 were pure technical collaboration agreement companies in India. Total foreign investment was Rs 189.5 crores in subsidiaries and Rs 116.31 crores in minority companies. Of the 4 public sector enterprises surveyed, 39 accounted for 163 technical collaborations.[7] Some of our large public sector corporations like BHEL had, as of 1974, as many as 15 collaborations, 12 of which were with MNCs.[8]

With increased industrialisation, the country's involvement with MNCs is likely to increase. We will probably continue to acquire technology from MNCs even if we do not seek direct foreign investment. More importantly, in most of our export markets we will meet them as our competitors. Our ability to export non-traditional and high value added items will depend on our ability to meet this competition. To manage our relationships with MNCs both internally and externally we have to start understanding the relative strengths and weaknesses of MNCs and Indian corporations.

Multinational corporations possess many of the strengths necessary to participate in world trade and investment. They also have some "soft spots." Compared with MNCs, India operates its export drive with several disadvantages, while also possessing some under-exploited strengths. An analysis of the relative strengths and weaknesses of MNCs and Indian industry reveals that these strengths and weaknesses are complementary.

Financial Strength: Ability to Invest

The financial strength of MNCs is well known. In 1975 the total foreign direct investments of the world's largest multinationals was $300 billion. The 20 largest corporations had a combined sales volume of $348.50 billion and a net income of $18.45 billion.[9] The growth in the level of foreign investment, sales volume and assets is unlikely to abate. For example, Japanese multinationals, a relatively new factor in direct investment abroad, are expected to increase their investment from $10.27 billion in 1973 to $44.87 billion in 1980. The value of production from their foreign investment is expected to be $78.75 billion in 1980.[10] Compared with the enormous financial strength and size of MNCs, Indian companies are minuscule. Two of India's largest corporations, Indian Oil Corporation and SAIL, reported sales of $1.25 billion and $0.727 billion in 1974. We are clearly at a disadvantage in terms of ability to invest in developing markets (investments in production, distribution, service, and marketing facilities), to derive the benefits of rationalised world-scale manufacturing, and to withstand sustained competitive price-cutting. Table 22.1 gives a summary analysis of the relative strengths and weaknesses of MNCs and Indian corporations.

Financial Strength: Ability to Disinvest

Because they operate in a large number of countries, MNCs are able to use disinvestment as a competitive weapon. Disinvestment is used in one of two ways: either to pull investments out of a politically undesirable situation or to move resources across countries to reduce manufacturing costs. For most multinationals, no one developing country represents a crucial market. For example, sales in India represented 0.4 per cent of the total sales for ICI, 0.7 per cent for Siemens, 0.74 per cent for Philips, 1.1 per cent for Unilever, and 2.2 per cent for Union Carbide.[11] The impact of losing a market is, in financial terms, not substantial. The primary interest of MNCs in India is in continuing their foothold in what is potentially one of the largest consumer markets in the world.

Several MNCs have recently begun a critical examination of their interest in developing countries and many have decided to pull out and seek ready markets in developed countries. Disinvestment by UK based MNCs in 1971 was around $715 million, of which $300 million was divested in developing countries.[12] At least 204 US based multinationals divested 561 foreign operations during 1967–1971, representing assets (book value) of $2.4 billion and a sales volume in excess of $3.68 billion.[13] This emerging pattern indicates that disinvestment is no more a result of corporate misjudgement, but a clearly thought out corporate strategy of *selective* investment. Multinationals can and do move resources around the globe and are increasingly exercising this option to avoid operating difficulties in some countries.

Indian corporations do not have the financial strength or the freedom to move resources across countries, to selectively exploit or to pull out of markets. Indian exports and foreign investments have so far been determined by available opportunities. While MNCs can use disinvestment as a competitive weapon, Indian corporations are far from acquiring this capability.

TABLE 22.1: RELATIVE STRENGTHS AND WEAKNESSES OF MNCS AND INDIAN CORPORATIONS

Aspects	MNCs	Indian Corporations
Financial	Sufficient financial strength to invest and/or divest. Can move resources across markets/countries.	Do not possess the strength to either invest or divest. Movement of resources across markets/countries severely restricted.
Marketing	Dominate markets like computers, machinery and chemicals. Possess strong distribution, service and brand advantages.	Market share is insignificant in world markets. Cannot afford major investments in market development. Do not possess strong brands.
Manufacturing	Can invest in and manage large-scale operations, choose locations, and rationalise manufacturing. But this leads to an inability to service protected and small markets.	No skills in developing large-scale plants. Little freedom to choose locations or rationalise production to achieve cost advantages. Have adapted imported technology to low-scale operations. Can service small markets by using adapted technology.
Technological	Have unique advantages in developing new products and processes and improving design and quality. Invest heavily in R and D.	Cannot effectively compete with MNCs in the development of new products and processes. Investment in R and D is negligible. Have advantages in the development of design and engineering specifications for standard processes.
Quality and Cost of Management	Very sophisticated and high cost management.	Not very sophisticated management, especially in managing international operations. Cost of management tend to be very low.
Support Skills	Very well developed.	Not developed at all.

Marketing Strength

Multinational corporations have attempted to control their markets through a variety of mechanisms. Most of the advanced technology industries—computers, electrical machinery, farm equipment, automobiles, chemicals, machine tools—are dominated by a few MNCs. They tend to use their collective strength to restrict "membership of the club." Indian industry has not yet faced competition from these giants in export markets, as it does not export sufficiently large amounts of non-traditional products to attract significant retaliation from them. Second, over the years, MNCs like Singer and Unilever have developed a large network of regional offices, distributors, agents and service centres. These marketing networks represent vested interests in each country and are hard to penetrate. Third, MNCs have, over the years, invested in building brand loyalties as well as loyalty to the company; Coca-Cola and IBM are notable examples. Indian corporations do not yet have the sales volume needed to invest and develop extensive marketing networks and brand loyalties in export markets.

Manufacturing Strengths

Manufacturing strengths of MNCs relate to the scale of operations, location of manufacturing activity, and the ability to move products around the globe based on a sophisticated logistics network. Multinationals tend to design their facilities with a view to achieving economies of scale. For example, 100,000-tonne-per-year capacity polyethylene plants, 1,300-tonne-per-day capacity fertiliser plants, one million units per year capacity air-conditioner and television plants are common. The demands that such plants impose on manufacturing skills are substantial. Indian corporations do not have the manufacturing skills needed to operate large-scale plants.

The development of rationalised global manufacturing has major implications for world trade. Essentially, it implies that transfers of products and components between the manufacturing divisions of a corporation constitute exports for one country and imports for another. The case of Ford illustrates this. "Ford has three main plants—at Basildon in England, at Antwerp in Belgium, and at Highland Park, a suburb of Detroit in the US. Antwerp makes all the transmissions for Highland Park and Basildon, while Basildon makes the hydraulics and engines for the other two. Both Basildon and Antwerp import the select-speed gear system from Highland Park and Basildon supplies engines to Highland Park for the giant tractors used on the North American prairies."[14] The list of such international rationalisation would include International Harvester, IBM, Philips, Olivetti, etc. These transactions between divisions of MNCs account for a substantial amount of world trade—22 per cent of Britain's exports in 1966.[15] More than 26 per cent of all imports to the US during 1971 was from the affiliates of US based MNCs.[16]

Several MNCs have devoted substantial attention to the location as well as the rationalisation of their manufacturing operations. Rationalised production enhances managerial control over product mix, production schedules, quality, costs and prices. It provides better utilisation and a sharper focus to R and D investments. It also enables multinational managers to move sub-assemblies and finished products across national boundaries at prices determined by them.

While the ability to rationalise manufacturing operations is a major competitive strength of MNCs, it is also one of their problems. Multinationals which have opted for rationalisation tend to lose their ability to penetrate markets which restrict imports and demand the production of these items on a small scale within the country. For example, take the case of a Japanese MNC which operated a totally automated refrigerator plant making close to one million units per year, and which yet found it hard to manage its joint venture in a Southeast Asian country with a capacity of 12,000 units per year. The "technological gap" between the two locations was so large that a substantial "technological reversal" was necessary before the problems of managing small-scale operations could be handled effectively by managers at the corporate office. In fact, attention has been drawn to problems that MNCs face in manufacturing if they "over automate" their foreign plants or use "inappropriate technologies."[17]

Indian industry is at a disadvantage when it has to compete with MNCs in products produced by them in their international production centres—in terms of quality, design or cost—in countries where these products are freely imported. But when, due to governmental pressure, a production unit has to be established for relatively small-scale production within the host country, Indian industry has tremendous advantages. India has successfully adopted technologies. It can now offer, for example, a one million tonne steel mill or a 600 tonne per day capacity fertiliser plant in competition with large MNCs.

Technological Strength

The technological strengths of MNCs arc generally accepted. Some large MNCs spend over $500 million per year on R and D. The R and D budget of IBM for 1972 was $726 million, and it operated 32 laboratories.[18] In 1971 in the US, large corporations in five industries—aircraft and missiles, chemicals and allied products, electrical equipment and communication, transportation and motor vehicles, and machinery—accounted for 81 per cent of the total resources spent on R and D.[19] IBM is supposed to have spent $5 billion in developing their system 360.[20] Not only do MNCs allocate substantial resources to R and D, but they also possess immense R and D management skills. Further, R and D in MNCs is closely tied to business needs. Due to these factors, they continue to be leaders in technology. Several large technology-intensive MNCs also perceive themselves as "traders in knowledge." Indian corporations in contrast do not have an R and D tradition. Less than Rs 14 crores was spent on R and D in the corporate sector in India in 1968. This represents less than 0.3 per cent of the sales volume of industry, both private and public, for that year.[21] The investments made by our government in national laboratories do not really enhance our fund of exploitable technologies as these laboratories lack the market orientation so necessary for the commercial exploitation of R and D. The relationship between Indian industry and research institutions continues to be unsatisfactory.

For a long time to come, MNCs will lead Indian corporations in product and process innovations, quality and consumer appeal. Even if we developed a new product or process, we would find it hard, in financial, marketing and manufacturing terms, to exploit it globally. Our opportunity in this area depends on our ability to understand and exploit the costs of technology transfer rather than develop new technologies. Typically, in the total cost of technology transfer, the cost associated with buying a proprietory process is small compared with the costs of designing and engineering a specific plant. In some chemical process plants, this cost could be as high as 10 to 15 per cent of the total cost. In most mature technologies, Indian companies can be cost effective with respect to this component of the total technology transfer process.

Quality and Cost of Management

Discussions on MNCs seldom deal with their real strength—the quality of management.[22] Over a period of time, MNCs have developed the skills needed to manage large and diverse operations in many countries. A typical diversified multinational like General Electric, Union Carbide or Philips might have as many as fifty businesses in a hundred countries. These corporations have evolved systems of managerial communication and control to cope with complexities inherent in managing such diversity.[23] Typically, MNCs invest heavily in management development. This results in the development of a large pool of managers with international business experience as well as sophisticated managerial expertise. In contrast, Indian corporations have had little exposure to managing international operations. Systems of management, even for domestic operations, are still evolving and tend to be inadequate. Our investments in management development are also small. As such, we have a long way to go before we can match the managerial skills of MNCs.

Indian corporations, however, have one distinct advantage. Most MNCs find it rather difficult to attract their own nationals to work in technical and craft-oriented jobs abroad. For example, there is a shortage of design engineers in the chemical industry in the US. It is difficult, for US-based MNCs, to attract engineers to Saudi Arabia or Iran for long periods of time. Second, the financial cost of building plants by using expatriates is very high. In both these areas—availability of technical manpower and costs of project management—Indian corporations have a decided edge over the MNCs.

Support Skills

Most MNCs have evolved substantial "support skills" needed for international operations. For example, MNCs have acquired considerable legal skills in devising patent protection systems, (Xerox and Polaroid are reported to have at least 600 to 700 patents protecting their basic processes.) Patent protection is an essential ingredient for the economic exploitation of industrial know-how.

Only a few of our large industrial undertakings and research laboratories have in-house patent/trademark expertise.

Expansion of MNC activities abroad is typically followed by multinational banks and shipping to support their operations. India has not yet developed adequate legal skills, financial institutional support, or shipping capabilities to sustain its export drive.

On the whole, Indian corporations are at a disadvantage with regard to several crucial dimensions. To be able to compete effectively, we have to build our strengths *vis-à-vis* MNCs in each one of these areas. This is a costly and time-consuming process. In the interim, it may be desirable to selectively collaborate with MNCs as some socialist countries are doing.

II

Socialist Countries and MNCs

Many East European countries face impediments, like those described in the previous section, in their export drive, especially to Western Europe and North America. They have to deal with MNC subsidiaries in Western Europe as well as with the exports of MNC subsidiaries in developing countries. Several developing countries which seem to have abandoned the protectionist "import substitution model" for a relatively open "export-intensive industrialisation model" of development have become competitors for East European manufacturers in the developed countries of the West.[24] This switch in the approach to industrialisation is noticeable among the city-states (like Hong Kong and Singapore) and Central American countries. Due to these changes in the pattern of trade—essentially the competition posed by MNCs and their subsidiaries—East European countries seem to be re-examining their position with respect to MNCs.

The critical problem faced by these countries is "their limited access to the hard-currency markets. This is chiefly the result of the inability of most socialist industries to meet product quality requirements of the highly competitive world markets."[25] In addition to product quality, design, packaging and such other skills, they also lack marketing networks abroad. Therefore, there has been a growing desire in socialist countries to develop joint venture marketing organisations with MNCs as well as the more traditional manufacturing-cum-marketing joint ventures. The established marketing networks of MNCs reduce the marketing costs and risks of international marketing and provide stability to socialist manufacturers who get into contractual agreements with them.

An equally interesting pattern of collaboration is emerging between MNCs and socialist manufacturers. Increasingly, MNCs are approached by these countries to "engage in the joint-manufacture and worldwide marketing of *dual trade-mark* products representing both the multinational corporations and the socialist economies. This aid is especially important in those product categories, such as machinery, chemicals, and transportation equipment, in which the East Europeans want to establish long-term world market shares but for which global competition is continually increasing. Hungarian economic officials told one of the authors that, in many cases while choosing multinational corporations for joint projects, marketing ability is the single most important selection criterion."[26]

A number of collaboration agreements have taken place recently between MNCs and East European countries. Massey Ferguson, a Canada based MNC, signed in late 1972 a production-cum-marketing agreement with the Romanian Mecano-export for manufacture of wheel-loaders, Romania has non-exclusive marketing rights for CMEA countries, exclusive marketing rights for Romania, and option to market their products anywhere in the world subject to prior consultation with Massey-Ferguson.[27] In 1973, Control Data Corporation set up a 20-year joint venture called Rom Control Data to produce printers, card punchers and other peripherals. Control Data will market 85 per cent of the output through its own distribution system; the remaining 15 per cent will be marketed by Romanians at home and in third countries, both in the east and the west.[28] General Motors is completing negotiations with Poland to convert an auto plant at Lublin, south east of Warsaw, to produce 50,000 lightweight vans per year. The deal is worth $300 million. General Motors will supply licenses, technology and equipment, and the Poles will operate the plant. General Motors will take out a part of the production as payment and sell it outside Poland.[29] Montedison of Italy is setting up six chemical plants in the Soviet Union. Six more are reported to be under negotiation. A substantial portion of the output is likely to be taken out of Soviet Union as part payment.[30] Western MNCs like International Harvester, Fiat, Volvo, MAN and Duetz of Germany, Pepsi Cola and GE are negotiating deals with East European countries. The pattern of these collaboration agreements indicates that East European and Soviet manufacturers also find it difficult to adopt a do-it-yourself approach to marketing in hard currency areas. As a result, they are engaged in innovative collaborative agreements with multinationals.

Some of the salient features of these agreements are:

(1) Marketing joint ventures to promote the sales of products manufactured in East Europe under licence from multinationals.
(2) Using dual-trademark agreements with MNCs to gain entry into competitive western markets.
(3) Part payment for foreign investment made by MNCs in East Europe in products manufactured in the host country. These products are earmarked for sale in western markets by the investing multinationals.

(4) One-shot payment for technical collaboration with MNCs for technology transfer.

These emerging patterns indicate that the strengths of MNCs in international marketing can be used to augment our exports as well. A critical and objective examination of national interests and the role of MNCs in furthering those interests is necessary. We may have to shift our orientation towards MNCs (as is done by the East Europeans)—away from the view that saw an MNC as always an adversary towards the view that the MNC can sometimes be an ally. The selectivity in our approach to MNCs must be based on our understanding of the MNCs concerned. We should ask ourselves the following questions: Are all MNCs alike? Whom should we confront and with whom should we collaborate? What should the basis for collaboration be?

III

Are All MNCs Alike?

If we consider MNCs as managerial systems rather than as mere economic and legal entities, we can segment them into groups by using managerially relevant criteria. The response of a specific MNC to our export/technology/investment demands may be predicted with a reasonable degree of confidence if we understand it managerially. Some of the dimensions along which such a managerially relevant classification can be developed are outlined below.

Managerial Organisation

Multinational corporations have adopted a variety of organisational forms. The pattern of evolution of organisational form in an MNC seems to depend on the nature, variety and extent of its involvement in international operations. For example, changes in the importance of international activities to the overall corporate, sales and profit of an MNC over a period of time tend to influence the organisational form the MNC adopts to manage its overseas operations.[31] Corporations start their international involvement by giving substantial freedom to the subsidiaries. This stage of development in the overseas operations of an MNC may be labelled the "autonomous subsidiary" stage. As the level of involvement in international operations increases, corporations tend to pool all overseas activities under one group. They create an international division at corporate headquarters to coordinate the activities of the various subsidiaries. This may be considered the second stage in the development of the management of overseas activities. Even at this stage the international operations of the corporations are not totally integrated with their domestic operations. When investments, sales and profit overseas as a percentage of the total become critical to the survival and profitability of the organisation, MNCs try to integrate their worldwide activities by using a variety of global structures. This may be labelled the "global stage." MNCs have adopted a variety of global structures. Some of them use a regional organisation structure to manage their worldwide network. In this structure, worldwide operations are divided into "regions" and all businesses in a region report to a central regional office. Some others operate with a worldwide product division structure. In this form of organisation, product divisions control decisions applicable to specific businesses worldwide from a central office, usually the corporate headquarters. Still others operate with mixed structures, i.e., they operate some of their businesses with worldwide product division structure and some others through the regional structure. A few of them have developed a matrix structure; this involves creative combinations of the benefits of the product and regional structures. In other words, based on the nature of the businesses they are involved in and the complexities in their respective business environments, MNCs have evolved a wide variety of global organisational forms.

An organisational form consists of the formal organisation structure, the pattern of internal communication, control and rewards, and the orientation of key executives. The organisational form adopted by an MNC influences the process of decision making within it.[32] For example, there are few corporate controls over overseas operations in the early stages of the international operations of a multinational. In contrast, when and if it adopts a worldwide product division structure, substantial central influence can be expected over a variety of managerial decisions like pricing, product mix, product movement across subsidiaries and markets, and level of technology. The influence of organisational form on the process of decision making suggests that the response of an MNC to innovative ideas for collaboration from a developing country is, in a manner of speaking, predictable.

The propensity of MNCs to form joint ventures is often related to the form of the corporate organization. As MNCs tend to centralise decision making on a worldwide basis, stresses in joint venture relationships inevitably develop.[33] This phenomenon indicates that compatibility of an MNC joint-venture partner relationship is as much a function of the overall corporate organisational form of the MNC as any other consideration. In dealing with MNCs, it is important, therefore, to carefully analyse their organisational form to assess what aspects of demands would be acceptable to them and what would not.

As a developing country India's primary interest should be in technology-intensive MNCs—more in the GEs and Hitachisthan in the Coca-Colas and General Foods. It is therefore important to examine whether there is a pattern in the organisational form adopted by the technology-intensive multinationals.

Technology Intensity

The level of technology that an MNC represents is a factor to consider. For example, companies operating in mature technologies like polyethylene or basic chemicals are more likely to be eager to accept joint venture or other forms of collaboration than those operating with advanced technologies like IBM, Texas Instruments or Hewlett-Packard. The level and life cycle of technology are good indicators of the ease with which mutually advantageous collaborative agreement may be negotiated.[34]

Closely related to the level of technology is the capital-intensity of technology. For example, in chemicals, farm machinery, automobiles and electrical machinery, the tendency of MNCs has been to centralise major resource allocation decisions. This pattern ensures corporate control over location, scale of operations, and product mix. The benefits of pooling resources and creating an interdependent global system are substantial in these industries. Capital intensity, and therefore the risk involved in the project, may also influence MNC behaviour.

Industry Concentration

Apart from technology intensity and capital intensity, industry concentration also influences the behaviour of multinationals. For example, the computer industry is dominated by IBM; the power industry by a few like GE, Westinghouse, Hitachi and Siemens. Consumer electronics industry, on the other hand, is fragmented. Entry into industries that are heavily concentrated is likely to be very difficult and expensive. Entry into industries like readymade garments, basic chemicals, light engineering, and consumer durables is less taxing. A major study of the behaviour of MNCs in oligopolistic markets suggests that while oligopoly conditions make it difficult for new entrants to gain a foothold, developing countries can gain advantages if they "play one against other."[35] The oil crisis had its genesis when Libya successfully seduced Occidental Petroleum to agree to its terms, and created conditions that led to the loosening of the hold of the "seven sisters."

Political Risk

The perception of MNC executives of the degree of political risk involved in various countries is yet another factor. This perception may or may not be based upon any detailed analysis of facts. It often is based on the feelings of key executives. If MNCs perceive the political risk to be high, they prefer to enter into collaboration agreements for technology transfer and/or equity participation.[36] Most analysts of MNC behaviour do not consider the importance of creating the right climate and educating prospective MNC executives.

Entry versus Post-Entry Behaviour

A substantial part of the problem for an MNC in accepting an Indian corporation arises in the "pre-entry stage," when the MNC does not have adequate experience of working with and operating within India as a base. Once the MNCs enter into a collaboration agreement with an Indian corporation and learn how to operate in this environment, they are much more amenable to the restrictions imposed on them. Hence, it might be desirable to enter into collaboration and then monitor them closely rather than impose restrictions even before they consider collaboration possibilities. The relative power of the state and an MNC changes as the MNC's involvement in the host country increases.[37]

IV

Opportunities for Collaboration with MNCs

A variety of opportunities exists for meaningful collaboration between Indian corporations and multinationals. Attempts at collaboration, however, must be based on a detailed analysis of the relative strengths and weaknesses of MNCs and Indian corporations as well as managerial understanding of the behaviour of specific multinationals. This suggests that our strategies must be industry and MNC specific. It is not in our interest to develop a regulatory framework which is general and which does not provide flexibility to exploit opportunities for useful collaboration. What are these opportunities? A few areas are outlined below.

Developing Export Platforms

We need to identify MNCs which are pursuing rationalisation of production activities and seeking low-cost production platforms because we can attract these MNCs to come and set up world-scale production centres for manufacture of components and finished products. Many Latin American countries, Taiwan, Korea and Singapore have used this device. We are ideally placed to attract these investments as we can provide low-cost but highly trained labour and suitable infrastructure facilities. However, we have to accept the freedom of MNCs to trade—to move resources across countries at prices determined by the corporate headquarters. If this freedom is denied to an MNC then the rationale for its setting up an international production centre is lost. The advantage of attracting MNCs to establish international production centres or world-scale plants using the most up-to-date technology in India is the substantial amount of value-added generated within the country. This strategy ensures that technology is transferred to India rather cheaply in that we not only attract a level of foreign investment in the country, but also introduce advanced technologies and skills in large-scale management. Such investments by MNCs also lead to the development of a pool of local vendors and sub-contractors. This enhances the sophistication of our infrastructure facilities. MNC exports from their export platforms in India contribute to our foreign exchange. A recent study showed that it was the export-oriented MNC investments that created a favourable trade balance for the LDCs. Of the 80 MNC investments researched, 21 were export-oriented. India was the base of 13 investments but none was export-oriented. The study underscored the need for a selective strategy based on an understanding of corporate investment behaviour.[38]

Sub-Contracting

Indian corporations can become sub-contractors for a substantial number of the projects in which MNCs are involved in Third World countries. Our skills in the area of civil engineering and construction, or process design for chemical plants using mature technologies, can be exploited in Third World countries in collaboration with multinationals. For the MNCs, we represent a relatively low-cost design and project management talent; for us, these sub-contracts with MNCs represent an entry into important markets of the world. While a few attempts have been made to develop joint projects with East European partners in Third World countries, there have been no attempts to sub-contract work with multinationals.

Further, the possibility of exporting machine tools as a sub-contractor to MNC projects in the Third World should also be explored. For example, several MNCs investing in developing countries to produce on a small scale have to develop "appropriate technologies." Several studies have shown that the corporate groups of most MNCs are ill-suited to develop appropriate technologies. Even if they did, they would find it hard to identify vendors who could supply them plant and machinery appropriate for that technology. Indian industry can, by carefully following the investment plans of MNCs in Third World countries, identify those MNCs which are likely to need this help.

Joint Venture Relationships

Joint ventures provide a basis for innovative collaborations. Typically, we have looked at joint ventures as a basis for manufacturing products for domestic consumption and as a mechanism for reducing the percentage of equity held by an MNC in India. Recently, we have attempted to explore the possibility of tying a certain level of export commitment with joint ventures. We should explore the feasibility of marketing joint ventures with multinationals. Such a joint venture has several advantages. It enables Indian industry to get access to the hard currency markets. It reduces the costs of entry into such markets as well as the risks associated with it. A marketing joint venture enhances our marketing skills in product design, packaging, branding, advertising and promotion. A marketing joint venture can develop into a channel (like our export houses) for the export of a variety of products produced by Indian industry as well as by Third World countries.

Closely related to marketing joint ventures is the potential for manufacturing joint ventures under licence from MNCs but with provision for dual trademarks. This would provide exposure to our products in international markets.

A third possibility is the development of project consortia where Indian industry can, in collaboration with MNCs, undertake projects in Third World countries. A sensitive matching of our skills and cost advantages in project management with the specific needs of MNCs is a prerequisite for developing this avenue.

The above listing is indicative of the types of collaborations with MNCs that are feasible. There are still many more types. What needs to be emphasised in these collaborative relationships is not the actual form which such relationships take but the belief and orientation that generates them. We have to be convinced that such relationships can benefit us and that we can manage these relationships without being unduly pressurised by the collaborating MNCs: that we have something to offer them as well as standing to gain from them.

V

Conclusion

In developing our export strategy we should recognise the following factors:

(1) Multinationals dominate world trade, especially trade in non-traditional manufactured products as well as exports to affluent and advanced countries.
(2) Multinationals possess significant strengths as compared with Indian industry, and an objective analysis of the relative strengths of the two must precede the development of our export strategy.
(3) Many socialist countries, recognising the dominant role of MNCs in world trade and especially in trade with hard currency areas, have started collaborating with multinationals. They have forged several collaborations with MNCs in the form of joint ventures in marketing, manufacturing and licensing.
(4) To develop a suitable national export strategy, we have to identify opportunities in world markets. This can be accomplished through a study of the worldwide industry structure and the identification of market niches

for development. We have to study the behaviour of MNCs in each of these industries to select a suitable national posture in the collaboration-confrontation continuum.

(5) Our strategy towards MNCs must be selective. It should be industry and MNC specific.

It is abundantly clear that while we can avoid MNCs at home, we will inevitably meet them abroad. It is also clear that we cannot wish away the dominant role of MNCs in world trade. To cope with these realities we should, without delay, initiate the following steps.

(1) Develop an inter-ministerial cell, coordinated by the commerce ministry, of competent industry analysts. This cell should analyse trends in selected industries worldwide for the next 10 years, and identify opportunities and market niches for exploitation by Indian industry. This cell should also recommend, on the basis of industry studies, the size of plants to be built in India. So far, licensing has not taken into account, explicitly, the scale of operations or the technology needed for our industry to be cost-effective in world markets. This cell should also develop a data bank on the behaviour of key MNCs in each one of these industries, in terms of their organisation, growth pattern, technological and marketing strengths, relationships with host governments, desire and ability to work with partners, etc. This data bank will indicate the MNCs with which we should deal, on what terms, and why.
(2) Create an "intelligence unit" to monitor the investment proposals of MNCs in the Third World countries. This data would provide the basis for exploring opportunities for sub-contracting, project management and sale of plant and machinery. The same unit should also monitor the investment behaviour of multinationals in industries that form the backbone of our export strategy to ensure that we are not caught unawares. For example, MNC investments in tea plantations in Kenya may affect Indian exports of tea in the long run.
(3) In its deliberations, the inter-ministerial cell should work in close collaboration with trade associations and factors. For example, idle capacity in the automobile ancillary industry is our strength as far as exports are concerned.
(4) Create a climate of mutual trust between Indian industry and government through a process of consultation. Similarly, we should change our orientation toward multinationals. The question is not: "Are MNCs our allies *or* adversaries?" The fact is: They are allies *and* adversaries; it depends on the specifics of a situation.

NOTES AND REFERENCES

[1] James W. Vaupel and Joan P. Curhan, *The World's Multinational Enterprises: A Source Book of Tables Based on a Study of the Largest US and Non-US Manufacturing Operations* (Harvard University, 1973).

[2] Estimates taken from the speech delivered by Orville Freeman, Chairman of the US delegation to the three-day session of the Indo-US Joint Council Meeting in Delhi, 2 February 1976.

[3] Estimates suggested in Surinder P. S. Pruthi (ed.), *Multinationals in Developing Countries* (New Delhi, 1974).

[4] Vaupel and Curhan, *The World's Multinational Enterprises.*

[5] Raymond Vernon, *Sovereignty at Bay: The Multinational Spread of US Enterprises* (New York: Basic Books, 1971), p. 156.

[6] *The Impact of Multinational Corporations on Development and on International Relations*, Report of the Secretary General, United Nations, 1974.

[7] *Foreign Collaboration in Indian Industry: Second Survey Report* (Bombay: Reserve Bank of India, 1974).

[8] *Bharat Heavy Electricals Limited: The Corporate Planning Process*, Case study of the Indian Institute of Management (Ahmedabad, 1974).

[9] "The Largest Corporations Outside the US," *Fortune* (August 1975), pp. 155–70.

[10] "New Light on Japan's Multinationals," *Multinational Business* (December 1975), pp. 33–40.

[11] Percentages based on annual reports of these corporations in India and data from the *Fortune* directory of the largest corporations outside the US in 1974. Also see, Peter F. Drucker, "Multinationals and Developing Countries: Myths and Realities," *Foreign Affairs* (October 1974), pp. 121–34.

[12] J. C. Sachdev, "Disinvestment: A New Challenge to Multinationals and a New Threat to Developing Countries," *Multinational Business*, Number 3 (1974).

[13] J. J. Boddewyn and Roger Torneden, "Foreign Divestment: Too Many Mistakes," *Columbia Journal of World Business* (Fall 1974), pp. 87–94. Also see, by the same authors, "US Foreign Divestment: A Preliminary Survey," *Columbia Journal of World Business* (Summer 1973), p. 25. They indicate that the total book value of divested assets is between $2 billion and $4 billion; the sales volume is over $3,675 billion.

[14] Christopher Tugedhat, *The Multinationals* (New York: Random House, 1972), Chapter 7.

[15] Ibid.

[16] Victor L. Korneev, "Multinationals and the Changing World Trade Structure," *Foreign Trade Review* (July–September 1975), pp. 113–21.

[17] Louis T. Wells (Jr), "Don't Over Auto-mate Your Foreign Plant," *Harvard Business Review* (January–February 1974). Wells makes a good case for MNCs to look at equipment produced by developing countries.

[18] Nancy Foy, *The Sun Never Sets on IBM* (New York: William Morrow, 1974).

[19] *Research and Development in Industry, 1971*, National Science Foundation, Washington, 1973.

[20] T. A. Wise, "IBM's $5,000,000,000 Gamble," *Fortune* (September 1966), p. 118. Also see, by the same author, "The Rocky Road to the Market Place," *Fortune* (October 1966), p. 139.

[21] *An Approach to the Science and Technology Plan*, National Committee on Science and Technology, New Delhi, January 1973, p. 34,

[22] Raymond Vernon, "Organization as a Scale Factor in the Growth of Firms," in *Industrial Organization and Economic Development*, eds J. W. Markham and G. F. Papanek (Boston: Houghton Mifflin, 1970).

[23] C. K. Prahalad, "The Strategic Process in a Multinational Corporation,"(Doctoral Dissertation, Harvard Business School, Boston, 1975).

[24] B. Kadar, *Recent Trends in the Industrialisation of the Developing Countries and the Global Strategies of the Leading Capitalist Countries* (Budapest: Hungarian Scientific Council for World Economy, 1974).

[25] G. Peter Lauter and Paul M. Dickie, "Multinational Corporations in East European Socialist Economies," *Journal of Marketing* (October 1975), pp. 40–46. Also see, for a similar line of argument, Leon Zarawicki, "The Cooperation of the Socialist State with the MNCs," *Columbia Journal of World Business* (Spring 1975), pp. 109–15.

[26] Lauter and Dickie, "Multinational Corporations," emphasis added.

[27] Ibid.

[28] Ibid.

[29] "Italy: Montedison expands its multinational role," *Business Week* (10 November 1975), p. 67.

[30] "East Bloc where the demand for trucks is booming," *Business Week* (20 October 1975), p. 60.

[31] John M. Stopford and Louis T. Wells (Jr), *Managing the Multinational Enterprise* (New York: Basic Books, 1972). Also see, Michael Z. Brooke and Lee H. Remmers, *The Strategy for Multinational Enterprise* (New York: American Elsevier Publishing Company, 1970).

[32] Prahalad, "The Strategic Process in a Multinational Corporation."

[33] Lawrence G. Franko, "Joint Venture Divorce in the Multinational Company," *Columbia Journal of World Business* (May–June 1971).

[34] The product life cycle approach is widely discussed in the literature on the subject. To assess the implications of product life cycle on the availability of technology to outsiders see, Robert B. Stobaugh, "Utilising Technical Know-how in a Forcing Investment and Licensing Program," *Proceedings of the Chemical Marketing Research Association*, Houston (February 1970).

[35] F. Knickerbroker, *Oligopolistic Reaction and Multinational Enterprise* (Boston: Harvard Business School, 1973).

[36] Yair Aharoni, *The Foreign Investment Decision Process* (Harvard University, 1966), especially Chapter 9.

[37] Ashok Kapoor, "MNC Negotiations: Characteristics and Planning Implications," *Columbia Journal of World Business* (Winter 1974), pp. 121–30.

[38] See, for example, the data presented in Harold Crookell, "Investing in Development—Corporate View," *Columbia Journal of World Business* (Spring 1975), pp. 80–88. Of the 80 foreign investment projects included in this sample, 21 were export-oriented, 33 market development-oriented (intended for sale in the host country only), and 25 were government-initiated (to displace imports). India was the base for 13 projects out of 80, none export-oriented. Seven projects were market development-oriented and six government-initiated. Only the export-oriented projects resulted in a positive trade balance for the developing countries. This study underscores the need for a selective strategy based on an understanding of corporate investment behaviour.

23

On Benefits of Tapping Foreign Portfolio Investments

An Indian Perspective*

Vihang R. Errunza

The linkages between capital market and economic development are well known to academics and policymakers. Accordingly, over the last two decades, many less developed countries (LDCs), including Brazil, South Korea, Thailand and Venezuela, embarked upon programmes designed to develop their local capital markets. The programmes generally consisted of fiscal policy reforms, regulatory measures, institution building, disclosure rules, etc. The results were encouraging but not spectacular. Hence, in recent years, these programmes have been reviewed and, as a result, some of the leading LDCs have begun selective liberalisation of rules governing foreign portfolio investments (FPIs) to provide further boost to capital markets and economic development, e.g., Mexico Fund and Korea Fund. This is of course not surprising given the important role of FPIs in economic growth of today's developed countries such as the US.

Over the past two to three years, India has also moved towards selective FPI liberalisation. The opening up of capital markets to non-resident Indians (NRIs) and the real possibility of an India Fund are concrete examples. Therefore it would be useful to review the benefits of FPIs as they pertain to India. Since any liberalisation effort would critically depend on mutual benefits, the chapter begins with a brief discussion of the benefits of portfolio investments in India from the viewpoint of the foreign investor and India's need for FPIs.

* Originally published in *Economic and Political Weekly* 21, no. 8, Review of Management (22 February 1986), pp. M17–M19.

We then discuss the general benefits and India-specific issues of liberalisation, following which some suggestions on tapping FPIs are put forward. Concluding remarks follow.

Benefits to Foreign Investors

Major benefits to investors include profit potential and risk diversification. Based on historical returns, future growth prospects of the Indian economy, as well as participation in worldwide competitive and pure play (one product/industry) firms suggest above average returns to foreign portfolio investors. Further, India offers substantial risk diversification opportunities. According to the IFC, World Bank data, Indian equities were least risky in terms of monthly standard deviation of US dollar returns over the 1976–1984 period in comparison to those from ten major developing countries. The low correlations between Indian and foreign equity returns also suggest significant benefits of including India in a global portfolio. Appropriately, India is a prime candidate for FPIs, and efforts to tap these funds as suggested in the last section would be mutually beneficial to both India and the foreign investor.

Need for FPI

Trade prospects, repayments of external loans coming due during the Seventh Plan and the resource requirements of continuing economic growth translate into increasing need for external finance. Over time, India's sources of external finance have undergone a dramatic change. In recent years, the traditional reliance on external (concessionary) assistance has been supplemented by credit from international official institutions and non-resident deposits. If one assumes reasonable prospects of modest growth in assistance flows (despite recent setbacks) and non-resident deposits, India would increasingly need to tap the international capital markets.

In view of her high credit rating, India is in a position to obtain both debt and equity financing. The debt financing would necessarily be commercial lending since bond markets have not been easily accessible to LDCs. The debt option for India will be discussed under India-specific issues of FPI. The equity financing can come from foreign direct investments by multinationals or portfolio investments. With respect to the equity options, multinational investments have a major disadvantage with respect to control and management of the firm. Also, one suspects that multinationals earn unreasonably high profits. However, their contribution especially on technology transfer may be indispensable in certain industries. On the other hand, portfolio investments can come either on an individual basis or via the international trusts/mutual funds.

General Benefits of FPI

FPI liberalisation would be beneficial on three counts: (1) the development effect, (2) the resource effect, and (3) the welfare effect.

Developmental Effect

Foreign portfolio investments would have three types of major development benefits. On the regulatory side, the foreign investors would demand more efficient market regulation, protection of minority interest, fair trading and brokerage practices as well as adequate disclosure/listing requirements. On the institutional side, foreign participation would necessitate development of new institutions and investments on one hand, and result in transfer of knowledge and training of local executives on the other hand. At the market level, long-term foreign investment would help dampen speculative movements and reduce imperfections that afflict many LDC markets. The improvement in regulatory, institutional and market environment in conjunction with private foreign capital would increase domestic investor confidence and participation, thereby providing further stimulus to LDC markets.[1]

Resource Effect

Foreign capital may substantially reduce the loss of domestic savings through capital flight by increasing domestic investor confidence as well as by making available a wider selection of securities initially designed to satisfy foreigners. Reduction in capital flight together with the capital inflows in the form of portfolio investments would augment total domestic savings and increase net external resources.

Welfare Effect

The welfare issue is very complex and as a result involves considerable simplification. Here we consider the impact on security pricing, the diversification benefit and the investor welfare under two liberalisation scenarios.[2]

Worldwide Removal of Barriers: Complete integration would mean that the prices of LDC securities will in general go up with a consequent decline in the cost of equity capital. Since market integration will expand the investment opportunity set, the ability to invest in the world market portfolio will result in a positive diversification effect. Finally, if LDC investors hold optimal portfolios, their welfare would increase following integration.

Introduction of a National Fund (e.g., India Fund): Partial integration of the world market leads to a somewhat weaker welfare result. The net effect on LDC security prices and investor welfare would likely be positive. The introduction of such a fund would, however, be favoured by all investors because it would not reduce their investment opportunity set.

India-specific Issues of FPI

In addition to the general benefits of FPI discussed above, the following India-specific issues are of interest.

Return to Foreign Investors

It is generally believed that returns on Indian equity and hence the cost of FPI to India would be much higher than commercial loans. This does not seem to be justified on the basis of either the historical returns on the rational expectations about future returns.

Historical Returns: Historical US dollar returns on portfolio equity investments in India cannot be considered high relative to debt, taking into account that lenders do not share interest, currency and economic risks with the borrowers and in general have not borne the political risk. On the other hand, international equity holders would bear currency risk and share economic, political and business risks with the Indian shareholders (see Table 23.1; note the volatility of equity returns). Finally, on the debt side, the borrowers are liable for cost of any new controls and may be exposed to IMF or foreign government interference. Also, due to the nature of the market, the risk of over borrowing has been greater in the case of debt than equity.

Future Returns: Notwithstanding the above, it is the future expected return that is of the most concern to India and the foreign investors. In this respect, if the Indian market is opened up, the world market integration effect would bring future Indian equity returns more in line with other major developed markets, i.e., future equity returns would be lower in comparison to the historical Indian average.

Diversification of External Sources

Although at present India has excess debt capacity, RBI projections suggest a rapid increase in the debt servicing ratio during the Seventh Plan. Hence it might be prudent to balance foreign debt and equity before long. There have been some proposals for converting debt to equity in the case of major Latin borrowers, which is expected to be very expensive. Thus, it might be in India's best interest to adopt the balanced diversified approach at the outset. Given the present high equity prices and excellent reputation, the time appears to be ripe for portfolio flow liberalisation.

TABLE 23.1: PER CENT US$ RETURNS TO FOREIGN HOLDERS OF INDIAN EQUITY AND DEBT

	1978	1979	1980	1981	1982	1983	1984	Mean
Portfolio Equity	51.2	21.1	42.3	23.5	–5.8	8.2	–3.9	18.0
Debt	10.7	13.7	15.5	18.1	15.0	11.3	12.7	14.0

Notes: Since equity investment is long-term, compounded mean is used. The data are from IFC, the World Bank. The debt figures are based on yearly average of six-month US$ LIBOR including a total of 1.5 per cent for spread, fees and effective tax sparing cost to India. The year 1978 is used as the initial year to reflect first Indian borrowings in the international market. IFC has not yet completed 1985 data but we know that equity return was high. However, the 1985 return was very atypical and not likely to be repeated. On the other hand, given high prices, this is probably an opportune time to rise equity from India's perspective.

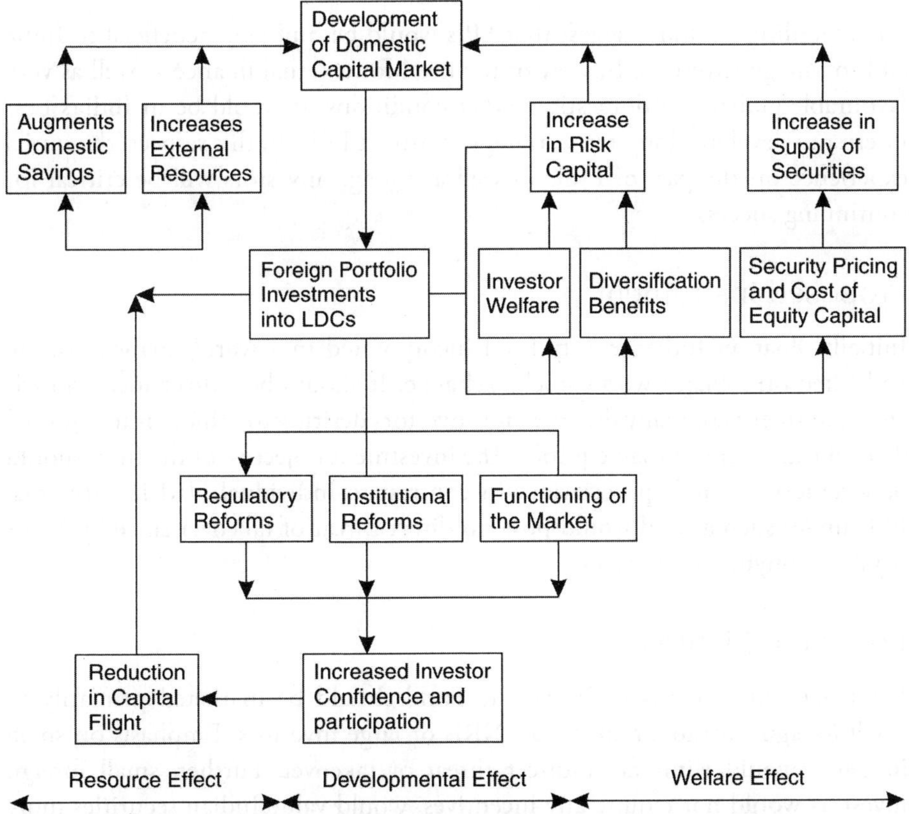

FIGURE 23.1: FOREIGN PORTFOLIO INVESTMENT AND CAPITAL MARKET DEVELOPMENT

Further Internationatisation

If in the future, Indian corporations would like to issue bonds and/or equity in the international markets, then portfolio investments by small individual foreign investors would provide the necessary exposure for Indian firms to the small investors who would subscribe to their bonds/equity.

Technical Assistance

FPI should be linked to technical assistance to the Indian investment community as in the case of the Korea Fund. The cost is borne by the foreign subscribers in the form of management fee to the fund manager.

Tapping FPI

The preceding sections suggest that FPIs would be mutually beneficial to India and to foreign investors. In view of the need for external finance as well as very favourable global and domestic market conditions, it would be in India's best interest to develop a long-term strategy to attract FPIs. In this respect, the initial experience on the part of India as well as foreign investors will be critical for continuing success.

Proposed Instrument

Initially, float an Indian equity fund incorporated in a world financial centre and listed on a major world stock exchange. It should be a diversified, closed-end investment company designed for investors desiring to achieve international diversification into Indian equities. The investment objective of the fund should be long-term capital appreciation. In contrast to individual NRI investments, FPIs under such a fund would pose no direct threat of takeover since investors would be buying fund shares.

Preferred Clientele

For maximum benefits to India, the Fund should be marketed primarily to small foreign investors rather than NRIs or large investors. Emphasis on small investors would eliminate indirect threat of takeover. Further, small foreign investors would not require any incentives, would value Indian securities more favourably than either the NRIs or the large investors and would constitute a preferred clientele in helping India's efforts to further internationalise her sources of finance.

Management and Underwriting

The Fund should be managed by a highly reputed investment counselling firm with an experienced research staff capable and willing to provide the necessary transfer of investment know-how to India. The Fund shares should be underwritten by a worldwide syndicate with a long-term commitment to meet India's needs. Since the success of the first (and subsequent) offering(s) would be critical from the Indian perspective, it would be prudent to objectively assess the placement ability of the various underwriters. Since in a dynamic world capital market the total cost across various contenders cannot be very different, given her strong bargaining position, India need not place undue emphasis on cost. The most important objective is long-term availability of portfolio funds and not cost minimisation.

Indian Task Force

Taking into account existing administrative apparatus, guidelines and policy initiatives within the Central government, it would seem prudent to nominate a task force with the directive to develop a long-term strategy that would facilitate portfolio flows into the Indian market under terms and conditions that would be most beneficial to India.

Concluding Remarks

The suggestion is to tap savings of small foreign investors as a complement to external borrowings. Such portfolio flows will earn reasonable returns and provide diversification of external sources, facilitate further internationalisation of the Indian market and help development of a competitive investment industry in India in addition to the general developmental, resource and welfare benefits associated with FPIs. India should move quickly but cautiously in tapping international portfolio funds. The time is ripe.

Notes and References

[1] For a detailed discussion of the Brazilian experience, see V. Errunza. 1979. "Efficiency and the Programmes to Develop Capital Markets: The Brazilian Experience." *Journal of Banking and Finance* 3: pp. 355–82.

[2] 2. For complete details, including mathematical proofs and economic rationale, see V. Errunza and E. Losq. 1985. "Capital Flow Controls, International Asset Pricing and Investors' Welfare: A Multicountry Framework." McGill University Working Paper.

24

Financial Scenario in the 1990s

Agenda for Reform*

N. A. Mujumdar

The financial sector plays a critical role in the process of economic development. The question naturally arises as to how a country's financial system should be developed—by relying heavily on the private sector and on market forces or by active state intervention? Economics seems to be a fashion-bound discipline and the great buzzword of contemporary financial policy discussions is "financial liberalisation." The *World Development Report, 1989* of the World Bank, which has "Financial Systems and Development" as its main theme, is not content by merely extolling the virtues of developing the financial system by market forces; it indicts the state-regulated financial system. To quote from the report: "In the past, governments' efforts to promote economic development by controlling interest rates, directing credit to priority sectors, and securing inexpensive funding for their own activities have undermined financial development."[1] In deriving this conclusion, the authors of the report appear to suffer from selective amnesia because there is enough empirical evidence to the contrary. In fact, in any analytical study with claims to objectivity, it should be realised that the discussion on whether the financial system should be ideally developed by market forces or by state intervention would hardly be meaningful without reference to a specific time frame.

I seek to draw some lessons from the Indian experience of building up the financial system—an experience which is unique in many respects. The main theme that emerges from the analysis is that in a developing country like India, the growth of the financial system can be divided into three distinct phases: the

* Originally published in *Economic and Political Weekly* 25, no. 14 (7 April 1990), pp. 731–37.

first phase is characterised by active state intervention with a view to building up the institutional infrastructure. Developing countries are in a hurry to catch up with modern banking and developments in money and capital markets; and they cannot afford to wait for the spontaneous or autonomous growth of the financial system to take place. In such a context, the performance of the financial system is judged by the test of "immediacy." Thus, in developing economies at this stage of development, state initiative and active participation in the building up of institutional infrastructure, as also in directing the flow of resources, become a historical necessity. Admittedly, this process of hurried growth may give rise to some distortions, and the system may also end up by being over-regulated. The second phase would therefore be a phase of deregulation, of rationalisation and simplification of controls, a phase in which distortions inherited from the first phase also need to be corrected. It is only after the system settles down to a new equilibrium in an environment of a good degree of autonomy for different financial institutions that one can begin to think in terms of the third phase of total liberalisation.

Looked at from a macroeconomic perspective, the 1970s and 1980s may be said to constitute the first phase in India's financial history. A quick review of the performance of the financial sector during this period also shows that the increased role of the public sector in the financial system has, far from retarding, actually accelerated financial growth. There is empirical evidence to support this thesis from the experience of other countries as well. Furthermore, it would be my endeavour to show that the Indian financial system is poised to enter the second phase of its development in the 1990s; and to think in terms of total financial liberalisation at this stage would be premature, notwithstanding the current fashion.

In the process of assessing the growth of the financial system, ushered in by *dirigiste* policies adopted during the last two decades, it has also been possible to sketch the broad contours of the financial scenario as it would emerge in the 1990s; as a corollary, an agenda for financial reform is also provided with a view to ensuring that the financial sector plays its supportive role in sustaining economic growth in the 1990s.

The outlook for growth in the 1990s is on the whole encouraging, notwithstanding the balance of payments constraints and persistence of inflation evidenced during the last two years of the Seventh Plan. The Seventh Plan period witnessed a record average annual growth of around 5.5 per cent in real national income, perhaps signalling a breakthrough from the so-called "Hindu rate of growth" of 3.5 per cent for the first three decades of planning. Industrial growth was around 8 per cent and export growth around 10 per cent. Both these indicators are perhaps suggestive of sustainability of high growth during the coming years, given the right mix of policies. The focus of our planning has been on "growth with equity," but recently some apprehensions have been expressed as to whether the acceleration of growth during these last four or five years following industrial liberalisation has resulted in a degree of de-emphasis on equity considerations. These characteristics of growth in the Seventh Plan period should therefore set the tone for shaping the financial system in the 1990s.

Banking Developments: The Indian Experience

The financial sector plays a crucial role in economic development. Monetary and credit policies accelerate the process of growth by influencing the supply and uses of credit, combating inflation, and maintaining balance of payments equilibrium. For monetary policy to be effective, however, developing countries must first improve their credit systems. Developing countries start with an initial handicap: their financial system is too narrowly restricted and is generally geared to provide credit only to large industries, plantations and foreign trade.[2] Such credit facilities are not available to the farm sector, small industries and retail trade. Banks and financial institutions should therefore both widen and deepen their operations so that credit facilities are greatly enlarged; and also that actual and potential savings are mobilised and channelled into productive uses.

At the initial stage of development of an economy, building up of the institutional framework thus needs to be accorded overriding priority. Extension of the commercial banking network, co-operative credit institutions and mutual funds are designed to remedy the situation. Such efforts are particularly warranted in the rural sector. By evolving a well-differentiated institutional infrastructure, the imperfections of the money and capital markets would be reduced. Furthermore, remodelling of the financial system is also needed with a view to ensuring that resources flowing through it are allocated among different sectors/sub-sectors in consonance with the development strategies.

It is against the background of this conceptual framework that the growth of the financial system in India needs to be assessed. The last two decades, the 1970s and 1980s, mark a distinct phase of active state intervention in the building up of the institutional infrastructure. Most remarkable is the progress that banking has made during the last two decades since the nationalisation of 14 major commercial banks in 1969. Banking has shed its erstwhile urban-elitist image and has emerged as a more potent instrument of economic growth and distributive justice. Even recognising the limitations of the ability of financial engineering to transform the economy, the dramatic growth of banking during this period deserves to be commended especially because, for the Indian pattern, there were no models to copy from or practices to emulate. The role of banks in India has been widened to such an extent that it has transcended the conventional concept of "financial intermediation."

Those of us who have been witnesses to the growth of banking in India during the last two decades do not seem to adequately appreciate the dramatic changes that have been brought about in the profile of Indian banking. Penetration of semi-urban and rural areas through extension of the branch network on a scale unprecedented in the history of world banking, bringing about a structural transformation in the sectoral distribution of credit, thereby augmenting sizeably the flow of credit to small farmers, small enterprises and the self-employed, and mobilisation of savings—these are substantial changes indeed. The total number of functioning bank offices was only 8,262 in June 1969; this number soared to more than 56,000 branches by June 1988. Moreover, nearly 60 per cent of the branches are in rural and semi-urban areas. The average population served by a bank office has declined from 64,000 in 1969 to 12,000 in 1988.

A significant structural transformation has also taken place in the sectoral distribution of credit.[3] The share of large and medium industries in total bank credit which was around 61 per cent in March 1968 has now declined significantly to about 38 per cent in 1982. Simultaneously, the share of priority sectors, which include agriculture and small industries, rose from a mere 11 per cent to nearly 46 per cent in 1988. Lending to the agricultural sector is particularly significant because in the pre-nationalisation era, commercial banks did not regard such lending as their legitimate business. Today, the banking system is servicing more than 17 million agricultural accounts, and the total number of borrower accounts under priority sectors adds up to 31.6 million. The procedures and practices of lending have therefore been suitably modified to attune banks to lend to the rural sector and to small businesses.

Over these two decades, commercial banks have also emerged as the single most important channel through which savings of the household sector are being mobilised. In fact, the role played by commercial banks has been critical in raising the rate of savings of the economy to an impressive level of 22 per cent of national income. The dramatic rise in the gross domestic savings from hardly 10 per cent in the 1950s to more than 20 per cent in 1970s is largely attributable to the contribution of commercial banks.[4] Two indicators of this role may be given in this context. First, commercial banks' deposits as a percentage of national income at current prices rose from 17 per cent in 1970 to about 47 per cent in 1988. Second, commercial banks' deposits as a proportion of gross financial savings of the household sector rose from 18 per cent to more than 62 per cent during this period.

The Indian experience of banking development may be regarded as unique for the following four reasons: first, for the Indian pattern of banking development there were no models to copy from or practices to emulate. Credit planning in the broad sense of planned allocation of credit among sectors has emerged as a strategic instrument for guiding both fixed and working capital allocation among sectors broadly in alignment with the plan priorities. Second, the role of banks has been widened to such an extent that it has transcended the conventional concept of "financial intermediation." In fact, banking has been converted into an instrument for economic and social development.[5] Banks are called upon to assume, and have actually assumed, a variety of tasks which in the pre-nationalisation period may not have been regarded as the legitimate responsibility of a credit institution. Support extended to the various anti-poverty programmes like the Integrated Rural Development Programme (IRDP), Self-Employment Programme for Educated Unemployed Youth (SEEUY) is a case in point. Third, an element of cross-subsidisation has been built into the administered interest rate structure. The extent of concessionality in interest rate is linked to the size of the loan and the degree of priority accorded to the sector. Lending to the rural sector in particular is characterised by a high degree of subsidisation. For instance, in contrast to the minimum lending rate of 16 per cent to large and medium industries, lending rates for agriculture vary from 10 to 14 per cent, depending on the size of the loan. The following sub-sectors attract only 10 per cent interest: short-term loans to farmers up to Rs 7,500; and also term loans for minor irrigation to small farmers; loans up to Rs 25,000 for small-scale industries in backward areas, and advances under the poverty alleviation programmes like the IRDP. Finally, this transformation in the profile of Indian banking has been brought about by conscious policy decisions. The growth of banking was supply-induced, rather than demand-following. The switch away from the magic of market mechanism guided by the criterion of maximisation of profit to *dirigiste* financing has been an important contributory factor in this transformation.

Thus, Indian banking in the last two decades provides a unique example of harmoniously blending commercial banking with social banking. Such blending was, in a sense, a historical necessity because commercial banking prior to nationalisation was highly elitist, catering primarily to large and medium industries, and wholesale trade. The agricultural sector, which used to contribute some 50 per cent of national income, was virtually bypassed. The conversion of elitist banking into mass banking during the last two decades can thus be regarded as a correction of historical distortion. The phenomenal expansion of bank branches, extension of credit at concessional rates of interest to priority sectors and to weaker sections, and coverage of a large number of small borrowers—all of these are achievements of which the banking system would justly be proud. In fact, wider disbursement of credit, both spatially and in terms of categories of borrowers, has to be viewed in the overall perspective of promoting a broad-based growth process in the sense of encouraging decentralised and dispersed development. The impact of banking development on the economy runs too deep to be measured by a couple of indicators; it could be regarded as part of the process of modernisation of the economy. It is easy to take these changes for granted now, but they seem mountainous in retrospect.

EMERGENCE OF OTHER FINANCIAL INSTITUTIONS

Over the years, the financial system in India has also become more sophisticated, in response to the varied needs of the economy. The system comprises of a wide range and a large number of financial institutions. At the apex is the Reserve Bank of India (RBI). Commercial banks have a dominant role, holding as they do 40 per cent of the total financial assets. Other important financial institutions include development finance institutions at the all-India, regional and state level, the insurance corporations, mutual funds such as the Unit Trust of India (UTI), and the Post Office Savings Bank.

This institutional framework was further streamlined by the emergence, during the last couple of years, of new institutions designed to cater to the increasingly sophisticated needs of the economy. To begin with, many banks set up in 1987–88 subsidiaries/joint ventures for undertaking specialised financial services such as merchant banking, leasing, mutual funds, venture capital and housing finance. The provision of these new financial services reflects the responsiveness of the financial system to the growing and varied needs of the economy, as also its endeavour to diversify and upgrade its services.

The National Housing Bank (NHB) was established in July 1988: its responsibilities include, *inter alia*, promotion and development of specialised housing finance institutions, mobilisation of resources for housing, provision of refinance facilities for housing finance institutions and scheduled banks, and extension of credit for housing, in particular for the economically weaker sections of society.

In April 1988, the RBI, in collaboration with commercial banks and financial institutions, set up the Discount and Finance House of India (DFHI) Ltd, as a first step towards developing a secondary market for money market instruments. DFHI commenced its operations by providing initially a secondary market in two money market instruments, namely 182-day treasury bills and short-term commercial bills. More recently, it has also been functioning as a broker in the inter-bank money market, attempting to equilibrate short-term surpluses and deficits of individual banks.

Yet another institution set up in 1988 was the Credit Rating Information Services of India Ltd (CRISIL), promoted jointly by the Industrial Credit and Investment Corporation of India (ICICI) Ltd., and the Unit Trust of India (UTI). Credit rating can play an important role in protecting investors by providing information on risk. It could also be beneficial to companies by helping them to raise funds more easily depending on their performance; companies with satisfactory performance would benefit in terms of lower costs of funds. Credit rating would thus foster financial discipline, improve financial information and facilitate larger direct mobilisation of funds by the corporate sector.

The Securities and Exchange Board of India (SEBI), which came into existence in April 1988, is designed to build up investors' confidence, which is a necessary pre-condition for enabling the corporate sector to raise larger resources from the capital market. Its establishment is a major step towards correcting structural weaknesses in the functioning of the stock exchanges, which have been largely responsible for the violent swings in share prices—swings which are unwarranted by the underlying fundamentals. With the effective functioning of SEBI—the necessary legislation is yet to be enacted—it is hoped that a more orderly growth of the stock exchanges would be ensured.

At this stage, a word about the capital market for which the 1980s have been a period of phenomenal growth. The impetus to growth witnessed in the past decade was provided in the early 1970s, when a revision of the Foreign Exchange Regulation Act (FERA) limited the expansion of the foreign-controlled companies and required them to dilute their equity. Spurred by this initial impetus, the market gained additional momentum in the 1980s, as a result of various measures introduced to stimulate both the demand for and supply of shares. These measures included incentives for equity and debenture issues, including a reduction in the corporate tax, and raising of the permitted interest rate of debentures well above that for time deposits of banks. General fiscal incentives were also provided to investors.

The sea change that has come about in the Indian capital market can be judged from the fact that resources raised jumped from only about Rs 220 crore in 1980 to some Rs 5,200 crore in 1988–89. The number of stock exchanges doubled from eight to 16. In fact, in 1987, India's stock exchanges listed more companies (6,017) than the stock markets of any other country except the United States (7,181). The buoyancy of the market during the decade is also reflected in the manifold rise in market capitalisation from about Rs 6,750 crore in 1980 to some Rs 52,000 crore in 1988. Equally impressive has been the growth in the shareholding population—from about three million in 1983–84 to an estimated 40 million in 1989.

Finally, data relating to the evolution of the financial system since 1969 show the increased "financialisation" of the Indian economy and indicate that the interventionist policy in the financial sector has, far from retarding development, actually assisted the acceleration of development. This is reflected in the ratio of assets of financial institutions to GDP, which rose gradually from 38 per cent in 1950 to 73 per cent in 1975, then sharply to 103 per cent in 1980.[6] Moreover, between 1968 and 1980 the growth rate of assets of financial institutions was 8.5 per cent per annum, as compared to the secular growth rate of 7.2 per cent for the period 1950–80. In fact, if the period 1975–80, when the impact of branch expansion of banks was at its peak, is taken separately, the growth rate proves to be as high as 10.7 per cent. This deepening of the financial system is largely attributable to increase in the assets of commercial banks and, to some extent, to emergence of other financial intermediaries discussed earlier.

DISTORTIONS IN GROWTH OF FINANCIAL SYSTEM

While the achievements in evolving a well-differentiated financial system during the last two decades have been undoubtedly impressive, it should be conceded, at the same time, that financial developments have tended to be episodic, fragmentary and structurally loose. This can be concretely illustrated with reference to some distortions which have erupted in the financial system. Again, in the first place, these are "dynamic distortions" in the sense of their being a result of over-zealous attempts to develop a particular segment of the financial market. Second, the scenario of policy-making in India is replete with instances of *ad hoc* measures taken in isolation from the macroeconomic parameters and the financial sector is no exception. Some of the distortions, which we will discuss shortly, are a result of this *ad hoc*ism. Three such distortions have been chosen for discussion here: de-emphasis on commercial banks, distortion in the interest rate structure, and mobilisation of resources by UTI. Although in terms of their impact there is an element of overlap, it is convenient to discuss them separately.

(i) De-emphasis of Commercial Banks

The starting point of the discussion is the de-emphasis on commercial banks witnessed in more recent years, as a result of which a sizeable slice of resources which would have in the normal course been mobilised by banks is now being diverted to mainly two areas: non-banking companies and the capital market.

In recent years, there has been a growth of the so-called finance companies. Such companies are classified as non-banking non-financial companies and non-banking financial companies, the deposit-taking activities of which have gained momentum, particularly in the southern states like Karnataka, Kerala and Tamil Nadu. These companies offer significantly more attractive deposit rates than banks are permitted to offer. Available data show that such deposits have doubled during the last four years to reach a level of around Rs 24,000 crore in 1988. What is more, in recent years, the average incremental deposits have ranged between Rs 3,000 and Rs 3,500 crore per year. Some in-depth studies have brought out clearly that, barring a few good companies, there are various undesirable features of the operations of other companies, particularly

TABLE 24.1: GROWTH OF COMMERCIAL BANKS—SELECTED INDICATORS

	June 1969	June 1980	Latest
Number of commercial banks	89	153	289 (June 1988)
Scheduled commercial banks	73	148	275 (June 1988)
Of which: Regional rural banks	–	73	196 (June 1988)
Non-scheduled commercial banks	16	5	3 (September 1988)
Number of offices in India	8,262	32,419	56,282 (December 1988)
Of which: Rural	183	15,105	31,641 (December 1988)
Population per office (in thousands)	64	21	12
Deposits of scheduled commercial banks in India (Rs crore)	4,646	33,37	1,39,430 (March 1989)
Credit of scheduled commercial banks in India (Rs crore)	3,599	22,068	83,805 (March 1989)
Advances to priority sector (Rs crore)	504	7,278	29,351 (April 1988)
Share of priority sector advances in total credit of scheduled commercial banks (per cent)	14.0	33.0	45.7 (June 1988)

the so-called blade companies in Kerala. Even apart from the flow of credit to non-priority areas and speculative activities, instances are not lacking where depositors have come to grief.

It is high time that such companies should be made to realise that permission given to them to accept deposits from the public is a privilege which should not be misused. The need for closer scrutiny and strict supervision of the operations of such companies cannot be overemphasised. Mere credit rating of such companies is not the answer, because credit rating provides only a snapshot picture of the financial position of the companies, whereas what is really required is a permanent machinery which conducts inspection and corrects the undesirable features on a continuing basis. At present, neither the government, nor the RBI, has such an inspection apparatus. It is high time that the RBI is invested with adequate powers to conduct such inspection on a continuing basis.

In fact, the situation is potentially explosive and if suitable regulatory measures are not put in place immediately, investors' confidence might be shaken. In this context, it would not be out of place to refer to the recent savings and loan industry crisis in the US. It may be recalled that plans for the biggest federal bailout of US savings and loan associations were given the go-ahead in

August 1988; the cost was estimated to exceed 200 billion dollars. In India, without adequate prudential supervision on a continuing basis, aggressive financial entrepreneurs are likely to rush into high-risk areas with all its dire consequences. This aspect of establishing a regular supervision apparatus should therefore be accorded high priority in the 1990s.

Turning to the capital market, the decade of the 1980s has clearly established the cult of equity in India. The widening and deepening of the capital market, tax incentives and tax liberalisation, and issue of tax-free securities and the emergence of new mutual funds have all helped the process of strengthening the capital market. During the last year of the Seventh Plan (1989–90) alone, total resources of about Rs 8,000 crore were raised. It is estimated that during the Eighth Plan period Rs 50,000 crore could be raised, the share of the private sector being Rs 35,000 crore and that of public sector undertakings some Rs 15,000 crore.

While efforts towards development of the capital market are indeed necessary and laudatory, what should not be overlooked is that such development should be on healthy lines. Two worrying features of the capital markets need to be underlined in this context. First, during the stock market boom in 1985 and 1986, some fly-by-night entrepreneurs were able to pass on sub-standard issues to gullible investors. The average investor in India is not yet sophisticated enough to discriminate between the good and the not-so-good scrips, with the result that the investor once bitten is twice shy, and this is hardly conducive to the promotion of savings in the long run. From this point of view, there was an imperative need to establish a machinery for verifying the claims of companies issuing new shares and also for regulating trading practices of brokers. SEBI, when it starts functioning effectively, should be able to fill this lacuna and build investors' confidence.

The second feature relates to a "kink" in the recent boom of the capital market. The so-called mega issues which figured prominently in 1989—for instance, a couple of issues in the month of October 1989 themselves exceeded Rs 1,900 crore—have resulted in the following distortions. First, resources raised are unrelated to the stream of investment expenditure, and hence, the corporate sector becomes highly liquid as a consequence of mega issues. The resources raised can be used for other purposes like takeover of existing companies rather than for development of new enterprises/companies. Second, such large issues at one point of time have unsettling effects on the banking sector's liquidity. Apprehensions have been expressed that the recent buoyancy in the capital market has led to dis-intermediation in the sense of resources raised through the capital market bypassing the banking system and directly entering the inter-corporate market. Third, resources raised by mutual funds, particularly the UTI, have also been sizeable; one scheme of UTI's alone was able to net about Rs 2,000 crore in

1989. Here is therefore a case of too much money chasing too few "blue chips," with all its consequent distortions. Fourthly, when these mutual funds deposit their funds temporarily with banks, this "hot" money itself causes "noise" in the even pace of accrual and disbursal of resources of the banking system, the dimensions of inflow and outflow being both unpredictable and sizeable.

Overall, the current euphoria of the development of the capital market needs to be tempered by more pragmatic considerations. The demands put forward by those who are overenthusiastic to develop the capital market—that banks should be encouraged to lend with a view to enabling the borrower to acquire shares/ stocks, or that they should be allowed to underwrite issues without any of the present limitations—should be eschewed.

To put the role of stock markets in a proper perspective, it should be underlined that throughout the capitalist world the bulk of corporate investment is financed by retained earnings. Studies by OECD and economists like Andrew Glyn of Oxford University suggest the irrelevance of the level of share prices for the determination of investment.[7] Thus, the role of stock markets in financing new investments, as against takeovers, and other speculative operations, is very slight. Even its barometric role as a measure of business confidence has diminished in the developed economies. Especially in India, the term-lending institutions continue to play the lead role in propelling new investment; for instance, financial assistance sanctioned by Development Finance Institutions (DFIs) rose from only Rs 1,360 crore in 1978–79 to Rs 14,200 crore in 1988–89. In such a context, it is all the more necessary to proceed cautiously in developing the capital market on healthy lines.

(ii) Distortions in the Interest Rates Structure

A number of new savings instruments have been introduced in recent years, such as the National Savings Scheme, deposits with the post office, Relief Bonds, and Indira Vikas Patra. In the case of many of these instruments, the element of fiscal concessions is substantial; the net return on some of these may work out to as high as 35 per cent for savers in the high income brackets. Even subsidiaries of commercial banks offer net yields of 15 to 18 per cent on deposits of five years, apart from company deposits to which a reference was made earlier. While the offer of a wide spectrum of savings instruments to cater to different target groups of savers is indeed welcome, what is undesirable is that the emerging yield pattern openly discriminates against banks.

If, in the past, commercial banks emerged as the single largest claimant of household sector's savings, this was due, to a great extent, to the fact that banks offered suitable avenues for investment of medium-term savings. In fact, over the years, the five-year deposit came to assume overwhelming importance in the deposit-mix of banks; deposits of three years and above formed only 25 per cent of term deposits in 1969, but this percentage rose to more than 70 in 1984–85. The average saver, particularly in the semi-urban and rural areas is a "one-institution man," and, over the years, banks have assiduously built up this relationship of trust and confidence. Unfortunately, this category of deposits of medium-term maturity was abolished in April 1987, after which date banks began to offer a ceiling rate of 10 per cent interest on all deposits for periods of two years and above. This had a destabilising impact and the deceleration in deposits growth in the subsequent period is largely attributable to this abolition. The crude elasticity of *real* deposits—that is, nominal deposits adjusted for inflation—with respect to real national income has declined perceptibly over the recent period; the elasticity which was around 2.9 per cent in the Fourth Plan period, declined significantly to 1.7 per cent in the Seventh Plan period. In modern banking, it is pointless to argue about the so-called mismatch between maturity profiles of assets and liabilities. After all, the "cash credit system" in India is a sort of perpetual credit system. In any case, taking the historical relationship between the average saver and the commercial banks, there is a strong case for restoring the five-year deposit category, with an appropriate rate of interest, say around 12 per cent.

At the same time, the net yields on the whole range of savings instruments should be brought broadly in alignment with this rate for medium-term deposits with banks. Some instruments of savings may have a marginal edge over medium-term deposits but certainly not the unjustifiably high differential as at present. In fact, it is preferable to offer a clearly set out structure of relatively high *nominal* interest rates reflecting maturity and liquidity, without excessive fiscal concessions.[8] Low nominal interest rates with large fiscal concessions, as at present, only unnecessarily raise the cost to the government of mobilisation of resources. This reform in the interest rate structure is overdue.

The trouble with the financial system is that notwithstanding the progress made in the sphere of "social banking," the system has continued to remain generous to the large and sophisticated clientele. Two instances may be cited to substantiate this point. First, the interest rate on savings deposits—a facility which the average individual saver uses—has remained frozen at 5 per cent since 1977, notwithstanding the inflation in the subsequent period of 12 years. On the other hand, the interest rate on three months' deposit has been raised to 8 per cent since 11 October 1989. Furthermore, under the facility of Certificates of Deposits (CDs), introduced recently, bulk deposits of one crore rupees and above would attract significantly higher rates of interest, for maturity periods between three months and one year. There is thus a premium on bigness. The second instance pertains to the cost of borrowing to the corporate entities. Under the prevailing corporate tax system, interest paid on borrowed capital is deductible as business expenditure, and hence the effective cost of borrowed capital to the company is substantially lower than the nominal rate of interest paid to banks or financial institutions. For instance, for working capital borrowed from banks, if a company is currently paying an interest of 16 per cent, it is effectively paying only about half of the rate. In contrast, take the interest rate charged to Food Corporation of India, whose operations of foodgrains procurement and distribution throughout the country form the sheet anchor of anti-inflationary policy. Distribution of foodgrains at fair prices is mainly designed to protect the vulnerable sections of the population from the ravages of inflation; and yet the interest rate was hiked up from the concessional rate of 10 or 12 per cent, to as high as 14 per cent. This was the impact of the new-fangled zeal for evolving a "market-related" interest rate regime!

(iii) Mobilisation of Resources by UTI

There is an imperative need to lend a proper perspective to the euphoria about the massive flow of funds to the UTI during the last couple of years. For instance, UTI's 1964 scheme alone is estimated to have netted in something like Rs 2,800 crore in 1989, as compared with about Rs 2,000 crore in 1988. How does one reconcile this massive flow with the macro-level state of stagnation in the savings rate at about 21 per cent for the last three years? If one probes underlying factors, the conclusion that emerges is that the fiscal concessions accorded to investment in UTI are a bundle of distortions and the massive flow is largely illusory.

Without going into the details of the technicalities, the main elements of distortions may be sketched. Paradoxically enough, although UTI's ostensible objective is to mobilise investible resources from the household sector, the bulk of the resources appears to flow, in recent years, from the private corporate sector; the corporate sector's share in the total resources mobilised for the 1964 scheme was reported to be as high as 75 per cent in 1989, as compared to about 35 per cent in 1988. This is so because investment in UTI schemes blesses the corporate investor twice. The first aspect relates to the ability of a company to claim deduction under Section 80(M) of the Income Tax Act, 1961; under this provision, if the gross total income of the domestic company includes income by way of dividend from another domestic company, a straight deduction of 60 per cent of the amount is allowed. In other words, on such dividend income from UTI, the company pays only about 20 per cent of the tax.

The second aspect relates to the losses that a company can incur in the course of doing business and the permissibility to set off such losses. It is possible for a company to purchase units of UTI in the secondary market, at a point of time nearer to the declaration of dividend by the UTI, collect the dividend, and claim the benefit of Section 80(M). Subsequently, the company can sell the units in the secondary market at a decidedly lower price and incur a loss. Such transactions are in the nature of "non-speculative business" and hence can be adjusted against other income.

Both these are unmerited fiscal concessions to the corporate sector since there is apparently no "additionality" element in the total genuine resources accruing to the UTI. The flow of funds from and to UTI, motivated by these considerations, represents "hot money" and not funds genuinely intended for investment. Such flows artificially inflate the magnitude of funds accruing to UTI and create an illusion of massive flows. The whole range of transactions also necessarily implies a large float of units in the secondary market, and movements of funds into and out of units also have an unsettling impact on the banking sector's resources.

What is saddening is that the fiscal distortions built into UTI investments are not so much a tribute to the ingenuity of the private corporate sector to outsmart the regulatory framework but concrete evidence of the authorities not taking an integrated view of the financial flows in the economy.

The earlier these *special* fiscal concessions accorded to UTI are done away with, the better it would be for the financial system. In fact, UTI should be placed on par with other mutual funds, so that only those fiscal concessions available to all other mutual funds should be available to UTI.

TABLE 24.2: CRUDE ELASTICITY OF REAL BANK DEPOSITS WITH RESPECT TO REAL INCOME

Period	Average Rate of Growth for the Period (Per Cent)		Crude Elasticity of Real Bank Deposits with Respect to Real National Income (1)/(3)
	Real Aggregate Deposits of Banks	Net National Product at Market Prices (1970–71 Prices)	
	(1)	(2)	(3)
Fourth Five-Year Plan (1969–70 to 1973–74)	10.3	3.5	2.9
Fifth Five-Year Plan (1974–75 to 1978–79)	15.2	5.4	2.8
Sixth Five-Year Plan (1980–81 to 1984–85)	7.9	5.3	1.5
Seventh Five-Year Plan (1985–86 to 1989–90)	10.6	6.1 (1980–81 prices)	1.7

Note: Aggregate deposits of banks are deflated by average wholesale price index (1970–71 = 100) to obtain real aggregate deposits.

Financial Liberalisation: Experience in Other Countries

While the correction of these distortions should be the pre-occupation of the financial policymakers in the 1990s, they have to contend with another important aspect of policy formulation, namely, the plea for financial liberalisation. The apostles of free market also advocate total financial liberalisation, as is clear from the *World Bank Report*, which I quoted earlier. It is contended that financial liberalisation would encourage efficient markets through "deepening" and elimination of "fragmentation" of markets, thereby leading to improvement in both mobilisation of savings and efficiency of investment. This current fashion in contemporary economic policy has also caught on in India, particularly in the wake of the wave of industrial liberalisation which swept the country in the mid-1980s. In this context, it is legitimate to pose the question: what has been the empirical experience? One in-depth study of financial liberalisation experiments of Argentina, Brazil and Uruguay in the 1970s comes to the conclusion that "the profound changes which financial liberalisation and opening up brought about did not translate themselves, despite intentions, into systematically higher savings, or, into clearly improved resource allocation. Indeed, the three experiences came to a close with their financial systems in a shambles."[9] It was realised, only later, that the advocates of liberalisation had totally ignored the unfavourable impact that it would have on savings and investment, through the release of the pent-up demand for consumption. The architects of financial reforms failed to take into account the inevitable increases in consumption that liberalisation would bring about.

Another study relates to Korea, which achieved a sustained growth of more than 8 per cent during the period 1962 to 1984. These growth rates are *not* explained by the existence of liberalised financial markets. To quote from the study: "the major commercial banks were all largely public enterprises... with the result that there was direct government control of virtually every aspect of banking operations. Second, as a means of allocating investment funds according to national priorities, the government resorted to strict control of interest rates and provided extensive preferential credit at subsidised rates."

Even the *World Bank Report* admits: "Korea's heavily regulated financial system was a key instrument in the government's industrial policy of the 1960s and 1970s. Interest rates were controlled and were kept low during this period. A substantial proportion of credit—well above one-third—was directed by the government to designated sectors!"[10] Although financial reforms were introduced in the early 1980s, the loans of commercial banks, even after privatisation, continued to be closely monitored and supervised. Full liberalisation of the financial system began only in late 1988, with most lending rates being freed, although deposit rates are still controlled.

Again, in the case of Japan, during the high growth period between 1953 and 1972, the GNP rose by an average annual rate of 9.2 per cent. "What was particularly interesting for researchers in money and banking was that this rapid economic growth had taken place within a highly regulated financial framework. The time-deposit rate was regulated, entry into bond issue market was regulated, international asset transactions were virtually forbidden and so on!" The "artificial low interest policy" pursued during this period appears to have promoted high growth rates.

These studies chosen from Latin America and Asia clearly indicate that financial liberalisation is not a simple panacea, as some would seem to believe, for improving financial efficiency. More importantly, the Korean experience, also chronicled by the *World Bank Report*, demonstrates the need for a properly phased programme of liberalisation—and in offering an omnibus prescription of liberalisation, the *World Bank Report* has chosen to ignore this lesson. Michel Camdessus, managing director of the International Monetary Fund (IMF) has summed up the position appropriately in the following words: "nowhere does there exist a final edition of the textbook describing the ideal role of the government; on the contrary, the action of the state has to be particularly mindful of the particular circumstances of the country and of the international context!"[11]

My submission is that the Indian financial system suffers from over-regulation and the task in the 1990s would be to deregulate or unshackle the system from myriad regulations. The various distortions that have erupted in the system, which we discussed earlier, clearly indicate that the system is not ripe for liberalisation. Thus, financial liberalisation, no; financial deregulation, yes. That brings us to the agenda for financial reforms in the 1990s.

AGENDA FOR REFORM

Financial reforms are necessary as we seek to raise our savings rate from the present stagnant level of about 22 per cent to, say, 24 per cent of national income, and to secure sustained non-inflationary growth. Some suggestions for reform have already emanated from the discussion on certain segments of the financial sector, and hence I would be content here by merely focusing on the more important of the reforms needed. Basically, the financial sector should continue to remain, in the 1990s, the handmaiden of growth in the real sectors as envisaged in the plans and also of our objective of achieving growth with equity. The financial system would therefore continue to function in a broad regulatory framework and there need be no apologies for adopting this approach.

Foremost among the reforms, it seems to me, is the need to restore the centrality of commercial banks in the financial system, primarily by correcting the distortions in the interest rate structure, discussed earlier. Briefly, the suggestions are that banks be permitted to accept, as in the past, medium-term deposits of say five-year maturity attracting a deposit rate of around 12 per cent. The interest rate on savings deposits could be raised to around 6 or 7 per cent. The net yields on other savings instruments should be brought into broad alignment with these rates. These changes in interest rates, coupled with the corrections of distortions in respect of investments in UTI discussed earlier, should go a long way towards restoring the pre-eminence of banks in the financial system.

There are two distinct advantages in restoring the pre-eminence of banks: first, the writ of the RBI in respect of sectoral deployment of credit runs on commercial banks and not on the resources mobilised by other institutions like the non-banking companies. Second, since the Statutory Liquidity Ratio (SLR) is applicable to resources mobilised by banks, the government would stand to gain; the cost of borrowing to government would be also relatively lower.

The concept of cross-subsidisation of interest rates, which appears to have taken a backseat in more recent years, should re-emerge as the idiom of the interest rate policy. This is the contribution the financial sector could make towards realising the objective of growth with equity. Illustratively, the interest rate on food credit, that is, credit extended for procurement and distribution of foodgrains through the public distribution system, should be brought down from the present level of 14 per cent to say 10 to 11 per cent. To the extent to which this would reduce the carrying costs, it may be possible to reduce the issue prices of foodgrains contributing thereby, directly and indirectly, to the containment of inflation.

Developments in the latter half of the 1980s appear to give the general impression that modernisation of banking means primarily mechanisation-computerisation and installation of automatic teller machines, credit cards and a host of new loan schemes designed to enable borrowers to purchase consumer durables. The stiff competition, as is evidenced by the intense publicity campaigns between foreign banks and some public-sector banks to finance purchase of cars, for instance, makes one wonder whether the consumer durables segment is exempt from the laws of credit restraint—the theme song of credit policy! This heady mixture of technological rhetoric and consumerism contrasts sharply with the banking system's commitments of the previous 15 years to priority sectors and the under-privileged sections of the population. Be that as it may, the minimum that could be done at this stage is to hike up the lending rates for consumer durables to say 18 per cent. This compares with the floor rate of 16 per cent to, say, large industries.

Turning now to the areas of deregulation, it should be conceded that over the years the regulatory framework governing banks has become highly rigid. While this may have been necessary in the period immediately after nationalisation, at the present stage of banking development the rigidity is hampering individual bank's initiative and innovative approach. The RBI has recognised the need to unshackle banks from the regulatory framework: this is reflected in its recent measures of removing the ceiling on lending rate, virtual abolition of the Credit Authorisation Scheme (CAS), and facilitating clientele mobility. This process of deregulation needs to be taken further. First, the present highly complex administered system of interest rates needs to be simplified. Illustratively, the prescribed interest rates which now number about 65 could be easily reduced to some 10 or 12 rates. Second, under selective credit control, an over-elaborate and complex framework has been evolved: the regulations cover some 20 pages of the printed document and even under one commodity, there may be some seven or eight categories to which different margins are applicable. Historically, this may have been a necessity, but over the years, bank executives are familiar with the basic principle of not permitting bank credit to be used for speculative holding of commodities. This document need not be abridged but could be easily scrapped. Starting on a clean slate, simple new regulations, whenever necessary, can be issued for a specific period, say a season or a year, after which the directive should stand automatically terminated. The main purpose in proposing these reforms is to permit a greater degree of operational autonomy to individual banks, within a very broad regulatory framework.

In our efforts to raise the savings rate, the thrust in the coming years will have to be on rural savings. The track record of financial institutions in the area of mobilisation of rural savings is far from satisfactory. For instance, the savings mobilised by rural branches of commercial banks and the regional rural banks have not been commensurate with the expansion in the number of branches. New rural and semi-urban offices accounted for 77 per cent of the total new offices opened between 1964 and 1984, but they accounted for only 37 per cent of the total incremental deposits during the period. Or, looking at the picture differently, although rural branches of commercial banks form some 60 per cent of the total number of offices, they account for only 14 per cent of total deposits.[12] There is a sizeable savings potential in the rural sector, particularly in the agriculturally affluent areas and pockets; and if innovative instruments suited to the pattern of flow of rural incomes and expenditure are devised, it should be possible to ensure larger mobilisation. The approach of financial institutions, particularly banks, to rural savings still remains somewhat alien to the rural milieu. This approach needs to be reoriented.

Finally, there is a medium-term problem which financial institutions have to address. This relates to employment generation. Employment in the organised sector is showing a decelerating trend: the compound growth rate of employment was 2.9 per cent per annum between 1970–71 and 1975–76; it declined to 2.6 per cent in the latter half of the 1970s. The rate fell further to

1.8 per cent in the first half of 1980s and to 1.5 per cent in the second half of the 1980s.[13] Even in the agricultural sector, as Hanumanth Rao has pointed out, there has been a significant decline in the elasticity of employment with respect to agricultural output for the country as a whole.[14] The point is that, in future, employment increases could come about primarily through the promotion of a broad-based growth process in the sense of encouraging decentralised and dispersed development of small industries, self-employment, services, etc. In fact, the whole range of issues relating to the question of bringing the informal sector into the fold of the banking system needs to be fully explored. Financial institutions would have to suitably reorient their lending procedures, practices and programmes to facilitate such growth.

This also raises a whole range of issues pertaining to streamlining rural credit institutions.[15] First, many regional rural banks, which had raised high expectations as low-cost institutions, have proved to be non-viable. In the case of co-operatives, the ardour of co-operative spirit has no doubt dimmed, and in some states that were in the forefront of the movement, the co-operatives have been superseded. Thus, the institutional structure supporting rural credit is passing through a critical stage, warranting a major reform: restructuring some of the non-viable institutions, establishing inter-institutional links, de-bureaucratisation of the co-operative institutions and so on.

The hope for the financial sector in the 1990s seems to lie in taking an integrated view of the flow of resources at the *macro* level and in correcting the distortions which have erupted in some segments. Only thus could we ensure larger mobilisation of financial resources, and their more efficient deployment in broad alignment with the priorities enshrined in the development plans.

Notes and References

(This chapter comprises the text of the author's Lala Lajpat Rai Memorial Lecture delivered in Bombay on 29 January 1990.)

[1] World Bank, *World Development Report, 1989* (Washington, DC: The World Bank, 1989).

[2] N. A. Mujumdar,"Credit Planning: Rationale and Techniques,"1984; included in the author's book, *Money, Savings and Economic Development* (Bombay, 1989).

[3] N. A. Mujumdar, "Structural Transformation in the Deployment of Credit: Some Implications,"1982; included in the author's book, *Money, Savings and Economic Development* (Bombay, 1989).

[4] N. A. Mujumdar, T. R. Venkatachalam, and M. V. Raghavachari, "The High Saving Phase of the Indian Economy, 1976–79: An Exploratory Interpretation,"1980; included in the author's book, *Money, Savings and Economic Development* (Bombay, 1989).

[5] N. A. Mujumdar, "Social Banking," *Economic Times* (Bombay), 15 February 1989.

[6] See Filipe Morris, "India's Financial System," World Bank Staff Working Paper, No. 739 (Washington, DC: The World Bank, 1985).

[7] Andrew Glyn, "The Crash and Real Capital Accumulation," *Frontline*, 16–29 April 1988; the role of the stock markets came in for unflattering comments in the editorial of the *Financial Times* (London), 17 October 1989.

[8] *Annual Report, 1987–88* (Bombay: Reserve Bank of India, 1988).

[9] Miguel Urrutia (ed.), *Financial Liberalization and the Internal Structure of Capital Markets in Asia and Latin America* (Tokyo: United Nations University, 1988).

[10] *World Development Report, 1989*, Box 9.2 on p. 126.

[11] "Role of Government is to Create Favourable Environment for Growth," *IMF Survey*, 11 December 1989, p. 369.

[12] N. A. Mujumdar, "The Emerging Savings Scenario—Some Key Policy Issues," *Economic Times*, 25 and 26 May 1988; included in the author's book, *Money, Savings and Economic Development* (Bombay, 1989).

[13] "Growth without Employment," *Economic and Political Weekly* 24, no. 48 (2 December 1989), p. 2628.

[14] C. H. Hanumantha Rao, *Technological Change in Indian Agriculture—Emerging Trends and Perspectives* (December 1989).

[15] N. A. Mujumdar, "Rural Credit Policy," *Economic Times*, 14 December 1989.

25

Federal Fiscal Transfers in India

Performance of Six Finance Commissions*

M. Govinda Rao

Introduction

Equity, allocative efficiency, growth and stability have been conceived of as the economic goals of federal finance.[1] In discussions of inter-governmental flow of funds, however, the criterion of equity has remained the mainstay, though some attention has also been given to its consequence on allocative efficiency and economic growth in the federations.

The claims on the equitable resource transfers in a federation have been made mainly in terms of equitable treatment of individuals[2] and of geographical units,[3] and the need to arbitrate against spill overs[4] and to provide for "merit wants."[5] Much of the discussion on equitable transfers, however, has centred around evolving objective distribution formulae to ensure "horizontal equity"[6] of individuals or geographical equity in a federation. The two approaches stem from two different philosophies of the state—"individualistic" and "organic." Whatever be the relative merits of the two approaches, the federal transfers thus effected are intended to be a corrective for the differences in relative fiscal capacities and expenditure needs of the states. This chapter attempts to evaluate the performance of the federal fiscal transfers effected by the six Finance Commissions in India in terms of fulfilling the objective of equity in the sense mentioned above.

* Originally published in *Economic and Political Weekly* 12, no. 31 (30 July 1977), pp. 1226–33.

II

SCOPE OF FINANCE COMMISSIONS

The framers of the Indian Constitution had foreseen the problems that can arise due to the existence of the gap between fiscal capacities and needs of the states and had provided for an impartial semi-judicial body to effect periodic assessment of the fiscal equilibrium of the Centre *vis-à-vis* the states in the Indian federation. Article 280(1) of the Constitution provides for the setting up of the Finance Commission every five years or earlier by the President, consisting of a Chairman and four other members. The Commissions are required to make recommendations to the President regarding:

> (i) the distribution between the Union and the states of the net proceeds of taxes which are to be, or may be, divided between them and the allocation between the states of the respective shares of such proceeds;
> (ii) the principles which should govern the grants-in-aid of the revenue of the states out of the consolidated fund of India;
> (iii) any other matter referred to the Commission by the President in the interest of sound finance.[7]

The Finance Commissions are thus required not only to bridge the gap between the fiscal capacities and needs of the states, but also to look into and arbitrate and settle various other issues which may cause irritation among and between the various constituent units of the federation.

As mentioned in Articles 280(1) (i) and (ii) above, the Finance Commissions are intended to provide a corrective to fiscal disequilibrium through (i) tax-sharing of income tax, which is obligatory, and of Union excise duties, which is permissive under Articles 270 and 272 of the Constitution, and (ii) grants-in-aid of revenue under the substantive clause of Article 275 of the Constitution. Though the Finance Commissions are also required to recommend the distribution of assigned taxes, it is implicit that they are required to distribute them according to the principles of derivation and, therefore, this cannot provide a handle to fulfil the objective of equity.[8]

While the intention of the framers of the Constitution was to bring about an effective corrective to the financial disequilibria of the Centre and the states by providing for the appointment of the Finance Commissions, the scope of the Commissions to a large extent was restricted due to the existence of multiple agencies effecting transference of resources from the Centre to the states. The grants made under Article 282 of the Constitution by the non-statutory permanent body, the Planning Commission, and sizeable loans from the Centre to states under Article 293 of the Constitution reduced the role of the Finance Commissions in the distribution of federal transfers, as can be seen from Table 25.1. Consequently, the role of the Finance Commissions has been relegated to the non-Plan revenue side of the budgets, to inquire into only the fiscal needs arising from the non-Plan expenditures within the revenue accounts of the states.

TABLE 25.1: FEDERAL TRANSFERS TO STATES

(Rs crores)

	Resources Transferred through		Other Transfers	Total
	Finance Commission	Planning Commission		
1951–56	447 (31.2)	880 (61.5)	104 (7.3)	1,431 (100.0)
1956–61	918 (32.0)	1,344 (46.9)	606 (21.1)	2,868 (100.0)
1961–66	1,590 (28.4)	2,738 (49.1)	1,272 (22.5)	5,600 (100.0)
1966–69	1,782 (25.0)	1,917 (27.0)	3,415 (48.0)	7,114 (100.0)
1969–74	5,316 (35.8)	4,230 (28.4)	53.7 (35.8)	14,853 (100.0)
1951–74	10,053 (31.5)	11,109 (31.1)	10,704 (33.4)	31,866 (100.0)

Note: Figures in brackets represent percentages to total transfer.
Source: *Report of the Finance Commission*, 1973, p. 6.

The preferable arrangement of assessing the fiscal gap (in the sense of the difference between the fiscal capacities and needs) of the states would be to have a single agency exercising command over the entire gamut of financial relations between the Centre and the states, encompassing the scrutiny of not only the revenue side of the budgets, but also the capital receipts and outlays of the states. Such a mechanism would enable the Commissions to ensure an effective compromise between the objectives of equity and growth. This is important because the distinctions made between Plan and non-Plan schemes do not really provide any indication as to the "developmental" and "non-developmental" expenditures of the states. Hence, grants recommended by the Planning Commission do not necessarily imply allocations made for achieving the objective of growth. The distinction between revenue and capital expenditures is based on the monetary ceiling of expenditure on a particular project rather than on the maintenance and creation of assets.[9] Besides, there exists a lot of interdependence between Plan and non-Plan expenditures on the one hand, and revenue and capital expenditures on the other.[10] Therefore, federal transfers, if they are to serve as an effective instrument of fiscal policy, should be comprehensively inquired into by a single non-political permanent and impartial body. The lack of such a body is a serious lacuna in the existing arrangement of federal-fiscal relations in India.[11]

Constitutionally, there is nothing that prevents the Finance Commissions from assessing the entire budgetary transactions of the states and recommending federal transfers to meet the excess needs (the needs which cannot be met from their own revenue sources) as a whole. In fact Rajamannar, chairman of the Fourth Finance Commission, observed "it may be said that the more or less arbitrary division of expenditure into capital and revenue does not find a place as such in the Constitution, though the Constitution draws a distinction between grants of capital and recurring sums and also between grants and loans. There is no indication either that the function of the Finance Commission is to be confined to the revenue part of the budgetary needs of a state."[12] He concluded, "There is no legal warrant for excluding from the scope of the Finance Commissions all capital grants; even the capital requirements of a state may be properly met by grants-in-aid under Article 275(1), made on the recommendations of the Finance Commission."[13] Nor is there any legal sanctity for leaving out Plan requirements in the revenue account because the Constitution never envisaged the emergence of the Planning Commission. Therefore, "the legal position... is that there is nothing in the Constitution to prevent the Finance Commission from taking into consideration both capital and revenue requirements of the states in formulating a scheme of devolution and the recommending grants under Article 275 of the Constitution."[14]

For practical considerations, however, the Finance Commissions have come to assess only the non-Plan revenue accounts of the states' budgets. This has been partly forced upon them by their terms of reference. A narrow interpretation of "grants-in-aid of revenue" to cover only the revenue accounts of the states' budgets, apart from the exigencies created due to the multiplicity of agencies with overlapping functions effecting federal transfers, has led to the Finance Commissions' confinement only to the revenue side of the states' budgets.

The emergence of the Planning Commission as a dispenser of Plan assistance has kept the Finance Commissions out of recommending Plan transfers for practical considerations. The terms of reference of the Finance Commissions cannot be entirely blamed in this regard. The terms of reference of the First Finance Commission did not make a mention of Plan requirements, nor did the Commission make any distinction between Plan and non-Plan requirements as it dealt with the revenue expenditure requirements of the states as a whole. But this was due to the fact that developmental planning had then only just begun and the effect of this was not felt by the Commission. The Second Commission was asked to take into account the need arising from the implementation of the Second Plan, and so it did, though it suggested that the roles of the two Commissions should be clearly delineated to avoid overlapping. The Third Finance Commission was also asked to enquire into the needs arising from the Third Plan, but their majority recommendation covering 75 per cent of Plan expenditures falling within the revenue account was rejected and the note of dissent of the member-secretary, leaving out the Plan side of the budgets altogether, was accepted. The Fourth Commission was not specifically asked to inquire into Plan needs. Though the chairman of the Commission felt that the Commission could go into the matter and recommend transfers to cover Plan assistance also, it abstained from doing so for the practical consideration that the Planning Commission specifically constituted for the purpose should have unhampered authority in this domain. The Fifth Finance Commission was specifically excluded, by its terms of reference, from taking account of Plan needs. Though the Commission felt, "As the language of Article 275 stands, there is nothing to exclude from its purview, grants for meeting revenue expenditures on Plan schemes nor is there any explicit bar against grants for capital purposes they did not do so, ... as it would blur the entire division of functions between the Commission and the Planning Commission."[15] The terms of reference of the Sixth Finance Commission required the Commission to recommend grants under Article 275, having regard to, among other considerations, "the existing practice of determining the distribution of Central assistance for financing state Plans." As the allocation of the revenue and capital components of expenditures between the states for the Fifth Plan was not available, the Finance Commission assessed the needs arising from the non-Plan revenue expenditures. The above amply demonstrates that the subdued role of Finance Commissions in deciding Centre–state financial relations was due mainly to hesitancy on the part of the Commissions themselves.[16]

It may be pertinent to refer to whether the Finance Commission can recommend transfers to raise the specific level of services to a "reasonable" level, particularly in backward states. The First, the Third and the Sixth Finance Commissions thought they could. The First Commission recommended grants under Article 275(1), for primary education to eight states.[17] The majority recommendation of the Third Commission provided substantial transfers for the development of communications, but the dissenting note of its member-secretary, G. R. Kamat—that any specific purpose transfer should be routed through the Planning Commission which can, as a permanent body, undertake continuous supervision of the utilisation of funds—was invoked by the government to reject the majority recommendation. Some of the states argued before the Fifth Finance Commission that though the Commissions are excluded from inquiring into the needs arising from the Plan schemes, they can recommend grants to improve the level of specific social services outside the Plan, but the Commission did not agree with this view as it thought it would blur the functions of the Finance Commission. The Sixth Finance Commission, however, interpreted broadly its terms of reference to consider the requirements of raising the standard of general administration in backward states to cover some administrative and social services and welfare of Scheduled Castes and Tribes (SCs and STs).

The rationale for recommending transfers to raise the standards of specific services may be either that these services are "meritorious" enough to justify interference with the choices of the states or that they involve substantial externalities so that their optimal provision will not come about without such interference. In either case, merely enabling the states to provide these services to reach the standard requirements by equalising average expenditures does not *per se* ensure the objective. First of all, the services chosen to be equalised by the Finance Commission are only the administrative heads. They do not represent functionally classified homogeneous expenditure categories and as such are not even strictly comparable between the regions. Further, the effect of specific purpose grants is not different from the effect of block grants, so long as the low level of services provided by the backward states has been essentially due to financial constraints. The necessity of making specific purpose grants arises only when the average level sought to be raised is so high that the removal of the financial constraint does not automatically ensure the desired average levels of these services.[18] But, in such cases, the amount of specific purpose grants that is required to be made should be the equivalent of the desired expenditure on the services because the recipient states would not spend any of their funds on the aided functions. Contrarily, the provision of the shortfall of expenditures from the all-state average level, as was done by the Sixth Finance Commission, would not ensure the average level of expenditure in the backward states which it was sought for.

It is also reasonable to suggest that the states should be enabled to meet the fiscal needs which they are not able to meet from their own resources in accordance with their preferences. This is achieved by devolving adequate funds by means of unconditional transfers rather than aiming at raising the standards of only a few services, which may in some cases distort the preferences of states.[19] Given adequate finances, the states can be expected to allocate the funds in an optimal manner without interference from the Centre.

In short, the chaotic developments in Indian federal finance have resulted in relegating the role of the Finance Commissions merely to considering the fiscal needs arising from non-Plan expenditures within the revenue accounts of the states taking account of the revenues available at the existing rates of taxation. This has seriously limited the employment of inter-governmental transfers as an effective instrument of fiscal policy.

III

Criteria for Federal Transfers

Given that the Finance Commissions' main role is confined to recommending federal transfers to encompass fiscal needs falling within the non-Plan revenue accounts of the states' budgets, it is pertinent to inquire to what extent the successive Finance Commissions have objectively determined federal transfers to attain the objective of effecting interregional equity. The Commissions have been equipped with various "handles" to attain the objective. They can be broadly classified as assigned taxes, shared taxes and grants-in-aid.

(i) *Assigned Taxes*: Assigned taxes, of which the Finance Commissions are required to recommend the *interse* distribution between the states, are the taxes which are levied and collected by the Centre, but which are distributable to the states wholly after deducting the cost of collecting these taxes. In essence, this arrangement is made for administrative convenience, and in effect they have to be considered on the same footing as taxes levied by the Centre but collected and appropriated by the states themselves, such as excise duties on medicinal and toilet preparations, inter-state sales tax, taxes under Indian motor vehicles tax act, etc. The taxes under Article 269 of the Constitution fall into the category of assigned taxes and of the seven taxes mentioned in this Article, only estate duty on non-agricultural property is in vogue at present. The tax on railway fares and freights levied under Railway Passenger Fares Tax Act, 1957, was repealed in 1961 and the tax was merged with the basic fares in accordance with the recommendations of the Railway Convention Committee, and in lieu of this an *ad hoc* grant has been made to the states; similar is the position of additional excise duties in lieu of sales taxes on mill-made textiles, tobacco and sugar in respect of which the states have voluntarily surrendered the right to levy the sales tax by an agreement reached in 1957. This is essentially a tax-rental arrangement wherein the states have voluntarily cleared the field of sales taxation on the said commodities in agreement to receive compensation to be paid by the Centre. In effect, the distribution of these assigned taxes is required to be in conformity with the principle of compensation, and therefore the Finance Commissions need not be expected to effect any interregional redistribution.

(ii) *Shared Taxes and Statutory Grants*: The position regarding the shared taxes and grants, however, is different. The Commissions enjoy unhampered authority in this domain and therefore can effectively employ these handles to bring about the desired objective. As for the tax shares, they can not only determine the distribution between the Centre and the states, but the *interse* distribution is also determined by them. The grants-in-aid of revenue to be made to the states from the consolidated fund of India under the substantive provision of Article 275 is entirely to be determined by the Finance Commissions.

Inconsistency between Objectives and Means

(i) *Method of Devolution*: In spite of the important handles, the working of the Finance Commissions presents a dismal picture. Consequent to the recommendations of the last three Commissions, some rich states ended up with sizeable surpluses in their non-Plan revenue account, as can be seen from Table 25.2. Punjab, Haryana and Maharashtra, the three richest states, have been enjoying sizeable surplus in their non-Plan revenue accounts under the awards of the last three Finance Commissions. The surplus arising in the case of the poorer states of Bihar and Uttar Pradesh on the other hand is due to the inability of these states to provide services at adequate levels, in comparison with other states. This may be broadly inferred from the fact that their per capita expenditures were lower than the states' average expenditures (Table 25.3). This tendency on the part of the Finance Commissions, far from mitigating the inequality in the public services provided between the states, is likely to aggravate it. As the richer states enjoy larger surpluses, their Plan outlay to that extent would be higher, which would further hasten their growth, while the poorer states continue to stagnate. Two reasons may be immediately adduced for this situation. First, rather than considering the financial needs within the revenue accounts of the states in totality, different criteria have been adopted for the distribution of shared taxes and grant-in-aid of revenue. Second, the criteria adopted for the distribution themselves have been inequitable.

There is no reason why different criteria should be adopted at all for tax-sharing and distributing grants. The overall purpose of this devolution being the attainment of interregional equity, measured in terms of providing adequate resources to meet the fiscal needs of the states, there is no reason why different criteria for tax sharing and grants should be applicable. The First Finance

TABLE 25.2: ESTIMATED SURPLUS IN NON-PLAN REVENUE ACCOUNT OF STATES

(Rs crores)

	States	Fourth Finance Commission	Fifth Finance Commission	Sixth Finance Commission
(1)	Bihar	89.25	199.46	–
(2)	Gujarat	8.00	158.99	355.46
(3)	Haryana	*	79.88	223.35
(4)	Madhya Pradesh	–	15.09	110.18
(5)	Maharashtra	215.66	419.29	748.42
(6)	Karnataka	–	–	232.74
(7)	Punjab	29.83	117.22	341.48
(8)	Tamil Nadu	–	–	184.53
(9)	Uttar Pradesh	17.02	280.87	–
(10)	West Bengal	13.97	–	–
		373.73	1,270.80	2,176.16

* Included in the composite state of Punjab.

Sources: Reports of Finance Commissions, 1965 (p. 59), 1969 (p. 65), 1973 (p. 73).

TABLE 25.3: PER CAPITA EXPENDITURES OF THE STATES

(*in Rs*)

States	1961–62	1965–66	1970–71
Andhra Pradesh	25.19	41.14	61.23
Assam	34.77	58.60	80.36
Bihar	17.44	24.95	42.30
Gujarat	31.20	49.61	79.35
Haryana	*	*	80.42
Jammu and Kashmir	53.48	82.20	127.57
Kerala	35.11	44.16	76.77
Madhya Pradesh	24.87	35.11	48.68
Maharashtra	31.93	55.43	88.15
Mysore	40.56	52.04	74.25
Orissa	34.96	47.61	57.70
Punjab	35.95**	60.98**	89.69
Rajasthan	25.79	45.18	82.42
Tamil Nadu	30.21	49.52	71.78
Uttar Pradesh	20.49	32.77	39.11
West Bengal	29.51	43.56	66.93

* Included in the composite state of Punjab.

** Includes Haryana also.

Sources: States' budgets. Population figures for 1965 and 1970 were calculated on the basis of growth rates between 1961 and 1971.

Commission itself, commenting on the weightage to be given to the factor of contribution stated that, "a proper scheme of the devolution of revenue to the states is to make larger funds available to them to meet their expenditure responsibilities."[20] The Fifth Finance Commission also noted, "taken together as a whole they can and must observe the overall purpose of providing the necessary assistance to the states on an equitable basis."[21] The actual approaches followed by the Finance Commissions of adopting different criteria for distributing tax shares and grants between the states, in the light of the above stated objective, seems to be wholly inconsistent.[22]

Even if the provisions of the Constitution are strictly interpreted to mean that different criteria should be adopted in regard to shared taxes irrespective of needs,[23] in contrast to the principles to be adhered to in the distribution of grants, the Finance Commissions can still recommend resource transfers to serve the overall purpose of interregional equity by keeping the tax-share components in the total devolution down to the barest minimum and expanding the share of grants-in-aid. Contrary to this approach, the suggestions made by the "Administrative Reforms Commission"[24] and endorsed by the Rajamannar Committee Report,[25] if followed, would lead to the furthering of the income disparities between the states if the criteria adopted for *interse* distribution between the states are not drastically changed.

(ii) *Criteria for Fiscal Devolution—Shared Taxes*: The shared taxes comprise obligatorily sharable income tax and permissively sharable Union-excise duties. Table 25.4 summarises the percentage distribution of the net proceeds from these taxes between the Centre and the states and the criteria adopted to distribute the states' share among the states by the six Finance Commissions constituted hitherto. Let us now examine how far the criteria adopted by the Commissions have been equitable.

TABLE 25.4: (A) AWARD OF THE FINANCE COMMISSION IN RESPECT OF DISTRIBUTION OF INCOME TAX

(in percentages)

Finance Commissions	Net Proceeds Distribution to the States	Criteria for Distribution	
		Population	Collection/ Assessment
First	50	80	20
Second	50	90	10
Third	66.67	80	20
Fourth	75	80	20
Fifth	75	90	10
Sixth	80	90	10

(B) AWARD OF THE FINANCE COMMISSIONS IN RESPECT OF DISTRIBUTION OF UNION EXCISE DUTIES

Finance Commissions	Coverage	States' Share (Per Cent)	Criteria for Distribution			Others
			Population	Per Capita Income	Economic or Social Backwardness	
First	Tobacco, matches and vegetable products	40	100	–	–	–
Second	Sugar, coffee, tea, paper, veg non-essential oils added to the above	25	90	–	–	10 adjustment
Third	All commodities yielding Rs 50 lakhs per year, except motor spirit	20	Population is major criteria; other are financial weakness, disparity in development, per cent of SCs			

(Contd)

Table 25.4 (Contd)

Finance Commissions	Coverage	States' Share (Per Cent)	Criteria for Distribution			Others
			Population	Per Capita Income	Economic or Social Backwardness	
Fourth	All items excluding regulatory duties, special excises and earmarked cases	20	80	–	20	–
Fifth	For 1969–70 to 1971–72 all items excluding regulatory duties, special excises and duties and cases earmarked cesses; for 1972–73 and 1973–74 all including special excises but excluding regulatory duties and cases earmarked cesses	20	80	13.3	6.7	–
Sixth	For 1974–75 and 1975–76 all articles levied excluding auxiliary duties for excise and cases levied under special acts and earmarked for special purposes. For 1976–77 to 1978–79 all including auxiliary duties but excluding cesses levied under special acts and earmarked for special purposes	20	75	–	25	–

The criteria for distributing the income tax share among the states have been in the main population and collection or assessment. Population was considered to be a broad measure of need, and collection or assessment was to compensate at least in part for the drain of incomes of local origin due to income tax. Similarly, in the case of Union excise duties population came to be accepted as the most important criterion. Indices of economic and social backwardness or financial backwardness also received some attention from the Finance Commissions.

"Population" is at best a neutral criterion and can serve as an index of need only when it is assumed that the existing discrepancies in fiscal capacities and needs of the states are in conformity with the social norm. Providing of compensation for the drain in incomes of local origin by assigning some weight to collection or assessment has consistently favoured by the rich urban states. This the Finance Commissions did in spite of the assertion by the First Finance Commission that "in our view, there is no question of considering distribution of the tax on the basis of returning to particular state the whole or part of the collection in its area or on the basis of the states having a notional right to the concurrent levy of income tax.... There is no question of any compensation or reimbursement in India where the former provinces, now part A states, at any rate, never possessed any right to tax incomes; even in part B states the integration did not countenance the theory of compensation either in respect of federal assets or federal revenues passing to the Centre."[26] When actually recommending distribution of income tax proceeds among states, the Commission, however, contended that "the relevance of the factor of contribution in the distribution of a shared tax will be generally acknowledged"[27] and assigned 20 per cent weightage to collection, in spite of its being aware of the shortcomings of this measure, to the sheer advantage of some rich urban states. The Second Commission also reiterated, "There is no legal basis for the ... claim that the Union is in some way required to return to the state the income-tax attributable to them after retaining its share,"[28] but in order not to cause a sudden break in continuity, it too assigned 10 per cent weightage to the factor of collection. The Third Finance Commission felt that with the exclusion of tax on income paid by the companies from the divisible pool, the shared tax on incomes of local origin in the total yield had increased substantially, and hence higher weightage should be given to the factor of contribution. It therefore gave 20 per cent weightage to collection. The Fourth Commission maintained the same position, while the Fifth took assessment instead of collection as a measure of contribution and reduced the weightage to 10 per cent. The Sixth Commission did not alter the recommendation of the previous Commission in respect of *interse* distribution of income tax proceeds.[29]

In respect of distribution of proceeds from Union excise duties, population has been assigned predominant weightage. The Third, Fourth, Fifth and Sixth

Commissions also gave weightage to some criteria of social, economic and financial backwardness of the states to compensate for their financial needs. Such an approach provides only a patchwork and does not consider comprehensively the needs of the states.

(iii) *Criteria for the Distribution of Statutory Grant*: If the criteria adopted by the Finance Commissions regarding the *interse* distribution of shared taxes have been to the advantage of the rich urban states, the "revenue gap" filling approach to the distribution of statutory grants cannot be said to be equitable either.

The procedure for determining the grants-in-aid under Article 275 of the Constitution was explicitly laid down by the First Finance Commission. Accordingly, the Finance Commissions start from the budgetary forecasts submitted by the states. After making adjustment in respect of "abnormal,""unusual" and "non-recurrent" items of receipts and expenditures to ensure inter-state comparability, the Finance Commissions, as laid down by the First Commission, are supposed to make allowances for "tax effort,""expenditure economy,""average standard of social services" achieved in states and special obligations of the states.[30] Finally, the budgetary gap is to be determined after devolving the assigned and shared taxes. Grants-in-aid to the states are then made to fill this residuary budgetary gap.

Even the method of determining the gap between the projected revenue and expenditure forecasts as adopted by the Finance Commissions is fraught with important weaknesses. First, the forecasts as provided by the individual states, which are accepted with only minor modifications by the Finance Commissions generally, are not comparable among the states. The states are not required to adopt a uniform methodology or concepts. Eventually, they are likely to provide forecasts to the Finance Commissions made with varying assumptions and employing different methodologies. Thus, the estimates of budgetary gap which form the basis of the Finance Commissions' federal transfers are really not comparable.

The second important weakness emanates from the procedure of considering only time as the "determinant" of the revenue and expenditures of the states. Different assumptions and methodologies apart, the states generally project their own revenues and expenditures to be supplied to the Finance Commissions on the basis of the expected growth rates. In fact, the Sixth Finance Commission, unlike the previous Commissions, practically re-estimated the states' revenues and expenditures on the basis of the observed, and in some cases expected, growth rates. Assuming relative price stability, the expenditures and revenues of the states are assumed to conform to their past behaviour with respect to time, and thus the forecasts for the relevant period are made. Such a procedure is objectionable on two grounds. First, it is not known to what extent the forecasts assuming time to be the only determinant of the states' revenues and expenditures are realistic and hence reliable. A host of economic, social, political and cultural factors determine the revenues and expenditures of the states, and subsuming all these factors into a single variable "time" may not explain the changes in revenues and expenditures as much as when these determinants are considered. Explanatory power being the main criterion of prediction, to get more accurate predictions, various "plausible determinants" of revenues and expenditures of the states should be included in the analysis of revenues and expenditures. Second, the devolutions made on the basis of the forecasts made by assuming price stability have been consistently found to have been eroded in real terms due to the continuous rise in the price levels.[31]

The major weakness, however, emanates from the fact that budgetary gap has been taken to be the bedrock of statutory grants. Though the "unexceptionable" principles such as "tax effort,""expenditure economy" and "standard of social services provided" have been approved by succeeding Finance Commissions, none, in fact, put them into practice satisfactorily. The First Commission did not consider the tax efforts of the states due to operational difficulties. The Second Commission assumed that "if a state raised additional revenue which it has promised for the Plan, it will have done its part,"[32] though it is not clear whether the defaulting states have been penalised at all for their laxity. The Third Finance Commission felt that to determine the states' relative tax effort "it has to be related to their tax potential, and this calls for a special study," and that therefore "an independent Commission should be constituted."[33] The Fourth Finance Commission abdicated responsibility in favour of the Planning Commission altogether. The Fifth Commission was the only one that considered tax efforts by relating the states' own tax revenues to the index of taxable capacity of the states—the states' income with some allowance made for agricultural incomes.[34] However, the Commission did not indicate the exact weightage given to this factor in distributing the grants. The Sixth Commission, rather than improving upon the effort index initiated by the previous Commission, ignored it, on the practical consideration that the application of a formula based on relative tax efforts, however designed, would place at a disadvantage some of the states faced with big gaps on non-Plan revenue accounts.[35] Thus all the six Commissions ignored the tax effort factor in recommendations of federal transfers. This fact is also true of another "unexceptionable" principle enunciated by the First Commission, the "expenditure economy."

There was nothing in the Constitution that called upon the Finance Commissions to recommend grants to cover budgetary gaps. Rather than covering the excess of fiscal needs of the states over their own revenue capacities objectively, the Commissions assumed the role of mere mechanical gap fillers. It may be very pertinent to ask what after all such an approach of mechanical gap-filling is intended to achieve. Mere establishment of budgetary balance on the non-Plan revenue accounts of the states cannot be expected to bring about attainment of the objective of equity, the role which the framers of the Constitution envisaged for the Finance Commissions.

If, on the one hand, the Finance Commissions did not consider the tax effort and economy in expenditures of the states, on the other hand they did not take into account the level of public services provided satisfactorily while determining the grants-in-aid of revenue. The First Finance Commission did recommend grants for the development of primary education. The Third Finance Commission by a majority recommended grants for the development of communications, but these recommendations were not accepted by the government on the strength of a dissenting note by G. R. Kamath, the member-secretary of the Commission. The Sixth Commission, however, broadly interpreted the terms of reference and recommended grants to provide the average level of some of the general and social services.[36] None of the six Finance Commission s ever took account of the level of overall services provided by the states in determining grants-in-aid of revenue. We have already pointed out the weaknesses of such specific purpose transfers.

Thus, the Finance Commissions have generally determined the grants-in-aid of revenue to be distributed to the states under Article 275 of the Constitution merely to fill the gap between revenues and expenditures, as projected by the states with only minor modifications.

Eventually, some states like Tamil Nadu and West Bengal could qualify for grants in spite of their higher per capita expenditures on the various services provided by them, consequent upon the recommendation of the Third, Fourth and Fifth Finance Commissions. On the other hand, due to the surpluses in its non-Plan revenue accounts, Bihar did not qualify for grants from the Third, Fourth and Fifth Finance Commissions in spite of low per capita expenditures on various services. Madhya Pradesh did not qualify for grants from the Fifth and Sixth Finance Commissions for the same reason. Uttar Pradesh, in fact, did not qualify for grants from the first five Finance Commissions.

As the recommendations pertaining to grants-in-aid are made to fill the gap between the predicted revenues and expenditures of the states, there is likely to be a serious disincentive for the states to raise revenue and economise on expenditures. As the states' own tax rates and unit costs of providing public "output" are entered into in the determination of grants, a state becomes eligible to receive grants if it consistently shows a large gap in its revenue account. This tendency has been strengthened by the Finance Commissions' approach of accepting the forecasts made by the states with only minor modifications and their failure to make an objective assessment of the states' revenue "capacities" and expenditure "needs." Apart from indulging in laxity in fiscal performance, the states may also succeed in obtaining sizeable grants by under-estimating their revenues, exaggerating their expenditures and thus manipulating a huge gap in their non-Plan revenue accounts.

The Finance Commissions have been aware of this danger. The First Finance Commission, for instance, stated: "If the amount of grants-in-aid were to be merely in proportion to the financial plight of the state, a direct premium might be placed on impervious policies and a penalty imposed on financial prudence less."[37] The Third Commission again opined, "secure in the knowledge that the annual budgetary gap would be fully covered by devolution of Union resources and grants-in-aid, the states are tending to develop, as we have noticed, an allergy to tap resources in the rural sector on many considerations and also a disinclination to make up the leeway in others. They do not also attach the same importance to a proper and adequate control on expenditures in the matter of services and supplies as before."[38]

To prevent the disincentive effect of federal transfers on the states' tax revenues and expenditures, it is necessary that the "tax rates" and "unit cost" of providing public output of the states should not enter into the formula adopted by the Finance Commissions. Therefore, rather than take the projected revenues and expenditures of the states, they should determine the fiscal gap by estimating the relative fiscal capacities and needs of the states,[39] which are determined on the basis of predetermined norms of tax rates and service levels. Thus, the grants as recommended by the Finance Commissions tend to promote fiscal irresponsibility either by changing the preferences in favour of private goods (substitution of states' own revenues by statutory grants) or by encouraging inefficiency in the provision of public services.

IV

CONCLUSIONS

We may now summarise the main issues discussed in the foregoing sections.

First, the fulfilment of the objective of equity, in the sense of effecting interregional flow of funds to compensate for the deficiency in "fiscal capacities" and unfulfilled "fiscal needs" is seriously hindered by the restricted scope which the Finance Commissions have come to accept over the years. Their confinement to recommending transfers to meet the needs arising from the non-Plan side of the revenue accounts of the states has been partly forced upon them by the terms of reference, but the Finance Commissions themselves also have to take a major part of the blame in not asserting their rightful role in effecting federal fiscal devolution. In any case, any attempt at rationalising the system of federal transfers should start with the determination of the entire federal fiscal devolution by a single agency so as to render federal transfers an effective instrument of fiscal policy. This issue should have been examined in detail while specifying the terms of reference to the Seventh Finance Commission which should be starting its work very shortly.

Even within the restricted scope the Finance Commissions have come to accept over the years, the federal transfers recommended by them have been found to be wanting in terms of fulfilling the objective of equity. As a consequence, some rich urban states have ended up with sizeable surpluses in their revenue accounts which could further benefit due to the matching provisions from the Plan grants. On the other hand, their poorer counterparts have had to resort to sizeable unauthorised overdrafts from the Reserve Bank of India, which had to be ultimately cleared by medium-term loans extended to these states by the Government of India. Some poor states, in spite of low level of public services, could not qualify for statutory grants due to the surplus in the revenue accounts, consequent upon the low levels of expenditures.

Two factors seem to have contributed to such an outcome. First, the adoption of different criteria for tax sharing and for the distribution of grants seems to have placed some doubts on the overall objective of federal transfers itself. The overall purpose of transfers being the attainment of equity, it is not clear why different criteria should be applicable to tax shares and grants-in-aid of revenue. Second, the criteria adopted by the Finance Commissions in recommending fiscal devolutions have themselves not been equitable. In fact, the weightage given to the factor of collection or assessment in the distribution of net income tax proceeds has meant the negation of equitable geographical redistribution. Besides, as the grants are distributed on the basis of projected budgetary gaps in the non-Plan revenue accounts of the states with no consideration given to fiscal performance of the states whatever, the whole scheme has tended to promote fiscal irresponsibility on the part of the states.

The Seventh Finance Commission should, therefore, comprehensively assess "fiscal capacities" and "needs" of the states and make that the basis of federal transfers. This would not only remove the disincentive effects such as on "tax efforts" and "expenditure economies" by the states, present in the prevailing scheme of the Finance Commissions' transfers, but also raise the level of public services in the backward states by removing the financial constraints on them.

Notes and References

[I am thankful to S. P. Gupta and R. S. Rao for useful discussions. S. P. Gupta also went through an earlier draft of the chapter and suggested some improvements. I also wish to acknowledge my gratitude to D. T. Lakdawala, with whom I had the opportunity to discuss some of the issues elaborated in the chapter.]

[1] See A. D. Scott, "The Economic Goals of Federal Finance," *Public Finance/Finances Publiques* (1964), pp. 242–88.

[2] J. M. Buchanan, "Federalism and Fiscal Equity," *American Economic Review*, Vol. 40 (1950); reprinted in *Readings in the Economics of Taxation*, ed. Richard D. Irwin.

[3] R. A. Musgrave, "Approaches to the Fiscal Theory of Political Federalism" in *Public Finances: Needs, Sources and Utilisation* (National Bureau of Economic Research, Princeton, 1961).

[4] Albert Breton, "A Theory of Government Grants," *Canadian Journal of Economics and Political Science* 31, No. 2 (May 1965), pp. 175–87.

[5] Lester C. Thurow, "Aid to State and Local Governments," *National Tax Journal*, Vol. 23 (1970), pp. 23–25.

[6] "Horizontal equity" is defined as "equal treatment of equals." This is in contrast to the concept of "vertical equity" which means "unequal treatment of unequals." The concept was first employed by Musgrave; see, R. A. Musgrave, *Theory of Public Finance* (New York: McGraw-Hill, 1959).

[7] Under this clause, the Finance Commissions have been asked to recommend the distribution of assigned taxes under Article 269 of the Constitution and additional excise duties in lieu of mill-made textiles, tobacco and sugar which are in the nature of tax rental arrangements. Besides, the Second Finance Commission was asked also to look into the modifications in the rate of interest and terms of repayment of loans made to the various states by the Government of India. The Fourth Finance Commission was asked to look into the creating of a fund for repayment of states' debt. The Fifth Finance Commission was required to inquire into the scope of additional revenue from the sources available to the states and to consider the problem of unauthorised overdrafts of the states with the Reserve Bank of India and the procedure to be observed to avoid such overdrafts. Finally, the Sixth Finance Commission was asked to make an assessment of the non-Plan capital gap of states to the financing of relief expenditures by the states affected by natural calamities.

[8] The only close similarity is with the Australian Commonwealth Grants Commission, which however does not enjoy the powers to change the percentage share of the shared taxes between the Union and Provinces, nor can it change the criteria for distributing tax-shares *interse* the provinces, unlike the Indian Finance Commissions. See D. T. Lakdawala, "Union-State Financial Relations."

[9] Since 1965, projects having individual works amounting to Rs 1 lakh and above and whose total cost is Rs 5 lakhs and above are debited to capital account.

[10] See K. Venkataraman, *States' Finances in India* (London: George Allen and Unwin), Chapters 2 and 3.

[11] On this issue, as many suggestions are available as there are authors on the subject. But mainly these suggestions boil down to either making the entire devolutions the responsibility of either the Finance Commission or the Planning Commission. See K. Venkataraman, *States' Finance in India*; Asok Chanda, *Federalism in India* (London: George Allen and Unwin 1965); K. Santhanan,"Union-State Relation in India", D. T. Lakdawala, "Union-State Financial Relations"; A. T. Eapen,"A Critique of Indian Fiscal Federalism," *Public Finance* 24, No. 4 (1969); V. V. Bhatt, "On the Magnitude and Allocation of Federal Assistance to the States in India: Some Rational Criteria," *Public Finance* 25, No. 4 (1970); P. K. Bhargava,"The Finance Commission," *Artha Vijnana*, Vol. 12 (1970).

[12] Report of the Finance Commission, 1965, p. 88.

[13] Ibid., p. 88.

[14] Ibid., p. 89.

[15] Report of the Finance Commission, 1969, p. 12.

[16] This is emphatically put in an article by an anonymous writer in *Economic and Political Weekly* thus: "if the Finance Commission, as an institution, has emerged as a mere filler of budgetary gaps for the states, little if any, of the blame for it lies with the Presidential orders appointing the Finance Commission every five years. The blame lay, really and truly, with the

Finance Commissions, themselves. They just abdicated their Constitutional obligations." See, "Centre-State Financial Relations—II," *Economic and Political Weekly* 8, no. 25 (1973), p. 115.

[17] Report of the Finance Commission, 1952, p. 103.

[18] This issue is extensively discussed in M. G. Rao, "Specific Purpose versus Block Grants—Sixth Finance Commission's Award in Retrospect" (unpublished). See also, James A. Wilde,"Grants-in-Aid: The Analytics of Design and Response," *National Tax Journal* 24, No. 2 (1971).

[19] See W. Z. Hirsch, *The Economics of State and Local Governments* (New York: McGraw-Hill, 1970), pp. 129–30.

[20] Report of the Finance Commission, 1952, p. 75.

[21] Report of the Finance Commission, 1969, pp. 72–73.

[22] V. V. Bhatt also comes to the same position. He opines, "I am of the view that since both tax sharing and grants-in-aid have to be governed on the basis of use, it should be possible to evolve rational criteria of allocation applicable to the total resources transfer from the federal to state governments.". See V. V. Bhatt, *op. cit.*, p. 566.

[23] Such an interpretation can be found in the memorandum submitted to the Sixth Finance Commission by V. K. R. V. Rao. He says,"Receipts from devolution constitute a right, their status is similar to that of the taxes directly levied and collected by the states, and all states, irrespective of their need or otherwise of special assistance, are entitled to a share in their proceeds." See his "Centre-State Financial Relations in India," Institute for Social and Economic Change Staff Papers—I, pp. 22–23.

[24] The Administrative Reforms Commission, for instance, opined, "Recognising that the needs of the states increasingly outstrip their resources and that funds have to be devolved by the Centre in some form or other, it is only realistic to grant the case for extending the base of devolution and bring other taxes also within the ambit of sharability" (pp. 41–42). Thus, "It... appears... necessary ... to secure for the states a larger devolution of taxes than at present, so that in actual practice the need for grants-in-aid under Article 275 either disappears or is minimised" (p. 41). See, Administrative Reforms Commission, *Report of the Study Team on Centre-State Relationships*, Vol. 1 (Government of India, 1971).

[25] Report on the Centre-States Relations Committee.

[26] Report of the Finance Commission, 1952, pp. 72–73.

[27] Ibid., p. 73.

[28] Report of the Finance Commission, 1957, p. 39.

[29] Report of the Finance Commission, 1961, p. 18.

[30] Report of the Finance Commission, 1952.

[31] See, I. S. Gulati, "Sixth Finance Commission's Award: An Appraisal in Retrospect," *Economic and Political Weekly*, Annual Number (1977), pp. 287–95.

[32] Report of the Finance Commission, 1957, p. 24.

[33] Report of the Finance Commission, 1961, p. 29.

[34] Report of the Finance Commission, 1969, p. 55.

[35] Report of the Finance Commission, 1973, p. 52.

[36] More specifically, grants to raise the level of services on general administration, justice, jails, police, primary education, medical and public health, welfare of schedule castes and tribes were recommended by the Sixth Finance Commission. See Report of the Finance Commission, 1973, Chapter XII.

[37] Report of the Finance Commission, 1952.

[38] Report of the Finance Commission, 1961, p. 38.

[39] See R. A. Musgrave, *op. cit.*, and also Grand Lullian, *op. cit.*

Notes on the Contributors

Satish K. Arora was a contributor to the *Economic & Political Weekly*.

Vimal Balasubrahmanyan was a contributor to the *Economic & Political Weekly*.

D. Banerji is Professor Emeritus, Centre of Social Medicine and Community, School of Social Sciences, Jawaharlal Nehru Unversity.

Jagdish Bhagwati is University Professor of Economics, Law and International Relations, Columbia University.

Pradip Kumar Bose is former Professor of Sociology, Centre for Studies in Social Sciences, Calcutta.

Vihang R. Errunza is Associate Dean of Research and holds the Bank of Montreal Chair in Finance and Banking at McGill University, Montreal.

Marc Galanter is Professor Emeritus, University of Wisconsin–Madison.

M. Govinda Rao is Counsellor, Takshashila Institution, Bangalore. He is former Director, National Institute of Public Finance and Policy and member of the Fourteenth Finance Commission.

Dipankar Gupta is former Professor in the Centre for the Study of Social Systems, School of Social Sciences, Jawaharlal Nehru University, New Delhi.

Surinder S. Jodhka is Professor, Centre for the Study of Social Systems, School of Social Sciences, Jawaharlal Nehru University, New Delhi.

Vijay L. Kelkar is Chairman, National Institute of Public Finance and Policy, New Delhi.

Rajni Kothari was founding director of the Centre for the Study of Developing Societies, Delhi.

Gopal Krishna is a member of Wolfson College, Oxford and former director of the Centre for the Study of Developing Societies, Delhi.

Rajiv Kumar is founding director of Pahle India Foundation, and Vice Chairman of NITI Aayog, New Delhi.

Amitabh Kundu is Distinguished Fellow at the Research and Information System for Developing Countries.

Gurpreet Mahajan is Professor, Centre for Political Studies, School of Social Sciences, Jawaharlal Nehru University, New Delhi.

N. A. Mujumdar was editor of the *Indian Journal of Agricultural Economics*, and a former principal advisor at the Reserve Bank of India.

Mahmood Mamdani is the Herbert Lehman Professor of Government at Columbia University, and Director, Makerere Institute of Social Research, Kampala.

Vina Mazumdar was the founding director of the Center for Women's Development Studies, New Delhi.

Oliver Mendelsohn is Emeritus Scholar, La Trobe University.

Ila Patnaik is Professor, National Institute of Public Finance and Policy (NIPFP).

C. K. Prahalad was the Paul and Ruth McCracken Distinguished University Professor of Corporate Strategy at the University of Michigan Stephen M. Ross School of Business.

C. Rajagopalan was a contributor to the *Economic & Political Weekly*.

Moin Shakir was Professor of Political Science at Dr Ambedkar Marathwada University, and author of many books on Muslims in India.

A. M. Shah is former Professor of Sociology, Delhi School of Economics, University of Delhi.

Kumud Sharma is Chairperson, Centre for Women's Development Studies, New Delhi.

Arun Shourie is a former economist with the World Bank, and former Minister of Communications and Information Technology.

Hira Singh is with the Department of Sociology, York University, Toronto.

K. S. Singh was an Indian Administrative Service officer, who served as a Commissioner of Chotanagpur and Director-General of the Anthropological Survey of India.

Jaspal Singh was a contributor to the *Economic & Political Weekly*.

T. N. Srinivasan was the Emeritus Samuel C. Park, Jr Professor of Economics at Yale University, and former chairman of the department of economics.

Alice Thorner was a social scientist and statistician who engaged with research on India for over six decades.